THE MONEY MARKET AND MONETARY MANAGEMENT

THE MONEY MARKET AND MONETARY MANAGEMENT

SECOND EDITION

G. WALTER WOODWORTH

Leon E. Williams Professor of Finance and Banking, Emeritus
The Amos Tuck School of Business Administration
Dartmouth College

HARPER & ROW, PUBLISHERS New York Evanston San Francisco London

This book is affectionately dedicated to my wife, Elizabeth C. Woodworth

THE MONEY MARKET AND MONETARY MANAGEMENT, Second Edition

Standard Book Number: 06-047216-2
Library of Congress Catalog Card Number: 79-188202

contents

part two MONETARY AND FISCAL MANAGEMENT

preface

Dynamic changes have occurred in the financial system since the first edition of this book in 1965. In addition to changes in institutions and practices, there have been important developments in monetary and fiscal theories which bear on effective monetary management. Institutional changes may be illustrated by the meteoric growth of the Eurodollar market, the further development of the market in negotiable time certificates (CDs), and the rejuvenation of the commercial-paper market. A significant development in theory has been rediscovery of the importance of money and its relation to output and prices by the "monetarists." At the same time, the predominance of fiscal policy as a method of economic stabilization has given way to greater emphasis on monetary management. In addition to updating tables, figures, and illustrations, I have added new chapters on the Eurodollar market and on recent financial developments. This thorough revision has required new sections and extensive rewriting of others.

This book is written to meet a two-fold need experienced by the author in teaching an advanced course in money markets and monetary-fiscal management: first, a lack of suitable teaching materials–books and articles too general and fragmentary or too detailed and technical; and second, a lack of integration between money markets and the intimately related field of monetary-fiscal management. It is virtually impossible to present either of the two latter topics effectively without drawing heavily on the other. There is also the hope that officers of banks and other financial institutions, executives of corporations, and government officials might find some parts of the work useful and informative.

Emphasis is placed on the theoretical framework and on the analytical approach to policy determination. However, real understanding of what transpires in this field requires considerable factual knowledge of the institutional setting; basic facts are presented in regard to practices, government regulation, and the several components of the money market.

Another feature of the book is its primary concern with the short-term money market rather than with the longer-term capital market. This procedure is justified by the closer relation of Federal Reserve policies and actions to the short-term markets, and also by the practical necessity of limiting the scope of the undertaking. The capital market is included when it has a significant bearing on the problem at hand.

It is quite impossible to give proper credit to all who have given me substantial assistance–many commercial bank officers, security dealers, and

Federal Reserve officials—all of whom were most cooperative and generous. My deepest debts are to Dean Karl A. Hill whose encouragement led to final completion, to Professor James C. T. Mao who provided constructive criticisms, and to my wife, Elizabeth C. Woodworth, who bore bravely the burden of neglect, typed the original manuscript, and suggested numerous improvements in style.

My debts in this edition are to Dean John W. Hennessey, Jr., for encouragement and financial assistance in pursuing research, and to many officers of New York City banks who were generous with interviews. I should also like to recognize the able assistance of Arline Wilson in preparing and typing the manuscript.

G. WALTER WOODWORTH

part one

THE MONEY MARKET

1

organization of the money market

NATURE AND FUNCTIONS

Financial literature provides no standardized definition of the term "money market." On the contrary, one encounters notable variations in usage. Some writers employ the term broadly to include the complex of arrangements by which lenders and borrowers of money capital are brought together, and by which outstanding bonds and other obligations are bought and sold. This usage includes long-term as well as short-term obligations, and therefore approaches the concept of *capital market,* although the market for equity capital is seldom included. At the other extreme, some authorities define money market narrowly to embrace only the objective open markets for near-money, liquid assets. Others, in-between, exclude long-term obligations, but include short-term loans of banks and other financial institutions to regular customers.

For the present purpose, the narrow definition serves best. That is, the money market embraces the various arrangements that have to do with issuance, trading, and redemption of low-risk, short-term, marketable obligations whose prices vary only moderately. Both long-term obligations and customer loans are excluded. Stated differently, the boundary line is drawn to include only those instruments that serve the secondary reserve needs of commercial banks and other investors—instruments that possess a high degree of liquidity and at the same time provide a moderate yield. While such a definition is conceptually useful, it is necessarily arbitrary and difficult to apply. Quality, maturity, and marketability are characteristics that change by fine gradations. Consequently, wherever a line is drawn, there is little difference in substance between assets in the immediate zone of the line, whether they be on one side or the other. For example, maturities under 5 years are included, whereas maturities of 5 years and over are excluded. But there is no significant difference between a maturity of 4 years and 364 days and one of 5 years. Nevertheless it is useful to draw a maturity line because there is a significant difference in price variations between 3-year and 6-year obligations of equivalent quality.

The fact that the center of interest in this study focuses on obligations with absolute liquidity (money) and with extraordinary liquidity (liquidity reserves) does not mean that their close relation to the broad capital market is unrecognized. Obviously, functional and competitive relationships exist. For example, a Treasury decision to offer more long-term and fewer short-term issues tends to raise long-term yields in relation to short-term yields. Again, a wave of business pessimism may lead to sale of stocks and second-grade bonds and to purchase of U.S. and other highest-quality obligations. In this event, prices of the former tend to fall and prices of highest-grade issues tend to rise. Such relationships as these are discussed when it seems analytically appropriate.

A more tangible idea of the place of money-market obligations in the capital market as a whole is given by Table 1-1. Credit- and equity-market instruments outstanding at the end of 1969 aggregated $2618 billion. Money-market obligations with maturities under five years outstanding on the same date totaled $316 billion. Thus, money-market obligations were about 12 percent of total capital instruments. The proportion is highest in U.S. securities in which four-fifths of marketable debt is represented by issues with maturities under five years. It is lowest in mortgage loans, consumer loans, and other customer loans of banks.

TABLE 1-1 / COMPARISON OF AGGREGATE CAPITAL-MARKET INSTRUMENTS AND MONEY-MARKET OBLIGATIONS OUTSTANDING ON RECENT DATES, END OF 1969 (billions of dollars)

Type of Security	Credit and Equity Market Instruments Outstanding	Money-Market Obligations with Maturities Under 5 Years
Federal obligations	235.9	191.4
Federal agency obligations	31.3	29.7
State and local obligations	132.2	35.0
Corporate and foreign bonds	183.3	11.9
Mortgages, home	266.9	0.0
Mortgages, other	157.9	0.0
Consumer credit	122.5	0.0
Bank loans n.e.c.	152.9	0.3[a]
Other loans	129.0	0.0
Bankers' acceptances		5.5
Commercial and finance-company paper		31.6
Bankers' time certificates		10.9
Miscellaneous financial instruments	278.3	0.0
Corporate stock (market value)	904.7	0.0
Total	2,617.6	316.3

[a]Call loans to U.S. security dealers.

Sources: *Federal Reserve Bulletin,* various issues; Board of Governors of the Federal Reserve System, *Financial Assets and Liabilities* (December 31, 1969).

The basic function of the money market is to provide efficient facilities for adjustment of liquidity positions of commercial banks, nonbank financial institutions, business corporations, and other investors. More specifically, this means that there be a nationwide market in high-grade, short-term obligations; that such obligations be available in sufficient amount and variety to meet investors' needs; and that the market mechanism provide quick mobility of money and securities throughout the country. Given these arrangements, banks and other investors holding surpluses of money can speedily put them to work by purchasing liquid earning assets; conversely, investors holding liquidity-reserve assets can readily convert them to money when the need arises. A smoothly functioning money market fosters the flow of funds to the most important uses throughout the nation and the world, and throughout the entire range of economic activities. In the process, interest-rate differentials are narrowed, both geographically and industrially, and economic growth is promoted. Moreover, individual banks and other enterprises gain from the opportunities for closer administration of liquid resources.

But while the foregoing services of the money market remain the same through time, important and frequently rapid changes in market institutions, instruments, and practices continuously take place. New institutions such as the Federal Reserve System (Fed), are developed; new instruments such as the Treasury bill, the certificate of deposit (CD), and the Eurodollar appear in volume; and practices are constantly adapted to these and other changes. Just as a description of the money market of the 1920s is far from representative of the 1970s, so today's description of institutions and practices will doubtless be obsolete a decade from now, despite the fact that market functions will remain about the same. This general observation also applies to money markets in different countries at the same time. The functions of the London and New York money markets are, generally speaking, the same, but institutions, instruments, and practices are quite different.

Although short-term loans of commercial banks to customers are excluded from this study, their close relation to money-market obligations requires preliminary comment. Customer loans are directly competitive with commercial paper and with bankers' acceptances. Also, as will be seen, they have replaced the most important division of the open market prior to the 1930s, viz., brokers' call loans. The chief distinction between customer loans and open-market paper lies in the nature of the lender-borrower relationship. Banks make business loans as a rule only to depositing customers. In fact, the amount and stability of a customer's deposit account has much to do with the size of his line of credit. Also, the borrowing customer must reveal the intimate details of his business, including balance sheets and income statements, as part of the relevant facts which bankers weigh in the loan-making process. If the customer's financial position, earnings, deposits, previous repayment record, and other relevant facts are satisfactory, the banker feels confident enough to lend a reasonable amount in accordance with needs. Thus, customer loans are made in an atmosphere of personal relationship, usually extending over many years. In most cases, there is mutual respect and trust. The customer values his credit line and seeks to maintain it; the bank values the customer's deposit account, loans, and other business, and strives to hold them. While the cost of borrowing is the dominant consideration, it is not the only factor entering into loan decisions. In fact, customer loan rates lag well behind open-market rates when market conditions change. This means that borrowing customers sometimes pay higher rates, and sometimes pay lower rates, than those quoted in the open market.

In contrast with customer loans, the open markets are entirely objective and free from personal considerations. Obligations are bought from dealers who offer lowest prices (highest yields) and are sold to dealers who bid the highest prices (lowest yields). Customer loans are seldom bought and sold, but are held by lending banks until repayment.

A notable feature of the money market is that trading in the various obligations takes place almost entirely in over-the-counter markets rather than on organized exchanges. Indeed, the only instruments on an exchange are U.S. bonds and some corporate obligations which are listed in the bond section of the New York Stock Exchange. Only rarely are Treasury securities traded on the exchange. Middlemen act as dealers rather than as brokers. That is, they buy for their own accounts and assume risks of holding positions during declining prices.

MONEY-MARKET INSTITUTIONS

While the broad functions of money markets are the same in different times and places, the institutions through which operations take place exhibit marked variations. The institutional environment is quite complex, and it significantly influences functional performance. All money-market transactions occur as a result of decisions by people utilizing existing instruments and institutions. Moreover, decisions and actions are often affected by the character of institutions and the limitations they impose. Therefore, a first requirement for understanding money-market operations is knowledge of the environment. This chapter is designed to meet this requirement by providing essential facts about the following main institutions: monetary laws and the stock of money; the commercial-banking system; the Fed; the U.S. Treasury; U.S. security dealers; dealers in other market instruments; lenders and borrowers; and the interest-rate structure.

monetary laws and the stock of money

The principal features of the monetary system are determined by laws pertaining to money and banking. The U.S. Constitution grants Congress the power "To coin Money, regulate the Value thereof . . . ."[1] Under this prerogative, Congress has passed monetary laws, notably the National Banking Act of 1864, the Federal Reserve Act of 1913, the Gold Reserve Act of 1934, the Banking Acts of 1933 and 1935, and the Employment Act of 1946. These laws, as amended, shape the character of our monetary system. Among other things, they define the monetary standard and the monetary unit; provide for coinage and printing of money; designate legal-tender money; arrange for issuance of coins and paper money by the Treasury and the Federal Reserve Banks; define reserve money and set legal-reserve ratios for member banks; permit commercial banks to issue the bulk of active money in the form of demand deposits; delegate a variety of mechanical monetary functions to the Reserve Banks; set forth the broad objectives of monetary policy; and grant the Board of Governors wide discretionary powers to control interest rates and the amount of money and total bank credit in order to achieve the stated objectives.

One should visualize this legal and institutional framework as the matrix from which the stock in trade of the money market arises. All transactions in this market are composed of purchases of high-grade, short-term obligations with money, or of sales of these obligations for money—the asset with absolute liquidity. In view of the large size of transactions, deposit money rather than currency is used in making payments.

the commercial-banking system

Commercial banks represent by far the most important class of buyers and sellers of money-market obligations, accounting for nearly half the number of resale transactions of dealers in U.S. securities and over one-fourth of transactions in state and local securities and in corporate obligations.[2] The proportions would no doubt be higher on the basis of values of securities traded. Confronted with wide variations of deposits and loans, the banks are continuously in process of liquid-reserve adjustments. Sometimes, and especially during recessions, the problem of the system is that of investing excess reserves. At other times, and particularly during cyclical booms, the general problem is one of meeting reserve deficiencies—often solved by sale of money-market assets or by borrowing. Individual banks, of course, have special reserve problems of their own and frequently sell when other banks are buying, and buy when others are selling.

While all commercial banks (13,664 in June 1970) buy and sell money-market obligations on occasion, the great bulk of such transactions is accounted for by a small number of large banks. The degree of concentration is

[1]Article I, Section 8.

[2]See Irwin Friend, G. Wright Hoffman, and Willis J. Winn, *The Over-the-Counter Securities Markets* (New York: McGraw-Hill, 1958), p. 84.

even greater when measured by holdings of deposits utilized in money-market payments, by debits to these accounts, by holdings of interbank and foreign bank deposits, and by financing of dealers in U.S. securities and other obligations.

There is no precise way of separating banks that have an active part in the national money market from those that are too small and too remote to play a significant role. In fact, any such classification is necessarily arbitrary because size, however measured, is not an accurate criterion of money-market participation. Nevertheless, a rough idea of the active group of banks may be gained from published information. To begin with, few actively participating banks are outside the reserve city group of member banks. While this group of 177 banks represented only 1.3 percent of the total number of commercial banks at midyear 1970, they held three-fifths of total deposits; and what is more important for the present purpose, they held 85 percent of interbank demand balances. Half of these balances was held by the 12 large money-market banks in New York City. A special *bank wire* links most of these (and a few other) banks in some 60 cities into an active, split-second communication system.

These bankers' balances experience the greatest turnover and the widest fluctuations of any class of accounts. They are a focal point of money-market operations, a large part of which arises from the continuous process of adjustment of bank reserves. In further support of the statement, it should be emphasized that most of the banking for money-market transactions is done by a few of the largest banks, and again with the spotlight on New York City. Payments for money-market obligations are made either by checks drawn on major banks or on Federal Banks, and debits to demand-deposit accounts are a much better basis for measurement of money-market importance than are total deposits. In addition, the great banks finance operations by loans to broker-dealers in U.S. securities and other securities; provide security custody services; act as agents for correspondent banks and other customers; participate directly as buyers and sellers of obligations, including Federal funds; maintain foreign departments which finance international trade, deal in foreign exchange, and act as middlemen in movements of international money capital; and serve the money market in various other capacities.

the federal reserve system

While commercial banks are the largest class of participants, the Fed occupies an even more basic position in the money market. At the highest level, the Board of Governors and the Open-Market Committee are responsible for determination of broad monetary policies. On the basis of general legislative directives, they have evolved a set of objectives (which will be discussed later): (1) high-level production and employment; (2) business stability; (3) healthy economic growth; (4) a relatively stable price level; and (5) international monetary cooperation, including a viable international balance of payments. The preeminent task of the Board of Governors is to determine and implement policies that continuously make the maximum contribution to achievement of objectives. This involves much more than resolution of whether policies shall be expansive, contractive, or neutral. It poses the difficult questions of timing and of degree of pressure on the market between the extremes of ease and firmness.

Once determined, policies are implemented mainly through the operations of the Federal Reserve Banks whose principal liabilities constitute the legal reserves of member banks in the forms of reserve balances and Federal Reserve Notes. However, most of the notes, which represent nine-tenths of our paper money, are in the hands of the public and are not held as vault cash reserves of commercial banks. Member-bank legal reserves are often called *high-powered money* when compared with commercial-bank demand deposits. This emphatic designation is fully deserved because one dollar of member-bank reserves is capable of supporting several dollars of commercial-bank deposits. The exact multiple depends on several factors, including minimum legal reserves, proportions of currency and demand deposits, and proportions of demand and time deposits. Speaking generally, the heart of Fed monetary management is control of the stock of money by regulation of member-bank reserve balances. In turn, changes in these balances are brought about by expansion and contraction of assets of the Reserve Banks.

The money market has two principal channels of access to Reserve Bank credit: (1) member-bank borrowing, known as *discounts and advances*; and (2) sale of U.S. and other securities to the Reserve Banks, usually called *open-market operations.* Borrowing at Reserve Banks represents a safety valve, especially for individual banks that experience legal-reserve deficiencies for various reasons. It is done at the initiative of member banks, although the Fed governs the discount rate and other terms, and also influences the amount of borrowing by open-market operations and legal-reserve requirements. Reserve Banks may also refuse to lend; that is, borrowing is viewed largely as a privilege instead of a right.

The open-market channel to Reserve Bank credit is governed entirely by Fed decisions. United States and other securities are purchased when policies call for creation of more bank reserves, and securities are sold when policies require reduction of bank reserves. A small part of Reserve Bank security holdings represents direct financing of nonbank U.S. security dealers, and to a lesser extent, of bankers' acceptance dealers. The securities are bought from dealers under repurchase agreements when the Open-Market Committee decides to release reserves to the market in this manner. The predominance of open-market operations as an instrument of monetary control is attested by the fact that Reserve Banks held $57.6 billion of Treasury securities at midyear 1970. By contrast, discounts and advances of these banks amounted to only about $1 billion on the same date, and they were less than $2 billion at their postwar peak in November 1952. But, as will be developed later, discounts and advances have far greater significance in money-market analysis than their volume indicates. They occupy a strategic position in view of their marginal character and of the general reluctance of banks to be in debt to Reserve Banks.

Another potent instrument of control in the hands of the Board of Governors is its power to set legal-reserve requirements for member banks. By raising percentage requirements, a net reserve surplus, which is associated with low interest rates, may be shifted to a net reserve deficit, which leads to high rates. By lowering reserve requirements, the opposite situation may be produced; that is, a firm money market may be transformed to an easy one.

Although less important than the general instruments of control, the Board's power to change margin requirements on loans to purchase or carry stock-exchange securities can be wielded to affect the market significantly. The use of borrowed funds to buy stocks has, on occasion, been shut off entirely by a requirement of 100 percent. At other times, the minimum margin has been as low as 40 percent.

Proceeding one step further, the Fed is responsible for the two media of money-market payments: Federal (Reserve) funds and clearing-house funds. Because Federal funds are deposits in Reserve Banks, or checks drawn thereon, they are immediately available and have been used increasingly in recent years in money-market settlements. Also, an active market in them exists, mainly among large member banks in adjusting reserve positions. Clearing-house funds are demand deposits of commercial banks, and checks thereon are not available for one or more business days.

In brief, the Fed is the most pervasive force in the money market. By regulating the reserve position of commercial banks, it controls the stock of money and also influences the level and structure of interest rates. These factors, in turn, affect the rate of spending for output, gross national product (GNP), employment, general business conditions, and the level of prices. In addition the Reserve Banks deal directly in money-market obligations and provide the major means of settlement in the form of Federal Reserve funds.

the u.s. treasury

The U.S. Treasury, like the Fed, occupies a central position in the money market, and similarly, it has various facets of connection with the market. Most important is its strategic influence on broad fiscal and monetary policies. While Congress and the Administration have final responsibility for the federal budget and the many underlying programs for revenues and expenditures, the Secretary of the Treasury and other Treasury officials materially affect final decisions. They suggest positive programs, and their advice is frequently sought in congressional hearings. In the end, they usually have a significant influence on the size of the deficit or surplus. Treasury officials are also in position to influence monetary policies. In fact, during World War II and until the Treasury-Federal Reserve Accord in 1951, their decisions in this area were dominant. Since that time, the Fed has taken primary responsibility for monetary policies, but the Treasury's influence in an advisory capacity has undoubtedly been very great.

Of nearly equal importance in the money market is the Treasury's role as manager of the federal debt. The size of the debt is inherited from past decisions of Congress and the Administration, but the Treasury determines the features of securities issued. It decides whether they shall be marketable or nonmarketable, whether they shall be bills, certificates, notes, or bonds, and what the maturity distribution shall be. In determining these features, it has much to do with ownership of the federal debt—by individuals, commercial banks, nonbank financial institutions, business corporations, or others. It also greatly influences the term structure of interest rates—that is, the relation between market rates and maturities. For example, by offering more short-term and fewer long-term issues, it raises short-term rates in relation to long-term rates. Taken together, these debt-management decisions shape the character of the predominant class of securities in the money market. At the end of May 1970, the amount of marketable Treasury issues maturing in less than one year was $109.4 billion, and in less than five years was $199.1 billion.[3]

Finally, the Treasury carries out various operations in the monetary sphere. For one thing, it issues Treasury currency—that is, coins, and all paper money except Federal Reserve Notes. Increases of Treasury currency tend to build up member-bank reserves and to lower rates, whereas decreases tend to reduce reserves and to raise rates. Another closely related operation pertains to the amount of Treasury currency in possession of the Treasury, technically known as *Treasury cash.* Increases of this item tend to reduce member-bank reserves, and decreases to enlarge reserves. Still another monetary operation has to do with administration of Treasury deposit accounts. The working balance of the Treasury is held by the Reserve Banks, but the great bulk of its balance is with depository commercial banks in *tax and loan accounts.* Transfer of Treasury deposits from commercial banks to Reserve Banks, other things equal, reduces member-bank reserves, whereas drawing down the Treasury's balance at Reserve Banks increases bank reserves. Other less important Treasury relationships with the market exist, but discussion is more appropriate at a later point.

dealers in u.s. securities

The role of dealers in U.S. securities in the money market is a far more basic and complex one than meets the eye. Full description requires considerable space and is reserved for Chapter 5. The purpose here is only a preliminary summary. To begin with, the huge market in U.S. securities is almost entirely

[3]*Federal Reserve Bulletin* (July 1970), p. A 43.

over the counter, or more accurately, *over the telephone.* While Treasury bonds are listed on the New York Stock Exchange, the amount of transactions is nominal. Between 15 and 20 major dealers maintain positions in most all Treasury securities and stand ready with bid-and-offer quotations. About 12 of these are nonbank dealers in New York City with branch offices in leading U.S. cities, and 6 are large commercial banks in New York and Chicago.

A central dealer group of this type is essential to the existence of a market of such magnitude, breadth, and variety. Otherwise, buyers and sellers could never adequately be brought together, and neither group would have assurance of representative market prices. Dealers not only facilitate the exchange of existing securities among investors, but also perform an underwriting function for the Treasury in distribution of new and refunding issues. In addition, they provide facilities for Federal Reserve open-market operations and quickly transmit effects of these operations and other credit control actions throughout the country.

The internal organization of U.S. security dealers, individually and collectively, provides a very close link with other divisions of the money and capital markets. Most dealers have a number of departments which trade in, or underwrite, other securities. For example, one large house handles, in addition to U.S. securities, state and local obligations, federal agency securities, bankers' acceptances, and bankers' CDs. Other dealers also have complementary specialties, including commercial paper, corporate obligations, foreign bonds, and over-the-counter stocks. Thus, all divisions of the national money and capital markets are welded together by the closely-knit dealer organization, with the result that changes initiated in U.S. securities, or elsewhere, are quickly imparted to all sectors of the market.

Finally, preliminary mention should be made of the dealers' role as a buffer between large money-market banks and the Reserve Banks. Dealers usually borrow the residual portion of funds needed to carry inventories from large New York City banks at rates somewhat above the cost of credit from other sources. The greater part of borrowing is ordinarily done under repurchase agreements from business corporations, banks outside New York, state and local governments, and other institutions. When the reserve position of New York City banks tightens, they are likely to raise the rate on call loans to dealers. This leads dealers to search more diligently for funds throughout the country, and to the extent they are successful, reserve positions of New York City banks are eased. But if reserve deficiencies still remain, the banks may then as a last resort have to borrow at the Reserve Banks. Thus, in this sense, dealers constitute a buffer between the large commercial banks and the Reserve Banks, and in the process they contribute to efficient utilization of legal reserves.

lenders and borrowers

Ownership of money-market obligations can best be analyzed by individual markets instead of on a consolidated basis. But while important differences exist between classes of investors in the separate instruments, the similarities of ownership are more striking. This results from the several features which these securities have in common. All are high-grade, short-term, readily marketable issues that meet investor needs for liquidity, and at the same time provide at least moderate yields. In general, commercial banks are the largest class of investors, followed in descending order by Federal Reserve Banks, nonfinancial business corporations, state and local governments, U.S. Government trust funds and other investment accounts, mutual savings banks, fire and casualty insurance companies, savings and loan associations, life insurance companies, private pension funds, educational and charitable funds, and individuals, including personal trust funds.

The pre-eminent borrower in the money market is the United States Treasury which at the end of 1968 had marketable securities outstanding with maturities under five years in the amount of $176.8 billion. This was almost two-thirds of total money-market obligations in this maturity class. Business corporations stood second with some $35 billion in the forms of bankers' acceptances, commercial paper, bonds and notes; state and local governments third with $32.7 billion; and federal agencies fourth with $20.3 billion. (See Table 1-1.)

INTEREST RATE STRUCTURE

The money rate of interest as conventionally expressed is the price for use of money capital for one year. Loan contracts are drawn in terms of monetary units which are homogeneous and standardized. From the standpoint of purchasing power, one dollar is like all others. That is, a gold dollar (13.714 grains of pure gold) has the same value as a dollar bill or a check for one dollar drawn on a bank. At first glance, these facts might lead one to expect a single rate of interest on all loans, just as there tends to be a single price in a competitive market for like units of a commodity. But such is not the case, as is shown in Table 1-2. Money rates are shown in comparison with midyear 1958, when monetary ease prevailed. Several significant facts are noted in Table 1-2.

First, with reference to 1970, yields on U.S. securities were lower than on other money-market obligations of comparable maturities. In ascending order, U.S. government agency securities came next, followed by bankers' acceptances, bankers' time CDs, commercial paper, and corporate obligations. The prime loan rate, which is the rate large banks charge their best business customers, fell between the rates on bankers' acceptances and on commercial paper. The Federal Reserve discount rate of 6 percent was well below all market rates.

Second, the low yields on state and local securities resulted from their exemption from the Federal income tax. On a tax-equivalent basis, their yields were the highest of all. Municipal bond prices were depressed because of large

TABLE 1-2 / THE MONEY-RATE STRUCTURE ON SELECTED DATES (percent)

Type of Security	June 1958	June 1970
U.S. Treasury		
Bills, 3-month[a]	0.85 (0.83)	6.97 (6.67)
Bills, 9-12-month	0.98	7.38 (7.07)
Notes and bonds, 3-5-year	2.25	7.86
Bonds, 10-year or longer	3.19	6.99
Bankers' acceptances, 90-day[a]	1.16 (1.13)	8.02 (7.78)
Commercial paper, 4-6-month[a]	1.59 (1.54)	8.67 (8.20)
Government agency securities		
9-month (FHLB)	2.10	7.04
3-5-year (FLB)	3.05	7.99
State and local securities[b]		
Under 1-year	1.1 [2.3]	7.00 [14.58]
3-5-year	1.6 [3.3]	7.81 [16.27]
Corporate obligations[c]		
1-3-year	2.65	9.07
3-5-year	3.55	9.87
Bankers' time certificates		
3-6-month	d	8.25
12-month and over	d	8.50
Bank prime loan rate	3.50	8.50
Federal Reserve discount rate	1.75	6.00
Federal (reserve) funds rate	0.5 to 1.63	7.50

[a]Adjusted to straight yield basis and a 365-day year from bank discount basis and a 360-day year; parenthesis indicates unadjusted rate.
[b]Moody's Aaa issues; bracket indicates tax-equivalent yields for corporations.
[c]Yields on Chesapeake & Ohio Ry. Co. equipment trust certificates, rated Aaa.
[d]Not available until 1961.
Sources: *Federal Reserve Bulletin* (July 1970), various pages; *Moody's Bond Survey* (July 22, 1970), various pages.

offerings of new issues at a time when commercial banks, which constitute about two-fifths of the market, were very illiquid and not in position to buy.

Third, perhaps the most striking feature was the precipitous rise of rates between midyear 1958 and midyear 1970. For example, the volatile 3-month Treasury bill rate was over 8 times higher in 1970, and the yield on 3-5-year Treasury issues was $3\frac{1}{2}$ times as high. A recession prevailed in 1958, with low loan demands and an abundant supply of loanable funds provided by an easy Fed policy. In 1970, loan demands were strong and loanable funds were scarce, largely because of a restrictive monetary policy. It should be noted that the general position of the various rates in the hierarchy remained about the same despite a marked change in the rate level. Yields on U.S. securities were lowest and yields on corporate obligations were highest in both cases, with other rates in the same relative positions. An exception was the rise in favor of U.S. government agency securities which moved from fourth to second place.

Last, attention is called to the significant change in the yield-maturity relationship—often called the *term structure of rates*—between the two dates. In

1958, short-term rates were much lower than long-term rates. For example, the 9-12-month Treasury bill rate was 0.98 percent, compared with 3.19 percent on long-term bonds. But in 1970, this relationship was reversed. The Treasury bill rate was 7.38 percent and the long-term rate was 6.99 percent. The reasons for this change, which is typical between periods of market ease and firmness, are complex; they are analyzed further in Chapter 11. The Federal Reserve discount rate was about the same as the Treasury bill rate but was below other market rates. Second, yields rose as maturities lengthened, being lowest in the very short maturities and highest in long maturities. Third, the low yields on state and local securities were a result of their exemption from the federal income tax. On a tax-equivalent basis, these yields were quite similar to those on other securities of like risk.

REFERENCES

Friend, Irwin, G. Wright Hoffman, and Willis J. Winn, *The Over-the-Counter Securities Markets* (New York: McGraw-Hill, 1958).

Madden, Carl H., *The Money Side of "The Street"* (New York: Federal Reserve Bank of New York, 1959).

Roosa, Robert V., *Federal Reserve Operations in the Money and Government Securities Markets* (New York: Federal Reserve Bank of New York, 1956).

2

forces governing the rate of interest

Aside from wage rates, interest rates are the most significant and pervasive prices in the economy. To business firms they represent one of the costs of operation and of new investment. Hence, low rates encourage business expansion, and high rates discourage it. Similarly, low rates encourage consumers to purchase houses and other durable goods with borrowed money, whereas high rates provide an obstacle to such outlays. On the supply side, interest rates significantly influence the flow of savings at any given level of income. High rates constitute a greater inducement to save rather than to spend on consumption, whereas low rates discourage saving. Thus, interest rates have a substantial influence on both the overall level of economic activity and the allocation of scarce resources among competing uses, including consumption.

The purpose of this chapter is to summarize the theoretical background of the forces governing the level of interest rates as a basis of subsequent analysis of the money market. For the sake of simplification, it is assumed that there is only one interest rate, representative of the entire market. This is, of course, an abstraction; the rate of structure is, in fact, highly complex, with many separate rates which cover a wide range because of varying contractual terms, risks, maturities, and degrees of liquidity. But the main forces governing the level of rates have a pervasive influence throughout the structure. Most individual rates increase and decrease along with the general level despite differences in timing and in degree. Hence, the assumption of a single rate can be made without seriously departing from realities.

The theory of interest has understandably occupied a large place in the literature of economics since the seventeenth century. Due to the great complexity of the phenomenon, many different theories have been developed. Before the 1930s, nonmonetary theories prevailed, with emphasis on real savings and real investment–productivity theories, use theories, abstinence theories, labor theories, time-preference theories, and others. Since the late 1930s, however, the monetary aspects of the problem have received greater emphasis.

This has led to classification of the two most widely accepted explanations as *monetary theories* of the rate of interest: (1) the liquidity-preference theory, and (2) the loanable-funds theory. Both are partial-equilibrium theories which are valid only under the assumption of no change in GNP or in the general price level. Despite the use of different concepts and emphasis on different variables, the two theories are reconcilable and arrive at the same destination. For the present purpose, the loanable-funds theory has definite advantages, mainly because it explicitly recognizes more of the forces determining rates, and because the concepts utilized are more commonly used in money-market parlance. Space does not permit an exposition of the liquidity-preference theory,[1] but only an abbreviated version of the loanable-funds approach.

The analytical method employed is the familiar one of the interaction of a demand schedule and a supply schedule for loanable funds, which results in the emergence of a market rate of interest. Thus, price determination follows the same procedure as in competitive commodity markets. However, special consideration must be given to the meaning of these schedules in order to attain reasonable precision and to avoid inconsistent interpretations. This becomes evident as one ponders the following questions: (1) Should demand and supply be defined broadly to include direct investment of savings by consumers and by businesses? (2) Should the schedules embrace all transactions in existing securities, or only those that pertain to new securities offered during the period? (3) Should investment, savings, and hoarding of money be treated as gross or net concepts? Specific answers to these questions can best be given as part of the discussion which follows. But, in general, the approach utilizes gross rather than net concepts. In this way, one is better able to understand the significance of all possible transactions in claims, and to see how certain transactions cancel out on opposite sides of the equation.

DEMAND FOR LOANABLE FUNDS

The aggregate demand schedule of loanable funds shows the amounts which seekers of money capital will take at each of a series of interest rates. The time period to which the schedule applies is a short one, say, a week, during which it is assumed that there is no change in expectations with respect to future income. In general, more will be demanded as the interest rate declines, and less will be taken as the rate rises. However, as will be seen, there are considerable differences in the interest-elasticity of demand for money capital among industries and under different economic conditions. (See figure 1, p. 25, for a graphic presentation of the demand schedule of loanable funds, *D*.) It is

[1]For an exposition of the liquidity-preference theory, see John Maynard Keynes, *The General Theory of Employment, Interest and Money* (New York: Harcourt Brace Jovanovich, 1936), chaps. 13, 14; Alvin H. Hansen, *A Guide to Keynes* (New York: McGraw-Hill, 1953), chap. 6.

desirable to divide the users of funds into three groups: (1) businesses, (2) consumers, and (3) governments. The funds are employed by these groups mainly for purposes of investment and consumption. Also, funds are demanded in some circumstances to increase money balances—that is, for hoarding (*H*).

1/The business sector is by far the most important source of demand for funds in peacetime. Net corporate debt increased $63 billion during 1968, and the amount outstanding at the end of the year was $605 billion.[2] Business firms use loanable funds principally to finance investment in plant, equipment, and inventories. Decisions to invest depend heavily on the prospect for profits, and on the availability and cost of investible funds. The demand schedule is interest-elastic because the higher the interest rate the greater the obstacle to exploitation of investment opportunities. Conversely, as the costs of borrowed funds decline, more and more projects come into the range of profitability. That is, the series of expected net returns from the new investment, allowing for risks and uncertainties, more than covers all costs, including those of borrowing. Business firms may also borrow in some cases to increase the size of their bank balances; in other cases, they may hold all or part of the proceeds of borrowing as deposits prior to subsequent investment expenditures. Such borrowing is prompted by the so-called finance motive and may be regarded as part of the increase in demand for money to hold—a part of the hoarding demand (*H*).

2/The growth of demand for consumer credit constitutes one of the outstanding financial developments since World War I. Largely liquidated during World War II, consumer credit rose from $5.7 billion at the end of 1945 to $121.3 billion at the end of May 1970. Four-fifths of the total was composed of installment credit to finance the purchase of automobiles and other consumer durable goods; the remainder was noninstallment credit in the forms of single-payment loans, charge accounts, and service credit.[3] Expenditures financed by the foregoing categories of consumer credit are classified as consumption expenditures in the national income accounts, and it is usual to treat a net increase in such credit as dissaving, and a net decrease as personal saving. The demand schedule for consumer credit is rather inelastic to the interest rate, at least within the range of actual rate changes. Most consumers who buy on credit are said to be influenced more by the size of monthly installment payments than by the interest rate which is only one of several elements determining installments. Nevertheless, there is doubtless some degree of interest-elasticity; that is, with income constant, consumers will borrow somewhat more as the interest cost declines.

Like businesses, consumers may also desire to hold larger money balances in relation to expected expenditures; if so, this becomes part of the hoarding demand for money (*H*). To some extent, consumers may borrow money for this purpose, but they may also express their desires by holding back on the spending of income, and by selling assets to build up money balances.

[2]*Economic Report of the President* (February 1970), p. 248.
[3]*Federal Reserve Bulletin* (July 1970), p. A 54.

Consumer outlays for residential construction are classified in the national income accounts as a component of private investment. They give rise to large amounts of mortgage borrowing. For example, mortgage debt on 1-4-family houses rose from $18.6 billion at the end of 1945 to $268.7 billion in the first quarter of 1970—an average annual increase of $10 billion. Most of these loans are payable in installments over long periods of between 10 and 30 years. Consequently, changes in the interest rate materially affect the total cost of the property, and also make an appreciable difference in the size of installment payments. The demand schedule of borrowers is, therefore, considerably more interest-elastic than that of borrowers of short-term consumer credit.

3/Since the early 1930s, governments—federal, state, and local—have greatly expanded their services and have assumed a much more important position in the market for loanable funds. When government purchases of goods and services (G) exceeds tax receipts less transfer payments, or net receipts (T_n), a budgetary deficit exists, and borrowing is necessary to cover the deficit. This has happened to the federal government in 31 of the 40 years during the period 1930-1970. During World War II, huge deficits were incurred, ranging from $19 billion to $54 billion in the consolidated cash budget. As additional evidence, it may be noted that the average annual increase of federal debt during the period 1950-1969 was $3.3 billion.[4] State and local securities were outstanding in the amount of $128.6 billion at the end of 1968, and increased on the average by $6.0 billion annually.

The demand schedule of the federal government for loanable funds is inelastic to changes in the interest rate. The amount of the federal deficit arises out of broad policies with respect to expenditure programs and revenue programs on which the interest rate has little bearing. This is particularly true of wartime deficits, but it is almost equally so in peacetime when, for example, a deficit may be planned to spur business recovery or to encourage economic growth. However, the demand schedule of state and local governments for loanable funds is generally held to be moderately interest-elastic. Like business firms, these governments postpone some construction projects if borrowing costs are high, and tend to move forward with certain projects when borrowing costs are low.

Looking back, it may be noted that all components of the demand schedule, with the exception of the federal government, are interest-elastic in varying degrees. Therefore, the aggregate demand schedule may reasonably be drawn with a moderate downward slope as in figure 1.

For those who prefer to think in mathematical terms it may be helpful to summarize the components of the demand schedule (D_y) for loanable funds as follows:

$$D_y = I + \Delta H + C_b + (G - T_n)$$

[4]*Economic Report of the President*, op. cit., pp. 248; 256.

where I represents both new and replacement investment by businesses and consumers; ΔH represents changes in demands by businesses and consumers for money to hold (i.e., changes in hoarding); C_b represents demands for mortgage credit and consumer credit, usually classified as personal dissaving $(-S_p)$; and $(G - T_n)$ represents government deficits which must be covered by borrowing when $G > T_n$ [this factor may also be designated as government dissaving $(-S_g)$].

SUPPLY OF LOANABLE FUNDS

The aggregate supply schedule of loanable funds indicates the amounts that lenders and investors will offer at each of a series of interest rates. Again, the time period assumed is very short, say, one week, during which expectations with respect to incomes and prices remain unchanged. In general, they will offer more in the market as the interest rate rises, and will offer decreasing amounts as it declines. (See figure 1, p. 25, for a graphic presentation of the supply schedule, S_y.) The various components of supply are (1) savings (S) which divides into (a) personal savings (S_p), (b) business savings (S_b) and (c) government savings (S_g); and (2) changes in the amount of money (ΔM).

personal savings

As defined in the national income accounts, personal saving is measured by the difference between disposable personal income and personal outlays. In 1969, these amounts were $631.6 and $593.9 billion, respectively, so that net personal savings were $37.7 billion.[5] This should be interpreted as the amount of realized savings on the supply schedule at the interest rate prevailing in 1969. In relative terms, 94 percent of disposable income was spent on consumption and 6 percent was saved. Part of personal saving is invested directly in capital goods such as houses, part is invested directly in securities by individual savers, but the largest part enters the capital markets indirectly through intermediary financial institutions–commercial banks, savings and loan associations, savings banks, insurance companies, investment companies, and others.

The exact relation between personal savings and the interest rate at a given level of income is unknown, but most economists believe that it is a positive one. That is, savings will rise at least moderately as the reward in the form of interest increases, and will fall as the interest rate declines. However, people respond differently to changes in the interest rate. Most individuals are doubtless disposed to save more of their incomes as the rate rises because they are motivated to build up larger future incomes and larger estates. The savings

[5] *Federal Reserve Bulletin* (August 1970), p. A 69.

decisions of others are probably not appreciably affected by changes of the rate within the range of market fluctuations. But a third group tends to react in opposite fashion—that is, to save more as interest rates decline, and to save less as rates rise. They do not wish to curtail current consumption in order to build up future income and wealth beyond certain rather limited amounts. Because these goals can be achieved more quickly at high interest rates, they will save less and consume more when rates are high; in opposite fashion, they will save more and consume less when rates are low. This group, however, is believed to be much less important than the first one, with the net result that personal savings at given income levels are positively related to the interest rate.

business savings

Gross business savings (S_b) are made up of undistributed corporate profits and depreciation allowances. In 1969 they amounted to $23.9 billion and $78.9 billion, respectively and aggregated $102.8 billion.[6] These amounts should be viewed as business savings realized at the prevailing interest rate. The supply schedule of business savings has a moderately positive relation to the interest rate. Corporations tend to retain a larger proportion of net profits as the interest rate (cost of outside funds) rises, and to retain a smaller proportion as the rate declines. But the size of depreciation allowances has little or no relation to the interest rate. Instead, such allowances are based on the estimated economic life of each type of capital asset, adjusted to conform with federal income-tax regulations.

It should be noted that gross business savings is consistent with the concept of gross business investment (I) included on the demand side of the equation. Depreciation allowances are largely used to finance the replacement category of investment, whereas undistributed corporate profits are more closely associated with financing new business investment. While gross business savings are large, they are mainly invested directly in capital assets, and they are not generally offered in the loan market. In fact, nonfinancial businesses as a whole borrow in much greater amounts than they lend. Corporate lending takes place chiefly in connection with administration of liquid assets which are invested in short-term federal securities, finance-company paper, CDs, and other near-moneys.

government savings

Just as government deficits give rise to borrowing to cover them when government purchases (G) exceed net receipts (T_n), so governments may save

[6] Ibid., pp. A 68-69.

and repay indebtedness when net receipts exceed purchases of goods and services. The amount of savings (S_g) is then represented by aggregate government budget surpluses ($T_n - G$). In fact, net savings by the federal government occurred in only 9 of the 40 years during the period 1930-1970.[7] The schedule of supply of total government saving doubtless shows a moderate degree of positive interest-elasticity. This is attributable to state and local governments which are inclined to defer construction projects when costs of borrowing are high, and to proceed with programs more freely when borrowing costs are low. The state of the federal budget, however, bears little relation to the interest rate level.

change in the amount of money

The remaining component in the supply schedule of loanable funds is change in the stock of money, designated ΔM. The appropriate concept of money is the active money stock (M), consisting of currency outside banks and adjusted demand deposits of commercial banks. At midyear 1970, the aggregate stock of money (seasonably adjusted) in the United States was $203.6 billion—$47.8 billion of currency and $155.9 billion of demand deposits.[8] Changes in the amount of money are governed principally by the policies of the monetary authorities, operating through the legal-reserve position of member (commercial) banks. An additional dollar of reserve money released to the commercial-banking system by Federal Reserve Banks provides the basis for a several-fold expansion of bank loans and investments, and thereby of deposits. Under the spur of the profit motive, banks usually put excess reserves to work. If acceptable loans are not available, they purchase U.S., municipal, and other securities in the open market.

When a new increment is added to the money stock, the supply schedule of loanable funds is correspondingly increased, and the interest rate tends to decline. Conversely, when the money stock declines, the supply of loanable funds decreases, and the interest rate tends to rise. Economists usually treat changes in the stock of money as an autonomous supply factor which is inelastic to the interest rate. This is a logical procedure because monetary policies are largely designed to achieve broad economic goals such as full employment, growth, and a stable dollar. Implementation of these policies is likely to exert a strong, and often dominant, influence on the interest rate. For example, high interest rates—as in 1969—may reflect a restrictive monetary policy, and low rates—as in 1958 and 1961—may be, in large part, the result of an expansionary monetary policy.

Having identified the various components of the supply schedule of loanable funds, we are now in position to summarize as follows.

[7]*Economic Report of the President,* op. cit., p. 249.
[8]*Federal Reserve Bulletin* (August 1970), p. A 17.

$$S_y = S_p + S_b + S_g + \Delta M$$

where S_p represents gross personal saving; S_b refers to gross business savings, which is the sum of undistributed corporate profits and depreciation allowances; S_g represents aggregate budget surpluses of governments [i.e., $(T_n - G)$]; and ΔM represents changes in the stock of active money.

EQUATION OF DEMAND AND SUPPLY OF LOANABLE FUNDS

We are now in position to bring together the demand and supply sides of the equation:

Demand for loanable funds = Supply of loanable funds (at the market interest rate)

$$I + \Delta H + C_b + (G - T_n) = S_p + S_b + S_g, \text{ or } (T_n - G) + \Delta M$$

By disregarding the government sector and combining the components of saving, this equation may be simplified to read:

$$I + \Delta H + C_b = S + \Delta M$$

This equation, for purposes of emphasis, presents investment and saving, on a gross rather than a net basis. A rise of consumer borrowing on the demand side is considered to be the measure of dissaving.[9] The interaction of the demand and supply schedules produces an interest rate at which the realized demand equals the realized supply of loanable funds.

Attention should be called to an additional aspect of the loanable-funds market. While the equation presented above utilizes gross concepts, they are gross in the national product sense, but not in an overall transactions sense. That is, the schedules of demand and supply do not include the huge volume of trading in existing securities. The seller of U.S. securities may be thought of as a demander of loanable funds, and when he reinvests in other securities he becomes a supplier of loanable funds. But because sellers and buyers are always on opposite sides of such transactions, their influence cancels out, and they may be disregarded in the determination of the interest-rate level. However, purchases and sales of existing securities greatly influence the relationships of the many separate rates which are quoted in the money and capital market. For example, a material decrease in corporate and personal income-tax rates would doubtless

[9]If investment, saving, and hoarding are treated on a net basis, the equation may be further simplified to a form which is generally used: $I + \Delta H = S + \Delta M$.

lead to a significant shift of investment funds out of tax-exempt municipal securities and into federal and corporate issues. In this event, yields on municipals would tend to rise and yields on federal and corporate obligations would tend to decline.

THE LOANABLE-FUNDS THEORY

Despite the fact that the degree of interest-elasticity of the demand and supply schedules for loanable funds is unknown, it may be helpful to present them schematically in graphic form, as in figure 1. As previously developed, and as shown on the demand schedule (D_y), the amount of loanable funds demanded increases as the interest rate declines. Schedule (D_y) is the aggregate of the separate schedules for investment (I), hoarding (ΔH), and consumer borrowing (C_b). Also, as indicated on the supply schedule (S_y), the amount of loanable funds offered increases as the interest rate rises. Schedule (S_y) is the aggregate of the separate schedules for saving (S) and changes in the stock of money (ΔM). The interaction of schedules D_y and S_y results in equality of the amount of loanable funds demanded and offered (O_p) at the interest rate of r_0. At any higher rate supply exceeds demand, and at any lower rate demand exceeds supply. Thus, r_0 is the only equilibrium rate for schedules D_y and S_y. If the schedule of supply increases to S'_y while demand remains at D_y, the equilibrium amount of loanable funds becomes O_s and the rate drops to r_1. Again, if the schedule of demand rises to D'_y while supply remains at S_y, the equilibrium amount is O_q and the rate rises to r_2.

The loanable-funds theory is usually known as a *partial-equilibrium* theory. While for succeeding short-planning periods the market for loanable funds may be in equilibrium, it is unlikely that equilibrium will also exist in the economy as a whole. For this to be the case, planned saving would have to be equal to planned investment at the market interest rate. Because it would be a coincidence if all these conditions were realized at the same time, it is likely that the seeds of change in income, savings, investment, and interest rates are sprouting in the current period even though equilibrium exists in the loanable-funds market.

Further explanation of the hoarding factor (ΔH) is desirable at this point. The concept refers to the disposition of businesses and consumers to hold a greater part of their assets in the form of money at the same interest rate. Such a development may occur when there is the prospect of a decline in the prices of commodities, real estate, common stocks, and bonds, and when there is uncertainty about future employment and income. With an increase in the hoarding demand for money (ΔH), the demand schedule for loanable funds shifts to the right and tends to raise interest rates. On a given demand schedule for loanable funds (D_y), the hoarding demand is interest-elastic—that is, people desire to hold more money as the rate declines, and less as the rate rises.

1 DETERMINATION OF THE INTEREST RATE.

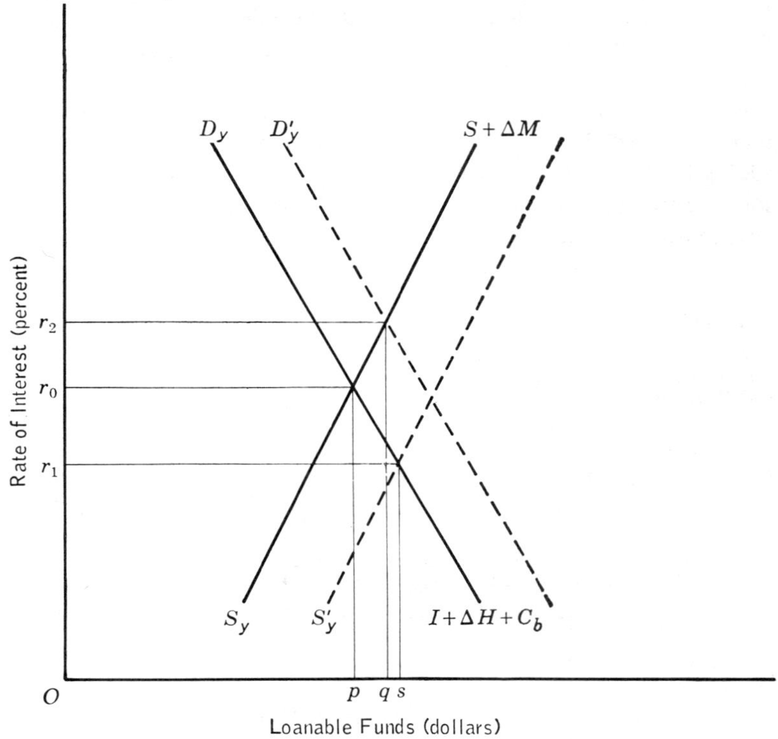

In the event that the hoarding demand declines—that is, businesses and consumers wish to hold a smaller part of their assets in the form of money—ΔH becomes a negative factor. This development may occur when people believe that the prices of commodities, real estate, and common stocks will rise, and when there is greater confidence in sustained or increasing future income. In the equation, ΔH may be treated negatively ($-\Delta H$) as an increase in the supply schedule (S_y) or positively (ΔH) as an increase in the demand schedule (D_y). For the sake of simplicity, ΔH is included only on the demand side of the equation.

Additional comment should also be made about the ΔM factor. The short-run effect of an increase of M is to lower interest rates, but the actual long-run result may be just the opposite. In the short-run, an increase of money may be provided by the Fed (central bank) without appreciably affecting the demand schedule for loan money, with a resultant decline in market rates. But if an expansionary monetary policy is pursued vigorously over a period of time, an inflationary psychology may develop in the minds of businessmen and consumers. Commodity prices may continue to rise materially when monetary demand for goods and services exceeds the economy's productive capacity. Under these circumstances, the demand schedule for loanable funds rises faster than the supply schedule, and consequently, market interest rates increase. When the idea becomes firmly implanted that the general price level will continue to rise substantially, all groups—businesses, consumers, and labor—attempt to hedge their positions. In particular, lenders discount the expected rise of prices by adding it to the rate at which they are willing to lend. A good illustration of this sort of situation is the period 1965-1969, when interest rates rose to the highest level in over a century.

REFERENCES

Board of Governors of the Federal Reserve System, *The Federal Reserve System: Purposes and Functions* (5th ed.; Washington, D.C., 1963), chaps. V, VI.

Conard, Joseph W., *An Introduction to the Theory of Interest* (Berkeley: University of California Press, 1959).

Fisher, Irving, *The Theory of Interest* (New York: Macmillan, 1930).

Homer, Sidney, *A History of Interest Rates* (New Brunswick, N.J.: Rutgers University Press, 1963).

Keynes, John M., *The General Theory of Employment, Interest and Money* (New York: Harcourt Brace Jovanovich, 1936), chaps. 13, 14.

Leigh, A. H., "Supply and Demand Analysis of Interest Rates," *American Economic Review*, XLI (September 1951), pp. 579-602.

Robertson, D. H., "Alternative Theories of the Rate of Interest," *Economic Journal*, 47 (1937), pp. 428 ff.

Sargent, T. J., "Commodity Price Expectations and the Interest Rate," *Quarterly Journal of Economics*, 83 (February 1969), pp. 127-140.

Tsiang, S. C., "Liquidity Preference and Loanable Funds Theories, Multiplier and Velocity Analyses: A Synthesis," *American Economic Review*, XLVI (September 1956), pp. 539-564.

3

sources and uses of reserve money

Additional light is cast on the supply and demand theory of the interest rate by analysis of the relation of Federal Reserve Banks and commercial banks to the money market. The Board of Governors and the Reserve Banks play a key role by determining the amount and cost of reserve money. They possess the power to increase, decrease, or just maintain member-bank legal reserves in accordance with current monetary policy. As previously stated, creation of more bank reserves provides the basis of a several-fold expansion of earning assets and deposits of commercial banks, whereas destruction of reserves may lead to multiple contraction of bank credit. As the dominant type of short-term credit retailers, commercial banks also hold a central position in the lending process—between the Reserve Banks as ultimate suppliers of reserve money and the mass of borrowers of all kinds. In connection with analyzing the roles of Federal Reserve Banks and commercial banks, it will also be necessary to consider other money-market factors such as gold movements, currency in circulation, and Treasury operations.

THE RESERVE-MONEY EQUATION

general nature

In order to facilitate more precise analysis of supply and demand factors in the money market, the Board of Governors developed a summary of these factors in the mid-1920s, presented in the form of a balanced statement, and here designated as the *reserve-money equation*. This equation is derived from the condition statement of the Federal Reserve Banks and from the Treasury circulation statement of United States money. Table 3-1 gives this equation as of January 1961 and January 1970, together with the changes that

TABLE 3-1 / THE RESERVE-MONEY EQUATION: SOURCES AND USES OF RESERVE MONEY (millions of dollars; monthly averages of daily figures)

Source and Use Items	January 1961	January 1970	Changes Increasing Member-Bank Reserves	Changes Decreasing Member-Bank Reserves
Sources of reserve funds:				
Total Reserve Bank credit	(28,484)	(60,833)	(32,349)[a]	
U.S. securities	26,942	56,273	29,331	
Discounts and advances	58	965	907	
Float and other	1,484	3,595	2,111	
Gold stock	17,567	11,296[b]		6,271
Treasury currency	5,401	6,856	1,455	
Total sources	51,452	78,985		
Uses of reserve funds:				
Currency in circulation	32,265	52,722		20,457
Treasury cash holdings	411	655		244
Treasury deposits with Federal Reserve Banks	482	1,206		724
Other deposits with Federal Reserve Banks[c]	638	812		174
Other Federal Reserve accounts[d]	941	0	941	
Member-bank deposits with Federal Reserve Banks	16,715	23,580		6,875
Total uses	51,452	78,985		
Member-bank cash reserves	2,600	5,278		
Total member-bank cash reserves	19,315	28,858		(+9,543)
Required legal reserves	(18,570)	(28,692)		(+10,122)
Excess legal reserves	(745)	(166)		(−579)
Total changes increasing member-bank reserves			34,745	
Total changes decreasing member-bank reserves				27,870
Net increase in member-bank reserves				6,875
				34,745
Addenda:				
Net surplus reserves (+) or net borrowed reserves (−) ("Excess reserves" less "Discounts and advances")	+687	−799		
Treasury bill rate (3 mos.)	2.24%	7.87%		
Commercial-paper rate (4-6 mos.)	2.98%	8.78%		

[a] Figures in parentheses are omitted in balancing the equation.

[b] Includes Special Drawing Rights on International Monetary Fund.

[c] Includes foreign central bank and nonmember bank deposits.

[d] "Other liabilities and capital" less "Other Federal Reserve" assets; beginning April 16, 1969, these items are included separately.

Source: *Federal Reserve Bulletin* (July 1961), pp. 790-791; (August 1970), pp. A 4-5.

occurred between the two dates. It will be noted that the sum of the sources of reserve funds (Reserve Bank credit, gold stock, and Treasury currency) equals the sum of the use factors (currency in circulation, Treasury cash, Treasury and nonmember deposits with the Reserve Banks, other Federal Reserve accounts, and member-bank reserve balances). In January 1961, this aggregate was $51.5 billion. Also, it follows that the change in any one item between two dates can be accounted for by the difference between the sum of changes that increase the given item and the sum of changes that decrease it. For analytical purposes, the changes are usually balanced in terms of member-bank deposits with Fed Banks. In the table, the sum of the item changes increasing reserves ($34,745 million) between January 1961 and January 1970 exceeds the sum of changes decreasing reserves by $6,875 million, thus accounting for the actual increase that took place in "Member-bank deposits with Federal Reserve Banks."

source items

The common thread uniting the source items—Reserve Bank credit, gold stock, and Treasury currency—is that increases in these items tend to augment member-bank reserves while decreases tend to reduce them.

Reserve Bank Credit / Reserve Bank credit is here viewed from the asset side of the balance sheet. When the Reserve Banks increase their credit in any form, whether security holdings, discounts, or float, reserve money is created and, in the absence of offsetting changes, member-bank reserves are built up by a corresponding amount. In opposite fashion, a reduction of Reserve Bank credit tends to extinguish member-bank reserves.

Since the early 1930s and particularly since World War II, the dominant earning asset of the Reserve Banks has been U.S. securities. These securities are purchased under direction of the Federal Open-Market Committee, and are held in the joint investment account. The total amount, type, and maturity distribution of this portfolio reflects the role of open-market operations as an instrument of Federal Reserve policy.

Discounts and advances are made almost entirely to member banks with legal reserve deficiencies. Member banks borrow principally on the basis of their promissory notes secured by U.S. securities. However, they may use other acceptable assets as collateral, or they may re-discount eligible promissory notes of customers. While discounts and advances constitute a small part of total Reserve Bank credit, they occupy a highly significant position in the money market. This follows from their marginal character, representing as they do the borrowed portion of member-bank legal reserves. Variations in the amount and distribution of borrowings at the Reserve Banks sensitively register the balance between forces of demand and supply of bank credit.

Technically speaking, the float is the excess of *cash items in process of collection* over *deferred availability cash items* for all Reserve Banks—an amount that usually fluctuates between $2.5 and $3.5 billion. The time schedule according to which member banks receive legal-reserve credit for checks sent to Reserve Banks for collection is, to the extent of the float, in favor of member banks. That is, on the average, the Reserve Banks give reserve credit before actual collection of checks from drawee banks. In reality, this represents a noninterest-bearing loan of reserve money to member banks. The amount of float—depending on the volume of checks presented for collection and the speed of the collection process—experiences wide short-term variations which register an intramonth range of up to $2 billion. The peak of float comes near midmonth, due to the prevailing practice of paying most bills during the second week, and the low point usually occurs near the first of the month. These variations, together with day-to-day changes associated with holidays and fortuitous events, present a continuous problem to Federal Reserve authorities in maintaining the desired condition of the money market. Compensating adjustments are made largely through open-market operations in U.S. securities. The remaining items of Reserve Bank credit—other security holdings and due from foreign banks—are ordinarily inconsequential for the present purpose.

Gold Stock / The U.S. monetary gold stock is owned entirely by the Treasury. The great bulk of it is represented by the gold-certificate reserves of the Reserve Banks, but a small part consists of gold against which no certificates have been issued—gold held against U.S. Notes (greenbacks), and gold in the Treasury's General Fund. Changes in the gold stock take place as a result of (1) gold transactions with foreign countries, (2) purchases and sales of domestic gold, and (3) other occasional influences such as devaluation of the gold dollar at the end of January 1934. The principal factors that govern gold imports and exports are summarized in the country's international balance of payments. Incidentally, it should be noted that gold held under earmark, or in safekeeping for foreigners, is not part of the gold stock, and that gold owned by the Treasury but held in safekeeping abroad is part of our gold stock. Thus, the gold stock may be increased by foreigners' release of earmarked gold that is already in this country (or increase of our earmarked gold abroad) as well as by physical gold imports; it may be decreased in opposite fashion. Purchases of domestic gold arise mainly from domestic mining operations, and domestic sales are largely for industrial consumption, including jewelry, plate, and dentistry. Before World War II, the gold stock was by far the largest source of reserve money, but since the war, Reserve Bank credit has become the principal source. Irrespective of relative size, the gold stock in a gold-standard country constitutes reserve money in a more ultimate sense than other reserve moneys.

Treasury Currency / Treasury currency outstanding is composed of the gross amounts of the various kinds of currency for which the Treasury is directly responsible—the permanent elements of which are silver dollars, subsidiary silver and minor coin, and U.S. Notes. It should be mentioned that neither Federal Reserve Notes nor gold certificates are a part of Treasury currency; the former are liabilities of the Reserve Banks and the latter represent the Treasury's gold stock. The bulk of Treasury currency outstanding is *in circulation*—that is, it is outside the Treasury and the Reserve Banks in the hands of individuals and businesses, including commercial banks. But a small part of each of the components of Treasury currency is always in the hands of the Treasury and the Reserve Banks—*outstanding* but not in circulation. Changes in Treasury currency have the same immediate effect on member-bank reserves as changes in the gold stock, but short-term changes in this item do not ordinarily exert a significant influence.

use-items

The use-items in the equation answer the question: Where are the reserve funds represented by the source items to be found? Currency in circulation accounts for about three-fifths of the total. Four relatively small items—Treasury cash, Treasury deposits with Reserve Banks, nonmember deposits with Reserve Banks, and other Federal Reserve accounts—represent 5 to 7 percent, and the remaining one-third resides in member-bank reserve balances at Reserve Banks. Increases of use-factors (other than member-bank reserves) tend to reduce member-bank reserves; decreases of use-factors augment member-bank reserves.

Currency in Circulation / Individuals and businesses, including commercial banks, decide from day to day, the amount of currency they wish to hold. These decisions taken together determine the amount of currency in circulation—that is, currency outside the Treasury and the Reserve Banks. The dominant current component at midyear 1970 was Federal Reserve Notes which constituted 88 percent of the total. Fractional coin accounted for another 10 percent, and the remaining 2 percent was distributed among silver dollars, U.S. Notes and currency in process of retirement. Currency in circulation is the principal factor using reserve money. Its variations, associated mainly with the volume of small payments in retail trade, are large. Between autumn and Christmas, the outflow of currency is in the vicinity of $2 billion, after which it returns during January and February. Sizable changes occur from day to day, particularly over holidays, and there is an underlying upward trend occasioned by the growth of retail trade and national income. Compensating adjustments, principally by open-market operations, must be made by the Fed in order to maintain the desired member-bank reserve position.

When the needs of trade draw more currency into circulation, member-bank reserves tend to be reduced by an equivalent amount as the Reserve Banks charge members' reserve accounts for currency sent to them.

However, due to the associated reduction of member-bank deposits and the release of required reserves, the decrease in excess legal reserves (or the needed increase in borrowed reserves) is somewhat less than the increase of currency in circulation. In opposite fashion, when the need for currency subsides, it is deposited in member banks whose reserves tend to rise by an equal amount. But excess reserves of member banks increase (or borrowed reserves decrease) by a somewhat smaller amount because required reserves against the new deposits must be provided.

treasury cash

In a sense, Treasury cash may be thought of as the Treasury's till money. It includes small amounts of all types of Treasury currency augmented by holdings of Federal Reserve Notes. In addition, it includes a small part of the gold stock against which gold certificates have not been issued. When Treasury cash increases, member-bank reserves tend to be reduced by the same amount. But when the Treasury pays its bills with these funds, member-bank reserves tend to increase. In fact, since 1953, the amount of Treasury cash has been quite stable, and changes in this item have been a minor influence on member-bank reserves. But this has not always been the case.

At irregular intervals during the period 1934-1953, changes in Treasury cash became a major factor in the money market. The first large change came as an incident to devaluation of the dollar at the end of January 1934, when the Treasury price of gold was raised from the traditional price of $20.67 to $35 an ounce. The gold stock was thereby written up overnight by $2,806 million. Because gold certificates were not issued at the time against this new increment, Treasury cash rose correspondingly—from $355 million to $3,161 million. In the three years that followed, over $800 million of gold certificates were issued against this increment in connection with operations of the $2 billion Gold Stabilization Fund created at the time of devaluation. When the Treasury deposited these gold certificates with the Reserve Banks, Treasury cash was reduced correspondingly and the Treasury's Stabilization Fund account at the Reserve Banks was increased. Then when the Treasury drew on this account to make payments—and not until then—member-bank deposits and reserves were increased.

Another notable increase in Treasury cash took place between December 1936 and February 1938, when the Treasury held new gold acquired in an inactive account and did not issue gold certificates against it. Under this *gold sterilization* program, designed to prevent the large inflow of gold from increasing member-bank reserves, Treasury cash rose by $1.3 billion to a peak of $3.6 billion in early 1938. When the program was abandoned in the spring of 1938, gold certificates were issued against this inactive gold and were deposited with the Reserve Banks. This reduced Treasury cash and increased Treasury deposits without any *immediate* effect on member-bank reserves. But as the Treasury drew on its deposit account in making payments, both deposits and legal reserves of member banks were increased.

The gold profit from devaluation was in large part utilized by November 1953—the bulk of it for two special purposes. The first was for payment of the gold portion—nearly $700 million—of the U.S. capital subscription to the International Monetary Fund (IMF). This payment was made in the spring of 1947. An additional gold subscription of $344 million was made to the IMF in June 1959. The second purpose was to provide needed funds for the Treasury when the legal debt limit precluded further borrowing. Gold certificates to the amount of $500 million were issued and deposited at the Reserve Banks in November 1953, with a corresponding reduction of Treasury cash. By midyear 1970, gold remaining in the Treasury cash account was only about $111 million.[1]

Treasury Deposits with Federal Reserve Banks / These deposits represent the Treasury's active checking account. Practially all disbursements are made from this account and almost all revenues and borrowed funds sooner or later flow into it. This account should not be confused with the Treasury's balances maintained with commercial-bank depositaries where most of its current balance is kept in tax and loan accounts. For example, at midyear 1970, Treasury deposits at Reserve Banks amounted to $1,005 million, while its balances with commercial and savings banks were $6,929 million.[2]

When the Treasury builds up its deposits at the Reserve Banks, either by transfer from depositary commercial banks or by borrowing from private investors, member-bank reserves are correspondingly reduced, if other factors remain unchanged. In reverse fashion, when the Treasury draws down its balance with Reserve Banks, member-bank reserves are increased. Therefore, in order to forestall serious disturbances to the money market, systematic cooperative efforts are made by the Treasury and the Reserve Banks to prevent wide variations in this account. In practice, these efforts have usually held this item within the $500-$1,300 million range since World War II, with a consequent reduction in the magnitude of offsetting open-market operations required to maintain desired money-market conditions. Thus, while changes in Treasury deposits with Reserve Banks have not been used significantly to influence member-bank reserves, they possess a large potentiality for this purpose and can be a focal point for Treasury cooperation or noncooperation with Federal Reserve policies.

Other Deposits with Federal Reserve Banks / All deposits held by the Reserve Banks besides those of the Treasury and member banks are classified as

[1] *Treasury Bulletin* (July 1970), p. 16.
[2] Ibid.

other deposits. The most important components of this account are (1) deposits of foreign central banks and governments and (2) nonmember-bank deposits which are maintained for clearing and collection purposes. The first component was relatively stable during the 1960s, with amounts usually between $150 and $250 million. But it has the potentiality of wide variations, especially in view of the huge volume of short-term dollar claims of foreigners which exceeded $42 billion at midyear 1970. The second component has varied more widely since 1959, ordinarily in the range of $400 to $850 million.[3]

When other deposits with Reserve Banks increase, member-bank reserves decrease unless offset by other factors. This results from the fact that this account is typically built up by depositing checks drawn on member banks. In opposite fashion, when the other deposits at Reserve Banks decline, member-bank reserves tend to increase because the checks drawn are usually deposited in member banks; or if not, the released reserves find their way indirectly to member banks. Thus, the Reserve Banks must be continuously alert in order to offset, by open-market operations, the variations that take place in this account; otherwise, these variations would cause easier or tighter money markets than currently desired.

interpretations

With definitions of items completed, we are now in position to undertake a preliminary interpretation of Table 3-1, which shows the amounts and changes in sources and uses of reserve money between the 1961 recession and January 1970, a high point of interest rates. It should be recalled that member-bank reserves, in terms of which changes are balanced, rise as a result of increases in reserve source items and as a result of decreases in reserve use-items; they decline as a consequence of decreases in source items and of increases in use-items. Between January 1961 and January 1970, the sum of the factors causing an increase of member-bank reserves exceeded the sum of the factors causing a decrease in reserves by $6,875 million—which corresponds with the actual change measured directly. While five items contributed to the increase, most of it came from the increase in holdings of U.S. securities. The principal offsetting items were an increase of $20,457 million of currency in circulation and a decrease of $6,271 million in the gold stock.

While total member-bank reserves rose $6,875 million, liquidity as measured by legal-reserve position deteriorated materially. Discounts and advances (borrowed reserves) increased $907 million and excess reserves declined $579 million—a combined change of $1,486 million. This was reflected in the market by a sharp rise of the rate on Treasury bills—from 2.98 to 8.78 percent; other rates rose in rough correspondence. The tighter money market was a result

[3]*Federal Reserve Bulletin* (August 1970), p. A 77.

of the Federal Reserve policy of restraint designed to check inflationary expansion combined with strong demands for loanable funds. The restrictive policy was implemented in the main by holding back on the release of reserve money through purchase of U.S. securities and by rationing discounts and advances. The additional currency drawn into circulation reduced bank reserves dollar for dollar, and the rise of about $150 billion in member-bank deposits caused an increase of $10.1 billion in required reserves.

While Table 3-1 focuses attention on the decline in member-bank liquidity as measured by legal-reserve position, it does not directly show diminished liquidity of bank earning assets. Member-bank holdings of U.S. Securities declined almost $12 billion, the bulk of which was short-term liquidity reserves, whereas their loans and other securities increased $138 billion. Stated differently, the ratio of cash assets and U.S. securities to total loans and investments declined from 54 percent in January 1961 to 32 percent in January 1970. This marked deterioration of liquidity of bank earning assets reenforced the decline in legal-reserve liquidity, and their combined influence was the immediate cause of the sharp rise of interest rates.

interrelationships of items

A firmer understanding of the reserve-money equation may be gained by further consideration of the interrelationships of the various factors.

1/It should be emphasized that member-bank reserves change in response to the combined influence of *all* other included items. Each factor is exerting an influence at all times even though it remains the same and even though the principal changes focus on a few items. Therefore, one is never justified in concluding that member-bank reserves will change in a particular direction or amount due to a change in just one factor. For example, with reference to Table 3-1, after noting only that the gold stock decreased $6,271 million and that currency in circulation increased $20,457 million, it would be erroneous to conclude that member-bank reserves declined. In fact, as a result of changes in U.S. securities and other factors, member-bank reserves actually increased. To carry this point further, one cannot infer that an increase or reduction of security holdings by the Reserve Banks signals a particular credit policy. Indeed, their portfolio may be reduced at times in the presence of an easy-money policy in order to compensate for some other change that would create an undesirable degree of monetary ease, such as a reduction in reserve requirements; on other occasions, their portfolio may be increased in the face of a policy of restraint in order to modify the effects of other factors.

2/Stated in terms of its dominant factors, the reserve-money equation becomes: Reserve Bank credit + gold stock = currency in circulation + member-bank reserves. Thus, the other five or six less important items are omitted. For rough approximation of changes, this simplified approach often tells the main story. But for precise analysis, it is necessary to consider all items. Each of the normally less important items may change significantly on occasion.

3/When there is an appreciable amount of member-bank borrowed reserves, changes in Reserve Bank discounts and advances and holdings of U.S. securities may largely offset one another in the short term, with the result that the change in *total* Reserve Bank credit is relatively small. That is, new reserves released by Reserve Bank security purchases will, in the absence of other factor-changes, be used mainly to repay member-bank borrowings; and reserves extinguished by Reserve Bank sales of securities may be replaced in large part, although not entirely, by member-bank borrowings. Thus, borrowing provides a channel through which member banks may secure needed reserves on their *own initiative,* but subject to Federal Reserve discretion as to both amount and cost. However, the form in which Reserve Bank credit is extended–whether as discounts and advances or as U.S. security holdings–has an important bearing on money-market conditions. This point is developed more fully in Chapter 4.

4/There are close interrelationships among the source factor, Treasury currency outstanding, and the use factors–currency in circulation, Treasury cash holdings, and Treasury deposits with Reserve Banks. For example, assume that the Treasury receives $1 billion of fractional coin from the U.S. mint. This would increase Treasury currency and Treasury cash holdings by an equal amount. Now assume that the Treasury deposits $950 million in coin at the Federal Reserve Banks. This would increase Treasury deposits with Federal Reserve Banks and would reduce Treasury cash holdings by the same amount, leaving a net increase of $50 million in this account. Assume further that the Fed Banks, in response to member-bank requests for $950 million in coin, send the currency to them. This transaction would reduce Member-bank deposits with Fed Banks and would increase currency in circulation, which means currency outside the Treasury and the Federal Reserve Banks.

5/Gold imports and exports have a very close connection with both member-bank reserves and foreign deposits with Federal Reserve Banks. Gold imports are made in two principal ways: (a) through large commercial banks and (b) directly by the Federal Reserve Banks. In the first case, member-bank reserves are increased almost immediately by a corresponding amount when member banks sell the gold to the Treasury which pays by a check on its account with the Reserve Banks. This account is rebuilt when the Treasury deposits gold certificates in the amount of purchased gold. Thus, upon completion of intermediate transactions, the accounts of the Reserve Banks show equal increases of gold-certificate reserves and of member-bank reserve deposits. In the second case, assume that the Bank of England ships $10 million of gold bullion to the Federal Reserve Bank of New York for deposit in its account. The Bank then turns the gold over to the Treasury and receives gold certificates (or gold-certificate credit) in exchange. Up to this point, member-bank reserves have not been affected. This happens later, if at all, when the Bank of England draws on its account to make some payment–say, for $10 million of

Treasury bills. When this check is collected by the member bank in which it is deposited, foreign deposits with Federal Reserve Banks are reduced by $10 million and member-bank cash reserves are increased by $10 million. Gold exports would have just the opposite effect on the positions of the Treasury, Reserve Banks, and member banks.

6/It is sometimes asked: If deposits of Reserve Banks are in the equation, why are Federal Reserve Notes not also included? The answer is that Federal Reserve Notes are included under Currency in circulation and are, in fact, the dominant component of that account.

7/Another question that arises is: What is the relation of member-bank earning assets and deposits to the reserve-money equation? The principal point of contact is through member-bank reserves. For example, with reference again to Table 3-1, the expansion of member-bank earning assets between 1961 and 1970 created about $150 billion of added deposits which, in turn, raised required legal reserves by over $10 billion. This constituted a deterioration of legal-reserve liquidity which had to be met, in the absence of other factor changes, by reducing excess reserves or by borrowing at the Reserve Banks. Thus, demand for bank credit was one of the important causes of the sharp rise in interest rates between the two dates.

8/The point should be underscored that the Fed does not have direct control over most of the factors in the equation, including gold stock, Treasury currency, currency in circulation, Treasury cash, Treasury deposits, and foreign and other deposits. The gold stock is determined, in the main, by the balance of international payments, gold production, industrial gold consumption, gold hoarding, and the price of gold as fixed by Congress. Treasury currency, cash, and deposits are in the hands of Congress and the Treasury, with only advisory influence from the Fed. The amount of currency in circulation is determined chiefly by decisions of individuals and businesses with respect to the part of their liquid assets they wish to hold in this form. These decisions ordinarily rest on the prospective amount of small payments to be made in the near future, and on the money habits of the community. Other deposits belong to foreign central banks and governments and to nonmember commercial banks—all of which make independent decisions concerning the size of their deposit accounts. Thus, the Fed's influence, if any, on the foregoing items is indirect and remote.

Federal Reserve policies and actions are brought to bear directly only on the components of Reserve Bank credit and on member-bank reserves. Changes in Reserve Bank holdings of U.S. securities is the most important instrument of Federal Reserve policy. While member banks take the initiative in borrowing, the Fed significantly influences these decisions by changing the discount rate, rationing Reserve Bank advances, and governing the amount of borrowed reserves by open-market operations and member-bank reserve requirements. The amount of Reserve Bank credit released as *float* has not been, and is not likely to be, employed as a means of giving effect to monetary policy.

Theoretically, this factor could be so utilized by changing the time schedule for checks in process of collection. But such changes are not administratively practicable, and whatever the schedule, the Reserve Banks always strive to process and collect transit items in the shortest possible time. Member-bank reserves are directly affected when the Board of Governors changes legal-reserve requirements. In the event that excess legal reserves are substantial and borrowed reserves are nominal, a change of reserve requirements alters only the distribution of member-bank reserves between the required and excess categories, with no change in aggregate amount. But if borrowed reserves are large, a rise (fall) in reserve requirements tends to cause an almost equal increase (decrease) in discounts and advances and in total member-bank reserves; the influence on excess reserves is small because under these conditions they approach a working minimum in the banking system.

NET RESERVE POSITION OF MEMBER BANKS

Money-market analysts often employ an extension or refinement of the foregoing analysis which may be designated as the *net reserve position of member banks,* and may be defined as *excess (legal) reserves minus discounts and advances (borrowed reserves).* When excess reserves exceed discounts and advances, the difference is called *net reserve surplus;* and when excess reserves are exceeded by discounts and advances, the difference is labeled *net reserve deficit,* or *net borrowed reserves.* Thus, net reserve position may be thought of as a single continuous statistical series with positive and negative values measured above and below zero. Net reserve deficit should not be confused with *legal-reserve deficiency* which means that reserves, usually of individual banks, are less than legally required reserves. Existence of a net reserve deficit does not imply that actual reserves are less than required reserves; instead, it means only that reserves borrowed from Reserve Banks exceed excess reserves for member banks as a whole. In recent years, the term "free reserves," which is identical with "net reserve position," has received wide usage. Positive free reserve, then, corresponds with net reserve surplus and negative free reserve is the same concept as net reserve deficit.[4]

The advantage of this refinement in analysis is that the condition of the money market is reflected at all times in a single summary factor—net reserve position. Without this, the analyst must always deal with two separate factors—borrowed reserves and excess reserves. In times of tight money, analysis must be mainly in terms of borrowings at Reserve Banks as excess reserves vary little from the operating minimum of member banks. In periods of easy money, analysis must be chiefly in terms of excess reserves as borrowed reserves are

[4]This author prefers the terms "net reserve position," "net reserve surplus," and "net reserve deficit" because their connotations are somewhat more precise and descriptive than free reserves, positive and negative.

nominal. When conditions within the limits of moderate ease and moderate firmness prevail, analysis should accord proper weight to both factors. Thus, the net-reserve-position approach applies equally well to all money-market conditions, and the particular situation under review can be delineated by interpretation. With reference to Table 3-1, the analyst can summarize the net effect of factor changes between 1961 and 1970 by pointing out that the net reserve position (legal-reserve liquidity) deteriorated by $1,486 million—the sum of the rise of $907 million in borrowed reserves and the decline of $579 million in excess reserves, and that this reflected an increased need for bank reserves against a limited amount, which brought about a sharp rise in interest rates.

Despite the advantages of the net-reserve-position approach, its use involves a definite analytical hazard. As in all averages, details are necessarily submerged, with the result that highly significant facts are often concealed. For one thing, the distribution of excess reserves may be as important as their amount. When they are held by large city banks, strong and immediate actions are taken to convert them to earning assets with accompanying downward pressures on rates. But when they are held by small- and intermediate-size banks, conversion to earning assets is likely to be a much slower process. Indeed, in many cases, it may not take place at all, so that hundreds of small pools of excess reserves (Federal funds) are withheld from affecting the money market. For another, the distribution of Reserve Bank discounts and advances among member banks has considerable bearing on their market influence. In general, large banks react more sensitively to borrowed reserves than small- and intermediate-size banks. That is, $100 million of discounts and advances of the former would have a materially greater effect on money rates than the same amount advanced to smaller banks. Still further, the reactions of the market to changes in net reserve position are not the same throughout the range between the extremes of large excess reserves and large borrowed reserves. This point requires further discussion under the next heading.

Some confusion in regard to net reserve position is implied in a question which is frequently posed: Does this factor summarize the conditions of supply or the conditions of demand for reserve money? At first glance, one may be inclined to say, "Supply, of course," because the term "reserve position" seems to connote supply. But further reflection reveals that the correct answer is that net reserve position is a single index of *both supply and demand* conditions. It is the net resultant of relationships of all source and use items in the reserve-money equation; demand factors and supply factors all have equal opportunities to impart their effects.

net reserve position and interest rates

The close inverse correlation between member-bank net reserve position and the interest-rate level is brought out by figure 2 which compares changes in

2 MONEY RATES AND THE RESERVE POSITION OF MEMBER BANKS, 1950-1970 (monthly averages of daily figures).
Source: *Federal Reserve Bulletin,* various issues

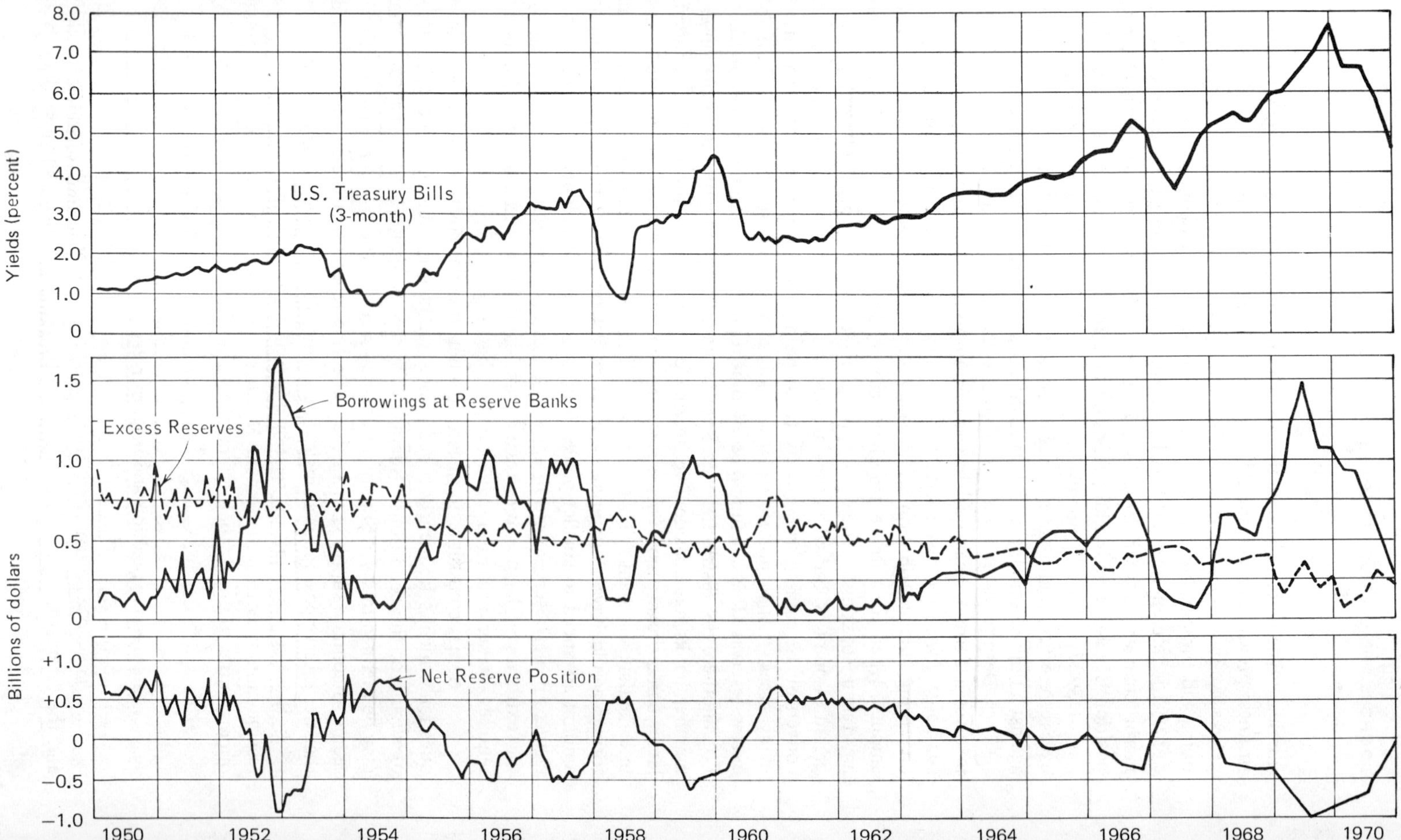

reserves and rates during the period 1950-1970. Rates are represented in the top panel by yields on three-month Treasury bills. Net reserve position, shown in the bottom panel, is the difference between excess reserves and member-bank borrowings at Reserve Banks, presented in the middle panel. A net reserve surplus exists when the values of net reserve position are positive, and a net reserve deficit obtains when these values are negative.

A number of significant facts and relationships may be observed.

1/When a net reserve deficit exists, rates are relatively high, as in 1956-1957, 1959, and 1969.

2/When a net reserve surplus prevails, rates are relatively low, as in 1954, 1958, and 1961.

3/When the net reserve position is deteriorating, rates move upward. Good examples are mid-1954 to mid-1956 and mid-1958 to the last quarter of 1959.

4/When the net reserve position is improving, rates move downward, as in mid-1953 to mid-1954, the third quarter of 1957 to mid-1958, 1960, and 1967.

5/Member-bank borrowings are far more important than excess reserves in bringing about changes in net reserve position. This is a logical expectation when the money market is characterized by conditions ranging from moderate ease to extreme tightness. Banks strive to keep excess reserves at work, with the result that they do not rise much above the operating level for the banking system. But during conditions of pronounced ease in the market, the opposite relationship prevails; that is, variations in excess reserves are much greater than in borrowings at Reserve Banks and are the predominant factor of change in net reserve position. Member banks repay discounts and advances as reserves accumulate, and borrowings remain at a nominal amount until pressures on reserves again appear. The prime illustration of this situation is the period 1934-1941, when excess reserves fluctuated in a range between \$1 and \$7 billion whereas member-bank borrowings seldom rose above \$25 million.

6/It should be observed that the degree of sensitivity of money rates rises as the net reserve position tightens, and diminishes as reserves become more abundant. While this relationship has been present since World War II, more striking illustrations are provided by prewar years. During the 1920s, when a net reserve deficit prevailed, changes in net reserve position brought immediate and substantial responses in rates, and rate sensitivity increased as the net reserve deficit became larger. The same was true in 1966 and 1969. At the other extreme, when a net reserve surplus existed, as in the 1930s and 1940s, changes in net reserve position brought sluggish and small rate responses, and rate sensitivity decreased as the net reserve surplus became larger. This raises the question: Why does rate sensitivity exhibit such variability? The answer can best be given by the simple analogy of stretching a rubber band. Little tension is created by stretching the first few degrees, but tension and resistance mount thereafter at an increasing rate until the breaking point. The same is true of a rising net reserve deficit. Member banks exhibit increasing resistance to borrowing a larger and larger portion of legal reserves, and their efforts to minimize indebtedness by selling securities result in a sharp rise in rates. To carry the analogy further, after tension is removed and the band returns to natural size, further pushing does not reduce its length but only changes its shape. Similarly, after the net reserve surplus rises to a substantial amount, say, about $1 billion, further steps to increase the amount find little or no response in lower rates. Costs of making and administering liquidity-reserve investments tend to establish minimum yields.

While there is a high degree of inverse correlation between net reserve position and interest rates, it falls considerably short of being perfect. The varying degrees of rate sensitivity have just been discussed; several other factors that reduce correlation are also present.

1/Net reserve position is measured only for member banks; nonmember banks are exluded.

2/Changes in the Federal Reserve discount rate exert a definite influence on the relationship.

3/Changes in the liquidity-reserve position of commercial banks affect the rate level, and such changes are only indirectly related to changes in net réserve position.

4/The distributions of excess reserves and of borrowings at Reserve Banks have a bearing on interest rates—that is, whether excess reserves and borrowings are found in large money-market banks, in intermediate-size banks, or in small country banks. In general, changes in excess reserves and borrowings of large banks have a stronger impact on rates than similar changes in banks in the smaller cities and towns.

5/The Treasury bill rate shown on figure 2 is not a perfect index of the entire money-rate structure. Rate relationships change from time to time, due to such factors as Treasury debt management, Federal Reserve open-market operations, commercial-bank changes in customer loan rates, and shifts in investor preferences among various investment media, including bonds, stocks, and real estate.

borrowings at reserve banks and interest rates

It was observed previously that the amount of member-bank borrowing at Reserve Banks is the most important single index of money-market conditions whenever the volume of such borrowing is substantial and excess reserves are at a working minimum, and that interest rates vary in close positive correlation with the amount of borrowing. A more complete explanation of why this is so follows. At first glance, the reader may be confronted with a dilemma in reasoning: Why do interest rates not fall, instead of rise, when Reserve Bank discounts and advances increase? Does not an increase in such advances constitute a release of *more* reserve money which, in the absence of other changes, should result in a larger supply of member-bank reserves? The answer to this apparent contradiction can best be given in terms of (1) reluctance of member banks to remain in debt to Reserve Banks and (2) the cost of borrowing.

1/Member banks by tradition have been reluctant borrowers from Reserve Banks. In part, this attitude arises from the fact that over nine-tenths of a bank's funds are normally represented by debts to depositors. Additional borrowing from the central bank, especially for extended periods, is therefore regarded as speculative by most bank officers and by many important depositors. In addition, Federal Reserve authorities have reenforced this attitude by stressing repeatedly that borrowing is a privilege, not a right, and that Federal Reserve accommodation should be for short periods and for nonspeculative purposes. As a consequence, most member banks borrow only when faced with a legal-reserve deficiency that arises from normal nonspeculative operations; moreover, they strive to repay indebtedness promptly. When repayment is made by sale of liquidity-reserve assets (mainly U.S. securities), prices of these securities are depressed and their yields rise; when repayment is made by cutting back loans, such restriction of the supply of loanable funds leads to higher rates. Moreover, the stronger the pure reluctance factor, the greater the rise of rates associated with an increase of member-bank borrowing; the weaker this factor, the less the rise of rates. If member banks felt no reluctance whatever to borrow and Reserve Bank discount rates were quite low, it would make little difference in the money market whether member banks obtained reserve money by borrowing or from open-market purchases by Reserve Banks.

2/Because borrowed reserves always involve some cost in the form of the Reserve Bank discount rate, pure reluctance to borrow is supplemented by the cost factor whenever the discount rate is above the yield on good liquidity reserves after deducting costs of making and supervising investments. A penalty discount rate in this relative sense represses borrowings and a premium discount rate encourages borrowings. Historically, the Fed has used the discount rate passively, and with a lag, so that it has been low in relation to market rates during periods of cyclical prosperity, and high in relation to market rates during recessions and depressions. Thus, its influence has been to reduce the degree of positive correlation between member-bank borrowing and interest rates.

Another aspect of the dilemma posed by the fact that rates rise and fall along with the volume of member-bank borrowings requires further comment. While the latter is true, the specific effect of new increments of borrowing is to *reduce* interest rates, not to increase them. That is, the new reserve money provided by Reserve Bank discounts and advances holds rates down to a lower level than would exist had borrowed reserves been unavailable. Without such borrowing, the enlarged demands for credit and currency would encounter a fixed supply of reserve money, and a much sharper rise of rates would result. This was, in fact, the situation in pre-Federal Reserve days when the call-loan rate on security loans not infrequently exceeded 10 percent.

In summary, interest rates rise along with member-bank borrowing despite the fact that such borrowing supplies additional reserve money, and therefore has the specific effect of reducing rates. The increase of borrowing is evidence that demands for credit and currency are in the ascendancy over the supply of loanable funds—a supply that is subject to mounting restrictive pressure from the reluctance factor. As a consequence, interest rates rise, but not so much as they would have risen had the discount windows of the Reserve Banks been completely closed.

Most discussions of this issue, however, fall into the error of according both the reluctance factor and the discount rate greater powers of restraint than they actually possess. One reason for this error is disregard for the fact that many banks have little or no reluctance to borrow and will do so, if permitted, whenever there is an opportunity to reinvest or relend at a profit. Another related reason is failure to analyze the issue in terms of the multiple expansion of bank credit. Consider first the nonreluctant banks—those that borrow for profit and are deterred little, if any, by either reluctance or cost. To the extent that these banks borrow reserve money to support loans and investments, *other* banks in the system receive new reserves that are neither borrowed nor costly. These recipient banks, many of which are reluctant borrowers, may then proceed as a group to lend and invest a multiple (four or five times) of their excess reserves just as if their new reserves had been derived from open-market operations, an increase in gold stock, or a reduction in reserve requirements.

Despite these limiting influences, however, the reluctance and cost factors potentially possess considerable power of restraint. The Reserve Banks ration or refuse Reserve credit to banks that seek to borrow in support of speculative operations and for extended periods. Also, there is rapid turnover of borrowing banks, so that most banks come under the pressure of indebtedness and the cost of borrowing at some time during a period of tight money and credit restraint. As in the past, therefore, the Fed may be expected to utilize both the reluctance and the cost factors as instruments of monetary management.

SUMMARY AND CONCLUSIONS

The reserve-money equation summarizes the sources and uses of reserve funds; that is, it shows whence such money comes and how it is employed. The chief purpose of the equation is to serve as a tool for more precise analysis of basic supply and demand conditions in the money market. The most important immediate indexes of the state of the market are *excess reserves* and *borrowed reserves* (discounts and advances of Reserve Banks) of member banks; the most important single index is the *net reserve position* which is the difference between excess reserves and borrowed reserves. The concept of net reserve position is identical with that implied by the term "free reserves" which has wide current usage. When excess reserves are larger than borrowed reserves, the net reserve position is positive, and the difference between the two items is known as *net reserve surplus.* When excess reserves are less than borrowed reserves, the net reserve position is negative, and the difference is labeled *net reserve deficit,* or *net borrowed reserves.*

A net reserve surplus reflects conditions in which the supply of loanable funds is large in relation to demand, so that interest rates are low. Rates show a close inverse correlation with net reserve surplus; that is, they fall as the net surplus rises, and they increase as it declines. In opposite fashion, a net reserve deficit mirrors a situation in which demand is in the ascendancy over supply, so that interest rates are high. When the net reserve deficit increases, rates usually rise, and when the deficit decreases, rates fall. Thus, explanation of the close correlation of net reserve position and interest rates lies in the changes it reflects in supply-demand relationships. Another way of viewing this phenomenon is in terms of bank liquidity. Net reserve position is a measure of legal-reserve liquidity. When bank liquidity increases, rates tend to decline, and when liquidity deteriorates, rates tend to rise.

A satisfying explanation of why rates usually rise and fall in direct correlation with the size of the net reserve deficit cannot be made without giving attention to (1) the reluctance of member banks to borrow from Reserve Banks even at nominal cost and (2) the Federal Reserve discount rate. A rising net reserve deficit indicates that the forces of demand for reserve money outweigh supply; rates rise until demand and supply are equated—although by not so much as would have occurred had borrowing been impossible. A declining net reserve deficit shows that demand factors are subsiding in relation to supply, with the result that rates usually decline.

Thus, in perspective, the reserve-money equation systematically brings together the factors that basically determine the degree of commercial-bank liquidity. By analyzing these factors, one is able to derive the most important single index of that liquidity—net reserve position—which, in turn, reflects quite accurately the state of the money market, including the level of rates.

REFERENCES

Board of Governors of the Federal Reserve System, *Banking and Monetary Statistics* (Washington, D.C., 1943), pp. 360-400.

Board of Governors of the Federal Reserve System, *The Federal Reserve System: Purposes and Functions* (5th ed.; Washington, D.C., 1963), chaps. IX-XIII.

Federal Reserve Bank of Chicago, *Modern Monetary Mechanics,* pp. 14-31.

Meigs, A. James, *Free Reserves and the Money Supply* (Chicago: University of Chicago Press, 1962).

Roosa, Robert V., *Federal Reserve Operations in the Money and Government Securities Markets* (New York: Federal Reserve Bank of New York, 1956), pp. 64-79.

4

the federal funds market

The Federal (Fed) funds market is a distinctive outgrowth of both the central banking system and the unit banking system of the United States. With about 13,600 commercial banks in operation, there is real need for adequate markets and other facilities for the efficient administration of liquid assets. The Federal funds market provides part of this mechanism, along with short-term Treasury securities, bankers' acceptances, commercial paper, and borrowing at Federal Reserve Banks, issuing certificates of deposit, and borrowing Euro-dollars. In essence, this market is in Reserve Bank deposits which are lent and borrowed, mainly overnight by large banks, at a specified rate of interest.

The market originated among major New York City banks in 1921 to satisfy a definite need. Some banks held sizable excess reserves whereas others were borrowing reserves from the Reserve Banks at between 5 and 7 percent. At the same time, attractive lending and investing opportunities were not readily available. Under these circumstances, the banks with excess reserves began lending them overnight to those with reserve deficiencies at rates below the Reserve Bank discount rate. This market developed rapidly in New York City and spread to other leading cities on a limited scale as the decade progressed. During 1925-1930, daily average volume of transactions ranged between $100 and $250 million.[1] The market all but disappeared during the 1930s and 1940s, due to the presence of large excess reserves during the 1930s, and to continuation of abnormal liquidity during and following World War II. Revival of the Fed funds market was an integral part of the new financial epoch ushered in by the Treasury-Federal Reserve Accord in the spring of 1951. From that point on, Federal Reserve authorities tightened the rein on bank liquidity until many banks encountered temporary reserve deficiencies. This was an environment once again in which the Federal funds market could breathe and grow.

[1]Board of Governors of the Federal Reserve System, *The Federal Funds Market* (Washington, D.C., 1959), p. 33. In the preparation of this chapter, the author has drawn heavily on this comprehensive research study.

NATURE OF FEDERAL FUNDS

Federal funds is a shorthand term for Federal Reserve bank funds, or more precisely, for legal-reserve balances of member banks on deposit with Fed Banks. Total legal-reserve balances are composed chiefly of *required* reserves, but a small part, between 1 and 2 percent, consists of *excess* reserves—that is, of reserves over and above requirements.[2] During the 1960s, excess reserves of member banks were usually in the range of $150 to $500 million, whereas total reserve deposits rose from about $20,000 to $28,000 million. On first view, one might conclude that the stock in trade of the Federal funds market is confined to excess reserves. But this is not the case. The stock also includes an indeterminate amount of required legal reserves. This follows from the facts that the legal-reserve settlement period is one week and that reserve requirements apply on an average daily basis during the week. Hence, individual banks often sell (lend) Federal funds on certain days of a week in which, on the average, they would have had no excess reserves in the absence of fund sales.

The active stock in trade of Federal funds possesses attributes that elevate it to a key position at the heart of the money market. As the highest form of member-bank reserve money, Federal funds are sometimes referred to as the *cashiest cash.* They are unsurpassed as a safe instrument for immediate payment throughout the country. When payment is required at once, the Federal Reserve wire transfer system may be utilized to shift funds between debtors and creditors. When haste is not imperative, payments may take the form of checks drawn on Federal Reserve Banks. In any case, creditors—whether they be banks, bond dealers, business corporations, or others—regard Federal funds as a preferred means of payment. Indeed, the advantages are such that important types of creditors, notably sellers of short-term Treasury securities, insist on settlement in Fed funds. The principal reason is to avoid loss of interest income on large sums. Payment by checks on commercial banks, known as *clearing-house funds,* involves loss of interest for at least one day, even within New York City or Chicago, because today's checks are presented for payment at tomorrow's clearing. Moreover, the loss of interest may be for two or more days if the drawee bank is located in a distant city.

While Federal funds have increasingly been utilized for settlement of transactions in the money and capital markets, the great bulk of trading takes place among leading money-market banks. These institutions exercise great care, on the one hand, to avoid the penalty of deficient legal reserves, and on the other, to prevent loss of income on excess reserves. The Federal funds market provides the most flexible and convenient facility for banks with excess reserves to lend them for a day at current rates to others whose reserves are temporarily deficient.

[2]For the present purpose, it is assumed that all excess reserves exist in the form of reserve balances. This assumption is not unrealistic because member banks typically minimize holdings of currency.

Up to this point, trading in Federal funds has been designated as lending and borrowing—terms that are accurately descriptive and doubtless most meaningful to the layman. But henceforth we must bow to the prevailing terminology of the marketplace, where a lender is known as a *seller* and a borrower as a *buyer* of funds.

STRUCTURE OF THE MARKET

Despite the enormous amount and number of transactions, the Federal funds market has no formal organization. There is no physical meeting place such as the New York Stock Exchange, and there is no dealer group that stands ready to buy and sell at bid and asked prices, as in the U.S. security market. Lenders and borrowers are brought together by (1) three New York stock brokerage firms; (2) a few large money-market banks that act in part as dealers and in part as brokers and clearing centers of information; and (3) the network of correspondent-bank relationships through which information on rates and on potential borrowers and lenders is transmitted. United States security dealers are also sources of information as well as important participants.

Each morning the money brokers receive reports by telephone and wire from banks all over the country about bids and offers of funds. On the basis of these reports, they quote rates, and match lenders and borrowers who, after being brought together, proceed with transactions on their own. Thus, the brokers do not buy and sell funds for their own accounts as dealers. No specific commission is ordinarily charged for these services, but the firms hope to be reimbursed by other security business from customers. If the volume of security business is inadequate, a supplementary service charge is made.

A number of leading money-market banks, mainly in New York City, serve as dealers in Federal funds, in addition to providing brokerage and informational services. One large New York City bank makes a two-way market continuously. It buys funds from all banks in appropriate amounts but sells only to banks whose loan lines have been established. The other major banks provide less extensive dealer services but buy and sell funds beyond their own reserve needs as an accommodation to correspondent banks. In fact, this service is largely undertaken as an aggressive method of building up correspondent-banking business. Some 40 leading banks that engage in it are sometimes called *accommodating* banks as opposed to others, known as *adjusting* banks, that deal in Federal funds only to adjust their own reserve positions. One other large bank, Irving Trust Company, is distinctive in that it has a separate brokerage department which arranges for active trading in Federal funds outside its money position. The operations of this department, which has over 150 regular banking contacts, resemble those of the three brokerage firms.

Beyond the orbit of accommodating banks, the network of relationships in the correspondent-banking system facilitates transactions in Federal funds.

Adjusting banks in leading cities disseminate market information to others in their trading areas, so that buying and selling banks are brought together. The largest regional market exists in San Francisco which is the clearing center for West Coast banks. A considerable part of this activity arises from the time lag compared with New York City where the market closes only a couple of hours after trading begins on the West Coast. The second largest regional market is the Midwest with its focus in Chicago. But these regional markets are small in comparison with New York City which is the hub of the nationwide market. Approximately one-half of total bank transactions takes place there, and a large part of trading outside New York is arranged by New York banks and brokers. In addition, the bulk of trading in Federal funds by U.S. security dealers centers in New York City.

Some conception of the huge volume of trading in Federal funds is conveyed by the fact that average daily volume of purchases in 1966 were estimated to be between \$3.5 and \$3.8 billion. On an annual basis, this would amount to between \$900 and \$1,000 billion.[3] Most transactions are in multiples of \$1 million. However, transactions of less than \$1 million, even as small as \$25,000, are often made as an accommodation to small correspondent banks.

reasons for buying federal funds

Large commercial banks, which account for the great bulk of transactions, use this market to maintain close adjustments of their legal-reserve positions. The nature of their business is such that they experience unpredictable changes of considerable size in reserve position from hour to hour and from day to day. These changes take place for a variety of reasons associated with changes in loans, investments, seasonal and other deposit movements, correspondent-bank balances, Treasury operations, Federal Reserve operations, float, foreign bank deposits, currency movements, and other factors. While large banks are permitted to meet legal-reserve requirements on an average basis over their weekly settlement period, most run a moderate cumulative deficiency, but with rather close daily reserve adjustments. This practice avoids the possible embarrassment from encountering a sizable deficiency or investing a large surplus on the last settlement day (Wednesday). Consequently, even though reserve-adjustment transactions reach peaks on Wednesdays and Fridays, they are, in large measure, spread throughout the week.

When a bank faces a reserve deficiency, it may make adjustment by deciding to (1) sell Treasury bills and other short-term liquidity reserves; (2) borrow from the Reserve Bank; (3) buy Federal funds; (4) sell longer-term investments; (5) call dealers' or brokers' loans; (6) issue more certificates of deposit (CDs); (7) borrow Eurodollars; and (8) curtail new loans. If the

[3]Parker B. Willis, *A Study of the Market for Federal Funds* (Washington, D.C.: Board of Governors of the Federal Reserve System, 1967), p. 10.

deficiency is diagnosed as temporary, the practical alternatives are usually limited to the first three, and many banks choose to buy Federal funds. Most are somewhat reluctant to borrow at the Reserve Bank, especially if they have been continuously in debt for several weeks. Moreover, even though they have not recently borrowed, they may prefer to save Reserve Bank borrowing for possible emergencies. Therefore, when Federal funds are available at a rate equal to or below the discount rate, most banks with reserve deficiencies buy them in preference to going to the Reserve Bank. However, this preference is not so firm that banks will pay more than the Reserve Bank discount rate when the discount window is open. Of course, if discounts and advances are strictly rationed, as in 1966 and 1969, the Federal funds rate may rise well above the Reserve Bank discount rate.

There are several aspects to the choice between selling Treasury bills and buying Federal funds to repair a temporary reserve deficiency. The most important consideration is relative rates. When the rate on bills is $\frac{1}{2}$ percentage point or more below the cost of Federal funds, most banks part with bills. But when the bill rate is equal to or higher, the typical procedure is to purchase funds that offer the advantages of freedom from interest rate risk and from the spread between bid and asked prices on bills. Also, partly for these reasons, Federal funds provide a larger measure of investment flexibility. For example, assume that bills are sold instead of buying Federal funds when rates are the same; assume further that rates are lower the next day when excess reserves accumulate. Then in this event, repurchase of bills could be executed only on a less favorable basis due to the lower rate and the dealer spread.

reasons for selling federal funds

On the other side, when a temporary surplus of bank reserves accumulates, the practical alternatives usually boil down to purchase of Treasury short-term securities, sale of Federal funds, or repayment of Reserve Bank borrowings. Most banks apply such a surplus to reduction of Reserve Bank borrowings, if they exist. In fact, this step is often taken even though Treasury bill rates are higher than the discount rate. But when banks are free from debt to Reserve Banks, the choice narrows to bills versus Federal funds. The primary considerations in the decision are relative rates, risks, and flexibility of position. In meeting day-to-day adjustments, Fed funds are commonly superior on all three counts. While the yield on bills is sometimes higher, its average is appreciably below that on Federal funds. But even if the bill yield is somewhat higher, many banks still prefer Federal funds because of their freedom from interest-rate risk and their greater flexibility. Bills are not well adapted to commitments for only a day or two in view of the dealer spread between bid and asked prices and the added risk that money rates may rise tomorrow or the next day. Such an unfavorable turn of events may, in case of the sale of bills by a bank to meet a reserve deficiency, reduce its net return well below the certain return on Federal funds. With these considerations in mind, most large banks sell Federal funds when temporary surplus reserves accumulate unless the rate is appreciably below rates on short-term U.S. securities. They may also reduce borrowings in the Eurodollar market.

mechanics of buying and selling federal funds

While details of practice in buying and selling Federal funds vary flexibly to meet different circumstances, there are two principal methods of making these transactions: (1) straight one-day loans and (2) repurchase agreements. Typical illustrations of each method are given to convey a more concrete understanding of operations.

As previously indicated, the Federal funds market is principally an interbank affair. Banks account for about 90 percent of the total amount of transactions in the process of adjusting reserve positions from day to day, and even from hour to hour. Moreover, the predominant type of bank transaction is the straight, unsecured, one-day loan. Assume, for example, that the First National Bank of Boston possesses $10 million of excess reserves which it wishes to sell in the Federal funds market, and that the Cleveland Trust Company has at the same time a reserve deficiency of $10 million, which it desires to repair by purchasing funds. Having been brought together by a money broker or a large money-market bank, the two banks arrange a rate of 6 percent and other terms over the bank wire and confirm by telegraph or letter. The First National telephones the Federal Reserve Bank of Boston to make immediate transfer of $10 million from its reserve account to the reserve account of Cleveland Trust in the Federal Reserve Bank of Cleveland. The next day Cleveland Trust reverses the process by instructing the Federal Reserve Bank of Cleveland to transfer $10 million to the First National's reserve account at the Federal Reserve Bank of Boston. Because there is a charge for sending odd amounts by wire transfer, the interest for one day ($1,666.67) is settled by a check sent by mail. In the event that one bank has a balance with the other or that they have mutual balances, settlement of interest may conveniently be made by debiting or crediting the proper account.

While the great bulk of straight Federal funds loans is unsecured, a small but significant part has been secured by short-term U.S. securities in recent years. Such loans were frequently used before 1963, when New York City banks purchased Federal funds from smaller outside banks whose unsecured loan limit is 10 percent of capital and surplus. In April 1958, the Comptroller of the Currency exempted loans secured by U.S. securities with maturities of 18 months or less from the 10 percent limit. As a consequence, the smaller banks, when secured, were often enabled to sell funds in large enough units to make purchases by money-market banks feasible. The securities were usually placed in custody in the trust department of the smaller bank's New York correspondent–often the fund-purchasing bank–and released when the loan was repaid. Otherwise, the procedure was the same as for an unsecured loan. On June 1, 1963, the Comptroller of the Currency further liberalized restrictions on national-bank transactions in Federal funds. Such transactions were interpreted to be sales and purchases, rather than lending and borrowing. As a consequence, there is no longer a legal limit on the amount of unsecured sales (loans) of Federal funds. This should enable large city banks to be of much greater service to smaller national banks because it is no longer necessary to secure purchases (borrowings) of Federal funds with U.S. securities. Also, the ruling means that the borrowing limit of a national bank of 100 percent of capital stock plus 50 percent of surplus no longer applies to Federal funds transactions.

The second principal method of buying and selling Federal funds is by repurchase agreements, or by a variant known as *buybacks*. The distinguishing feature of this method, compared with straight loans, is that title to securities actually changes hands for the duration of the loan. Assume, for example, that the First National Bank of Kansas City has a $2 million reserve surplus which it desires to sell for a day and that the Irving Trust Company of New York wishes to purchase this amount; also assume that the Morgan Guaranty Trust Company is the New York City correspondent of First National. After reaching agreement on terms, First National sends $2 million by wire transfer to Morgan Guaranty and instructs the latter to pay this amount in Federal funds to Irving Trust upon receipt of securities which are to be held in custody. The agreement calls for sale of $2 million of U.S. securities by Irving Trust today and for repurchase from First National tomorrow at the same price plus interest at 6 percent per annum. Accordingly, on the next day, Irving Trust draws a check on its Federal Reserve account for $2,000,333.34 payable to Morgan Guaranty, in return for which the securities are given back to Irving Trust. Thus, while the transaction takes the form of sale and repurchase of securities, in reality it is a loan of Federal funds for one day at the going rate.

In the foregoing illustration, the operation would be a buyback if the agreement between Irving Trust and First National took the form of two *separate* contracts: one covering the initial sale of securities by Irving Trust for Federal funds; the other providing for repurchase (and resale) on the next day. Buybacks are frequently used when discount-type securities, mainly Treasury bills, are sold and repurchased. One contract typically calls for sale at a given discount rate, 6 percent, with payment in Federal funds. The other contract provides for repurchase at the same rate of discount the next day. In this way, the seller of Federal funds (initial buyer of securities) receives one day's interest at the agreed rate.

Repurchase agreements and buybacks are used extensively by nonbank U.S. security dealers in purchasing Federal funds from business corporations and smaller banks outside New York City. Large banks prefer the straight unsecured loan when possible because this method avoids the considerable inconvenience and expense of handling and transferring securities. This disadvantage for money-market banks, which predominantly engage in overnight transactions, loses much of its force for dealers who usually borrow for longer periods. Repurchase agreements also have the substantial advantages of eliminating credit risk for the seller of Federal funds and enabling dealers to borrow up to market value of securities.

RATES ON FEDERAL FUNDS

Like other free-market prices, rates on Federal funds emerge from interaction of the forces of supply and demand, and tend toward a level at which these forces are equated. Because Federal funds occupy a key position at the heart of the money market, their rate reflects most of the broad forces that govern the market as a whole. Nevertheless, the analyst must bear in mind that the Federal funds market is highly specialized and therefore mirrors most closely the state of its particular sector. In the main, this is the market for overnight loans of funds by large banks to adjust reserve positions.

Federal fund rates are quoted from hour to hour by the money brokers and by a few large money-market banks which serve as dealers and brokers. Quotations are based on a continuous flow of information from all parts of the nation with respect to amounts offered and demanded at various rates. Quotations reported daily in the press include opening, high, low, and closing rates. The Federal Reserve Bank of New York also publishes the so-called effective rate which is the most common one at which transactions take place.

relation to other rates

The Federal funds rate bears a close relationship to all rates in the money market because all are basically influenced by common causes. Also, as indicated, the focal position of Federal funds often establishes this rate as the most sensitive indicator of money-market conditions. However, the Federal funds rate is most closely related to the Federal Reserve Bank discount rate and the rate on shortest-term Treasury securities. This follows from the fact that these rates are the prices of the principal competitive alternatives in the reserve adjustment processes of large banks.

As a rule, the Federal Reserve Bank discount rate sets the upper limit of the Federal funds rate. Only under exceptional circumstances will banks pay more for Federal funds than the cost of borrowing at the Reserve Bank. The most notable exception occurred in the late 1920s, when many banks were so heavily committed to stock-exchange security loans that their ability to borrow at the Reserve Bank was impaired or exhausted. As a consequence, during the tight-money period of 1928-1929, the funds rate moved appreciably above the discount rate. Also, during the firm periods of 1956-1957 and 1959, a few transactions in Federal funds took place at rates above the discount rate. Again, during the 1968-1970 period of tight money and strong loan demands, the Federal funds rate rose well above the discount rate. During the autumn peak in 1969, the disparity exceeded 3 percentage points—over 9 percent compared with the discount rate of 6 percent. These transactions represented borrowing by banks unable or unwilling to borrow from Reserve Banks, and borrowing by bond dealers to carry inventories of U.S. and other securities. But despite these occasional exceptions, the Reserve Bank discount rate usually sets the upper limit, and during moderately firm money periods, the effective funds rate is typically identical with the discount rate.

At the other extreme, when substantial surplus bank reserves accumulate, the Federal funds rate commonly drops well below the Reserve Bank discount rate to a minimal level of $\frac{1}{8}$ to $\frac{1}{4}$ percent. Such a low rate barely covers the cost of transactions, so that banks reach a point of indifference whether they hold or lend excess reserves. Under these circumstances, borrowings at Reserve Banks become very small because individual banks with reserve deficiencies can obtain reserves more cheaply by purchasing Federal funds or by selling short-term Treasury securities. This situation prevailed most of the time between 1934 and 1951, and reappeared in the recessions of 1954 and 1958.

Between the two extremes and especially in the zone of moderate ease to moderate tightness, the Federal funds rate fluctuates responsively from day to day and week to week. At one time, it may bump the ceiling of the discount rate; at another, it may rest on the floor established by transactions costs.

Comparison of the shortest Treasury bill rate with the Federal funds rate reveals a reasonably close competitive relationship; they usually rise and fall together. However, both rates exhibit individuality as reflected by independent movements. While bills are not a perfect substitute for Federal funds for reasons previously indicated, there is a definite tendency for banks to purchase bills when their rates are above Federal fund rates. Such decisions, of course, have the equalizing effect of lowering bill rates and raising fund rates. Conversely, there is a disposition to sell Federal funds in preference to buying bills when fund rates are relatively high, again with an equalizing influence. The lower average rate on bills may be explained by the facts that bills are relatively free from credit risk, enjoy worldwide investor familiarity, are legal investments for various purposes, and are more readily available to many investors. Independent variations in the two rates are to be expected in view of different features of the instruments, individual conditions of supply and demand, and lack of perfect substitution. For example, Treasury debt-management policy may substantially increase or decrease the amount of bills outstanding. Or such factors as changes in Federal Reserve Bank holdings of securities, float, currency outside banks, and gold stock may materially increase or decrease the volume and distribution of excess reserves of banks.

effects on the money market

The principal effect of the Federal funds market is its contribution to efficient utilization of excess reserves in the banking system. This effect has several facets, including (1) prompt transmission of Federal Reserve policies and operations throughout the country; (2) reduction of direct dependence of member banks on Reserve Bank borrowing as a method of repairing reserve deficiencies; (3) reduction of aggregate member-bank reserve balances; and (4) increase of earning power of commercial banks and bond dealers.

With some 13,600 commercial banks in the nation, most of them small, mobility of reserves is far from perfect. Pools of excess reserves accumulate in small- and medium-size banks, so that even in the presence of substantial member-bank borrowing at Reserve Banks, a hard core of $200 to $300 million in excess reserves exists. This amount would be much larger in the absence of Federal Reserve transfer facilities, the U.S. security market, the Federal funds market, and other divisions of the money market which promote mobility. From the standpoint of effective monetary regulation, it is highly important that the effects of Federal Reserve open-market operations and other monetary actions be transmitted quickly throughout the country. The Federal funds market materially contributes to effective monetary regulation by providing a ready facility for redistribution of bank reserves.

Closely associated with enhanced nationwide mobility of bank reserves is their more efficient utilization, as excess reserves find their way through the Federal funds market to banks with deficiencies. This has the effect of reducing member-bank dependence on Reserve Bank borrowing because banks in need of reserves can more readily locate and borrow excess reserves. Another allied effect of the Federal funds market is significant reduction in total member-bank reserve balances, and of aggregate Reserve Bank credit. This follows from the fact that less total reserve is needed to support the amount of money and the level of money rates that Federal Reserve authorities regard to be consistent with basic objectives.

Still a further incidental influence of the Federal funds market is an increase in net earnings of banks and bond dealers. The market enables banks to maximize income from liquid assets by minimizing holdings of nonearning reserves. It also reduces expenses at times by reducing costs of borrowed reserves and by avoiding penalties on reserve deficiencies. Bond dealers enjoy larger earnings as a result of increases in sales made possible by greater credit availability to carry more adequate inventories. In addition, the funds market often enables dealers to reduce costs of borrowing.

POSTWAR PATTERN OF GROWTH

Analysis of postwar activity in Federal funds reveals both a strong trend of growth and considerable cyclical variation. Several factors are responsible for this pattern of change.

trend of the market

A Federal Reserve study of the Federal funds market finds that average daily volume of transactions more than doubled between the periods 1950-1953 and 1955-1957, from $350-$450 million to $800-$1,100 million.[4] This strong growth trend continued through the 1960s. Another Fed study estimated average daily purchases of funds in 1966 at between $3.5 and $3.8 billion, and on some days as high as $5 billion.[5] A notable feature of the development during the 1960s was the growth of regional markets with focal points in the larger cities. This was largely a result of city banks competing for interbank balances of the smaller banks in their trade areas by offering Fed fund services. As a consequence, some 2,500 country member banks participated in the market in 1967, compared with only about 400 in 1961.[6]

Several factors have been responsible for this vigorous uptrend, the most important of which are the following:

1/A material expansion in the dollar size of the economy has taken place. Hence, a considerable part of growth in funds transactions represents merely keeping pace with GNP.

2/Bank management has become increasingly sophisticated with respect to careful administration of liquid assets. This is, in part, a consequence of growing concentration in banking through mergers, branching and holding companies; it is also a result of improved management techniques through education.

3/A marked increase in volume of trading in U.S. securities has taken place. This is associated with the increase in marketable federal debt, and particularly with the rapid expansion of short-term Treasury securities in which trading chiefly occurs. Settlement is largely made in Federal funds.

4/The practice of making settlements and payments in Federal funds has developed rapidly in New York City in recent years. Large creditors actively bargain for payment in such funds, rather than in clearing-house funds, in order to avoid loss of one or more day's interest.

5/The sizable increase in Reserve Bank float beginning in 1951 led to wider variations in member banks' day-to-day reserve positions, with a consequent greater need for liquidity adjustments through Fed funds or otherwise. Float was increased when the maximum period before reserve credit given for checks

[4]Board of Governors of the Federal Reserve System, op. cit.

[5]Willis, op. cit., pp. 10, 19.

[6]Ibid., p. 19.

in process of collection was reduced from three to two days after receipt by a Reserve Bank.

6/Growth of the funds market has been promoted by improvements in trading facilities. A few large banks have assumed dealer functions in addition to serving as brokers and information centers. Also, more complete middleman services have been provided by the three money brokers, and improvements have been made in the Federal Reserve wire transfer system. Partly as a consequence, nonfinancial corporations and a layer of medium-size banks have become important suppliers of Federal funds.

In addition to the foregoing factors, the Federal funds market has expanded to fill a void in the money market created by reform legislation of the early 1930s, which prohibited interest payments on demand deposits and severely restricted call loans secured by stocks. The result was elimination of two of the principal methods by which banks previously adjusted reserve positions—that is, by increasing or decreasing balances with correspondent banks and by making and calling brokers' loans. Short-term Treasury securities do not fill this void in view of price changes and the spread between bid and asked prices. But Federal fund purchases and sales do fill the gap in part by enabling banks and others to lend or borrow for a day or more at a specified rate and with no risk of price changes.

cyclical variations in transactions

The volume of trading in Fed funds exhibits a fairly definite cyclical pattern. Cyclical bulges occur during periods of average to moderately easy-money conditions such as 1954, 1958, and 1960-1961. On the supply side, a medium-size fund of mobile excess reserves becomes available and therefore for sale. On the demand side, sufficient credit stringencies exist in particular areas and banks to cause substantial needs for borrowed reserves. Also, credit demands of U.S. security dealers and of other bond dealers are usually high in view of favorable markets.

Cyclical troughs in fund transactions develop during periods of extremely tight credit conditions such as 1953, 1957, and 1959, and periods of extremely easy conditions such as 1934-1940. When credit stringencies develop, the fund of mobile excess reserves shrinks so much that Fed funds are available, if at all, only in small amounts. Thus, even though demand for them is larger than usual, the amount of transactions materially declines. The years 1965-1970 provide an important exception to this generalization. Loan demands were so intense that commercial banks borrowed Federal funds not only for adjustment of reserve positions, but also to support their rapidly expanding loan portfolios. The strict rationing of discounts and advances by the Reserve Banks also contributed to the high level of fund-borrowing.

Under conditions of extreme credit ease, trading volume also drops, but for quite different reasons. An abundance of mobile excess reserves exists so that Federal funds are readily available at very low rates. However, on the demand side, few banks encounter even day-to-day reserve deficiencies, so that little need for borrowed reserves exists. These conditions characterized the entire period 1934-1947.

REFERENCES

Board of Governors of the Federal Reserve System, *The Federal Funds Market* (Washington, D.C., 1959).

Brandt, Harry, and Paul A. Crowe, "The Federal Funds Market in the Southeast," Federal Reserve Bank of Atlanta, *Monthly Review* (January 1968), pp. 7-13.

Madden, Carl H., *The Money Side of the Street* (New York: Federal Reserve Bank of New York, 1959).

Miles, Mark H., "Federal Funds and Country Bank Reserve Management," Federal Reserve Bank of Philadelphia, *Business Review* (September 1968), pp. 3-8.

Willis, Parker B., *The Federal Funds Market: Its Origin and Development* (3d ed.; Boston: Federal Reserve Bank of Boston, 1968).

Willis, Parker B., *A Study of the Market for Federal Funds* (Washington, D.C.: Board of Governors of the Federal Reserve System, 1967).

5

the united states government-security market

Because the subject receives little publicity, and because few individuals purchase and sell Treasury securities, it is not widely known that the U.S. government securities market is by far the largest and broadest in the world. Quotations of these securities occupy only a six-inch column in the *Wall Street Journal* compared with three or more entire pages devoted to stock quotations. There is no physical meeting place for this market to dramatize trading as in the New York Stock Exchange, the American Stock Exchange, and other organized exchanges. By contrast, the market is over the counter, or better, over the wire. It is made by some twenty major dealers most of whom have head offices in New York City—where the great bulk of trading is concentrated—and branches in other leading cities. Dealers also maintain a network of private wires connecting them with each other and with their larger customers—commercial banks, Federal Reserve Banks, and other financial institutions. By these means, this informal market is not only nationwide but worldwide. The vast size of the market is indicated by the fact that total sales in 1969 amounted to $283 billion, or one-third of the entire GNP and about five times the total volume of the New York Stock Exchange.[1]

The huge federal debt is largely a heritage of World War II, augmented by large budget deficits during the Great Depression and by a substantial net deficit during the postwar years. At midyear 1970 the interest-bearing federal debt amounted to $369 billion, consisting of $136.4 billion of nonmarketable obligations and $232.6 billion of marketable securities. The latter category, which is the principal concern here, provides investors with a wide variety of maturities and types of securities. There were 117 separate issues of Treasury bills, Notes, bonds, and tax-anticipation bills with maturities ranging from a few

[1] See Table 5-3, p. 76.

days to 28 years. In contrast with private obligations, federal securities are free from credit risk. They are backed by both the taxing power and the money-creating power of the federal government, so that investors have no misgivings about receipt of interest and principal. In addition, short-term government securities are highly liquid. They can be converted to cash in a few minutes without appreciable loss of principal. Hence, they are held to meet liquidity needs by commercial banks, other financial institutions, business corporations, foreign banks, and others.

Attention should also be given to other aspects of the market that contribute to its great importance. First, it occupies a position at the heart of the money and capital markets. The interest rate structure that applies to the various types and maturities of government securities forms a basis to which all other rates are continuously in process of adjustment. These rate relationships provide the mechanism by which current savings are transmitted to those industries, areas, and companies that offer the highest promise of profitable investment. In other words, the market significantly helps to provide the mobility of capital that is necessary for effective utilization of basic resources and for a satisfactory rate of economic growth. Second, the U.S. securities market is the principal medium for implementation of monetary policies. Federal Reserve open-market operations, the dominant instrument of credit control, consist mainly of purchases and sales of U.S. securities. Moreover, the effectiveness of such operations depends on transmission of yield-price responses of these securities throughout the national money and capital markets.

GROWTH OF THE FEDERAL DEBT

Under what circumstances does the federal debt increase, and under what circumstances does it decline? A superficial answer to this question may be given in terms of the Treasury's cash balance. When this balance falls below a desired working level, the Treasury usually borrows; when the balance rises above current needs, the Treasury pays off debt with its extra cash. The Treasury's balance seldom falls below $1 billion or rises above $10 billion. While $1 billion is a tidy sum, it represents less than 2 days' expenditure with a $200 billion annual budget. As a rule, borrowing operations are therefore undertaken when this uncomfortably low level is reached.

In terms of the federal *cash* budget, when cash expenditures exceed cash receipts from the public, the deficit must be met by Treasury borrowing or by reduction of the cash balance. When cash expenditures are less than receipts, the cash balance rises and debt may be retired. An illustration may be drawn from the cash budgets of fiscal 1967 and 1970. The tax and loan account balance declined by $5,778 million between 1966 and 1967 because total cash withdrawals of $97,160 million exceeded total receipts from taxes and sales of securities of $91,382. Treasury borrowing was insufficient to close the gap. But in 1970, the reverse was true. Receipts of $151,721 million exceeded withdrawals of $149,317 million, with the result that the cash balance increased by $2,404 million–from $4,525 to $6,929 million. Proceeds from borrowing were larger than needed to maintain the same cash balance.[2]

A more fundamental explanation would have to delve into policies of the Congress and the Administration in regard to expenditure and taxation programs. One would also have to consider the economic and political conditions that underlie these policies. However, these basic issues are beyond the scope of this chapter.

Prior to World War I, federal securities occupied a secondary place in the financial markets. The first important peak in the federal debt came during the Civil War when it reached $2.3 billion; previous to that time, it was never so much as $100 million. Conservative financial policies reduced the debt to below $1 billion in the late 1880s, where it remained until World War I. Moreover, special-purpose issues represented a large part of this modest amount, so that during these years federal securities were not an important medium for general investment.

The dominant position of the U.S. security market dates back to World War I. About two-thirds of wartime expenditures was financed by borrowing, with the result that the gross federal debt reached the unprecedented total of $25.8 billion at the end of 1919. However, in the following eleven years, the debt was steadily reduced so that by the end of 1930, it stood at $16 billion, a reduction of 38 percent. It is thus significant that the high-level prosperity of the 1920s was sustained in the presence of substantial surpluses in the federal budget.

In sharp contrast with the 1920s, a series of uninterrupted budget deficits occurred during the 1930s. By 1934, the former peak of the debt was exceeded, and by the end of 1940, it amounted to $50.9 billion (see figure 3). This enormous increase was largely a consequence of the longest and deepest depression in the nation's history. Federal tax revenues shrank along with personal incomes and corporate profits. Federal expenditures rose to meet relief programs for the unemployed and public-works programs to promote recovery.

But the deficits of the 1930s, which seemed large at the time, were destined to appear small in comparison with those of World War II. Nearly three-fifths of federal expenditures during the war was financed by borrowing, so that the debt rose to a new peak of $279 billion in February 1946.

Some progress was made in debt reduction until midyear 1948, when the debt declined to $252.3 billion. This was made possible by budget surpluses in fiscal 1947 and 1948, and by drawing down the huge cash balance that accumulated from the final Victory Loan. Since 1948, the general course of the debt has been upward with the exceptions of fiscal 1956, 1957, 1960, and 1969, when budget surpluses accrued. At midyear 1970, the federal gross debt amounted to $370.9 billion (see figure 3).

While the federal debt reached an all-time peak at midyear 1970, it

[2] *Treasury Bulletin* (August 1970), p. 17.

3 GROSS DEBT OF U.S. GOVERNMENT (end of June and December).
Source: Board of Governors of the Federal Reserve System

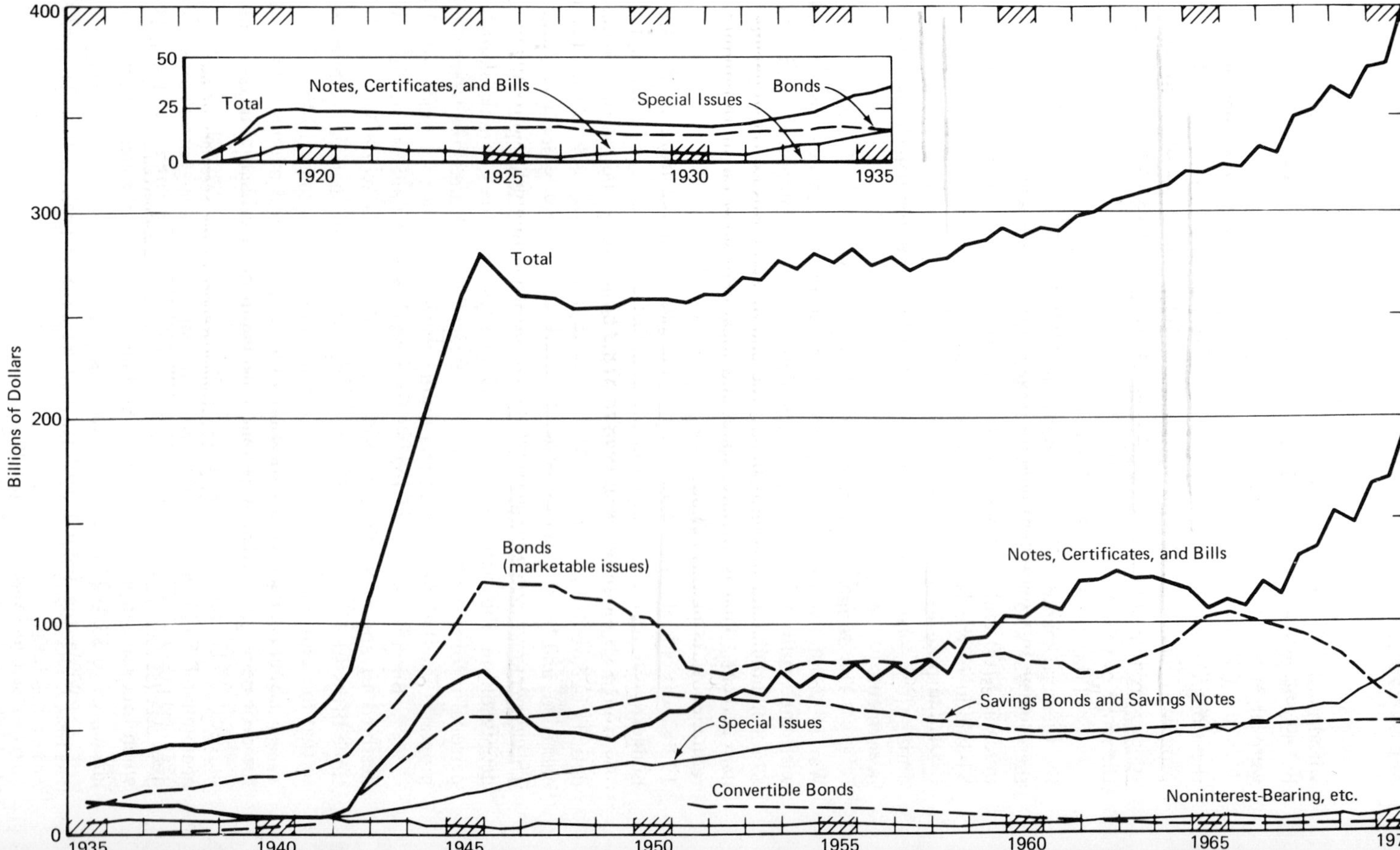

should be noted that some progress has been made since World War II in reducing its relative importance. At midyear 1948, the debt of $252.3 billion represented 97 percent of GNP; by midyear 1970, this proportion had declined to 38.2 percent of GNP.[3] As a matter of fact, gross federal debt considerably overstates its own real importance because securities held by government investment accounts and by Fed Banks are included. These duplicative elements should be deducted in calculating federal debt held by private investors, which is a more relevant measure of real debt. They should not be included because the government owes this amount, and pays interest thereon, to itself.[4] There was little change in federal debt held by private investors between midyear 1948 and midyear 1970–it rose from $195.2 to $218 billion–despite the increase of $118.6 billion in the gross debt. That is, the growth of debt was largely accounted for by increases in holdings of U.S. securities by government investment accounts and by the Reserve Banks.[5] Hence, federal debt held by private investors declined more in relation to GNP between 1948 and 1970 than did gross federal debt–from 75 to 22.4 percent.[6]

The federal debt also has declined since World War II in relation to total public and private debt. At the end of 1948, net federal debt was 50 percent of total net public and private debt; by the end of 1968, this ratio had declined to 18.6 percent.[7] That is, private, state, and local debt grew far more rapidly than federal debt during this period.

Growth of the federal debt should also be viewed from the standpoint of its interest cost. As reported in the administrative budget, interest payments rose from $5.5 billion in fiscal 1948 to $18.3 billion in 1970, or by 233 percent. This was partly a consequence of the increase in federal debt, but mainly the result of higher interest rates. A better measure of interest costs is provided by the national *flow of funds* account which shows net interest paid by the federal government, excluding intragovernmental transfer payments of interest to trust funds and agencies. Net interest paid rose from $4.3 billion in calendar 1948 to $13.1 billion in 1969, or by 205 percent.[8] This was primarily a result of the rise of rates because federal debt held by the public rose only about 11 percent. Net interest paid, however, declined moderately in relation to national income–from 1.9 percent in 1948 to 1.7 percent in 1969.[9]

[3]Federal debt ($370.9 billion) ÷ GNP ($971.1 billion) × 100.

[4]Federal Reserve Banks return 90 percent of net profits to the Treasury as taxes on Federal Reserve notes not backed dollar for dollar by gold certificates.

[5]*Treasury Bulletin* (August 1970), p. 67; *Annual Report of the Secretary of the Treasury* (Washington, D.C., 1969), Statistical Appendix, p. 61.

[6]1948: debt ($195.2 billion),÷ GNP ($259.4 billion) × 100 = 75 percent.
1970: debt ($218.0 billion) ÷ GNP ($971.1 billion) × 100 = 22.4 percent.

[7]1948: net federal debt, $216.5 billion; total net public and private debt, $433.6 billion (ratio, 50 percent).
1968: net federal debt, $291.9 billion; total net public and private debt, $1,568.5 billion (ratio 18.6 percent).
Data from *Economic Report of the President* (February 1970), p. 248.

[8]*Federal Reserve Bulletin* (May 1970), p. A 71.5.

[9]$4.3 billion ÷ $223.5 billion × 100 = 1.9 percent.
$13.1 billion ÷ $769.5 billion × 100 = 1.7 percent.

In summary, although gross federal debt has grown considerably since World War II, the publicly-held category has risen only moderately. Both categories have declined in relation to GNP and to total net private and public debt. Also, while interest payments by the federal government have risen markedly in absolute terms, they have declined in relation to national income. Thus, U.S. productive capacity has more than kept pace with the debt and with the interest payments on it, so that the burden rests somewhat more easily on American shoulders.

CLASSIFICATION OF U.S. SECURITIES

The total interest-bearing federal debt divides into two broad classes: marketable and nonmarketable. Table 5-1 summarizes the subdivisions of each class as of

TABLE 5-1 / INTEREST-BEARING DEBT OF THE U.S. GOVERNMENT AS OF JUNE 30, 1960 AND JUNE 30, 1970 (billions of dollars)

Type of Security	1960	1970	Amount of Change
Bills	33.4	76.2	+42.8
Certificates of indebtedness	17.7	0.0	−17.7
Notes	51.5	93.5	+42.0
Bonds	81.3	63.0	−18.3
Total marketable issues	183.9	232.6	+48.7
Convertible bonds	6.3	2.4	− 3.9
Savings bonds and notes	47.5	52.0	+ 4.5
Special issues	44.9	76.3	+31.4
Other nonmarketable bonds	0.7	5.7	+ 5.0
Total nonmarketable issues	99.4	136.4	+37.0
Total interest-bearing debt	283.3	369.0	+85.7

Source: *Federal Reserve Bulletin* (August 1970), p. A 42.

midyear 1960 and 1970. Marketable issues amounted to $232.6 billion in 1970, or about three-fifths of the total; nonmarketable issues totaled $136.4 billion. Both types increased between the two dates, and the proportion of marketable debt to total debt declined somewhat. Before undertaking analysis of marketable securities, with which we are primarily concerned, a brief consideration of nonmarketable issues is necessary.

nonmarketable securities

United States savings bonds, which were first issued in 1935, are primarily designed to attract savings of individuals, especially those of small investors. While a number of series have been issued, only two types have been sold since April 1957—Series E, on sale since 1941, and Series H, offered since mid-1952. Payroll-savings plans during and since World War II have mainly utilized Series E which constituted about 86 percent of outstandings at midyear 1970. The total of $51.5 billion was distributed as follows: Series E, $44.2 billion, and Series H, $7.3 billion.

Series E bonds are sold to nonbank investors on a discount basis at 75 percent of maturity value in denominations ranging from $25 to $10,000. They are not transferable but may be redeemed by the owner after two months' holding according to a fixed schedule of values. If held to maturity, their redemption at par provides an annual yield of 5 percent. But if the investor redeems his bond before maturity, he must accept a yield penalty which is large at first but declines as the holding period lengthens.

Series H savings bonds are similar to Series E except that they are designed for the small investor who desires current income. They are sold at par, and interest is paid semiannually on a graduated scale—low at first but with yield progressively rising to 5 percent at maturity which is ten years from date of issue. They are nontransferable, but are redeemable at par on one month's notice after six months from date of issue.

Analysis of the savings-bond program reveals three significant developments: (1) cash sales exceeded cash redemptions in every fiscal year from 1935 to 1950; (2) cash redemptions exceeded cash sales in every fiscal year from 1951 to 1963; and (3) the amount outstanding reached a peak of $58.6 billion at midyear 1955 and declined to $51.5 billion by 1970. The Treasury has, therefore, constantly faced the problem of selling other securities to meet this cash outflow. As Table 5-1 reveals, replacement issues were mostly marketable bills and notes.

It is significant that the net cash outflow arose mainly in connection with liquidation of the discontinued Series F, G, J, and K. These issues were held by institutions and wealthy individuals alert to the rise of market interest rates after 1951. When yields of marketable U.S. securities rose above fixed yields on savings bonds, many investors redeemed the latter and purchased marketable issues.

Special issues include securities issued directly by the Treasury to various government agencies and trust funds. Their amount grew rapidly between 1960 and 1970 from $44.9 billion to $76.3 billion. Almost seven-eighths of the total in 1970 was accounted for by only three of the funds—Federal Old-Age and Survivors Insurance Trust Fund, $25.9 billion; Federal Employees' Retirement Fund, $18.9 billion; and Unemployment Trust Fund, $10.5 billion. Special issues may be redeemed whenever the fund or agency needs money. Rates paid by the Treasury are usually in line with the average rate on publicly-held government securities.

marketable securities

In order to meet demands of various types of investors, the Treasury issues marketable securities in the forms of bills, certificates of indebtedness, notes, and bonds. All are bought and sold in the market, but each type has certain distinguishing features. Altogether, these issues aggregated $232.6 billion at midyear 1970, nearly two-thirds of the federal debt.

Treasury Bills / Treasury bills have emerged since their legal authorization in 1929 as the most important short-term instrument in the money market. During the 1950s, their amount approximated that of certificates of indebtedness, their nearest rival, but certificates were of less importance in the 1960s, and were discontinued in July 1967 (see Table 5-2). Bills are held largely by

TABLE 5-2 / MARKETABLE INTEREST-BEARING DEBT IN SELECTED YEARS, 1950-1970 (billions of dollars)

Midyear	Total	Bills	Certificates	Notes	Bonds
1950	155.3	13.5	18.4	20.4	103.0
1955	155.2	19.5	13.8	40.7	81.1
1960	183.8	33.4	17.7	51.5	81.3
1965	208.7	53.7	—	52.5	102.5
1966	209.1	54.9	1.7	50.6	101.9
1967	210.7	58.5	5.6	49.1	97.4
1968	226.6	64.4	—	71.1	91.1
1969	226.1	68.4	—	78.9	78.8
1970	232.6	76.2	—	93.5	63.0

Source: *Treasury Bulletin* (August 1970), p. 21.

commercial banks, business corporations, foreign banks, and other investors to meet liquidity requirements. They are also the chief instrument bought and sold by the Federal Reserve Banks in monetary-management operations. In 1970 the dollar volume of trading in bills was about three-fourths the total volume in the government-securities market and about four times the volume of stock and bond trading on the New York Stock Exchange.

Treasury bills, which have a maturity not to exceed one year, are issued on a discount basis. That is, they are sold at prices below par (100) and are redeemed at par on date of maturity. The market rate of discount is determined by the amount of discount and the length of the period until maturity. For example, the average price on 182-day bills sold on July 30, 1970 was 96.786, which corresponds to an annual discount rate of 6.429 percent. Having paid $96.786, the investor received $100, 182 days later. However, the bank discount rate of 6.429 percent should not be confused with actual investment yield to maturity, which is 7.09 percent.[10]

The Treasury has developed a systematic procedure in offering and redeeming bills. Each Thursday the regular weekly offering of 91-day (13-week) and 182-day (26-week) bills is announced. Tenders must be received by a Federal Reserve Bank on the following Monday by 1:30 P.M. New York time, and bidders are apprised of awards the next morning. The highest competitive bids (lowest rates) are accepted in order until the desired amount is reached. Small noncompetitive bids for $200,000 or less–mainly from small banks and other small investors–are allotted in full at the average price of competitive bids. Payment for the bills, which are issued in denominations ranging from $1,000 to $1,000,000, must be made in Federal (Reserve) funds, or in maturing bills, on the following Thursday. Between January and July 1970, the weekly amount of accepted bids for 13-week bills ranged between $2.4 and $3.0 billion, and for 26-week bills between $1.9 and $2.9 billion.

Since August 1963, monthly offerings of 1-year bills have been made and tenders of $1 billion or more have been accepted.[11] Thus, there are three cycles of bills, with rollovers of 13 weeks, 26 weeks, and 52 weeks, respectively. Investors requiring liquidity therefore have a wide choice of maturities for their convenience.

In addition to the regular weekly and monthly offerings, the Treasury makes important use of *tax-anticipation bills* which mature near quarterly tax dates (mid-March, June, September, and December) and are receivable for tax payments. Their sale helps to iron out the uneven flow of tax receipts to the Treasury. Under present arrangements, there is a marked seasonal tendency for a large cash deficit to develop in the first half of the fiscal year (July-December) and for a large cash surplus to accumulate during the second half (January-June). Thus, the cash deficit of $2.9 billion in fiscal 1970 was the net result of a deficit of $8.1 billion during the first half and a surplus of $5.2 billion during the second half. Sale of tax-anticipation obligations during the July-December period, mainly to corporations, correspondingly reduces the cash inflow during the second half. While certificates of indebtedness were used more largely for this purpose prior to fiscal 1957, the Treasury has shifted its preference to tax-anticipation bills. The amount of tax-anticipation bills issued in fiscal 1970 was $14.5 billion.

The auction method of selling Treasury bills at regular weekly and monthly intervals has definite advantages. Most important, it minimizes

[10]While Treasury bills are quoted on a bank discount basis, their actual yield is appreciably higher. Two adjustments of the bank discount rate are required: (1) to allow for the fact that computation of bank discount is based on a 360-day year, and (2) to adjust for the fact that the investor earns his return not on face value (100), but on face value minus the discount. Thus, the annual discount rate of 6.429 percent in the example is equivalent to an investment yield of 7.09 percent; that is:

$$6.429\% \times \frac{365}{360} \times \frac{100}{(100 - 6.429)} = 7.09\%$$

[11]*Treasury Bulletin* (August 1970), pp. 33-34.

interference of Treasury financing with effective monetary management by the Fed. Knowledge of regular forthcoming offerings on a discount basis is less upsetting to the money market than irregular offerings of fixed-rate securities which may, directly or indirectly, require Federal Reserve support. There are also advantages from the standpoint of Treasury debt management. (1) The cost of borrowing is somewhat lower. This follows from (a) maximum competition among investors who bid prices up (rates down), (b) acceptance of only the highest prices offered as opposed to a single price which calls forth the least willing investors, and (c) freedom from the tendency to overprice fixed-rate securities in order to assure success of the offering. (2) Treasury officials are not faced with the difficult problem of setting a coupon rate at which investors will buy the amount of securities that the Treasury wishes to sell. (3) Allotments to all subscribers on some arbitrary basis, and the associated huge volume of paper work, are largely avoided.

u.s. certificates, notes, and bonds

Certificates of indebtedness, notes, and bonds have more similarities than differences, so that it is desirable to discuss them as a group. Following are the various features they have in common.

1/In contrast with Treasury bills which are sold on a discount basis, certificates, notes, and bonds are all offered with a set coupon rate and at a fixed price.[12] Prior to 1958, the fixed price was always face value (par), but since then the Treasury has, on occasion, fixed a premium price (above par) or a discount price (below par). For example, in November 1960, a 4 percent bond maturing October 1, 1969 was offered at $100\frac{1}{2}$; then in July 1961, a $3\frac{7}{8}$ percent bond maturing May 15, 1968 was offered at $99\frac{3}{8}$. The new practice of pricing at a premium or a discount, as well as at par, is advantageous in that it permits closer adaptation of yields on new issues to those of similar existing securities, because by convention, coupon rates vary by not more than $\frac{1}{8}$ percentage point. In addition, this practice permits the Treasury to reopen subscriptions to outstanding issues whose coupon rates are no longer in line with market rates. Both offerings just mentioned were reopenings of outstanding issues.

2/The general procedure is the same in a new offering, whether the security is a certificate, note, bond, or some combination thereof. The usual approach to new financing involves extensive investigation of the market by the Treasury, including consultation with authorities from Federal Reserve Banks, investment banks, commercial banks, savings banks, and life insurance companies. On the basis of these findings, the features of the offering are determined—types of securities, maturity dates, call options, coupon rates, timing, and pricing. If refunding is involved, the issues to be retired and the

[12]This difference exists only because of conventional practice; by law the Treasury is authorized to issue all types of securities at a discount.

securities to be offered in exchange must be selected. At the appropriate time, the Treasury releases a formal announcement, giving details of the offering. This includes the period during which subscriptions may be tendered to Federal Reserve Banks and branches, or directly to the Treasury. After the books are closed, the final problem of allotment arises because subscriptions are usually between two and four times larger than cash sales. Small subscriptions are ordinarily allotted in full and the remainder is allotted proportionally by size of subscription. Preferential treatment is sometimes accorded to savings institutions in allotments of long-term bonds; allotments of such securities to commercial banks are occasionally restricted. Thus, there is a distinct contrast with Treasury bills which are allotted automatically by competitive price bids, whereas other marketable securities are offered at fixed prices, and usually enough above the market to call forth heavy oversubscriptions. Therefore, rationing among subscribers on some rather arbitrary basis becomes necessary.

3/Commercial banks may ordinarily pay for allotments of cash offerings of certificates, notes, and bonds by credits to Treasury tax and loan accounts—in contrast with regular bill offerings which must be paid for with Federal funds. This is an important advantage to banks because they can count on a period of about three weeks before Treasury withdrawal, and during which their only cost is maintenance of the fractional-reserve requirement (17.5 percent for city banks in October 1970). Partly as a consequence, commercial banks serve as underwriters, reselling a large proportion of their purchases to other investors. In recent years, commercial banks have been granted over two-thirds of total public allotments of certificates and notes and over one-third of bond allotments.

4/Certain other similarities among these types of securities may be summarized by the following three points. All are issued in coupon form, but only bonds are invariably offered in both coupon and registered form. (Only certain issues of certificates and notes are available in registered form.) Certificates and notes have never been made callable before maturity, whereas several existing bonds are callable, usually 5 years before maturity—for example, the $4\frac{1}{4}$s of 1992-1987. These securities are all quoted on the basis of 100 and in $\frac{1}{32}$ of 1 percent gradations, although short-term issues are sometimes quoted in $\frac{1}{64}$s. For example, the bid price in early October 1970 on 8 percent notes maturing August 15, 1977 was 102-00, and on $3\frac{1}{2}$ percent bonds maturing November 15, 1998, was 67.06. (Note that by convention the fractions denote 32s, rather than 100s.)

The significant differences between certificates, notes, and bonds almost all arise from variations in original maturities. Certificates have maturities not exceeding 1 year, and vied for many years with Treasury bills as instruments of liquidity. Notes are issued with maturities of not less than 1 year nor more than 7 years. Treasury bonds have original maturities in excess of 5 years.[13] The

[13]These differences in original maturities are conventional only, because there is no legal restriction on issuing bonds with any desired maturity.

longest bond outstanding at midyear 1970 was the $3\frac{1}{2}$ percent bond of 1998. Of course, with the passage of time, the structure of actual maturities markedly changes. Long-term bonds move into both the 1-5-year and the under-1-year categories, and notes move toward and into the under-1-year classification. There is usually little practical difference between certificates, notes, and bonds of the same maturity.

Due to differences in original maturities, the prices of long-term bonds (say, 20-year) fluctuate more widely than those of typical notes (say, 3-year), and in turn the price of a 3-year note varies more than that of a 9-month note. For example, a bond table tells us that with a rise of 1 percent in the market rate of interest, a 3 percent, 20-year bond would drop from 100 to 86.32; a 3 percent, 3-year note would drop from 100 to 97.20; and a 3 percent, 9-month note would decline from 100 to 99.26.

Some idea of the amount and variety of U.S. marketable securities available to investors is provided by the following list of outstanding issues at midyear 1970.[14]

61 issues of bills,	total	$ 76.2 billions
31 issues of notes,	total	93.5 billions
25 issues of bonds,	total	63.0 billions
Grand total		$232.6 billions

U.S. SECURITY DEALERS

The great importance of the U.S. security market in the financial system places a unique responsibility on the dealers that serve investors and traders. While there are hundreds of small retail dealers throughout the country, the bulk of transactions is concentrated in some twenty wholesale security dealers. In 1967, twenty such dealers were identified, of which twelve were nonbanks and eight were commercial banks. Most of the dealers had headquarters in New York City; the rest were located in Chicago.[15] Thus, the great bulk of transactions–90 percent according to some estimates–occurs in New York. However, these dealers have branches in leading cities and a network of correspondent dealers throughout the country. The market is an over-the-wire, negotiated one, in contrast with an organized auction market. There is no common meeting place, such as the New York Stock Exchange, but each dealer is connected with the others and with the Federal Reserve Bank of New York by private wire. Also, there are direct telephone connections with leading institutional customers such as large commercial banks and insurance companies.

[14] *Treasury Bulletin* (July 1970), pp. 28-29.
[15] *Joint Treasury-Federal Reserve Study of the U.S. Government Securities Market* (Washington, D.C., April 1969), p. 14.

functions of dealers

Stated very generally, the function of dealers is to offer and stand ready to purchase all types and maturities of U.S. securities at prices that truly reflect demand and supply conditions. Making a market in this sense means that they are obliged to quote bid and asked prices at which they are prepared to buy and sell significant amounts of each security. This necessarily requires an inventory of most issues, and arrangements for ready acquisition of other issues either by purchase or borrowing transactions. Some idea of the magnitude of this problem may be gained from the facts that dealer positions (inventories) ranged between \$2.2 and \$4.5 billion in 1969-1970, and that the number of outstanding issues of bills, notes, and bonds exceeded 115. With such a complicated structure of securities, and with buyers and sellers located all over the nation and in foreign countries, the need for an efficient dealer system is clear. Without it, no seller can be assured that he is receiving the highest bids, and no buyer can be assured that he is tapping the lowest offers.

Dealer operations are most concerned with secondary transactions—that is, in buying and selling the various outstanding marketable securities which at the end of June 1970 aggregated \$232.6 billion. Commercial banks are by far the most important customers in view of their continuous need to adjust reserve positions. Banks with excess reserves usually put them to work at once by purchasing short-term Treasury securities. But banks with reserve deficiencies may sell securities. Other financial institutions—especially savings banks, insurance companies, savings and loan associations, and pension funds—are also large customers. Nonfinancial corporations buy short-terms heavily to meet their needs for liquid assets in advance of tax payments, dividend and interest payments, construction expenditures, and other cash outlays. Foreign banks and governments invest the greater part of their dollar claims in bills and other short-term obligations. According to estimates, Federal Reserve open-market operations account for around 5 percent of average dealer volume. Interdealer trading is said to amount to between 10 and 25 percent of total transactions. Volume is concentrated heavily in the short-term sector, with about three-fourths in bills alone and over four-fifths in obligations with maturities of under one year. Miscellaneous investors of all types, including individuals and trust funds, account for the rest of transactions throughout the maturity range.

A significant part of total transactions arises from dealer underwriting operations associated with new Treasury offerings. Dealers purchase in the vicinity of one-fifth of Treasury bill issues and then resell them to customers. Sales of allotted notes and bonds account for nearly one-tenth of total dealer sales of such securities.[16] Dealers play a particularly important role in Treasury refunding operations when holders of maturing issues have the privilege of exchanging them for new securities. In this case, the maturing securities are

[16]Joint Economic Committee, 86th Congress, 2nd sess., *A Study of the Dealer Market for Federal Government Securities* (Washington, D.C., 1960), p. 2.

known as *rights.* They are traded heavily during the subscription period and sometimes in advance of the Treasury announcement of refunding terms. Dealers buy the rights for immediate resale and for exchange into the new securities—part of which may be sold at once on a when-issued basis, the rest after date of issue. Thus, dealers lay the groundwork for successful refunding by accumulating maturing securities (rights) from holders who do not want the new securities, and by distributing the new issues among investors who do want them.

Dealers also make a material contribution to execution of current monetary policies. As previously stated, Federal Reserve open-market operations are the most important instrument of control. Treasury securities are sold by the Reserve Banks to absorb member-bank reserves and thereby to restrict credit expansion; they are purchased to enlarge bank reserves and to promote monetary expansion. These transactions are largely in bills and other short-term securities, although on occasion intermediate- and long-term securities are bought and sold. The Reserve Banks depend entirely on qualified dealers, selling to the highest bidders, and taking the lowest offers; consequently, they seek an efficient market having breadth, depth, and resiliency. Arbitrage operations by dealers and their customers are the chief means by which a change of monetary policy is quickly transmitted to the entire structure of rates. For example, the immediate impact of a purchase of $50 million of bills by Reserve Banks is to raise their prices (lower their yields). The secondary effect of such a purchase is far more potent because the system of commercial banks may then use the new reserves to purchase a multiple amount, say, $200 million. At this stage, some of the banks, attracted by relatively higher yields, purchase intermediate-term securities and perhaps a few long-terms; other investors do the same. Meanwhile, dealers may enlarge inventories of intermediate- and long-terms for speculative resale at higher prices. It should be emphasized that this transmission process may take place without holders of bills shifting directly to long-term securities. All that is required is that marginal investors in each maturity class somewhat lengthen maturities. That is, holders of under-1-year issues may shift to 1-3-year securities; holders of 1-3-year issues may convert them to 4-5-year securities; and so on. Thus, arbitrage operations by dealers and their customers promote quick responses in the rate structure and thereby contribute to the effectiveness of flexible monetary policies.

Finally, security dealers serve a basic role in the economy by facilitating the saving-investment process. An adequate flow of savings and their commitment to productive investment is the prime condition for a satisfactory rate of economic growth. Dealer operations provide responsive adjustments of the rate structure to changes in demand and supply of money capital. This enables new savings to flow to areas, industries, and companies where highest returns are promised, all risks considered.

Ingenious methods of clearing and transferring U.S. securities traded by dealers have been developed. As previously indicated, some nine-tenths of total transactions are executed in New York City. For convenience, these securities are largely held in safekeeping by Wall Street banks to expedite physical deliveries. A large part of security transfers takes place on the day of the transaction with payment in Fed funds; most of the rest are delivered the day after the transaction with payment in clearing-house funds (checks on Wall Street banks); and the remaining deliveries are delayed a few days to suit the convenience of the parties. Most of the clearing of money claims and securities for nonbank dealers was handled in 1970 by three New York City banks which specialize in this business–Manufacturers Hanover Trust, Irving Trust Company, and Marine Midland Trust Company. Debits and credits to dealers' accounts in both money and securities are recorded and arrangements for transfer and deliveries are made. More ingenious, the Fed provides a telegraphic transfer service for U.S. securities to Federal Reserve Banks and most of their branches throughout the country. Assume, for example, that a dealer in New York purchases $10 million of U.S. securities from a bank in San Francisco and immediately transfers Federal funds to the San Francisco bank in payment. This bank then delivers the securities to the Federal Reserve Bank of San Francisco which retires them and wires their amount and description to the Federal Reserve Bank of New York. The latter reissues the securities and delivers them to the New York dealer.

financing dealers

A primary condition to successful operation by government-security dealers is that they be able to borrow most of the funds required to carry their security inventories at rates approximating yields realized on securities held. Their net worth is small in proportion to total sources of funds, ranging between 2 and 5 percent for most dealers; in fact, this ratio has to be very low in order to realize a fair return on capital because the narrow spreads between bid and asked prices closely limit net revenues. In 1965 nonbank dealers reported aggregate net worth of $261 million of which $86 million was specifically allocated to operations in U.S. securities.[17] Supplementing this, the dealers must obtain on the average between $3 and $7 billion to finance their net inventory position–three-fourths of which by nonbank dealers. The two principal sources of nonbank dealer financing are (1) collateral loans from Wall Street and other city banks and (2) sales of government securities under repurchase agreements. Before 1951, collateral loans were the dominant source, but since that time repurchase agreements have become the more important.

The bulk of collateral loans to nonbank dealers is made by New York City banks, but they are also made by city banks outside New York, including some foreign institutions. In view of the riskless nature of the collateral, dealers

[17]*Joint Treasury-Federal Reserve Study of the U.S. Government Securities Market,* op. cit., p. 29.

can borrow on very narrow margins—ranging from no margin at all on very short-term bills to about 5 percent on long-term bonds. Each morning New York money-market banks post both the renewal and new rates at which they will lend on call to dealers. Their rates are usually somewhat higher than those offered by banks in other cities, and higher than rates on repurchase agreements. Proceeds of such loans are ordinarily in clearing-house funds (credits to checking accounts) instead of in Federal funds. As a result, dealers also may have to borrow Federal funds for one day to make payment for the day's net cash purchases. For these reasons, collateral loans are usually the least desirable source of funds and are utilized when sufficient credit under repurchase agreements is not forthcoming.

The development of repurchase agreements for nonbank dealer financing during the past decade illustrates the ready adaptability of the money market to changing requirements. When for various reasons the New York money-market banks were unable adequately to meet the financing needs of government-security dealers, the latter aggressively sought to tap small pools of surplus funds throughout the country. In a repurchase agreement, the dealer contracts to sell government securities at a definite price to the provider of funds and to buy them back in the future at a specified price with allowance for interest. The rate is often above that available on Federal funds, but usually below the bank loan rate to dealers. The securities are ordinarily held in trust by a New York bank for the benefit of the lender (buyer) and are returned to the dealer at the time of repurchase. Payments are made in Federal funds.

Repurchase agreements are mutually advantageous to both nonbank dealers and lenders. To the dealer, they usually are a means of obtaining Federal funds more cheaply than they can be borrowed from New York banks, and also a way to arrange convenient maturity dates. To a business corporation, they are a method of realizing a yield on liquid assets that is often higher than yields on Federal funds, Treasury bills, or time deposits in banks. At the same time, maturity dates can be arranged to meet taxes, dividends, and other scheduled payments, and risks of security price fluctuations are entirely avoided. For these reasons, nonfinancial corporations are one of the major sources of nonbank dealer financing. Dealers also enter significantly into repurchase agreements with commercial banks, especially with smaller city banks outside New York. These banks often choose this form of investment because of a higher yield than on Federal funds, because the minimum unit for Federal funds is too large, and because they can eliminate the price risk on short-term government securities.

There are also broad advantages to the money market arising from the use of repurchase agreements. The increased mobility of reserve money removes slack, and thereby contributes to responsiveness of the financial system to changes in monetary policies. In addition, by marshaling pockets of surplus liquidity from all over the country, repurchase agreements assist in developing a truly national money market with greater equalization of money capital and with narrower rate differentials.

A further important source of funds for nonbank dealers is the Federal Reserve Bank of New York, which utilizes repurchase agreements in administration of monetary policies. Reserve funds are released through this channel only at the volition of the Bank, and usually to relieve undue pressure on dealers in financing their security inventories. The amount of government securities held under repurchase agreement by Reserve Banks varies widely, but at times it is not only the largest single source of dealer funds, but also a larger source of Reserve Bank credit than their discounts and advances to member banks. When the Federal Reserve Bank of New York chooses to release reserves in this manner, it may purchase government securities from dealers under agreement that they will repurchase them on call, and at most within 15 days. The repurchase price is usually fixed so that the dealer pays a rate that equals the Reserve Bank discount rate which is the cost of borrowing for bank dealers. On occasion, however, the rate is set in relation to the Treasury bill rate. Reverse repurchase agreements are also used on occasion by the Reserve Banks. In these transactions, the Reserve Banks sell U.S. securities to the dealers under a repurchase agreement.

size and character of the market

Few people are aware of the huge volume of transactions in U.S. securities and of the fact that this market dwarfs all others. This is understandable because most trading is done by commercial banks, Reserve Banks, other financial institutions, nonfinancial corporations, foreign banks and governments, and security dealers. Moreover, transactions in this market receive little publicity. The total amount of transactions ranged between two and seven times the value of transactions on the New York Stock Exchange during the period 1948-1968 (see Table 5-3). Two other features are also evident from the table: (1) the rising trend of trading volume and (2) the declining proportion of the amount of transactions in U.S. securities to transactions on the New York Stock Exchange.

A further question of interest is the composition of transactions by types and maturities of securities. During the period 1969-1970, about 85 percent of total transactions took place in securities with maturities under 1 year, and nearly three-fourths of total trading was in Treasury bills alone. Trading in bonds with maturities over 5 years has shown a declining proportion during the last two decades, in large part a consequence of the declining average maturity of marketable debt. Note also that the annual turnover ratios (sales to securities outstanding) are highest for short-term issues and lowest for long-terms. The average ratio during the period for bills was 0.79; for Notes and bonds with maturities of 1 and under 5 years, 0.34; and for bonds 5 years and over, 0.21.[18] Size of individual transactions also declines as maturities lengthen.

[18]Joint Economic Committee, 86th Congress, op. cit., p. 59.

TABLE 5-3 / TOTAL VALUE OF TRANSACTIONS: U.S. SECURITIES MARKET COMPARED WITH NEW YORK STOCK EXCHANGE (billions of dollars)

Year	Dealer Transactions in U.S. Securities[a] (1)	New York Stock Exchange Transactions[b] (2)	Proportion of (1) to (2) (3)
1948	88.7	11.9	7.44
1951	97.2	19.0	5.12
1954	142.7	25.2	5.66
1957	143.5	28.5	5.03
1961	197.1	54.3	3.63
1963	233.1	56.4	4.15
1965	223.3	76.2	2.93
1967	270.6	129.3	2.09
1968	303.5	148.8	2.04
1969	283.1		
1970	298.7[c]		

[a]Joint Economic Committee, 86th Congress, 2nd Sess., *A Study of the Dealer Market for Federal Securities* (Washington, D.C., 1960), p. 58; *Federal Reserve Bulletin,* various issues. These data combine purchases and sales and are therefore halved for comparison with the amount of transactions on the New York Stock Exchange.

[b]*Fact Book,* New York Stock Exchange, 1969.

[c]Estimated on basis of first half of 1970.

In the case of bills, $1 million is a small transaction and $25 to $50 million is regarded as large, while in long-term bonds, a transaction of $500,000 to $750,000 is considered large, and $250,000 is typical.

OWNERSHIP OF U.S. SECURITIES

total federal securities

As Table 5-4 reveals, the pattern of ownership of the federal debt has shown marked changes during and since World War II. The following developments are especially important.

1/The total federal debt was over four times larger at the end of the war than at the beginning. All types of investors increased holdings several-fold, with commercial banks, Reserve Banks, nonfinancial corporations, state and local governments, and miscellaneous investors showing the largest percentage gains.

2/The total federal debt grew materially between 1947 and 1970 from $258 billion to $371 billion, or by 43.5 percent.

3/The total private-held federal debt increased very little between 1947 and 1970—by only 7 percent during the 23 years. Government investment

TABLE 5-4 / OWNERSHIP OF U.S. SECURITIES ON SELECTED DATES, MIDYEAR, 1940-1970 (billions of dollars)

Type of Investors	1940	1947	1960	1970	Percentage Distribution 1970
Commercial banks	16.1	70.0	55.3	53.0	14.3
Individuals	10.1	66.6	69.2	81.0	21.8
Insurance companies	6.5	24.6	12.0	6.8	1.8
Mutual savings banks	3.1	12.1	6.6	2.9	.8
Nonfinancial corporations	2.1	13.7	20.7	13.6	3.7
State and local governments	.4	7.1	18.1	25.9	7.0
Miscellaneous investors[a]	.7	9.6	22.7	34.8	9.4
Total private-held debt	38.9	203.7	204.7	218.0	58.8
U.S. government investment accounts	7.1	32.8	55.3	95.2	25.7
Fed Banks	2.5	21.9	26.5	57.7	15.5
Total government-held debt	9.6	54.7	81.8	152.9	41.2
Total government securities outstanding	48.5	258.4	286.5	370.9	100.0

[a]Includes savings and loan associations, nonprofit institutions, corporate pension trust funds, dealers and brokers, and foreign investment accounts.
Sources: *Treasury Bulletin* (August 1970), p. 66; *Federal Reserve Bulletin,* various issues.

accounts and Reserve Banks took up over nine-tenths of the increase in total debt. This is significant because government-held debt cancels, and interest costs on this portion are recovered by the Treasury.[19]

4/The holdings of Federal securities by three important types of investors—commercial banks, insurance companies, and mutual savings banks—declined materially between 1947 and 1970. This is explained by the tremendous growth in private demand for short- and long-term credit. These institutions sold government securities in order to make loans. They were overloaded with low-yielding U.S. securities just after the war, and welcomed the opportunity to exchange them for loans at higher rates. The added loans of insurance companies and mutual savings banks were principally real-estate mortgages. Commercial banks experienced the largest increase in business loans, but also recorded large increases in real-estate loans and in consumer loans.

5/The ownership of U.S. securities by individuals was by far the most important category of private-held debt; it represented over one-fifth of the total debt in 1970.

6/Notable increases took place in holdings of three types of investors—nonfinancial corporations, state and local governments, and miscella-

[19]Federal Reserve Bank holdings are included with government-held debt because these banks are in essence government institutions, and 90 percent of net profits after the 6 percent dividend is returned to the Treasury.

neous owners. Business corporations increasingly developed the practice of using short-term government securities to meet liquidity needs. State and local governments held long-terms in their rapidly growing pension funds, and also owned short-term issues for liquidity. The miscellaneous category grew so rapidly because of inclusion of savings and loan associations, private pension funds, and foreign investment—all of which experienced dynamic development.

7/The percentage distribution of total government securities in 1970 is of interest. Private-held obligations represented 59 percent, and government-held debt the remaining 41 percent. Government investment accounts held the largest part of the total debt, 25.7 percent, followed by individuals with 21.8 percent, and the Reserve Banks with 15.5 percent.

marketable securities

It is of further interest to analyze ownership of marketable federal securities by types of securities and investors. These data (as of midyear 1970) are summarized in Table 5-5. The following features may be noted.

TABLE 5-5 / U.S. MARKETABLE SECURITIES BY TYPES OF SECURITIES AND INVESTORS, MIDYEAR 1970 (millions of dollars)

Types of Investors[a]	Bills	Notes	Bonds	Total Amount Outstanding
Commercial banks (5,743)	4,384	22,458	15,609	42,451
Mutual savings banks (495)	147	1,205	1,496	2,848
Life insurance cos. (290)	112	168	2,959	3,238
Fire and casualty ins. cos. (458)	138	891	1,602	2,631
Savings & loan assns. (488)	201	1,468	1,896	3,564
Nonfinancial corporations (468)	1,257	1,018	1,365	3,640
State and local governments:				
General funds (316)	4,424	2,608	2,772	9,804
Pension funds (187)	340	152	2,940	3,432
Fed Banks	22,407	32,420	2,887	57,714
U.S. govt. investment accts.	968	6,472	9,264	16,974
All other investors[b]	41,777	24,359	20,167	86,303
Total	76,154	93,489	62,956	232,599

[a]Parentheses indicate number of reporting institutions.
[b]Included are those banks, insurance companies, savings and loan associations, corporations, and state and local government funds not reporting in the Treasury survey.
Source: *Treasury Bulletin* (August 1970), p. 72.

1/Differences in distribution of holdings of the various types of investor are less than one would expect. This may be explained by the abnormally short average maturity of the marketable federal debt (under four years), and by the fact that with the passage of time, many notes and bonds have relatively short maturities.

2/Commercial banks, the largest private type of investor, distribute their holdings more widely among bills, notes, and bonds than others. Their primary need for liquidity is indicated by the fact that bills and notes represented over three-fifths of total holdings.

3/Mutual savings banks, insurance companies, and savings and loan associations hold small proportions of bills and notes, with a preference for bonds.

4/General funds of state and local governments prefer short-term bills and notes; their pension funds show a preference for bonds.

5/The Federal Reserve Banks hold principally bills and notes.

6/While the foregoing conclusions are justified from the Treasury data as given, their validity is somewhat modified by the fact that over one-third of marketable securities resided in the category "All other investors."

MATURITY DISTRIBUTION OF U.S. SECURITIES

Because one of the goals of Treasury debt management is a proper maturity distribution, it is pertinent to analyze what has happened in this regard since World War II. Table 5-6 summarizes the maturity distribution of marketable

TABLE 5-6 / AVERAGE LENGTH AND MATURITY DISTRIBUTION OF MARKETABLE U.S. SECURITIES, 1947-1970 (billions of dollars)

End of Fiscal Year	Amount Outstanding	Maturity Classes[a]					Average Length
		Within 1 yr.	*1-5 yrs.*	*5-10 yrs.*	*10-20 yrs.*	*20 yrs. and over*	
1947	168.7	51.2	21.9	35.6	18.6	41.5	9 yrs. 5 mos.
1952	140.4	46.4	47.8	13.9	25.7	6.6	5 yrs. 8 mos.
1957	155.7	72.0	40.7	12.3	26.4	4.3	4 yrs. 9 mos.
1962	196.1	88.4	57.0	26.0	9.3	15.2	4 yrs. 11 mos.
1967	210.7	89.6	71.4	24.4	8.4	16.8	4 yrs. 7 mos.
1968	226.6	106.4	64.5	30.8	8.4	16.6	4 yrs. 2 mos.
1969	226.1	103.9	62.8	34.8	8.4	16.2	4 yrs. 0 mos.
1970	232.6	105.5	89.6	15.9	10.5	11.0	3 yrs. 8 mos.

[a]All issues classified to final maturity except partially tax-exempt bonds, which are classified to earliest call date.

Sources: *Treasury Bulletin* (August 1970), p. 21; *Economic Report of the President* (January 1961), p. 185.

federal debt during the period 1947-1970. The outstanding development is a steady decline in the average maturity from 9 years, 5 months in 1947 to 3

4 YIELDS OF U.S. GOVERNMENT SECURITIES, 1944-1970.
Source: Board of Governors of the Federal Reserve System

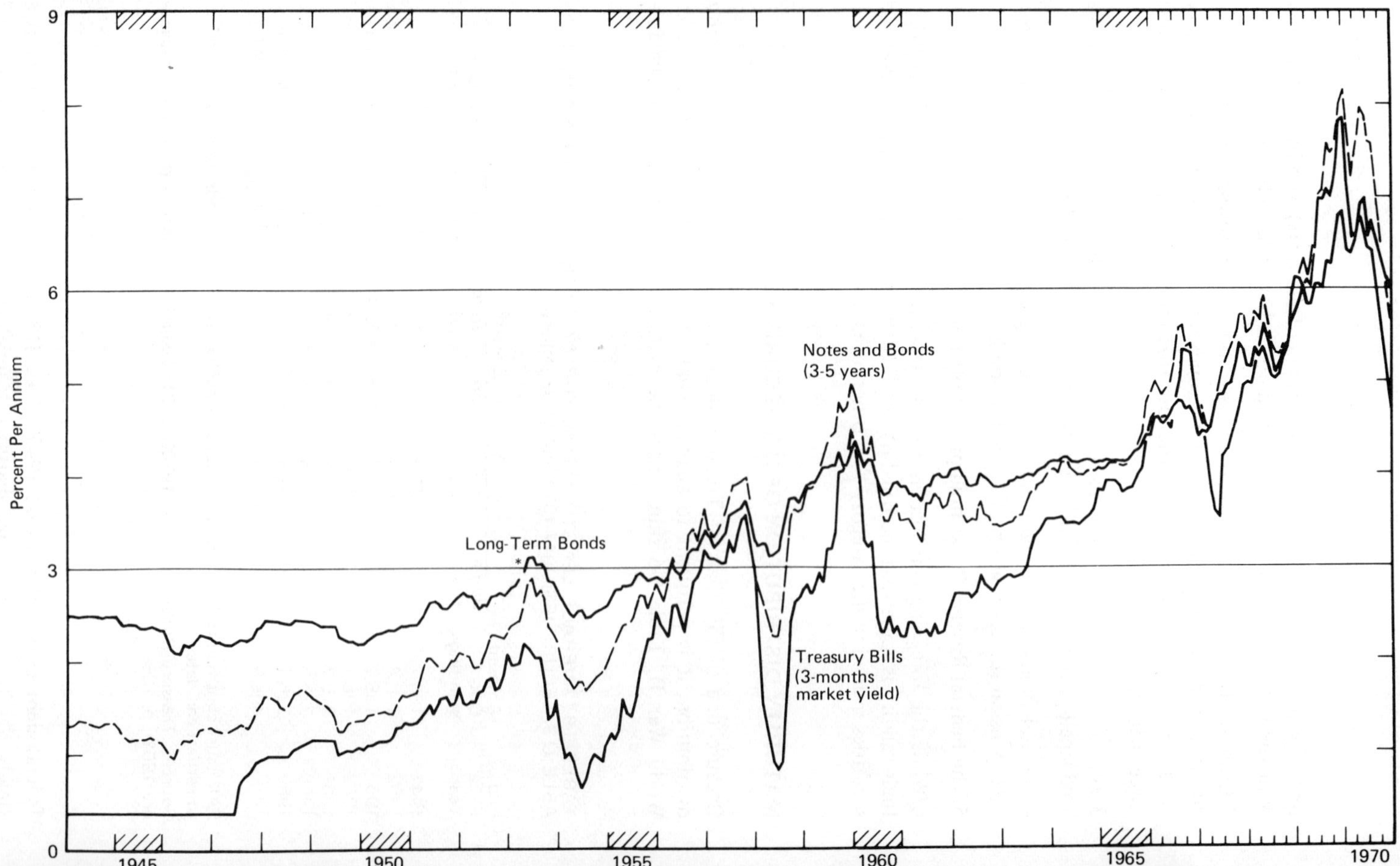

years, 8 months in 1970. A better understanding of what transpired is gained by looking beyond the average to the several maturity classes. The proportion of debt in the under-5-years category in 1947 was 43 percent, and the proportion in the 10-years-and-over category was 36 percent. By 1970, the proportion in the under-5-years category had increased to 84 percent, and the proportion in the 10-years-and-over category had declined to 9 percent.

The material reduction of average debt maturities after the mid-1950s is in part to be explained by the interest rate ceiling of $4\frac{1}{4}$ percent which dates back to the Third Liberty Bond Act during World War I, and which applies to bonds with initial maturities in excess of five years. Since market yields on long-term U. S. bonds often exceeded this ceiling, the Treasury could not sell bonds with a $4\frac{1}{4}$ percent coupon rate except at a discount from par—a practice viewed as illegal. As a consequence, all borrowing was at short-term during this period. Despite repeated requests by the President and the Secretary of the Treasury, Congress refused to remove the rate ceiling.[20]

A little progress in lengthening average maturities was made in the early 1960s. This was achieved by use of *advance refunding,* a new technique in debt management as applied to long-term marketable issues. For example, in September 1960, three new bond issues with maturities ranging from 1980 to 1998 and with coupon rates of $3\frac{1}{2}$ percent were offered in exchange for four outstanding issues with call and maturity dates from 1962 to 1969. About $4 billion of old bonds was exchanged. This, and subsequent advance refundings, account for the increase of the 20-years-and-over category in 1961-1963. Advance refunding is a promising method of lengthening debt maturities with minimum impact on the government-security market and on other capital markets because it offers the new issues mainly to long-term investors. Such an exchange is less likely to be successful when bonds are approaching maturity because by that time they have largely moved into the hands of short-term investors who seek liquidity.

YIELDS ON U.S. SECURITIES

Yields on U.S. securities form a structure characterized by close, yet changing, interrelationships. These features are graphically presented in figure 4, which depicts yields during the period 1942-1970. Comprehensive interpretation would require a complete recounting of economic and financial developments; space permits only a summary of the main features.

First, the yield on three-month Treasury bills is lowest on the average as a consequence of widespread demand for bills as instruments of liquidity. Also, the bill rate is most variable and sensitive to changing market conditions.

[20]The practical effects of this restriction were largely removed in early 1961 by an opinion of the Attorney General that the limit applied only to the coupon rate, not to the effective rate.

This is not surprising in view of the facts that the weight of trading volume centers there, that Federal Reserve open-market operations are conducted largely in bills, and that Treasury financing involves weekly rollovers and frequent changes in the outstanding amount of bills.

Second, the yield on long-term bonds is higher on the average than short-term yields. The greater price stability of short-term issues makes them more valuable as liquid investments, so that their rates are normally lower. It may also be noticed that the spread between long-term and short-term rates is wider before 1955 than afterward. There are two principal reasons for this development: (a) the abnormally low level of rates before 1955—a condition commonly associated with a wider spread between short-term and long-term rates; and (b) the proportion of long-term marketable debt declined significantly during the period (see Table 5-5). The relative scarcity of long-term securities and the relative abundance of short- and intermediate-term issues is reflected in the narrowed spread of yields.

A third feature of the yield structure is the change in relationships as the general level of rates increases—for example, 1958-1959, 1965-1966, and 1968-1969. Using 1958-1959 for illustration, the wide differentials that existed at midyear 1958 decreased materially during the second half of the year and the first half of 1959 as rates moved upward. Then during the second half, when the market tightened further, the short- and intermediate-term rates successively crossed and rose above long-term rates—first 3-5-year obligations, then certificates, and finally bills; the differentials were reversed.[21]

Fourth, an opposite pattern of yield relationships develops during cyclical downturns—for example, 1953-1954, 1957-1958, and 1960-1961. For illustration, with the advent of somewhat easier money during the first half of 1960, short- and intermediate-term rates retreated from their 30-year peak, crossed and dropped below long-term rates, and resumed their typical easy-money relationship. In June 1963, rates on 3-month bills, 3-5-year issues, and long-term bonds were, respectively, 2.99 percent, 3.67 percent, and 4.00 percent.

Fifth, figure 4 shows clearly the pegging of rates by the Fed during World War II and until the Treasury-Federal Reserve Accord in the spring of 1951. Bills were held at $\frac{3}{8}$ percent and certificates at $\frac{7}{8}$ percent until mid-1947, after which both rates were allowed to seek a higher level. The ceiling on long-term bond yields was set at $2\frac{1}{2}$ percent by an open offer of the Fed to purchase at that yield-price. However, actual bond yields dropped below this peg during 1945-1947, due to strong demand by banks and other investors. After 1951, when artificial support by the Fed was largely withdrawn, the general level of rates began an uptrend which carried through to 1969. This was in the more healthy environment of a flexible Federal Reserve policy designed to foster high-level production, business stability, and a steady value of the dollar.

[21]The explanation of yield-maturity relationships is complicated and cannot be undertaken here (see Chapter 11).

In addition to analysis of the rate structure of U.S. securities, it is of interest to see the relation of these rates to other rates in the money and capital markets (see figures 5 and 8). The former compares yields on long-term U.S. bonds with those of long-term corporate and state and local government issues during the period 1942-1970. Perhaps the most important feature is the similarity among the various yields in broad cyclical movements and in trend. This attests to the national character of the capital market, and also underscores the mobility of marginal funds and the competition of borrowers for investors' dollars. United States long-term yields are lowest among taxable issues, due mainly to absence of credit risk and to superior marketability. Highest-grade (Aaa) corporates provide yields ranging between 0.2 and 0.5 percentage points higher than U.S. securities. The spread is somewhat wider since 1956 because of the relative scarcity of U.S. long-term securities and the heavy offerings of corporate bonds. In turn, fourth-grade (Baa) corporates usually provide yields of between 0.6 and 1.0 percentage point higher than Aaa corporates. This is explained by greater credit risk.

However, highest-grade state and local bonds ordinarily yield between 0.5 and 1.0 percentage point less than U.S. long-terms. This is because of their exemption from federal income taxation, which is a feature of varying value to different investors. To banks and other corporate investors subject to the 48 percent federal tax (1970), the after-tax yield of U.S. bonds is well below that of tax-exempt issues. For example, the yield of 7 percent on long-term U.S. bonds in July 1970 was the equivalent of an after-tax yield of 3.64 percent[22] compared with 7 percent on Aaa municipals. It may be further noted that the differential between state and local and federal government yields usually narrows in prosperous years when interest rates are high, as in 1957, 1959, and 1969. This is a consequence of heavy offerings of municipals combined with the fact that the market for tax-exempt issues at highly preferential rates is limited to banks and other corporate investors and to individuals enjoying large incomes. Offerings beyond this market area must be made to investors unfamiliar with tax-exempt bonds, and to whom the feature has much less value. These extramarginal investors can be induced to buy them only at materially higher yields.

Figure 8 compares rates on Treasury bills, 4-6-month commercial paper, and the Federal Reserve Bank discount rate. Again, the most significant feature is the similarity in cyclical movements and in trends of the various rates. This indicates responsiveness to changing conditions, competition, mobility of funds, and the national character of the markets. The rate on 3-month Treasury bills is lowest on the average and also shows the greatest sensitivity to change. The commercial-paper rate averages about $\frac{1}{2}$ percentage point higher than the bill rate because of a higher degree of credit risk and less liquidity. The Federal Reserve Bank discount rate is ordinarily set at a level slightly higher than the bill rate. However, both upward and downward adjustments of the discount rate typically

[22] $7.00 - (.48 \times 7.00) = 3.64$.

5 BOND YIELDS.
Source: Board of Governors of the Federal Reserve System

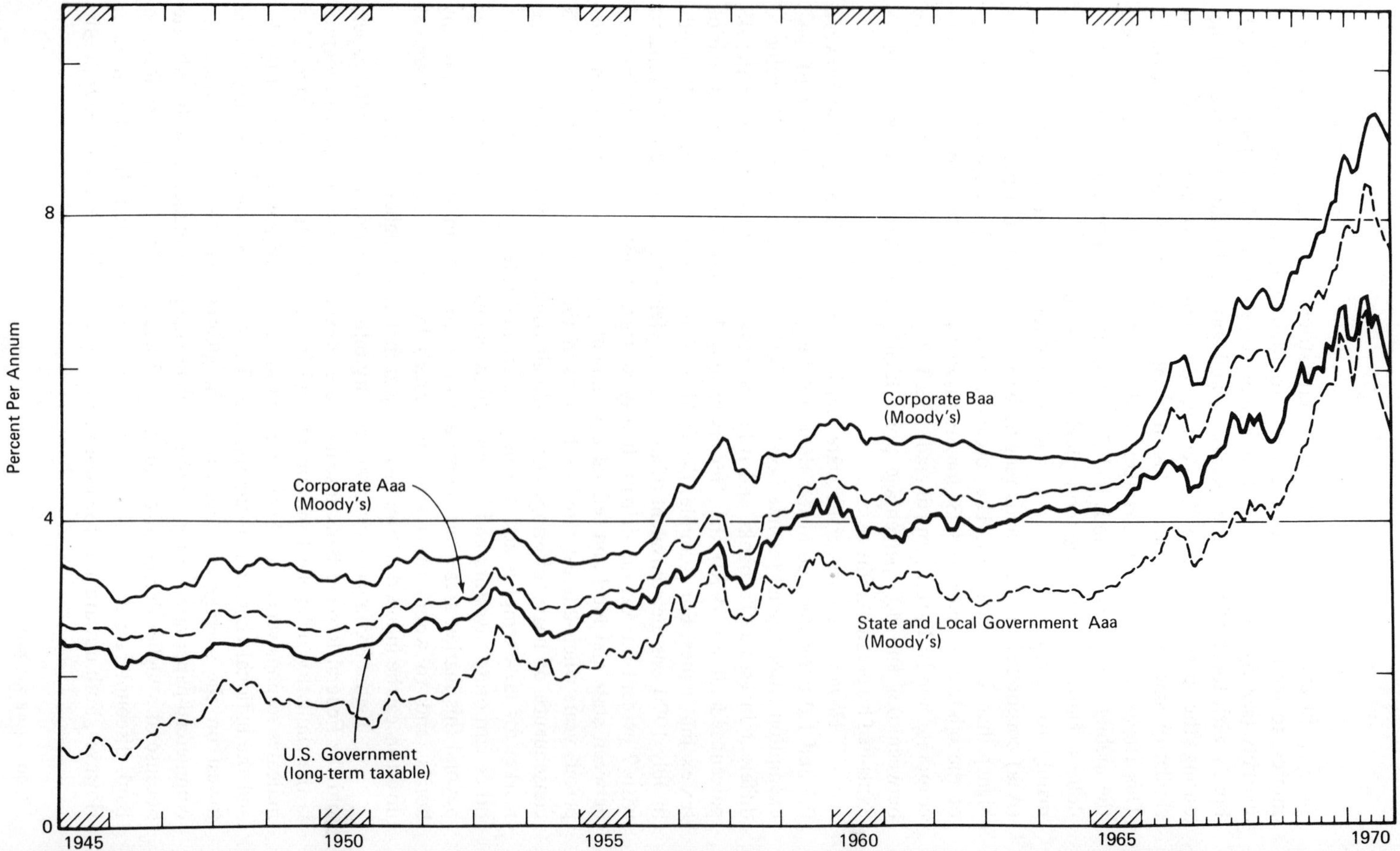

lag behind changes in open-market rates. Thus, it plays a passive not a positive role as an instrument of monetary management. In periods of firm money such as 1957, 1959, 1966, and 1969, the bill rate rises well above the discount rate, and the differential between the discount rate and other open-market rates widens. However, when easy-money conditions develop, as in 1958 and 1961, the bill rate drops well below the discount rate; even the commercial-paper rate usually falls below it.

TREASURY DEBT MANAGEMENT AND THE MARKET

The largest single influence on the U.S. security market is Treasury debt management—a topic of such importance that Chapter 18 is entirely devoted to it. Here the purpose is only to summarize its dominant influence. Congress, with the advice of the Administration, is responsible for the size of the debt by virtue of its Constitutional authority over federal expenditures and revenues. Aside from the opportunity for advice and recommendations in regard to the budget, the Treasury inherits the current deficit or surplus, and all past deficits and surpluses which together account for the size of the federal debt. But the Treasury has almost complete responsibility for the character of the debt. The following are the main areas of policy and decision.

1/Proportion between marketable and nonmarketable securities.

2/Sector of the investment market to be tapped by nonmarketable issues. Shall it include only low- and middle-income savers, or shall it be extended to securities designed for high-income groups, financial institutions, and other investors?

3/Division of the marketable debt among types of securities—bills, certificates of indebtedness, notes, and bonds.

4/Features and terms of each type of security—for example, callability, convertibility, redeemability by owner, restrictions on ownership by banks or others, receivability for tax payments, coupon or registered form, denominations, sale on discount basis or on fixed coupon and price basis, coupon rates, offering prices, and maturities.

5/Maturity distribution of the marketable debt. Shall a well-balanced distribution be a dominant objective? Or shall the maturity distribution be altered to foster economic stabilization by changes in the amount of liquid assets in the economy?

6/Ownership of the marketable debt. Shall aggressive efforts be made to achieve widespread ownership of the debt? Shall ownership of the debt be shifted to and from commercial banks in order to promote the basic objectives of the economy?

7/Interest cost of carrying the debt. Shall the distribution of the debt by types of securities, and by maturities, be determined largely by the objective of minimizing interest costs? Or shall minimization of interest cost be a secondary aim as compared with the basic objectives?

8/Tables 5-1 to 5-6 illustrate the sweeping powers of the Treasury to alter the character of the debt and to influence the U.S. security market. With $105.5 billion of the marketable debt maturing within one year at midyear 1970, and $195.1 billion maturing within five years, a major alteration in types of securities and in maturities can shortly be made. Moreover, by use of advance refunding and by exercising the call option, an even more rapid change can be effected. In addition, the character of the debt is continuously changing as a result of decisions about current developments—borrowing new money to cover cash deficits, using cash surpluses to retire debt, and buying and selling marketable issues for government trust and agency accounts. All such operations and transactions have an important effect on the structure of rates by types and maturities and may also influence the general level of rates.

THE FED AND THE MARKET

The Fed stands second only to the Treasury in weight of influence on the U.S. securities market; in fact, at times its influence transcends that of the Treasury. Federal Reserve influence is exercised directly, through the large volume of its purchases and sales of U.S. securities. Most of these operations are undertaken to implement broad monetary policies. But some are taken to assist Treasury financing programs, to prevent disorderly conditions in the government-security market, and to perform agency functions for foreign governments, central banks, and federal agencies. The Fed also exerts significant indirect influence on the market by using its other instruments of monetary management and by financing U.S. security dealers under repurchase agreements.

Some idea of the magnitude of Fed open-market operations is given by the fact that in June 1970, the Reserve Banks held $57.7 billion of U.S. securities, which represented one-fourth of aggregate marketable federal securities. Moreover, the gross amount of purchases of U.S. securities in 1969, including repurchase agreements, was $58.3 billion.[23] While all types of marketable government securities were bought and sold over the years, transactions were largely in Treasury bills. This was especially true between 1953 and 1960 when a policy of *bills only* or *bills preferably* was followed by the Federal Open-Market Committee. In 1961, the bills-preferably policy was modified, and moderate purchases of intermediate- and long-term securities have since been made.

The volume of Federal Reserve transactions in U.S. securities as an agent for the Treasury is almost beyond comprehension. Issues, redemptions, and exchanges of U.S. securities in 1969 amounted to $1,151 billion.[24] In

[23]Board of Governors of the Federal Reserve System, *Annual Report* (Washington, D.C., 1969), p. 334.

[24]Ibid., p. 340.

addition, the Reserve Banks act as agent for foreign central banks and governments and for the several federal agencies. Thus, when agency transactions are combined with monetary-management operations, the effects on the money market are always important, and sometimes dominant.

The indirect influences of Federal Reserve actions should be emphasized because they are often far more important than direct transactions. This is true mainly because of fractional legal-reserve requirements for commercial banks. Consider first the case of Fed purchase of U.S. securities, which tends directly to increase prices and lower yields of the specific issues. But this is only the beginning. The excess reserves of member banks, which may realistically be assumed to rise almost as much as the amount of purchased securities, serve as a basis for multiple expansion of bank earning assets and deposits. Depending on circumstances, $1 of new bank reserves may permit asset additions of between $4 and $8, part or all of which may be U.S. securities. Thus, the downward pressure on rates from secondary purchases of securities by member banks is likely to be far greater than the downward pressure from the initial Federal Reserve purchase.

A similar indirect influence may arise from a lowering of member-bank reserve requirements by the Board of Governors. The newly created excess reserves may lead to commercial-bank purchases of U.S. and other securities amounting to several times the excess reserves. A sharp rise in prices and a drop in yields therefore tends to take place.

Another indirect effect may spring from Federal Reserve discount policies—changing discount rates and administration of advances to member banks. This effect is not so potent as that of open-market purchases or of lower reserve requirements, due to the reluctance of banks to borrow. Nevertheless, it may in some circumstances be substantial.

While the foregoing illustrations of indirect influence of Federal Reserve actions on the market have all looked toward lower rates and the associated changes in rate structure, they may with equal force be directed toward higher rates. That is, sales of U.S. securities by Reserve Banks, prescription of higher member-bank reserve requirements, and higher Reserve Bank discount rates combined with reserve credit rationing all point to a higher level of interest rates and to associated changes in rate structure.

Finally, the Fed exerts indirect influence on the government-security market by financing nonbank dealers under repurchase agreements. In tight-money markets, the amount of this financing often exceeds $500 million, thus providing a substantial part of their entire borrowing needs. However, the significance of Reserve Bank repurchase agreements arises more from their marginal character than from their amount. The Federal Reserve Bank of New York offers to release reserve funds through this channel when such action is in harmony with general credit policies, and when dealers have special credit requirements to carry security inventories. These funds flow directly to the points of need and they may be withdrawn flexibly as soon as needs subside.

REFERENCES

Gaines, Tilford C., *Techniques of Treasury Debt Management* (New York: Free Press, 1962).

Joint Economic Committee, 86th Congress, 2nd sess., *A Study of the Dealer Market for Federal Government Securities* (Washington, D.C., 1960).

Joint Treasury-Federal Reserve Study of the U.S. Government Securities Market (Washington, D.C., April 1969). Also, see 13 staff studies, including Lawrence Banyas, *New Techniques in Debt Management Since the Late 1950s,* and Paul Meek, *The Changing Structure of the Dealer Market in Government Securities.*

Roosa, Robert V., *Federal Reserve Operations in the Money and Government Securities Markets* (New York: Federal Reserve Bank of New York, 1956).

Treasury-Federal Reserve Study of the Government Securities Market, Part I, 1959; Part II, 1960; Part III, 1960.

6

the commercial-paper market

The open market for commercial paper is a distinctive feature of the financial system of the United States. No other country has such a market worthy of mention. Since the early part of the nineteenth century, a significant amount of open-market borrowing for working capital purposes has been done by business firms of high credit standing. Such borrowing has been an alternative to customer bank loans–usually supplementary, but in some cases subtitutional.

The peculiar need for such a market in the United States is attributable mainly to the unit system of commercial banking, which lacked facilities for the ready transfer of surpluses of banking funds in one section of the country to other areas experiencing shortages. England, Germany, France, and other important nations had little need for this type of market because of their nationwide, branch-banking systems by which transfers of bank reserves could be made quickly and effectively within each of the large banking institutions.

In the broadest sense, commercial paper includes all short-term evidences of indebtedness used in the financing of business operations–bankers' acceptances, trade bills of exchange, promissory notes of business firms that borrow from their own banks, as well as open-market commercial paper. The term is used here in a narrower meaning to include (1) notes sold to investors through commercial-paper dealers and (2) notes placed directly with investors by large finance companies, and more recently by large bank holding companies. Directly-placed paper is a relatively recent development, mainly since the mid-1930s, but beginning in the early 1920s. Although these two divisions of the market have much in common, they differ in several important respects, and it is therefore desirable to discuss them separately. Consideration is first given to the open market in which dealers serve as middlemen to bring borrowers and lenders together.

DEVELOPMENT OF THE OPEN MARKET

The modern commercial-paper dealer and market are the product of a gradual development stretching over a century and a half. It is well established that brokers handling promissory notes and trade bills were operating in the important commercial centers of the country as early as 1790. The rapid expansion of industry, trade, and banking during the early part of the nineteenth century was accompanied by further growth in note brokerage. The increased importance of the market was indicated by the fact that rates on open-market commercial paper in leading cities were quoted in the *Financial Register of the United States* during the 1830s.

In the period before the Civil War, New York City became the leading market for commercial paper, with Boston and Philadelphia in second and third places, respectively. Smaller markets existed in the thriving cities of the Midwest and South, including St. Louis, Cincinnati, Baltimore, and New Orleans. The bulk of borrowing was done by textile mills (in New England), dry-goods jobbers, wholesale hardware dealers, and wholesale grocers. The buyers were principally banks, although some paper was purchased by wealthy individuals and merchants. Middlemen in this era were typically brokers instead of dealers. Just before the Civil War, dealers began to buy notes outright from borrowers, rather than handling them for brokers' commission. This practice developed rapidly after 1880 and became the prevailing method by 1910.

Closely allied to outright purchase of notes was the development of more systematic methods of credit investigation. With acceptance of greater responsibilities and risks, dealers became more discriminating in their selection of paper. Around 1900, the larger dealers created departments that kept files of relevant information about borrowing customers. Detailed financial statements were required from prospective borrowers as a basis for intelligent credit decisions.

A more definite idea of the development of the market is conveyed by Table 6-1 and figure 6, which present the amounts of commercial paper outstanding since World War I. Note that dealer-placed paper reached a peak of about $1 billion in 1920, but declined steadily thereafter to around $100 million at the bottom of the depression in 1933. Little revival of the market occurred during the 1930s, World War II, or the early postwar years. Real revival awaited the 1950s, when credit demands rapidly expanded and the supply of bank credit was restricted by tighter Federal Reserve monetary policies. The upsurge between 1960 and 1970 brought the amount to nearly $14 billion in May of the latter year.

What were the reasons for the decline and subsequent revival of the dealer market in commercial paper? During the 1920s, the principal cause of decline was a shift to sale of stocks and bonds as a means of providing working capital. The growth in size of firms opened the capital markets to a wider sector

6 COMMERCIAL PAPER OUTSTANDING, 1953-1970.
Source: Federal Reserve Bank of New York

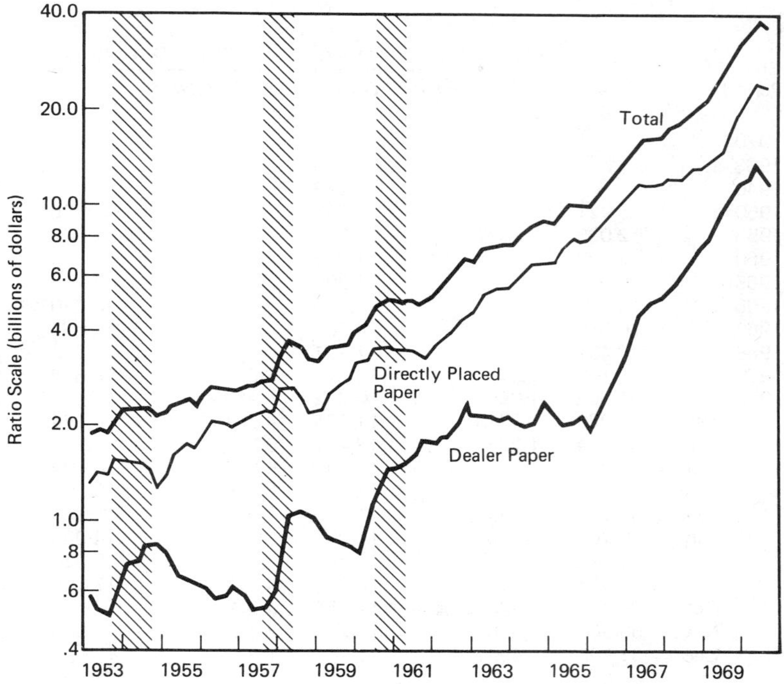

of business which took advantage of a favorable stock market to reduce dependence on banks. Also, there was a growing tendency to finance working capital by retained earnings. Still another reason was the progress made by management in economizing inventories whose proportion to sales declined significantly. During the Great Depression, the small volume of paper was linked to the drastically reduced level of business and the fact that commodity prices declined over one-third. Also, bank reserves were so abundant and customer loan rates were so low that there was little advantage in open-market borrowing.

Revival of the market during the postwar period was part of the large growth of the economy in terms of all value measurements. The GNP was almost 11 times as large in 1970 as in 1939—one-third of which was real, and two-thirds a result of the rise of commodity prices. The market's expansion paralleled the vigorous growth in loan demand as evidenced by the fact that commercial-bank loans rose from \$26.1 billion at the end of 1945 to \$314 billion at the end of 1970, and that business loans of banks increased during the same period from \$9.6 to \$110 billion. Expansion of dealer paper was also closely associated with the dynamic development of installment financing of automobiles and other durable consumer goods. While the largest finance companies placed their notes

TABLE 6-1 / COMMERCIAL AND FINANCE-COMPANY PAPER, 1920-1970
(millions of dollars)

End of Period		Total	Placed Through Dealers		Placed Directly		Number of Borrowers Through Dealers
			Bank Related	*Other*[a]	*Bank Related*	*Other*[b]	
1920				948			4,395
1933				109			538
1940				218			734
1950		921		345		576	400
1955		2,035		510		1,525	417
1960		4,497		1,358		3,139	327
1965		9,058		1,903		7,155	n.a.
1966		13,279		3,089		10,190	n.a.
1967		16,535		4,901		11,634	n.a.
1968		20,497		7,201		13,296	335
1969		31,709	1,216	10,601	3,078	16,814	561
1970	Jan.	34,362	1,266	10,772	4,262	18,062	n.a.
	Feb.	36,020	1,271	11,604	4,781	18,364	n.a.
	Mar.	37,164	1,223	12,411	5,295	18,235	n.a.
	Apr.	38,011	1,088	12,647	5,584	18,692	n.a.
	May	39,724	1,126	12,826	6,474	19,298	n.a.
	June	37,798	1,044	11,945	6,559	18,250	n.a.
	July	36,961	986	11,048	6,834	18,093	n.a.
	Aug.	36,570	802	11,242	6,501	18,025	n.a.
	Sept.	33,958	505	12,013	4,115	17,325	n.a.
	Oct.	34,401	520	12,564	3,179	18,138	n.a.
	Nov.	33,966	526	12,775	2,600	18,065	n.a.
	Dec.	31,765	409	12,262	1,940	17,154	633

[a] Includes finance-company paper as well as other commercial paper sold in the open market.
[b] As reported by finance companies that place their paper directly with investors.
Sources: *Federal Reserve Bulletin,* various issues; National Credit Office, Inc., for number of borrowers.

directly, the smaller companies raised a substantial part of requirements in the dealer market. In fact, finance companies accounted for over one-half of dealer paper after 1958. Finally, it should be emphasized that revival of the dealer market did not occur until the Treasury-Federal Reserve Accord in early 1951. A rising tide of credit demand combined with a tighter Federal Reserve rein on bank reserves resulted in an uptrend of interest rates. The spread between customer loan rates of banks and commercial-paper rates widened, especially during recession conditions, so that open-market borrowing afforded a significant cost advantage.

Table 6-1 illustrates the striking contrast of the number of borrowers and the amount of outstanding commercial paper during the postwar period. While the number of borrowing firms increased only moderately between 1950 and 1970, the amount of outstandings rose 38-fold. This meant, of course, that average outstandings per firm increased substantially—from about $750,000 to

$3.5 million. This development is attributable to a material increase in size of firms using the market.

Finally, Table 6-1 and figure 6 show the relative importance of both the dealer market and directly-placed paper. With the rapid growth of installment financing of consumer durables during the postwar years, large finance companies turned increasingly to direct placement of short-term notes. In fact, this was the outstanding development with respect to commercial paper. From only a nominal amount in 1945, directly-placed paper increased steadily to nearly $26 billion in 1970. Its rate of growth was far more rapid than dealer paper through 1957, when the amount was nearly four times larger. But vigorous growth of dealer paper after 1959 reduced the ratio to between two and three to one. Their combined amount reached a record peak of $39.7 billion at midyear 1970. Looking back over the entire period since World War I, the striking factor is the change in character of the market. Before 1920, there was no directly-placed finance company paper, and dealer paper was composed largely of seasonal borrowing by industrial and trading firms. In sharp contrast, by the early 1960s, borrowing by the smaller finance companies had come to occupy the dominant position in the dealer market, accounting for over 85 percent of total outstandings according to estimates. The extremely tight credit conditions of 1969 and 1970 brought commercial banks into the dealer market as borrowers. Bank-related paper exceeded $1 billion, and represented between 8 and 10 percent of total outstanding dealer paper.

THE DEALER MARKET

The open market for commercial paper embraces three groups: (1) commercial-paper dealers, (2) borrowing business firms, and (3) investors. Each group requires separate consideration.

commercial-paper dealers

Virtually all commercial paper has been handled in recent years by six dealers, four of whom do over 90 percent of the total business.[1] The largest dealers have main offices in New York, Chicago, and Boston, with branches in other leading cities. They usually combine the commercial-paper business with other operations such as investment banking, security brokerage, and commodity trading.

Practically all open-market paper is composed of single-name, unsecured promissory notes of prime borrowers. To qualify for open-market borrowing, the firm's credit standing must be high enough to make collateral

[1]A. G. Becker & Co., Chicago; Goldman, Sachs & Co., New York; Salomon Brothers, New York, and Weil, Pearson & Co., Boston.

security unnecessary. In special cases, however, the notes are secured by warehouse receipts or other collateral, or are guaranteed by another party. As figure 7 indicates, a note is typically made payable to bearer on a given date at a designated bank. The bearer form contributes to ready transferability without the need for endorsement.

Notes are issued in round denominations to suit requirements of banks and other investors. The most common denomination is $1 million, but denominations range between $25,000 and $5 million. For example, a loan of $25 million might be made up as follows:

Denomination	Number of Notes	Total Amount
$5,000,000	1	$ 5,000,000
1,000,000	14	14,000,000
500,000	10	5,000,000
100,000	7	700,000
50,000	5	250,000
25,000	2	50,000
		$25,000,000

Commercial paper sold by dealers usually falls in the maturity range of three to six months; occasionally, firms borrow for only three days or for as long as nine months. Original maturities do not exceed nine months because registration with the Securities and Exchange Commission is required for longer maturities—with all the expense and delay involved. Maturities are mainly determined by working-capital needs which are governed by such factors as the period of inventory turnover, the collection period for receivables, and the seasonal character of the business.

7 EXAMPLE OF OPEN-MARKET COMMERCIAL PAPER.

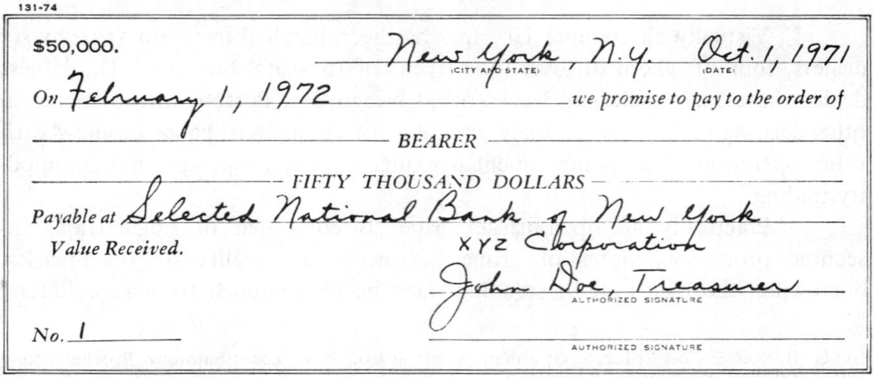
131-74

$50,000. New York, N.Y. (CITY AND STATE) Oct. 1, 1971 (DATE)

On February 1, 1972 we promise to pay to the order of

BEARER

FIFTY THOUSAND DOLLARS

Payable at Selected National Bank of New York

Value Received.

XYZ Corporation

John Doe, Treasurer

AUTHORIZED SIGNATURE

No. 1

AUTHORIZED SIGNATURE

Dealers exercise great care in origination of commercial paper because they wish to minimize credit risk and to maintain the almost spotless reputation enjoyed by this instrument. They cannot afford to sully their reputations by selling inferior paper. Consequently, a thoroughgoing credit investigation should, and usually does, precede the actual purchase of notes from a borrower. The procedure is very similar to that of a large bank when it determines the line of credit for a customer. Space precludes more than an indication of its general nature. But suffice to say that it includes among other things a survey of the industry, the position of the firm in the industry, analysis of balance sheets and operating statements over a 5-10-year period, and careful appraisal of the integrity and capability of management. In short, the object is to analyze all relevant information that bears on the ability and willingness of the firm to meet its obligations according to contract.

Commercial-paper dealers procure most of their paper by outright purchase. That is, the borrowing firm is immediately paid the face value of the notes less the discount and commission. This method ensures the borrower a specific amount of funds at a definite time. The dealer assumes the risk that he may not be able to dispose of the notes profitably, either because of a general rise of money rates or of unfavorable reaction to the notes. However, he may gain by selling the notes for an amount larger than the purchase price plus the normal commission.

Finance-company paper is sometimes *bought as sold,* and a small amount of industrial and trade paper is also handled in this manner. The dealer sells the notes at the best price obtainable and remits the proceeds less commission *after* the sale is completed. In this case, which accounts for less than 5 percent of dealer-placed notes, the dealers are really brokers.

A third method, which is a compromise between the first two, is the *open-rate* basis. The dealer advances a substantial amount, usually 90 percent or more of the face amount, upon receiving the notes. Later, when the notes are sold, the remainder with adjustment for discount and commission is turned over to the borrower. In this way, the dealer shifts the risk to the borrower who realizes the gain or stands the loss arising from a favorable or unfavorable market. A variant of this method is sometimes employed whereby the dealer extends limited protection to the borrower by assuming the loss if the rate of discount exceeds a stipulated maximum.

The standard commission of dealers of $\frac{1}{4}$ percent per annum is paid by borrowers as part of the cost of credit. However, departures from the standard commission occur from time to time as a result of bargaining. For example, when the spread between bank loan rates and commercial-paper rates narrows, dealers may be forced to shade their commission to prime borrowers to $\frac{1}{8}$ percent.

Commercial-paper dealers finance their inventory of notes with their own capital and by loans from banks. Loans are usually arranged with large banks in New York City and other leading cities where dealers keep deposit accounts and where rates are lowest. Most loans are on a demand basis, although some dealers borrow partly on time. Loans are nearly always secured by the notes being offered. Banks expect a margin of about 5 percent of face value for their protection, although the strongest houses borrow with less margin or even with no margin at all. Rates charged are among the lowest in the money market in view of the high quality of the collateral security and the short duration of the typical loan. They are usually somewhat above the open-market rate on commercial paper and about the same as the prime rate on business loans.

Dealers sell commercial paper with an option period of usually ten days during which the buyer has the opportunity to check its quality. If he so desires, he may return the paper during the option period for repurchase at the original annual discount rate. Settlement is usually in Federal (Reserve) funds.

BORROWERS IN THE OPEN MARKET

Commercial-paper dealers set very high credit standards for borrowers. In fact, it is estimated that less than 5 percent of business firms are able to meet the test. The remaining firms fail to measure up due to some weakness–whether it be earnings prospects, capital structure, current position, condition of the industry, quality of management, or some other factor. These high standards are essential to preserve the reputation of open-market paper as an almost riskless short-term investment. This reputation passed the acid test during the Great Depression when losses were negligible. Even near the bottom of the depression in 1932, the rate of loss on outstandings was less than 0.1 percent. Investors enjoyed complete freedom from losses between 1936 and 1969.

However, a near crisis occurred in the market when the Penn Central Transportation Company entered bankruptcy in June 1970, with $82 million of outstanding commercial paper. In addition, Mill Factors, a finance company, defaulted. The losses to investors from these defaults will doubtless be substantial. These events created considerable investor apprehension, which was magnified by the generally low level of corporate liquidity at the time and the erratic performance of the stock market. As a result, a run on the commercial-paper market developed, and nonbank outstanding paper declined by $3 billion (about 10 percent) in the three weeks ended July 15, 1970. But by the end of the month, the crisis had subsided, and the volume outstanding began to rise again. This was a stern warning to the dealer group that had been lulled by the prosperity of the late 1960s and had become rather lax in regard to thorough credit analysis. Likewise, investors ceased to accept notes solely on the dealer's recommendation and began to insist on notes of firms of high credit standing.[2]

[2]See F. C. Schadrack and F. S. Breimyer, "Recent Developments in the Commercial Paper Market," Federal Reserve Bank of New York, *Monthly Review* (December 1970), pp. 289-290.

type of borrowers

Borrowers with the intermediation of dealers are characterized by wide diversity. The common denominator is high credit standing rather than engagement in particular lines of business. Table 6-2 indicates that at the end of

TABLE 6-2 / NUMBER OF BORROWERS IN THE OPEN MARKET FOR COMMERCIAL PAPER

Type of Borrower	December 1968	Percentage Distribution	December 1970	Percentage Distribution
Industrial companies	149	44.5	289	45.6
Public utility companies	82	24.5	157	24.8
Finance companies	96	28.6	92	14.5
Bank holding companies	0	0.0	53	8.4
Mortgage companies	3	0.9	22	3.5
Insurance companies	1	0.3	12	1.9
Railroad companies	4	1.2	8	1.3
Total	335	100.0	633	100.0

Source: National Credit Office, Inc.

1970, 46 percent of commercial-paper borrowers were industrial corporations. Producers of grains, flour, fertilizers, meat, canned products, sugar, petroleum products, chemicals, rubber products, and electronic products were among the important industrial borrowers. Public utilities accounted for 25 percent and finance companies for 15 percent. Bank holding companies, which were not in the market before 1969, rose to 8 percent. Automobile finance companies are the most important in the finance area, but companies financing other durables and making small loans are also represented. Retail chain and department stores are important borrowers, as are wholesalers of hardware and groceries.

Borrowers are widely distributed over the country, with the heaviest concentration in the New York and Chicago Fed districts and along the Atlantic seaboard. With respect to size, few borrowers have net worth below \$50 million, with most in the \$350-\$800 million range; some are multibillion dollar companies.

advantages to borrowers

The open market provides definite advantages to qualified firms with fluctuating working-capital requirements. Most important is the lower cost of borrowing. During the 1950s and 1960s, the commercial-paper rate was $\frac{1}{2}$ to 2 percentage points below the customer loan rate on business loans of banks, although in 1969 it rose above this rate (see figure 8, p. 108). This differential, however, is not a precise measure of the cost advantage because allowance must be made for two offsetting factors—dealers' commission and reduction of compensating bank balances—as well as for certain intangibles. The dealers' commission, which is typically $\frac{1}{4}$ percent per annum, is borne by the borrower and must be added to the open-market rate. However, it is possible that use of the open market may enable a firm to reduce somewhat its lines of bank credit and the amount of compensating balances. But this economy is not certain because the amount of bank balances may be determined entirely, or largely, by liquidity needs instead of by compensating balance requirements. If so, a shift of part of current borrowing to the open market would justify little or no reduction of bank balances. Also, dealers typically insist that the borrower maintain bank credit lines in the amount of outstanding paper, or at least to a high proportion of it. Thus, generalization in regard to the effect on compensating balances is unwarranted; each firm must analyze this factor for itself.

Closely allied to the cost advantage is the fact that open-market borrowing improves a business firm's competitive position in the credit market. In bargaining with banks on rates and other loan terms, the firm can point out a convenient alternative. Moreover, the prestige that goes with open-market borrowing increases competition among banks for the borrower's account.

A third advantage to the borrowing firm grows out of financial recognition and publicity received. Recognition as an open-market borrower is likely to open the door to the capital market for sale of stocks and bonds on a more favorable basis. In fact, the commercial-paper dealer may also be an underwriter of long-term securities. Moreover, the publicity received is sometimes good advertising for the sale of products.

Finally, open-market borrowing is viewed by many firms as a desirable supplement to direct bank borrowing. In some cases, the 10 percent loan limit may prevent depositary banks from advancing the full amount of needed funds. In other instances, it may prove more convenient to deal with one dealer than to borrow from many depositary banks. A program frequently followed is that of alternating bank and open-market borrowing, so that periodic cleanups can be effected even though some debt may constantly be outstanding. Another practice is to borrow concurrently from both sources, with variable proportions depending on rates and other terms.

Opponents of the open market for commercial paper enumerate several alleged disadvantages for borrowers. Only two of these have real substance, viz., inflexibility and impairment of bank relationships. Once the maturity, rate, and other terms have been set and notes have been purchased by a dealer, nothing can be done to change the contract. The principal and interest must be paid at the designated time and place; prepayment, renegotiation of terms, and extension of maturity are no longer possible. In contrast, the rather intimate bank-customer relationship often affords much greater flexibility. An unforeseen change of circumstances may be accommodated by prepayment, extension of maturity, adjustment of compensating balance, or other alterations of terms. This greater adaptability of direct bank borrowing may be of considerable value to some businesses; others may find it of little or no significance.

Under some circumstances, open-market borrowing may impair valuable personal bank-customer relationships. When a firm gives its depositary bank all loan business, the bank in return is more likely to respond with every possible accommodation, including favorable loan terms and loyal support during adversity. Such a bank relationship may be very valuable and well worth cultivation. At the other extreme, if a firm shifts borrowing to the open market whenever a rate advantage develops, the friendly bank relationship may be strained or seriously impaired. It is natural for bank officers to resent the loss of profitable loan business, to carry over this attitude in future relations, and to give extra services and accommodations to their best customers. Hence, a business firm must at times evaluate the bank relationship in comparison with the cost advantage of open-market borrowing. Frank discussion with loan officers often resolves the problem on a friendly basis by some combination of rate adjustment and allocation of borrowings.

With the cost advantage of open-market borrowing as large as it has been, the question may well be raised: Why has the amount of such borrowing not increased even faster in recent years? One part of the answer is found in the decisions of qualified borrowers; the other part in the attitudes of investors. As previously indicated, businesses prefer to borrow from their banks in order to enjoy the continuing benefits of cordial relationships, and at times the greater flexibility of direct loans. An appreciable saving in interest cost is required to induce borrowers to forsake their banks. Businesses are mindful of the fact that bank lines of credit must be maintained in reserve for periods when the open market may provide only part of their needs, or even be closed to them. Another reason why dealer-placed paper did not rise more rapidly during the 1950s and 1960s is the limited capacity of commercial paper to attract investible funds. Short-term Treasury securities and other high-grade issues compete for investors' dollars, and the supply of investible funds attracted by commercial paper is limited and somewhat immobile. Investors would not purchase more paper except at higher rates. In turn, rising rates would narrow the difference from bank loan rates, and thereby remove the main inducement for open-market borrowing. In conclusion, it may be observed that the size and growth of the open market are closely related to the spread between open-market rates and customer loan rates. That is, the size of the market much depends on the degree of competitiveness of banks. They can encourage growth of the market by permitting the rate spread to widen; they can limit growth of the market by narrowing the rate differential and by keeping customer loan rates sensitively responsive to money-market conditions.

The foregoing conclusion is supported by Table 6-3 and figure 6. Analysis of the data reveals high correlation between commercial paper

TABLE 6-3 / COMMERCIAL PAPER OUTSTANDING COMPARED WITH SPREAD BETWEEN MARKET RATES AND CUSTOMER LOAN RATES OF BANKS, 1957-1970

Year and Month		Commercial Paper Placed Through Dealers (millions of dollars) (1)	Rate on 4-6-Mo. Commercial Paper (percent) (2)	Rate on Short-Term Business Loans, $200,000 and over, NYC (percent) (3)	Rate Spread—(3) − (2) (percent) (4)
1957	Mar.	489	3.63	4.11	0.48
	June	454	3.79	4.12	0.33
	Sept.	501	4.00	4.60	0.60
	Dec.	551	3.81	4.62	0.81
1958	Mar.	862	2.33	4.17	1.84
	June	965	1.54	3.74	2.20
	Sept.	958	2.93	3.87	0.94
	Dec.	840	3.33	4.18	0.85
1959	Mar.	883	3.35	4.18	0.83
	June	729	3.83	4.61	0.78
	Sept.	763	4.63	5.06	0.43
	Dec.	627	4.88	5.12	0.24
1960	Mar.	805	4.49	5.10	0.61
	June	1,021	3.81	5.10	1.29
	Sept.	1,263	3.39	4.62	1.23
	Dec.	1,358	3.23	4.66	1.43
1961	Mar.	1,525	3.03	4.64	1.61
	June	1,460	2.91	4.63	1.72
	Sept.	1,730	3.05	4.64	1.59
	Dec.	1,711	3.19	4.66	1.47
1962	Mar.	1,876	3.25	4.68	1.43
	June	1,878	3.25	4.68	1.43
	Sept.	2,228	3.34	4.65	1.31
	Dec.	2,088	3.29	4.68	1.39
1963	Mar.	2,260	3.34	4.70	1.36
	June	2,049	3.38	4.68	1.30
	Sept.	2,098	3.88	4.71	0.83
	Dec.	1,928	3.96	4.65	0.69
1964	Mar.	2,038	4.00	4.66	0.66
	June	1,948	4.00	4.68	0.63
	Sept.	2,220	3.89	4.61	0.72
	Dec.	2,223	4.17	4.66	0.49
1965	Mar.	2,070	4.38	4.62	0.24
	June	1,965	4.38	4.62	0.24
	Sept.	2,194	4.38	4.64	0.26
	Dec.	1,903	4.65	4.99	0.34
1966	Mar.	2,066	5.21	5.34	0.13
	June	2,090	5.51	5.57	0.06
	Sept.	2,773	5.89	6.05	0.16
	Dec.	3,089	6.00	6.09	0.09
1967	Mar.	4,360	5.24	6.08	0.84
	June	4,934	4.65	5.88	1.23
	Sept.	5,124	5.00	5.88	0.88
	Dec.	4,901	5.56	5.95	0.39
1968	Mar.	5,832	5.64	6.39	0.75
	June	5,822	6.25	6.82	0.57
	Sept.	7,737	5.82	6.87	1.05
	Dec.	7.201	6.17	6.59	0.42

TABLE 6-3 / Continued

Year and Month		Commercial Paper Placed Through Dealers (millions of dollars) (1)	Rate on 4-6 Mo. Commercial Paper (percent) (2)	Rate on Short-Term Business Loans, $200,000 and over, NYC (percent) (3)	Rate Spread—(3) – (2) (percent) (4)
1969	Mar.	9,033	6.82	7.30	0.48
	June	10,159	8.23	7.81	–0.42
	Sept.	11,871	8.48	8.83	0.35
	Dec.	11,817	8.84	8.83	–0.01
1970	Mar.	13,634	8.33	8.89	0.56
	June	12,989	8.21	8.53	0.32
	Sept.	12,518	7.32	8.24	0.92
	Dec.	12,671	5.73	7.83	2.10

Source: *Federal Reserve Bulletin,* various issues.

outstanding and the spread between the open-market rate and customer loan rates on short-term business loans of banks. For example, the widened rate spread in the first three quarters of 1958 was associated with an increase of some $500 million in the amount of dealer commercial paper. This relation was repeated in the first three quarters of 1961. These were periods of recession when commercial banks failed to adjust rates downward in step with open-market rates. As a consequence, business loans of banks declined both because their customers shifted borrowings to the open market and because business firms repaid a part of working-capital loans. A good example of the reduction in amount of paper associated with a narrowed rate spread is provided by the period 1956-1957. More specifically, a reduction of the rate differential of roughly 1 percent from its previous peak in 1954 was linked with a decline of around $250 million, or one-third, in the volume of paper. This relationship reappeared in 1959. These were periods of high prosperity when open-market rates rose much more rapidly than the less responsive bank loan rates. Business loans of banks rose both because of growing working-capital requirements and because customers returned from the open market.

The late 1960s provide an exception to the foregoing generalization. The inflationary boom generated a more intense loan demand than the banks were able to satisfy, with the result that more and more firms turned to the open market despite a narrowed rate spread.

INVESTORS IN OPEN-MARKET COMMERCIAL PAPER

The various features of open-market commercial paper meet the needs of a wide range of investors. As already indicated, credit risk is at a minimum so that safety of principal is almost assured. Such paper also provides a large measure of liquidity. While there is little or no secondary market, the holder always receives payment at maturity even though the borrower may, on occasion, refund his debt by sale of a new issue of notes. In the event that investors need money before maturity, there is some possibility of resale. Most dealers do not stand ready to repurchase, although they are willing to assist in finding other buyers. One large dealer, however, has recently offered to buy back its paper at market price before maturity. Also, member banks may rediscount it at Reserve Banks, and both member and nonmember banks sometimes sell it to city correspondent banks. In addition, commercial paper usually produces a satisfactory yield for those who desire a rather high degree of safety and liquidity in combination. Its yield ordinarily exceeds that of Treasury bills by about $\frac{1}{2}$ percentage point, and that of bankers' acceptances by $\frac{1}{4}$ percentage point. Thus, commercial paper well meets requirements of investors who seek safety and liquidity, but who desire somewhat less of these and a higher yield than is provided by short-term Treasury issues and bankers' acceptances. The greatest limitation of commercial paper, especially for large investors, is lack of availability in desired amounts and maturities.

A notable broadening of investor interest in open-market paper developed during the 1960s. In the 1920s and early 1930s, the great bulk of it was owned by commercial banks in the "country" and "reserve city" classifications—usually over 90 percent. The large money-market banks in New York and Chicago held only small amounts, preferring instead short-term Treasury issues, bankers' acceptances, brokers' call loans, and other liquid assets. Small- and intermediate-size banks bought commercial paper to cover part of liquidity requirements, to augment earning assets when loan demands were low, and to provide diversification of asset risks. While these banks continue to hold such paper, other investors—notably nonfinancial corporations—have also discovered its merits. This fact is indicated more specifically in Table 6-4, which

TABLE 6-4 / DISTRIBUTION OF DEALER-PLACED COMMERCIAL PAPER BY TYPE OF INVESTOR, 1960-1970 (percent)

End of Period	Nonfinancial Corporations and Others	Commercial Banks	Investment Companies	Total
1960	21.4	71.4	7.2	100.0
1965	21.1	52.6	26.3	100.0
1966	16.7	50.0	33.3	100.0
1967	34.7	44.9	20.4	100.0
1968	43.0	40.3	16.7	100.0
1969	50.0	29.7	20.3	100.0
1970-Q1	50.0	29.4	20.6	100.0
1970-Q2	46.2	33.8	20.0	100.0
1970-Q3	48.8	40.8	10.4	100.0

Source: Board of Governors of the Federal Reserve System.

presents a percentage distribution by type of investor. Nonfinancial corporations have held between two-fifths and one-half since 1967. The share of commercial banks dropped from 71 percent in 1960 to 29 percent in early 1970, when their liquidity reached its nadir. But their proportion rose materially during 1970, reaching 41 percent in the third quarter, as liquidity positions improved. Investment companies also represent a significant part of the market—ranging between 7 and 33 percent during the period. Their proportion rises with the desire for liquidity and when commercial-paper yields are relatively attractive.

A notable service to both investors and dealers has recently been offered by Standard & Poor's Corporation in the form of quality ratings of issuers of commercial paper. The ratings range from A-1 for highest quality on down to A-2, A-3, B, C, and D in descending order. An A rating indicates that liquidity ratios are better than the industry average, that the issuer has access to at least two additional channels of borrowing, that net earnings exhibit an upward trend, that the issuer occupies a strong position in its industry, and that the quality of management is unquestioned. B-rated companies are acceptable on the above counts but are lower in quality. C indicates high risk, and D indicates failure to qualify on any of the criteria.

DIRECTLY-PLACED FINANCE-COMPANY PAPER

One of the notable developments in the money market since World War II has been direct placement of short-term notes by large finance companies. Small- and intermediate-size finance companies have remained an important type of borrower in the open market, but the large sales finance companies have bypassed commercial-paper dealers, and have developed staffs and departments of their own to reach investors. This development has had its counterpart in the long-term capital market in shunting investment bankers by direct placement of bonds with life insurance companies and other institutional investors. General Motors Acceptance Corporation began to place its short-term notes directly in the early 1920s. The other two largest finance companies—C.I.T. Financial Corporation and Commercial Credit Company—adopted the practice during the mid-1930s. More companies joined the movement during the postwar years, so that 21 companies holding over four-fifths of total receivables of all U.S. finance companies were engaged in direct placement of short-term notes in 1970. One large conglomerate corporation, Gulf and Western, also made direct placements.

features of directly-placed paper

Directly-placed paper is issued as unsecured promissory notes payable to bearer at a designated time and place. As with open-market paper, there is no stated interest rate on the notes. The rate depends on the amount of discount from face value at which notes are purchased and the time until maturity. Denominations are arranged to suit convenience of buyers, usually in multiples of $10,000. Small investors sometimes prefer notes in the $10,000-$25,000 range, whereas large investors desire denominations of from $1 to $10 million, and on occasion to as much as $100 million. An attractive feature to many investors is the fact that maturities can be arranged flexibly to correspond with specific needs such as tax or dividend payments. Maturities ordinarily range between one and nine months, with some concentration on the short side. However, significant amounts of borrowing take place outside these maturity limits.

In view of highly competitive conditions, all finance companies commonly offer their notes on the same discount-rate basis. A change in open-market rates on Treasury bills, commercial paper, and bankers' acceptances soon evokes a corresponding adjustment by finance companies which must remain competitive with alternative investments. However, there is usually not a single rate but rather a structure in which rates rise somewhat as maturities lengthen. For example, on August 21, 1970, the quoted rates were as follows:[3]

5-14 days	7.50%
15-89 days	7.75
90-239 days	7.25
240-270 days	7.38

At the same time, the rate on prime open-market commercial paper, 30-180 days, was 8 percent. This is a quite typical relationship because rates on dealer-placed paper are almost always between $\frac{1}{8}$ and $\frac{1}{2}$ percentage point higher than those on directly-placed notes in corresponding maturities.

growth of directly-placed paper

Reference is again made to Table 6-1 and figure 6, which provide a record of growth of directly-placed finance paper. From less than $600 million at the end of 1950, it rose almost steadily to nearly $26 billion in 1970. This was about twice as large as the open market for commercial paper and more than four times the size of the bankers' acceptance market. In 1970, the combined amount of open-market commercial paper and directly-placed finance paper approached $40 billion.

There are four main reasons for the rapid growth of sales finance-company paper: (1) growth of consumer installment credit; (2) growth of

[3]As reported in Manufacturers Hanover Trust, *Financial Digest* (August 21, 1970).

finance-company requirements for short-term credit; (3) inadequacy of bank credit lines for large finance companies; and (4) growth of nonbank investor demands for liquid assets.

1/The strong growth of consumer installment credit represents one of the notable financial developments of the postwar period. From $2.5 billion at the end of 1945, the amount outstanding increased steadily to $98.7 billion at midyear 1970. Over one-third of this total was held by finance companies, which required huge amounts of borrowed funds because their equity capital was relatively small.

2/In view of the cyclical variability of installment credit, sales finance companies at times used short-term borrowing to carry nearly one-half the amount of receivables. They sought to keep a flexibly balanced relationship between maturities of receivables and maturities of their own debt. Until the end of 1950, bank loans were the larger source of short-term funds, but after 1950, directly-placed paper became the more important source. In fact, during the 1960s, directly-placed paper of finance companies was approximately twice as large as their bank loans.

3/Another reason for the more rapid growth of directly-placed paper was the inadequacy of bank credit lines to meet expanding needs of finance companies for short-term borrowing. National banks and most state banks are prohibited by law from lending more than 10 percent of capital and surplus to one borrower, and even in the absence of such a law, most banks would hesitate to go much beyond this limit as a matter of policy. Consequently, any one of the three largest finance companies would find it impossible to meet its short-term borrowing needs of between $1 and $1.5 billion by bank loans. Credit lines of this magnitude would require the full lending capacity of several hundred of the largest banks in the country. Moreover, the financial policy of most finance companies would call for holding a comfortable portion of bank credit lines in reserve for emergencies, including fluctuations in availability of open-market funds.

4/Directly-placed finance-company paper could not have increased so rapidly without a corresponding growth of investor demand for this type of liquid asset. The reasons for this development are discussed below.

A significant development in the market occurred in 1969 and 1970, when bank holding companies borrowed heavily (see Table 6-1). Bank liquidity was at its lowest level since the late 1920s and the early 1930s as a result of strong Federal Reserve restraint and customers' intense loan demands. One aspect of Federal Reserve policy was setting the rate ceiling on interest payable on time deposits (Regulation Q) well below competitive market rates. As a consequence, negotiable CDs were not renewed at maturity, and the amount outstanding declined about $14 billion between December 1968 and January 1970. For the individual bank, this meant an equivalent loss of legal reserve. For the banking system, it meant a shift of time deposits to demand deposits with an associated increase in percentage-reserve requirements. Faced with this squeeze, the banks borrowed heavily in the Federal funds market, the Eurodollar market, and the commercial-paper market.

If the banks had sold paper directly, the amount would have been subject to legal-reserve requirements and to the interest-rate ceilings of Regulation Q. But by forming holding companies, they were able for a time to issue paper indirectly without the penalties of reserve requirements and Regulation Q.

Reference to Table 6-1 indicates that holding-company note issues increased dramatically in 1969 and 1970, reaching a peak of $7.8 billion in July of the latter year. The bulk of the borrowing was done by holding companies of large city banks on a direct-placement basis. But a significant amount—more than $1 billion—was arranged through open-market dealers by smaller holding companies which lacked the organization for direct placements. During the second half of 1970, such borrowing declined as rapidly as it had previously risen, and amounted to only $2.3 billion at the year-end. This was a consequence of the more liberal Federal Reserve policy initiated in early 1970, including an increase of the Regulation Q ceilings, the more moderate demand for bank loans, and the application of legal-reserve requirements to bank-related commercial paper in August of that year.

investors in directly-placed paper

As just indicated, one of the main factors in the rapid growth of directly-placed paper was the development of nonbank investor demand for this kind of liquid asset. In the 1920s and the 1930s, commercial banks provided over 90 percent of the market for commercial- and finance-company paper. But for reasons already developed, they could not be expected to absorb more than a small part of the huge new volume of directly-placed paper. Finance-company credit lines of large banks were already nudging the legal upper limit of credit extension to these companies. Reliable estimates place bank holdings of directly-placed paper in 1970 at about 5 percent of the total.

The new market was largely developed among nonfinancial corporations, which owned over one-half of directly-placed paper after the mid-1950s, and over four-fifths of outstandings in 1970. Table 6-5 gives a more detailed picture of the investor distribution since 1960. Large petroleum corporations were by far the largest investors, but other industries were also represented—notably steel, automobile, chemical, and electrical manufacturing companies. Liquid assets of these companies grew rapidly during these years, and corporate financial officers were increasingly alert to realize maximum earnings on liquid funds. At the same time, the large finance companies achieved recognition as high-quality credit risks and investors were willing to buy their notes at lower rates than on prime commercial paper placed through dealers. The differential

TABLE 6-5 / DISTRIBUTION OF DIRECTLY-PLACED COMMERCIAL PAPER BY TYPE OF INVESTOR (percent)

End of Period	Nonfinancial Corporations and Others	Commercial Banks	Life Insurance Companies	Total
1960	65.6	25.0	9.4	100.0
1965	85.9	9.9	4.2	100.0
1966	78.4	17.7	3.9	100.0
1967	70.9	24.8	4.3	100.0
1968	85.7	11.3	3.0	100.0
1969	87.4	7.1	5.5	100.0
1970-Q1	88.1	5.1	6.8	100.0
1970-Q2	88.7	5.3	6.0	100.0
1970-Q3	89.3	3.7	7.0	100.0

Source: Board of Governors of the Federal Reserve System.

was a result of the higher credit standing of large finance companies, tailoring of maturities and denominations to the investor's needs, availability in larger amounts, and the willingness of finance companies to repurchase paper in emergencies. Other important types of investors in directly-placed paper were life insurance companies, pension funds, trust funds, endowment funds, and state governments. Settlement for borrowings and repayments is usually made in Federal (Reserve) funds.

MONEY RATE COMPARISONS

While some reference has already been made to relationships between commercial-paper rates and other money rates, it is desirable to present these comparisons more systematically. This is done in figure 8, which shows the rates on open-market commercial paper, the Fed Bank discount rate, the yield on Treasury bills, and the prime loan rate of commercial banks since 1954. Several significant relationships are evident.

1/The similarities of movement in the rate series were perhaps even more important than their differences. All responded to major changes in money-market conditions, and with a high degree of correlation. This gives emphasis to the basic unity and the nationwide character of the money market.

2/Each rate series maintained a level that was consistent in relation to the others, although rate differentials varied considerably as conditions changed. The rate on open-market commercial paper occupied a median position between the Treasury bill rate and the rate charged by banks on large short-term business loans. As would be expected, the Treasury bill rate was appreciably below the commercial-paper rate, usually from $\frac{1}{4}$ to $\frac{1}{2}$ percentage point. Investors were willing to pay this premium for complete freedom from credit risk, greater assurance of ready marketability without loss, wider choice of maturities, and legal advantages for certain purposes such as cover for Treasury deposits. The prime-loan rate of banks was materially higher than the commercial-paper rate, with a widely varying differential of between $\frac{1}{2}$ and 2 percentage points. Explanation of this large discrepancy is difficult, but it mainly lies in the absence of keen rate competition among banks, costs of bank loan administration, a higher risk factor attached to the average bank loan, and the lower degree of loan liquidity. Directly-placed notes of finance companies commanded a moderately lower rate than dealer-placed paper, usually in the range of $\frac{1}{8}$ to $\frac{1}{2}$ percentage point. This premium doubtless reflected the exceedingly high credit standing of large finance companies, greater flexibility of maturity terms, and somewhat lower marketing costs. The discount rate of the Reserve Banks and

8 MONEY RATES, 1954-1970.
Source: Board of Governors of the Federal Reserve System

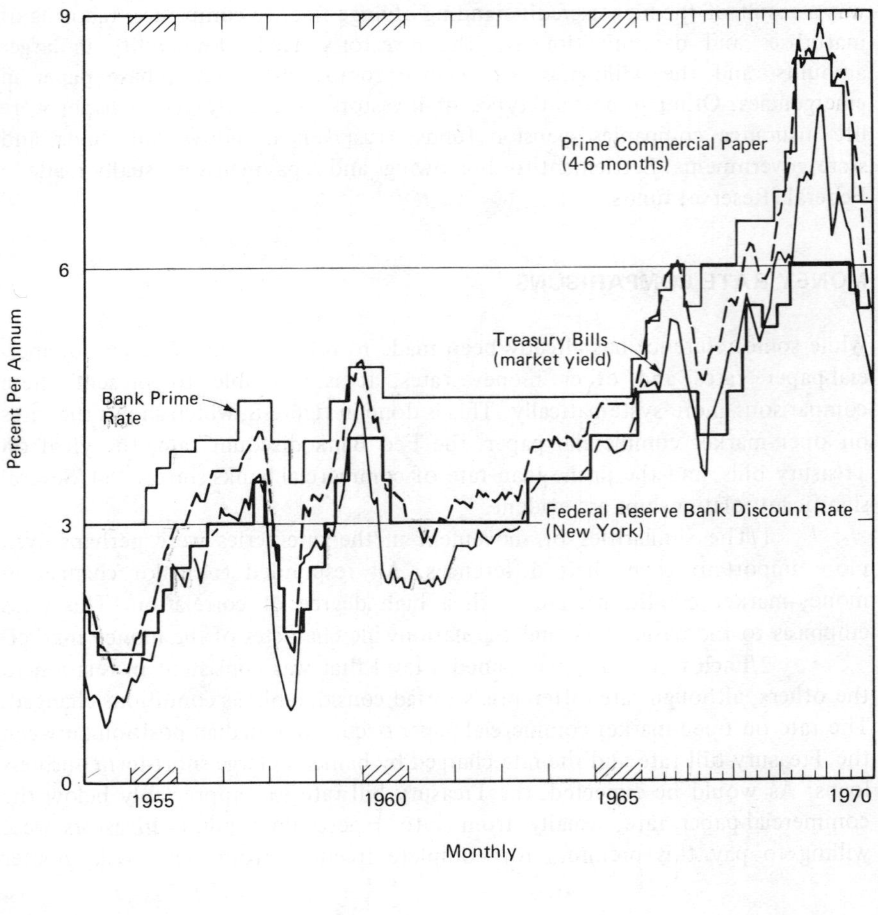

the yield on Treasury bills averaged about the same. However, the discount rate was passively adjusted to changing market conditions after a lag of one to three months, and the bill rate fluctuated more widely—rising well above the discount rate during tight-money periods and falling well below during recessions.

3/There were notable differences among the rate series in speed of response to changing money-market conditions. Treasury bill rates exhibited the greatest sensitivity and typically led open-market commercial-paper rates by one or two months at turning points. The almost simultaneous changes of the latter two rates emphasizes the keen competition between the dealer market and the direct-placement market. Moreover, the alacrity of adjustments in both divisions of the commercial-paper market to changes in Treasury bill rates underscores the fact that all offer competing alternatives to investors who seek liquidity. The most striking difference in rapidity of response, however, applied to rates on business loans. As a rule, this series lagged behind Treasury bill rates by two to four months at major turning points.

4/There was a marked contrast between the amplitudes of cyclical variations of rates on business loans and of the other rate series as a group. Commercial-paper rates and bill rates reacted strongly, and in about the same degree, to cyclical changes. By comparison, the cyclical responses of business loan rates were moderate—ranging between one-third and one-half as much percentagewise. It has already been noted that failure of banks to make downward adjustments of rates in 1958, 1960-1963, and 1967-1968, in keeping with declines in open-market rates set the stage for large increases in open-market borrowing.

SIGNIFICANCE OF THE COMMERCIAL-PAPER MARKET

Despite its relatively small size, the market for commercial and finance company paper is an important element in the financial system of the United States. This was more conspicuously true before establishment of the Fed, which contributed greatly to the mobility and availability of credit throughout the country. But it is still true, and will doubtless continue to be so for many decades to come. For the importance of this market should be measured by the *flow* of funds through it rather than by the amount of paper outstanding at any one time, and perhaps even more by its contribution to the most effective use of credit resources.

The market affords a facility, nationwide in scope, through which borrowers of high standing and banks and others with investible funds are brought into contact. Open-market borrowers gain because they can usually obtain funds at lower rates and other borrowers benefit from the competition of the open market even though they actually borrow directly from their own banks. The beneficial effects arising from its contribution to active competition in the credit market are seldom appreciated by borrowers. In particular, during the 1950s and 1960s, the marked growth of directly-placed finance-company paper has aided both companies and consumers by increasing credit availability and lowering credit costs.

Banks and other investors are rewarded in that the market provides an investment which is safe, quite liquid, and at the same time yields a comparatively high return. Large city banks often denounce the open market as an unfair competitor, taking away business and depressing loan rates. But such a viewpoint is exceedingly shortsighted in terms of the larger welfare of banks. The business of banking carries such a heavy public responsibility that banks must face the alternatives of meeting legitimate credit needs at competitive rates or of submitting to more government intervention. Hence, in a very real sense, the market is a genuine friend because it exerts a strong influence in the direction of a healthier banking system.

The general public benefits by the contribution of the market to effective employment of the country's credit resources. Business activities of many industries and areas have been stimulated by the availability of credit at reasonable rates; at the same time, areas from which funds were transferred have been protected from a temptation to overexpand. That is to say, the nationwide equalizing influence of the market on the distribution of credit and on interest rates has contributed over the years to the economic welfare of all.

REFERENCES

Baxter, Nevins D., *The Commercial Paper Market* (Boston: Bankers Publishing Co., 1966).

Dailey, D. M., "The Early Development of Note Brokerage in Chicago," *Journal of Political Economy* (April 1938), pp. 202-217.

Federal Reserve Bank of Cleveland, "Use of Commercial Paper to the Fore," *Monthly Business Review* (October 1960), pp. 3-9.

Federal Reserve Bank of Kansas City, "Renaissance of the Commercial Paper Market," *Monthly Review* (August 1957), pp. 3-8.

Federal Reserve Bulletin, "Directly Placed Finance Company Paper" (December 1954), pp. 1245-1252.

Greef, A. O., *The Commercial Paper House in the United States* (Cambridge, Mass.: Harvard University Press, 1938).

Schadrack, F. C., "Demand and Supply in the Commercial Paper Market," *Journal of Finance,* Vol. XXV (September 1970), pp. 837-852.

Schadrack, F. C., and F. S. Breimyer, "Recent Developments in the Commercial Paper Market," Federal Reserve Bank of New York, *Monthly Review* (December 1970), pp. 280-291.

Selden, Richard T., *Trends and Cycles in the Commercial Paper Market* (New York: National Bureau of Economic Research, 1963).

7

the bankers' acceptance market

Since the mid-1950s, the bankers' acceptance market has, like the mythical phoenix, risen from its ashes. After reaching a peak of $1.7 billion in 1929, the amount outstanding declined steadily during the depression of the 1930s and World War II to barely $100 million. But the postwar revival in acceptance financing brought the volume to a record $7 billion at the end of 1970.

In contrast with the commercial-paper market, which is indigenous and dates back to this nation's early developments, the bankers' acceptance market was consciously created when the Fed was established. It was patterned after the bankers' acceptance market in London, which represented an evolutionary development of more than two centuries in the financial center of the world. The bulk of international trade, whether inside or outside the British Empire, was financed through London in terms of the pound sterling which was recognized as the principal international money unit. With a network of overseas connections, British banks offered acceptance credits throughout the commercial world. The sale of silk to the U.S. by Japan or the sale of coffee by Brazil to Sweden, for example, usually gave rise to a sterling bill in London even though the goods never touched British shores.

Briefly stated, the function of the bankers' acceptance is as follows: A borrower may, under certain circumstances, obtain short-term credit by arranging for his bank to "accept" a time draft upon it. The bank stamps its official "accepted" across the face of the draft and thereby converts it into a bankers' acceptance. The instrument, now being a bank obligation, may be sold to an acceptance dealer who, in turn, may sell it to an investor who seeks liquidity. Before the acceptance matures, the borrower puts the bank in funds to redeem it in accordance with the agreement. Thus, the borrower is enabled indirectly to borrow at a low rate in the open market from both domestic and foreign investors. The accepting bank in effect underwrites the borrower's credit for a commission, but without burdening its reserve position unless it chooses to hold the acceptance.

ESTABLISHMENT OF THE MARKET

For various reasons, there was general agreement among founders of the Fed that the new banking machinery should include a bankers' acceptance market. It was felt that (1) the great actual and potential importance of New York City as a center of international commerce called for a correspondingly important financial position; (2) U.S. foreign trade would be encouraged by such a market; (3) U.S. banks would enjoy a part of the commission previously collected by banks in London and other financial centers; (4) an active bankers' acceptance market would provide a superior liquid investment; (5) an acceptance market would tend to equalize interest rates domestically and internationally; and (6) greater mobility and availability of credit would contribute to economic development.

The task of establishing the new market was a major one. National banks were not empowered by the National Bank Act to accept time drafts, so that the small amount of acceptance business was confined at the time to a few private and state-chartered banks. It was therefore necessary to encourage development of all groups and institutions essential to such a market: (1) accepting banks with well-staffed foreign departments; (2) borrowers of this type of credit; (3) investors in acceptances; and (4) dealers to serve as intermediaries. Also, it was necessary to encourage establishment of foreign branches of American banks and American branches of foreign banks, and to provide special support to dealers and the infant market. The Federal Reserve Act conferred the needed legal powers: national banks were enabled to accept time drafts under certain restrictions, and Federal Reserve Banks were permitted to rediscount or purchase eligible acceptances. The legal framework, however, was only a prerequisite to actual development of the market.

ACCEPTING BANKS

Acceptance operations are restricted in several respects by the Federal Reserve Act and Regulation C of the Board of Governors. Member banks, which account for about nine-tenths of acceptances, may accept time drafts arising from (1) foreign trade, (2) domestic shipment of goods, (3) domestic or foreign storage of readily marketable staples, and (4) provision of dollar-exchange credit to banks in designated countries. With a special permit from the Board, a bank may accept commercial drafts in aggregate up to the amount of capital and surplus, and in addition it may accept dollar-exchange drafts up to one-half capital and surplus. When properly secured, acceptance credit to one borrower is not subject to the limitation of 10 percent of a bank's capital and surplus; otherwise this rule applies.

Acceptance credit is highly concentrated in large money-market banks. This is a consequence of the size and specialized nature of the underlying transactions—chiefly in the field of international trade. Only banks with properly staffed foreign departments are qualified to do this type of business. In 1970, a dozen banks accounted for over four-fifths of all acceptances outstanding, and only some 80 banks reported acceptance liabilities. The New York Federal Reserve district was responsible for three-fourths of the total, mainly banks in New York City. The San Francisco district claimed another 15 percent, leaving only 10 percent for the rest of the country.

When a bank accepts a time draft, it underwrites the credit of the borrower, and it is responsible for payment of the face amount of the acceptance at maturity. For assumption of this credit risk and to cover costs, the bank charges a commission which is customarily at the rate of $1\frac{1}{2}$ percent per annum, applied on the basis of $\frac{1}{8}$ percent per month. A somewhat lower commission of about 1 percent per annum is charged for acceptance credits to foreign correspondent banks. The commission is paid by the borrower, although its actual incidence may fall in part on the seller through pricing and other terms of sale.

DEMAND FOR ACCEPTANCE CREDIT

As indicated in Table 7-1, acceptance credit is used predominantly in financing foreign-trade transactions, including foreign storage of staple products and creation of dollar exchange. Since the mid-1950s, it will be noted, foreign-trade financing has been responsible for between 80 and 90 percent of outstandings, and domestic shipment and storage have accounted for only 5 to 20 percent.

Several developments may be cited to explain the rapid expansion of acceptances to finance international trade. First, there has been an upsurge in foreign trade, due both to growth in dollar value of world output and to a rise in the proportion of trade to output. Second, the proportion of privately financed foreign trade has increased since the early postwar years when government financing prevailed. Third, more liberal credit terms have emerged as competition in world markets has become keener and as confidence among countries has improved. One aspect of this has been substitution of acceptance credit for sight drafts and immediate cash payment. Fourth, elimination of many foreign-exchange controls and establishment of freer convertibility of foreign moneys into dollars have provided a healthier environment for trade and acceptance financing. Fifth, the cost of acceptance credit relative to that of direct bank borrowing, its chief competitor, has declined in recent years. Finally, lower interest rates in New York City than in London and the position of the dollar as

TABLE 7-1 / BANKERS' ACCEPTANCES OUTSTANDING IN UNITED STATES, BY USE OF FUNDS, 1924-1970 (millions of dollars)

End of Year	Total	Imports into United States	Exports from United States	Foreign Shipment and Storage	Domestic Shipment and Storage	Dollar Exchange
1924	821	292	305		200	23
1929	1,732	383	524	441	308	76
1935	397	107	94	84	110	2
1940	209	109	18	27	44	10
1945	154	103	18	7	26	[a]
1950	394	245	87	32	28	2
1955	642	252	210	100	63	17
1960	2,027	403	669	524	308	122
1961	2,683	485	969	819	293	117
1962	2,650	541	778	974	171	186
1963	2,890	567	908	1,317	41	56
1964	3,385	667	999	1,565	43	111
1965	3,392	792	974	1,564	35	27
1966	3,603	997	829	1,595	80	103
1967	4,317	1,086	989	2,042	162	37
1968	4,428	1,423	952	1,934	68	52
				All Other		
1969	5,451	1,889	1,153	2,408		
1970	7,058	2,601	1,561	2,895		

[a] Less than $500,000.
Source: *Federal Reserve Bulletin*, various issues.

the leading international monetary unit have combined to draw a larger share of international financing to the United States.

Most acceptances that finance international trade are drawn under authority of commercial letters of credit which importers and other borrowers arrange with their banks. Such a letter provides that the bank will accept time drafts drawn by the exporter-seller in connection with sale and shipment of specified products up to a stated amount and within a specified time. It also provides that the importer-borrower will pay the face amount of the acceptance to the bank just prior to maturity. This enables the bank to redeem the acceptance without drawing on its own resources. Having received a letter of credit from an American importer, the foreign exporter ships the goods and draws a time draft on the importer's bank. The exporter then discounts this dollar draft at his own bank which credits his account with the proceeds in domestic money. Next, the exporter's bank through its New York correspondent presents the draft, accompanied by proper shipping documents, to the American bank on which it is drawn. After detaching the bill of lading and other documents for security, the American bank stamps the draft with its duly signed "accepted," and the instrument becomes a negotiable bankers' acceptance payable to bearer. The foreign bank may direct the correspondent either to hold the acceptance as an investment, or to sell and credit the proceeds to its deposit account. At maturity, the investor presents the instrument to the accepting bank for redemption at face value. Meanwhile, the importer sells the goods and discharges his obligation to the accepting bank shortly before the acceptance matures.

Similarly, a foreign importer of goods from the United States or from another country may finance the transaction by use of dollar acceptances. With assistance from his bank, he may arrange for a letter of credit from a New York bank which agrees to accept dollar drafts of the exporter to cover specified transactions. The American or foreign exporter may then receive payment in dollars immediately by sale of the acceptances. The marked increase since the mid-1950s of acceptances generated by exports from the United States and from trade between foreign countries took place largely through arrangements of this type. The best single example is that of financing the booming foreign trade of Japan by dollar-acceptance credits (see Table 7-1). At the end of 1970, acceptances for the account of Japanese firms amounted to $2.1 billion.

Dollar-exchange acceptances have usually been the smallest category, ranging between $50 and $200 million. They are time drafts of foreign banks (usually central banks) drawn on and accepted by banks in the United States. By this method, dollar exchange can be provided for specified countries—mostly Latin American—during seasons of low exports and deficient dollar holdings. Repayment of such acceptance credits is expected during months of high exports from the borrowing country.

A wide variety of internationally traded products are financed by bankers' acceptances which are used most extensively in connection with trade in marketable raw materials adapted to storage. While acceptances are often used in financing trade in manufactured products, the great bulk of such trade is financed by direct bank loans and by capital resources of large corporations. Export acceptances most frequently arise from the sale of cotton, foodstuffs, automotive products, oil, ores, scrap metal, chemicals, iron, and steel. Import acceptances are most often generated by purchase of coffee, sugar, wool, rubber, cocoa, metals and ores, crude oil, jute, automobiles, and textiles.

Bankers' acceptances have never occupied an important position in domestic finance. The main reason is the high state of confidence among businesses, which permits the great bulk of transactions to be carried out on an open-account basis. Another reason is that direct bank borrowing can be more flexibly adapted to most short-term credit needs, and without appreciably higher cost. In addition, Federal Reserve regulations restrict the use of bank acceptances. Domestic shipments can be financed in this manner only if accepting banks are firmly secured by title to the specific goods; domestic-storage financing by acceptances is limited to readily marketable staples.[1] In 1960 and 1961, this amount was in the vicinity of $300 million, mostly for storage of cotton, tobacco, grain, and wool. The sharp drop to only under $75

[1] Board of Governors, Regulation C.

million after 1962 is largely a result of the fact that the Commodity Credit Corporation has provided cheaper financing of cotton storage than the banks have offered in the acceptance market (see Table 7-1).

The stringent credit conditions of 1969-1970 were responsible for a substantial increase in the amount of acceptances. Bank holding companies and affiliates drew acceptances on their hard-pressed banks as a means of raising funds in the market. These working-capital acceptances were then sold to dealers, usually in $100,000 denominations, and the proceeds were loaned back to the operating banks.

At this point, the reader may gain a more tangible understanding of acceptance practices by reference to figure 9, which illustrates the use of an acceptance in financing the importation of coffee from Brazil.

The decision to use acceptance credit involves comparisons with alternative methods of financing, the most important of which are direct bank loans and book credit. Both alternatives enjoy features of simplicity and familiarity, and are therefore likely to be chosen unless acceptance credit offers appreciable cost saving, availability in larger amount, or other distinct advantages. Another alternative since the mid-1960s has been Eurodollar financing. As already indicated, the scope for acceptance credit in domestic finance is very limited in view of the predominant use of book credit, greater flexibility of bank loans, and legal obstacles. But in international trade, acceptance credit provides specialized advantages. Intercession by well-known accepting banks enables exporters to sell to foreign buyers whose credit standing, money, trade practices, and legal environment would otherwise present unsurmountable obstacles. Also, dealers in readily marketable international goods are usually able to borrow larger amounts by use of acceptance credit than

9 EXAMPLE OF BANKERS' ACCEPTANCE.
Courtesy of Federal Reserve Bank of New York

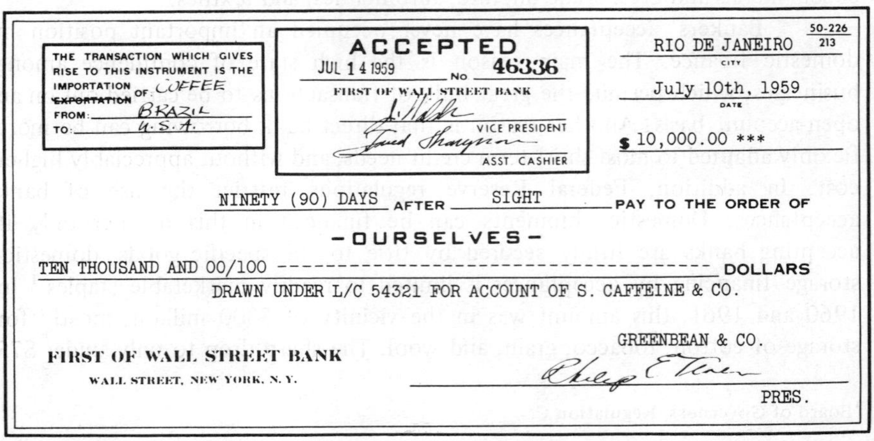
THE TRANSACTION WHICH GIVES RISE TO THIS INSTRUMENT IS THE IMPORTATION ~~EXPORTATION~~ OF: COFFEE
FROM: BRAZIL
TO: U.S.A.

ACCEPTED
JUL 14 1959 No. 46336
FIRST OF WALL STREET BANK
VICE PRESIDENT
ASST CASHIER

50-226
213
RIO DE JANEIRO
CITY
July 10th, 1959
DATE
$ 10,000.00 ***

NINETY (90) DAYS AFTER SIGHT PAY TO THE ORDER OF
-OURSELVES-
TEN THOUSAND AND 00/100 -- DOLLARS
DRAWN UNDER L/C 54321 FOR ACCOUNT OF S. CAFFEINE & CO.

FIRST OF WALL STREET BANK
WALL STREET, NEW YORK, N.Y.

GREENBEAN & CO.
PRES.

by direct bank loans. In addition, there is typically some cost saving by use of acceptances. This saving may be substantial during periods of recession, when the bankers' acceptance rate declines much more than the prime rate on bank loans. For example, the spread between the two rates more than doubled in both 1958 and in 1960-1961 (see figure 10, p. 124).

An approximation of the relative costs of acceptance credit and bank loans can be made by comparing the customer loan rate of money-market banks on large short-term business loans with the dealers' bid rate on 90-day bankers' acceptances plus the $1\frac{1}{2}$ percent per annum commission typically charged by accepting banks. At the end of 1961, acceptance credit afforded a significant cost saving of about $\frac{1}{3}$ percent per annum on this basis. By contrast, during the tight-money market at the end of 1959, the rate spread favored bank loans by about $\frac{7}{8}$ percent (see figure 10). Beyond doubt, this marked change in relative credit costs was one of the important reasons for the fact that the amount of bankers' acceptances more than doubled between 1959 and 1963—from $1.2 billion to $2.7 billion. It should be noted, however, that the foregoing basis of cost comparison is no more than an average approximation, and that other influences are relevant in choosing one or the other alternative in specific cases. The fact that a borrowing business firm can sometimes reduce its compensating bank balance by using acceptance credit may be a definite cost advantage. However, the fact that prepayment of acceptances is usually impossible without penalty, and that prepayment of bank loans is permitted, may be an offsetting item in favor of loans. The importance of these factors cannot be generalized; each firm must apply them to its own circumstances.

INVESTORS IN BANKERS' ACCEPTANCES

In contrast with short-term U.S. securities and commercial paper, the market for bankers' acceptances has been a highly concentrated one. Most acceptances have been owned by one of three groups: (1) foreign central and commercial banks; (2) large city banks in the United States (mainly accepting banks); and (3) Federal Reserve Banks. Table 7-2 provides a classification of ownership of acceptances for the period 1925-1970.

foreign-bank investors

The investment qualities of bankers' acceptances have special appeal to foreign central and commercial banks which usually hold between one-half and two-thirds of total outstandings. Safety of acceptances purchased by these institutions is almost beyond question because two of the obligors are leading money-market banks, and because a Federal Reserve Bank adds its guarantee on acceptances bought by foreign central banks. Liquidity is also high in view of

TABLE 7-2 / OWNERSHIP OF BANKERS' DOLLAR ACCEPTANCES, 1925-1970
(millions of dollars)

End of Year	Total	Held by Accepting Banks: *Own Bills*	*Bills Bought*	*Total*	Held by Fed Banks: *Own Account*	*Account of Foreign Correspondents*	Held by Others[a]
1925	774	38	55	93	372	70	239
1929	1,732	59	132	191	391	548	603
1935	397	183	185	368	0	0	29
1940	209	100	67	167	0	0	42
1945	154	64	48	112	0	0	42
1950	394	114	78	192	0	21	180
1955	642	126	49	175	28	33	405
1960	2,027	490	173	662	74	230	1,060
1961	2,683	896	376	1,272	51	126	1,234
1962	2,650	865	288	1,153	110	86	1,301
1963	2,890	1,031	260	1,291	162	92	1,345
1964	3,385	1,301	370	1,671	94	122	1,498
1965	3,392	1,094	129	1,223	187	144	1,837
1966	3,063	983	215	1,198	193	191	2,022
1967	4,317	1,447	459	1,906	164	156	2,090
1968	4,428	1,344	200	1,544	58	109	2,717
1969	5,451	1,318	249	1,567	64	146	3,674
1970	7,058	1,960	735	2,694	57	250	4,057

[a]Mainly foreign banks.
Source: *Federal Reserve Bulletin,* various issues.

short maturities, a large measure of Federal Reserve support, and the opportunity for resale to dealers. In addition, the relatively high yield of bankers' acceptances appeals to foreign investors. Gross yields are $\frac{1}{8}$ to $\frac{1}{2}$ percentage point higher than on Treasury bills. Also, acceptances have, in some cases, provided a tax advantage to nongovernmental foreign investors. Earnings on acceptances and interest on time deposits have been exempt from a federal withholding tax of up to 30 percent that applies, in general, to interest received, including interest on Treasury bills and other federal securities. However, the extent of this tax advantage of acceptances has been substantially modified by reciprocal tax treaties with most nations whose dollar investments are significant. Also, foreign central banks were specifically exempted from taxation of interest received from U.S. securities by an amendment to the Internal Revenue Act in 1961. Taken together, these qualifications have greatly reduced the tax advantage of acceptances to foreign investors.

With reference to Table 7-2, acceptances "Held by Others" are principally owned by foreign central and commercial banks, and acceptances held by Federal Reserve Banks for "Account of Foreign Correspondents" are largely owned by foreign central banks. Note the sharp increase in foreign acceptance holdings between 1960 and 1970, for which two developments are mainly responsible: the large deficit in the U.S. balance of payments, which rapidly built up foreign dollar holdings; and the growth in dollar acceptances available for investment, the reasons for which are discussed later.

domestic-bank investors

Ownership of acceptances by domestic banks is highly concentrated in large city banks, and principally in the great money-market banks that do the bulk of acceptance business. Table 7-2 indicates that accepting banks usually hold between one-fourth and one-third of total outstandings; also, that up to four-fifths of their holdings consist of "Own Bills" which more closely resemble customer loans than open-market paper. Own bills may, of course, be converted to open-market status at any time by sale to dealers, correspondents, or other customers. The remaining one-fifth of bank holdings is composed of acceptances of other banks, often swapped with dealers for own bills. Small- and intermediate-size banks seldom purchase acceptances, preferring instead to hold short-term U.S. securities and other alternative investments.

federal reserve bank holdings

The Federal Reserve Banks as sponsors of the acceptance market have given it a large measure of support from the beginning. Their close relationship may well be divided into three separate periods: (1) 1914-1933, when strong and continuous support was given and the Reserve Banks held a substantial part of outstandings; (2) 1934-1954, when potential support was given, but when other investors absorbed all acceptances at high prices (low yields); and (3) 1955-1970, when Reserve Bank purchases of acceptances were resumed under a policy of moderate support.

During the first period, 1914-1933, the Reserve Banks posted buying rates at which they stood ready to purchase all bank-endorsed acceptances offered. These rates were low relative to other open-market rates, so that the Reserve Banks usually owned between one-fourth and one-half of outstandings. That is, at these low discount rates (high prices), other investors were willing to hold only between one-half and three-fourths of them, and the overflow gravitated to the Reserve Banks. During this period of strong support the open-market rate on bankers' acceptances was governed by the Reserve Bank buying rate. The market rate could not rise above the buying rate because sellers would eliminate the differential by selling to the Reserve Banks. Nor could it fall below the buying rate because investors would not take all offerings at such a low discount rate.

The second period, 1934-1954, was one of *potential* support because the Reserve Banks continued to post a schedule of rates at which they would buy all eligible acceptance offerings. But no actual support was given the market because the buying rates were well above market rates. Other investors absorbed the entire amount of outstandings at abnormally low discount rates until after the Treasury-Federal Reserve Accord in 1951.

Finally, after an interlude of two decades, during which no acceptances were bought, the Fed Open-Market Committee directed resumption of Reserve Bank purchases in 1955. However, the practice of posting a schedule of buying rates at which all qualified offerings would be bought was discontinued. Under traditional practice, control was exerted by changing buying rates, and was less effective than desired. Under the revised practice, amounts and timing of purchases were brought under direct control. In addition to regular purchases, the Fed at times buys acceptances from dealers under repurchase agreements of 15 days or less. The charge for this method of financing is ordinarily, although not necessarily, the same as the discount rate on member-bank borrowing. Unlike open-market operations in U.S. securities in which all 12 Reserve Banks participate, bankers' acceptance transactions are, for the sake of simplicity, handled through the accounts of the Federal Reserve Bank of New York. During the period 1955-1970, total acceptance holdings of Reserve Banks ranged between $25 and $200 million.

Domestic investors, other than the Fed and commercial banks, purchase few bankers' acceptances. However, many types of investors are represented, including savings banks, insurance companies, pension funds, trust funds, investment companies, and nonfinancial corporations. The main limitation on acceptances for these investors is lack of availability in suitable denominations and maturities. Also, competing alternatives are more familiar and are usually more attractive. Short-term U.S. securities, in particular, provide a more active secondary market with a smaller spread between bid and asked prices. Commercial and finance-company paper offers higher yields. However, with the marked expansion in volume of acceptances in 1960-1970, these limitations receded somewhat, and nonfinancial corporations–notably oil and automobile companies–purchased larger amounts.

DEALERS IN BANKERS' ACCEPTANCES

The function of dealers in bankers' acceptances is, in general terms, the same as that of middlemen in other markets, viz., to provide adequate facilities so that bids of buyers and offers of sellers may be brought together and transactions may take place at a fair market price. Dealers stand ready to buy and sell acceptances at all times at quoted prices for each maturity. In order to do so, they maintain a portfolio that in the aggregate ranges between $100 and $500 million.

Open-market transactions in acceptances are handled by eight dealers, all in New York City. The seven largest of these are "recognized" in the sense that the Fed accepts their endorsement of acceptances.[2] In order to acquire this status, a dealer must have adequate capital and facilities, a satisfactory financial position, and reputable management. Most dealers do not restrict their activities to this one field. In fact, all but one are primarily dealers in U.S. and other securities.

Dealers purchase acceptances outright at a discount from face value determined by rate and maturity. They hope to realize a profit by selling at a still lower rate (higher price). The usual trading profit is $\frac{1}{8}$ percent per annum, but if money rates change, or the particular purchase varies from standard, the profit may increase, disappear, or turn to a loss. Dealers seek their profit by rapid turnover instead of by holding acceptances to maturity. If requested, they endorse the acceptances for which they charge between $\frac{1}{16}$ and $\frac{1}{8}$ percent per annum. The Federal Reserve Banks require a dealer endorsement unless the acceptance already bears satisfactory bank endorsement.

A part of dealer transactions consists of so-called swapping operations with accepting banks. The banks commonly discount their own acceptances at the prevailing bid rate, sell over one-half of them to dealers at the same rate and buy back acceptances of other banks at the dealer's asked rate which is $\frac{1}{8}$ percent lower. The banks are then in position to add their endorsements, for which they charge $\frac{1}{8}$ percent per annum, and to provide foreign correspondent banks and other customers with acceptances having three names, two of which are banks. Thus, investors in such acceptances receive a yield of $\frac{1}{4}$ percentage point less than the prevailing bid rate of dealers on acceptances with one bank name. Dealers also sell acceptances to the Federal Reserve Bank of New York and to a wide variety of others, but the greater part of sales is to accepting banks. Trading is not very active in the secondary market. For example, during the third quarter of 1970, total weekly sales by dealers were in the vicinity of \$150 million, representing an annual turnover of about 1.3 times for total outstanding acceptances.[3]

Acceptances that are not swapped with dealers by accepting banks fall into two categories. The greater part is held by accepting banks and never reaches the market. During 1960-1970, own bills of accepting banks constituted between one-fourth and one-third of total acceptances. The second category is composed of bills that after acceptance are turned back to the drawer's bank or its city correspondent. Such acceptances may then be sold to dealers, to customer investors directly, or they may be held as an investment by the drawer's bank.

Because equity capital of dealers is often small in relation to their acceptance inventory, they need to borrow short-term funds. This need is met mainly by borrowing from large commercial banks, and by selling acceptances to

[2]Briggs Schaedle & Co., Discount Corporation of New York, The First Boston Corporation, M. and T. Discount Corporation, Merrill Lynch, Pierce, Fenner & Smith, Inc., New York Hanseatic Corporation, and Salomon Brothers.

[3]Based on data reported by the Federal Reserve Bank of New York.

the Federal Reserve Bank of New York under repurchase agreement. Bank loans are usually arranged with the dealer's bank and are secured by acceptances whose face value exceeds the loan by 2 percent or more. The call-loan contract is ordinarily used, although banks seldom enforce it unless collateral security becomes inadequate, or some other hazard develops. Substitution of acceptance collateral is permissible. Rates charged on such loans are posted daily by New York City banks. They are typically $\frac{3}{4}$ to $\frac{7}{8}$ percentage point lower than the prime rate on short-term business loans, but somewhat above the market yield on bankers' acceptances. Also, rates charged have often been $\frac{1}{8}$ to $\frac{1}{4}$ percentage point above loan rates on Treasury bills, although this differential disappeared in the 1960s. Unsecured *day loans* are often employed to finance the requirements of dealers during the day. Such loans bear no interest and are taken up at the end of each day by the proceeds of sales or by secured call loans.

RATES ON BANKERS' ACCEPTANCES

The published rate on bankers' acceptances is ordinarily the dealers' offering discount rate on prime 90-day, unendorsed acceptances. The dealers' bid rate is $\frac{1}{8}$ percent higher. Also, there is a maturity structure in which rates usually rise as maturities are extended. For example, closing quotations on September 14, 1970 were as follows:

	1-90 days	91-120 days	121-180 days
Bid	$7\frac{1}{4}$%	$7\frac{3}{8}$%	$7\frac{1}{2}$%
Asked	$7\frac{1}{8}$%	$7\frac{1}{4}$%	$7\frac{3}{8}$%

Bankers' acceptances constitute one segment of a huge and complex short-term money market. Investors continuously compete with each other and decide whether to purchase acceptances, commercial paper, short-term Treasury securities, CDs, tax-exempts, or other open-market obligations. In addition, commercial banks choose between granting acceptance credit and making direct customer loans. On the other side, borrowers compete for lenders' dollars and determine whether to use acceptance credit, direct bank borrowing, or some other source of funds. Important alternatives in international trade finance may be a choice among dollar-acceptance credit, sterling-acceptance credit, Euro-dollar financing, or financing through some other international center. This illustrates the fact that bankers' acceptance rates emerge from demand-supply conditions in a worldwide money market. When credit conditions tighten, interest rates in general rise and acceptance rates move upward as part of the broad development. However, when credit conditions ease, interest rates in general fall and acceptance rates similarly decline. Thus, the explanation of major movements of acceptance rates is the same as that for rate movements in general.

However, the acceptance market is a specialized one with certain unique features. Consequently, against the backdrop of the entire market, special conditions of demand and supply influence acceptance rates. But even so, these divergences from the general rate pattern are quite limited because of competitive influences.

A more concrete view of the points just made is given in figure 10, which compares rates on bankers' acceptances with their closest competitors—rates on Treasury bills, and on large short-term bank loans in New York City for the period 1949-1970. Since 1953, the acceptance rate has usually been from $\frac{1}{4}$ to $\frac{1}{2}$ percentage point higher than the Treasury bill rate. Exceptions to this rule occurred occasionally during periods of firm money and rising rates, notably in 1952-1953, when the Treasury bill rate moved above the acceptance rate, and during the credit crunch of 1969, when the acceptance rate rose $\frac{3}{4}$ to $1\frac{1}{2}$ percentage points above the Treasury bill rate. The higher average level of acceptance rates is in line with expectations because Treasury bills are subject to less risk; are more readily marketable without loss; are available in larger amounts, in more convenient denominations, and in a wider selection of maturities; and are legal holdings for more purposes. Acceptance rates also exhibit less sensitivity to changes in money-market conditions. This was conspicuously true before 1955, when acceptance rates often remained unchanged for many months, and adjusted upward or downward only after a lag of four to six months. In this period, also, the range of fluctuation of acceptance rates was narrower. However, the material growth in volume of acceptances since the mid-1950s has been accompanied by much greater rate sensitivity. Adjustments usually lag only a few weeks, and the range of variation in rates has been about the same as that of Treasury bills.

While the Federal Reserve Bank discount rate is not shown in figure 10, its relationship to bankers' acceptance rates is a significant one. As a rule, the 90-day acceptance rate has stood $\frac{1}{8}$ to $\frac{1}{4}$ percentage point below the Reserve Bank rate. However, since the mid-1950s, the acceptance rate has usually closed the spread during periods of tightening credit, and has moved above the discount rate at the peaks. For example, the acceptance rate was $\frac{1}{4}$ percentage point or more above the discount rate of $3\frac{1}{2}$ percent during the fall of 1957. This pattern was repeated in 1959, when the acceptance rate rose over $\frac{1}{2}$ point above the discount rate of 4 percent, and again in 1969, when the acceptance rate exceeded the discount rate by over $2\frac{1}{2}$ percentage points.

Comparison of the bankers' acceptance rate with the dealer commercial-paper rate may be made by reference to figure 10 and figure 8 (p. 108). It will be noted that the acceptance rate is typically $\frac{1}{4}$ to $\frac{1}{2}$ percentage point lower. This differential is chiefly attributable to the risk factor. Acceptances are obligations of the largest and strongest banks in the country as well as of the drawing bank or firm. This gives them a near-riskless status superior to that of commercial paper, even though the latter represents obligations of firms with superior credit standing. Also, the moderate support given to bankers' acceptances by Reserve Bank purchases tends to lower acceptance rates. There appears to be little difference between the two rates in responsiveness to changing conditions since the mid-1950s. Both rates react quickly and show about the same deviations from their respective averages.

10 RATES ON BANKERS' ACCEPTANCES, TREASURY BILLS, AND BUSINESS LOANS OF BANKS, 1949-1970.
Source: *Federal Reserve Bulletin,* various issues

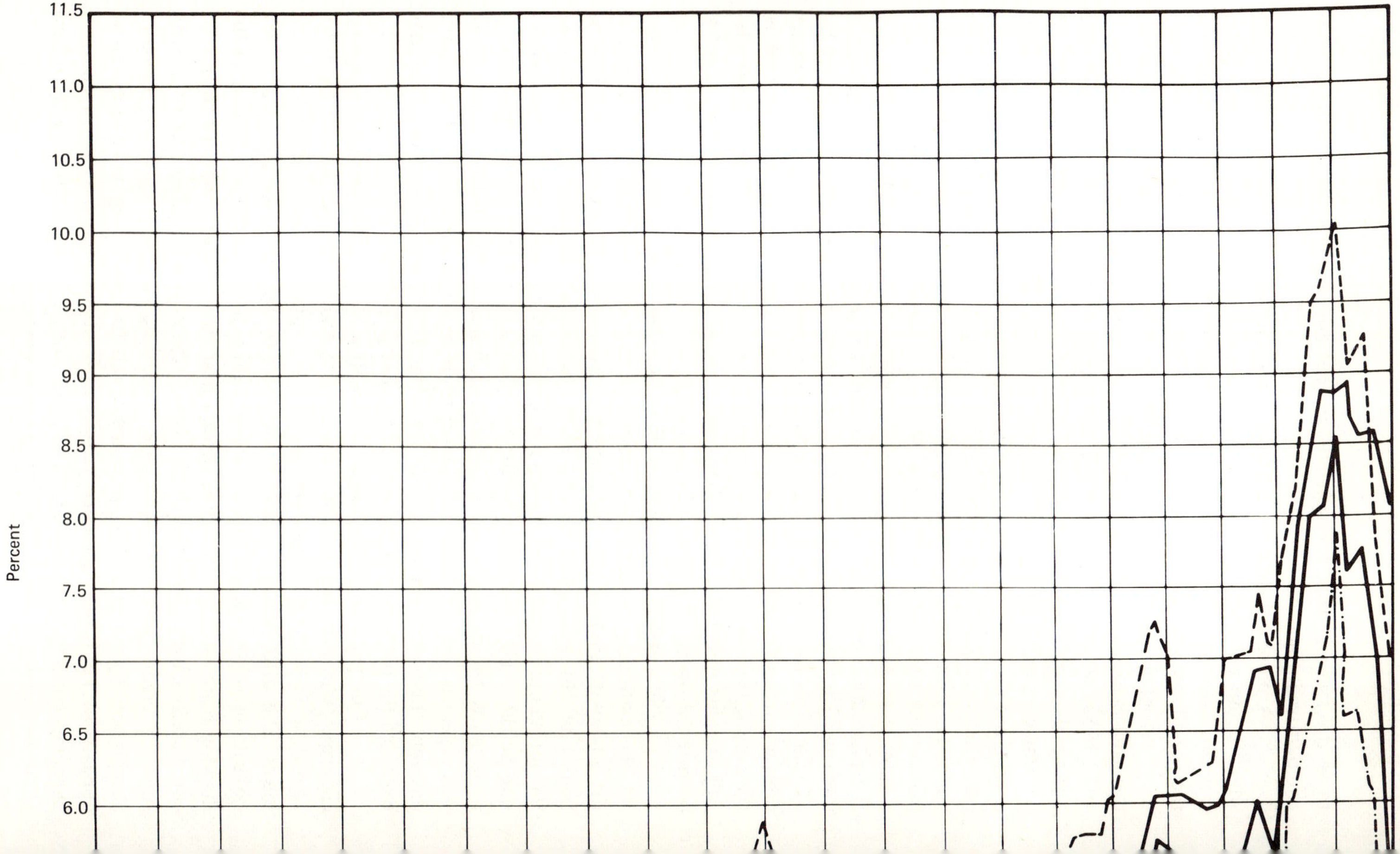

[a]New series beginning February 1965: N.Y.C., $100,000-$499,000 class.

Comparison of acceptance rates with those on large short-term business loans of banks in New York City is of particular interest because these rates constitute costs of an important alternative method of financing international trade and allied transactions. The acceptance rate averages approximately $1\frac{1}{2}$ percentage points lower than the bank loan rate, a spread that corresponds roughly to the prevailing commission charged for use of acceptance credit. In order to sharpen this comparison, figure 10 shows the acceptance rate plus $1\frac{1}{2}$ percent and the rate on short-term business loans of $200,000 and over in New York City. It will be observed that the cost of acceptance credit is considerably more responsive to changing economic and money-market conditions. At cyclical turning points, the acceptance rate leads by four to six months. Also, in tight-money periods, the cost of acceptance credit rises well above the loan rate, whereas in easy-money periods, it declines well below the loan rate. These cyclical swings in relative costs of acceptance credit and customer loans have much to do with the volume of acceptances outstanding. For example, the marked increase of acceptance credit in 1954, and again in 1960-1961, may be attributed, in large part, to its low cost. Evidence is not so clear that the amount of acceptances has been suppressed by the relatively high cost of acceptance credit. But analysis of monthly data indicates that this factor was an important deterrent during 1955-1956 and 1959—periods of sharply rising relative cost.

With the emergence since the late 1950s of free convertibility of foreign moneys into dollars, comparison of the dollar-acceptance rate in New York with the sterling-acceptance rate in London has become increasingly significant. Bankers' acceptances have the unique feature of being an equalization agent for international money rates through operations of both investors and borrowers. For example, when the rate on sterling acceptances in London is materially higher than the rate on dollar acceptances in New York, two actions occur: (1) An outflow of short-term funds from the United States to Britain tends to occur as investors seek the higher yields in London, and (2) borrowers tend to finance a larger part of international trade by means of dollar-acceptance credits, thus increasing the amount of dollar acceptances offered in New York and diminishing of sterling acceptances offered in London. These forces have an equalizing influence, tending to raise rates in New York relative to those in London.

However, the process of rate equalization in New York and London markets through the medium of bankers' acceptances is not entirely a question of relative interest rates, even if perfect mobility of funds is assumed. Investors must also consider the forward-spot relationship in sterling and dollar exchange. American investors would ordinarily sell sterling exchange for future delivery in dollars at the time of investment in sterling acceptances to cover return of funds when the sterling acceptances mature. A $1\frac{1}{2}$ percent discount of such forward exchange over the current spot rate nullifies a $1\frac{1}{2}$ percent spread in London-New York money rates, and a $1\frac{1}{2}$ percent premium of forward sterling exchange over spot exchange adds correspondingly to profitability of investment in sterling acceptances. Foreign borrowers in the dollar-exchange market are similarly affected by the forward-spot relationship of foreign-exchange rates because they usually cover their future need for dollars at the time of borrowing. Their cost of borrowing acceptance credit in New York is increased when dollar forward exchange costs more in sterling than spot exchange. Conversely, their borrowing cost in New York is reduced when dollar forward exchange costs less than spot exchange. In addition, borrowers must allow for whatever differences exist in bank commissions and taxes when financing in one market or the other. New York has enjoyed some advantage over London on this score in recent years. Dollar acceptances are not subject to a stamp tax of 0.2 percent per annum, which is levied on sterling acceptances. Also, New York banks quote a minimum commission of 1 percent on acceptance credit for foreigners when a foreign bank assumes the obligation, compared with 1.2 percent charged by London banks. Offsetting this, a foreign borrower may have to pay a commission to his bank as well as the New York bank when he uses dollar-acceptance credit.

All things considered, dollar-acceptance credit has been much cheaper than sterling-acceptance credit since the mid-1950s, and this has been one of the major reasons for the rapid growth of dollar acceptances outstanding. The dollar-acceptance rate has continuously been lower than the sterling-acceptance rate, although the differential has varied widely – from as little as 0.2 percent in late 1952 and early 1970 to over 3 percentage points in 1967. But the incentive for short-term investment by Americans in sterling acceptances and the incentive to borrow in the dollar-acceptance market have been substantially modified by the discount which has usually been present on sterling forward exchange.[4] While small or even negative at times, this discount ordinarily fell in the range of $\frac{1}{4}$ to $1\frac{1}{2}$ percent of the spot rate. But it was seldom enough to neutralize the effect of lower money rates in New York than in London.

In retrospect, it should be noted that the upsurge in amount of dollar acceptances outstanding during the mid-1960-1970 period was a result of two major factors: (1) the lower cost of dollar-acceptance financing compared with sterling-acceptance financing; and (2) the lower cost of dollar-acceptance financing compared with direct borrowing from New York banks.

REFERENCES

Board of Governors of the Federal Reserve System, "Bankers' Acceptance Financing in the United States," *Federal Reserve Bulletin* (May 1955), pp. 482-494.

Federal Reserve Bank of Cleveland, "Rebound in Use of Bankers' Acceptances," *Business Review* (January 1961), pp. 5-10.

Federal Reserve Bank of New York, "Bankers' Acceptances," *Monthly Review* (June 1966), pp. 127-135.

Ganoe, C. S., "Working Capital Acceptances," *Journal of Commercial Bank Lending,* Vol. 52, No. 5 (January 1970), pp. 50-53.

Ward, Wilbert, and Henry Harfield, *Bank Credit and Acceptances* (4th ed.; New York: Ronald, 1958).

[4]Notable exceptions to this generalization were the last quarter of 1954 and the period of the dollar scare of 1960 and early 1961, when sterling forward exchange stood at a premium.

8

federal agency securities and bankers' certificates

Two new members have joined the money-market family in recent years. One is federal agency securities, the other is negotiable time certificates of deposit (CDs) of leading commercial banks. Little is popularly known about these markets because they are given almost no space in the financial press, and because borrowers and lenders are chiefly confined to large institutions. Nevertheless, both markets have outgrown their older brothers, bankers' acceptances and dealer-placed commercial paper, and have come to occupy positions of real importance.

FEDERAL AGENCY SECURITIES MARKET

A visitor to the quotation room of a large government-bond dealer may note that a section of the board is allocated to securities of five federal government agencies. Three are farm credit agencies–Federal Land Banks (FLB), Federal Intermediate Credit Banks (FICB), and Banks for Cooperatives (COOP). Two are housing credit agencies–Federal National Mortgage Association (FNMA) and Federal Home Loan Banks (FHLB). While these agencies are under federal supervision, their securities are not guaranteed by the government with respect to either principal or interest. Nevertheless, they are very highly rated by investors, and provide pretax yields only a step above those on Treasury securities of comparable maturities. Growth of agency securities has been notably rapid since 1954–from under $2 billion to $35.6 billion at midyear 1970. Before undertaking analysis of agency markets, brief summaries of functions are in order.

federal agency functions

Farm Credit Agencies / All three farm credit agencies are under supervision of the Farm Credit Administration (FCA). Its job is to see that dependable sources of credit at reasonable rates are available to farmers. More specifically, FCA assists in planning the financing for each group of banks, coordinates their borrowing with that of the Treasury and other agencies, and certifies that securities are issued in accordance with law.

The twelve FLBs were organized in 1917 to provide dependable long-term credit to farmers at reasonable rates through local federal land-bank associations. At midyear 1970, loans of $7 billion were outstanding, made through some 640 associations. Funds to finance these loans were raised principally in the money and capital markets by sale of consolidated Federal farm-loan bonds which were outstanding in the amount of $6.2 billion.[1]

A major source of short- and intermediate-term credit for farmers is the cooperative system composed of twelve FICBs, organized in 1923. They do not lend directly to farmers, but advance funds to local production credit associations. Farmers borrow from the associations to meet operating expenses, operating capital requirements, and family needs. At midyear 1970, such loans of the 450 associations amounted to $5.1 billion. Maturities were from a few months to three years. In turn, the FICBs raise funds to lend to the associations by sale of consolidated collateral trust debentures which were outstanding in the amount of $4.9 billion.[2]

Another significant, though less important, source of farm credit is the system of twelve district COOPs and the Central Bank for Cooperatives in Washington, D.C., organized under the Farm Credit Act of 1933. Farmers' cooperatives engaged in storing and marketing farm products, purchasing supplies, and providing business services may borrow from the district COOPs. Loans are classified as *commodity, operating capital,* and *facility* loans. At midyear 1970, they totaled $1.7 billion, made to some 3,000 cooperatives. The Central Bank for Cooperatives participates in large loans to cooperatives made by the twelve district COOPs, and also lends directly to the district banks in case of need. The COOPs raise funds in the money market by sale of consolidated collateral trust debentures which were outstanding in the amount of $1.5 billion at midyear 1970.[3]

Federal Housing Agencies / While the Federal National Mortgage Association (FNMA) dates back to 1938, its status as a constituent agency of the Housing and Home Finance Agency was established in 1954 by amendment of the National Housing Act. The principal function of FNMA is to provide a nationwide secondary market in residential mortgages insured by the Federal

[1]*Federal Reserve Bulletin* (August 1970), p. A 39.
[2]Ibid.
[3]Ibid.

Housing Administration (FHA) and guaranteed by the Veterans Administration (VA). It also provides special assistance by purchasing mortgages to finance programs such as urban renewal, housing for the elderly, and cooperative housing. The special assistance function further extends to purchase of mortgages in order to prevent a cyclical decline in home building.

The primary function of providing liquidity to mortgage investment was supposed to be accomplished by purchasing mortgages in areas and times of short supply of mortgage money, and by selling in areas and times of plentiful supply. In fact, purchases have greatly exceeded sales. More specifically, during the period 1954-1962, aggregate purchases were $4.8 billion whereas sales were only $1.4 billion. Sales were nominal in all years except 1958, 1961, and 1962, when credit was easy and mortgages became more attractive to investors than bonds and other alternative investments. Purchases reached highest levels in boom periods, particularly in the late 1960s, when mortgage money was scarce, interest rates were high, and investors preferred bonds and stocks. At midyear 1970, the mortgage portfolio amounted to $13.7 billion. Borrowings of FNMA from private investors have been principally in support of secondary marketing operations; other functions have usually been financed by Treasury borrowing. At midyear 1970, debentures and notes outstanding totaled $13.2 billion.[4]

The eleven Federal Home Loan Banks (FHLB), established in 1932, provide reserve credit for thrift institutions that are members, principally savings and loan associations. The FHLBs make advances to members to meet customer withdrawals, seasonal lending requirements, and local mortgage loan demands that exceed members' resources. At midyear 1970, such advances amounted to $10.2 billion.[5] The chief source of FHLB funds to support advances to members is sale in the money market of consolidated obligations which aggregated $9.9 billion at midyear 1970.

farm credit bank securities

Features in Common / While each group of farm credit bank securities has distinctive characteristics, they have several features in common. First, all security issues are under overall FCA supervision. This means that FCA is responsible for organizing the whole process of security issuance and retirement, including planning committees, fiscal agency, coordination of financing operations among the three groups and with the Treasury, and arranging for services of Federal Reserve Banks. In addition, it is responsible for legality; in fact, each obligation bears signatures of the governor and a deputy governor of FCA, attesting that it has been issued in accordance with law.

Second, all farm credit bank securities are consolidated obligations of the banks within the respective groups. That is, the separate banks within each

[4]Ibid.
[5]Ibid.

group do not issue securities; instead, each group issues securities which are the joint and several obligations of all. None of the securities is guaranteed by the federal government.

Third, all securities are safeguarded by collateral consisting chiefly of underlying mortgage loans. Collateral is assigned to farm loan registrars, one in each of the twelve districts.

Fourth, the three groups of banks jointly employ a single fiscal agent whose office is in New York City. The agent's main task is to arrange for successful sale of new issues. This is done through nationwide selling groups of selected bond dealers. A continuing agreement between the fiscal agent and each dealer defines the responsibilities of both parties. Among other things, the fiscal agent agrees to notify dealers by telegram concerning the details of new offerings. Dealers assume no underwriting liability, but agree to make prompt payment in Federal funds for securities sold. Separate selling groups exist for the three groups of banks, although a majority of dealers belong to all three. There are about 450 members in the selling group of the FLB, some 300 in that of the FICB, and 250 in that of COOP.

Fifth, delivery of all farm credit securities takes place at the Federal Reserve Bank of New York against payment in Federal funds. Dealers arrange for direct delivery to many of their large customers who usually leave securities in safekeeping in New York City even though they are located elsewhere. This practice simplifies delivery in case of sale, saves shipping expense, and facilitates redemption.

Sixth, farm credit securities enjoy wide investment eligibility. They are lawful investments for all government trust funds, and are eligible as security for Treasury deposits. In addition, these securities are eligible investments for trust funds, insurance companies, commercial banks, and mutual savings banks in most states.

Finally, most farm credit securities are redeemed, and interest is paid thereon, at the Federal Reserve Bank of New York. However, they are redeemable at any Federal Reserve Bank or branch, the Treasury, and the individual farm credit banks.

Federal Land Bank Securities / The FLBs first sold consolidated bonds in 1933. Since that time, they have been marketed at irregular intervals to redeem maturing issues and to provide funds for lending operations. Original maturities have covered a wide range—from under 1 year to over 16 years. During the fiscal year ended June 30, 1969, FLBs issued bonds to the amount of $1,907 million and retired $1,507 million.

Table 8-1 presents the maturity distribution of FLB bonds outstanding at midyear 1970. It will be noted that nearly one-third of the amount had maturities of under one year, and that 86 percent had maturities of under five years. The 28 separate issues aggregated $6.2 billion.

TABLE 8-1 / FEDERAL LAND BANK CONSOLIDATED BONDS OUTSTANDING AT MIDYEAR 1970

Maturity	Number of Issues	Amount (millions of dollars)	Percentage Distribution
Under 1 year	9	1,910	31.0
1-3 years	9	2,340	37.9
3-5 years	5	1,073	17.3
5-9 years	5	856	13.8
Total	28	6,179	100.0

Federal Intermediate Credit Bank Securities / FICBs have sold consolidated debentures since 1935. Proceeds are used to redeem maturing issues and to meet lending requirements. A new issue is offered every month with a maturity almost invariably of nine months. During the fiscal year ended June 30, 1969, new issues aggregated $5.4 billion. A detailed list of outstanding issues at the end of June 1970 is presented in Table 8-2. The ten issues totaled $4.9 billion, and maturities ranged from one to nine months, with the exception of one three-year issue maturing in 1973.

TABLE 8-2 / FEDERAL INTERMEDIATE CREDIT BANK DEBENTURES OUTSTANDING, MIDYEAR 1970

Date of Issue	Face Rate (percent)	Maturity	Amount (millions of dollars)
10/1/69	8.20	7/1/70	419
11/3/69	7.95	8/3/70	499
12/1/69	8.75	9/1/70	498
1/5/70	8.80	10/1/70	593
2/2/70	8.65	11/2/70	656
3/2/70	8.10	12/1/70	348
4/1/70	7.50	1/4/71	560
5/4/70	7.40	2/1/71	592
6/1/70	8.15	3/1/71	511
3/2/70	8.15	3/1/73	203
Total			4,879

Source: *Federal Reserve Bulletin* (August 1970), p. A 39.

Banks for Cooperatives Securities / Consolidated debentures of COOPs were first issued in 1955. They are offered monthly or bimonthly with maturities of six months. On this regular schedule, the amount of each new issue is gauged to meet the rollover of the maturing issue, modified by lending operations and other cash requirements. During the fiscal year ended June 30, 1969, new issues totaled $2.8 billion. Table 8-3 lists the issues outstanding at the end of June 1970, which totaled $1.5 billion.

TABLE 8-3 / BANKS FOR COOPERATIVES CONSOLIDATED DEBENTURES OUTSTANDING, MIDYEAR 1970

Date of Issue	Face Rate (percent)	Maturity	Amount (millions of dollars)
1/5/70	8.65	7/1/70	298
2/2/70	8.65	8/3/70	423
4/1/70	7.45	10/1/70	279
5/4/70	7.25	11/2/70	221
6/1/70	7.70	12/1/70	288
Total			1,509

Source: *Federal Reserve Bulletin* (August 1970), p. A 39.

federal housing agency securities

Federal National Mortgage Association Securities / The FNMA sold its debentures in the private investment market for the first time in 1955. Since that time, its outstanding securities have increased steadily until they totaled $13.2 billion at the end of June 1970. At that time, there were 32 separate issues of debentures, two of mortgage-backed bonds, two of subordinated capital debentures, and a large amount of discount notes ($3.2 billion). Over half the total amount had maturities of under one year, and 98.5 percent had maturities under five years.

TABLE 8-4 / FEDERAL NATIONAL MORTGAGE ASSOCIATION NOTES, DEBENTURES, AND BONDS OUTSTANDING, MIDYEAR 1970

Maturity	Number of Issues	Amount (millions of dollars)	Percentage Distribution
Under 1 year	12	6,764	51.4
1-3 years	18	4,603	35.0
3-5 years	6	1,600	12.1
5-7 years	1	198	1.5
Total	37	13,165	100.0

Source: *Federal Reserve Bulletin* (August 1970), p. A 39.

A new method of borrowing was introduced in April 1961, when short-term discount notes were issued. These notes are offered at a stated interest rate in maturities from 30 to 270 days to suit investors' preferences. Thus, the method closely resembles that in use for many years by large finance companies. The advantages are a saving in borrowing costs and greater flexibility of financial position. For example, in the event that FNMA should sell part of its mortgage portfolio, as in 1958, the proceeds can be used to retire notes, and the problem of investing surplus cash is avoided. Also, short-term borrowing can be used for interim financing until conditions become favorable for longer-term offerings. During 1969, FNMA sold $9 billion of notes and redeemed $7.8 billion; there were $3.2 billion outstanding at midyear 1970.[6]

A special problem in regard to maturities confronts FNMA, arising from its function of providing a secondary mortgage market. Because maturities of most mortgages in its portfolio fall in the range of 15 to 30 years, the casual observer might conclude that maturities of its debentures could be designed to match mortgage maturities without risk of financial embarrassment. But this is not so. Mortgage maturities are not so relevant as times of purchases and sales. Mortgage purchases are most likely during periods of active demand for credit and high interest rates. Borrowing long-term under these conditions would commit FNMA for many years at high rates. Hence, it is frequently wise to borrow at short-term, which preserves the option of selling long-term securities under more favorable conditions. Mortgage sales are most likely when the supply of investible funds is large relative to demand, and therefore when interest rates are low. Proceeds of sales would have to be invested at low rates if obligations take the form of noncallable long-term debentures. A better alternative often is to use sales proceeds to retire maturing short-term obligations. Thus, in view of the fact that FNMA cannot predict the timing of mortgage purchases and sales, there is need to maintain financial flexibility by keeping a substantial part of borrowing on a short-term basis. It is also advisable to hedge against rising interest rates by borrowing long-term for part of requirements when rates are relatively low.

Like the farm credit banks, FNMA maintains a fiscal agency in New York City. The principal job of the agent is to market debentures and notes on a favorable basis. This is done by arranging a nationwide selling group of dealers and dealer banks. Dealers do not underwrite new issues, but receive a commission on sales of allotted securities. Most of the redemptions and interest payments are made at the Federal Reserve Bank of New York.

Federal Home Loan Bank Securities / Consolidated obligations were first marketed by FHLB in May 1937. Since that time, several issues of notes, with maturities of one year or less, have been offered on an irregular schedule during most years. Recently, the principal means of borrowing has been

[6]Federal National Mortgage Association, *Annual Report* (Washington, D.C., 1969), p. 9.

intermediate-term bonds with maturities from one to ten years.

Securities are marketed through a fiscal agent in New York City in much the same manner as other federal agency securities. That is, the fiscal agent assists the FHLB Board and the banks in planning the amount, timing, and terms of new issues to meet operating requirements. He also has a continuing arrangement with a countrywide selling group of dealers who sell new issues for a concession of about 0.1 percent of face value. The Board serves as coordinator in plans for new issues, including consultation with the Treasury in regard to timing, amounts, maturities, rates, and other terms.

TABLE 8-5 / FEDERAL HOME LOAN BANK CONSOLIDATED BONDS AND NOTES OUTSTANDING, MIDYEAR 1970

Maturity	Number of Issues	Amount (millions of dollars)	Percentage Distribution
Under 1 year	15	7,250	73.4
1-3 years	5	1,300	13.2
3-5 years	4	980	10.0
9 years, 8 months	1	350	3.4
Total	25	9,880	100.0

Source: *Federal Reserve Bulletin* (August 1970), p. A 39.

Table 8-5 presents a distribution of FHLB bonds and notes outstanding at midyear 1970. There were 3 issues of short-term notes totaling $1,550 million, and 22 issues of bonds ranging in maturity from 1 to nearly 10 years. Almost three-fourths of the total had maturities of under 1 year, and 96.6 percent had maturities under 5 years.

The safety of FHLB obligations is protected in various ways. To begin with, they are the joint and several obligations of the eleven banks in the system, and the banks have statutory liens against their stock held by borrowing member institutions. Beyond this, consolidated obligations cannot be issued in excess of (1) twelve times the total paid-in capital stock and reserves of the banks, and (2) the sum of unencumbered cash, U.S. direct or guaranteed securities, and secured advances of the FHLBs. In addition, although it has never done so, the Treasury may purchase up to $1 billion of these obligations and is authorized to deposit public funds in the FHLBs.

The practice of borrowing principally at short-term is consistent with the fluctuating financial needs of the FHLBs. When demands for residential mortgage credit are high in relation to supply, as in 1959 and 1969, the resources of member savings institutions are insufficient, and they seek FHLB advances. Under these circumstances, members usually reduce deposits maintained with FHLBs. Hence, a sizable increase in open-market borrowing becomes necessary. Under opposite conditions, when credit demands subside, members ordinarily repay advances and increase deposits. The banks are then able to retire part of their obligations.

summary of agency security maturities

While the maturity distribution of securities of each federal agency has been analyzed, it is of interest to summarize the combined distribution. This is done as of the end of June 1970 in Table 8-6. The aggregate of agency securities

TABLE 8-6 / MATURITY DISTRIBUTION OF FEDERAL AGENCY SECURITIES, JUNE 30, 1970[a] (millions of dollars)

	Under 1 yr.	1-3 yrs.	3-5 yrs.	5-10 yrs.	Total
FLB					
Amount	1,910	2,340	1,073	856	6,179
Percent	30.9%	37.9%	17.4%	13.9%	100%
FICB					
Amount	4,879	0	0	0	4,879
Percent	100%	0	0	0	100%
COOP					
Amount	1,509	0	0	0	1,509
Percent	100%	0	0	0	100%
FNMA					
Amount	6,764	4,603	1,600	198	13,165
Percent	51.4%	35.0	12.2	1.5	100%
FHLB					
Amount	7,250	1,300	980	350	9,880
Percent	73.4%	13.2	9.9	3.5	100%
Total					
Amount	22,312	8,243	3,653	1,404	35,612
Percent	62.7%	23.1%	10.3%	3.9%	100%

[a] In addition to federal agency securities included, the Tennessee Valley Authority had securities outstanding as follows: short-term notes, $331 million; 3-5 years, $150 million; 5-25 years, $525 million.

Source: Tables 8-1 to 8-5.

outstanding was $35.6 billion, of which $22.3 billion—over three-fifths—had maturities of under one year, and $30.6 billion, or 86 percent, had maturities of under three years. This portion of the agency market is of particular interest because this study is mainly concerned with the short-term money market. These issues compete with short-term Treasury securities, commercial paper, finance-company paper, bankers' acceptances, bankers' certificates, and other liquid investments.

comparative yields

Some idea of comparative yields on federal agency securities and Treasury securities is given in Table 8-7, which presents quotations on

TABLE 8-7 / COMPARATIVE YIELDS OF FEDERAL AGENCY AND TREASURY SECURITIES, SEPTEMBER 18, 1970 (percent)

Maturity	Agency Securities	Treasury Securities	Difference in Yield[a]
3-mo.	6.51	6.28	+0.23
6-mo.	6.93	6.59	+0.34
9-mo.	6.88	6.66	+0.22
1-yr.	6.83	6.58	+0.25
2-yr.	7.18	6.60	+0.58
3-yr.	7.39	6.82	+0.57
4-yr.	7.48	7.19	+0.29
5-yr.	7.45	7.12	+0.33
10-yr.	7.79	7.25	+0.54

[a]Offering yields before taxes, based on yield tables.
Source: Aubrey G. Lanston & Co., *Quotation Sheet* (September 21, 1970).

comparable maturities in September 1970. It will be noted that the investment market gave a very high quality rating to agency securities even though they were not guaranteed by the Treasury. Yields fell in a range of between 0.22 and 0.58 percentage points higher than on Treasuries. The amount and maturity pattern of the spread differ with changing supply-demand conditions. Also, the spread measured in percentage points tends to widen as interest rates rise and as maturities lengthen, and to narrow as rates and maturities decline.

ownership of federal agency securities

Growth in the amount and variety of federal agency securities has been accompanied by a broadened distribution of ownership. Commercial banks have been the most important class of investor. At midyear 1970, the 5,743 commercial banks reporting in the Treasury survey held 14 percent of all outstanding federal agency securities.[7] They are attracted by the predominantly short maturities, existence of a secondary market, safety, and the fact that yields are usually higher by 0.2 to 0.5 percentage points than on Treasury securities of comparable maturities. Because banks hold these securities for liquidity

[7]*Treasury Bulletin* (August 1970), pp. 76-77; the Treasury survey accounts for about 90 percent of total commercial-bank investments.

purposes, both the amount and proportion of their holdings vary widely with changes in credit conditions. They rise during easy-money markets such as 1958 and 1961, when bank reserves are abundant; they decline during firm markets such as 1969, when bank reserves become deficient.

The analyst may gain further information on ownership of agency securities from the Treasury's monthly survey. Mutual savings banks, savings and loan associations, insurance companies, trust funds, individuals, endowments, and state and local governments—all hold significant amounts.

BANKERS' CERTIFICATES OF DEPOSIT

The great adaptability of the money market to changing conditions is demonstrated by the development of an entirely new market in negotiable time certificates of deposit (CDs) since early 1961. In essence, CDs are equivalent to borrowing funds by sale of short-term notes or debentures. In its first decade the new instrument has been issued in volume by leading banks, secondary trading by dealers has been instituted, and the market has become roughly twice as large as the long-established market for dealer-placed commercial paper and three times larger than the market for bankers' acceptances. This market enlists keen interest not only because of its meteoric rise, but also because of its potentiality for substantial further growth.

development of new market

Credit for devising and launching the CDs belongs to the First National City Bank of New York which announced in February 1961 that

> We are prepared to accept time deposits from nonfinancial corporate customers, maturing on any date from 90 days to approximately a year, and will provide as evidence thereof a Negotiable Certificate of Deposit payable to the order of the named depositor, or to bearer. The deposits will be established in minimum units of $1 million and will pay interest at maturity calculated for the actual days to maturity and based on a 360-day year. Interest rates will vary from time to time with changes in the money market, subject to the ceilings imposed by Regulation Q of the Federal Reserve Board. At this time, we are quoting the maximum rates payable: $2\frac{1}{2}$% for maturities of 90 days to less than 6 months and 3% for maturities of 6 months to one year inclusive. . . . These Bankers' Certificates will give the holder the advantage of a time deposit, plus the liquidity resulting from potential sales to interested parties because of their negotiable form. Negotiability may be arranged through several of the Government bond dealer firms, including Discount Corporation, First Boston Corporation and others, who are actively dealing in these certificates.

Other major banks in New York City and in other leading cities soon followed with similar offerings. Investors—principally nonfinancial corporations—responded promptly with substantial purchases of the new CDs, and dealers soon created a secondary market. By midyear 1963, total CDs outstanding exceeded \$8 billion, and rapid growth continued until August 1968, when a peak of \$22.3 billion was reached.

As background it should be recalled that time deposits in the broadest sense are those subject to 30 or more days' notice before the bank is obliged to pay. Regular savings (book) accounts amounted to \$89.9 billion in January 1970, over one-half of total time deposits, and were composed chiefly of long-term savings of individuals in the middle- and lower-income groups. The other half of total time deposits falls into three categories: (1) time deposits on open account, which amounted to \$19.1 billion in insured commercial banks in January 1970; (2) time deposits of \$45.8 billion, largely nonnegotiable, and held mostly by individuals; and (3) negotiable CDs of \$13.6 billion, belonging mainly to corporations and institutions.[8]

In offering time CDs to domestic corporations in early 1961, the New York City banks were not presenting something that had no precedent in American banking. The new ingredients were increased negotiability and marketability. The major New York City banks reversed a policy in force since the 1920s of paying no interest on time deposits of domestic corporations.

Motivation for establishment of the new market came from the declining share of the nation's total commercial-bank deposits in New York City banks during and since World War II. In 1941, their share was 25 percent, but by 1960, it was only 15 percent. In part, this decline was a consequence of the lower rate of economic growth in the New York trading area than in the rest of the country. However, in larger measure, it was the result of a marked change in administration of liquid assets of large corporations. Financial officers became highly sophisticated in regard to realization of maximum income from liquid assets, and their efforts in this direction were spurred by the uptrend of interest rates. Deposit balances that paid no interest were pared to a working minimum, and the remainder of needed liquidity was kept in short-term *earning* assets. At the end of 1960, estimates of holdings of such assets by business corporations were in the neighborhood of \$30 billion—\$20 billion in short-term U.S. government securities, \$1.5 billion in short-term state and municipal obligations, \$1 billion in federal agency securities, the rest in commercial and finance-company paper, bankers' acceptances, short-term corporate obligations, and loans to government bond dealers and others under repurchase agreements. Indeed, these extensive lending operations of nonfinancial corporations were popularly known as the *second banking system.* The major banks of New York City, as chief depositaries of large nationwide corporations, suffered most severely from these developments. In addition to being unwilling participants in

[8]*Federal Reserve Bulletin* (September 1970), p. 682.

the general reduction of deposits that accompanied these operations, New York banks also lost deposits to other banks throughout the country. Thus, the principal motivation for initiating the CDs was to stem and reverse the drain on deposits and reserves that had been operative for two decades in New York City banks. In this way, it was hoped that their lending capacity and their earning power might be materially improved. Another motive, though less important, was development of greater stability of deposits. There was good reason to believe that this would follow from inducing corporate treasurers to place surplus cash in CDs rather than in Treasury bills or other liquid assets.

investors in certificates

A Federal Reserve survey has provided more specific information on investors in CDs as of December 5, 1962. Domestic business corporations were the predominant original purchasers—accounting for 69 percent of total outstandings. State and local governments stood second with 15.3 percent, and foreign interests was third with 6.9 percent. The remaining 8.6 percent was purchased by insurance companies, commercial banks, pension funds, mutual savings banks, endowed institutions, individuals, and savings and loan associations.

features of certificates

A more concrete understanding of the form of CDs may be gained from

11 EXAMPLE OF NEGOTIABLE CERTIFICATE OF DEPOSIT.
Courtesy of First National City Bank, New York

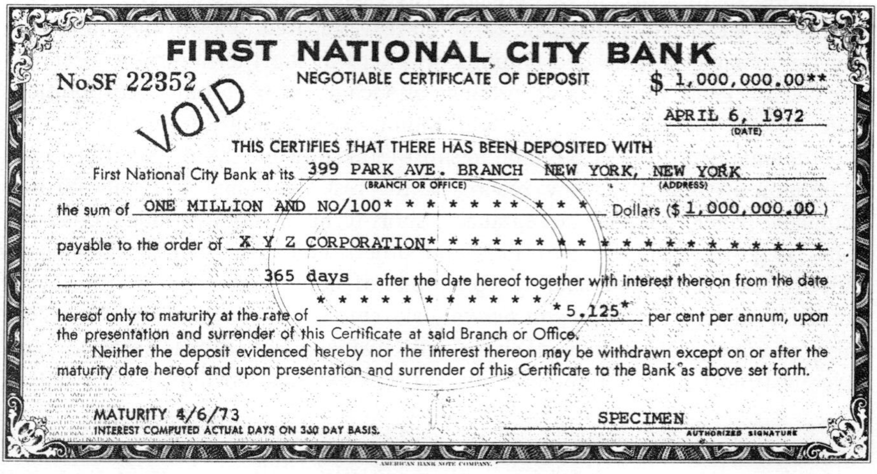

FIRST NATIONAL CITY BANK

No.SF 22352 VOID NEGOTIABLE CERTIFICATE OF DEPOSIT $ 1,000,000.00**

APRIL 6, 1972 (DATE)

THIS CERTIFIES THAT THERE HAS BEEN DEPOSITED WITH

First National City Bank at its 399 PARK AVE. BRANCH (BRANCH OR OFFICE) NEW YORK, NEW YORK (ADDRESS)

the sum of ONE MILLION AND NO/100* * * * * * * * * * Dollars ($ 1,000,000.00)

payable to the order of X Y Z CORPORATION* * * * * * * * * * * * * * * * *

365 days after the date hereof together with interest thereon from the date hereof only to maturity at the rate of * * * * * * * * * * * * * *5.125* per cent per annum, upon the presentation and surrender of this Certificate at said Branch or Office.

Neither the deposit evidenced hereby nor the interest thereon may be withdrawn except on or after the maturity date hereof and upon presentation and surrender of this Certificate to the Bank as above set forth.

MATURITY 4/6/73
INTEREST COMPUTED ACTUAL DAYS ON 360 DAY BASIS.

SPECIMEN
AUTHORIZED SIGNATURE

figure 11. In essence, it is a receipt for deposit of a stated sum in the bank on a given date, together with a promise to redeem this sum plus interest at the indicated rate on a designated date. The instrument is negotiable because it is payable either to bearer or to the order of the depositor. As the market has developed, the bearer form has become most common in view of its greater convenience in the secondary market. The most common denomination is $1,000,000 in the larger money market banks where the CDs are designed to appeal to large corporations that would not be interested in smaller amounts. Banks outside New York City, which serve local and regional markets, issue CDs in units of $100,000 or less. In April 1970, 2,750 banks had negotiable CDs in denominations of $100,000 or more outstanding in the total amount of $8.8 billion.[9]

The original maturities of CDs have been significantly affected by the interest rate ceilings enforced by the Board of Governors. Very few have been issued with maturity under 6 months because market rates were, until mid-July 1963, above the maximum rates that banks could pay. But banks have been able to compete with Treasury bills and other alternative investments in maturities of 6 months and beyond. At the time of the Federal Reserve survey in December 1962, nearly half the dollar volume fell in the 6-9-month category. The 1-year maturity was next in popularity, although the 9-12-month class was utilized rather heavily by larger banks. Issues maturing in over 1 year were moderately important, and a few extended beyond 2 years.[10] Investors desiring maturities of under 6 months had to purchase them from dealers in the secondary market. It should be emphasized that the entire scale of original maturities between 6 months (3 months after July 1963) and over 1 year has been utilized in order to suit investor requirements as precisely as possible. In fact, the feature of carefully tailored maturities is one of the significant advantages of CDs to investors in comparison with short-term government securities.

Rates quoted on original issues of CDs change rather flexibly with general money-market conditions; however, like rates on finance-company paper, they sometimes remain unchanged for several weeks at a time. Within the maximum limits fixed by the Board of Governors, rates are set competitively with other instruments in the money market. When the ceiling is inoperative, rates are usually about 0.25 percentage point above the market rate on Treasury bills, and about the same as yields on finance-company paper. Different yields are quoted for different maturities in rough correspondence with the yield-maturity curve of the money market. The yield structure and maximum rates permitted by Regulation Q on July 10, 1970 were as follows.

[9]*Federal Reserve Bulletin* (September 1970), p. 682.
[10]*Federal Reserve Bulletin* (April 1963), p. 465.

Days to Maturity	Bank Rates on Original Issues	Dealer-Offering Rates	Maximum Rates, Regulation Q
30-59	6¼%	8%	[a]
60-89	6½	8	[a]
90-179	6¾	8⅛	6¾
180-1 yr.	7	8¼	7
1 yr. and over	7½	8½	7½

[a]Effective June 24, 1970 maximum rates on these maturities were suspended.
Source: Manufacturers Hanover Trust Co., *Financial Digest* (July 10, 1970).

the secondary market

One of the essential elements in successful development of CDs is a healthy secondary market. Because a bank is prohibited from redeeming CDs before maturity, quick liquidity depends on resale to dealers. Such a market was initiated by Discount Corporation of New York, and entered soon thereafter by four additional large security dealers—C. J. Devine & Co., First Boston Corporation, New York Hanseatic Corporation, and Salomon Brothers. These dealers after 1963 usually carried sizable individual inventories, ranging between $40 and $70 million. The total dealer inventory position ranged between $164 and $396 million during the period July-September 1970.[11] By midyear 1970, several large commercial banks and a number of smaller nonbank dealers had also entered the field. Dealers stand ready to quote bid and asked rates on various maturities. The dealers' spread is between 2 and 3 basis points. That is, when the bid rate is 8.00 percent, the asked rate may be 7.97 to 7.98 percent. The spread widens in tight-money markets and narrows in easy markets. Rates are usually quoted on a regular yield basis, but on a 360-day year. Hence, an adjustment must be made when comparing them with quoted rates on Treasury bills, bankers' acceptances, and commercial paper which are quoted on a discount basis and a 360-day year. That is, the Treasury bill rate must be adjusted upward by multiplying it by the fraction, $100/100 - d$, when d is the amount of annual discount. In addition, both certificate rates and Treasury bill rates must be multiplied by $\frac{365}{360}$ to be comparable with bond table yields.

The level of rates is basically determined by general conditions of supply and demand for loanable funds. But in this setting, dealers adjust quotations to those in competing sections of the money market. More specifically, rates are kept in proper relation to those on Treasury bills, finance-company paper, commercial paper, repurchase agreements on government securities, and to rates offered by banks on original certificates. As indicated, quoted rates are usually about 0.25 percentage point above Treasury

[11]Federal Reserve Bank of New York, *Weekly Release.*

bill rates, but in periods of tight money, as in 1969, they rise to as much as $1\frac{1}{2}$ percentage points above the bill rate. Also, rates usually rise directly with maturities. For example, in early July 1970 rates on certificates in the 30-89-day and the 360-day-and-over categories were 8 percent and $8\frac{1}{2}$ percent, respectively, and they rose by gradations within this range. However, the yield-maturity relationship must be kept in step with that of the money market in general.

Rates quoted by dealers also vary somewhat depending on a number of factors that deserve mention. For one thing, quoted rates apply to prime CDs of some 30 major banks; rates on lesser-prime certificates of about 45 somewhat smaller banks are about 10 points higher; and rates on still smaller banks (off-prime CDs) are some 25 basis points higher than prime rates. For another, quoted rates apply to standard units of $1,000,000; they are somewhat higher on smaller denominations (odd lots) which are occasionally traded. Finally, CDs purchased from dealers usually yield a shade more than original CDs. This arises from the fact that the maturity of original issues can be precisely matched with investor needs.

Dealers estimate that aggregate volume of sales was in the vicinity of $1 billion during the new market's first year. During the period July-September 1970, sales were at the annual rate of $5.5 billion. The bulk of trading takes place in CDs of some 30 leading banks, the rest in CDs of about 45 others. The typical transaction is for $2 to $3 million in units of $1 million, although many large corporations will not trade for less than $5 million. The supply of CDs in the market comes directly from banks and from corporate investors who need funds before maturity date. Dealers also acquire an important part of their inventory by prearranged *takeouts* with customers. That is, the customer will buy the CDs from the issuing bank and immediately sell them to a dealer at an agreed price that allows the customer a profit of 1 or 2 basis points.

Dealers usually make delivery of CDs sold on the next business day. Clearing of CDs is largely handled by Manufacturers Hanover Trust Company, but one large dealer does its own clearing. Payment for CDs purchased by dealers is made in Federal funds, and it is also customary for major banks to redeem maturing certificates in Federal funds rather than in clearing-house funds.

the rate ceiling: regulation q

The most threatening obstacle to development of the new market has been, and continues to be, the regulatory ceiling on rates. The Banking Act of 1933 directed the Board of Governors to set limits on interest payable on time deposits, and the Board has done so under Regulation Q. No change was made in the schedule of maximum rates during the twenty years preceding 1957, when rates actually paid were almost universally below the ceiling. But following 1957, seven upward adjustments were made in line with the general rise of interest rates.

Comparison of the ceilings with yields on Treasury bills and commercial paper reveals that CDs could not have competed with these alternative investments between mid-1955 and mid-1960, with the exception of a few months during the recession of 1958. Upward adjustment of the ceiling in January 1962 opened the way for competition in the maturity range of 6 months and over, but precluded issuance of CDs in less than 6 months, because yields on Treasury bills and other competing instruments were well above the ceiling of $2\frac{1}{2}$ percent. The further upward adjustment in July 1963 permitted banks to compete effectively in original issues throughout the maturity range of 3 months and beyond, but still kept the door closed to them in the under-90-days category. However, raising the ceiling from $2\frac{1}{2}$ to 4 percent in the 3-6-month area, and from $3\frac{1}{2}$ to 4 percent in the 6-12-month class constituted a material increase in freedom of action for the banks to compete for liquid funds. With obstacles removed by the Fed, the amount of CDs outstanding grew steadily to a peak of $18.6 billion in August 1965.

But in the third quarter of 1965, a marked change in Federal Reserve policy became apparent. During the following months and throughout the credit crunch of 1966, rates on other money-market instruments rose well above the maximum rates permitted on CDs, with the result that by December 1966, outstandings had declined by over $3 billion. Thus, the rate ceiling became a new instrument of restrictive monetary policy. Such a large loss of time deposits by the large banks sharply reduced their liquidity and their ability to expand loans, investment, and, thereby, deposits.

Maximum Rates on CDs, $100,000 and Over	Effective Date			
	July 20, 1966	*April 19, 1968*	*Jan. 21, 1970*	*June 24, 1970*
30-59 days	5½	5½	6¼	none
60-89 days		5¾	6½	none
90-179 days		6	6¾	6¾
180 days-1 year		6¼	7	7
1 year or more		6¼	7½	7½

Source: *Federal Reserve Bulletin* (September 1970), p. A 11.

The increase of maximum rates in April 1968 (see accompanying schedule) gave the CD market a new lease on life. Expansion began again in 1967 with the decline of open-market rates, and continued to a new peak of $22.3 billion in August 1968. But the worst was yet to come. As the money market tightened in 1968 and 1969, open-market rates rose to their highest level in a century, again well above the official ceiling. The result was readily predictable. By the end of 1969, the volume of CDs had declined to $10.9 billion, or by over one-half.

With the turn of 1970, a more liberal policy toward the CD market was adopted by the Fed, with an increase in maximum rates payable in January, and complete removal of restrictions on maturities under three months in June 1970. The market responded immediately, and by late September, it had almost retraced its steps, with outstandings of $22 billion.

Looking back, the use by the Board of Governors of rate ceilings as an instrument of monetary management was an unwise decision. Having given the CD market its blessing, and having permitted it to grow to a position second only to Treasury bills, it was a gross mistake to put it nearly out of business in 1966 and 1969. The Fed has adequate powers to restrain credit expansion through its other general instruments—open-market operations, legal-reserve requirements, the discount rate, and rationing the discount window. Use of the rate ceiling served only to add to uncertainties and to create a near crisis. A viable CD market requires the assurance of the Fed that the rate ceiling will be kept in close relation to competitive market rates, or better yet, the complete removal of maximum interest rates payable. Banks and dealers can justify the outlays for promotion and development of the CD market only if they are permitted to offer competitive rates at all times. Otherwise, the amount of CDs will fluctuate so widely that profitable lending and investing of the funds will be impossible. Also, unless a stable market is assured, the CD will be regarded as an instrument inferior to commercial paper and bankers' acceptances. Under these circumstances, investors can be induced to buy them only at higher yields than would otherwise obtain.

effects on the money market

Growth of the CD market may have significant effects on the money market, on Federal Reserve operations, and on management policies of large city banks. The actual effects cannot be accurately anticipated because they depend on amount and character of asset shifting to CDs. Nevertheless, it is of interest to analyze possibilities and to estimate the most likely course of events.

1/Insofar as growth of CDs represents a shift from other forms of commercial-bank time deposits, there should be no significant repercussions. It is unlikely that regular savings accounts would lose to CDs because the former belong principally to small individual savers. However, there may be some shift from time deposits on open account to CDs because a large part of such accounts belongs to business corporations and other institutions.

2/If growth of time CDs comes from demand deposits, several results of importance may follow. The initial effect would be a reduction in demand deposits, an equivalent increase of time deposits, and release of required legal reserves, due to lower reserve requirements against time deposits. Assuming that the banking system subsequently utilizes the released reserves to support expansion of credit, the ultimate result would be an increase in *total* deposits but a reduction in *demand* deposits—unless the Fed provides additional bank reserves. Whether such a change, involving a decrease in the active money supply, would tend to reduce spending for output is indeterminable, although many economists would expect this result. In such an event, levels of employment, income, and prices would be depressed unless countered by expansionary monetary and fiscal policies. The growth of CDs on which interest is paid, at the expense of demand deposits on which no interest is paid, would be a most unwelcome development to bankers.

There will undoubtedly be both direct and indirect shifting of demand deposits to CDs. The direct shift within one bank will take place whenever a corporation has a larger demand balance than needed for working purposes. Indirect shifts will occur when competitive money-market instruments are sold and the proceeds are used to purchase CDs. For example, bank A would welcome the decision of its customer, corporation X, to convert $10 million of Treasury bills into time CDs. But if the bills are purchased by a nonbank investor, it is likely that he will pay by drawing down demand deposits in *other* banks. That is, the consolidated balance sheet of the banking system would in this case show a decrease of demand deposits and an increase of time CDs. The release of reserve requirements would *in part* save the day provided attractive loan and investment opportunities exist. In fact, this would be likely because banks might purchase the Treasury bills which were sold by their corporate customers. But even after full utilization of released reserve, demand deposits would remain well below their former amount, and their ratio to time deposits would decline. Moreover, while bank A might not shed tears over loss of demand deposits by other banks, it could not, as a member of the system, avoid for long the impact of a pervasive development such as this. Its tears might come later when another of its large customers, corporation Y, drew down demand deposits to purchase Treasury bills which were being converted to time CDs of bank B. Thus, because the largest potentiality for growth of CDs appears to be through shifts from Treasury securities and other short-term investments, it is likely that development of the CD market would be in large part at the expense of demand deposits. This conclusion assumes, however, that the total amount of member-bank legal reserves was just sufficient to meet requirements before the shift to CDs occurred, and also that Federal Reserve authorities would not permit additions to bank reserves. Of course, if the Fed should respond by releasing a new increment of legal reserves, bank-credit expansion could replace the extinguished demand deposits. In fact, such action would be most likely if the monetary authorities interpreted the shift from demand deposits to CDs as undesirably deflationary.

Consideration should also be given to another possible development. Assume in the foregoing example that corporation X sold the $10 million of Treasury bills to commercial banks which paid by checks drawn on their balances at Reserve Banks. For the banking system, the net effect would be an increase of Treasury bill holdings and of time CDs. In the event that excess reserves existed, their amount would be decreased by the added reserve requirement of $500,000. But if legal reserves were just sufficient at the outset, a reserve deficiency would develop. This, in turn, would initiate a multiple contraction of bank credit to repair the deficiency unless new reserves were released by the Fed or became available from other sources.

3/While the banking system as a whole would be affected along the foregoing lines, what of the distribution of deposits and reserves? The probabilities are high that successful growth of the CD market would move deposits and reserves toward large banks in money centers—particularly toward New York City—and away from smaller banks that do not issue CDs. However, this movement would not be likely to take the form of direct shifts of deposits. Instead, the process would probably be an indirect one, growing out of sale of Treasury securities and other investments by depositor-customers to other nonbank investors and placement of the proceeds in CDs. After the initial stage, the process might most often involve decisions of large customers initially to buy CDs rather than Treasury bills. But regardless of the process, the effects on smaller banks throughout the country would be significant. The extent of the drain on smaller banks will depend on the countermeasures they can take, such as promoting their own consumer-type CDs, and—in the case of intermediate-size banks—issuing their own CDs to compete in local and regional markets.

4/Development of a sizable new CD market may have some effects on the money-rate structure. Because CDs compete most directly with Treasury bills, commercial paper, finance-company paper, and bankers' acceptances, the relative demand for these instruments by corporations and others should be somewhat less than before, and therefore their relative yields should rise. However, to the extent that banks find released legal reserves as a consequence of shifts from demand to time deposits, their demands for these instruments may, in part, replace reduced corporate demands. On balance, there should be a tendency for these rates to rise slightly in relation to other market rates. The influence of major banks in committing funds gained from CDs is less clear. Almost certainly, a part would be invested in tax-exempt municipals, thereby causing a relative decline in tax-exempt yields. Beyond this, visibility is too poor to justify even a guess. Presumably, the new funds would find their way into all forms of loans and investments with the possible exception of real-estate loans.

SUMMARY AND CONCLUSIONS

1/A new money-market instrument, the negotiable time CD, was offered by major banks beginning in early 1961. By midyear 1963, this new division of the money market had grown phenomenally to more than twice the size of the dealer commercial-paper market and of the bankers' acceptance market. In the last quarter of 1970, the amount of CDs outstanding exceeded $22 billion.

2/Most of these CDs were issued in denominations of $1 million or more by large banks in New York City and other leading cities and with maturities ranging between three months and one year.

3/Investors in CDs were principally large business corporations, but significant amounts were also held by state and local governments and by a wide variety of other investors.

4/Several large bond dealers in New York City made a market in CDs by quoting bid and asked rates at which they stood ready to buy and sell.

5/The rate level on CDs averages about 0.25 percentage point above the rate on Treasury bills, although in tight-money periods such as 1966 and 1969, the spread exceeded 1 percent.

6/The principal obstacle to substantial further development of the new market is regulation of maximum interest rates payable on time deposits by the Board of Governors. Repeal of rate regulation, or a policy of setting the ceiling sufficiently high to permit bank competition with alternative investments, is a prime requisite to healthy growth, or even survival, of the market.

7/If the barrier of rate ceilings is removed, a promising further development of the new market almost certainly lies ahead. When allowed to compete freely for money-market funds, the major banks are able to issue CDs that provide many investors with an attractive combination of liquidity, safety, and yield.

REFERENCES

federal agency securities market

Farm Credit Administration, annual reports (Washington, D.C.).

Farm Credit Administration, *Marketing Farm Credit Bank Securities* (Washington, D.C., January 1962).

Federal Home Loan Bank Board; annual reports (Washington, D.C.).

Federal Home Loan Banks, *The Federal Home Loan Bank System* (Washington, D.C.: Federal Home Loan Banks, 1961).

Federal Reserve Bank of Chicago, "Federal Agency Securities," *Business Conditions* (August 1960), pp. 12-16.

Federal Reserve Bank of Cleveland, " 'Fannie Mae' in the Secondary Mortgage Market," *Business Review* (August 1963), pp. 2-9.

First Boston Corporation, *Securities of the United States Government and Federal Agencies* (Boston, 1970).

Moody's Investors Service, municipal and government manuals.

U.S. Housing and Home Finances Agency, annual reports (Washington, D.C.).

bankers' certificates of deposit

Board of Governors of the Federal Reserve System, "Negotiable Certificates of Deposit," *Federal Reserve Bulletin* (June 1963), pp. 458-468.

Federal Reserve Bank of New York, "Certificates of Deposit," *Monthly Review* (June 1963), pp. 82-87.

Federal Reserve Bank of San Francisco, "Twelfth District Participation in the Expanding Secondary Market for Negotiable CD's" (June 1963), pp. 82-91.

Fieldhouse, Richard, *Certificates of Deposit* (Boston: Bankers Publishing Co., 1962).

Willis, Parker B., *The Secondary Market for Negotiable Certificates of Deposit* (Washington, D.C.: Board of Governors of the Federal Reserve System, 1967). (A staff study for the Committee for the Fundamental Reappraisal of the Discount Mechanism.)

9

brokers' loans and other market components

BROKERS' LOANS

While brokers' loans are no longer a constituent of the open money market, their dominant position for nearly a century prior to the 1930s requires at least brief consideration. In a history of the money market, they would doubtless merit more space than any other subdivision—certainly if measurement is based on their place in financial literature.[1] From the 1840s until the 1930s, the brokers' call-loan market was the principal facility for adjustment of reserve position by commercial banks. This era ended with the regulatory financial legislation of the early 1930s. In the paragraphs that follow, a summary of features of the call-money market as it existed in the 1920s is presented first, followed by a brief description of the current status of brokers' loans.

The brokers' loan market was an adjunct of the organized security markets, and particularly of the New York Stock Exchange. It represented only a part, though usually the larger part, of loans for the purchase or carrying of securities. The other part of such loans was made directly by banks to nonbroker customers who wished to borrow for this purpose. Brokers' loans were of two standard types: call loans and time loans. A call loan could be repaid by the broker or called by the bank on any day following its origination. Time loans had a definite maturity, most commonly 90 days, when they were repaid or renewed. They were usually made to broker customers, but in active markets they were frequently made on an objective, open-market basis. Money brokers brought major banks and brokers together for a small commission. But call loans

[1]Several books, major parts of other books, and hundreds of articles have been written about brokers' loans. Also, they have been a topic for extensive congressional hearings, followed by regulatory legislation in the Banking Act of 1933, and in the Securities Exchange Act of 1934. See references at the end of this chapter.

were better adapted to the day-to-day variations of both brokers' credit needs and banks' reserve positions. Consequently, they constituted between 75 and 90 percent of aggregate brokers' loans during the 1920s, and time loans accounted for only 10 to 25 percent.

call-loan procedures

Open-market call loans were typically arranged through the money desk of the New York Stock Exchange. Brokers listed their credit needs at the desk and banks reported their offerings of funds. The clerk then paired brokers and banks. All details of making a loan were left to the broker and the bank. In most cases, the facilities of the Stock Clearing Corporation for delivery of securities and of money were utilized. Loans were made under a blanket loan agreement which brokers signed and filed with all important lending banks. This agreement was designed to provide complete protection to the banks and at the same time to facilitate trading operations of brokers. Banks could sell collateral securities without notice if the broker failed to meet a call for an increase in protective margin. Brokers could substitute acceptable collateral as securities in their possession changed in the daily course of trading.

In arranging a call loan, the broker prepared a loan envelope on which was recorded names of parties, amount, rate, and a list of enclosed stocks and their values. Loans were made in round denominations of $100,000 and multiples thereof, so that one broker usually had many separate loans outstanding with a number of different banks. There were generally recognized standards for acceptable collateral. Banks preferred a diversified list of actively traded, quality stocks because they provided greater protection than inactive issues of secondary companies. Although margin requirements varied, brokers were typically expected to maintain a minimum margin of 20 percent of the value of collateral. Stated differently, the maximum loan value of acceptable securities was about 80 percent. Termination of a call loan was made at the initiative of either the borrowing broker or the lending bank, provided notice was given before 12:15 P.M. In either case, the broker repaid the loan with interest and the bank returned the collateral, usually through the Stock Clearing Corporation. Most call loans, however, were renewed from day to day at the renewal rate posted daily at the money desk.

demand and supply of call money

Brokers borrowed in the call market principally to finance customers' margin purchases of stocks. A small part of such purchases could be financed by the brokers' own capital, and a much larger part by customers' credit balances. But the highly fluctuating amount of customers' debit balances—that is, borrowing to buy—above this level, necessitated brokers' loans. Brokers also borrowed at times to purchase securities for their own account. As previously indicated, the bulk of borrowing took the form of call loans rather than time loans, in view of their ready adaptability to changing needs.

The supply of call-loan money came from three sources: (1) New York City banks; (2) correspondent banks outside New York City; and (3) others. Before the stock-market boom of 1927 to 1929, New York City banks were by far the largest source of brokers' loans. But as call-loan rates rose, correspondent banks and nonbank lenders were drawn into the market. Call loans placed by Wall Street banks for the account of correspondents became almost as large as their "own account" loans. The out-of-town banks looked upon brokers' loans and balances with New York City banks as alternative liquid assets because New York banks usually paid about 2 percent interest on such balances. Whenever call-loan rates rose well above this level, the out-of-town banks shifted part of their balances to call loans. Under opposite circumstances of relatively low call-loan rates, these banks tended to reduce loans and to increase balances. Over one-half of brokers' loans in the "others" category was made by domestic business corporations and the rest by nonbank fincancial institutions, individuals, foreign banks, and other foreign interests. Between midyear 1926 and 1930, this classification was the largest of all, and at the speculative peak in 1929, it exceeded three-fourths of aggregate brokers' loans.

call-loan rates

There were two interest rates on call loans. One was the market rate on new loans which often changed several times during the day. The other was the renewal rate which was determined each morning by the Stock Clearing Corporation after accumulating information from principal lenders and borrowers on the supply-demand situation. The great bulk of loans was renewed each day at the posted renewal rate because it usually reflected the market and was satisfactory to both lenders and borrowers.

Comparison of the call-loan rate with other rates during the 1920s may be made on the bases of both level and sensitivity to changing conditions. The call rate averaged about the same as the open-market rate on commercial paper. It was usually well above the Federal Reserve Bank discount rate and rates on bankers' acceptances and on short-term U.S. securities; it was commonly below rates on brokers' time loans.

With respect to sensitivity, the call rate displayed both quicker responses and wider fluctuations than other money-market rates. Speedy responses were an outgrowth of nationwide use of this market by banks to adjust reserve positions. Accumulation of surplus reserves was quickly reflected by declining rates even from hour to hour as call money offerings rose. However, reserve deficiencies soon led to higher rates. Similarly, changes in demand for brokers' loans were promptly transmitted to rates. The range of fluctuation of the call-loan rate was also considerably wider than that of other open-market rates. For example, during the easy-money period of 1924, the call-loan rate dropped in August to an average of 2 percent, compared with $3\frac{1}{4}$ percent on commercial paper and 2.13 percent on bankers' acceptances. Then during the tight-money period in 1929, the call rate rose in July to an average of 9.23 percent compared with 6 percent on commercial paper and 5.13 percent on bankers' acceptances.[2]

These wider fluctuations of the call rate were a consequence of both demand and supply conditions. Demand for stock-exchange credit was highly volatile, declining to nominal amounts during periods of pessimism and becoming very insistent during waves of optimism. From the standpoint of supply, banks became increasingly reluctant to make call loans as reserve positions tightened. They desired to give priority to commercial-loan customers, and they responded to Federal Reserve opposition to excessive speculative credit. In the opposite situation, when demand for call loans was small, the banks were commonly flooded with surplus reserves which they offered freely at low rates.

regulation of brokers' loans

There was general recognition that the effects of the speculative orgy in stocks during 1927 to 1929 were harmful. Authorities differed on the nature and extent of these effects. But most of them agreed that brokers' loans and other loans for the purpose of trading in stocks should be brought under regulation. This was done by provisions of the Banking Acts of 1933 and 1935, and of the Securities Exchange Act of 1934 which applied to both the supply and demand for speculative credit. The Board of Governors was empowered to limit security loans of member banks by Fed districts, and to suspend discount privileges of member banks that made excessive security loans. Also, brokers' loans by nonbank interests, which accounted for over three-fourths of brokers' loans at the peak, were prohibited. Speculative credit demand was subjected to control by giving the Board power to fix margin requirements on borrowing by brokers, their customers, and others for carrying or trading in listed stocks.

The foregoing regulations, combined with prohibition of interest payments on demand deposits by the Banking Act of 1933, led to the demise of the open market for brokers' loans. High margin requirements—between 50 and 100 percent during the 1950s and 1960s—curbed demand for brokers' loans and set a low ceiling on their amount. Prohibition of interest on bankers' balances eliminated them as earning assets for correspondent banks, and therefore reduced their amount to an operational minimum. As a consequence, one of the principal sources of funds for brokers' loans dried up.

[2]Board of Governors of the Federal Reserve System, *Banking and Monetary Statistics*, (Washington, D.C., 1941), p. 450.

brokers' loan market today

The primary difference between the brokers' loan market today and in the 1920s is that it is no longer an objective, open market. This has been the situation since 1933-1934, when comprehensive legal regulation was instituted. Since that time, brokers' loans have been made only on a customer-loan basis—that is, to brokers who are depositing customers. For this reason, large brokerage firms maintain deposit accounts and general loan agreements with several money-market banks in order to assure adequate borrowing power. The call-loan form is used for the most part, but the call option is exercised by banks only in exceptional cases. Thus, in contrast with the situation before the 1930s, the brokers' loan market is seldom utilized to adjust bank reserve positions.

The shift of brokers' loans to a customer basis has led to rather general use of the accordion-type loan which in 1970 accounted for about nine-tenths of total brokers' loans. Under this arrangement, the broker has all indebtedness to one bank centered in a large loan under a general loan agreement. The amount of the loan from day to day, and the applicable rate, are then changed flexibly in keeping with the broker's needs and market conditions. A diversified package of listed stocks is pledged as security to meet margin requirements. Substitutions of stock are necessarily frequent in view of changes in a broker's holdings. Also, the bank has the right to sell pledged stock in the event the broker fails to meet the required margin. However, this new type of loan has not entirely displaced the old individual loans in units of $100,000 and multiples thereof, where each loan is an entity with separate collateral. This traditional-type loan is still preferred by some brokers to meet specific requirements.

Another aspect of replacement of open-market brokers' loans with customer loans is sluggishness of rate movements. In contrast with the 1920s and before, when the rate on brokers' loans was the most sensitive one in the market, its movements are now much less responsive to changing conditions than open-market rates on short-term Treasury issues, bankers' acceptances, commercial paper, and Federal funds. Since the 1960s, it has been about the same as the prime rate on business loans.

The great New York City banks represent the largest source of brokers' loans, but banks in other leading cities also lend substantial amounts. More specifically, brokers' loans of member banks in leading cities in 1970 were divided between banks inside and outside New York City in a ratio of approximately 55 to 45.

Margin requirements on brokers' loans are a net result of standards set by (1) the Board of Governors of the Fed, (2) lending banks, and (3) the New York Stock Exchange. As already indicated, the Board of Governors was empowered to fix margin requirements by the Securities and Exchange Act of 1934. The Wall Street banks arrange for brokers' loans by outside banks for a service charge which is usually $\frac{1}{4}$ percent per annum. Also, New York City banks are generally willing to grant participations in their brokers' loans to correspondent banks throughout the country in amounts as small as $25,000 for a service charge of $\frac{1}{2}$ percent per annum. The maturity of such participations is usually between one and three months, and there is a firm understanding that the New York bank will buy back the participation at any time. Thus, while brokers' loans are not liquidity reserves to New York City banks, the participations therein by smaller correspondent banks have a high degree of liquidity and therefore qualify as liquidity reserves.

Margin requirements are stated as a percentage of the current value of stocks, and have varied during the postwar years between 50 and 100 percent. In October 1970, they stood at 65 percent, which meant that borrowings were limited to 35 percent of current value of securities. The margin requirement applies to *initial* loans made by brokers to their customers—known as customer *net debit balances*. This requirement does not apply to brokers' loans secured by customers' collateral. On these loans, which represent the bulk of total brokers' loans, lending banks determine the *initial* margin, which in recent years has been between one-fourth and one-third of market value. The New York Stock Exchange margin regulation of 25 percent is the minimum requirement for all brokers' loans and for customers' net debit balances. That is, if the margin falls below this figure, the broker must repair the deficiency, or the lending bank must sell enough pledged securities to do so.

The strong rise in common-stock prices during the 1950s and 1960s was accompanied by a sizable increase in brokers' loans. Between the end of 1950 and the end of 1968, customers' net debit balances of the members of the New York Stock Exchange rose from $1,356 million to $9,790 million. The reason for this large increase was to provide credit to their margin customers.[3]

In conclusion, the question may well be raised whether the brokers' loan market may one day regain its place as an important component of the open money market. The answer appears to be in the negative. Most authorities agree that the rampant stock speculation in the late 1920s, largely with borrowed funds, was a harmful and disrupting influence on the economy. Also, while they may not approve all details of existing security regulations, they recognize the imperative need for effective stock-exchange control. As long as these controls are enforced, it is likely that brokers' loans will continue on a customer basis. However, there is a possibility of sufficient relaxation of controls in the years ahead to permit rebirth of open-market brokers' loans on a modest scale. An environment conducive to such a development might grow out of more liberal margin requirements, relaxation of prohibition of loans to brokers by nonbank interests, and removal of the interdiction on banks to pay interest on demand deposits. These are possibilities, not probabilities.

[3]*Federal Reserve Bulletin* (March 1951), p. 303; (March 1969), p. A 34.

OTHER MARKET COMPONENTS

A notable feature of the money market is the absence of a sharp peripheral boundary line. Any such line purporting to separate near-money assets from other marketable obligations would be highly artificial. Instead, the degree of liquidity recedes by small gradations from money at the center to such assets at the other end of the scale as conventional real-estate mortgages. It is therefore desirable, in the interest of completeness, to give brief consideration to three components on the edges of the market, viz., call loans to dealers in U.S. securities; the market in short-term state and local securities; and the market in short-term corporate obligations.

call loans to dealers in u.s. securities

Money-market banks look upon call loans to U.S. security dealers as part of their liquidity reserve. Because the large dealers have deposit accounts at several of the major banks, these loans are usually to customers. This means that a bank feels some responsibility to provide its share of credit to dealers if they have no alternative sources. But, in fact, each dealer ordinarily has alternative sources, including loans from other large banks inside and outside New York City, repurchase agreements with corporations and banks, and repurchase agreements with the Federal Reserve Bank of New York. As a consequence, with understanding between the banks and dealers, there is considerable objectivity in the relationship. Rate changes are used positively to ration credit. Instead of calling dealer loans, the banks raise rates enough to bring about voluntary reductions in amount. When excess reserves accumulate, they lower rates to encourage borrowing.

The rate on dealers' call loans is a sensitive indicator of demand-supply conditions in the market. The principal money-market banks post two rates each morning after estimating reserve positions—the *renewal* rate and the *new* rate. A quotation of $7\frac{1}{4}$-$7\frac{3}{8}$ means that outstanding loans will be renewed at $7\frac{1}{4}$ percent, and that new loans will be made at $7\frac{3}{8}$ percent. Rates frequently change during the course of the day in reflection of fund flows that affect bank reserves.

Rates on dealers' call loans by New York City banks are usually $\frac{1}{8}$ to $\frac{1}{2}$ percentage point higher than the cost of funds borrowed under repurchase agreements from corporations, out-of-town banks, the Federal Reserve Bank of New York, and others. This means that dealers borrow residually from Wall Street banks after exhausting alternative sources. Dealer loans of New York City banks tend to be highest (1) when dealer inventories are high because of large Treasury offerings or when there is a consensus that declining yields are in prospect, and (2) when alternative sources of dealer credit diminish. These circumstances lead to wide variations in amount of dealer loans of New York City banks—sometimes over $1,000 million, sometimes under $100 million. Ordinarily, they represent the larger half of such loans by banks in all leading U.S. cities, but this proportion varies between nominal and three-fourths.

Money-market banks also make call loans to dealers in state and local securities, corporate obligations, bankers' acceptances, commercial paper, and CDs. These loans are also on a customer basis, with rates often a shade higher than those on loans secured by Treasury obligations.

short-term state and local securities

While precise information is fragmentary on the volume of trading in short-term state and local securities, there is ample evidence that this market is a substantial one. Some conception of its ownership distribution is given by Table 9-1. There were $132.2 billion of state and local securities outstanding at the

TABLE 9-1 / OWNERSHIP DISTRIBUTION OF STATE AND LOCAL BONDS, MIDYEAR 1967 (billions of dollars)

Type of Investor	Amount	Percentage Distribution
Individuals[a]	39.8	35.2
Commercial banks	45.6	40.3
Insurance companies	15.3	13.5
State and local governments[b]	4.2	3.7
Other corporations	4.8	4.2
Mutual savings banks	0.3	0.3
U.S. government agencies and trust funds	1.0	0.9
Miscellaneous investors[c]	2.1	1.9
Total	113.3	100.0

[a]Includes partnerships and personal trust funds.
[b]Sinking, trust, and investment funds.
[c]Includes savings and loan associations, corporate pension trust funds, dealers and brokers, etc.
Source: U.S. Treasury, as reported in Moody's Investors Service, *Municipal and Government Manual*, 1969, p. a 15.

end of 1969, of which commercial banks owned about 40 percent, individuals 35 percent, and insurance companies 14 percent.[4] From this, one may safely reach the preliminary conclusion that a very considerable volume of trading

[4]Board of Governors of the Federal Reserve System, *Financial Assets and Liabilities* (Washington, D.C., December 1969).

takes place. Further evidence on amount of short-term state and local securities may be deduced from a compilation of the U.S. Bureau of Census on maturity distribution. The Bureau reports that as of midyear 1962, the proportion of state and local securities maturing in 1 year was 5.0 percent; in 3 years, was 14.5 percent; and in 5 years, was 23.6 percent.[5] Because these proportions are relatively stable, they may be applied with reasonable accuracy to the aggregate of such securities at the end of 1969, with the following results: maturing in under one year, $6.6 billion; in under 3 years, $19.2 billion; and in under 5 years, $31.2 billion.

Less information is available on activity in the secondary market, but there are a few relevant facts. To begin with, the Blue List of Current Municipal Bond Offerings[6] contains between 600 and 800 names of dealers who maintained positions in state and local issues during the period 1960 to 1970. The firms that underwrite new issues typically maintain a continuing secondary market interest. This constitutes a nationwide market facility whose considerable use is confirmed by the decisions of these firms to pay for expensive advertising space. A more specific estimate of volume of sales may be derived from Professor Irwin Friend's comprehensive study of activity in over-the-counter markets. He found that resales of state and local securities in a quarterly test period in 1949 were at the annual rate of $4,224 million.[7] This represented 20.6 percent of total outstandings of $20,538 million at midyear 1949.[8] Applying this percentage to aggregate outstandings of $136 billion at midyear 1970 gives an estimated resales volume of $28 billion.

In addition to volume, the character of the secondary market is of interest. Professors Friend, Hoffman, and Winn in the Wharton School study of over-the-counter markets found that 40.4 percent of the *number* of transactions in state and local securities in 1949 were among dealers.[9] This reflects the fact that with over 35,000 separate issues outstanding, dealers can meet a large segment of customer demands only by acquiring securities from other dealers who hold positions in them. The nondealer proportions of transactions were as follows: commercial banks, 27.3 percent; individuals, 20.9 percent; other financial institutions, 8.9 percent; and others, 2.5 percent.[10] Commercial banks keep the bulk of their non-U.S. security investments in state and local issues which provide the highest after-tax yields. In fact, these holdings of commercial banks at the end of 1969 amounted to $59.2 billion.[11] Banks engage in a

[5]Moody's Investors Service, *Municipal and Government Manual,* 1969, p. a 17; interpolations of semiannual values from the given data were made by the author.

[6]Blue List Publishing Company, 130 Cedar St., New York, N.Y. 10006; daily.

[7]Irwin Friend, *Activity on Over-the-Counter Markets* (Philadelphia: University of Pennsylvania Press, 1951), p. 17.

[8]U.S. Treasury, as reported in Moody's Investors Service, *Municipal and Government Manual,* op cit., p. a 16.

[9]Irwin Friend et al., *The Over-the-Counter Securities Markets* (New York: McGraw-Hill, 1958), p. 183.

[10]Ibid.

[11]*Federal Reserve Bulletin* (September 1970), p. A 24.

considerable amount of tax-swapping operations. They also shift holdings for investment purposes, and to an increasing extent for adjustment of reserve positions. Individuals, insurance companies, and other investors engage in a significant amount of purchases and sales, mainly for investment and liquidity reasons.

Some indication of types of securities traded in the secondary market is provided by the Blue List which regularly publishes all bond offerings. As would be expected, large issues of states and cities appear most frequently. In general, obligations of smaller cities and political units are inactive and tend to have limited local markets. A considerable volume of trading also takes place in revenue bonds of turnpikes and bridges, if one may judge by frequency of listings. Some of these issues have speculative appeal in view of uncertainties concerning coverage of operating expenses, interest, and sinking-fund requirements. Another type of issue that appears often, especially in relation to amount outstanding, is Public Housing Administration obligations. In addition to the tax-exemption feature, these issues are also guaranteeed by the federal government.

short-term corporate obligations

There is even less information available on the secondary market in corporate obligations than on the market in state and local issues. Nevertheless, it is possible to see the broad outlines by piecing together certain disconnected, though relevant, facts. First, the total amount of corporate and foreign bonds outstanding is reported in the Fed "flow of funds" accounts. At the end of 1969, this aggregate was $183.3 billion, as compared with $132.2 billion of state and local obligations.[12] Second, a rough estimate of the amount of such securities in the short-term area may be made from data provided in Professor Hickman's study of corporate bonds. This study gives a maturity distribution of outstanding issues in 1944, as follows: 1 year or less, 0.7 percent; 1-3 years, 2 percent; and 3-5 years, 3.8 percent.[13] Applying these percentages to total outstandings at the end of 1969 ($183.3 billion), we have: 1 year or less, $1.3 billion; under 3 years, $4.9 billion; and under 5 years, $11.9 billion. Whether the 1944 maturity distribution is reasonably representative of maturities in 1969 is unknown. However, in view of the continuity and long-period stability of corporate bond maturity distributions, the results provide a useful approximation. Attention is called to the marked difference in the maturity distributions of corporate bonds and state and local obligations. Despite the larger aggregate of corporate bonds, the amount of short-term securities was much smaller than that of state and local issues—$\frac{1}{6}$ as much under 1 year; $\frac{1}{5}$ as much under 3 years; and less than $\frac{1}{3}$ as much under 5 years.[14]

[12]Board of Governors of the Federal Reserve System, *Financial Assets and Liabilities*, op. cit.

[13]W. Braddock Hickman, *Statistical Measures of Corporate Bond Financing Since 1900* (Princeton: Princeton University Press, 1960), p. 60.

[14]See p. 156 for amounts of state and local obligations.

Third, an estimate of volume of sales of corporate bonds may be made from Professor Friend's study by the same method used for state and local issues. He found that resales of corporate bonds in a quarterly test period in 1949 were at the annual rate of $3,796 million.[15] This amounted to 10 percent of total outstandings of $38.3 billion at the end of 1949.[16] If this percentage is applied to total outstandings of $101.1 billion at the end of 1962, we have an estimated secondary-market volume of $10.1 billion, which compares with resales of $16.5 billion in the state and local securities market. It will be noted that the rate of turnover of outstanding corporate bonds is about one-half that of state and local obligations—10 percent compared with 20.6 percent.

Fourth, trading in corporate bonds takes place predominantly in over-the-counter markets, although a significant volume occurs on organized security exchanges. Professor Friend found that during the quarter-year test period in 1949 the proportion was: over-the-counter sales, 82.4 percent; exchange sales, 17.6 percent.[17] At that time, there were approximately 3,000 dealer-brokers that formed the nucleus of the nationwide over-the-counter market. In the three-month period, they executed 180,000 transactions in 1,600 separate issues of corporate bonds.[18]

Finally, it is of interest to note the types of investors and traders that engage in the secondary market for corporate bonds. Professor Friend found that during the quarter-year test period of 1949, the distribution of resale transactions was as follows: broker-dealers, 32 percent; commercial banks, 27 percent; individuals, 26 percent; and nonbank institutions, 15 percent.[19] As with state and local securities, dealers can meet customer demands only by purchasing from other dealers who hold particular issues. This largely accounts for the high proportion of interdealer transactions. It is likely that the 1969 distribution of resale transactions differs appreciably from that of 1949 in view of shifts in ownership. In particular, the proportion of total corporate bonds owned by commercial banks has declined sharply since 1949, and the proportion of corporate bonds owned by nonbank institutions, notably life insurance companies and pension funds, has materially risen.

SUMMARY OF MONEY-MARKET COMPONENTS: SIZE AND RATE STRUCTURE

It remains to summarize the size and rate structure of the various components of the money market. This is done as of the end of 1969 in Table 9-2, which brings out the following significant facts.

[15]Friend, op. cit., p. 17.
[16]*Federal Reserve Bulletin* (August 1959), p. 1056.
[17]Friend, op. cit., p. 17.
[18]Friend et al., op. cit., pp. 56-57.
[19]Ibid., p. 84.

TABLE 9-2 / COMPONENTS AND RATE STRUCTURE OF THE MONEY MARKET AT END OF 1969

	Amount Outstanding (billions of dollars)	Rates (percent)
U.S. government securities		
Under 1 year	118.1	
Bills, 3-month		7.81
Bills, 6-month		7.89
Bills, 9-12 month		7.64
1-5-year	73.3	
Notes and bonds, 3-5-year		7.98
Total under 5 years	191.4	
Bankers' acceptances	5.5	
3-month		8.58
Commercial paper, dealer-placed	11.8	
4-6-month		8.84
Finance-co. paper, directly-placed	19.8	
3-6-month		7.93
Bankers' time certificates (original issues)	10.9	
3-6-month		9.00
6-9-month		9.125
9-12-month		9.125
12 months and over		9.25
Federal agency securities		
Under 1 year	19.9	
3-month (FICB)		8.55
6-month (COOP)		8.66
9-month (FICB)		8.60
1-3-year	8.5	
1-year (FLB)		8.60
3-5-year	1.3	
3-year (FNMA)		8.40
Total under 5 years	29.7	
State and local securities—Aaa[a]		
Under 1 year	6.6	5.55 (11.56)[a]
1-3-year	12.6	5.70 (11.87)[a]
3-5-year	12.0	5.90 (12.30)[a]
Total under 5 years	31.2	
Corporate obligations—Aaa[b]		
Under 1 year	1.3	
1-3-year	3.6	9.00[a]
3-5-year	7.0	8.10[a]
Total under 5 years	11.9	
Federal (Reserve) funds		8.97
Call loans, leading banks to U.S. security dealers	0.3	8.50
Federal Reserve Banks discount rate		6.00
Prime-loan rate of commercial banks		8.50
Total amount	316.3	

[a]Rates are on Moody's Aaa issues; parenthesis indicates after-tax equivalent yields for corporations.
[b]Amounts estimated as of end of 1969.

1/Open-market obligations with maturities under five years totaled $316 billion at the end of 1969.

2/Three-fifths of these obligations consisted of marketable U.S. securities. The remaining two-fifths was distributed among six other open markets, the largest of which were (a) state and local securities, (b) federal agency securities, and (c) commercial and finance-company paper.

3/With allowance for explainable differentials, yields of all obligations of comparable maturity were held closely in line by active competition among borrowers and among lenders.

4/The most basic rates were those on short-term U.S. securities, the Federal Reserve Bank discount rate, and the Fed funds rate–the cost of borrowing additional reserve money.

5/The most sensitive rates were the Federal funds rate which reflected hour-to-hour changes in demand and supply of loanable funds, Treasury bill rates, and the rate on call loans to U.S. security dealers.

6/Yields of comparable maturities were lowest in U.S. securities and highest in corporate securities. Yields of obligations in other market-subdivisions found their places somewhere within this range.

7/Yields on tax-exempt state and local securities were highest of all when adjusted for the corporate income-tax rate of 52 percent. This can be accounted for by the extremely illiquid position of commercial banks which normally hold one-third or more of outstanding state and local securities, combined with large offerings of such issues. At this point, when interest rates were at the highest level since the Civil War, the banks were selling, rather than buying, securities.

REFERENCES

on brokers' loans

Beckhart, Benjamin H., *The New York Money Market* (New York: Columbia University Press, 1932), Vol. III, pp. 1-211.

Cooke, Gilbert W., *The Stock Markets* (Rev. ed.; Cambridge, Mass.: Schenkman, 1969), chap. 20.

Griffis, Bartow, *The New York Call Money Market* (New York: Ronald, 1925).

Haney, L. H., L. S. Logan, and H. S. Graves, *Brokers' Loans* (New York: Harper & Row, 1932).

Madden, John T., and Marcus Nadler, *The International Money Markets* (Englewood Cliffs, N.J.: Prentice-Hall, 1935), pp. 178-197.

Leffler, George L., *The Stock Market* (2d ed.; New York: Ronald, 1957), chap. 17.

New York Stock Exchange, *Fact Book* (annual).

Woodworth, G. Walter, *The Monetary and Banking System* (New York: McGraw-Hill, 1950), chap. XXXII.

on the state and local securities market

Friend, Irwin, *Activity on Over-the-Counter Markets* (Philadelphia: University of Pennsylvania Press, 1951).

Friend, Irwin, G. Wright Hoffman, and Willis J. Winn, *The Over-the-Counter Securities Markets* (New York: McGraw-Hill, 1958).

Robinson, Roland I., *Postwar Market for State and Local Government Securities* (Princeton: Princeton University Press, 1960). (A study by the National Bureau of Economic Research.)

on the corporate bond market

Hickman, W. Braddock, *Statistical Measures of Corporate Bond Financing Since 1900* (Princeton: Princeton University Press, 1960). (A study of the National Bureau of Economic Research.)

10

the eurodollar market

The Eurodollar market is a prime illustration of the great ingenuity of bankers in developing new institutions in response to changing conditions. In a decade, this market rose like a meteor from about $1 billion in 1959 to $37.5 billion in 1969. Other recent illustrations of banker ingenuity and adaptability are the CD market, the Federal funds market, and utilization of the commercial-paper market as sources of liquidity. In view of its international character and its awesome complexity, the Eurodollar market has been shrouded in mystery to the layman, and while better understood by bankers and monetary economists, it gives rise to many important controversial issues which still remain unresolved—some pertaining to bank-liquidity management and others to broad economic and monetary policies. It is the purpose of this chapter to throw additional light on the topic by presenting the best current thought in the rather extensive literature on the subject.

BASIC FACTS ABOUT THE MARKET

Eurodollars are ordinary dollars deposited in foreign commercial banks. Anyone owning a sizable demand deposit in a U.S. bank, whether resident or nonresident, can create Eurodollars by transferring his deposit to a Eurobank. After completion of the transaction, the depositor holds an interest-bearing claim on the Eurobank; in turn, the Eurobank holds the transferred demand deposit in the U.S. bank and is liable for the new Eurodollar deposit. While anyone can make such a deposit, the market is a wholesale, institutional one in typical units of $1 million. However, sizes of transactions vary widely to serve the convenience of customers—up to $10 million and more, and as small as $100,000. The standard maturities are at call, overnight, 7 days, 90 days, and 180 days, although it is possible to arrange any maturity up to 2 years, and even longer, to meet specific customer needs. Interest rates offered by Eurobanks are usually higher than in most national money markets and constitute the principal inducement to investors. Rates are typically lowest on short-term money and rise as maturities lengthen. But in periods of intense credit demand, such as 1969, short-term rates may rise above long-term rates in conformance with the downward-sloping yield curve in national money markets.

Having received and pooled deposits from all over the world, Eurobanks are in position to loan these funds to worldwide borrowers, usually at rates below the cost of available funds elsewhere. The principal borrowers are commercial banks, multinational corporations engaged in trade and production, domestic firms, local governments, and sometimes central banks and national treasuries.

London is the predominant center of the market where Eurobanks quote rates both ways—on deposits and loans. As the leading world financial center, apart from New York City, it was natural that the new market would develop there. No other center offered comparable financial knowledge, experience, international contacts, and long-established banking institutions. But smaller Eurodollar markets exist in other countries. Switzerland is second in importance, with markets in Basle, Geneva, and Zurich; Paris probably ranks third. Other smaller markets are found in Europe, the Middle East, and Canada, with centers in Brussels, Amsterdam, Frankfurt, Vienna, Rome, Milan, Beirut, Cairo, Tel Aviv, Montreal, Toronto, and Nassau. While few Eurodollar deposits are received in Tokyo, Japan is a large borrower in London.

The premier position in the London market is occupied by branches of large U.S. banks, which account for between one-half and two-thirds of Eurodeposits in the City. The remaining one-third to one-half is held by affiliates of the great London joint stock banks, merchant bankers, British overseas banks, and London branches of large banks on the Continent and elsewhere. There is no central meeting place for this market such as the New York Stock Exchange. Instead, it is organized through a worldwide network of communication by long-distance telephone and telex. Transactions take place directly between banks and customers, and also by intermediation of Eurodollar brokers who operate in all important centers.

While we are concerned here only with the Eurodollar market, attention should be called to the fact that this market is a member of a larger family—the Eurocurrency market. There are markets in Eurosterling, Euromarks, Eurofrancs (Swiss), and Eurofrancs (French). Paris is the leading center for Eurosterling; London for Euromarks and Eurofrancs (French); and both London and Paris for Eurofrancs (Swiss). These markets are all dwarfed, however, by the Eurodollar market which accounts for about 80 percent of aggregate Eurocurrency deposits.[1]

The Eurodollar market is characterized by freedom from regulations that hamper most national money markets, its international scope, a high degree of competition which narrows the margin between deposit rates and loan rates,

[1]In preparing this section I have drawn heavily on an interview with Fred H. Klopstock, Manager, International Research Department, Federal Reserve Bank of New York; also, on Paul Einzig, *The Euro-Dollar System* (3d ed.; London: Macmillan, 1967).

and by depth, which makes the schedules of supply and demand highly sensitive to rate changes. Lenders and borrowers are linked together from all over the world, including Russia and other Communist nations. The rate structure which emerges is influenced by competitive rates in the various national markets, but it has a measure of independence arising from worldwide inflows and outflows of liquid funds. These flows tend to make credit more readily available, at loan rates below alternative sources, while at the same time offering investors higher yields than can be obtained in most national markets. As a consequence, the new market stimulates world trade and production, promotes more efficient utilization of world resources, and thereby contributes to higher standards of living.

EVOLUTION OF THE MARKET

There are four conditions essential to the existence and development of the Eurodollar market. First, there must be a leading national monetary system that enjoys a high degree of international prestige and confidence. After World II, the dollar definitely replaced the pound sterling as the predominant international currency. The United States held over one-half the world's monetary gold stock, and it was the only important nation that provided international convertibility of its money into gold at a fixed ratio. Thus, for all practical purposes, the dollar met this first requirement.

Second, there must be significant interest-rate differentials in the money markets of leading nations. This condition was also present. In 1958-1959, when the market began its rapid development, the Eurobanks in London were paying up to 4 percent on time deposits compared with the maximum of $2\frac{1}{2}$ percent prescribed by Regulation Q in the United States. In addition, U.S. banks were prohibited by law from paying interest on deposits with maturity of less than 30 days. Likewise, Eurobanks offered dollar loans at rates in the vicinity of $4\frac{1}{2}$ percent, whereas comparable loan rates in the United States were from $\frac{1}{2}$ to 1 percentage point higher.

Third, there must be reasonable freedom from foreign-exchange controls in leading nations. This condition was also approaching fulfillment in 1958. The rigid structure of exchange controls which developed during and after World War II in the United Kingdom, France, Germany, Italy, and other important nations had gradually been modified until relatively free dollar convertibility was emerging. Without freedom of movement of liquid funds among nations, an international market in Eurodollars would be stifled.

A last essential condition to development of the market is freedom from regulation of interest rates payable by Eurobanks on dollar deposits, and of rates charged on Eurodollar loans. There can be no Regulation Q to set interest-rate ceilings as in the United States. This condition was also realized. Eurodollar rates are determined in a highly competitive setting with worldwide sources of supply and demand. As a consequence, unique features of the market are its responsiveness to change, breadth, depth, and interest-rate elasticity. Indeed, the progressive development of these features has become an additional cause of its phenomenal growth: The market can absorb much larger amounts on short notice than existing domestic money markets.

An additional comment is required on the deficit in the U.S. balance of payments. Many analysts have insisted that sizable deficits are an essential condition of the Eurodollar market. This is not the case. As long as commercial banks, central banks, corporations, and others wish to hold Eurodollar deposits for liquidity and investment purposes, the market can exist and develop regardless of whether the balance shows deficits or surpluses. However, it is true that the long series of payments deficits since World War II strongly contributed to the growth and size of the market. The deficits added to the pool of foreign short-term dollar claims, and made possible the gradual lifting of foreign-exchange controls, one of the basic conditions listed above.

The origins of the market can be traced to the early 1920s, when European banks, notably in Berlin and Vienna, accepted dollar deposits on an extensive scale during the hyperinflation following World War I. But these banks typically converted their dollar claims to domestic currency, and they did not make dollar-denominated loans. Also, in the 1950s, Russia and other Communist countries deposited their dollar claims in London and Paris rather than in the United States—motivated no doubt by the fear that balances in U.S. banks might be blocked in case of a political crisis. But as already indicated, it was not until about 1958 that foreign-exchange controls were sufficiently liberalized to permit rapid development of the Eurodollar market. The other basic conditions were already present—the leading international status of the dollar, rate differentials in national money markets, and freedom from regulation of Eurodollar rates.

Impetus to growth of the market was also given by a number of banking regulations in Britain and the United States. In 1957, the British government restricted the use of sterling in financing nonsterling trade as a consequence of continuing balance-of-payments deficits and the loss of monetary reserves. Eurodollar financing largely filled the vacuum. In the United States, a major market stimulus has been the fixing of maximum rates payable on time deposits at below-free-market levels (Regulation Q), and the prohibition to pay interest on deposits with maturities of less than 30 days. With Eurodollar rates frequently 2 or more percentage points higher in London than time-deposit rates in New York, business corporations, nonbanking financial institutions, and commercial banks have had a strong incentive to seek the higher return. A further stimulus to the market occurred in September 1964, with passage of the Interest Equalization Tax Act. As the title indicates, it was designed to equalize the cost of raising capital in the United States with that in other important foreign financial centers by a tax applied to securities purchased from foreigners by U.S. residents.[2] The basic purpose was to improve the U.S. balance-of-

[2]See *Annual Report of the Secretary of the Treasury* (Washington, D.C., 1963), pp. 335-345, for Secretary Douglas Dillon's explanatory statement.

payments position temporarily by reducing the capital outflow and the payments deficit (estimated then at $1.5 billion annually by the U.S. Treasury). The influence of this tax was to shift foreign borrowing from the United States to the Eurodollar market. Still a further impetus to the market was the Voluntary Foreign Credit Restraint Program instituted by President Johnson in early 1965. The Federal Reserve Board issued guidelines to commercial banks and other financial institutions restricting the increase of their foreign loans and investments.[3] The purpose was similar to that of the interest equalization tax: to reduce the payments deficit. The influence on the market was also similar: to shift foreign loan demands from the United States to Eurodollar loans.

STRUCTURE OF THE MARKET

The Eurodollar market has experienced a spectacular growth—from less than $1 billion in 1959 to $9 billion in 1964, and on to $37.5 billion at the end of 1969. This is shown in Table 10-1, which also gives some idea of the geographic distribution and the flows of funds through the market. It will be noted that in 1969, by far the largest source of funds—about three-fifths—was western Europe; another fifth came from the United States and Canada; and almost all the remainder from Latin America, the Middle East, and eastern Europe.

sources of funds

Institutionally, the principal sources of Eurodollar deposits are central banks; commercial banks, insurance companies, and other nonbank financial institutions; and large international business corporations. Central banks, including the Bank for International Settlements, are attracted by the relatively high rates of return, and also for monetary-policy reasons they release or withdraw dollar reserves from their commercial-banking systems which, in turn, deposit or withdraw Eurodollars. Moreover, large commercial banks from all over the world invest a part of their liquidity reserves in Eurodollar deposits with suitable maturities. Insurance companies and other financial institutions and large business corporations are attracted to the market as the best alternative for investment of liquid assets. These corporations may be parent firms or their subsidiaries in foreign countries.

An additional source of Eurodollars is the accumulation of interest on accounts, which has amounted to between $3 and $4 billion annually since 1968. Part of interest earned is, of course, withdrawn, but a substantial part is left to build up aggregate deposits.

[3]See *Annual Report of the Board of Governors of the Federal Reserve System* (Washington, D.C., 1965), pp. 22-26, for a description of this program.

TABLE 10-1 / NET SIZE AND GEOGRAPHIC DISTRIBUTION OF EURODOLLAR MARKET[a], (billions of dollars, end of year, 1964-1969)

Items	1964	1965	1966	1967	1968	1969
Sources						
United States	1.5	1.3	1.1	1.7	3.2	3.8
Canada			0.6	0.9	1.3	2.9
Total	1.5	1.3	1.7	2.6	4.5	6.7
Western Europe						
Inside area[b]			8.4	9.6	13.2	18.6
Nonbanks	1.8	2.2	2.8	4.0	5.2	9.4
Banks	2.6	4.4	5.6	5.6	8.0	9.2
Other western Europe	n.a.	n.a.	1.1	1.4	1.9	2.7
Total	4.4	6.6	9.5	11.0	15.1	21.3
Japan	—	—	—	0.1	0.1	0.4
Eastern Europe	0.3	0.3	0.4	0.4	0.6	1.0
Other	2.8	3.3	2.9	3.4	4.7	8.1
Total	3.1	3.6	3.3	3.9	5.4	9.5
Grand total (net size)	9.0	11.5	14.5	17.5	25.0	37.5
Uses						
United States	2.2	2.7	4.4	5.2	9.5	16.5
Canada			0.6	0.7	0.9	1.3
Total	2.2	2.7	5.0	5.9	10.4	17.8
Western Europe						
Inside area[b]			6.3	6.9	7.9	11.7
Nonbanks	2.3	3.3	3.7	4.1	4.7	5.6
Banks	2.7	3.0	2.6	2.8	3.2	6.1
Other western Europe	n.a.	n.a.	0.9	1.2	1.5	1.6
Total	5.0	6.3	7.2	8.1	9.4	13.3
Japan	0.4	0.5	0.6	1.0	1.7	1.5
Eastern Europe	0.5	0.5	0.7	0.8	0.9	1.0
Other	0.9	1.5	1.0	1.7	2.6	3.9
Total	1.8	2.5	2.3	3.5	5.2	6.4
Grand total (net size)	9.0	11.5	14.5	17.5	25.0	37.5
Net[c]						
United States	+0.7	+1.4	+3.3	+3.5	+6.3	+12.7
Canada			—	−0.2	−0.4	−1.6
Western Europe: inside area	+0.6	−0.3	−2.1	−2.7	−5.3	−6.9
Other western Europe	—	—	−0.2	−0.2	−0.4	−1.1
Japan	+0.4	+0.5	+0.6	+0.9	+1.6	+1.1
Eastern Europe	+0.2	+0.2	+0.3	+0.4	+0.3	—
Other	−1.9	−1.8	−1.9	−1.7	−2.1	−4.2

[a]Net of interbank balances.

[b]Area includes Belgium-Luxembourg, France, West Germany, Italy, the Netherlands, Sweden, Switzerland, and the United Kingdom.

[c]Minus sign indicates net supplier of funds; plus sign indicates net user of funds.

Source: Bank for International Settlements, Basle, Switzerland, *Fortieth Annual Report* (1968), p. 149; *Forty-First Annual Report* (1969), p. 158.

uses of funds

By far the largest borrowers of Eurodollars in recent years have been U.S. corporations, notably commercial banks. Such loans increased sixfold between 1965 and 1969—from $2.7 to $16.5 billion. Faced with intense loan demands and a highly restrictive monetary policy in 1966 and 1969, the banks turned to the Eurodollar market for reserve funds. In fact, the liabilities of large commercial banks to their foreign branches exceeded $15 billion in November 1969—90 percent of total Eurodollar borrowing in the United States. As discussed more fully in a later section, the legal-reserve position of our commercial banks as a whole is eased only a small fraction of the amount of Eurodollar borrowing. While the individual bank may temporarily gain reserves, this is largely at the expense of other banks in the system.

The second largest use of Eurodollars was in western Europe where such loans amounted to $13.3 billion at the end of 1969. The government of Belgium has on occasion borrowed sizable amounts, as have businesses in Italy and West Germany. However, nonbank loans, mainly to finance international trade and other working-capital needs, exceeded loans to banks in the four preceding years, 1965-1968. The remaining $6.4 billion of loans in 1969 was made to resident firms in Japan, eastern Europe, and many other countries. A significant type of loan, made indirectly by merchant banks or other intermediaries, was to British local authorities. These and many other Eurodollar loans are converted to sterling or another domestic money before payments are made. It is also of interest that central banks seldom borrow Eurodollars, with the exception of several institutions in the Communist bloc.

the flow of funds

Analysis of the flow of funds accents the close linkages of all important national money markets into a truly international market through which liquid capital moves to areas where it can be employed most efficiently. The net movements to and from selected areas and nations are shown in Table 10-1. The United States has been the largest net user of Eurodollars. Under the abnormally tight credit conditions of 1969, it absorbed 90 percent of the net flow, while the remaining 10 percent went to Japan. During the preceding four years, 1965-1968, the United States accounted for about three-fourths, Japan and eastern Europe, the remaining one-fourth. The predominant net supplier of funds since 1965 has been western Europe, with about three-fifths. Canada, Latin America, the Middle East, and other nations have provided the other two-fifths. In general, the most impressive aspect of the market has been the intermediation by the United Kingdom between continental Europe as a supplier of funds and the United States as a borrower.

It should be emphasized, however, that the foregoing pattern of net flows does not permanently characterize the Euordollar market. For example, in 1964, the United States and Canada absorbed less than two-fifths of the net flow, with Europe and Japan accounting for the rest. The net suppliers were all located in the Middle East, Latin America, and other countries. We may generalize that the net flows will go to the areas and nations that at the time exhibit the strongest demand for capital because of the dynamic nature of their economies. Obviously, these relationships can be expected to change over the long term, and to show considerable cyclical and other short-term variations. The associated net-flow pattern will change with them. Whatever the pattern, in the foreseeable future London is likely to remain the predominant focal point into which Eurodeposits flow and from which Eurodollars are loaned throughout the world.

the eurodollar rate structure

As stressed earlier, the primary condition for the existence and development of the Eurodollar market is a significant premium between the rates offered by Eurobanks on dollar deposits and the rates offered by domestic banks on time deposits in important money markets of the world, and also between yields of competitive short-term instruments in the various financial centers. Such a differential has existed since the early beginnings of the Eurodollar market in 1958. Figure 12 shows the relation between the Eurodollar rate and the comparable CD rate in the United States since 1967. The spread in the earlier years—about $\frac{1}{2}$ percentage point—was similar to that in 1967, with the exception of 1966, when the credit squeeze in the United States widened the premium to well over 1 percentage point. Again, during the credit crisis in 1969 the spread exceeded 2 percentage points, but narrowed to about 1 with the moderation of Federal Reserve policy in 1970.

Further light is thrown on the relation between the Eurodollar rate and yields in selected national money markets by Table 10-2. It will be observed that the Eurodollar rate exceeded rates in the several national money markets in 1969 by a wide margin, ranging from 1.5 percentage point in the United Kingdom to 8.5 in Italy on time deposits, and from 3.5 percentage points in Belgium to 6.25 in Switzerland on other market instruments. The differentials were not so wide in 1967 and 1968, but the Eurodollar rate was significantly higher than domestic rates with the single exception of the United Kingdom in 1968, and with two exceptions in 1967—the United Kingdom and Canada. These comparisons are made before any adjustment for the discount or premium in the forward-exchange rate between the dollar and the respective national moneys. The covered interest advantage of Eurodollar deposits is shown at the bottom of Table 10-2. For example, the covered advantage of a Eurodollar deposit over purchase of a Treasury bill in Netherlands guilders was 4.55 percent; that is,

11.25 – 6.30 – 0.40 = 4.55. To be more specific, when the Netherlands investor purchased spot (current) dollar exchange of, say, $1 million, for deposit in a Eurobank, he would at the same time sell $1 million payable three months hence in order to safeguard against adverse change in the dollar-exchange rate. Because the guilder was at a discount (–0.40 percent), this deduction from the unadjusted spread of 4.95 percent was necessary to arrive at the true net advantage. However, in countries where forward dollar exchange was at a premium in relation to the spot price in local money, the covered advantage would exceed the unadjusted differential. For example, the net advantage of a Eurodollar deposit in Belgium was 14.08 percent (11.25 – 7.75 + 10.58).

In the preceding discussion, we have dealt only with the 3-month Eurodollar rate. But, in fact, a rate structure by maturities exists for the convenience of investors–ranging from call to 1 year, and even beyond by negotiation. The rates offered usually rise as maturities lengthen. For example, the rates quoted for the week ended March 5, 1971 by Dominion Securities International, Ltd., were as follows: 1 month, $4\frac{3}{4}$-$4\frac{7}{8}$; 3 months, 5-$5\frac{1}{8}$; 6 months, $5\frac{5}{8}$-$5\frac{3}{4}$; 12 months, $6\frac{5}{16}$-$6\frac{7}{16}$. But the term structure varies with conditions, and in tight markets such as 1969, rates may decline as maturities lengthen; that is, the slope of the yield curve may be downward in conformance with national markets.

12 INTEREST RATES ON DOLLAR DEPOSITS IN LONDON AND NEW YORK, 1967-1970.
Source: Bank for International Settlements, *Fortieth Annual Report* (1968), p. 161

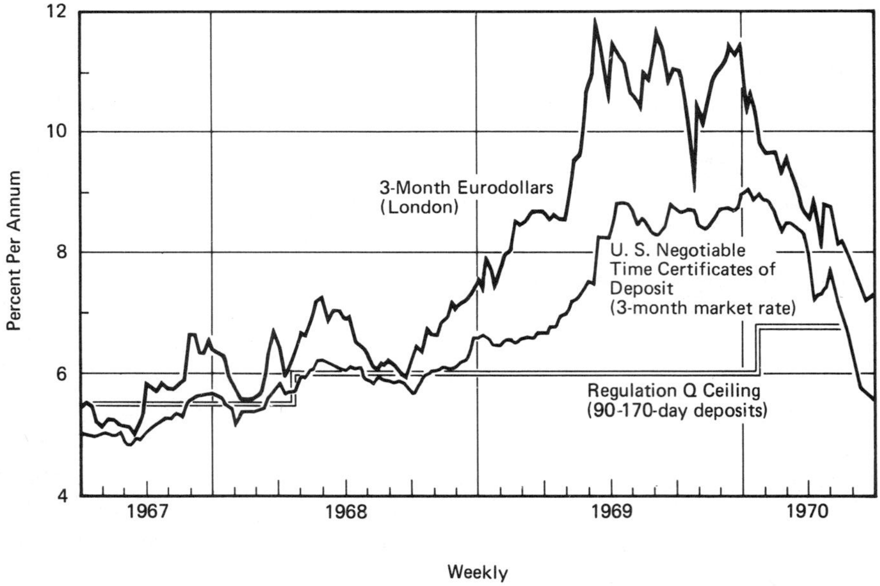

TABLE 10-2 / COMPARATIVE RATES OF INTEREST ON THREE-MONTH FUNDS IN SELECTED COUNTRIES, 1967-1969 (at or near end of period; in percent per annum)

Type of Instrument	December 1967	December 1968	August 1969
Eurodollar deposit	6.25	7.44	11.25
Large-size time deposit in domestic currency			
Belgium	4.75	7.25	7.38
France	2.75	3.00	3.00
Germany	4.00	4.38	6.63
Italy	2.75	2.75	2.75
Netherlands	5.75	6.25	9.00
Sweden	5.25	4.25	6.25
Switzerland	4.00	4.25	5.00
United Kingdom	7.88	7.63	9.75
Canada	6.25	6.50	7.50
Japan	4.00	4.00	4.00
Money-market instruments			
Belgium: Treasury bill	4.40	5.00	7.75
Germany: Interbank loan	3.96	4.46	6.50
Netherlands: Treasury bill	4.60	5.00	6.30
Switzerland: Interbank deposit	4.00	4.25	5.00
United Kingdom: Treasury bill	7.26	6.63	7.64
Canada: Treasury bill	5.82	6.06	7.42
Premium or discount (–) of 3-month dollar against			
Belgium franc	–2.00	0.20	10.58
German mark	–3.00	–4.47	–5.49
Netherlands guilder	–1.33	–0.83	–0.40
Swiss franc	–2.13	–1.89	–0.24
United Kingdom pound sterling	2.83	3.79	8.13
Canadian dollar	0.49	0.45	–0.57
Covered interest advantage of Eurodollar deposit over market instruments in			
Belgium: Treasury bill	–0.15	2.64	14.08
Germany: Interbank loan	–0.71	–0.27	–0.25
Netherlands: Treasury bill	0.32	1.61	4.55
Switzerland: Interbank deposit	0.12	1.30	6.01
United Kingdom: Treasury bill	1.82	4.60	11.74
Canada: Treasury bill	0.92	1.83	3.26

Source: *Federal Reserve Bulletin* (October 1969), p. 777.

The level of Eurodollar rates is governed by the international forces of supply and demand for liquid funds as focused in national money markets and through them in the Eurodollar market. On the supply side, the rate of creation of reserve money by central banks and the IMF is crucial, along with the rate of savings; on the demand side, the rates of growth of capital investment the world over and of international trade are vital. The lower limit of Eurodollar rates is determined by competitive rates offered on time deposits in the United States and in other national money markets, and by yields on other competitive money-market instruments such as Treasury bills. If Eurodollar rates were not higher than domestic rates, the principal motivation would be eliminated, and the amount of Eurodollars would decline sharply. Of course, allowance must be made for premiums or discounts of forward-exchange rates on the dollar in relation to the spot rate in terms of the various national moneys.

While published data focus on rates offered Eurodollar depositors, there is also a structure of Eurodollar loan rates. Keen competition results in narrow margins between deposit and loan rates because costs are low in such a large-scale, low-risk market. Prime-name banks can borrow at margins of between $\frac{1}{32}$ and $\frac{1}{4}$ percent; the best commercial and industrial firms, at a margin of about $\frac{1}{2}$ percent. Beyond that, the margin may rise along with risks and costs to as much as $2\frac{1}{2}$ percent. The ceiling on Eurodollar loan rates is set by competitive bank loan rates in the United States and in other financial centers. Unless Eurodollar loan rates are somewhat lower than rates on alternative domestic sources, borrowers will prefer domestic loans in terms of their own national money. This assumes, however, that there are practical borrowing alternatives. If credit is unavailable elsewhere because of domestic controls, the Eurodollar rate may rise above alternative loan rates. Assuming repeal of the Voluntary Credit Restraint Program in the United States, many foreign and domestic borrowers would prefer to borrow directly from U.S. banks when there is no rate advantage in Eurodollar loans. In comparing loan rates, allowance must, of course, be made for the premiums or discounts of the dollar in the forward-exchange market in terms of the relevant local money in transactions that require a hedge.[4]

LIQUIDITY MANAGEMENT OF LARGE U.S.BANKS AND THE EURODOLLAR MARKET

Some indication of the extent to which large U.S. money-market banks have utilized the Eurodollar market in the management of their liquidity positions is given by Table 10-3, which shows borrowings from their overseas branches. These Eurodollar branches, largely in London, but also in Paris, Nassau, Beirut, and a few other centers, account for well over half of total Eurodollar deposits. In turn, the head-office borrowing from such branches has, since 1967, absorbed over half of branch Eurodollar deposits. From a level of about \$1 billion in the first half of 1964, these borrowings rose steadily to \$4 billion at the end of 1966. The pace quickened markedly during 1966 when the banks were faced with intense loan demands and a highly restrictive monetary policy. In addition to

[4]See Jane S. Little, "The Euro-Dollar Market: Its Nature and Impact," Federal Reserve Bank of Boston, *New England Economic Review* (May-June 1969), pp. 3, 5-7.

TABLE 10-3 / GROSS LIABILITIES OF LARGE U.S. COMMERCIAL BANKS TO THEIR FOREIGN BRANCHES, 1964-1970 (last Wednesday of month; billions of dollars)

	1964	1965	1966	1967	1968	1969	1970
January	1.0	1.4	1.7	3.7	4.3	8.7	13.9
February	1.1	1.6	1.9	3.4	4.5	8.8	13.4
March	1.0	1.4	1.9	3.4	4.9	9.6	12.4
April	1.1	1.4	1.9	3.0	5.0	9.4	12.5
May	1.1	1.4	2.0	2.8	5.9	9.8	13.0
June	0.9	1.4	2.0	3.2	6.2	13.3	12.7
July	1.0	1.6	2.8	3.7	6.2	14.4	10.9
August	1.2	1.8	3.1	4.0	7.0	14.7	10.7
September	1.2	1.6	3.5	4.1	7.1	14.3	10.8
October	1.2	1.7	3.7	4.3	7.1	13.6	9.4
November	1.4	1.7	3.8	4.2	7.2	14.5	8.6
December	1.2	1.3	4.0	4.2	7.0	12.8	7.7

Source: *Federal Reserve Bulletin,* various issues.

traditional instruments of control, the Fed held the ceiling on rates payable on CDs well below yields on other competitive market instruments. As a consequence, the amount of outstanding CDs shrunk over $3 billion, with an associated increase of demand deposits subject to much higher reserve requirements. Under these pressures, the banks sought relief in the Eurodollar market. During the economic pause of 1967, when Federal Reserve policy was relaxed, the amount of borrowing declined significantly in the first half of the year not so much because of pressing need as of a desire to take a part of the increasing supply of Eurodollar deposits, and thereby maintain the flow for possible future requirements. Having developed contacts and lines of communication, the banks were reluctant to sever them, and thus were willing to borrow more Eurodollars at the expense of Fed funds, CDs, and other liquidity sources. Also, the large banks were becoming more familiar with procedures in the market and were more confident of its breadth and depth as a source of reserves.

After a further steady rise in 1968, borrowings reached a peak of about $15 billion in the last half of 1969. The intensity of loan demands combined with harsh monetary restraint produced a credit crisis far more severe than that of 1966. Priced out of the CD market by Regulation Q, the amount of CDs declined over $14 billion. Again the banks turned to the Eurodollar market in frantic efforts to borrow liquidity. During the last half of 1970, Eurodollar borrowing was sharply reduced as a consequence of lagging loan demands and a substantial easing of Federal Reserve policy.

The principal incentives for Eurodollar borrowing by U.S. banks have been the relatively low rates at which funds could be obtained and the ready availability of Eurodollars during periods of great credit stringency such as 1966 and 1969. The net cost of funds has usually been lower than that on Federal funds, CDs, and other domestic alternatives. Even when the gross rate on

Eurodollars is higher than that paid on CDs, the net rate may be lower because Eurodeposits are subject to neither legal-reserve requirements nor FDIC fees. The availability of Eurodollars at a price arises from the worldwide depth of the market. An increase in offering rates typically draws funds from one or more national money markets. Moreover, there is no legal upper limit such as Regulation Q on rates payable.

There are, however, some obstacles to borrowing Eurodollars, especially for day-to-day adjustments of reserve position. One is the time factor. By the time New York City banks open, it is noon in London; and by the time West Coast banks open, London banks are closed. Hence, the normal lag in receiving Reserve Bank credit for borrowed Eurodollars is two days. Other impediments are lack of information, the difficulty of estimating liquidity needs several days ahead, and the problem of Eurobanks' estimation of the amounts and maturities available in the future. As a consequence of these obstacles, large U.S. banks generally prefer Fed funds, CDs, Treasury bills, and at times borrowing from the Fed to Eurodollars as methods of day-to-day adjustment of liquidity positions.

The most important use of Eurodollar borrowing is provision of a hard core of reserve money to support a larger amount of loans than would otherwise be possible. Although borrowing is mainly overnight or very short term, the breadth and depth of the market permits a continuous rollover of such loans, with the result that the pool of borrowed reserves is maintained at the desired level. In addition, Eurodollars are borrowed by U.S. banks to provide their branches with working balances needed in international finance.

An interesting, although not basic, short-term feature of the market is the weekly bulge of overnight borrowing on Thursdays by U.S. money-market banks—amounting to between $100 and $400 million. This phenomenon arises from technical aspects of the U.S. clearing and collection system. Assume that Chase Manhattan borrows $25 million overnight from its London branch on Thursday, is paid by a check on Morgan Guaranty, and receives credit in its reserve account on Friday. Chase then repays the branch on Friday with a London or *bills-payable* (nondeposit) check.[5] Before July 1969, such checks were typically not included in deposits subject to reserve requirements, even though they were and still are deductible from gross demand deposits, so that an appreciable saving in required reserves was realized. The 1969 amendment of Regulation D partly closed this loophole by including London checks and bills payable in demand deposits and thereby subjecting them to reserve requirements. The upshot of the foregoing transaction is that Chase holds the reserve credit over the weekend (three days) because the bills-payable check is not charged to its reserve account until Monday.

Because all large banks play the game, partly in defense, the surge of demand for Eurodollars drives the rate up on value-Thursday borrowing to nearly three times the Fed funds rate in New York, after which it returns to

[5]Liabilities of the head office to a foreign branch are recorded as "due to overseas branches" rather than as "deposits."

normal on Friday and the other days of the following week. A similar situation develops before bank holidays. In most cases, reserve credit is enjoyed two days (instead of three over weekends), so that the Eurodollar rate in London rises on the bulge day to almost twice the Fed funds rate.

Closely associated with borrowing Eurodollars are two types of loan transaction by foreign branches and by other Eurobanks: (1) purchase of loans from head offices under repurchase agreement; and (2) direct loans by branches to affiliates of multinational firms and to other businesses that customarily borrow directly from U.S. banks. Sale of loans to branches or to other Eurobanks under repurchase agreement has usually arisen to avoid violation of the voluntary credit-restraint program without denying credit to valued international customers. On occasion, but less frequently, money-market banks have sold loans to their Eurodollar branches to release resources for the accommodation of domestic customers.

Direct dollar loans by foreign branches to customers that would ordinarily be financed by U.S. banks is a more important category than sale of loans under repurchase agreement. This method also enables U.S. banks to observe voluntary restraint guidelines and at the same time meet loan demands of valued international and domestic customers.[6]

ANALYTICAL ISSUES

A number of important analytical issues, some of which are highly controversial, have arisen in regard to the Eurodollar market. What is the effect on the reserve position of U.S. banks? How do chain redeposits with other Eurobanks influence the market? To what extent are Eurodollars created by a multiple expansion process on the basis of fractional reserves? How does the market influence world trade, production, and capital movements? And finally, what are the implications of these issues for Fed monetary policies?

effect on reserve position

There is widespread confusion among bankers and academicians concerning the effects of Eurodollar borrowing on the reserve position of U.S. banks. At one extreme, some bankers and analysts view the market as an almost inexhaustible pool from which the banks can draw reserve money at will to negate a Federal Reserve policy of monetary restraint. At the other pole, another group believes that Eurodollar borrowing by one bank is at the expense of others in the system, with no increase in aggregate bank reserves.

[6]For an excellent and more comprehensive discussion of these issues, see Fred H. Klopstock, "Euro-Dollars in the Liquidity and Reserve Management of United States Banks," Federal Reserve Bank of New York, *Monthly Review* (July 1968).

The truth appears to lie between these extremes, but much closer to the second viewpoint.

With the exception of nondeposit liabilities of U.S. banks to their foreign branches and other Eurobanks, there is a counterpart demand deposit on the books of American banks for the greater part of the *net* amount of Eurodollar deposits. The net amount is utilized to cancel the considerable volume of duplication present in gross deposits arising from the redeposit of Eurodollars among Eurobanks. As already indicated, Eurodollars are initially created when owners of demand deposits in U.S. banks transfer them by check to Eurobanks. The latters' assets in the form of demand-deposit claims against U.S. banks are increased, and their Eurodollar liabilities (predominantly time deposits) are correspondingly enlarged. Subsequent Eurodollar loan transactions merely shift the counterpart U.S. demand deposits to borrowers and to their payees. Hence, when Bankers Trust Company borrows $1 million of Eurodollars from its London branch, it is likely to receive the proceeds in the form of a check on another New York City bank, say, First National City. Thus, the gain of reserve money by Bankers Trust is offset by First National City's loss of reserves, and the banking system's aggregate reserves remain the same.

However, prior to October 1969, the net reserve position of the whole banking system was fractionally improved by the foregoing transaction as a consequence of the reduction in aggregate required reserves—even though total reserves were left undisturbed. More specifically, the new $1 million liability of Bankers Trust to its branch was recorded as a nondeposit liability, instead of a deposit subject to reserve requirements. Consequently, the legal reserve formerly required against the $1 million deposit in First National City ($175,000) was released. If this released reserve was not absorbed by Federal Reserve action, it would then serve as the basis for a multiple expansion of loans and investments, and thereby of deposits, in the banking system. Assuming a multiple of 5, additional bank-credit expansion of $875,000 could take place. Because most of the liabilities of head offices to foreign branches and to other Eurobanks are recorded as "due to overseas branches," this quirk of reserve requirements opened a sizable loophole. For example, liabilities of U.S. banks to foreign branches during the period mid-1968-mid-1970 ranged between $6 and $15 billion—not to mention their liabilities to other Eurobanks.

The Federal Reserve Board has twice taken action by amending Regulation D. In October 1969, a 10 percent reserve requirement was applied to Eurodollar borrowings in excess of a specified reserve-free base. Then, in January 1971, the required-reserve ratio was raised from 10 to 20 percent.[7] These steps were effective in preventing further releases from reserve requirements by additional Eurodollar borrowing, but they did not erase the reduction in reserve requirements associated with the existing volume of borrowing. Whether this reduction was, in fact, offset by a compensatory sale of U.S. securities by the

[7]*Federal Reserve Bulletin* (August 1969), p. 657; (January 1970), pp. 35-37; (December 1970), pp. 940-941.

Reserve Banks or by other restrictive action, it is impossible to divine. But a complete offset is unlikely. Consequently, it is probable that bank-credit expansion was significantly greater because of the dramatic growth of the Eurodollar market.

In addition to release from reserve requirements, the total reserve base of U.S. banks may be enlarged by induced expansion of Fed Bank credit. This may develop from the network of reciprocal currency arrangements which exist between the Federal Reserve and 15 other central banks. In September 1970, these swap arrangements totaled $11.2 billion and ranged individually between $130 and $2,000 million.[8] In effect, each of these banks has a call on dollars up to an agreed limit in return for an equal Federal Reserve call on pounds, francs, marks, lira, and other currencies. The basic purpose is to smooth the effects of temporary disequilibria in balances of payments on the international financial mechanism, including foreign-exchange rates. An example of the expansion of dollar reserves in this manner may be drawn from swap transactions with the Bank of England in 1969. The so-called Federal Reserve swap line ranged between $650 and $1,415 million, which meant that the Fed had purchased sterling (provided dollars) to these amounts. The effect of this purchase of sterling was to increase total member-bank reserves in the same manner as if the Reserve Banks had purchased U.S. securities. It is quite impossible to estimate whether, and to what extent, this represented a *net* increase in Reserve Bank credit—that is, to what extent the Fed took compensatory actions, mainly through open-market operations, to offset the purchases of sterling. But it is possible that overall monetary policy was somewhat modified by these international pressures, and that a significant addition was made to total member-bank reserves.

Thus, in conclusion, the only way the Eurodollar market can, at present, increase aggregate reserves of the U.S. banking system is through induced expansion of Reserve Bank credit. Such expansion may have occurred consciously or unconsciously in the overall environment created by the phenomenal growth of the market. Internationally, it may have taken place through swap arrangements with other central banks when dollars were loaned under pressure to various central banks. Domestically, it may have occurred as an outgrowth of the shift of reserve money to large money-market banks associated with their Eurodollar borrowing. Because large banks have access to this market, they gain reserves from smaller banks that cannot borrow there in defense. The Reserve Banks then may come to the rescue of the pressured smaller banks by releasing more reserve money through open-market operations, or otherwise.

In addition, prior to October 1969, when Eurodollar borrowing was free from reserve requirements, a significant amount of bank-credit expansion may have occurred on the basis of released reserve requirements—that is, from

[8]Federal Reserve Bank of New York, *Monthly Review* (September 1970), p. 199.

the shift of demand deposits to nondeposit liabilities, unaccompanied by full compensatory Federal Reserve actions. Also, it is likely that the presence of the Eurodollar market with relatively attractive yields contributed to more efficient utilization of the U.S. reserve base—that is, to a somewhat lower level of excess legal reserves. Thus, under the combined influence of larger total reserves and a reduction of reserve requirements, it is probable that a significant increase in total bank deposits was generated in the United States as an incident to development of the Eurodollar market.

interbank eurodeposits

The size of the Eurodollar market is sometimes considerably overstated as a result of using gross, rather than net, figures. For example, the dollar liabilities of reporting European banks to nonresidents were $46.1 billion at the end of 1969; liabilities to residents were unknown. On the same date, the estimated dollar liabilities on a net basis to both residents and nonresidents were estimated at $37.5 billion—$21.3 billion to residents and $16.2 billion to nonresidents.[9] Obviously, the amount of duplication is very large because the gross figure for both residents and nonresidents would be $106.7 billion on the basis of proportions in the net estimate—that is, (46.1 × 37.5) ÷ 16.2.

This duplication arises from the common practice of Eurobanks redepositing with other Eurobanks. Sometimes the chain includes three or more banks. Rate differentials are the motivating force, and the process can continue until the last institution cannot find another that offers a significantly higher rate. The practice moves funds to areas of most efficient utilization, allowing for risks, and reduces rate differentials. It should be emphasized that there is no corresponding duplication of Eurodollar loans. There is only one final-use loan made by the last Eurobank in the chain.

multiple expansion of eurodollars

Perhaps the most controversial theoretical issue pertaining to Eurodollars has to do with their origin and creation. How did the gross amount at the end of 1969 (over $100 billion) and the net amount ($37.5 billion) come into existence? The difference between the gross and net figures, which results from interbank redeposits, was explained in the preceding section; only the net amount concerns us here.

Expositions of the market during its first decade viewed the Eurobanking system as basically similar to our savings and loan and mutual savings bank systems which do not create demand deposits when lending, but only transfer existing demand deposits to borrowers. Eurobanks were regarded as

[9]Bank for International Settlements, *Fortieth Annual Report*, op. cit., pp. 156, 158.

pure intermediaries as opposed to money creators, like commercial banks which create deposits by expansion of their loans and investments. More specifically, instead of direct ownership of demand deposits in U.S. banks by foreign banks and corporations, one or more tiers of deposits in Eurobanks were interposed. The foreign corporation then had an interest-bearing claim on the Eurobank, and the Eurobank owned a demand deposit in New York, which it subsequently loaned to a company needing dollars.

But in the late 1960s the idea developed that the Eurobanks resembled commercial banks rather than savings banks, and that on the basis of fractional reserves the system had the capacity to create several Eurodollar deposits by expansion of loans and investments. That is, Eurobank A, having received a Eurodeposit of $100, is in position to loan $90 after retaining, say, $10, as a prudential reserve; Eurobank B receives the loan proceeds as a transferred deposit and can loan $81 after retaining $9 as reserve; Eurobank C receives loan proceeds of $81 and can loan $72.90 after retaining $8.10 as reserve; and so on, until the original $90 of excess reserve supports $900 of new loans and Eurodeposits. In fact, this example understates the expansion potential because (1) Eurobanks are not subject to legal-reserve requirements and a prudential cash reserve of well under 10 percent may be sufficient, and (2) there is no drain of reserves into currency circulation in this wholesale-type operation.

The leading exponent of this theory is Professor Milton Friedman who states: "The correct answer for both Euro-dollars and liabilities of United States banks is that their major source is a bookkeeper's pen."[10] He concludes that most of the $37.5 billion Eurodollars, just as the aggregate deposits (over $400 billion) of U.S. banks at the end of 1969, were created by loan and investment expansion. Most monetary analysts agree with the statement as applied to deposits of U.S. banks, but only partially agree in regard to the origin of Eurodollars. They disagree because they cannot wholly accept the analogy between the process of deposit creation in a commercial banking system and the creation of Eurodollars in the Eurobanking system. The basic reason is that the only important leaks of reserves in a domestic banking system are the currency drain from the banks and a possible loss of reserves to other countries; in the Eurodollar system there are many such leaks which stall the loan-expansion (and deposit-creation) process. Fred H. Klopstock, Manager of the International Research Department of the Federal Reserve Bank of New York, has convincingly refuted Professor Friedman's thesis in two recent articles.[11] A summary of his argument follows.

[10]Milton Friedman, "The Euro-Dollar Market: Some First Principles," *The Morgan Guaranty Survey* (October 1969), p. 4; also see Fritz Machlup, "Euro-Dollar Creation: A Mystery Story," Reprint No. 16, International Finance Section, Department of Economics, Princeton University, 1970.

[11]"The Euro-Dollar Market: Some Unresolved Issues," *Essays in International Finance,* No. 65, International Finance Section, Department of Economics, Princeton University (March 1968); and "Money Creation in the Euro-Dollar Market—A Note on Professor Friedman's Views," Federal Reserve Bank of New York, *Monthly Review* (January 1970), pp. 12-15.

1/Eurobanks as a group, unlike a commercial banking system, can expect only a small fraction of their loans and investments to return to them as deposits; this fact becomes clear from analysis of Eurobank assets.

2/A large and often dominant part of Eurobank loans consists of loans of foreign branches of U.S. banks to their head offices in New York and other large cities in the United States. These funds are rarely returned as Eurobank deposits because they are used by the banks and their borrowing customers in the United States.

3/In addition to the foregoing branch loans to head offices, a significant amount of Eurodollar loans is made by other Eurobanks to smaller U.S. banks which do not have foreign branches. These funds are also employed by U.S. banks and their customers.

4/Eurobanks also lend substantial amounts to foreign banks in Japan, Latin America, and elsewhere. These funds are largely used to finance their customers' payments to the United States and third countries. Often, the dollar-loan proceeds are sold in the foreign-exchange market for local or third currencies. Few, if any, of these proceeds are redeposited in Eurobanks.

5/A further sizable part of Eurodollar loans to corporations, banks, and other customers is converted immediately into sterling, marks, francs, and other moneys in the foreign-exchange market. These funds increase deposits in the respective countries and are rarely returned to Eurobanks.

6/Only a small fraction of Eurodeposits consists of overnight and call deposits similar to demand deposits in U.S. banks; the great bulk is composed of time deposits against which checks are not drawn. In fact, the typical Eurodollar loan is not credited to the customers' deposit account as in the United States; instead, the proceeds are immediately transferred to a bank of the customers' choosing in the United States or another country, and often converted to another currency at the same time.

7/The rather small fraction of Eurodollar loans that does return to Eurobanks as deposits consists of (a) loans to customers to finance purchases where the seller is a depositing customer of a Eurobank (rare in a worldwide market); (b) deposits of central banks that have come into possession of Eurodollar loan proceeds in excess of the amount they wish to hold as direct claims on the United States; and (c) miscellaneous redeposits which do not fall in categories (a) and (b). Mr. Klopstock estimates that in view of the massive leakages listed above, the Eurobank multiplier is very low, in the range of 0.5 to 0.9.

8/What then is the real source of primary Eurodollar deposits which constitute, according to this estimate, between 53 and 67 percent of the total? It lies in the decisions of holders of claims on dollars, both foreign and domestic, in the forms of deposits and securities to shift such claims to Eurodollar deposits–induced by the higher yields obtainable and by the superior facilities and liquidity provided by this international market for the dollar. Demand depositors in U.S. banks can readily make this transfer by check. Time depositors and owners of securities must, of course, first convert their holdings to demand deposits, after which the shift can be made with equal ease. While the shift is not dependent on deficits in the balance of payments, the long series of deficits since the 1950s built up foreign dollar claims and heavily contributed to decisions to make Eurodollar deposits. These deposits were made by commercial banks, central banks, nonbank financial institutions, business corporations, and others. This portion of Eurodeposits—roughly between one-half and two-thirds—may be likened to primary deposits in mutual savings banks and savings and loan associations. The remaining one-third to one-half was created by the loan and investment expansion of Eurobanks—the multiple expansion process described in an earlier section. However, the actual size of the multiplier is little more than an educated guess.

effect on economic development and world trade

Just as the development of a truly national money market in the United States has fostered economic growth and domestic trade, so the development of the Eurodollar market has promoted worldwide growth and trade. Liquid capital has been drawn in myriad streams from national money markets seeking the higher yields offered by Eurobanks. These banks, in turn, have loaned these pooled funds to credit-worthy borrowers in nations and areas that are in the greatest need for capital. Basically, this freer flow of funds means that savings and other resources have been put to more efficient use than would otherwise have been possible. Real world output has been stimulated, and the marked expansion of trade has distributed a larger amount and a greater variety of goods to consumers all over the globe. For example, real international trade, measured by imports, almost doubled between 1961 and 1969, rising from $124.3 to $231.3 billion in constant dollars.[12] This represented an annual rate of increase of over 9 percent, which exceeded the 6 percent growth rate of world production by one-half. The presence of the Eurodollar market contributed materially to these developments by providing machinery for the ready flow of funds and by financing trade and production at lower costs. In the process, the market served as an equalizer of interest rates, reducing the differentials in national money markets.

Finally, there is no doubt that the market has affected the character of the flows of trade and capital among nations, as well as increasing the aggregate amount. In other words, the balances of payments of the United States and other countries have been somewhat different because of the existence of the market. Space precludes analysis of the year-to-year effects on these balances, but there is no doubt that the pattern of annual surpluses and deficits of nations

[12] Bank for International Settlements, *Fortieth Annual Report,* op. cit., p. 79; *Thirty-fourth Annual Report* (1962), p. 79.

has been quite different from the pattern that would have evolved in the absence of the market. The existence of Eurodollar facilities has encouraged international inflows of Eurodeposits and outflows of loans and investments that otherwise would not have occurred. For example, on a liquidity basis, there was a shift from a $0.2 billion surplus in 1968 to a $7.1 billion deficit in the United States in 1969.[13] A large part of this change resulted from the circular flow of funds from the United States to the Eurodollar market and then back again as U.S. banks borrowed heavily from their branches. Another part was a consequence of American discontinuance of the practice of encouraging foreign official holders of dollars to shift from liquid to nonliquid claims. Both factors led to a misleading overstatement of the actual deterioration of the balance of payments. While it is certain that the market has significantly influenced these short-term changes in the balances of payments of all important nations, it is impossible to measure the extent of this influence or to trace all the complicated interrelationships of trade and capital movements. Over periods of three to five years, most of the short-term movements of funds induced by the market cancel out. Consequently, intermediate changes attributable to the Eurodollar market are likely to be insignificant, aside from the overall increase in the volume of trade and capital flows.

effects on monetary policies

Development of the Eurodollar market has magnified the problems of monetary management by central banks in various ways. In order to achieve their domestic and international objectives, they need to understand the complex interrelationships in the market, including its effects on domestic banking systems. In addition, adequate current analysis of developments requires comprehensive statistical information—much more, in fact, than is now available.

Most important, the central bank (Federal Reserve) should be fully aware of the influence of the market on the reserve position of domestic banks. As developed earlier, while aggregate bank reserves need not be significantly affected, they may be changed by the response of the central bank to the new environment created by the market. This response may be conscious, as in acceding to loan dollars to another central bank under a swap agreement; or it may be unconscious, as in lending to smaller member banks whose reserves have moved to New York City banks as an incident to borrowing Eurodollars. Moreover, even if total bank reserves are unaffected, legal-reserve requirements may be altered. The fact will be recalled that when Eurodollar borrowing by U.S. banks increased, required reserves were released. This was a result of the laws and regulations defining U.S. reserve requirements and the clearing and collection system. While these loopholes were partially closed in 1969, the bulk

[13]Bank for International Settlements, *Fortieth Annual Report,* op. cit., p. 83.

of nondeposit liabilities is still free from reserve requirements. Thus, it is clear that the central bank needs to be fully aware of Eurodollar operations in order to compensate through other instruments of control, or to make appropriate amendments to regulations. Otherwise, its intended program of monetary management will to a degree be negated.

The central bank should also have complete understanding of the effects of the enormous increase in the international mobility of liquid funds developed by the Eurodollar market. While the long-range character of balances of payments is not materially influenced by the market—aside from larger trade and investment movements—the short-term flows of funds are profoundly affected. The central bank must be alert to these movements in order to maintain the desired stance of domestic monetary policy as well as to meet its international responsibilities. Decisive action may be called for to moderate a strong outflow of funds induced by higher Eurodollar interest rates in relation to domestic rates, or to moderate an inflow under opposite conditions. An example of such action was *operation twist* in the early 1960s, when the Fed attempted to raise short-term rates in relation to long-term yields. The purpose was to reduce the outflow of liquid funds and at the same time to encourage investment and economic expansion. This technique was employed again in the spring of 1971 for the same purpose.

Other more drastic steps may be required by the central bank to reduce deficits or surpluses in the balance of payments under a system of fixed foreign-exchange rates. For example, the central banks in West Germany and Italy have at times reduced domestic liquidity by selling claims to dollars in the domestic market for marks and lira. Then by offering to purchase forward dollars simultaneously at above-market prices, they have encouraged their commercial banks to make Eurodollar deposits rather than domestic loans. At other times, these central banks have increased domestic liquidity by depositing dollars in the banks without requiring local currency in exchange.[14] Other central banks have employed a variety of direct controls, including administrative control or prohibition of depositing Eurodollars, of bank or corporate lending of dollars at home or abroad, and of conversion of Eurodollars into domestic currency. In the United States, the best illustration is the Voluntary Credit Restraint Program (discussed above) instituted in 1965. Most of these direct controls, established partly in response to the short-term effects of the Eurodollar market, represent obstacles to its development.

Another illustration of the influence of the market on a method of credit control may be drawn from the program of fixing maximum rates payable on time deposits by U.S. banks (Regulation Q). As already indicated, the high yields available in the Eurodollar market constituted one of the important alternatives to domestic time deposits and CDs. Consequently, when the Federal Reserve Board set the interest-rate ceilings well below market yields in 1966 and

[14]See Francesco Masera, "International Movements of Bank Funds and Monetary Policy in Italy," Banca Nazionale del Lavoro, *Quarterly Review* (December 1966).

1969, maturing CDs were not renewed, and their amounts declined some $3 billion in 1966 and some $13 billion in 1969. The resultant credit restriction fell most heavily on residential construction and state and local government projects. This experience led many monetary economists to oppose the entire idea of fixing maximum rates, and particularly the use of Regulation Q as a method of bank-credit control.

A final example of the need for central-bank alertness to the influence of the Eurodollar market relates to definition of the money supply. This issue has assumed far greater importance since the late 1960s, when the rate of change in the money supply became one of the leading targets for Federal Reserve policy. Prior to revision of the money-supply series in August 1969, the series was somewhat understated because of the regulation governing bank clearings and collections. In the computation of adjusted demand deposits, "cash items in process of collection" is one of the items deductible from gross demand deposits. The huge increase in volume of transactions of large banks with their branches after 1966 led to a sharp rise in these cash-collection items in the forms of bills payable checks and London checks. Yet such checks were classified as nondeposit liabilities and were not included in gross deposits. This meant that the money supply was understated by as much as $3.3 billion. The revised series increased the annual growth rate by 0.5 percentage point in 1968 and 1.6 percentage points for the first half of 1969.[15] While this is not a large discrepancy, it is enough to cause a significant difference in the Board's decision in regard to the rate of expansion of Reserve Bank credit.[16]

REFERENCES

Altman, Oscar L., Euro-Dollars," International Monetary Fund, *The Fund and Bank Review: Finance and Development*, Vol. IV, No. 1 (March 1967), pp. 9-16.

Bank of International Settlements, annual reports, Basle, Switzerland.

Block, Ernest, "An Emerging International Market," New York University, *The Bulletin*, No. 39 (April 1966), pp. 1-32.

Board of Governors of the Federal Reserve System, "Euro-Dollars: A Changing Market," *Federal Reserve Bulletin* (October 1969), pp. 765-784.

Chase Manhattan Bank, N.A., "Euro-Dollar Financing," 2d ed., New York (1968).

Einzig, Paul, *The Euro-Dollar System* (3d ed.; London: Macmillan, 1967).

Federal Reserve Bank of Chicago, "Eurodollars–An Important Source of Funds for American Banks," *Business Conditions* (June 1969), pp. 9-20.

Friedman, Milton, "The Euro-Dollar Market: Some First Principles," *The Morgan Guaranty Survey* (October 1969), pp. 4-14.

[15]See *Federal Reserve Bulletin* (October 1969), pp. 787-789, for an analysis of revision of the money-supply series; also Federal Reserve Bank of St. Louis, *Review* (January 1971). The revised series includes other minor adjustments, but the principal one was for Eurodollar float.

[16]In addition to the works cited under References, this chapter is based on interviews with leading authorities on the Eurodollar market, including T. J. Devine, Vice President, Manufacturers Hanover Trust Company; A. James Meigs, Vice President and Economist, First National City Bank; Fred H. Klopstock, Manager, International Reserach Department, Federal Reserve Bank of New York; and Wolfgang Schoellkopf, Vice President, The Chase Manhattan Bank. I am particularly indebted to Mr. Klopstock whose criticisms of the manuscript led to a number of improvements.

Freidrich, Klaus, "A Quantitative Framework for the Euro-Dollar System," *Princeton Studies in International Finance, No. 26*, International Finance Section, Department of Economics, Princeton University (1970).

Johnson, Norris O., "Euro-Dollars in the New International Money Market," First National City Bank (1965), pp. 1-21.

Klopstock, Fred H., "The Euro-Dollar Market: Some Unresolved Issues," *Essays in International Finance, No. 65*, International Finance Section, Department of Economics, Princeton University (March 1968).

Klopstock, Fred H., "Money Creation in the Euro-Dollar Market–A Note on Professor Friedman's Views," Federal Reserve Bank of New York, *Monthly Review* (January 1970), pp. 12-15.

Klopstock, Fred H., "The Wiring of the Euro-Dollar Market," *Euromoney* (August 1970), pp. 16-20.

Kvasnicka, Joseph G., "Euro-Dollars–An Important Source of Funds for American Banks," Federal Reserve Bank of Chicago, *Business Conditions* (June 1969), pp. 9-20.

Little, Jane S., "The Euro-Dollar Market: Its Nature and Impact," Federal Reserve Bank of Boston, *New England Economic Review* (May-June 1969), pp. 2-31.

Machlup, Fritz, "Euro-Dollar Creation: A Mystery Story," Reprint No. 16, International Finance Section, Department of Economics, Princeton University (1970).

Mayer, Helmut W., "Some Theoretical Problems Relating to the Euro-Dollar Market," *Essays in International Finance, No. 79*, International Finance Section, Department of Economics, Princeton University (February 1960).

Massaro, Vincent G., National Industrial Conference Board, *The Record* (October 1970), pp. 15-22.

Morgan Guaranty Trust Company, "The Financing of Business with Euro-Dollars," New York (1967), pp. 1-39.

Prochnow, Herbert V., ed., *The Eurodollar* (Skokie, Ill.: Rand McNally, 1970).

Scott, Ira O., Jr., "That Controversial Euro-Dollar Market," National Westminister Bank, *Quarterly Review* (August 1969), pp. 2-22.

Schaffner, P. P., "Euro-Bank Credit Expansion," *Euromoney* (July 1970).

Swoboda, Alexander K., "The Euro-Dollar Market: An Interpretation," *Essays in International Finance, No. 64*, International Finance Section, Department of Economics, Princeton University (February 1968).

11

the term structure of interest rates

The term structure of interest rates has rightfully received considerable attention in recent years from both financial economists and managers of investment portfolios. Prior to the 1930s, economists were chiefly concerned with forces determining the general level of rates, rather than with the changing relationship of yields and maturities. Similarly, few bank and investment officers had more than superficial knowledge of yield-maturity relationships, or had ever heard of a *yield curve.* In sharp contrast, a considerable body of literature on this topic has appeared during the past four decades, and practical men have found yield-curve analysis to be very useful in reaching decisions on investment policies.

It is the purpose of this chapter to explain the fundamentals pertaining to bond yields and prices, the use of time series in analyzing rate structure, the underlying theory of different types of yield curves, and the practical applications of such curves in the field of investment and finance.

BOND YIELDS AND BOND PRICES

There is need at the outset to review certain fundamentals with respect to bond yields and prices: definitions of terms; computation of yields and prices; relationships between yields and prices; relative movements of short-term and long-term interest rates; and relative movements of prices of obligations with different maturities.

definitions

A *bond* is a long-term promissory note which is subdivided into convenient denominations, usually $1,000 and multiples thereof. The issuer contracts to pay the owner the amount of the *face value* on a definite future date, and to pay interest at a specified rate and at regular intervals, usually semiannually. Most bonds are payable to *bearer,* are negotiable, and have interest coupons attached which must be clipped and presented for payment. Many bonds are also available in *registered* form to investors who prefer to hold obligations in their own name. Registration eliminates the danger of loss from theft; it also provides the convenience of interest payments by check and eliminates the nuisance of clipping and presenting coupons. A bond sells at a *premium* when the market price is above face value;[1] it sells at a *discount* when the market price is below face value.

The *coupon rate*[2] is designated on the face of the bond, is fixed at the original time of issue, and remains the same throughout the life of the bond. This is in contrast with the *market yield* which varies inversely with market price. That is, when a bond sells at a premium, the market yield is below the coupon rate; and conversely, when a bond sells at a discount, the market yield is above the coupon rate. Market yield, however, may refer either to *current yield* or to *effective yield.* Current yield is the simple relation between the annual interest payment and market price. For example, the current yield of a 4 percent bond maturing in 25 years and selling for 80 is 5 percent; that is, $\frac{\$\ 4}{\$80} \times 100 = 5$ percent. But while the concept of current yield is relevant in the case of stocks and with respect to bonds with no maturity dates (annuity bonds), it is not applicable to bonds with definite maturity dates. This means, in fact, that current yield has very little relevance to the bond market in this country because virtually all bonds have fixed maturities.[3]

The reason that current yield is not applicable to a fixed maturity obligation is that it fails to take into account the *accumulation of discount* over the life of a bond that sells below face value, or the *amortization of premium* in the case of a bond that sells above face value. In the foregoing example, the investor would realize not only the annual \$4 interest payment, but also an average accumulation of discount of \$.80 per annum; that is, $\frac{\$20}{\$25} = \$.80$. His average total return each year would therefore be \$4.80. His average investment would be about \$90; that is, $\frac{\$80 + \$100}{2}$, so that the *effective yield* to maturity would be about 5.33 percent. This method of computation of effective yield, however, is only an approximation and is too inexact for most practical purposes. Giving effect to the compound-interest aspects, the annual accumulation of discount is not a uniform amount but rises from year to year, and the

[1]Also called *par value.*
[2]Also called *nominal rate.*
[3]The outstanding illustration of annuity bonds is the government consols of Great Britain. This type of bond has been used by the British Treasury for over two centuries.

average investment is somewhat higher than stated. The exact effective yield as computed from a bond table is 5.478 percent.

calculation of bond prices and yields

Investors in bonds are frequently faced with two problems in regard to prices and yields. First, given the coupon rate, maturity, and effective yield, they wish to know the corresponding price. Second, given the coupon rate, maturity, and price, they wish to know the corresponding effective yield.

Mathematically, the price of a bond is the sum of (1) the present value of the principal due at maturity, and (2) the present value of the scheduled series of interest payments during the remaining life of the bond. The present value of the principal is determined by discounting the redemption value on a compound basis at the prevailing market yield for the period until maturity. It may be calculated from the formula, $V_p = \frac{A}{(1+i)^n}$, where V_p is the present value of the principal, A is the amount of the principal due at maturity, i is the market yield, and n is the number of years or interest periods to maturity.

The present value of the series of expected interest payments (V_a) is found by discounting each payment for the proper period and at the prevailing market yield, and then by adding the discounted values. The present value of the first payment is $\frac{A_1}{(1+i)}$; of the second payment, $\frac{A_2}{(1+i)^2}$; of the third payment, $\frac{A_3}{(1+i)^3}$; and so on. Hence,

$$V_a = \frac{A_1}{1+i} + \frac{A_2}{(1+i)^2} + \frac{A_3}{(1+i)^3} + \cdots + \frac{A_n}{(1+i)^n}$$

Now, combining results, the price of a bond, designated

$$P = V_p + V_a = \frac{A}{(1+i)^n} + \left[\frac{A_1}{(1+i)} + \frac{A_2}{(1+i)^2} + \frac{A_3}{(1+i)^3} + \cdots + \frac{A_n}{(1+i)^n}\right]$$

For example, if the price desired is that of a 20-year, 4 percent bond whose effective yield is 5 percent, substitution in the formula is as follows:

$$P = \frac{100}{(1+.025)^{40}} + \left[\frac{4}{1+.025} + \frac{4}{(1+.025)^2} + \frac{4}{(1+.025)^3} + \cdots + \frac{4}{(1+.0025)^{40}}\right]$$

Solution by use of logarithms establishes that

$V_p = \$37.24$
$V_a = \$50.21$
$P = \$87.45$

It will be noted that because interest is paid semiannually, there are 40 interest periods at the semiannual rate of 0.025 percent. This laborious calculation is obviated by use of a bond table from which the price can be read directly or derived by a simple interpolation. Selected values from such a table are presented in Table 11-1; the price of $87.45 is found in the 5 percent column and the 20-year row.[4]

TABLE 11-1 / PRICES OF 4 PERCENT COUPON BONDS WITH SELECTED MATURITIES AND MARKET YIELDS

Years to Maturity	Current Market Yields					
	2%	*3%*	*4%*	*5%*	*6%*	*8%*
1/12	100.16	100.08	100.00	99.91	99.83	99.71
1/2	100.99	100.49	100.00	99.51	99.03	98.22
1	101.97	100.98	100.00	99.04	98.09	96.36
5	109.47	104.61	100.00	95.62	91.47	84.28
10	118.05	108.58	100.00	92.21	85.12	73.50
20	132.83	114.96	100.00	87.45	76.89	60.41
30	144.96	119.69	100.00	84.55	72.32	54.75
50	163.03	125.81	100.00	81.69	68.40	50.99
100	186.33	131.64	100.00	80.14	66.76	50.02
Infinity	200.00	133.33	100.00	80.00	66.67	50.00

Source: *Comprehensive Bond Values Tables* (Boston: Financial Publishing Co., 1958) various pages.

The second problem of the investor can also be solved by use of a bond table. That is, given the price of $87.45 on a 4 percent 20-year bond, he can readily read the yield of 5 percent directly, or derive it by interpolation.

relationships of bond yields, prices, and maturities

The purpose of Table 11-1 is to summarize several of the basic relationships between bond yields, prices, and maturities. One of the most important principles is that *yields and prices move inversely*. For example, if the market yield declines to 3 percent the price of our 20-year, 4 percent bond rises to $114.96, and if the yield drops even further to 2 percent the price goes up to $132.83. Conversely, a rise of market yield to 6 percent is associated with a price of $76.89, and a further increase of yield to 8 percent corresponds with a

[4]It is suggested that readers who are unfamiliar with the mathematics of bond valuation read a more comprehensive treatment of this topic. See *Financial Handbook*, Jules I. Bogen, ed. (3d ed.; New York: Ronald, 1948), pp. 1210-1223; R. E. Badger and H. G. Guthman, *Investment Principles and Practices* (4th ed.; Englewood Cliffs, N.J.: Prentice-Hall, 1951), chap. 22; also consult a bond table such as *Comprehensive Bond Values Tables* (Boston: Financial Publishing Co., 1958).

price of \$60.41. This relationship is explained mathematically by the general formula for capitalization. That is, $P = \frac{A}{i}$ where P is the value of principal, A is the annual income return, and i is the market rate of return on this type of investment. It is clear that P becomes larger when A is divided by (capitalized at) a lower rate, and that P becomes smaller when A is capitalized at a higher rate. To use the simplest case from Table 11-1—the 4 percent bond with no maturity date—when market yield is 2 percent, $P = \frac{\$4}{.02} = \$200$, but when yield is 8 percent, $P = \frac{\$4}{.08} = \$50$. It is also helpful to explain this relationship by comparison of new bond issues with old bonds outstanding. If market yield has risen to 6 percent, a new bond with this coupon rate can be sold at face value (100). Under these conditions, the price of the 4 percent, 20-year bond would have to decline to \$76.89 in order to provide a competitive alternative for the investor. Thus, price is the adjusting factor that enables outstanding bonds, with coupon rates that differ from market yields, to keep in step with each other and with new issues.

In this connection, the statement is often made that yields have risen *because* bond prices have fallen, or that yields have fallen *because* bond prices have risen. This is a misleading interpretation of causation because changes in yields do not *cause* changes in prices any more than changes in prices cause changes in yields. They are simply different aspects of the same phenomenon and necessarily have a precise, inverse mathematical relationship. The *causes* of changes in yields and prices lie deeper and are found in conditions of supply and demand for investible funds.

Another basic relationship highlighted by Table 11-1 is that with a given change of market yields, prices of long-term bonds fluctuate far more widely than prices of short-term securities. Stated more precisely, *the variability of bond prices with a given change of interest rates increases as maturities lengthen, and decreases as maturities shorten.* For example, a rise in market rate from 4 to 6 percent is associated with only a nominal decline in price of an obligation which matures in 1 month—from 100 to 99.83. At the other extreme, the bond with a 100-year maturity declines from 100 to 66.76. Conversely, a decline in market rate from 4 to 3 percent corresponds with a minimal rise in price of a 1-month obligation—from 100 to 100.08—but with a very large increase in price of a 100-year bond—from 100 to 131.64. The explanation of this relationship is found in the time element and in the nature of the bond contract. In the case of a 100-year bond, the market discount rate is applied to (1) the principal over a span of 100 years, and (2) the entire series of interest payments. A change of market rate is therefore associated with a relatively large change in present value. By contrast, in the case of the 1-month security, the discount rate is applied for such a short period that even a large rate change cannot move the price far from the imminent redemption value.

Still another basic relationship is that *the variability of bond yields with a given change of prices decreases as maturities lengthen, and increase as maturities shorten.* In fact, this relationship is the same as the previous one, but it is stated reciprocally. It is evident from Table 11-1 but cannot be read therefrom directly. Reference to a bond table indicates that a decline in price from 100 to 98 of a 4 percent coupon bond is associated with yield increases by maturities, as follows: 1 year, 2.02 percent; 5 years, 0.45 percent; 10 years, 0.24 percent; 20 years, 0.15 percent; and 100 years, 0.08 percent. The explanation is that the entire effect of accumulation of the $2 discount is centered in 1 year in the first case, so that yield has a marked increase. In contrast, discount accumulation is spread over many years in the case of long-term bonds; the yield effect per year diminishes as maturities lengthen.

A final significant relationship is that yields on short-term obligations exhibit far wider cyclical variations than yields on long-term bonds. More explicitly, *yield variations through time tend to diminish as maturities lengthen, and to increase as maturities shorten.* Yields on obligations with maturities under 3 years rose about 4 percentage points during the cyclical recovery between May 1958 and December 1959, whereas yields on 10-year securities rose $1\frac{3}{4}$ percentage points, and yields on 30-year securities rose only 1 point. Then during the subsequent period of declining rates between December 1959 and September 1960, short-term yields dropped about 2 percentage points; 10-year yields, 1 point; and 30-year yields, only $\frac{1}{2}$ point.

The foregoing pattern of yield changes may be explained in part by the mathematical fact of maturity differences, and by reactions of lenders and borrowers to these differences in light of expectations concerning future yield changes. Full discussion of this question is undertaken later in this chapter.

actual bond price movements by maturities

Two highly significant relationships between bond yields, prices, and maturities have already been noted: (1) that with a given change of interest rates, fluctuations of bond prices vary directly with maturities, and (2) that variations of actual market yields decrease as maturities lengthen; in other words, short- and intermediate-term yields move through a considerably wider range than long-term yields. For investors, this poses the important practical question of the extent to which (2) above offsets (1), whether in part, in whole, or in excess. Stated differently, do short- and intermediate-term bonds provide, in fact, a higher degree of price stability than long-term bonds? This question may be partially answered by reference to Table 11-2 which shows changes in prices and yields of selected U.S. securities between May 1958 and December 1959. The former date marked a high point in bond prices during recession, and the latter a low point in bond prices during prosperity.

Several significant facts are evident from Table 11-2. First, price

TABLE 11-2 / CHANGES IN PRICES AND YIELDS OF SELECTED U.S. GOVERNMENT SECURITIES BETWEEN MAY 1958 AND DECEMBER 1959

	May 29, 1958		Dec. 31, 1959			
Securities	*Price[a] (dollars)*	*Yield to Maturity (%)*	*Price (dollars)*	*Yield to Maturity (%)*	*Decrease in Price (%)*	*Increase in Yield (% pts.)*
1½% note 4/1/60	99.28	1.57	99.05	4.96	− .72	+3.39
1½% note 4/1/61	98.26	1.93	96.18	4.39	− 2.28	+2.46
1½% note 4/1/62	97.30	2.06	92.24	4.96	− 5.30	+2.90
1½% note 4/1/63	97.04	2.13	89.26	4.94	− 7.53	+2.81
3% bond 2/15/64	103.06	2.40	92.20	5.01	−10.24	+2.61
3% bond 8/15/66	102.26	2.61	90.14	4.70	−12.04	+2.09
4% bond 10/1/69	109.06	3.04	94.06	4.74	−13.74	+1.70
3½% bond 2/15/90	106.10	3.18	84.22	4.42	−20.34	+1.24
3% bond 2/15/95	98.00	3.09	79.24	4.10	−18.62	+1.01

[a]Bid prices; decimals are 32s.
Source: *Treasury Bulletin* (July 1958, pp. 45-46; February 1960, pp. 59-60).

declines were small for issues with short maturities, but increased with maturity until they amounted to 20 percent for the $3\frac{1}{2}$ percent bonds of 1990. However, it should be noted that correlation between price variations and maturity changes is less than perfect. For example, the 3 percent bond of 1995 declined less than the $3\frac{1}{2}$ percent bond of 1990 due mainly to the fact that the prices of deep-discount bonds are buoyed by the feature of acceptance at face value by the Internal Revenue Service in payment of estate taxes. It will also be noted that price declines of short- and intermediate-term issues are greater and declines of long-terms are less than would be predicted on the basis of maturity differences alone.

Second, increases in yields were largest for short-term issues and declined as maturities lengthened. For example, the yield increase of the $1\frac{1}{2}$ percent note of 1960 was 3.39 points compared with 1.01 points for the 3 percent bond of 1995. But again, correlation was not perfect between yield and maturity changes. This may be illustrated by the fact that the rise of 2.46 points in yield of the $1\frac{1}{2}$ percent note of 1961 was less than that of other issues maturing during the following three years.

Third, a corollary fact should be emphasized: The marked tendency of increases of yield to diminish as maturities lengthen was not sufficient to offset the basic tendency of price fluctuations to increase with maturities. For example, the price of the 3 percent bond of 1995 declined 18.6 percent compared with 5.3 percent for the $1\frac{1}{2}$ percent note of 1962, even though the rise in yield of the former was nearly three times larger. But as already noted, exceptions to this general rule occasionally occur as a result of special conditions of supply and demand in the capital market.

Finally, Table 11-2 draws attention to the common error of overstating price fluctuations of long-term bonds compared with prices of short- and intermediate-term securities. This error arises quite naturally from use of bond tables which show price changes that correspond with yield changes over the range of maturities. The usual approach is to raise the question: What are the effects on prices of bonds of different maturities of a *given* change of interest rates? But the answer is a misleading overstatement of what actually takes place since, as Table 11-2 shows, it is highly unrealistic to assume that the change in yields is the *same* for all maturities. Between May 1958 and December 1959 yields of short-term issues rose about three times as much, and yields of intermediate-term issues rose twice as much, as those of long-term bonds. As a result the actual declines in long-term bond prices were materially moderated and the actual price declines of relatively short-term issues were magnified. For illustration, assume that yields of all maturities rose 2 percentage points between May 1958 and December 1959. Consultation of a bond table shows that in this event the price of the 3 percent bond of 1995 would have fallen 32.8 percent instead of its actual decline of 18.6 percent, and that the price of the $1\frac{1}{2}$ percent note of 1962 would have dropped 3.6 percent instead of its actual decline of 5.3 percent.

It is also pertinent to analyze the actual price performance of obligations with varying maturities during the recession phase of the cycle when yields are moving downward. This is done in Table 11-3 which shows changes in prices and yields of selected U.S. securities between December 1959

TABLE 11-3 / CHANGES IN PRICES AND YIELDS OF SELECTED U.S. GOVERNMENT SECURITIES BETWEEN DECEMBER 1959 AND APRIL 1961

Securities	Dec. 31, 1959 Price[a] *(dollars)*	Dec. 31, 1959 *Yield to Maturity (%)*	April 28, 1961 *Price (dollars)*	April 28, 1961 *Yield to Maturity (%)*	Increase in Price (%)	Decrease in Yield (% pts.)
$3\frac{5}{8}$% note 5/15/61	98.10	4.92	100.02	1.85	+ 1.78	−3.07
4% note 2/15/62	97.08	5.01	100.20	2.83	+ 3.47	−2.18
$2\frac{5}{8}$% note 2/15/63	92.28	5.13	99.09	3.04	+ 6.90	−2.09
$4\frac{3}{4}$% note 5/15/64	99.25	4.80	104.10	3.25	+ 4.54	−1.55
3% bond 2/15/64	92.20	5.01	99.16	3.19	+ 7.42	−1.82
3% bond 8/15/66	90.14	4.70	98.02	3.41	+ 8.43	−1.29
4% bond 10/1/69	94.06	4.74	102.10	3.68	+10.86	−1.06
$3\frac{1}{2}$% bond 2/15/90	84.22	4.42	94.24	3.81	+11.19	−0.61
3% bond 2/15/95	79.24	4.10	88.10	3.61	+11.07	−0.49

[a]Bid prices; decimals are 32s.

Source: *Treasury Bulletin* (February 1960, pp. 59-60; June 1961, pp. 56-57).

and April 1961. The former date marked a peak in yields, and the latter marked the recession low point. In general the relationships revealed are opposite to those of the preceding phase of rising yields during economic expansion, so that a summary of the significant facts should suffice.

First, price increases were small for obligations with short maturities, but rose as maturities lengthened. For example, the price of the 4 percent note of 1962 rose only 3.47 percent, whereas that of the 3 percent bond of 1995 rose 11.07 percent. Second, decreases in yields were largest for short-term issues and smallest for long-terms, with intermediate changes graduated downward as maturities lengthened. As an illustration, the yield of the $3\frac{5}{8}$ percent note of 1961 declined 3.07 percentage points compared with a decline of only 0.49 point for the 3 percent bond of 1995. Finally, the marked tendency of yield decreases to decline as maturities lengthened was not strong enough, in general, to offset the basic tendency of price fluctuations to widen along with maturities. However, there were occasional exceptions to this price-maturity relationship. For example, the price of the $2\frac{5}{8}$ percent note of 1963 rose 6.9 percent between the two dates compared with 4.5 percent for the $4\frac{3}{4}$ percent note of 1964.

For emphasis, attention is again called to the prevalent error of misstating the comparative price fluctuations of long-term and short-term obligations. With reference to Table 11-3, assume that yields of all maturities decline a uniform $1\frac{1}{4}$ percent—the usual illustrative approach to this problem. Reference to a bond table reveals that in this event, the price of the 3 percent bond of 1995 would have risen by 29.6 percent instead of the actual 1.07 percent, and the price of the $2\frac{5}{8}$ percent note of 1963 would have risen by only 5.3 percent instead of the actual 6.9 percent.[5]

TIME SERIES OF RATES

Much can be learned about the term structure of interest rates from a graph comparing yields of different maturity classes over a long period of time. Such a graph showing yields of U.S. securities, 1919 to 1970, is presented in figure 4, p. 80. Several significant features of the structure may readily be observed.

1/Long-term rates were typically higher than intermediate-term rates which, in turn, were usually higher than short-term rates. That is, yields showed a high degree of direct correlation with maturities.

2/Short-term rates fluctuated through a far wider range than long-term rates. During the upswing of the business cycle, short-term rates rose more rapidly than long-term rates, and drew well above them at the peak of the boom.

[5]The reader may well question whether the yield, price, and maturity relationships shown in Tables 11-2 and 11-3 can be generalized, because the observations are drawn from only one business cycle. After analyzing in a similar manner other interest-rate cycles in the postwar period, the author concludes that, in general, the patterns of relationship described above also apply to them. One notable exception to the tendency of long-term bond prices to move through a materially wider range than prices of intermediate-term prices occurred during the recession of 1957-1958. Prices of obligations with maturities of 3½ to 5 years rose as much or more than long-term prices. For example, between September 30, 1957 and May 29, 1958, the price of the 1½ percent note of 1962 rose 9.5 percent compared with a rise of 10.8 percent for the 3 percent bond of 1995.

This was conspicuously true in 1920, 1928 to 1929, 1956-1957, 1959, 1966, and 1969. Conversely, during the downward phase of the cycle, the more rapid decline of short-term rates widened their differential from long-term rates until the bottom of depression was reached. Conspicuous examples were 1930-1933, 1954, 1958, and 1960-1961.

3/Yields of all maturities were responsive to changes in business and money-market conditions. Even though intermediate- and long-term rates showed less absolute change, the timing and direction of their movements were similar to those of short-term rates. This fact testifies to the unity which characterizes the entire market despite existence of certain maturity compartments. The strong thread of unity is explained by the mobility of marginal investment funds, and by the disposition of borrowers to choose the most favorable contract, after giving due regard to both rates and maturities in light of their credit needs.

relation of time series to yield curves

In contrast with a time series, a yield curve shows the relation between yields and maturities at a given *point in time.* Yields are conventionally measured on the vertical axis and maturities along the horizontal axis of the grid. All available yields of different maturities are plotted and a free-hand curve is drawn through the plots to approximate a line of best fit.

The three yield curves in figure 13 illustrate the relation to the time series in figure 4. The plots are taken from selected points in time in figure 4. These three curves—the upsweeping, downsweeping, and normal—represent the three broad categories of yield curves. But between the extremes, an almost infinite variety of curves of different levels, slopes, and contours appear over any long period.

The statistical rule of homogeneity of data needs careful application in the construction and interpretation of yield curves. Ideally, all features of the obligations whose rates are compared should be identical, except for differences in maturity. This requirement can be fulfilled for practical purposes in the case of U.S. securities because all are obligations of the Treasury, although care must here be taken to avoid differences arising from tax features, callability, and eligibility for purchase by commercial banks. However, a satisfactory degree of homogeneity for corporate, state, and local obligations is difficult to attain. In addition to different obligors, there are differences of quality, callability, collateral, protective features, legality for purchase, and so on—all of which affect yields. Consequently, the analyst must be on guard to avoid attributing to maturity what in fact are yield differences arising from other factors. For this reason, yield-curve analysis of corporate, state, and local obligations should be used with special care. It is a very useful tool, however, in determination of offering prices, coupon rates, and yields of serial bonds which are used extensively in the state and local field.

13 YIELDS OF TREASURY SECURITIES.
Source: *Federal Reserve Bulletin,* various issues

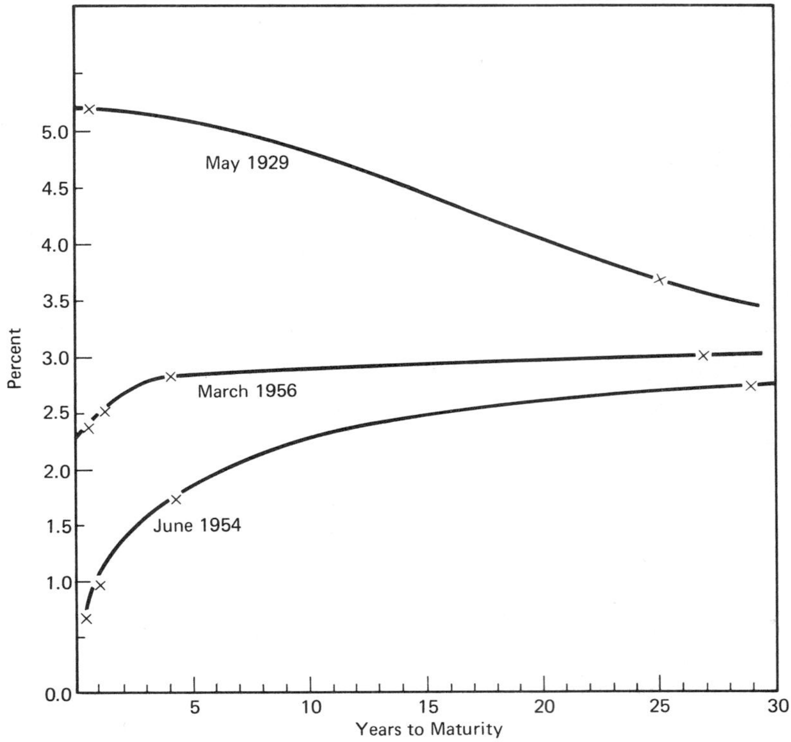

THEORY OF TERM STRUCTURE OF RATES

To this point we have not gone beyond the relation between time-series curves and yield curves, and identification of the three main types of yield curves. The next task is that of developing a theoretical explanation of these varying rate patterns. This can be done most realistically by reference to figure 14, which presents three more recent yield curves. One is the upsweeping curve of May 29, 1958; another is the downsweeping curve on December 31, 1959; and the third is the relatively normal curve on September 30, 1960. In all three cases, a satisfying explanation requires proper blending of two theories: (1) the expectational theory and (2) the segmented-markets theory. These theories will now be applied to each of the broad types of yield curve.

upsweeping yield curves

The upsweeping yield curve on May 29, 1958 rose very rapidly from yields of 0.6 percent on 3-month issues to 1.9 percent on 3-year obligations.

14 YIELDS OF TREASURY SECURITIES ON SELECTED DATES.
(Treasury bill rates adjusted)

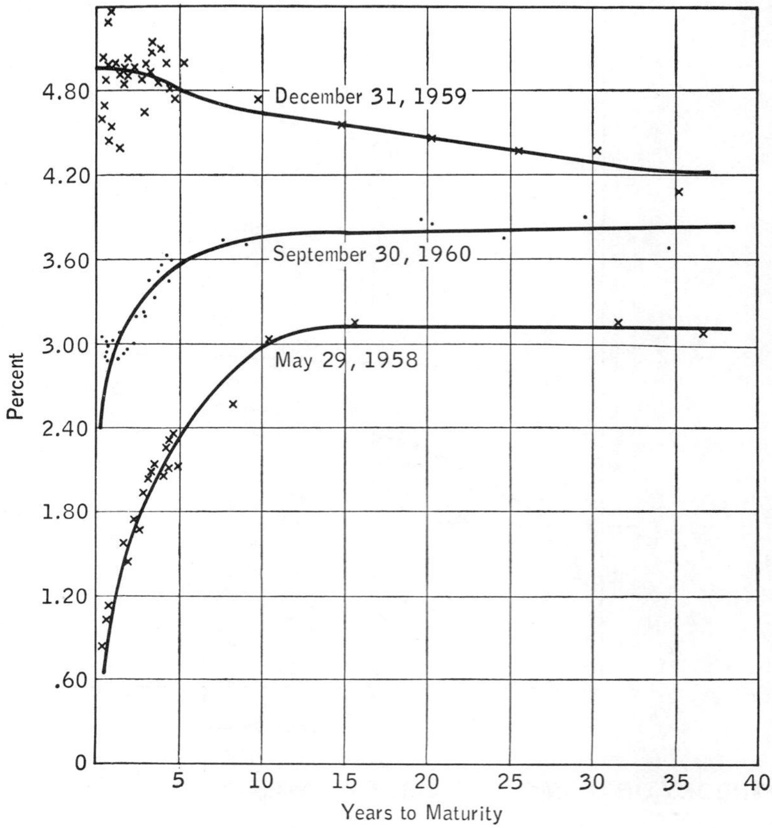

Thereafter, the rate of increase declined until maturities reached about 12 years when yields were 3.1 percent. From this point on, the curve was flat. This curve belongs to a family that prevails when interest rates are abnormally low—a phenomenon that almost always occurs during depressions. Witness 1921-1922, 1924, 1930-1940, 1954, 1958, and 1960-1961 in figure 4. A low level of rates and rising yield curves may also be produced during prosperous years by expansionary monetary policies. The best example is the ceiling on yields of government securities enforced by the Fed during World War II and afterward until the Treasury-Federal Reserve Accord in the spring of 1951. Indeed, rising yield curves prevailed without exception from 1930 to 1955, a fact that led many observers to the erroneous conclusion that this pattern would henceforth prevail and that downward-sloping curves belonged only to history.

This brings up the question: What are the underlying reasons for a rising yield curve? A large part of the explanation is provided by the expectational theory. Lenders and borrowers, according to this theory, carry in mind a rough image of a normal interest rate level. When market rates fall substantially below this normal, the general consensus is that they will rise in the near future and perhaps move well above normal before reaching the next cyclical peak. With this expectation, investors prefer to hold short-term rather than long-term securities for two reasons. (1) Those who primarily seek income and expect to hold securities until maturity avoid committing themselves to long-term contracts with abnormally low yields. They prefer, instead, to hold short-term issues temporarily, even at substantial sacrifice of current income. Later, when yields have risen and bond prices have declined, they expect to purchase long-term bonds. (2) Investors who are more speculative-minded wish to avoid the substantial price decline that long-term bonds will suffer if interest rates rise. For example, a rise of market yield from 3 to 4 percent means a price decline from $100 to $82.62 for a 3 percent, 30-year bond. These investors, therefore, prefer to accept temporarily a lower yield on a short-term issue that will experience little loss of value. They will then be in position to buy long-term bonds at much lower prices during the anticipated period of above-average rates. Thus, the expectations of investors that rates will rise lead them to bid up prices (bid down yields) of short-term securities relative to prices and yields of long-term securities.

An important influence is also exerted by borrowers' expectations of higher rates, which reenforce those of investors. In general, their preferences shift from short-term to long-term contracts. Borrowers who can use long-term money seek to arrange such loans at prevailing low rates. This has the effect of bidding long-term rates higher in relation to short-term rates, and of widening the spread between them. Thus, expectations of both lenders and borrowers that rates will be materially higher in the near future provide one explanation of upsweeping yield curves such as those of June 1954 and May 1958.

The expectational theory views all debt maturities as perfect substitutes for each other. On this assumption, the price of each obligation will be at a point that will promise the same return in future periods as all other obligations differing only with respect to maturity. For example, assume that a 1-year Treasury bill yields 5 percent when a 2-year note yields 6 percent. The general expectation of the market is then that at the end of 1 year the 2-year note will decline in value by roughly 1 percent so that both securities will give a realized yield of 5 percent. Or, from the point of view of the holder of the 2-year obligation, the yield of 1-year Treasury bills during the second year will be 7 percent, with a 2-year average of 6 percent.

But the expectational theory alone is not sufficient; it needs to be supplemented by the segmented-markets theory. With reference to demand, this theory holds that the purpose of borrowing largely determines maturities. For example, short-term funds are needed by businesses to finance working capital, by brokers and dealers to carry security inventories, and by federal, state, and local governments to meet expenditures in anticipation of tax revenues.

Intermediate-term credit is needed by businesses to finance purchases of equipment, by consumers for purchases of automobiles and other durable consumers' goods, and by farmers for purchases of equipment and livestock. Long-term funds are needed by businesses to build plants, by farmers to purchase and improve land, by individuals to finance houses, and by public bodies to build highways, water systems, school buildings, and other capital improvements. These purposes compartmentalize borrowers to a large extent with respect to maturities. This is particularly true of borrowers with fluctuating short-term credit needs. They will not borrow for intermediate or long terms, even though rates are materially lower, because they are uncertain whether funds will be needed. Similarly, borrowers who need intermediate-term credit will not borrow for long terms even though long-term rates are lower. However, borrowers for long-term purposes enjoy greater flexibility. They may, to some extent, take advantage of low short- and intermediate-term rates. That is, they may borrow temporarily in these markets with the expectation of renewing loans or of shifting later to long-term loans on a more favorable basis. Then, too, borrowers who need intermediate-term credit may take advantage of low short-term rates. But despite these possible flexibilities, necessity, conventional practice, and inertia combine to produce substantial rigidities in the structure of borrowers' demands. In general, they tailor the maturity to the term for which credit is needed.

Analysis of outstanding credit reveals that the amount of short-term credit experiences rather wide cyclical fluctuations, whereas the amount of long-term credit remains quite steady. During the decline phase of the business cycle, short-term loans of businesses are reduced as inventories and receivables are liquidated, and as current expenses decline. By contrast, installment payments on long-term loans represent a small proportion of their outstanding amount, so that the principal is reduced only moderately during recessions. Also, residential mortgage loans may actually increase during recessions, as they did during the 1950s and in 1961 and 1967. Thus, the cyclical change in the structure of demand for credit explains, in part, the upsweeping pattern of yield curves during depressions. That is, the scarcity of short-term obligations and the abundance of long-term obligations, relatively speaking, tends to produce low short-term rates in relation to long-term rates.

Turning to the supply side, if there were perfect mobility of investment funds along the maturity scale, investors might compensate for the change in structure of loan demand. That is, rate differences attributable to the change in loan demands could be eliminated by the shift of investment funds toward obligations with longer maturities. But perfect mobility of investment funds does not, in fact, exist; instead, there is considerable rigidity in the structure of supply. Financial institutions, notably commercial banks, have real liquidity needs which they largely fulfill by holding short-term obligations. Nonfinancial corporations, individuals, and other institutions likewise hold short-term securities for liquidity purposes. In fact, because of greater uncertainties about incomes and prices, the disposition to hold liquid assets rises during depressions. These investors look primarily to the liquidity characteristics of securities, and only secondarily to yield. They are likely to hold about the same amount even though short-term rates decline in relation to long-term rates. At the other end of the maturity scale, institutions and individuals typically investing in long-term securities are, in general, disposed to continue their conventional maturity policies despite a wider yield differential between short-term and long-term issues. This group includes life insurance companies, mutual savings banks, trust funds, state and local pension funds, private pension funds, and individuals. Some of them shift to longer maturities to realize higher present yields, and thus tend to reduce long-term yields in relation to short-term yields. But this is more than offset by others who shorten maturities because they anticipate a higher level of rates.

A special institutional factor on the supply side should also be emphasized, viz., Federal Reserve policy and the response thereto of commercial banks. When a recession develops, Federal Reserve policy is typically expansionary in order to foster business recovery. Net surplus bank reserves are provided by Reserve Bank purchases of U.S. securities and/or by lowering reserve requirements. Commercial banks typically respond by adding substantially to holdings of short-term U.S. and other securities. For example, the low yields of short-term Treasury securities on May 29, 1958 are, in part, to be explained by the fact that commercial banks increased their holdings by $6 billion during the first half of 1958.

Another important institutional influence is Treasury debt-management policies and operations. During depressions, the Treasury usually tries to further its aims of lengthening maturities and reducing interest costs. To the extent that a shift toward longer maturities is made, long-term rates tend to rise relative to short-term rates.

Thus, in summary, upsweeping yield curves during periods of depression and easy money can, in part, be explained by the change in structure of demands for credit combined with rigidities in the structure of supply of investible funds. There is reason to expect a smaller amount of outstanding short-term obligations both absolutely and in relation to the amount of long-term securities. There is also reason to expect an increase in investor demands for short-term issues and a reduction in demands for long-term bonds. Under these conditions, short-term rates are depressed relative to long-term rates; the gap between them widens.

downsweeping yield curves

The downsweeping yield curve at the end of 1959 may also be explained by expectations, the structure of demand and supply of credit, and by institutional factors. With rates at the highest level in 30 years, both lenders and borrowers expected them to decline in the not too distant future. Income-minded investors viewed this as an opportunity to secure an attractive yield for many years to come. Speculative-minded investors saw a good chance to realize substantial appreciation in bond prices during the months ahead. Thus, investors bid up prices (reduced yields) of long-term obligations relative to prices and yields of short-term issues. They chose to forgo the higher yields obtainable on short-term securities in order to obtain more favorable long-term contracts.

The actions of borrowers further explain the downward slope of the curve. Expecting a decline in rates, they wished to avoid long-term commitments. Their strong demands for short- and intermediate-term credit bid these rates well above long-term rates. They preferred to pay higher rates temporarily with the belief that long-term credit, if needed, could be borrowed later at lower rates.

The theory of segmented markets also contributes to the explanation. The cyclical recovery in 1959 was accompanied by rapid accumulation of inventories and a rise of receivables. Short-term loans to business therefore expanded to finance current assets; the total amount of short-term credit outstanding reached a new peak. Meanwhile, the rate of expansion of long-term credit was more moderate. These developments, which are typical of this stage of the cycle, tended to raise short-term rates relative to long-term rates. While less important, rigidities of supply of investible funds doubtless reenforced the downward-sloping rate pattern. Most investors were slow to alter their conventional maturity distribution, so that a substantial yield inducement was required to bring about an important shift to short maturities. In fact, the schedule of demand for liquid assets probably declined in 1959, due to the prevailing optimism at this stage of recovery. If so, it tended to drive short-term rates upward and to produce a steeper downward slope. The fact that some long-term investors shifted to high-yielding short- and intermediate-term securities prevented these rates from moving even further above long-term rates.

In addition, the institutional factors of Federal Reserve policy and Treasury debt management had an important bearing on the shape of the curve. A restrictive monetary policy was in effect at the time with the result that commercial-bank liquidity was under pressure during 1959. This is evidenced by the fact that member-bank borrowed reserves averaged \$906 million in December, and that all commercial banks reduced holdings of U.S. securities by \$7.4 billion during 1959. Selling of short- and intermediate-term securities by banks thus gave a strong upward thrust to yields in this maturity sector. The hump in the yield curve may also be explained, in part, by Treasury debt-management operations. Due to the $4\frac{1}{4}$ percent legal ceiling on coupon rates of U.S. bonds, the Treasury was forced to issue securities with maturities under five years. Because market yields of securities with maturities over five years exceeded this ceiling, bonds could be sold only at a discount—a practice the Treasury rejected as possibly illegal. Even without a legal rate ceiling, the Treasury is disposed to borrow short-term in periods of high market rates because it is reluctant to make long-term commitments at such times. Hence, borrowing to meet the large current deficit and to cover heavy refundings of maturing issues was mainly in the forms of bills, certificates and notes, and the shift in the maturity structure of federal debt toward short-term issues contributed to the downward pattern of the curve.

normal yield curves

With the exception of the short-term sector, the yield pattern of September 30, 1960 approximates a normal curve; that is, it rises very gently as maturities increase. When rates are at a normal level, their deviation from average by maturities approaches a minimum. This feature is evident in figure 14, but it is more apparent on the time series in figure 4, page 80, which includes a number of cycles.

Why does the normal yield curve follow a moderately upward course? A satisfying explanation must consider attitudes of both investors and borrowers. In general, liquidity is valuable to investors; they have a liquidity preference, and they are willing to pay a premium for it. Short-term issues whose maturities are near, and whose price variations are small, tend to command the lowest average yields. At the other extreme, long-term bonds whose maturities are remote, and whose price fluctuations are much greater, normally provide the highest average yields. A modifying factor is that some investors have small need for liquidity, prefer the convenience of long-term contracts, and wish to avoid the trouble and expense of frequent reinvestment. But, on balance, investors prefer liquidity to illiquidity.

It is not enough, however, to analyze the position of investors. Consideration must also be given to borrowers' attitudes. They, too, prefer the luxury of a liquid position. But in contrast to lenders, their liquidity is maximized by long-term obligations and minimized by short-term debts. The borrower who provides for long-term needs with long-term debts is free from worry in this regard. But the borrower who provides for long-term requirements with short-term loans faces the possibility of embarrassment. The lender may refuse to renew the loan in whole or in part, and he may also set a high renewal rate. For these reasons, borrowers who need long-term credit are willing to pay a higher rate for it than for intermediate- or short-term credit; and similarly, borrowers who require intermediate credit will pay a higher rate for it than for short-term credit. Thus, the preferences of both investors and borrowers for liquidity reenforce each other to produce a moderate upward trend in the normal yield curve.

The departure of the yield curve of September 30, 1960 from normal in the short-term area requires further explanation. Why does it rise sharply from about 2.4 percent for very short-term issues to 3.7 percent for seven-year obligations before reaching the extended level of the long straight-line trend?

The answer is found in the structure of demand and supply of credit and in Fed and Treasury operations. Liquidity needs of investors were heavy so that the supply of investible funds in the short-maturity sector was very large. On the other side, Treasury offerings and outstanding issues in this area were not large enough to maintain rates at the level of the straight-line trend. Investors bid yields down until demand and supply were equated. Perhaps, also, investors at this stage of the business cycle harbored the general expectation that interest rates would rise further.

An interesting view of the wide variations in yield-maturity relationships in 1969-1970 is provided by figure 15. The yield curve on December 29, 1969 represented the peak of the credit stringency with rates at the highest level in a century. Two months later, the curve had dropped 150 basis points in the 3-4 year area and 60 points in the 20-25 year segment. This sharp decline reflected a quick psychological change in expectations—that monetary policy would be relaxed, that the economy would slacken, that credit demands would become less intense, that price inflation would be curbed, and that the level of interest rates would decline.

During the next three months, the yield curve retraced most of its steps and changed its shape, with yields beyond 12 years rising well above the December 1969 level, and with yields in the short and intermediate maturities remaining well below those of December. This move resulted largely from the realization that there was little foundation for the sanguine expectations held in February. But by July, expectations were again more optimistic, and the curve returned to approximately the February level, but with short-term rates lower and long-term rates higher than in February.

15 YIELD CURVES OF U.S. GOVERNMENT SECURITIES ON SELECTED DATES, 1969-1970.
Source: Manufacturers Hanover Trust Company, *Financial Digest* (July 31, 1970)

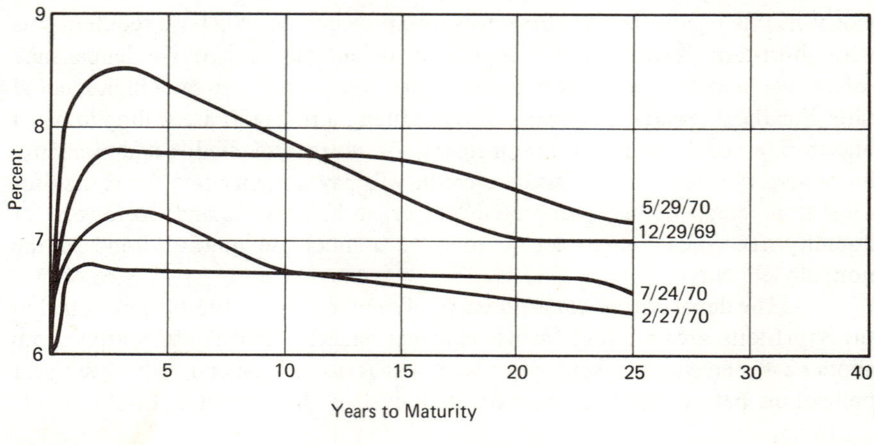

PRACTICAL USES OF YIELD CURVES

The preceding discussion provides ample illustration of the usefulness of yield curves as tools of theoretical analysis in explaining relationships between yields and maturities under varying conditions. This is the most practical general use of such curves, because all sound practices should follow principles set forth by basic theory. But in addition to this broad application, officers of banks, investment houses, life insurance companies, and other financial institutions; financial officers of corporations; and Treasury and Federal Reserve officials make substantial use of this graphic tool in decision-making processes.

Many financial officers use charts similar to figures 14 and 15 as a means of gaining perspective in arriving at their continuing forecast of the level and structure of market yields, and of shaping the desired maturity distribution of their security portfolios. The current yield curve can be interpreted more meaningfully when it is compared with other curves representing strategic points in time. These points usually include the last preceding cyclical high point and the last preceding low point in rates. It may also be helpful to include one or more other curves that are clearly relevant under the circumstances. The current level and maturity pattern of rates can then be seen against the backdrop of past experience.

Referring again to figure 14, attention is called to some of the more specific practical applications of yield curves. First, suppose that after careful study the analyst concludes that the curve of May 1958 is likely to persist for five or more years. In this event, he may well decide to enlarge holdings in the 5-12-year sector by (1) selling longer-term issues and reinvesting the proceeds, (2) selling shorter-term issues, and (3) investing new money from maturities and other sources. He can then "ride the yield curve" downward and reap the rewards of appreciation by selling at appropriate times. He will sacrifice little in current interest by shifting 15-40-year bonds to 12-year issues, and in addition he can expect a substantial return from appreciation. For example, if the yield curve remains unchanged, a 3 percent, 12-year bond bought at par can be sold 5 years later at $103\frac{1}{2}$. The investor will thereby realize a net return of about 3.7 percent compared with 3.1 percent on longer bonds. At the other end of the scale, he can realize a current interest return of 2.3 percent on 5-year maturities compared with less than 1 percent on issues maturing in under 1 year. Also, if he desires, he can augment total returns by selling at a profit as time passes. For example, at the end of 3 years he can sell for about $101\frac{1}{2}$, and thereby realize a total net return of 2.8 percent. Still another conclusion follows from the investor's forecast of no change in the May 1958 curve, namely, that it is unwise to invest in securities with maturities beyond 12 years because expected returns do not compensate for risks assumed. Little more interest return is offered and no appreciation will be realized unless the general level of rates falls even lower. Moreover, if the rate level should rise, long-term bonds are most vulnerable to price decline.

Second, suppose that the investor holds a firm conviction in May 1958 that rates will rise during the next two years to the approximate level and pattern shown by the December 1959 curve in figure 14. In this case, he may well concentrate holdings in the under 3-year category. The temporary sacrifice of income—about 2 percent at the outset—is a small price to pay for avoidance of depreciation of between 12 and 20 percent in principal, or of being committed to a low yield on long-terms for many years to come. Having made this sacrifice, he is then in position to sell short-terms at little or no loss of principal, and to purchase intermediate- and long-term issues at low prices and high yields as opportunities develop. In fact, if the investor's expectations are realized, the short-term position may involve only a nominal loss of current income because short-term rates typically rise more sharply and equal or exceed long-term yields during the last phase of the upward movement. As long as he firmly believes that rates are destined to move higher, he will continue to hold short issues to benefit from their rising yields and to avoid depreciation of long-term bonds.

Third, assume now that the investor determines in December 1959 that the period of abnormally high rates has been reached and that the outlook is for materially lower yields in the period immediately ahead. He may then decide to forgo the higher current return of short-terms and to shift his holdings to the intermediate- and long-term sectors. This will enable him to receive a relatively high return until maturity, or if he desires, to realize a substantial profit by selling later at higher prices. This phase of the cycle may be illustrated by the September 1960 curve in figure 14.

Fourth, suppose that the investor believes that the December 1959 curve will obtain for 5 or more years. His strategy then is to concentrate holdings in the short-term sector. In this way, he not only receives the highest possible current return, but also avoids riding the yield curves in the wrong direction on intermediate- and long-term bonds. For example, a $4\frac{3}{4}$ percent, 10-year bond bought at par would decline to $98\frac{1}{2}$ in 5 years if the yield on 5-year bonds is 5 percent.

Fifth, yield curves are a useful tool in spotting overpriced and underpriced securities. The former appear as plots below the line, and the latter as plots above the line. Such knowledge has many practical uses, including profitable arbitrage operations, investment of new money, subscription to new issues, and selection of issues to buy and sell when executing a change of policy concerning maturity distribution of the portfolio. It should be noted, however, that the usual before-tax yield curve is not sufficient for investors subject to high income tax rates and to whom after-income-tax yields have special significance. Such investors often find an after-tax yield curve useful in conjunction with the usual curve.[6]

Sixth, investment banking houses make extensive use of yield curves in

[6]See Federal Reserve Bank of Kansas City, *Monthly Review* (December 1960), pp. 3-8, for an illuminating analysis of this point.

planning for new issues and refundings of high-grade bonds. This device is essential to finely-drawn decisions in regard to maturities, prices, and coupon rates—especially for issues of municipal and other serial bonds which have different prices, coupon rates, and yields in the various maturity classes.

Finally, Treasury officials prepare and study yield curves in reaching decisions on various aspects of federal debt management such as planning to raise new money, developing refunding programs, and determining maturities, prices, and coupon rates on offerings.

REFERENCES

Conard, Joseph W., *An Introduction to the Theory of Interest* (Berkeley: University of California Press, 1959), pp. 287-367.

Culbertson, J. M., "The Term Structure of Interest Rates," *Quarterly Journal of Economics,* LXXI (November 1957), pp. 485-517.

de Leeuw, Frank, "A Model of Financial Behavior," in J. S. Dusenberry et al., eds., *The Brookings Quarterly Econometric Model of the United States* (Skokie, Ill.: Rand McNally, 1965), pp. 465-530.

Federal Reserve Bank of Kansas City, "Taxes and the Term Structure of Yields," *Monthly Review* (December 1960), pp. 3-8.

Granger, C. W. J., and H. J. B. Rees, "Spectral Analysis of the Term Structure of Interest Rates," *Review of Economic Studies,* 35 (January 1968), pp. 67-76.

Hicks, J. R., *Value and Capital* (2d ed.; Oxford: Clarendon Press, 1946), chap. XI.

Johnson, Ramon E., "Term Structure of Corporate Bond Yields as a Function of Risk of Default," *Journal of Finance,* XXII (May 1967), pp. 313-345.

Kane, Edward J., "The Term Structure of Interest Rates: An Attempt to Reconcile Teaching with Practice," *Journal of Finance,* XXV (May 1970), pp. 361-374.

Kessel, Reuben A., *The Cyclical Behavior of the Term Structure of Interest Rates,* Occasional Paper 91, National Bureau of Economic Research (New York: Columbia University Press, 1965).

Luckett, D. G., "Multi-Period Expectations and the Term Structure of Interest Rates," *Quarterly Journal of Economics,* 81 (May 1967), pp. 321-329.

Lutz, F. A., "The Structure of Interest Rates," *Quarterly Journal of Economics,* LV (November 1940), pp. 36-63.

Malkiel, B. G., and E. J. Kane, "Expectations and Interest Rates: A Cross-Sectional Test of the Error-Learning Hypothesis," *Journal of Political Economy,* 77 (July 1969), pp. 453-470.

Malkiel, Burton G., "The Term Structure of Interest Rates," *American Economic Review,* LIV (May 1964), pp. 532-543.

McCulloch, Huston J., "Measuring the Term Structure of Interest Rates," *The Journal of Business,* 44 (January 1971), pp. 19-31.

Meiselman, David, *The Term Structure of Interest Rates* (Englewood Cliffs, N.J.: Prentice-Hall, 1962).

Pye, G., "Markov Model of the Term Structure of Interest Rates," *Quarterly Journal of Economics,* 80 (February 1966), pp. 60-72.

Scott, Robert H., "Liquidity and the Term Structure of Interest Rates," *Quarterly Journal of Economics,* LXXIX (February 1965), pp. 135-145.

Van Horne, J., "Interest Rate Risk and the Term Structure of Interest Rates," *Journal of Political Economy,* 73 (August 1965), pp. 344-351.

part two

MONETARY AND FISCAL MANAGEMENT

12

objectives of monetary and fiscal management

The major mistakes in economic decisions can usually be traced to a failure to weigh relevant facts in terms of well-defined goals. For this reason, it is imperative in the discussion of monetary, fiscal, and debt management that adequate attention be given to goals and criteria as a background for consideration of the means of fulfilling particular policies.

BROAD OBJECTIVES OF THE ECONOMY

Most people in the United States would agree that the broad objectives of the economy are substantially as follows:

> To maintain full employment, stable employment, growth in production, widely-shared distribution, a relatively stable price level, and international equilibrium—all within the environment of political and economic freedom, and the conservation of natural and human resources.

This summary statement raises many questions which require further analysis, such as: What is the precise meaning of full employment, and of unemployment? How are economic progress and a rising standard of living attained? How are we to interpret the concept of equitable distribution of the national income? What behavior of the price level do we really want? Is there conflict among the various goals, and can these aims be achieved without undue sacrifice of our systems of political democracy and free competitive enterprise? We now turn to consideration of these issues.

full employment

It is not surprising that the mass unemployment of the 1930s elevated full employment to the dominant goal of our times. In the worst month of

1933, nearly one-third of the U.S. civilian labor force was unemployed, and for the whole decade, unemployment averaged about one-fifth. These proportions were even larger in areas dominated by the durable-goods industries–iron and steel, nonferrous metals, construction equipment, industrial equipment, transportation equipment, household durables, and others. The catastrophe was worldwide; it spawned the fascist dictatorships of Hitler and Mussolini, and nurtured socialistic experiments in Great Britain, France, and many other nations. In the field of political economy, what later became known as the "Keynesian Revolution" had its beginnings in 1936 with publication of John Maynard Keynes' *The General Theory of Employment, Interest and Money*. This book was chiefly concerned with the theoretical conditions of employment and unemployment, and with public policies that would assure full employment. It inspired the myriad books and articles written by followers and critics of Keynes.

The philosophy of the Keynesian school, in which the central government assumes large responsibility for the level of employment, provided the rationale for government deficit-spending programs in Great Britain, France, the Scandinavian countries, the United States, and several other nations. At the end of World War II, Congress passed the Employment Act of 1946 which explicitly proclaimed "maximum employment, production, and purchasing power" henceforth to be a basic national policy. The large majority in both parties supporting this bill reflected fear of a severe postwar depression when the government reduced its spending in peacetime.

Meaning of Full Employment / When full employment is cited as a goal of economic policy, there is need for more precise definition; the concept, as it stands, is vague. For example, does it mean no unemployment whatever? Or that some arbitrary proportion of the civilian labor force–say, 96 percent or more–is employed, so that unemployment is less than 4 percent? Again, are part-time workers to be classified as employed, and if so, how long does one have to work per week or per month to be so classified? Should the "unemployed" category include workers on strike, those temporarily laid off, and those who are not working because of illness? These are only samples of the many questions requiring rather arbitrary quantitative answers before the employed and unemployed can be counted.

According to the official definition of the Bureau of the Census, the civilian labor force includes the civilian noninstitutional population 14 years of age and over, who are able and willing to work. Thus, it does not include the *voluntarily* idle. *Employed* persons comprise those who (1) are at work 15 hours or more per week, and (2) are not at work but have jobs to which they expect to return within 30 days. *Unemployed* persons are those who have no jobs to which they expect to return within 30 days, and who are looking for jobs at going wages. Thus, this category includes only the *involuntarily* idle. The *civilian labor force* is defined as the sum of the employed and unemployed categories. For examples, the employed averaged 77.9 million in 1969, the unemployed 2.8 million, and the civilian labor force 84.2 million. The average rate of unemployment was therefore 3.5 percent.[1]

Types of Unemployment / For the present purpose, involuntary unemployment may well be separated into two types: one that is not appreciably affected by monetary and fiscal policies, and another that is largely dependent on such policies. The greater part of the first type is commonly known as structural unemployment; it is the minimum unemployment that can be expected under conditions of maximum output without price inflation. The largest part arises from the continuous technological and other changes that characterize a dynamic economy. New products, new processes of production, changes in methods of distribution, and changes in demands all combine to destroy jobs as well as to create new ones. It takes time for displaced workers to move to other locations, acquire new skills, and obtain other occupations. Thus, a reasonable amount of this kind of unemployment is a necessary aspect of growth and progress. Another part of unemployment arises from monopoly pricing by business, labor, and agriculture; from labor disputes; and from inept government regulations. Still another portion is seasonal in nature.

The second type of unemployment—that susceptible to monetary and fiscal control—is largely cyclical and represents the most basic aspect of an economic recession or depression. It may also include *chronic unemployment* during periods of stagnation, such as the 1930s, when effective monetary demand is insufficient to induce full use of labor and other resources.

Practical Full Employment / The question now arises: How may full employment be defined as a practical goal of the economy and as a guide for monetary and fiscal policies? In general, it is the civilian labor force less the first type of unemployment as just defined. But irreducible unemployment defies precise measurement. Estimates of leading authorities vary between 3 and 5 percent of the civilian labor force. For several years, the Council of Economic Advisers has used 4 percent in calculating the level of GNP consistent with noninflationary growth. In terms of the civilian labor force of 85.8 million in August 1970, this would represent unemployment of 3.4 million compared with actual unemployment of 4.2 million, or 5.1 percent of the labor force.

The proportion of irreducible unemployment also varies with conditions. It is undoubtedly higher in a large, dynamic country such as the United States with its wide geographic, industrial, and racial differences than in smaller, more homogeneous nations such as Denmark and Great Britain. The proportion should show a slowly declining trend as progress is made in retraining, moving, and adapting displaced workers to new jobs.

[1]*Federal Reserve Bulletin* (September 1970), p. A 64.

16 EMPLOYMENT AND UNEMPLOYMENT IN THE UNITED STATES, 1929-1970.
Source: Board of Governors of the Federal Reserve System

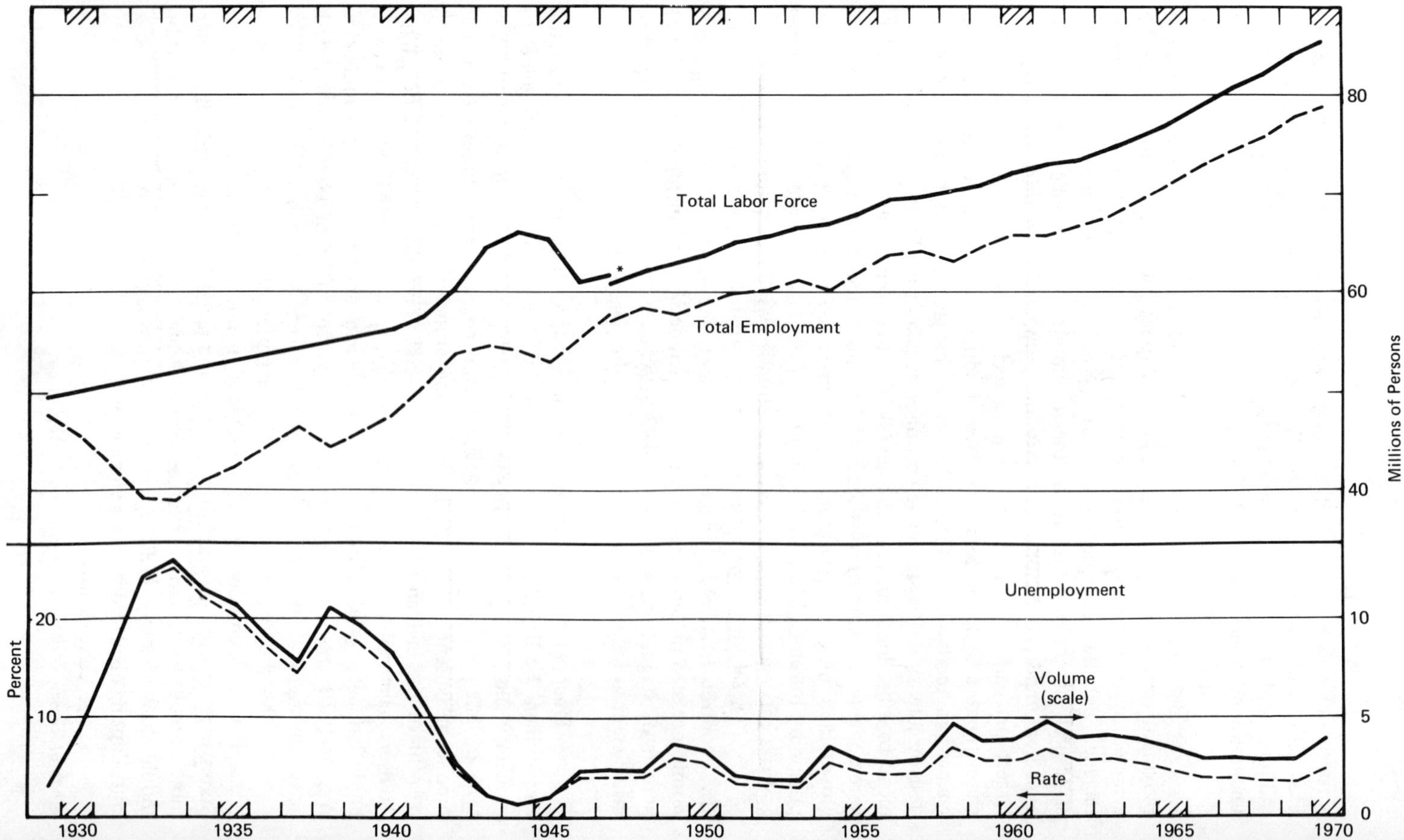

Official U.S. unemployment rates during the postwar years suggest that a realistic annual full-employment rate is about 95 to 96 percent of the civilian labor force, with inflexible unemployment about 4 or 5 percent. During the four-year period 1952-1955, when there was only nominal change in retail and wholesale price levels, the unemployment rate averaged under 4 percent. But prices edged upward during 1956 and 1957 when the unemployment rate was 4.3 percent. During the seven-year period 1958-1964, wholesale prices remained steady and consumer prices moved moderately upward in the presence of annual unemployment rates ranging between 4.5 and 6.8 percent. In the final period, 1965-1970, both wholesale and retail prices rose at an increasing rate—between 2 and 6 percent per annum. The fact that the associated unemployment rate ranged between 3.5 and 3.9 percent suggests that intolerable price inflation develops under existing economic and political conditions when the rate of unemployment drops below 4 percent[2] (see figure 16). Insofar as "practical full employment" is used as a guide for monetary and fiscal policies, it is highly important that an accurate quantitative measure be developed. Setting the employment goal too high leads to price inflation; setting the goal too low results in the waste of needless unemployment.

Further light is thrown on this issue by figure 17, which shows a Phillips curve relating the annual rate of unemployment to annual changes in the U.S. wholesale price index.[3] The vertical scale on the right is included to show the corresponding changes in hourly wage rates on the assumption that real output per man-hour increases at 3 percent per year. It will be observed that a stable wholesale price level is roughly associated with a $5\frac{1}{2}$ percent rate of unemployment. As the rate of unemployment declines to 4 percent, the price level rises on the average at a rate of $3\frac{1}{2}$ percent; and when unemployment approaches 3 percent, prices rise abruptly at an increasing rate—sometimes called *hyperinflation.* At this point, the economy is operating at its practical capacity, and further increases in monetary demand have responses almost entirely in higher prices.

While the chart does not show so conclusively the effects of rising unemployment on prices, it suggests that as unemployment rates rise above about $5\frac{1}{2}$ percent the price level declines. Inclusion of the 1930s would have brought out this relationship more clearly, but comparable data are not available. Suffice it to say that between 1929 and 1932, when the unemployment rate rose from about 4 percent to over 20 percent, wholesale prices

[2]There is nothing final about the practical percentages of employment and unemployment that may be used as one guide for monetary and fiscal policies. In the event that progress can be made in retraining the unemployed and in moving them more quickly into job opportunities, that the degree of monopoly in business and labor can be diminished, and that government policies in general become more conducive to enterprise and employment, it is quite possible that the practical rate of unemployment may be reduced to between 3 and 4 percent.

[3]The Phillips curve is named after Professor A. W. Phillips of the London School of Economics, who is the pioneer in analysis of this relationship.

declined 32 percent. However, after this precipitous decline, the price level crept upward until 1937 in the presence of an unemployment rate of over 10 percent. This represented a snapback from the wholesale liquidation of assets, which took place during the period 1929-1933.

A final comment should be made on the relation between the wholesale price index and the consumer price index. The latter increases about $1\frac{1}{2}$ percent

17 THE PHILLIPS CURVE RELATING THE RATE OF UNEMPLOYMENT TO CHANGES IN THE PRICE LEVEL AND WAGE LEVEL, ANNUALLY, 1948-1970.
Sources: *Economic Report of the President* (February 1970); *Federal Reserve Bulletin* (October 1947), p. 1294

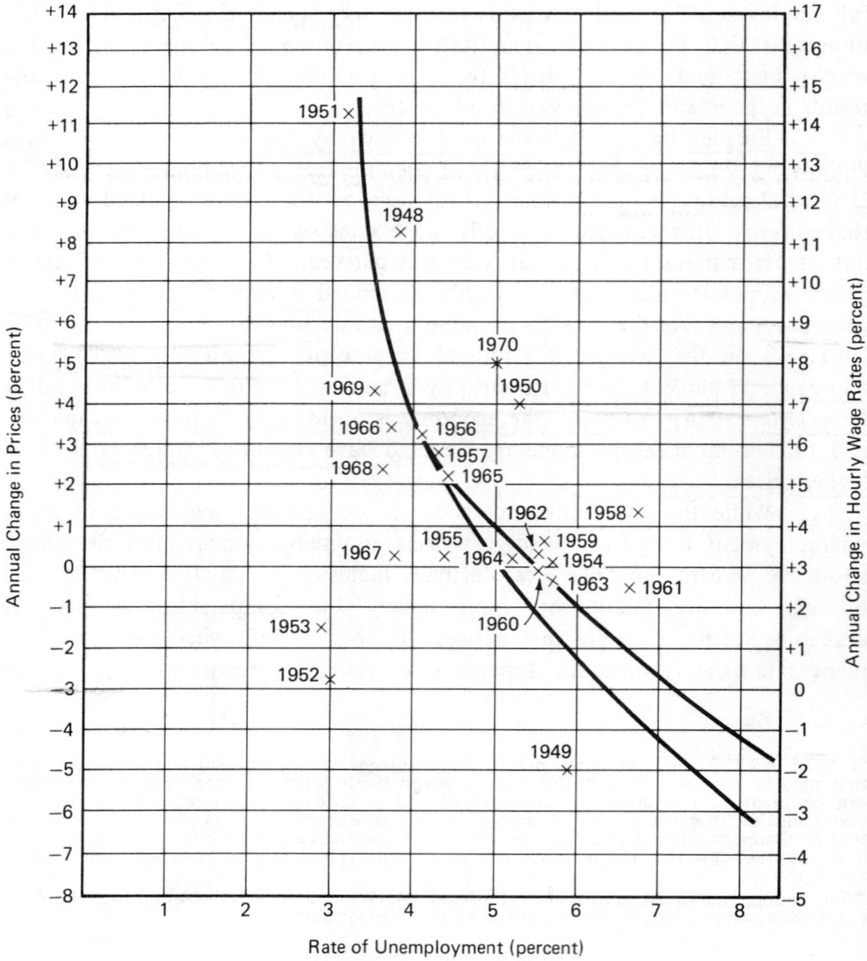

per annum when the index of wholesale prices is stable.[4] Hence, a higher unemployment rate, between 6 and $6\frac{1}{2}$ percent, would be necessary to stabilize consumer prices under existing conditions.

While full employment, realistically interpreted, is beyond doubt one of the basic objectives, a note of warning should be sounded against the mechanical use of official employment (or unemployment) rates as accurate measures of the concepts. Careful study of the statistical difficulties of arriving at the amount of employment and unemployment leaves one uneasy about the margins of error. In addition to the numerous arbitrary decisions concerning definitions, the sampling process must be utilized in assembling basic information. When the sample was enlarged in early 1954, the new sample indicated unemployment to be 700,000, or 31 percent, larger than the former sample.[5] Also, entries and withdrawals from the civilian labor force show large changes from year to year, due to such factors as changes in size of the armed forces, age distribution of the population, and labor-force participation by housewives, teen-agers, and older workers. Abnormal variations in the rate of unemployment are the result. Finally, it is often hazardous to look only at an average or aggregate. A rise in the rate of unemployment may not reflect a widely distributed condition, but instead a special situation in a particular area, industry, racial group, or age group. If so, the proper remedy may be specific, rather than monetary. The rate of unemployment also needs to be interpreted in the light of changes in part-time work and in weekly hours of work.

Full Employment Versus High-Level Output and Consumption / With so much emphasis on full employment in recent years, it is sometimes forgotten that the more basic goal, after all, is high-level output as the only means of achieving widely-shared, high-level consumption. Jobs alone are not enough; we cannot eat and wear them. Enterprisers must effectively combine labor with capital resources to produce and distribute a maximum of goods and services. Dictators can forcibly bring about full employment, but this is a long step from maximum output in accordance with consumer choices. In order for full employment to be converted to maximum output, laborers must give their best efforts, must work an optimum number of hours, and the supply of labor of all types and skills must be matched with the great variety of jobs in factories, mines, trade, transportation, public utilities, personal and professional services, government services, and so on. For this happy result to be realized, enterprisers must assume business risks, organize productive processes, and tailor their products to market demands; that is, they must have ideas with respect to potentially successful ventures, and must risk their time and capital in activating them. Otherwise, the engine of production will idle or misfire.

[4]At midyear 1970, the consumer price index was 135.2 and the wholesale price index stood at 117, when 1957-1959 = 100.

[5]U.S. Bureau of the Census, *Annual Report on the Labor Force* (Washington, D.C., 1954), p. 11.

The concept of full employment of labor should, in fact, be expanded to include the other basic productive factors. Maximum output cannot be realized unless there is also high-level utilization of producers' capital, natural resources, and enterprise. The assumption is usually made—sometimes without justification—that this will occur when labor is fully employed. It should also be noted that full employment in a free economy does not imply *forced* labor, as it may under dictatorship. In a free society, people enter or leave the civilian labor force voluntarily; they make their own choices between leisure and higher income.

In a static economy—where the size and quality of the labor force, the efficiency of management, and methods of production remain the same—full employment would yield a constant volume of real output. But this is obviously not the case in a progressive economy such as that of the United States. Productive efficiency has increased more rapidly than population, with the result that the rate of increase of real output has been about double that of population—about $3\frac{1}{2}$ percent per annum compared with $1\frac{3}{4}$ percent.

Over short periods, there is a very close correspondence between the number employed and the volume of real output. This follows from the fact that changes in technology, management, labor, and other factors take place slowly.

18 INDEX OF INDUSTRIAL PRODUCTION IN THE UNITED STATES, 1919-1970.
Source: Board of Governors of the Federal Reserve System

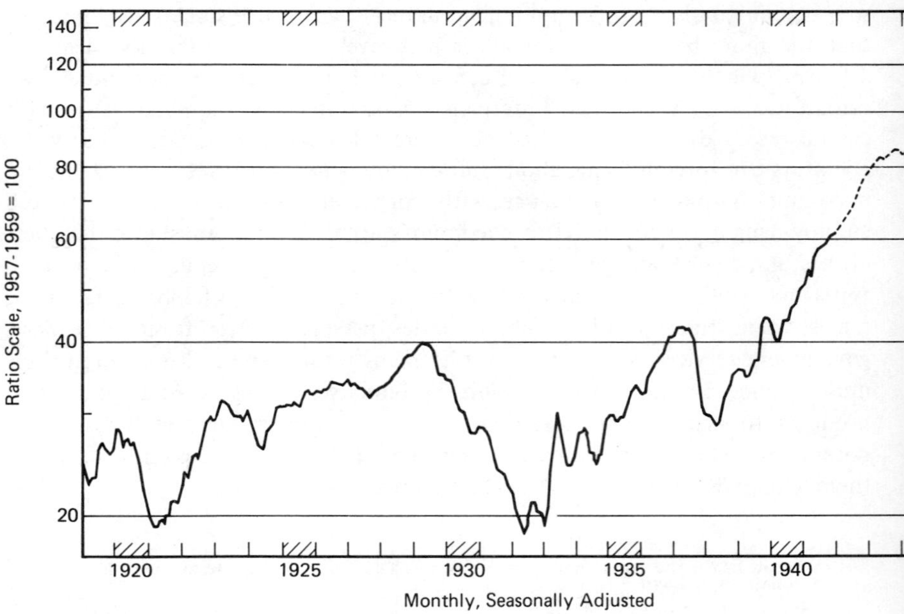

But correlation between employment and output is less than perfect, because of cyclical changes in hours worked per week. Work is spread during depressions and overtime is utilized in prosperous periods. As a consequence, the percentage variations of employment are suppressed as compared with those of output. Also, some conflict between full employment and high-level output may arise from the deterioration in quality of products and services during an extended period of prosperity. The disciplines of competition are relaxed for both labor and enterprise in a sellers' market. These limitations do not detract seriously, however, from the usefulness of employment and unemployment data as measures of business conditions.

stable employment

While maintenance of full employment implies *stability*, the ruling importance of steady employment requires separate discussion. The strongest indictment that can be brought against the free-enterprise system is its susceptibility to depressions. Cycles of depression, recovery, prosperity, and decline are a feature of U.S. business annals as far back as records are available (see figure 18). A short cycle of about $3\frac{1}{2}$ years and a longer cycle of approximately 9 years on the average were identifiable before World War II. From peak to trough, the shorter cycles declined between 10 and 20 percent as

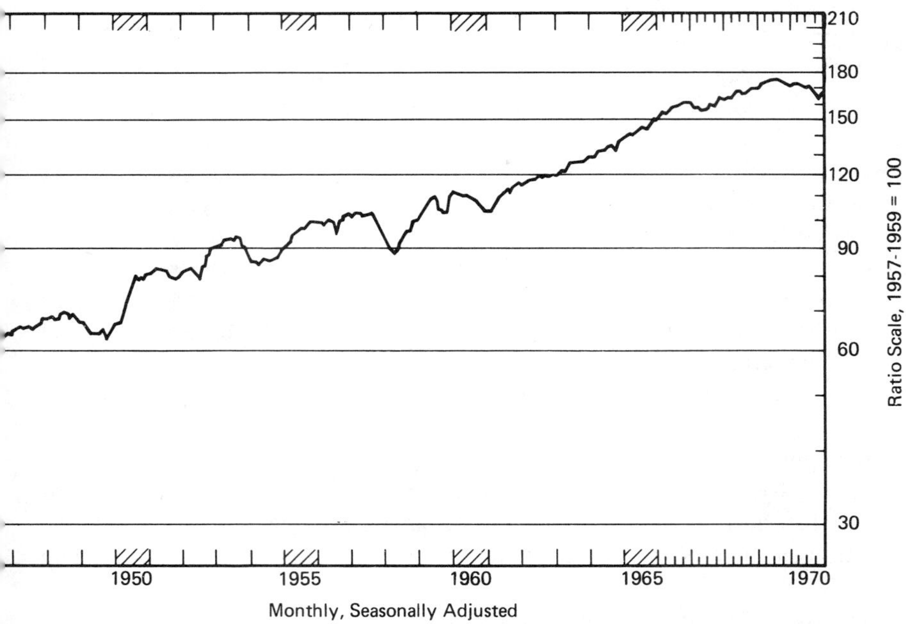

measured by industrial production; the longer ones, between 25 and 50 percent. In the quarter-century since World War II the U.S. economy has experienced five recessions in which the decline of the Federal Reserve Index of Industrial Production has ranged between 6 and 11 percent. The absence of a major depression suggests that the monetary and fiscal authorities have made real progress in stabilizing the economy. But most economists would hasten to add: at the cost of an unacceptable degree of price inflation.

Some changes that are taking place in the economy magnify its susceptibility to severe depressions and inflationary booms. In general, as a nation becomes wealthier and as luxuries occupy a larger place in consumers' lives, a wave of pessimism may lead to a greater reduction in spending than was possible when necessities more completely dominated the budget, and when a smaller share of disposable income was discretionary in nature. Another development is the growing habit of consumers to become heavily indebted for houses, automobiles, and other durables. For example, between the end of 1950 and the first quarter of 1970, home mortgage debt (nonfarm, 1-4-family) rose from $45.2 billion to $268.7 billion; and consumer credit increased from $21.5 billion to $119.7 billion.[6] Business and government debt also expanded rapidly. Beyond a doubt, the large postwar expansion of debt contributed to the longest period of general prosperity in U.S. history, and to the rising level of prices. On the other side, the existence of a heavy debt burden aggravates a business decline. Uncertainties about jobs and incomes lead consumers and businesses to curtail current purchases in order to reduce indebtedness.

However, certain other postwar developments tend to reduce the susceptibility of the economy to wide cyclical swings. For example, consumer expenditures for services have represented a growing proportion of total consumer outlays since World War II. Also, consumer expenditures for nondurable goods have risen more rapidly than outlays for durable goods. Still another stabilizing influence has been the rising part of GNP represented by government (federal, state, and local) purchases of goods and services. This proportion rose from one-twelfth in 1929 to one-seventh in 1940, and to just over one-fifth in 1970. Authorities differ as to whether the endogenous forces making for wider cyclical fluctuations or those having a moderating influence have been the stronger during postwar years. A good case can be made that they have been largely offsetting, and that there has been little change in natural cyclical amplitudes.

But whether or not our susceptibility to fluctuations is greater than in the past, there are three additional reasons why control of cyclical swings has become increasingly imperative. First, the political tolerance for depression conditions has narrowed since the 1930s. Many people suffered great hardships during this "lost decade" and quite understandably shrink from its recurrence. At the same time, they are convinced that the government can do something

[6] *Federal Reserve Bulletin* (September 1970), p. A 54.

about it in view of relatively full employment during and since the war. It is, in fact, doubtful whether either democracy or free enterprise would survive a repetition of the 1930s.

Second, removal of the specter of major depressions not only would reduce cyclical losses but also would tangibly quicken the rate of economic progress. With stronger confidence in the future, consumers, businesses, and state and local governments would proceed more vigorously with long-range plans. Moreover, banks and other lenders, influenced by the same outlook, would be more justified and more willing to finance new projects. This point is frequently overlooked, or given inadequate emphasis.

Finally, as the leading nation of the free world, the United States has a special responsibility to foster economic stability. A depression, or even a recession, in this country has severe repercussions in many smaller countries heavily dependent on exports to the United States. The countries of western Europe and South America provide good illustrations, and many nations of Asia and Africa are in the same position. Our stake in developing strength and free institutions in these nations is so large that we can ill afford to export depression conditions. Nor should we fail to grasp the opportunity to foster their confidence in free institutions by setting an example of stable progress.

Fortunately, much can be done to moderate instability by monetary and fiscal management, and without impairing free enterprise. These methods of stabilization are discussed in the chapters that follow.

economic growth

Few would deny that economic growth represents one of the primary aims of a good society. Just to maintain the standard of life of the average person, output must grow apace with population. But this goal is too modest; output should expand at a materially faster rate than population, so that the average person can enjoy rising standards of consumption, and each generation can live better than the preceding one.

Growth a Reasonable Goal / There are two principal reasons why economic growth deserves a high priority. First, despite the amazing improvement in living standards of the Western world during the past two centuries, poverty remains the world's number one economic problem. Even in the United States, where the real income of the average person is many times higher than in Asia and Africa, real poverty stalks at least one-third of the people and another one-third is denied many of the comforts in life. Increased income makes possible more leisure as well as higher consumption, with the result that new vistas of self-expression and development are opened to the individual. These include better education, better medical care, more travel, more cultural enjoyments, more recreational activities, and more time for hobbies.

Second, growth is an essential ingredient of free economic and political institutions. There are several threads to this proposition. Equality of opportunities—a basic feature of free enterprise—leads to inequality of incomes because people with varying abilities are rewarded mainly on the basis of contribution. Savings by the higher-income groups and by businesses are largely invested in producers' capital goods which bring about *growth* in output. Again, the combination of equality of opportunities and inequality of incomes arouses the basic human urge to live as well as, or better than, one's neighbors. This provides a continuous pressure for growth to higher and higher levels. Still again, the ever widening flow of new inventions, new products, and improved technologies in this age of science contributes mightily to productive efficiency. A forward stride by one firm is forced on others by competition. Thus, there is a clear mutual dependence: equality of opportunity begets growth, and growth widens and deepens the scope of opportunity.

The question now arises: What is the optimum rate of growth of output in a free society? At first, one might answer, "As fast as possible." But such an answer overlooks the fact that growth requires sacrifice of present satisfactions to the future, and also leaves debris strewn in its wake. A prime essential of growth is increased investment in the latest forms of producers' capital. This, in turn, involves saving—the decision not to spend current income. Also, growth involves hard work—imaginative planning, the risk of time and resources, and vigorous action to bring forth new products and methods. Then, too, growth is a destroyer of old jobs, old plants and equipment, even industries and communities. Like profit, whether its value is positive or negative can be determined only after deduction of costs. Growth can thus be pressed too vigorously to serve the best interests of those living today. Curtailment of consumption, temporary loss of jobs and other disequilibria that are the price of change may cause undue suffering, or even starvation, as under one five-year plan in Russia.

However, few would be satisfied with no improvement at all in the standard of life of the average person—that is, for output to increase at the same rate as population. Thus, while the optimum rate lies somewhere between the extremes of no per capita growth and growth that levies unwarranted hardships, there is no absolutely correct rate. The optimum rate in a free peacetime economy is the one that emerges automatically from individual choices and decisions with respect to consumption, saving, leisure, investment, enterprise, desired government services, and so on. These decisions, however, should be made in a governmental environment that fosters expansion. The government should follow policies that are unbiased and fair to enterprise, labor, and capital; it should also expressly assume responsibility for maintaining conditions of relatively full employment of resources and a relatively stable dollar.

Conditions of Growth / Space precludes more than the following list of the essential conditions of healthy economic growth in a free society.

1/Political, economic, social, and religious institutions that foster freedom of the individual and equality of opportunity.

2/Continuous improvement in the amount and quality of education and training.

3/A population that responds energetically to the basic human urge to improve its lot.

4/A labor force with constantly rising abilities and motivations to work efficiently.

5/Ready availability of good natural resources. It is not necessary that such resources be located in the country if they can be obtained freely in trade with other nations.

6/A gradually rising proportion of savings to GNP.

7/Sufficient confidence in long-range profit prospects on the part of entrepreneurs to commit the flow of savings to producers' capital goods.

8/A growing number of people with the spirit of enterprise and with special abilities to undertake the risks and responsibilities of production.

9/A private-enterprise economic system guided largely by consumers' choices and characterized by competitive markets and the absence of monopoly.

10/Vigorous programs of pure and applied scientific research by business firms, government agencies, universities, and other institutions with the object of promoting new inventions, products, and technologies.

11/A strong democratic system of government that performs its functions efficiently and pursues policies conducive to expansion.

12/Adequate public investment in highways, streets, bridges, educational facilities, hospitals, recreational facilities, and other needed public works.

13/Relatively free international trade and capital movement.

14/Monetary and fiscal policies that foster high-level employment, business stability, and a relatively stable price level.

While no country has provided this ideal environment for growth, there is little doubt that the United States has over the years come the nearest to doing so. What, therefore, has been its record of economic growth? The most authoritative estimate is that of the National Bureau of Economic Research.

> Net national product in the decade 1944-53 stood about thirteen times as high as it had in 1869-78. This increase implies an average rate of growth of 3.5 per cent per annum. Population, however, more than tripled in the same period. Net product per capita, therefore, approximately quadrupled, implying an average rate of growth of 1.9 per cent per annum.[7]

[7]Moses Abramovitz, *Resource and Output Trends in the United States Since 1870,* National Bureau of Economic Research, Occasional Paper 52, 1956, p. 7.

A rough measure of the rate of growth in more recent years may be made on the basis of GNP in constant 1958 dollars, which rose from $203.6 billion in 1929 to $727.7 billion in 1969. This is at the annual rate of 3.2 percent. On a per capita basis, the rate per annum is about the same as for the longer period—1.9 percent.[8]

Growth and Monetary Policies / While economic growth is unquestionably a primary goal of the economy, there is heated controversy in regard to its qualifications as an object of monetary policies. Since World War II, the Federal Reserve Board of Governors has officially accepted it as one of their principal policy guides. Whenever objectives are discussed by the Board, this concept variously appears as "orderly economic growth," "stable economic progress," "steady development of the nation's resources," "rising standard of living," "rising level of consumption," and "sustainable economic progress."[9]

Whether this new emphasis is desirable or unfortunate depends on the Board's interpretation of this goal and on application in practice. It is desirable if the monetary authorities do no more than give proper consideration to the country's growing productive capacity in applying the guide of sustained full employment. Full employment is not a static concept, but is a moving short-term relation between actual employment and current employment capacity. Observance of this guide implies little more than passive recognition of the growth that is taking place largely because of nonmonetary forces.

But this new emphasis on growth is unfortunate if it represents an aggressive aim of the Fed to promote more rapid growth than would occur when monetary influences are neutral. This aim would constitute unwise interference with basic economic forces; it would also call for oracular judgments with respect to a "proper" or "ideal" rate of growth when there is no accurate way to measure it. Pressed too hard by excessive monetary expansion, this aim would magnify the danger of price inflation, and would be in conflict with the goal of a stable dollar.

That this aggressive aim would represent unwise interference with nonmonetary forces is suggested from the summary of conditions of growth given on page 223. Of the 14 conditions listed, only the last one is strictly monetary in nature. And in this regard, the monetary authorities will have done their job well if they meet their fair share of the governmental responsibility for relatively full employment, moderation of cyclical fluctuations, and relatively stable purchasing power of the dollar.

Some elaboration of the problem (previously mentioned) of determining a "proper" or "ideal" rate of growth is desirable. Statistical studies of the historical rate of growth provide only moderate help. While the study of the National Bureau of Economic Research found an average rate of growth of 3.5

[8] *Economic Report of the President* (February 1970), pp. 183, 201.
[9] See Board of Governors of the Federal Reserve System, *The Federal Reserve System* (4th ed.; Washington, D.C., 1961), pp. 1, 123; *Federal Reserve Bulletin* (June 1957), p. 649.

percent per annum in real net national product during the period 1869-1953, it also found wide variations in the long-term rate during alternating upswings and downswings:

> The curve mounts relatively steeply for a time and then exhibits retardation in a pattern which has repeated itself roughly every twenty years. . . . The average rate of growth in upswing periods was about five times as rapid as in the down-swing periods.[10]

If nonmonetary causes are responsible for varying rates of growth in succeeding decades, ranging between about 1.5 and 7.5 percent, how can the monetary authorities confidently know whether the current rate of growth is the "right" rate? Adoption of the average 3.5 percent rate would evidently be repressive during a rapid-growth era and inflationary during a slow-growth period. Moreover, there is no way of forecasting whether the average rate of growth in decades to come will be higher or lower than that of the past. In view of these facts, it follows that the monetary authorities should adopt a facilitating, rather than an aggressive, attitude toward growth. That is, they should accept the fact of growing capacity and make ample allowance as it appears, but they should not actively sponsor some arbitrary growth rate, say, 5 percent per annum, of their own choosing. In a free economy, the wise course in peacetime is to let the rate of growth emerge naturally from individual decisions to spend, save, invest, venture, borrow, and lend. This statement assumes that governmental functions are being efficiently performed, including active promotion of the basic conditions of growth.

economic and equitable distribution of income

Meaning of Concepts / In a free-enterprise system, economic distribution means that each individual receives an income that approximates his contribution to society by personal services or by owned property. This income reward, however, does not represent contribution in the absolute sense of loss sustained by society if each individual's services were withdrawn and were not replaced. Rather, it represents the value of contribution at the margin of the group or type of service. Recognizing the principle of substitution, workers of the same skill can replace each other, and therefore tend to receive the same compensation. The rate of pay approximates the value of the *least* important service rendered by a member of a homogeneous group. This is an aspect of the general economic law that a single price tends to emerge for all standard units of the same product in a free market.

If society approves the private-enterprise system of economic organization, then it in general sanctions the *equitableness* of the distribution of income which is an integral part of that system. While the free-market principle

[10] Abramovitz, op. cit., pp. 19-21.

dominates distribution of personal income in the United States, important modifications of this principle are made by the government for humanitarian and practical reasons. These modifications have the effect of significantly reducing differences in disposable personal income. Rates of personal income taxation rise steeply as the amount of income increases, with the result that tax receipts from higher income groups are utilized to improve the welfare of the less fortunate. Graduated estate-, inheritance-, and gift-tax rates have the same effect.

Thus, *equitable* distribution for our purposes means distribution of income in accordance with the system legally approved in a free society. It is the job of the monetary authorities to foster conditions that permit realization of equitable distribution in this sense. It should also be noted that equitable distribution does not mean *equal* division of personal income, as advocated under some forms of socialism or communism. Rather, in a free society, the goal is not equality of income regardless of contribution, but equality of *opportunities* for individuals to develop and to utilize their talents. Some people respond with large contributions, and are rewarded accordingly; others contribute little, and therefore receive low incomes.

Monetary Policies / Granted that economic and equitable distribution of income is an important objective of the economy, to what extent should it be an aim of the monetary authorities? The answer is similar to that previously given concerning economic growth: They contribute most tangibly to this goal by fostering high-level employment, business stability, and steady purchasing power of the dollar. Beyond this, nonmonetary influences largely govern distribution.

An unstable dollar plays havoc with equitable distribution. When the price level rises sharply, as in the periods 1940-1951 and 1965-1970, all persons whose incomes and property are fixed in dollars are impoverished (see figure 19). This includes holders of money, owners of savings accounts, pensioners, annuitants, beneficiaries of life insurance, and owners of government and corporate bonds. At the same time, debtors and owners of common stocks, real estate, commodities, and other appreciative assets reap windfall gains. The real terms of all money contracts, amounting to some $1,800 billion in 1970 are changed without consent of the parties. In addition, those groups whose incomes lag behind the rise in consumer prices suffer heavily. These include nonunion labor, white-collar workers, government employees, teachers, and employees of industries or of endowed institutions who lose ground when prices rise rapidly.

An unstable dollar also undermines the productive power of the economy, and consequently the standard of living of the people. This process takes place in various ways. For one thing, the delicate relationships within the price structure are thrown out of adjustment. In the case of fast-moving inflation, prices rise at varying rates. In general, industrial raw-material and farm-product prices go up first and farthest, whereas some sticky prices such as public utility rates remain the same or move up slowly with a lag. For example, figure 19 shows the sharp increase in farm-product prices during both World Wars. Prices of cost factors get out of line with final-product prices. Some companies and industries profit handsomely; others are victims of the maladjustments. But on the whole, dollar profits increase sharply because costs tend to lag behind selling prices and thereby to widen profit margins. In part, however, profits are illusory, because of conventional accounting methods which charge depreciation of plant and equipment on original cost instead of on replacement value. Appreciation of inventory values may also appear as profits.

Whatever the cause, the artificially stimulated money profits create in many businesses an unfounded optimism which may result in overexpansion of capacity. This error is superimposed on numerous mistaken decisions in regard to current operations—decisions that spring from maladjustments in the price-cost structure just described. For the whole economy, these mistaken decisions constitute wasteful uses of limited resources. They may be corrected by *rolling adjustments*, but in the past they have frequently led to recession or depression.

Another unfortunate aspect of price inflation is the fact that real personal savings are reduced and diverted from their normal channels. Anticipating higher prices, people spend a larger proportion of disposable income on consumer goods; indeed, they may go one step further by borrowing to buy. They become increasingly wary of investing in government bonds, savings deposits, life insurance, and other high-grade obligations in view of anticipated further erosion of the dollar's real value. Instead, savers become more speculative-minded and progressively seek appreciative-type investments such as common stocks, real estate, and commodities. With this stunting of voluntary real savings, a normal volume of real investment can be financed only by borrowing a larger part of investment outlays from commercial banks. This, in turn, creates new money and induces further price inflation. Thus, the impasse is reached: either more price inflation, or a reduced rate of real investment and economic growth.

It may be concluded, therefore, that, in addition to causing inequities, a rapid rise of prices impairs the economy's long-run performance; that is, it reduces productive capacity and the level of real output compared with what might be the case under stable monetary conditions.

Some economists advocate mild price inflation, say, 2 or 3 percent per annum, as an aim of monetary policy. They argue that such a policy would increase business profits and that with better profit prospects, the rate of investment and of economic progress would be stimulated. The practical argument is also advanced that the strong bargaining position of union labor will inevitably increase wage rates faster than the rise in product per worker. Consequently, holding prices steady will create unemployment. A little inflation, so these economists say, is preferable to a chronic layer of unemployment. While

19 INDEX OF WHOLESALE PRICES.
Sources: U.S. Bureau of Labor Statistics; Board of Governors of the Federal Reserve System

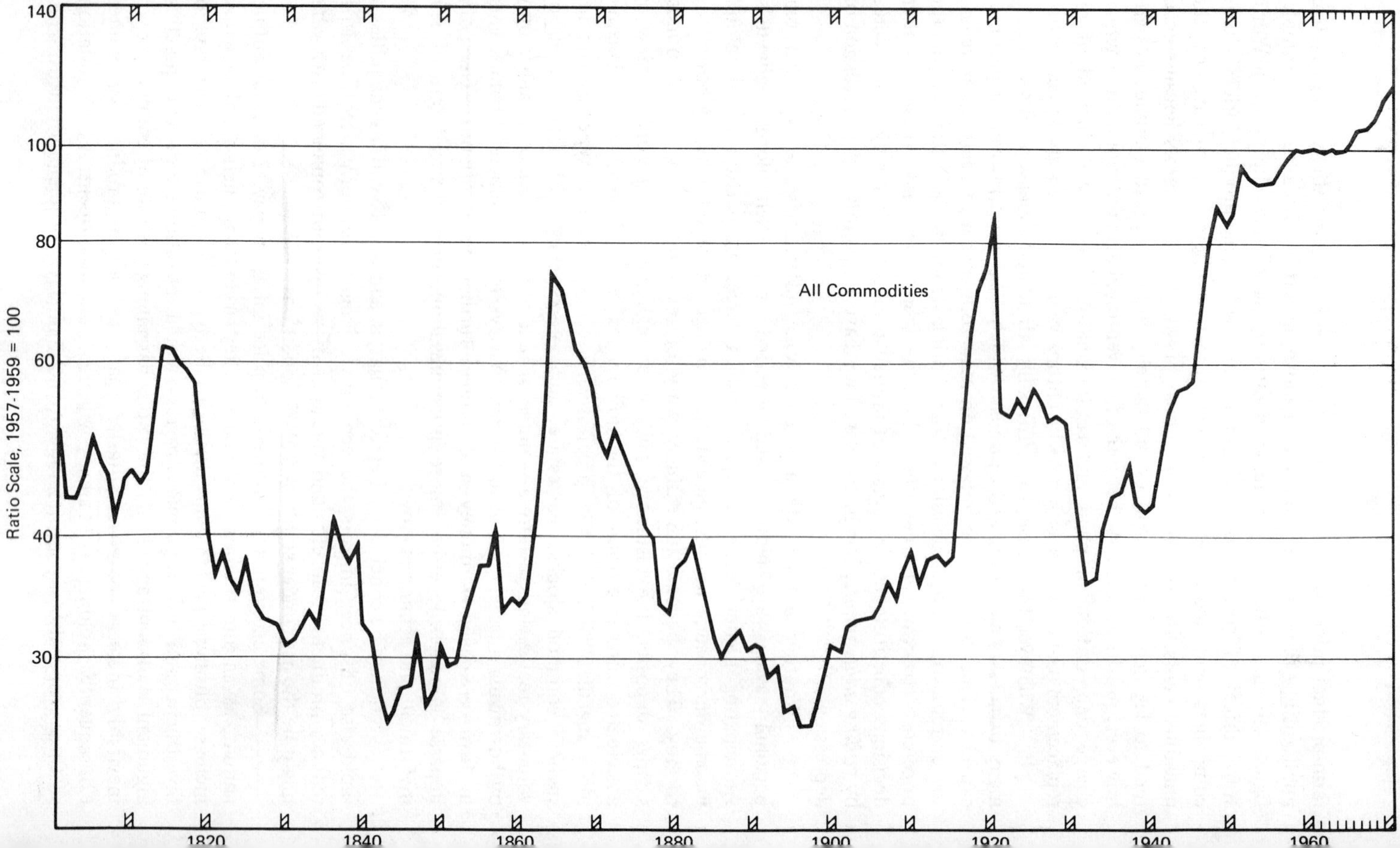

this argument has some appeal, the weight of economic opinion favors a relatively stable price level. It is pointed out, first, that even a rise of 2 or 3 percent per annum is a severe penalty on owners of bonds, deposits, and other dollar claims. At 2 percent the price level doubles (value of dollar halves) in 35 years; at 3 percent this happens in 24 years and at 5 percent in 14 years. The interest return on savings deposits or U.S. savings bonds would be largely or wholly eroded. In fact, from the standpoint of justice alone, the price level in a growing economy, instead of rising, should decline gradually in inverse proportion to the rate of increase of productivity. This would permit suppliers of financial capital in the form of obligations to share in economic progress along with labor and enterprise. That is, their fixed dollar income would rise in purchasing power. Second, a criterion of mildly rising prices contains a progressive upward bias; it is next to impossible to have "just a little" inflation. When people generally become aware of government-induced inflation, they seek speculative protection. Prices of common stocks, real estate, and commodities are bid up and prices of bonds decline (interest rates rise). This happens when holders of dollar obligations shift to appreciative-type assets and current savings also flow in this direction.

If price inflation is not in harmony with equitable distribution and economic progress, neither is its opposite, price deflation. Full development of the arguments is unnecessary because they are, in reverse, almost the same as those just presented. In general, a sharply falling price level constitutes a levy on debtors and those whose incomes decline flexibly in favor of creditors and those whose incomes are fixed or slow to decline. This statement assumes that debts will be paid and that jobs will be held. But this is not, in fact, the case, because of the sharp decline of incomes. Net profits of business decline when selling prices drop more rapidly than costs, business spending for capital and current purposes is reduced, unemployment rises, consumer spending declines, and general depression develops. Even the aim of a mild decline of prices to match rising productive efficiency would not be a practical one. As previously indicated, the strong bargaining position of union labor introduces an upward bias in money wage rates. Accepting this stubborn fact, a declining price level would dampen profit prospects, induce more labor strife, and create chronic unemployment.

From the foregoing analysis, we may conclude that neither inflation nor deflation, but price-level stability is the aim most consistent with the broad goal of economic and equitable distribution of income and wealth. It is just as important to provide a stable unit to measure values as it is to have stable units of physical measurement—the pound, foot, gallon, and so on. Consider the confusion that would follow the creation of a variable yardstick! Yet we try to live with, and adjust to, the uncertainties and confusion that arise from an unstable dollar. Price-level stability, therefore, should stand as one of the important goals of monetary policy.

A strong case is made by those economists who believe that the *sole* criterion of monetary policy should be price-level stability. In addition to stressing its reasonableness, they emphasize the importance in the economy of an atmosphere of monetary stability. If a stable dollar were one of the expressed objects of government policy, a large element of uncertainty would be removed from decision-making by businesses and consumers. Long-range plans could be made with greater confidence and schedules for project completions would stand more firmly. Relatively stable business conditions would, so they believe, emerge as a by-product of stabilizing the price level.[11]

environment for a healthy economy

The specific economic goals discussed in preceding pages can be attained only in a favorable economic environment. Moreover, in order to serve the basic values cherished by most citizens of the United States, this environment must be characterized by a large measure of individual freedom and equality of opportunity. Responsibility in this area rests principally on the shoulders of representative government. Space permits only a summary of the role of government in providing for (1) political democracy, (2) private enterprise, (3) economic stability, (4) wise regulation of the economy, and (5) peace and friendly international cooperation. Monetary and fiscal policies do not bear directly on some of these objectives, but they should always be in harmony with them.

Political Democracy / Harsh experiences with dictatorships since World War I have made an indelible impression on the American people. Most of them want no part of such systems, whether they be fascist or communist in nature. Abraham Lincoln's famous saying "government of the people, by the people, and for the people" has assumed a new meaning to this generation. Government should, therefore, play its role under a system of political freedom, and more effective government should be achieved by making democracy work. Monetary policies should function in this framework.

Private Enterprise / Private enterprise is an essential constituent of any social system that is designed to foster the dignity, development, and independence of the individual. A man should be free to start his own business, choose his occupation, decide where and for whom he shall work, spend, save, borrow, and invest in accordance with his own choice–limited only by infringement of the rights of others. History reveals, even if theory does not, that political freedom withers and dies unless accompanied by economic freedom. Economic collectivism, whatever its initial form or avowed purpose, gravitates toward political dictatorship. Moreover, healthy economic progress is most likely to occur under spur of the high incentives afforded by free

[11]For an effective presentation of this general viewpoint, see Lloyd W. Mints, *Monetary Policy for a Competitive Society* (New York: McGraw-Hill, 1950).

competitive enterprise. It follows, then, that economic activities should dominantly be private in nature. The government should directly provide only those goods and services in the production of which it has clear superiority.

Fair Government Relations with Business, Labor, and Capital / Scarcely a business or personal decision can be made without giving consideration to some aspect of government—federal, state, or local. Laws, taxes, regulations, subsidies, bonuses, purchases, public services, courts, and national defense are some of the words that suggest the myriad contacts with government. By its policies and activities, therefore, government may create a hospitable environment for a private-enterprise economy; or at the other extreme, it may produce a stifling and unfriendly atmosphere. It is highly important that the latter extreme be avoided, and that the relations of government to business, labor, and capital be fair and unbiased. In addition, it is the function of government to protect and conserve our natural and human resources. To illustrate, scarce natural resources such as timber and oil should be controlled, water and air should be protected from pollution, and the working conditions of labor should be adequately safeguarded.

In general, the provisions of all laws should be tested in terms of their consistency with a free economy and the basic economic goals as discussed above. Equally important, administration of laws by government agencies should be firm, honest, and fair. Tax laws should be revised with the object of fostering a high-incentive economy, as well as equitably raising needed revenues. Government should maintain effective competition in the private sector of the economy as an essential feature of healthy private enterprise. Areas of monopoly should be carefully defined, and where permitted, should be brought under strict regulation in regard to price, quality, and business practices. Social-security benefits should be adequate not only from a humane standpoint, but also to remove forebodings and to free men's minds for productive effort; at the same time, unemployment compensation should not be so liberal as to undermine high incentives to work. Government should expressly accept responsibility for maintaining relatively full employment, for moderating cyclical variations, and for maintaining a stable price level.

International Cooperation / Since World War II, the United States has emerged with heavy responsibilities of political and economic leadership in the noncommunist world. This circumstance elevates international cooperation to a higher priority than ever before among our basic politico-economic goals. All domestic and international policies and programs should be tested for consistency with this objective. While the economic policies that bear on international relations have a wide range, those most vitally involved relate to trade barriers, foreign investment, foreign aid and technical assistance, economic stabilization, and monetary issues, including viable equilibrium in the international balance of payments.

Real progress has been made under the Reciprocal Trade Agreements Act in reducing tariffs and other trade barriers. Well over one-half the value of imports is duty free, and the tariff rate on other imports averages about 10 percent. However, rates are still so high on specific products as to restrain severely, or to prohibit, sales in this country. Because a system of unobstructed trade contributes to the output and living standards of all nations, a vigorous and continuous effort should be made to move in this direction, including removal of foreign-exchange controls and positive development of free foreign-exchange markets. Private foreign investment should be fostered insofar as practicable. Just as the growth of the American economy was promoted by foreign investment during the nineteenth century, so the growth of underdeveloped areas can today be speeded by their borrowing U.S. savings. Equilibrium in the U.S. international balance of payments can be fostered by maintenance of a relatively stable price level and by worldwide adoption of a more flexible system of foreign-exchange rates.

Government economic aid to foreign countries, except in great emergencies, should largely take the form of educational and technical assistance, and help in raising funds from private sources. In addition to private investment, utilization of the resources of the Export-Import Bank, the International Bank for Reconstruction and Development, and the Inter-American Bank is possible. A program of providing the talents of engineers, economists, business experts, and other technical personnel is relatively inexpensive in terms of the probable long-range benefits both to underdeveloped nations and to the United States.

One of the most substantial contributions that the United States can make to the economic health of other nations is maintenance of relative stability of employment and prices. Depression in the United States severely affects the economies of many smaller nations that normally sell a large part of their exports to us. Sweden and New Zealand are examples. Maintenance of stability depends in large part on the implementation of proper monetary and fiscal policies.

conflict of objectives

To this point, the various goals of the economy have been considered separately. Now the question arises: Are they in harmony or in conflict with one another? More specifically: (1) Is full employment consistent with a stable price level? (2) Is economic progress in harmony with business and price stability? (3) Do economic stability and price stability conflict with international cooperation?

Some monetary economists hold the view that the goal of full employment embraces an inflationary bias. This belief is based chiefly on the institutional setting—the facts of union labor and practical democracy—rather than on theoretical grounds. They argue that the powerful bargaining position of union labor will result in pushing money wage rates up faster than the rise of output per worker. This means either a reduction in business profits accompanied by mounting unemployment or a rise in the price level. Political necessities, they say, will force the monetary authorities to resolve this dilemma in favor of higher prices. Voters will not tolerate the presence of substantial unemployment as a method of holding the price line.

A closely related argument is that, in practice, the level of full employment will be set too ambitiously. Structural unemployment, including trouble in specific industries, will be mistaken for cyclical or chronic unemployment. It is argued that the monetary authorities will then increase the amount of money more rapidly than is consistent with a stable price level, and fiscal policies will similarly become inflationary.

Although these arguments are based on very real facts and tendencies, it does not follow that the issues can be resolved only by giving way to higher prices. Intelligent recognition of the problem is half the battle. If the general public becomes better informed in regard to the dangers and burdens of price inflation, more political support can be mustered in support of relative price-level stability. Practical full employment may then come to be defined as a level compatible with price stability. It is not inconceivable that union wage demands would be substantially toned down, and that business resistance to wage increases would be materially strengthened, if it were believed by both parties that the monetary and fiscal authorities were determined to hold the price line. This leads to the conclusion that, while there may be an inflationary bias in the goal of full employment, there is no controlling reason why this bias cannot be neutralized, or significantly moderated, given the desire to do so.

Next, is economic progress in harmony with business and price stability? The course of progress, as already noted, has not been a smooth one; rather, it has occurred rapidly for about a decade, followed by a period of much slower growth. It is true that the surging optimism of an expansion period magnifies inflationary pressures and makes price stabilization a more difficult task. In the opposite situation, the economy is more recession-prone in a period of slow growth. But whatever conflict exists between these aims is, practically speaking, unimportant. It is unlikely that long-range progress will be deterred by restraints to rising prices in a period of capacity output. More likely, such restraints will prevent overemployment and speculative excesses, and will thereby reduce the danger of corrective recessions. In the slow-growth phase, more monetary and fiscal nudging may be required to maintain full employment and to prevent a declining price level, but this too can readily be provided.

A rapid rate of economic growth also conflicts with stability in some measure because of the very nature of change. A high wind creates a choppy sea, and sometimes a tidal wave. New products, industries, methods, and technology necessarily involve destruction of the old. For example, oil and natural gas for a time turned coal into a declining industry, and in years to come nuclear or solar power may largely replace oil and gas. While, as indicated above, such developments may, at times, magnify the threat of cyclical fluctuations, readjustments take place in the main without much disturbance to overall stability. In conclusion, there is no serious conflict between progress and stability. Indeed, there is reason to believe that economic and price-level stability positively contribute to progress by removing psychological uncertainties and shoring up confidence. As a consequence, a higher level of savings and capital investment—the well-springs of growth—should emerge.

Finally, are domestic business stability and price-level stability in harmony with international cooperation? To a large extent, the answer depends on whether the nations have independent monetary standards, or adhere to a common standard such as gold. In the case of independent monetary standards and flexible foreign-exchange rates, there should be a minimum of disturbance to other nations if an important country such as the United States stabilizes the economy and the dollar. The beneficent effects of American stability would be exported to other nations by a steadier demand for their products. American demands would be sustained both by stable growth of income, and the tendency of foreign-exchange rates to fall when U.S. imports decline in relation to exports. Also, price stability would remove variations in foreign-exchange rates occasioned by changes in the value of the dollar. At the same time, flexible exchange rates would permit adjustments to changes in international balances of payment, and thereby greatly reduce current deficits and surpluses.

Under the international gold standard, foreign-exchange rates are relatively fixed, their variations above and below par being confined to the cost of shipping gold between countries. The price level of one country is tied closely to prices in other nations; that is, to the international price level. It follows that one nation cannot stabilize its price level when prices in other countries are moving persistently downward or upward. To do so would result in exhaustion of its gold stock when international prices were falling. Thus, price-level stability is consistent with the gold standard over long periods only if all countries cooperate in adopting a policy to stabilize the international purchasing power of gold. Such a proposal was made by the Genoa Monetary Conference in 1922, with a view to providing both stable prices and stable foreign-exchange rates. This worthy aim is perhaps not a too ambitious one for the United Nations and the International Monetary Fund. Attainment, however, would require a very large measure of international cooperation. Short of this, if a choice must be made between stable growth and prices with flexible foreign-exchange rates, on the one hand, and unstable business and prices with fixed foreign-exchange rates, on the other, the former alternative is the more attractive. The contribution, if any, of fixed exchange rates to the volume of international trade and investment is small compared with the far-reaching benefits that arise from stable business and a steady price level. Moreover, these benefits would expand progressively as the nations more nearly achieved the goal of stability. Foreign-exchange rates would become more stable over long periods as a result of relatively constant purchasing power of leading monetary units over goods in general.

In summary, it is manifest that the basic goals of the economy form a complex and interrelated structure; there is no single, simple objective. Maximum economic welfare is attained by a sagacious blending of high-level output and growth with stability of business and the dollar. The amalgam should be forged in an environment of political and economic freedom and in an atmosphere of international cooperation. On occasion, some conflict is bound to arise among these objectives, but the problem is not too serious; given wisdom and perspective, it can be satisfactorily resolved.

GOALS OF MONETARY MANAGEMENT

The basic goals of the economy were discussed at some length because some of them are identical with the criteria of monetary management, and all of them provide guidelines for wise economic policies in general, including monetary policies. The maintenance of capacity output and a stable price level are, at the same time, basic goals and practicable, although very broad, monetary criteria. Similarly, international responsibilities and cooperation may, at times, call for specific monetary policies. While the essential conditions for growth and political and economic freedom are largely nonmonetary, they should be facilitated, and certainly not jeopardized, by monetary actions.

goals and criteria of congress

The monetary objectives of Congress are found mainly in the Gold Acts of 1900 and 1934, and the Federal Reserve Act of 1913, as amended, and in the Employment Act of 1946. A summary and brief discussion of the relevant provisions follows.

Gold Acts of 1900 and 1934 / The Gold Standard Act of 1900 represents a landmark in our financial history in view of its declaration of monetary policy. The gold standard was expressly recognized by law for the first time, after a long experience with bimetallism and a heated political struggle between bimetallism and gold after the Civil War. A gold dollar containing 23.22 grains of pure gold was designated the ultimate monetary standard and the Treasury was directed to maintain other forms of currency at parity with the gold dollar.

The Gold Reserve Act of 1934 is also a financial landmark because it laid the groundwork for a return to gold after defaulting in the crisis of March 1933. In accordance with its provisions, devaluation of the gold dollar took place on January 31, 1934, when its weight was reduced to 13.714 grains of pure gold, equivalent to $35 per troy ounce. Other forms of legal-tender money were to be kept at parity with the standard gold dollar. Thus, before 1965, the discretionary range of policy of the monetary authorities was not very wide. Their primary obligation was presumably to maintain the existing monetary standard—in other words, to maintain the fixed relation between gold dollars and circulating dollars. Full employment, economic stability, a steady price level, and growth could not be pursued to the point of threatening the standard. That is, the monetary gold stock and the minimum legal-reserve ratio of the Federal Reserve Banks were foundational facts that conditioned, and dominated, monetary policies unless and until monetary laws were changed. In fact, the prescription of Treasury purchase and sale of gold at $35 per ounce did not impose an effective limit on Federal Reserve policies between devaluation of the dollar in 1934 and 1959 in view of the huge U.S. gold stock. But the large and persistent loss of gold since 1959 joined the issue. In 1962 and 1963, the predominant monetary question was whether to combat an unemployment rate of 5.6 percent and to promote more rapid growth by easy money, or to reduce the deficit in the balance of payments and stem the gold outflow with a firm monetary policy.

In 1965, Congress saw fit to reduce the restraint of gold on bank-credit expansion. The continuous decline of the gold stock from nearly $23 billion in 1957 to $15 billion in early 1965, combined with the growth of Federal Reserve credit, brought the legal-reserve ratio of the Reserve Banks near to its minimum of 25 percent. At this juncture Congress amended the Federal Reserve Act in March 1965, to eliminate legal requirements against Federal Reserve Bank deposits.[12] As a consequence, the ratio of gold-certificate reserves to legally defined liabilities rose from 27.2 percent at the end of February 1965 to 41.3 percent at the end of March.[13] With the requirement applying only to Federal Reserve Notes, the Reserve Banks were relieved of pressure, at least for a time.

Further action was taken by Congress in March 1968, when the Federal Reserve Act was again amended to eliminate all legal-reserve requirements of the Federal Reserve Banks.[14] This step was prompted by the continued reduction of the gold stock—to under $12 billion—and a sizable increase in Federal Reserve Notes, so that the legal-reserve ratio was again approaching the 25 percent minimum. By this action, the restraint of gold on monetary expansion was completely removed in the domestic economy. Henceforth, the rate of growth of money and of Federal Reserve credit was to be determined solely by the judgment of the monetary authorities. The only role left for gold was that of a reserve for settlement of deficits in the balances of international payments among nations. The Treasury price of $35 per ounce was retained as a basis for valuation of monetary gold stocks. This official price provided a measure of restraint on monetary expansion in nations that attempted to keep a fixed parity between their monetary units and the dollar. But because the dollar is the predominant international reserve money, the discretionary expansion of dollars

[12]*Federal Reserve Bulletin* (March 1965), p. 413.
[13]Ibid., pp. 439, 555.
[14]Board of Governors of the Federal Reserve System, *Annual Report* (Washington, D.C., 1968), p. 333.

can provide the basic reserve for discretionary monetary expansion in other countries. Contemplation of this point underscores the great importance of adopting monetary policies in the United States that are consistent with a relatively stable price level. Otherwise, the United States is in the position of exporting an undesirable rate of price inflation to the international community with a subsequent feedback of mounting inflation at home.

Federal Reserve Act / The founders of the Fed had little conception of monetary management as it has developed since World War II. Rather, they viewed the aims of the Fed quite narrowly in terms of overcoming certain defects in the banking system, namely, inelasticity of currency, inelasticity of credit, undue concentration of legal reserves in New York City, and ineffective supervision of banking.[15] Even as amended, the Federal Reserve Act contains nothing but vague and general criteria which can, by interpretation, be given different meanings. For example, discounts and advances must be made with due regard for "the maintenance of sound credit conditions, and the accommodation of commerce, industry, and agriculture."[16] This same general phrase is also used in stating the aims of the discount rate and open-market operations.[17] A somewhat more specific purpose is expressed in directing Federal Reserve Banks to ascertain whether "undue use is being made of bank credit for the speculative carrying of or trading in securities, real estate, or commodities"[18] before extending discounts and advances. Also, reserve requirements of member banks are to be changed by the Board "in order to prevent injurious credit expansion or contraction."[19]

But this is as far as the Federal Reserve Act goes in establishing criteria for guidance of the monetary authorities. High-level employment, business stability, a steady price level, and economic growth are nowhere mentioned. The idea of business stability is perhaps implied in the directive "to prevent injurious credit expansion and contraction," but to read into this directive the concepts of full employment, price-level stability, and growth requires an interpretative tour de force. In fact, Congress has repeatedly refused to direct the Federal Reserve authorities to use their powers to stabilize the price level, and it refused in the 1930s to designate business stability and full employment as Federal Reserve responsibilities.

From time to time, the Board has attempted to interpret the foregoing broad directives in terms of more specific guides to policy. During the 1920s one of the dominant aims was restriction of commercial-bank and Reserve Bank credit to "productive" uses. The best statement of this aim is found in the Board's 1923 *Annual Report*.

[15]See the Preamble of the Federal Reserve Act.
[16]Ibid., Section 4, par. 8.
[17]Ibid., Section 12A, par. 3; Section 14, par. 5.
[18]Ibid., Section 4, par. 8.
[19]Ibid., Section 19, par. 6.

> It is the belief of the Board that there will be little danger that credit created and contributed by the Federal Reserve banks will be excessive in volume if restricted to productive uses. . . . Credit for short-term operations in agriculture, industry and trade, when these operations are genuinely productive and nonspeculative in character, that is to say, credit provided for the purpose of financing the movement of goods through any one of the successive stages of production and distribution into consumption, is a productive use of credit. . . . The withholding of goods from sale when there is a market or the accumulation of goods for an anticipated rise of price is not a productive use. It is the unproductive use of credit that breeds unwarranted increase in the volume of credit; it also gives rise to unnecessary maladjustment between the volume of production and the volume of consumption, and is followed by price and other economic disturbances.[20]

The *productive-credit* theory proved to be unworkable and fallacious; fortunately, it was abandoned in the 1930s. Other names for this doctrine are the *commercial-loan* and *real-bills* theories. It is based on the view that the *right* amount of bank credit (or money) will emerge as a by-product if commercial banks confine their earning assets to short-term, self-liquidating loans for nonspeculative, working-capital purposes. This proposition has little or no logical foundation. For one thing, the definition of productive uses of bank credit is quite arbitrary. In the large sense, any credit-worthy loan is *productive* if it finances the creation of additional utilities in the economy as a whole. Loans to finance consumers, construction, fixed-capital requirements of business, and even moderate speculation are as productive as working-capital loans. For another, circular reasoning is involved. When the economy is operating at capacity, additional credit-worthy loans create more deposit money, which may lead to higher prices and increased earnings and asset values. These, in turn, validate additional credit-worthy loans. The circle in reasoning is also present during the downswing of business. A reduction of loans extinguishes money, which may lead to lower prices, earnings, and asset values. This development, in turn, removes previously credit-worthy loans from that category and, thereby, may lead to a further round of reductions in money, prices, and loans. Thus, the productive-credit theory provides no reasonable standard for the right amount of money. This standard is found principally in the more basic goals of high-level production, healthy growth, stable business, and a steady price level.

A second aim of the Board at times has been to stabilize interest rates at a "reasonable" level. In the 1920s, it took the form of attempts to prevent excessive costs of credit to legitimate business. The best example may be drawn from the 1928-1929 experience, when the use of general control instruments to curb the speculative boom was limited by the fear of unduly penalizing business

[20]Federal Reserve Board, *Annual Report* (Washington, D.C., 1923), p. 34.

borrowers. In 1937, this aim took another form, viz., assumption of responsibility for maintenance of an orderly market for U.S. securities. In practice, this meant the moderation of yield and price variations in these securities by Reserve Bank purchases and sales. During World War II, the support of Treasury finance became dominant, and the Federal Reserve Banks stood ready to buy all U.S. securities offered at prices corresponding to yields ranging between $\frac{3}{8}$ percent on bills to $2\frac{1}{2}$ percent on long-term bonds. This support, although somewhat less complete, continued until the Treasury-Federal Reserve Accord in March 1951. Moreover, stabilization of yields on U.S. securities was transmitted indirectly to all interest rates by competitive forces. With the abandonment of Reserve Bank support after the Accord, the aim of stabilizing interest rates receded into the background. The Fed regained its authority over monetary policy, and the use of general instruments of control was accompanied by wide changes in rates.

The goal of interest-rate stabilization is a false one in view of its inconsistency with the economy's basic goals. When price inflation threatens, high rates are an integral part of a program of monetary restraint. Central-bank measures to keep rates artificially low at such a time only provide more fuel to promote inflation. Conversely, when business recession threatens, easy-money policies to spur recovery necessarily include low interest rates. Thus, when the choice of Federal Reserve authorities is between use of their powers to stabilize interest rates or to stabilize the economy, it is clear that the latter goal is far more important.

Another objective of the Board has been to prevent "undue use . . . of bank credit for the speculative carrying of or trading in securities, real estate, or commodities."[21] The best example of vigorous use of general controls to this end was during the period 1928-1929, when stock speculation was rampant. Several reasons were given by the Board at that time for its policy of restraint. First, it feared that the rapid increase of security loans of banks would lead to overexpansion of the amount of money, and also to more active turnover of money. The resulting rise in money expenditures, so it believed, would lead to an unsustainable inflationary boom with the danger of subsequent depression. Second, because the Board held to the productive-credit theory of banking, it viewed with special alarm the growing proportion (about three-fifths) of bank assets in the forms of security loans and investments. The departure from self-liquidating, working-capital loans was regarded to be unsound in principle. Third, it deplored the "absorption" of credit by speculative activities. Legitimate business borrowers, in its view, were being penalized by both higher interest costs and the unavailability of bank credit. In fact, while security-loan demands bid rates upward, the Board was overimpressed with the idea that security loans absorbed credit from other uses. Credit was not absorbed or impounded by the stock market. Instead, brokers' and other security loans were channels for distribution of funds to businesses and investors throughout the country.

[21]Federal Reserve Act, Section 4, par. 8.

Finally, it was concerned lest high interest rates would adversely affect the economies of foreign countries. More specifically, it feared that funds would be drained from foreign money markets, and that the gold standard—especially in the sterling area—would be threatened.[22]

In order to forestall a repetition of the speculative excesses of 1928-1929, Congress granted the Board authority in 1933-1934 to apply selective control to security loan credit.[23] This mainly took the form of setting margin requirements on loans secured by stocks. Notable increases in these requirements were made in 1936, 1945, 1958, and 1968, when the Board desired to curb excessive speculation.

Still another aim that has always more or less influenced Federal Reserve policy has been international financial cooperation. One evidence of such cooperation was the maintenance of easy credit conditions in order to assist many countries in returning to, or adhering to, the gold standard after World War I. The liberal credit policies in both 1924 and 1927 were, in part, motivated by this purpose. Another method of assistance was by direct loans to foreign central banks. Many such loans, ranging between $100 and $1,000 million, have been made since the first one to the Bank of England in 1925. The best illustration of international financial cooperation is the reciprocal currency arrangements of the Fed with other central banks. Established in 1962 with only a few central banks and with total arrangements of under $1 billion, this network had grown by March 1970 to 15 central banks with total arrangements of $11 billion.[24] The largest swap line of credit was $2 billion with the Bank of England, under which either central bank can draw on the other for that amount to support its international reserve position. Rather active use of these lines has occurred in every year since 1962 for the purpose of stabilizing the international monetary system.

Finally, the Board has summarized its postwar interpretation of objectives as follows: "Today it is generally understood that the primary purpose of the System is to foster growth at high levels of employment, with a stable dollar in the domestic economy and with over-all balance in our international payments."[25]

There is no solid reason why the broad objectives of monetary policy should not be spelled out more precisely in the Federal Reserve Act in place of existing directives that are so broad as to be almost meaningless. The monetary authorities could then follow a well-marked highway instead of an uncertain wilderness trail. The dangers of taking a by-path such as supporting U.S. security prices and tolerating price inflation would, thereby, be greatly reduced.

[22]Federal Reserve Board, *Annual Report* (Washington, D.C., 1928), pp. 7-8; 1929, pp. 2-4.
[23]Banking Act of 1933; Securities Exchange Act of 1934.
[24]*Federal Reserve Bulletin* (March 1970), pp. 225-245.
[25]Board of Governors of the Federal Reserve System, *The Federal Reserve System: Purposes and Functions* (5th ed.; Washington, D.C., 1963), p. 2.

D *Employment Act of 1946*/ Passage of the Employment Act of 1946 marked an epoch in the definition of goals of the economy and in the establishment of federal responsibility for achieving them. The broad declaration of policy was, as follows:

> The Congress hereby declares that it is the continuing policy and responsibility of the Federal Government to use all practicable means consistent with its needs and obligations and other essential considerations of national policy, with the assistance and cooperation of industry, agriculture, labor, and state and local governments, to coordinate and utilize all its plans, functions, and resources for the purpose of creating and maintaining, in a manner calculated to foster and promote free competitive enterprise and the general welfare, conditions under which there will be afforded useful employment opportunities, including self-employment, for those able, willing, and seeking to work, and to promote maximum employment, production, and purchasing power.[26]

This statement of general policy embodies several strands which merit separation and comment. (1) There is the idea of *maximum employment*. That this means voluntary, rather than compulsory employment is indicated by the phrase, "there will be afforded useful employment opportunities . . . for those able, willing, and seeking to work." Definition of maximum employment is left to the Executive Branch and to Federal Reserve authorities. (2) The concept of *maximum production* goes beyond maximum employment by implying the promotion of efficiency of both management and labor. Business stability is implied as a by-product of maximum employment and production. Economic growth is also implied, although it is not explicitly stated. (3) These ends are to be sought "in a manner calculated to foster and promote free competitive enterprise." Thus, a philosophy of individual freedom is implied—a free economy as opposed to collectivism in any form. (4) The stated goals are to be attained by "all practicable means consistent with its needs and obligations and other essential considerations of national policy." That is, although important, these goals are not to be reached at any cost. (5) The meaning of "maximum purchasing power" is not clear. If real purchasing power is indicated, the concept might be regarded as synonymous with *maximum production*, and therefore repetitious. If GNP in dollars is meant, the implication is a highly inflationary one and is inconsistent with a stable dollar. (6) The goal of price-level stability is not mentioned.

discretionary authority versus rules

A sharp difference of opinion exists about whether the monetary authorities should be given broad discretion in the determination of policies, or

[26]Employment Act of 1946, Section 2.

whether they should be completely guided by an appropriate, nondiscretionary legal rule. The Federal Reserve Act was based on the former view, and the Board of Governors has always officially adhered to this philosophy. Because of the complexity and ever-changing character of the economy, it has taken the position that no fixed statutory rule nor automatic method can be devised that will apply to the future. It holds that there is no substitute for good judgment and discretion.[27]

In reaching a decision on the proper monetary policy, the authorities need to have all relevant information at hand. This includes, among other things, employment and unemployment statistics, labor hours, indexes of production, trade and distribution data, inventories, new orders, unfilled orders, savings, investment, government expenditures, national income data, changes in gold stock, amount of money, velocity of money, bank loans and investments, reserve position of Federal Reserve Banks and commercial banks, indexes of commodity prices, wage rates, interest rates, new security issues, federal debt and financial position, and international trade and financial information.

Monetary economists have, in general, supported this view of the Board, but it is not shared by an important minority, whose original leaders in the 1930s were Professors Lloyd W. Mints and Henry C. Simons of the University of Chicago. Their argument may be summarized as follows:

1/Bank-credit expansion has created more money in prosperous years and its contraction has reduced the money stock in bad years, with the result that booms and depressions have been greatly magnified. That is, money has had a perverse influence on business stability.

2/The record of the monetary authorities reveals gross policy errors which have contributed to instability at times, rather than to stability. Examples are the failure to take vigorous expansionary steps during the 1929-1933 period, the inflationary support of U.S. security prices during the 1946-1951 period, and permitting the money stock and Federal Reserve credit to expand excessively in 1968—at annual rates of 7.3 percent and 10.3 percent, respectively—while price inflation was gaining momentum. The inaccuracy of economic forecasts and the fallibility of any group of men make the granting of discretionary authority unwise.

3/A healthy environment for private enterprise requires monetary stability and certainty. The normal risks of enterprise are enough without having to add those of inflation and deflation, and of uncertainties about future monetary policies.

[27]For example, in a statement to the Chairman of the Senate Committee on Agriculture and Forestry in 1937, the Board stated: "...the broader objective of maximum-sustainable utilization of the Nation's resources cannot be achieved by attempting to maintain a fixed level of prices, and ... therefore, price stability should not be the sole or principal objective of monetary policy.... Inasmuch as the management of the country's monetary system is not an exact science, since it involves forecasting and dealing with many uncertainties, it is essential in determining an objective to leave scope for judgment and discretion." *Federal Reserve Bulletin* (September 1937), pp. 827-828.

4/What is most needed is a simple, definite, and appropriate rule to guide the actions of the monetary authorities. Businesses would then know what to expect in the monetary field, and they could make plans with added confidence.

5/Stabilization of the price level is the monetary guide most widely advocated by this group, but certain other rules would be acceptable. More important than the particular rule (among several possibilities) is the certainty of having a definite, practicable rule.

6/A private-enterprise economy is inherently stable in nature if monetary disturbances are removed. Stabilization of the price level would also create, as a by-product, relative business stability.

7/Stabilization of the price level would be brought about by changes in the amount of money. To this end, the monetary authority would be given more precise and direct control of the stock of money than it now possesses. A 100 percent legal reserve against deposits, instead of the present fractional reserve system, is often advocated.[28]

nondiscretionary rules: the monetarists

Building on the general philosophy of Mints and Simon, a new school of thought evolved whose members have become known as "monetarists." The leader is Professor Milton Friedman of the University of Chicago.[29] Their principal thesis is that change in the rate of growth (decline) in the stock of money is the predominant factor governing variations in the levels of output, employment, and prices. This view diametrically opposes that of the Keynesian school, which was widely accepted between the late 1930s and 1950s: that "money doesn't matter" much more than other types of assets, and that changes in its amount affect income and prices only indirectly through its influence on interest rates. The intellectual basis for the monetarist position is a monumental historical and analytical study published in 1963.[30] Professor Friedman concluded in this study that "peaks in the rate of change in the stock of money tend to precede peaks in general business by about 16 months and troughs in the rate of change in the stock of money to precede troughs in general business by about 12 months."[31] However, there was wide variability among specific cycles

[28]See Mints, op. cit.; also see Henry C. Simons, "Rules Versus Authorities in Monetary Policy," *Journal of Political Economy,* XLIV (1936), pp. 1-30.

[29]Other prominent members are Leonall C. Anderson; Research Department, Federal Reserve Bank of St. Louis; Professor Karl Brunner, Ohio State University; Phillip D. Cagan, National Bureau of Economic Research; Keith M. Carlson, Research Department, Federal Reserve Bank of St. Louis; David I. Fand, Wayne State University; Jerry L. Jordan, Research Department, Federal Reserve Bank of St. Louis; E. James Meigs, Vice President, First National City Bank; and Professor Allan Meltzer, Carnegie-Mellon University. Clark Warburton, formerly Economist, Federal Deposit Insurance Corporation, is also a monetarist, but his views differ importantly from those of the Chicago school.

[30]Milton Friedman and Anna J. Schwartz, *A Monetary History of the United States, 1867-1960* (New York: National Bureau of Economic Research, 1963).

[31]Milton Friedman, *A Program for Monetary Stability* (New York: Fordham University Press, 1960), p. 87.

in the lead of monetary changes–between 6 and 29 months at peaks and between 4 and 22 months at troughs. Thus, having observed that an increase in the rate of growth of money has always preceded periods of economic expansion and price inflation, and that a decrease in the rate of growth (or an absolute decline) in the stock of money has preceded periods of business contraction and price deflation, the next step logically followed: to stabilize the rate of growth of money as a means of producing business and price stability.

The monetary rule that Professor Friedman proposes is that the stock of money be increased month-by-month at a rate that will produce a relatively stable price level. The rate applied should take into account the rate of economic growth and the trend in the velocity of money. Over the past century, this would have required annual monetary growth of just over 4 percent–a little more than 3 percent to allow for growth in production, and 1 percent to offset a secular decline in the velocity of money. On the basis of this evidence, Professor Friedman estimates that for the intermediate future an annual monetary growth rate of between 3 and 5 percent would roughly stabilize the price level. The definition of money he utilizes includes currency outside banks and demand and time deposits of commercial banks. If the narrower definition of currency plus demand deposits were employed, a somewhat lower annual growth rate for money would be consistent with a stable price level, say, about 3 percent. Whether money is defined broadly or narrowly is not vital, according to Friedman; the important thing is that a reasonably acceptable monetary aggregate be increased at a steady rate. Elimination of the wide swings in the rate of monetary changes, which have characterized the past, is the main objective. Only in this way can the cyclical fluctuation of business and prices, produced by the preceding monetary swings, be stabilized.

Underlying the monetarists' philosophy is the hypothesis that a private, capitalistic economy with relatively free markets tends strongly toward stability at capacity production. This view is in conflict with the traditional one held by the majority of economists and by our monetary authorities: that cyclical swings in the economy are self-generating and inevitable, and that a major function of the Fed is to "lean against the wind"–that is, to reduce the rate of growth (or the amount) of money during expansionary periods, and to increase the rate of growth during periods of economic contraction. Friedman believes that this cyclical stop-go policy of the Fed has been a major destabilizing force, with the current policy creating a cyclical response after an average lag of some 12 to 16 months. He also holds that in the present state of knowledge we are unable to predict economic conditions a year or more ahead with enough accuracy to know what monetary actions should be taken today. This leads to his conclusion that a rule calling for a proper, steady increase in the amount of money will better serve ultimate objectives than the discretionary actions of Federal Reserve authorities.

Some members of the monetarist school, while in general agreement with Professor Friedman, would apply the rule more flexibly over time. That is, they would attempt to keep the chosen monetary aggregate within a predetermined range by quarters or half-years, rather than by months. This method would permit the Fed some discretion in regard to short-term changes in interest rates, member bank borrowing, and net reserve position of the banks.[32]

Those who oppose the monetarist view do so for a wide variety of reasons. Space precludes more than summary identification. First, adherents of the Keynesian school, which is large, are not impressed. Money plays a rather minor role in their system, and they rely mainly on fiscal policy as a method of economic stabilization. Another group of non-Keynesian neoclassicists is unable to accept the predominant position of money in the economy. They recognize its unique importance as an asset, but believe that many other factors that influence output and prices must be given due consideration. In particular, they emphasize the cyclical significance of the forces that govern the velocity of money, and note that in past cycles the percentage variations of velocity have usually exceeded those of money. They also stress the effects of changes in consumer tastes, industrial technology, and prevailing psychology on the levels of output and prices. In general, they regard the monetarist approach to be an oversimplification of a highly complex set of forces. Hence, they prefer that Federal Reserve authorities be given discretion in the determination of proper monetary policies—based on continuous analysis of all relevant factors, including money, and guided by the broad objectives of the economy. In their judgment, this approach, rather than a rigid rule, provides the best hope of achieving stable economic growth and a steady price level.

SUMMARY AND CONCLUSIONS

The broad objectives of the economy are: (1) full employment of labor and other resources; (2) stable employment and production; (3) healthy economic growth; (4) economic and equitable distribution of income, which requires a relatively stable price level; and (5) a favorable environment for a vigorous economy, which calls for (a) effective representative government, (b) private competitive enterprise, (c) unbiased government regulation of business and labor, (d) protection of natural and human resources, and (e) international cooperation, including reasonable equilibrium in the international balance of payments. While some conflict among these basic goals exists, it is not very serious from a practical standpoint if each goal is realistically interpreted.

These basic goals of the economy provide the principal criteria for guidance of monetary management. Monetary policies should always promote them and be consistent with them, although their contribution is a facilitating one in regard to the rate of economic expansion and the general environment of political and economic freedom. Frequently, the desirability of international

[32]For example, see Allan H. Meltzer, "Controlling Money," Federal Reserve Bank of St. Louis, *Review* (May 1969), pp. 16-24.

cooperation modifies monetary policies. This was true in the 1920s, when we wished to assist other nations in returning to gold. It was the case during both World Wars, when war finance became dominant; and it has been true in the postwar period with the necessities of free-world leadership, foreign military and economic aid, and since 1959, the outflow of gold associated with the current deficit in the balance of payments.

When a nation adopts a nondiscretionary monetary rule, or standard, it becomes the primary guide. The authorities cannot directly pursue the basic economic goals, but must proceed according to plan with the hope that these objectives will indirectly be realized. Good examples of this proposition are the automatic international gold standard and the stable-price-level standard. Once such a standard is established, the job of the authorities is to live by the rules and to maintain the standard in accordance with the law.

Under special circumstances, adherence to a managed gold standard may not conflict appreciably for long periods with full employment or the stability of business and prices. This was the case after our return to gold in 1934 and until 1958. Devaluation and the huge gold inflow that followed gave us much more gold than was needed to support the monetary system. Although the money supply nearly trebled during World War II and bank credit expansion continued during the postwar years, it was not until 1959-1970 that our gold standard came into practical conflict with basic objectives. By that time, the balances of payments of other leading nations had become readjusted and their moneys were rather freely convertible into dollars. The previous dollar shortage of foreign countries was transformed to a dollar surplus. Between the end of 1949 and December 1966, gold reserves and dollar holdings of foreign countries and international organizations rose from $18.7 billion to $61.7 billion.[33] Meanwhile, the U.S. gold stock declined slowly from $24.6 billion in 1949 to $22.8 billion at the end of 1957. Thereafter, it dropped steadily to $10.5 billion in April 1968 as a consequence of the substantial deficit in the balance of payments in each year after 1957. The upshot of these developments was that the gold problem became the leading monetary and fiscal issue facing Congress, the Administration, and the Federal Reserve authorities in 1961-1963. Should the balance-of-payments deficit and the gold outflow be attacked by a firm policy leading to rising interest rates, and by a surplus in the federal budget? Or should the existing business recession, excessive unemployment, and the unsatisfactory rate of growth be opposed by easy money and a federal deficit? This was the dilemma. In the end, Congress resolved the issue by eliminating gold-reserve requirements of the Fed Banks in March 1968, thereby removing the restraints of gold on monetary expansion and on the domestic economy.

The monetary criteria provided by Congress are contained in the Gold Acts of 1900 and 1934, the Federal Reserve Act, and the Employment Act of 1946. Under the Gold Acts, the dollar is defined as a fixed weight of gold, and

[33]*Federal Reserve Bulletin* (April 1967), p. 667.

other legal-tender moneys are to be kept at parity with the gold dollar.

The Federal Reserve Act states only the vaguest criteria, such as "sound credit conditions," the "accommodation of commerce, industry and agriculture," and prevention of "injurious credit expansion or contraction." It would be a constructive forward step if the Act were amended to give the Board more precise and basic criteria in terms of high-level employment and output, economic stability, reasonable growth, and a steady price level.

The Employment Act of 1946 proclaims a general policy of fostering "maximum employment, production, and purchasing power" and "free competitive enterprise." Lacking, however, is explicit recognition of the goals of stability of employment, stability of the price level, and economic growth. These basic objectives should be added by amendment.

The controversy in regard to whether the monetary authorities should be allowed wide discretion in the determination of policies, or whether they should be guided by a simple, definite rule, is one that is destined to continue. Experience in this and other countries may eventually provide the basis for a more confident answer. As previously indicated, the most pressing task is a more precise and complete statement of goals and criteria to guide the authorities. When this is done, the best end result will doubtless be realized by able authorities exercising judgment in policy determination. This approach provides for needed flexibility to meet changing conditions, but more plainly marks the boundaries of discretion.

REFERENCES

The American Assembly, Columbia University, *The Report of the President's Commission on National goals* (Englewood Cliffs, N.J.: Prentice-Hall, 1960).

Board of Governors of the Federal Reserve System, annual reports.

Commission on Money and Credit, *Report on Money and Credit* (Englewood Cliffs, N.J.: Prentice-Hall, 1961), chap. 2.

Edwards, Edgar O., ed., *The Nation's Economic Objectives* (Chicago: University of Chicago Press, 1964).

Friedman, Milton, *A Program for Monetary Stability* (New York: Fordham University Press, 1960).

Friedman, Milton, "The Role of Monetary Policy," *The American Economic Review,* LVIII (March 1968), pp. 1-17.

Friedman, Milton, and Anna J. Schwartz, *A Monetary History of the United States, 1867-1960* (New York: National Bureau of Economic Research, 1963).

Horvitz, Paul M., *Monetary Policy and the Financial System,* (Englewood Cliffs, N.J.: Prentice-Hall, 1969), chap. 23.

Mayer, Thomas, *Monetary Policy in the United States* (New York: Random House, 1968).

Mints, Lloyd W., *Monetary Policy in a Competitive Society* (New York: McGraw-Hill, 1950).

Simons, Henry C., "Rules Versus Authorities in Monetary Policy," *Journal of Political Economy,* XLIV (1936), pp. 1-30.

U.S. Congress, Hearings before the Subcommittee on Economic Stabilization of the Joint Committee on the Economic Report, 83rd Congress, 2nd sess., pursuant to Sec. 5(a), Public Law 304, especially pp. 3-30.

U.S. Congress, Senate, *Report of the Joint Economic Committee,* "Standards for Guiding Monetary Action" (Washington, D.C., 1968).

13

general instruments of monetary management: discount mechanism

The broad economic goals just discussed require careful and thoughtful definition, and they should always provide the basis for wise decisions in action. But they are of little practical significance unless they can be made effective by various means. This chapter and those that follow are mainly concerned with means and methods of implementation of objectives. Monetary instruments are of two types: general and selective. In turn, the general instruments divide into three categories: (1) the discount mechanism, (2) open-market operations, and (3) changes in legal-reserve requirements. All three methods bring their influence to bear mainly on the flow of spending (total monetary demand) by altering the liquidity—and thereby the money-creating power—of commercial banks. When monetary demand is inadequate, it should be stimulated; when excessive, it should be curbed; when correct, it should be maintained.

THE DISCOUNT MECHANISM

The discount mechanism of the Fed was looked upon by its founders as the main contribution of the new central-banking system. In their view, the former inelasticity of currency and reserve money would be eliminated by the opportunity of member banks to borrow from Federal Reserve Banks in case of need, and to repay indebtedness when the need subsided. Federal Reserve credit would be lent at a price—the discount rate—which would be varied to govern its cost. Thus, there were two strings on this new instrument: (1) administration (rationing) of Reserve credit lent to member banks and (2) the price at which such credit would be extended. Discount policies of ease or restraint could be applied by tuning one or both of the strings. While new in this country, these techniques had long been employed by foreign central banks, notably the Bank of England.

federal reserve credit administration

Under the Federal Reserve Act, each Reserve Bank is authorized to:

> extend to each member bank such discounts, advancements, and accommodations as may be safely and reasonably made with due regard for the claims and demands of other member banks, the maintenance of sound credit conditions, and the accommodation of commerce, industry and agriculture. . . . Each Federal Reserve Bank shall keep itself informed of the general character and amount of the loans and investments of its member banks with a view to ascertaining whether undue use is being made of bank credit for the speculative carrying of or trading in securities, real estate, or commodities, or for any other purpose inconsistent with the maintenance of sound credit conditions; and in determining whether to grant or refuse advances, rediscount or other credit accommodations, the Federal Reserve Bank shall give consideration to such information.[1]

The Board of Governors is empowered to prescribe regulations with respect to the use of discount facilities, and it has done so in Regulation A. It also has power to deny discounts and advances to member banks which make undue use of Reserve Bank credit.

There are three ways by which a member bank may borrow from its Reserve Bank: (1) by discounting eligible customers' notes and commercial paper; (2) by giving its own promissory note secured by collateral consisting of eligible customers' notes and commercial paper, U.S. securities and other securities eligible for purchase by the Reserve Banks; and (3) by giving its own promissory note secured by satisfactory, though ineligible, assets.

1/The first method was the only one originally available. It requires a definition of "eligible" commercial paper, which is provided, in general terms, by the Federal Reserve Act and is interpreted more specifically in regulations of the Board of Governors. In general, eligible paper includes notes and drafts (including bankers' acceptances) which are drawn to finance the short-term working capital needs of business and agriculture. It includes neither paper that finances fixed investments such as land and buildings, nor paper that finances speculative transactions such as carrying or trading in stocks. To be eligible, the maturity of business paper at the time of discount is limited to 90 days, and that of agricultural paper to 9 months.[2] Thus, in order to borrow in this manner, a

[1]Federal Reserve Act, Section 4, par. 8.

[2]Board of Governors of the Federal Reserve System, Regulation A, February 15, 1955 revision, Section 3.

member bank must endorse a batch of eligible customers' notes of varying amounts and maturities and send them to the Reserve Bank. The proceeds of the discount operation are credited to the member's legal-reserve account. Each note must then be returned before maturity by the Reserve Bank so that collection can be made. This process is so cumbersome that banks borrow in this manner only in exceptional cases.

2/In practice, almost all borrowing at Reserve Banks is done by the second method; that is, by the banks' promissory notes secured by U.S. securities or other securities eligible for purchase by the Banks.[3] This method was made possible by an amendment to the Federal Reserve Act in 1916, designed to enable members to borrow conveniently for short periods. The greater part of borrowing is done to correct a temporary deficiency in legal reserves, and therefore has a maturity of only a few days or weeks. Member banks usually place enough U.S. securities in safekeeping at the Reserve Bank to cover the probable limit of borrowing. Then it is a simple matter to instruct the Reserve Bank to use these securities as collateral for a note of the desired amount. When signed promissory notes are on file at the Reserve Bank, a telephone call of instructions is all that is usually required to arrange for immediate Reserve credit. Advances of this type to member banks cannot be made for longer than 15 days, but when the collateral consists of eligible customers' notes and commercial paper, the maturity may be as long as 90 days.[4] Such advances may be renewed at maturity unless the member bank has been abusing its borrowing privilege. When the banks were under extreme liquidity pressure in 1969 and the first half of 1970, many of them held only enough U.S. securities to secure Treasury deposits. Under these circumstances they reverted to the use of eligible customer loans to secure their borrowing at the Reserve Banks.

3/During the worst of the Great Depression, the liquidity of many banks was so undermined that they no longer held U.S. securities or eligible paper, with the result that Reserve credit was not available when most needed. This emergency was met by an amendment, known as the Glass-Steagall Act, in February 1932, which raised the discount window to its top notch.[5] Reserve Banks were authorized to make advances for a period not exceeding four months on the basis of member banks' promissory notes secured by *satisfactory* collateral. This meant that any sound bank asset–including consumer loans, term loans, real-estate loans, and corporate bonds–could, in an emergency, be converted to legal reserves. Little use is ordinarily made of this method because

[3]A September 1968 amendment to the Federal Reserve Act broadened the definition of obligations eligible as collateral for advances to member banks to include all "such obligations as are eligible for purchase under Section 14(b) of the (Federal Reserve) Act." Regulation A was amended at the same time, interpreting the amendment to include direct Treasury securities, obligations guaranteed by the United States or an agency thereof, and municipal obligations issued in anticipation of taxes or assured revenues, and with a maturity not to exceed six months. Board of Governors of the Federal Reserve System, *Annual Report* (Washington, D.C., 1968), pp. 93-94.

[4]Federal Reserve Act, Section 13, par. 8.

[5]Federal Reserve Act, Section 10(b).

such advances bear a penalty discount rate not less than $\frac{1}{2}$ percent above the regular rate. Nevertheless, it is an important standby facility both for the banks and for the economy as a whole. Member banks have greater assurance of Reserve Bank support in the event of currency hoarding or other drains on their reserves. Businesses and consumers have less reason to harbor fears of a general liquidity crisis.

Regardless of the method of borrowing, the Reserve Banks observe certain rules in the administration of discounts and advances. These principles have been succinctly stated.

> Access to the Federal Reserve discount facilities is granted as a privilege of membership in the Federal Reserve System in the light of the following general guiding principles.
>
> Federal Reserve credit is generally extended on a short-term basis to a member bank in order to enable it to adjust its asset position when necessary because of developments such as a sudden withdrawal of deposits or seasonal requirements for credit beyond those which can reasonably be met by use of the bank's own resources. Federal Reserve credit is also available for longer periods when necessary in order to assist member banks in meeting unusual situations, such as may result from national, regional, or local difficulties or from exceptional circumstances involving only particular member banks. Under ordinary conditions, the continuous use of Federal Reserve credit by a member bank over a considerable period of time is not regarded as appropriate. In considering a request for credit accommodation, each Federal Reserve Bank gives due regard to the purpose of the credit and to its probable effects upon the maintenance of sound credit conditions, both as to the individual institution and the economy generally. It keeps informed of and takes into account the general character and amount of the loans and investments of the member bank. It considers whether the bank is borrowing principally for the purpose of obtaining a tax advantage or profiting from rate differentials and whether the bank is extending an undue amount of credit for the speculative carrying of or trading in securities, real estate, or commodities, or otherwise.[6]

Certain features of the foregoing statement of principles are worthy of note. Borrowing is viewed as a privilege, rather than an unqualified right. The application of a member for credit may be refused entirely, or in part, due either to the circumstances of the bank itself, or to a general system policy of restraint, as in 1966 and 1969. Improper use of Reserve credit includes undue extension of speculative credit, borrowing in order to profit from reinvesting in securities that yield more than the discount rate, borrowing to gain an income-tax advantage, and borrowing continuously for an extended period. Long-term borrowing is frowned upon except in emergencies, and is regarded as evidence

[6]Board of Governors of the Federal Reserve System, Regulation A, op. cit.

that a bank needs more capital funds, or that it should reduce its loans and investments. The approved borrowing transaction is to meet a temporary primary reserve deficiency. All this means that a member bank can usually borrow reasonable amounts for approved purposes provided it holds adequate collateral in the form of U.S. securities, eligible notes of customers, or other eligible securities. The first request for funds is almost never refused. But it also means that a member faces uncertainty in regard to continued Federal Reserve support during periods when the general monetary policy is a restrictive one. In general, discounts and advances represent the release of Reserve Bank credit with strings in contrast with open-market operations which release it without strings.

fed bank discount rate

In addition to Reserve credit rationing, the discount mechanism includes the complementary instrument, discount-rate changes—that is, regulation of the cost of borrowed reserves. The Federal Reserve Act requires each Reserve Bank to establish the discount rate for its district every 14 days, or sooner if deemed necessary by the Board of Governors. Because the rate is also subject to the Board's review and determination, the final authority rests with it in case of dispute.[7] In the early experience of the Fed, varying rates often applied to different classes of paper, and rates varied among the Federal Reserve districts. But the drift since the 1920s has been toward uniformity of the discount rate both within and between districts. Exceptions to this rule, however, have occurred from time to time. For example, a preferential rate was established during World War II on advances secured by Treasury obligations maturing within one year; also, rate changes have sometimes been initiated in one, or a few, districts rather than being made simultaneously in all.

The theory of the discount rate is relatively simple; it rests on an assumed elasticity of demand for bank loans and on cost-price relationships. When the rate is raised, member banks tend to reduce their borrowed reserves because of the higher cost. A reduction of primary reserves, in turn, requires a several-fold contraction of bank loans and investments and, thereby, of deposits. This process takes place by restrictive loan policies, higher loan rates which reduce customer loan demands, and the sale of investments to nonbank investors. Expenditures of businesses and consumers are restrained by reduction in the stock of money and by higher interest rates, and the higher rates also provide a greater incentive to save. It should be stressed, however, that effectiveness of a rise in the discount rate depends on conditions in the money market. When large excess reserves exist, as in the 1930s and until 1951, there is little or no occasion for borrowing, so that the level of the discount rate is of small concern to the banks. But when the volume of borrowed reserves is

[7]Federal Reserve Act, Section 14, par. 5.

substantial, members are sensitive to rate changes and the discount rate is said to be "effective."

The response of member banks to the discount rate depends more on its position in the structure of money rates than on its absolute level. If it is raised well above the yield on short-term Treasury obligations, members strive to repay Reserve Bank indebtedness, and are likely to sell Treasury bills and other short-term securities to do so. This, in turn, raises yields (lowers prices) on these securities, and the effects are transmitted to competitive securities throughout the market. However, when the discount rate is appreciably below the yields on short-term Treasury obligations, the banks have a profit motive for borrowing, which becomes stronger as the rate differential widens. When confronted with a primary-reserve deficiency, they are more inclined to borrow than to sell liquidity reserves. Some banks may attempt to go one step further by borrowing to buy short-term U.S. securities and tax-exempt municipals. Under these circumstances, the task of Reserve Bank credit administration becomes very difficult. Illustrations of this situation may be drawn from 1959, 1966, and 1969, when yields on short-term Treasury obligations exceeded the discount rate (see figure 4, p. 80). Thus, it is true that member banks are deterred from borrowing not so much by the absolute height of the discount rate as by a high discount rate in relation to yields on short-term U.S. securities and other liquid investments.

A sharp difference of opinion exists with respect to the elasticity of demand for loans by businesses and consumers as interest rates rise and fall. Some economists take the position that within the usual range of rate changes, loan demands are highly inelastic. That is, borrowers may demand almost as much credit at 8 percent as at 4 percent. This argument is based on the fact that interest is, in general, a small part of total costs, and particularly so in the presence of high income-tax rates. Despite these facts, other authorities hold the view that a high loan rate remains a strong deterrent to a fringe of borrowers, especially in certain fields. They contend that an important effect arises from the decline in prices of all long-lived income bearing assets as interest rates increase. These prices gravitate toward an amount represented by their net income capitalized at the prevailing rate of return (risk included) on the particular type of asset. For example, a rental property whose net income in a year is $1,000 would be worth $20,000 if the income is capitalized at 5 percent, but only $16,667 if the income is capitalized at 6 percent. When the cost of building a comparable new property is $19,000, an investor or enterpriser might decide to build if the prevailing rate is 5 percent, but to purchase an existing property if the rate is 6 percent. Perhaps, as usual, the truth in regard to the elasticity of the demand for credit lies between these two extremes. The fields in which loan demands are most interest-elastic are those in which long-term borrowing is necessary and the interest cost is substantial, such as residential construction and the building and equipping of public utility and industrial plants.

Because the influence of lowering the Federal Reserve discount rate is, in general, just the reverse of raising it, only a summary is required. In a period of business expansion, reduction of the rate—especially when it is below the yields on short-term Treasury issues—encourages member banks to borrow. The added increment to primary reserves forms the basis for a multiple expansion of earnings assets and deposits—that is, for an increase in the stock of money. This expansion process develops as lower interest rates and a larger supply of bank reserves combine to encourage borrowing and lending. Expenditures of businesses and consumers are also stimulated with a consequent spur to employment, production, and prices. But during a period of business decline and mounting pessimism, there is little response to lowering the discount rate. Instead of borrowing, businesses and consumers strive to repay indebtedness. This, combined with the return of currency from circulation, enables banks to repay borrowings from the Federal Reserve and to accumulate excess primary reserves. Under these conditions, they are unlikely to borrow even at a very low discount rate, and the rate is said to be "ineffective." Nevertheless, readily available credit at low rates fosters recovery and diminishes the impact of the deflationary forces at work.

In general, the Federal Reserve discount rate has not been used as an aggressive instrument of monetary management, as evidenced by the facts that it has seldom been raised to a penalty level, and that it has typically lagged three or more months behind changes in open-market money rates. For example, the money-rate structure may move upward, in response to increased credit demands and reduced bank liquidity, until the discount rate is well below its usual position in the structure. When the Reserve authorities are convinced that the higher structure has some permanence, they are likely to raise the discount rate to its normal relationship. Illustrations of this process are provided by the rising interest-rate periods, 1966 and 1969, and by the declining rate period in 1967, when lagging adjustments were made in the discount rate. The range within which adjustments of the discount rate usually occur is between the rate on three-month Treasury bills, which averages about $\frac{3}{8}$ percent below it, and the rate on 4-6-month open-market commercial paper, which averages about $\frac{3}{8}$ percent above it. When the bill rate rises to or above the discount rate, an upward adjustment of the latter is likely; and when the commercial-paper rate declines to, or below, the discount rate, a downward adjustment of the latter is usually made. An exception to these relationships existed during the inflationary period 1966-1970, when both the Treasury bill rate and the commercial-paper rate were well above the discount rate (see figure 4, p. 80).

There has been considerable confusion in regard to what levels of the discount rate represent a neutral, penalty, or premium position. A neutral rate may be defined as one that, in general, neither encourages nor discourages borrowing by member banks. A penalty rate places the cost of borrowing high enough to be regarded as a losing operation by most banks, while a premium rate sets the cost low enough to make borrowing profitable. In the early experience of the Fed, many held the view that in order to be neutral the rate should be the same as that realized by member banks on their loans and discounts eligible for rediscount at Reserve Banks. This idea was in part based on the assumption that the proceeds of the reserve borrowing were used by member banks for similar purposes. Experience proved this assumption to be unrealistic. Some banks might borrow to make high-yielding speculative loans; others to buy U.S. or other securities. Another erroneous aspect of this view was that a neutral rate meant equality between the discount rate and the gross, instead of the net, rate of return on loans. The facts were disregarded that a bank must make an allowance for loan risks, and that there are service and other costs involved in making loans. In view of these costs, a neutral discount rate is appreciably below (between 1 and 2 percent) the average rate on customer loans.

The most realistic conception of a neutral discount rate in normal times is in terms of riskless liquidity reserve assets, the sale or purchase of which represents alternatives to borrowing or repaying Reserve Bank credit. When the rate is equal to the prevailing yield on such assets there is little or no profit incentive either to borrow or to repay Reserve credit. When the rate is above these yields with allowance for investment costs, it is in a *penalty* position; that is, banks with deficient primary reserves gain by selling liquidity reserve assets instead of borrowing at the Reserve Bank. When the rate is below these yields with allowance for investment costs, it is in a *premium* position; that is, there exists a profit incentive to borrow. Banks that are already in debt may delay repayment, or even try to borrow more. Those with no indebtedness may seek to borrow with a view to investing at a higher yield. Because the great bulk of liquidity reserve assets of commercial banks consists of short-term U.S. securities, the relative position of the discount rate can best be judged in terms of yields on Treasury bills, and short-term notes.

However, under conditions of inflationary expansion, when loan and investment opportunities of the banks are especially inviting, the most realistic conception of a penalty discount rate is one that neutralizes the prospective profit from these tempting commitments. That is, the discount rate must be high enough, allowing for loan and investment costs, to discourage materially the expansion of loans and the purchase of tax-exempt securities. The fact that the Reserve authorities fixed the discount rate at a premium (relatively low) level during the inflationary period 1965-1970 explains the rigid rationing at the discount window and the relatively small amount of member-bank borrowing in those years.

theories of member-bank borrowing

There are two distinct theories of member-bank borrowing, which are often labeled the profit theory and the need theory. The *profit* theory is based on the proposition that member banks borrow from Reserve Banks when it is profitable to do so, and strive to repay when use of the borrowed reserves promises no profit, or perhaps a loss. That is, the cost of borrowing is regarded as an important determinant of its amount. But emphasis is placed on the *relative* level of the discount rate rather than on its *absolute* level. When open-market rates on liquidity reserve assets (now mainly short-term U.S. securities) are above the discount rate, Federal Reserve funds are cheap, with the result that banks are disposed to repair reserve deficiencies by borrowing rather than by selling secondary reserves. Conversely, when yields on liquidity reserve assets are below the discount rate, Federal Reserve funds are dear, so that banks tend to adjust reserve deficiencies by selling liquidity reserves rather than by borrowing. This theory contemplates active use of the discount rate as an instrument of monetary control. The amount of member-bank borrowing would be restricted by raising the rate, just as demand for any commodity is reduced by raising its price. Borrowing would be encouraged by lowering the rate. In applying this theory, nonprice rationing of Reserve credit would not be attempted, or would be held to a minimum. In general, sound member banks could borrow reasonable amounts at the quoted rate, provided the contemplated use of the proceeds would not impair their safety or liquidity. This theory of cost-price guidance of the volume of member-bank borrowing resembles the traditional one that was applied by the Bank of England and other foreign central banks long before the Fed was established.

In contrast, the *need* theory minimizes the importance and use of the discount rate. Member banks are said to borrow at Reserve Banks when they need reserve money and to repay when the need no longer exists, regardless of whether the discount rate is high or low. The profit motive for borrowing, according to this view, has been largely destroyed by a strong tradition against such indebtedness. The origin of this tradition antedates the Fed when most commercial banks on occasion borrowed primary reserves from large city correspondent banks. Because deposits (debts), rather than equity capital, are the principal source of a bank's funds, the officers were reluctant to contract additional debt and thereby weaken solvency. This attitude was reenforced by the attitude of depositors–especially corporate depositors–who looked upon correspondent borrowing as a sign of weakness. When the Fed was established, both the Board and the Reserve Banks strengthened this tradition, and have continued to do so. From the beginning, they developed the philosophy that Reserve Bank credit should normally be borrowed only for short-term adjustments; never for speculative purposes nor for long-term use, except in emergencies.

Since the early 1920s, Federal Reserve officials have proceeded largely on the basis of the need theory. The reluctance of member banks to borrow, or to remain long in debt to the Reserve Banks, has occupied a key position in implementing restrictive credit policies. Far more emphasis has been placed on regulating the volume of member-bank borrowing than on raising the discount rate. The typical restrictive procedure has been to create a deficiency in required reserves by open-market sales of U.S. securities by Reserve Banks. This has forced member banks to borrow in order to meet reserve requirements. But their reluctance to be in debt has usually led them to sell liquidity reserve assets and to adopt more restrictive loan policies. With the supply of loanable funds thus curtailed, open-market money rates and customers' loan rates have risen. The desired degree of firmness in the market has been gauged mainly by the amount of borrowing at the Reserve Banks, changes in bank loans and investments, changes in the amount of money, and the behavior of money rates. After the emergence of higher market rates by this process, the discount rate has then been raised from its premium (low) position to a neutral place in the new rate structure. The amount of member-bank borrowing has also been actively held in check at times, as in 1966 and 1969, by the rationing of Reserve Bank advances.

Sharp differences of opinion exist with respect to the validity of the need and profit theories of member-bank borrowing. The strongest case for the need theory was made by Winfield W. Riefler, an influential economist with the Board for over three decades and for many years assistant to the chairman of the Board of Governors.[8] In a study which has become a classic, he compared variations of open-market rates, Reserve Bank discount rates, and the volume of member-bank borrowings during the period 1917-1928. While correlation existed between open-market rates and Reserve Bank discount rates, it was not close, and there was a definite lag of discount rates. By contrast, correlation was high between open-market rates and the amount of member-bank borrowing at Reserve Banks. From this he concluded:

> Because of the hesitation of individual member banks in borrowing at the reserve banks and their prompt repayment of such borrowing as is necessary through withdrawals from the open markets, changes in aggregate volume of indebtedness at the reserve banks are the most important single factor in *fluctuations* of money rates in the market. The absolute volume of this indebtedness, furthermore, is one of the important factors in the level of money rates and probably the most important factor in the margin between money rates in the market and discount rates.[9]

Dr. Riefler recognized, however, that the profit theory was valid within limits, and that the Reserve Bank discount rate played an influential role. It affected the *level* of market rates, and also exerted a *stabilizing* influence on them through the lending, investing, and borrowing operations of member banks. That is, when market rates rose in relation to the discount rate, some member banks borrowed more than they otherwise would have borrowed, and the added supply of reserve money moderated the rise of market rates. The opposite was true when market rates declined in relation to the discount rate.

[8]Winfield W. Riefler, *Money Rates and Money Markets in the United States* (New York: Harper & Row, 1930).
[9]Ibid., p. 35.

Nevertheless, the far closer correlation between member-bank borrowing and open-market rates than between the Reserve Bank discount rate and open-market rates established Federal Reserve open-market operations as a much more important instrument of control than the discount rate. Purchase and sale of U.S. securities could be used to govern the amount of member-bank borrowing, and thereby to influence money-market and business conditions.[10]

The validity of the need theory has been roundly criticized by other authorities in three respects: (1) tradition against member-bank borrowing at the Reserve Banks is less potent than formerly; (2) reluctance to borrow is a variable and indeterminate factor; and (3) the term "need" is vague and difficult to define.

Several reasons are given in support of the view that tradition is no longer an important deterrent to member-bank borrowing. First, the belief is widespread among member banks that they are entitled to borrow from the Reserve Banks within reasonable limits if proper collateral can be furnished. One of the principal aims in establishing the Fed was to provide elasticity of currency and credit. The discount window, which originally accepted only eligible customer loans and commercial paper, has been opened to borrowing with U.S. securities and other satisfactory bank assets as collateral. Also, the technique of borrowing has become increasingly convenient, and the borrowing relationship has become less personal than it was under correspondent banking. Furthermore, many member banks feel that they have a right to borrow because their legal reserves are on deposit, and also because they own the stock of Reserve Banks. Second, it is pointed out that certain factors which restrain borrowing are often erroneously confused with the tradition against borrowing. One is the discount rate itself. Another is the cost of lending, which includes assuming risks of loss and the servicing of loans. Still another is the inertia of many banks to take advantage of loan and investment opportunities that arise because of a relatively low discount rate. A final one is the fact that banks sometimes fear that market rates will go higher, once they have moved upward. Consequently, they sell bonds before prices decline further, rather than borrow to meet reserve deficiencies.[11] Finally, the tradition against borrowing almost certainly became weaker during the period 1934-1951—nearly two decades when most banks had no occasion to borrow.

But even if the force of the reluctance factor be granted, it is contended that the variability and the indeterminate nature of this factor make it an undependable instrument of monetary management. In a period of prosperity, when an optimistic outlook prevails, banks become less reluctant to borrow. However, during major depressions, when liquidity and solvency requirements are of greater concern, they are more reluctant to assume indebtedness. Thus, the intensity of the reluctance factor varies perversely during the business cycle

[10]Ibid., pp. 33-34.
[11]See Robert C. Turner, *Member-Bank Borrowing* (Columbus: Ohio State University, 1938), pp. 75-82.

from the standpoint of monetary management. There is also a substantial difference in the degree of reluctance to borrow among the 5,800 member banks at any one time. Some have no reluctance whatever; others always refrain from borrowing as a matter of principle; and the rest fall between these extremes, but with a wide range of attitudes. Important differences exist on the bases of location and size. There is doubtless a stronger tradition against being in debt for long periods in the larger city banks than in small- and intermediate-size banks, particularly when the latter are located in agricultural regions.

Another aspect of dependence on the reluctance factor in monetary management arises in regard to the fractional-reserve feature of commercial banking. One dollar of member-bank legal reserve under average conditions forms the basis for a potential multiple expansion of bank earning assets and of deposits and currency of $4 or $5. If the nonreluctant banks borrow the initial dollar of reserves at Reserve Banks and expand their loans by that amount, the reluctant banks will then gain free reserves by favorable clearings and collections. They are likely to join in the expansion process even though they remain reluctant to borrow directly. To them, the new increment of reserves is non-borrowed and not unlike a similar amount released by open-market operations or a reduction in required reserves. Thus, the lack of uniformity among member banks regarding reluctance to borrow constitutes a serious limitation on the dependability of this factor as an instrument of monetary management.

When the term "borrowing for need" is analyzed, it becomes apparent that it is extremely vague, and that any definition of "need" must be an arbitrary one. The broadest sort of concept of need is implied by the statement that member banks borrow only when they need reserves, because of a deficiency that has developed. The deficiency may have arisen from a wide variety of underlying transactions, including currency withdrawals, gold exports, Federal Reserve policies, expansion of loans of any type, and purchase of securities of any kind. The narrowest concept of need is implied by the traditional view that bank earning assets should be restricted to short-term working-capital loans to business. In this context, borrowing to support consumer loans, security loans, real-estate loans, term loans to business, or to purchase bonds would be for profit, rather than for need. As a compromise, need might be given a variety of definitions between these two extremes. But in any case, the choice is based on some rather arbitrary conception of what is, and what is not, a proper commercial-bank asset.

The validity of the profit theory of member-bank borrowing during the period 1922-1938 was tested statistically in a valuable study by Robert C. Turner.[12] He found that a high correlation existed between the volume of member-bank borrowing and the profit spread between the Reserve Bank discount rate and short-term open-market money rates. That is, borrowings were usually high when the yields on open-market paper were high in relation to the

[12]Ibid. (complete volume).

discount rate, and borrowings were typically low when yields on open-market paper were low in relation to the discount rate. The short-term open-market rates were those on prime 4-6-month commercial paper, the renewal rate on stock-exchange call loans, and the rate on 60-90-day stock-exchange time loans. While this study failed to establish conclusively the fact that high open-market rates in relation to the discount rate *caused* increased borrowings, it nevertheless provided reason to believe that the profit theory had considerable validity as applied to bank administration of liquidity reserve assets. If applied to the postwar period, such a study should recognize the fact that U.S. securities have become the dominant type of liquidity reserve asset. Therefore, an analysis should be made of the relation between Fed borrowings and the spread between the discount rate and yields on short-term U.S. securities. Interpretation of the results, however, would be less conclusive than in the former periods in view of the much greater disposition of the Reserve Banks to ration advances to member banks.

In fact, a good case can be made for the view that since the Treasury-Federal Reserve Accord of March 1951, and especially since 1965, the discount mechanism, including the discount rate, has not been a method of monetary control at all. Rather, it has been a mechanism to protect individual member banks from liquidity hardships which may arise from a variety of causes—failure of the market system to provide perfect mobility of funds, day-to-day variations in liquidity needs, seasonal behavior of deposits and customer loan demands, cyclical fluctuations, and emergency conditions such as a long strike or a crop failure. To the extent that reserve money is released or withdrawn through the discount window as an accommodation to member banks, the Fed must compensate appropriately by its other general controls in order to achieve the desired rate of growth of money and bank credit and the desired conditions in the money market. Open-market operations, discussed in the next chapter, have been the principal compensating method, supported by changes in legal-reserve requirements to create the proper money market environment. In addition, changes in maximum interest rates payable by banks (Regulation Q) have been utilized since 1965, especially in 1966 and 1969. Further support for the view that the discount mechanism has not, in fact, been a method of monetary control is provided by the passive role of the discount rate and by the stringent administration of discounts and advances.

REFORM OF THE DISCOUNT MECHANISM

collateral for advances

For several years, the Board of Governors has recommended legislation authorizing Federal Reserve Banks to lend reserve money to member banks on sound, although ineligible, collateral without the penalty of a higher discount rate. Under present (1970) law, Reserve Banks can lend on any satisfactory collateral, but they must set the rate at least $\frac{1}{2}$ percentage point above the basic discount rate. In the Board's view, this is an inequitable penalty on those banks that hold sound assets, but have a scarcity of eligible assets because of special local or regional conditions, or because of a general liquidity squeeze. Also, the Board regards the existing law to be an unnecessary limitation on its ability under all conditions to provide for the legitimate credit needs of the economy.[13] Despite the Board's repeated recommendations, Congress has thus far failed to respond.

Most financial economists would endorse the foregoing proposal, and recommend, in addition, that collateral requirements for member-bank borrowing be removed from the Federal Reserve Act and be left to the discretion of the Reserve Banks. Although such requirements might have been justified in the early days of the Fed, they no longer serve a useful purpose. Moreover, they occasion unnecessary cost, inconvenience, and inequity among member banks. The risks of lending to member banks on an unsecured basis are certainly minimal, and constitute no threat to the solvency of the Reserve Banks. If a safeguard is needed at all, a much better one would be a prior lien on the assets of borrowing banks.

proposed redesign of the discount mechanism

A proposal for fundamental redesign of the discount mechanism was made by a Fed steering committee in July 1968. It was the outgrowth of extensive research beginning in 1965 by the staffs of the Board and the Banks as well as by academic economists, who together prepared over twenty valuable studies. The probable adoption of this proposal, perhaps with some refinements, when monetary policy becomes more expansionary, merits a summary of its provisions.

The essence of the proposal is to open the discount window a notch wider for accommodation of the short-term liquidity needs of member banks under conditions of certainty at a discount rate that would be adjusted closely to other competitive market rates. Short-term borrowing at the Reserve Banks, which traditionally has been an uncertain privilege, becomes a right within carefully defined limits. Also, equality of treatment of banks wishing to borrow is assured by guidelines which will be standardized and applied uniformly throughout the Federal Reserve System.

More specifically, discounts and advances are classified under three headings: (1) short-term adjustment credit, (2) seasonal credit accommodation, and (3) emergency credit assistance.

[13]Board of Governors of the Federal Reserve System, *Annual Report* (Washington, D.C., 1968), p. 337; 1969, p. 300.

Short-term adjustment credit has two components: (a) basic borrowing privilege and (b) other adjustment credit. Under the basic borrowing privilege, a firm line of credit for each member bank (a specified percentage of capital and surplus) will be established. Thus, the banks will be able to count on borrowing within this limit during half of the weeks of the preceding quarter (or half year). Other adjustment credit will be supplemental to the basic borrowing privilege, recognizing that under some circumstances member banks will need to borrow in larger amounts and for longer duration. This segment of borrowing will be subject to administrative discipline, but member banks will be able to expect satisfaction of their justifiable needs.

Seasonal credit accommodation is designed for banks whose deposits and customer loan demands vary widely during the year–for example, in one-crop agricultural regions and resort areas. A member bank that can demonstrate a need for specific amounts of seasonal liquidity will be given a firm commitment by the Reserve Bank over and above short-term adjustment credit. However, such credit will not be available if the period of need is too short or the amount is too small–more than four weeks, and a certain proportion of deposits (5 to 10 percent), respectively.

Emergency credit assistance has three facets: (a) lending to member banks, (b) lending to nonmember institutions, and (c) support of distressed financial markets. Under this heading, the Fed, as the ultimate source of liquidity, will recognize its responsibility to deal with emergency situations as they affect both member banks and the economy in general. Reserve credit will be provided promptly and sympathetically to member banks in emergencies after assurance from the chartering authority that the bank is solvent and that a promising solution is anticipated. However, such assistance will be under extensive administrative review. Lending to nonmember institutions–limited to depositary institutions except under the most extraordinary circumstances–will be approved only when the probable impact of failure threatens the economy's financial structure. Distressed markets will be supported by loans to member and nonmember banks as well as by open-market operations, where crisis conditions threaten the financial system. Marks of such conditions would be the necessitous dumping of federal, state, local, and other securities in disorganized markets.

Proponents of the proposed mechanism believe that the foregoing changes would substantially improve Reserve Bank services to member banks and the economy without reducing the effectiveness of monetary management. They anticipate that more member banks would use the discount mechanism more frequently and more extensively in making liquidity adjustments. While the average level of borrowed reserves would be appreciably higher, total member-bank reserves would not be significantly affected because offsetting open-market operations would be undertaken to create the desired rate of monetary expansion and the desired money market conditions.[14]

[14]For a more comprehensive account of the proposed redesign of the discount mechanism, see Board of Governors of the Federal Reserve System, *Report of a System Committee* (Washington, D.C., 1968); see also the reports of members of the staff committee listed under References at the end of Chapter 15.

Those who oppose the proposal belong for the most part to the monetarist school of thought. Believing in the importance of precise control of the amount of money, they would prefer to see the discount mechanism abolished instead of expanded. To them, the proposal is yet another obstacle—along with Treasury financing, money market conditions, and individual bank supervision—in the pathway of realizing effective monetary management.

REFERENCES

See references at the end of Chapter 15.

14

general instruments of monetary management: open-market operations

While the founders of the Fed contemplated that the discount mechanism, including discount rate changes, would be the principal instrument of monetary management, subsequent developments elevated open-market operations to the predominant position. In contrast with borrowing at Reserve Banks, in which initiative rests with member banks, open-market operations are an alternative method of releasing and withdrawing Reserve credit at the initiative of the Reserve authorities.

LEGAL BASIS AND ORIGIN

As will shortly be explained, open-market operations consist of purchases and sales of securities by the Reserve Banks. When securities are purchased, Reserve Bank credit is expanded and member-bank legal reserves tend to be increased. Conversely, when securities are sold, member-bank reserves tend to be extinguished. Thus, by changing directly the amount of primary reserves of member banks, open-market operations constitute a powerful weapon of control over money-market conditions, bank credit, the stock of money, and the state of the real economy.

The legal basis of open-market operations is provided in the Federal Reserve Act.[1] The Federal Reserve Banks are empowered to buy and sell a variety of securities including U.S. obligations, bankers' acceptances, foreign exchange, and obligations of the states and political subdivisions and of selected

[1]Federal Reserve Act, Sections 12A and 14.

federal credit agencies. For practical purposes, this long list may be reduced to U.S. securities because transactions in others are usually inconsequential. Policies and operations are governed by the Open-Market Committee, a body of twelve members composed of the Board of Governors and five presidents of the Fed Banks. Each Reserve Bank is required to participate in operations of the Open-Market Account in proportion to its resources, and is prohibited from engaging in independent open-market operations without Committee approval.

The gradual evolution of open-market operations as an instrument of control represents a significant chapter in financial history. There is good evidence that the founders of the Fed and its early officials did not understand the power of these transactions in the money market, even though they had long been used by the Bank of England. Before 1922, the individual Reserve Banks bought and sold U.S. securities without consultation, usually motivated by the need for earnings instead of monetary control. This led to disturbances in the U.S. security market and in the money market as a whole. Recognizing this fact, the heads of the Reserve Banks appointed a committee of five in the spring of 1922 to execute centralized purchases and sales of securities. A year later, the Federal Reserve Board appointed an Open-Market Investment Committee of five representatives of the Reserve Banks to supersede the former committee. This new committee was under supervision of the Board and was to coordinate operations according to definite rules. In the fall of 1923, arrangements were made to establish the first Fed open-market investment account. While participation was voluntary, important changes in Reserve Bank holdings of U.S. securities after that date reflected changes in the System Account. This was a significant step because it marked the first effective use of open-market operations as an instrument of national credit policy.

The Open-Market Committee was first given legal status by the Banking Act of 1933, which provided that each Reserve Bank should select one member. Operations were subject to Board regulations and were to be "governed with a view to accommodating commerce and business and with regard to their bearing upon the general credit situation of the country."[2] This Act recognized by law the organization and procedure that had actually been effective since the spring of 1930.

The present organization of the Open-Market Committee, as described above, was provided by the Banking Act of 1935.[3] In addition to giving the seven members of the Board of Governors a dominant position in the Committee, individual Reserve Banks were required to participate in all Fed operations. Complete coordination of operations was at last achieved.

The operating arm of the Committee is the manager of the Open-Market Account and his assistants at the trading desk in the Federal Reserve Bank of New York. It is the manager's responsibility to translate the policy

[2]Ibid., Section 8.
[3]Ibid., Section 205.

decisions of the Open-Market Committee into concrete actions in the money market—whether to buy or sell U.S. securities, in what amounts, types, and maturities. This creates a communications problem of the first order because many people are involved from the Committee, the Board, and the Reserve Banks.

The Committee is basically concerned with the conditions and objectives of the real economy as reflected in employment, production, prices, stability, growth, the international position of the dollar, and so on—as developed in Chapter 12. But these general guides must be supported by more proximate ones in the fields of money, credit, banking, and money market conditions. Consequently, on the basis of a consensus at each meeting of the Committee (every three or four weeks in Washington, D.C.) a summary of conditions, together with a formal directive, is prepared for the manager's guidance until the next meeting. As an example, at the meeting of the Committee on July 21, 1970, the directive issued to the trading desk was as follows:

> The information reviewed at this meeting indicates that real economic activity changed little in the second quarter after declining appreciably earlier in the year. Prices and wage rates generally are continuing to rise at a rapid pace. However, improvements in productivity appear to be slowing the rise in costs, and some major price measures are showing moderating tendencies. Since mid-June long-term interest rates have declined considerably, and prices of common stocks have fluctuated above their recent lows. Although conditions in financial markets have improved in recent weeks uncertainties persist, particularly in the commercial paper market where the volume of outstanding paper has contracted sharply. A large proportion of the funds so freed apparently was rechanneled through the banking system, as suggested by sharp increases in bank loans and in large-denomination CD's of short maturity—for which rate ceilings were suspended in late June. Consequently, in early July bank credit grew rapidly; there was also a sharp increase in the money supply. Over the second quarter as a whole both bank credit and money supply rose moderately. The over-all balance of payments remained in heavy deficit in the second quarter. In light of the foregoing developments, it is the policy of the Federal Open-Market Committee to foster financial conditions conducive to orderly reduction in the rate of inflation, while encouraging the resumption of sustainable economic growth and the attainment of reasonable equilibrium in the country's balance of payments.
>
> To implement this policy, while taking account of persisting market uncertainties, liquidity strains, and the forthcoming Treasury financing, the Committee seeks to promote moderate growth in money and bank credit over the months ahead, allowing for a possible continued shift of

credit flows from market to banking channels. System open market operations until the next meeting of the Committee shall be conducted with a view to maintaining bank reserves and money market conditions consistent with that objective; provided, however, that operations shall be modified as needed to counter excessive pressures in financial markets should they develop.[4]

It will be noted that the directive is couched in broad, general terms and emphasizes continued moderate growth in money and bank credit and on money market conditions consistent with such growth. In converting this directive into concrete operations, the manager is assisted by the supporting discussion at the meeting, by the daily statistical analyses and projections of the staffs of the Board and the Banks, and by daily communication with the Board and the presidents of the Reserve Banks.

EFFECTS ON BANK RESERVES AND DEPOSITS

In view of the complex technicalities of open-market operations, a full understanding of their influence can be gained only by tracing results on the balance sheets of both member banks and Reserve Banks. The effects vary significantly depending on who owns securities that are purchased by Reserve Banks and who buys securities that are sold. Because the trading desk of the Open-Market Committee deals only with some twelve large nonbank U.S. security dealers, the following examples take this into consideration.

open-market purchases

First assume that the trading desk purchases $100 million of Treasury bills from a nonbank dealer with the object of providing member banks additional legal reserves. Assume also that excess legal reserves and borrowings of member banks at the Reserve Banks are both zero, and that the dealer buys the securities from business corporations and other nonbank holders. Under these conditions, there would be the effect shown in Case I, p. 269.

In step 1, the dealer delivers the securities to the Federal Reserve Bank of New York and receives an officers' check in payment. In step 2, the dealer deposits the check in a member bank which places the item in its collection account. Step 3 indicates transfer the next day from the collection account to the legal-reserve account of the member bank and also the increase of member-bank reserves on the books of the Reserve Bank. Holdings of Treasury bills by business corporations are reduced $100 million, and it may be assumed that the dealer's checks in payment for the bills were deposited by the

[4] *Federal Reserve Bulletin* (October 1970), pp. 762-763.

CASE I

Federal Reserve Banks

Assets	*Liabilities*
(1) U.S. securities + 100	(1) Officers' checks + 100
	(3) Officers' checks – 100
	(3) Deposits – member banks + 100

Member Banks

Assets	*Liabilities*
(2) Federal Reserve collection account + 100	(2) Demand deposits + 100
(3) Federal Reserve collection account – 100	
(3) Reserve with Federal Reserve Bank + 100	

corporations. Thus, the net effect on member banks is an increase of both legal reserves and deposits in the amount of the open-market purchase. The increase in excess legal reserves, however, is less than that in total legal reserves, because of the additional required reserve against the new deposits. That is, if the legal-reserve requirement is 20 percent, required reserves would increase $20 million and excess reserves would rise $80 million.

Next assume that the security dealer buys the Treasury bills from member banks instead of from nonbank owners. The following transactions would occur:

CASE II

Federal Reserve Banks

Assets	*Liabilities*
(2) U.S. securities + 100	(2) Officers' checks + 100
	(4) Officers' checks – 100
	(4) Deposits – member banks + 100

Member Banks

Assets	*Liabilities*
(1) U.S. securities – 100	(1) Demand deposits (dealer) – 100
(3) Federal Reserve collection account + 100	(3) Demand deposits + 100
(4) Federal Reserve collection account – 100	
(4) Reserve with Federal Reserve Banks + 100	

In step 1, the dealer buys the bills from member banks and pays by check. Step 2 includes delivery of the securities to the Reserve Bank which pays with an officers' check. In step 3, the dealer deposits the officers' check, and the member bank enters it in the collection account. Step 4 shows the effect of collection of the item on the books of both the Reserve Bank and the member bank. This case differs from Case I in that there is no immediate increase in member-bank demand deposits, and in that excess legal reserves rise by the full amount of the purchase of securities.

Finally, consider the case of direct purchase of U.S. securities from the Treasury, which is an exception to the general rule of buying only from dealers.

CASE III

Federal Reserve Banks

Assets	*Liabilities*
(1) U.S. securities + 100	(1) Deposits – U.S. Treasury + 100
	(3) Deposits – U.S. Treasury – 100
	(3) Deposits – member banks + 100

Member Banks

Assets	*Liabilities*
(2) Federal Reserve collection account + 100	(2) Demand deposits + 100
(3) Federal Reserve collection account – 100	
(3) Reserve with Federal Reserve Bank + 100	

In step 1, the Reserve Banks pay for the bills by crediting the Treasury's deposit account. At this point, there is no effect whatever on member-bank reserves. Step 2 includes Treasury spending of the money for goods and services, and deposit of the Treasury checks in member banks by sellers of the goods. Step 3 embraces collection of the checks from the Reserve Banks by member banks. Final effects on member-bank deposits and legal reserves, it will be noted, are the same as in Case I.[5]

It should be underscored that in all three cases the purchase of securities by the Reserve Banks creates new reserve money that forms the basis for a *potential* multiple expansion of member-bank loans and investments, and, thereby, of deposits. Demand deposits may increase to the same amount in all three cases when the expansion process is completed. But Case II differs from Case I and Case III in that no deposits arise from the initial purchasing operation. Of course, the potential expansion will be realized only if the banks are able and willing to make loans and/or purchase securities.

open-market sales

Consider now the opposite situation when the monetary authorities decide to implement a restrictive policy by selling securities. In order to observe the extreme consequences, assume that member-bank excess reserves and

[5]While the Reserve Banks have authority to puchase direct or fully guaranteed U.S. obligations from the Treasury, this method of financing is used infrequently. However, the line of credit at the Fed provides desirable flexibility in cash and debt management by the Treasury. This authority is conveyed by Public Law 90-300.

Reserve Bank borrowings are zero; also that the trading desk sells $100 million of Treasury bills to dealers who resell them to nonbank interests—for example, business corporations. The following would be the effect:

CASE IV

Federal Reserve Banks

Assets	*Liabilities*
(1) U.S. securities – 100	(2) Deposits – member banks – 100
(1) Uncollected items + 100	
(2) Uncollected items – 100	

Member Banks

Assets	*Liabilities*
(2) Reserve with Federal Reserve Bank – 100	(2) Demand deposits – 100

The dealer pays the Reserve Bank by a check on a member bank, after which the Reserve Bank collects by reducing the latter's reserve account. When the dealer subsequently sells the bills to business corporations, there is no accompanying change in total deposits; only a shift among existing accounts. Thus, both legal reserves and demand deposits are extinguished by the amount of the sale. But because legal-reserve requirements are reduced by, say, $20 million, the deficiency in member-bank legal reserves would be only $80 million.

Again, the results would be somewhat different if the dealers resell the bills to member banks:

CASE V

Federal Reserve Banks

Assets	*Liabilities*
(1) U.S. securities – 100	(2) Deposits – member banks – 100
(1) Uncollected items + 100	
(2) Uncollected items – 100	

Member Banks

Assets	*Liabilities*
(2) Reserve with Federal Reserve Bank – 100	(2) Demand deposits – 100
	(3) Demand deposits + 100
(3) U.S. securities + 100	

In step 1, the dealer pays for the bills by a member-bank check which is temporarily held for collection by the Reserve Bank. Step 2 includes the collection process in which the dealer's deposit account and member-bank reserves are reduced. In step 3, the dealer sells the securities to the member bank and is paid by credit to his account. Thus, there is no immediate change in total deposits, and member-bank legal reserves become deficient by the entire amount of the sale transaction.[6]

[6]In the foregoing cases it is assumed that settlement is made in clearing-house funds instead of Federal funds. With the latter, the deferred collection transactions would be eliminated.

If member banks as a whole are not able to borrow at the Reserve Banks nor to gain reserves in other ways, their only alternative is to reduce deposits by a multiple of the reserve deficiency. More concretely, assuming a legal-reserve requirement of 20 percent and no change in currency or time deposits, they would have to dispose of earning assets in the amount of five times the reserve deficiency. In Case IV, this amount would be $400 million, and in Case V, $500 million. But in reality, the harshness of the contraction process is usually cushioned by member-bank borrowing at the Reserve Banks, and the extent of bank-credit contraction depends on current conditions. Such factors as the reluctance to borrow, height of the discount rate, holdings of liquidity reserves, intensity of loan demands, and rationing of Reserve credit are determinative.

relation of operations to the national credit market

At first glance, one might gain the impression that because open-market operations are centered in New York City, their influence is largely confined to this small geographical area. Quite the contrary. The effects of Reserve Bank purchases and sales are quickly transmitted through the national credit market to all areas of the United States, and indirectly even to foreign countries. Primary reserves and demand deposits of commercial banks possess a very high degree of mobility. Three aspects of institutional arrangements are chiefly responsible. First, while the government-security market centers in New York, it is nationwide—even worldwide—in scope. A large part of the transactions is, directly or indirectly, for the account of banks, financial institutions, and business corporations located in other parts of the country. For example, open-market sales to buyers located in Los Angeles, San Francisco, and Seattle reduce bank reserves in the West Coast region. Second, bank-reserve positions are tied together by the network of correspondent-bank relations as reflected in interbank balances. These balances are shifted on short notice in response to changing conditions. Finally, the mobility of reserves is greater because of their easy transfer through the Fed, and because of the existence of the Federal-funds market in which excess reserves in certain areas are lent to banks in other regions with deficient reserves.

A notable feature of open-market operations is their objectivity. Sales are made to the highest bidders in a broad market, regardless of location or types of buyers; purchases are made from those who come forward with the best offers. When ultimate purchasers are nonbanks, the checks drawn in payment drain reserves alike from banks with excess reserves and from banks that are borrowing reserves. When ultimate purchasers are member banks, the initial effect is, of course, to absorb excess reserves in their possession. In the opposite case, when the Reserve Banks purchase securities from nonbanks, the checks in payment find their way to both borrowing banks and banks with excess reserves, with the result that borrowings are reduced by the former and excess reserves of the latter are enlarged. Purchases from member banks are almost always from the borrowing group with a consequent reduction in borrowings because banks with excess reserves seldom desire to sell liquidity reserve assets.

Another significant feature of open-market operations is their dependence on flows of funds through the national money market to achieve their ultimate purpose. A purchase or sale of U.S. securities executed through large bond dealers initially releases or absorbs reserves of a relatively few (mostly large) banks. The distribution of easier or more stringent credit conditions throughout the nation follows by virtue of the market processes described just above. However, these processes are subject to frictions and obstacles, with the result that some individual banks, certain localities or regions, and specific industries may not share proportionately in the desired effects. This is the principal reason why the discount mechanism is needed as a supplement to open-market operations. When a member bank with deficient reserves borrows at the Reserve Bank, the funds flow directly and immediately to the point of need; and when the need subsides, the member bank directly repays the Reserve Bank. Thus, the discount mechanism provides a safety valve to prevent hardships and to assist the Federal Reserve authorities in effective transmission of monetary policies throughout the country.

REPURCHASE AGREEMENTS WITH U.S. SECURITY DEALERS

A phase of open-market operations that requires separate discussion is the purchase of U.S. securities from nonbank government security dealers by the Federal Reserve Bank of New York under agreement that the dealers will repurchase the same securities in 15 days or less. The repurchase price is the same as the sale price, and the interest rate paid by the dealer usually corresponds with the discount rate of the Reserve Bank.

This is a method of providing funds to dealers to finance the carrying of their security inventory at times when commercial banks and others are not in position to lend the amounts needed without unduly tightening the market. Repurchase operations are made at the request of dealers, but only when the Open-Market Committee, which supervises these agreements, is so disposed. Such transactions are made only for the account of the Federal Reserve Bank of New York; they are not part of the Fed Open-Market Account.

The initial effect of a repurchase agreement is mechanically the same as a regular open-market purchase from nonbank holders, described on pages 268-269. That is, such a transaction to the amount of $100 million tends to increase demand deposits and member-bank reserves by the full amount and to increase excess reserves by $80 million when the legal-reserve requirement against demand deposits is 20 percent. In opposite fashion, when repurchase agreements run off and dealers buy back the securities, the effect is, in general, the same as a regular open-market sale to nonbank interests. That is, demand deposits and member-bank reserves tend to decrease by the amount of the run-off, and a legal-reserve deficiency of a somewhat smaller amount develops.[7]

Repurchase agreements with the large U.S. security dealers provide a useful supplement to regular open-market operations. They represent a flexible and sensitive means of meeting the temporary financing requirements of individual dealers when their inventories of the various types and maturities of securities become abnormally large. This is likely to occur during tight-money periods, and especially when Treasury offerings are large or when seasonal and other factors reduce bank liquidity. Repurchase agreements have distinct advantages over regular open-market operations in meeting day-to-day shortages of dealer-loan money. The funds are provided for specific dealers who need them, whereas a regular open-market purchase may not do so. Also, repurchases are less disturbing to the U.S. security market because Federal Reserve officials accomplish their purpose without alternately buying and selling in the market. In this way, they avoid bidding prices up and down and passing judgment on what is a right price for different issues.

Furthermore, repurchase agreements contribute to the development of a broader and smoother government-security market, which assists in effective administration of regular open-market policies. Nonbank security dealers are encouraged by the knowledge that they have direct access to Reserve credit at low rates, even though some uncertainty exists in regard to how much and when. Moreover, they are placed on about the same footing as large bank dealers in U.S. securities who can borrow at the Reserve Bank at the discount rate. Despite the constructive and convenient features of repurchase agreements, the Open-Market Committee continuously faces the problem of keeping them within the bounds of general monetary policy. It would be easy during a period of credit restraint to accede to dealer requests for Reserve credit to such an extent that the general policy was negated. In the opposing situation, a too rapid withdrawal of funds released through repurchases could cancel other actions designed to effectuate an easy-money policy.

Since 1965, the Fed has at times found the *reverse repurchase agreement* a useful device to tighten the money market. In this operation, U.S. securities are sold to the large bond dealers with an agreement to repurchase in from 1 to 15 days at a fixed price. Unlike the outright sale of securities, this method has the advantages of absorbing excess reserves immediately at the point of existence, and of less direct disturbance to the U.S. securities market. In 1969, the combined amount of repurchase and reverse repurchase agreements was $100 billion.[8]

Repurchase operations are, in fact, much more significant than the

[7]For a more comprehensive description of repurchase agreements see Robert V. Roosa, *Federal Reserve Operations in the Money and Government Securities Markets* (Fed Reserve Bank of New York, 1956), pp. 25-26, 83-87. Also see Edward C. Simmons, "Sales of Government Securities to Federal Reserve Banks Under Repurchase Agreements," *The Journal of Finance,* IX, no. 1, pp. 23-40.

[8]Board of Governors of the Federal Reserve System, *Annual Report* (Washington, D.C., 1969), p. 210.

amount outstanding indicates because they represent marginal Reserve credit which supports a multiple of bank deposits, and also directly finances large turnover of government securities. In view of the nature of requirements, wide variations take place. For example, during the first 8 months of 1970, no repurchases at all were outstanding during 13 weeks, and the amounts in the remainder of the period ranged between $13 million and $756 million.[9]

EFFECTS ON U.S. SECURITY MARKET

The huge volume of open-market operations necessarily raises important questions of policy in regard to their relation to the U.S. security market. Some idea of the large responsibility of the Open-Market Committee to this market is conveyed by the fact that at the end of August 1970, they were administering a portfolio of about $60 billion, the largest in the world, and representing $1 out of every $4 of marketable federal debt.

At one extreme, the Open-Market Committee may take large, or even complete, responsibility for prices and yields in every sector of the market—short, intermediate, and long. This was the case during World War II, when prices of government obligations were supported all along the line at par or above. At the other extreme, open-market operations may be confined entirely to short-term issues, leaving market forces to determine the prices and yields of intermediate- and long-term issues. Or the Committee may adopt a middle-ground policy that contemplates normal transactions in short terms, but occasional transactions in notes and bonds when necessary to correct a disorderly market.

During the period 1953-1960, the actual policy of the Committee was much closer to the second extreme than to the first. In the sharp controversy concerning the question, their policy came to be known as the bills-only, or bills-preferably, doctrine. That is, they confined operations to bills or other short-terms unless a clearly disorderly condition developed. The Fed did not directly support new Treasury financing by purchasing when-issued securities, securities that were exchangeable into new issues, or outstanding issues with comparable maturities to the offered securities. When support was given, it took the form of releasing Reserve credit by bill purchases, or of repurchase agreements with nonbank government-security dealers.

A major change in open-market policy made in February 1961 remained in force in 1970. The Committee authorized the manager of the Open-Market Account to acquire intermediate- and longer-term U.S. securities and to make shifts in types and maturities of holdings.[10] Briefly stated, the

[9]*Federal Reserve Bulletin,* various issues.

[10]In the administration of this policy, the Federal Reserve Banks held $22.3 billion of bills, $31.4 billion of notes, and $3.5 billion of bonds at the end of 1969. The maturity distribution on the same date was as follows: within 90 days, $13.3 billion; 91 days-1 year, $22.7 billion; 1-5 years, $12.8 billion; 5-10 years, $7.6 billion; and over 10 years, $0.7 billion—Board of Governors of the Federal Reserve System, *Annual Report* (Washington, D.C., 1969), pp. 326, 333.

purpose of this change in policy, popularly known as *operation nudge,* and later as *operation twist,* was to spur business recovery and growth by lowering long-term interest rates, and at the same time to restrain the outflow of short-term funds and of gold by maintaining a relatively high Treasury bill yield. Thus, the Fed assumed an active role in determination of the term structure of rates.

Space precludes more than a summary of the arguments, pro and con, with respect to the bills-only policy. The principal argument in its favor turns on the importance to monetary management, Treasury finance, and the entire private economy, of a U.S. security market that functions effectively under conditions of maximum possible freedom—a market with depth, breadth, and responsiveness. Experience demonstrates that such a market cannot develop in the presence of uncertainties as to whether, when, and on which side the trading desk may operate in the intermediate and long sectors. Dealers cannot be expected under such uncertainties to risk their capital to maintain an adequate position in each issue, to provide firm offers to buy and sell the various issues at quoted prices, and to engage in active arbitrage transactions. Interference with the market is at a minimum when open-market operations are restricted to short-term issues where price fluctuations are small and trading volume is large.

The foregoing argument is buttressed in theory by the fact that the pattern of yields for different maturities largely depends on market *expectations* in regard to the level of interest rates. If higher rates are expected to prevail, long-term issues will be sold and short-term issues will be purchased, thereby raising long-term yields in relation to short-term yields. Conversely, if lower rates are the expectation, intermediate- and long-term issues will be purchased and short-terms will be sold with the result that longer-term yields decline in relation to short-term yields. It follows that when the Fed operates in all maturity sectors, it becomes more or less committed to the established rate pattern, which may be markedly affected by changing expectations of investors. This unwisely limits its freedom, so the argument runs, in discharging its main responsibility of monetary management. When Reserve Bank dealings are limited to short-term issues, forecasts of interest-rate levels are left to buyers and sellers and the maturity structure of yields is determined in a relatively free market.

Another argument advanced by the Committee was that operations in the short end of the market are less likely to be interpreted as signaling a basic change in credit policy than transactions in the longer issues. This follows from the fact that dealers and other financial specialists know that the Reserve Banks engage more or less continuously in buying and selling short-terms to compensate the day-to-day changes in float, currency in circulation, Treasury balances, gold stock, and other factors affecting member-bank reserves.

Those who oppose the bills-only doctrine present the following arguments. For one thing, they deny that limited operations in longer issues will disrupt the market and seriously diminish its breadth, depth, and resiliency. For another, they point out that concentration of operations at the short end necessarily magnifies fluctuations in short-term yields and thereby causes wide variations in rate-maturity relationships (i.e., in the yield curve). In this connection, they also stress that larger purchases and sales are often required to achieve desired results when they are massed at the short end. In turn, this results in greater disturbance to bank-reserve positions and to rates than would occur if transactions were made in all maturities. In support of the positive side of their program, they contend that strategic operations in the intermediate- and long-term area will, with greater speed and certainty, influence the cost and availability of credit all along the maturity scale, and will thereby more effectively achieve the aims of monetary management. The opponents of the bills-only doctrine do not wish to rely completely on private arbitrage transactions to transmit the effects of releasing or absorbing bank reserves at the short end to the longer sectors of the market.[11]

The issue of proper techniques in open-market operations still remains a controversial question both inside and outside the Fed. Much can be learned from past experiences, notably, (1) the epoch of a relatively fixed pattern of rates during World War II and until the Treasury-Federal Reserve Accord in 1951, (2) the eight-year reign of bills only-bills preferably, 1953-1960, which was an extreme reaction from the former era, and (3) the current policy which has been underway since the first quarter of 1961. The proper relation of the Fed to the market should emerge more clearly, and a wider area of agreement should develop, as experience with the current phase unfolds and is analyzed in light of the two earlier phases.

OPEN-MARKET OPERATIONS IN BANKERS' ACCEPTANCES

Since the spring of 1955, a small part of open-market holdings of the Federal Reserve Bank of New York has consisted of bankers' acceptances. The Federal Open-Market Committee authorized purchases at that time in recognition of their rising volume and the likelihood of their further growth as an instrument of foreign-trade finance. While acceptance holdings were substantial during the 1920s, this step marked a change in policy because, with a minor exception in 1946, they were not purchased in the long interval 1934-1954. After acceptance by the city bank on which they are drawn, bankers' acceptances may be sold in the market, represented in 1970 by five or six active dealers who resell them to commercial banks and others as liquidity reserve investments. Most of them arise out of foreign-trade transactions. Being short-term obligations of the strongest U.S. banks and eligible for discount at the Reserve Banks, bankers' acceptance yields are among the lowest in the money market—only a small fraction above that of Treasury bills.

Bankers' acceptances are purchased from dealers at the going rate for the account of the Fed Bank of New York, but under supervision of the

[11]For a more comprehensive presentation of the issues pertaining to the bills-only doctrine, see Hearings before the Subcommittee on Economic Stabilization of the Joint Committee on the Economic Report, U.S. Congress, December 6 and 7, 1954, especially pp. 15-25; 223-227.

Open-Market Committee. Under current practice, they are held to maturity, not resold. The maturity distribution is arranged so that some acceptances mature every day or so. During 1955-1970, the amount of Reserve Bank holdings has usually been between $20 and $75 million.

In order to aid dealers in financing acceptance holdings, the trading desk also enters into repurchase agreements under approximately the same arrangements as exist with respect to U.S. securities. Most of the time, no funds are loaned to dealers in this manner. But on occasion, and especially during firm money-market conditions, such repurchases sometimes amount to as much as $30 million.

Before the spring of 1955, the practice of the Reserve Banks in connection with the bankers' acceptance market differed in one important respect from current practice. Instead of buying the amounts desired on their own initiative, they posted buying (discount) rates at which they would purchase all prime acceptances offered. A low buying rate (high price) in relation to other money rates caused acceptances to flow to the Reserve Banks; a high buying rate (low price) reduced the flow or even cut it off entirely. Thus, the amount of Reserve Bank holdings was largely determined by the level of the buying rate in the market-rate structure. In fact, the buying rate was kept at a low level during the 1920s in order to encourage development of the infant American acceptance market. Consequently, in that period the Reserve Banks held between 25 and 50 percent of all outstanding bankers' acceptances, and their portfolios usually exceeded $300 million. But after 1933, when the amount of outstanding acceptances greatly declined and easy-credit conditions prevailed, the buying rate was set above the market rate, with the result that Reserve Bank holdings were negligible.

RELATION OF OPEN-MARKET OPERATIONS TO DISCOUNTS AND ADVANCES

The relationship between open-market operations and discounts and advances of the Federal Reserve Banks is close and significant. First, they are the two principal channels through which reserve money is released or withdrawn from the commercial-banking system. As indicated in Chapter 13, discounts and advances are made only at the initiative of member banks, although the discount rate charged is set by the Fed. A high (penalty) rate in relation to alternative rates in the money market makes member-bank borrowing less attractive compared with other options available to adjust legal-reserve deficiencies. And a low (premium) discount rate in relation to other relevant rates makes borrowing at the Reserve Banks more attractive. In this case, for example, banks are inclined to borrow at the low rate rather than to sell Treasury bills to adjust a reserve deficiency. However, firm administration of the discount window since 1951 has strictly limited the ability of member banks to borrow. Consequently, the amount of discounts and advances has been held down to a relatively insignificant level–in the range of $0.8 to $1.5 billion in 1969-1970 compared with holdings of $54 to $60 billion of U.S. securities.

Second, in contrast, open-market operations are undertaken at the initiative of the Fed. Sale of U.S. securities absorbs legal reserves, and if carried far enough when a policy of restraint exists, the member banks are forced to borrow. At the same time, the discount rate is likely to be raised in successive steps and to be made effective against an increasing amount of discounts and advances. On the other side, purchase of U.S. securities releases legal reserves and, if pursued aggressively, leads to repayment of indebtedness by member banks, followed by creation of a rising amount of excess reserves.

This calls attention to the third aspect of the relationship: the tendency for discounts and advances to move inversely with the Reserve Banks' U.S. security holdings. If open-market purchases are made when the amount of member-bank borrowing is substantial, the repayment of indebtedness may largely offset security purchases, so that there is little increase in total Reserve Bank credit. A significant increase in total Reserve Bank credit will come only if purchases are continued after indebtedness is repaid; excess reserves will then accumulate. In reverse, sale of securities by the Reserve Banks will not decrease total Reserve Bank credit very much when net free reserves are in the vicinity of zero. Under these conditions, rising discounts and advances will largely offset the reduction in U.S. securities. The extent of this offset depends on the degree of credit rationing at the discount window, and the extent to which the discount rate is changed to a penalty position in the money-rate structure.

Last, open-market operations represent a shotgun approach by releasing or withdrawing reserve money from the market. The mobility of reserves through market processes is then depended on to distribute the effects nationwide. In contrast, discounts and advances are like a rifle aimed at a specific target. Reserve money is released only to the bank that needs it, and withdrawn only from the bank that does not need it.

REFERENCES

See references at the end of Chapter 15.

15

general instruments of monetary management: legal reserve requirements and rate ceilings

Changes in legal reserve requirements were no more contemplated by the founders of the Fed than were open-market operations. Before 1933, the basic reserve percentages required against member-bank deposits by the Federal Reserve Act were not subject to administrative changes by the Board. Although emergency powers to change requirements were granted by the Inflation Act of May 1933, permanent authority to make such changes was not granted until the Banking Act of 1935.[1] Legal reserves of member banks had to be kept on deposit with the Reserve Banks, and requirements were expressed as a percentage of net demand deposits and a percentage of time deposits. The Board has discretion in 1970 within percentage ranges, as follows:

Location of Banks	Net Demand Deposits	Time Deposits
Reserve city	10-22	3-10
Country	7-14	3-10

Another significant amendment to the Federal Reserve Act with respect to legal reserves was passed in July 1959. The most important provision gave the Board power to count vault cash of member banks as legal reserves. The Board granted this privilege, by stages, and since November 1960, all vault cash has counted as

[1]Federal Reserve Act, Section 19.

legal reserve. The amendment also removed the legal distinction between central-reserve cities and reserve cities, and set the minimum and maximum ratios against net demand deposits for all reserve city banks at 10 and 22 percent, respectively. A further amendment to Section 19 of the Federal Reserve Act, approved in September 1966, set the minimum and maximum reserve ratios against time deposits at 3 and 10 percent.[2]

FUNCTION OF RESERVE REQUIREMENTS

Monetary economists and Federal Reserve officials have changed their views in regard to the functions of legal reserves of commercial banks since World War I. Prior to that time, reserves were mainly required to assure at least a minimum of asset liquidity and safety. But it was soon realized that (1) there was little liquidity provided by a minimum reserve which could not be used when needed; (2) individual banks had to depend on liquifying loans and investments and on borrowing funds to meet reserve deficiencies; and (3) commercial banks as a whole had to depend on the central bank or the Treasury to provide needed additional liquidity. It was also realized that legal reserves make only a small contribution to safety of bank deposits because they are only a fractional part of total assets, and that safety depends primarily on the quality of bank loans and investments, efficiency of bank management in general, protection provided by capital funds, and an effective system of deposit insurance.

The modern purpose of legal reserves, viz., to serve as an instrument of monetary management, evolved and gained acceptance after World War I. More specifically, by changing the amount of member-bank reserves, the amount of required reserves, and the cost of borrowed reserves, the monetary authorities can exert a strong influence on the amount of money, total bank credit, on total money expenditures, employment, production, and prices. Creation of excess reserves by lowering requirements, or otherwise, promotes a multiple expansion of bank loans, investments, and deposits. Creation of reserve deficiencies by raising requirements, or otherwise, tends to bring about contraction of loans, investments and deposits, or at least to act as a brake on further expansion. This follows from the general reluctance of banks to borrow at the Reserve Banks, from administration of the discount window, and from the higher interest-rate structure that is associated with borrowed reserves.

COMPUTATION OF LEGAL-RESERVE REQUIREMENTS

Computation of a member bank's required legal reserve is a complicated procedure. The legal-reserve percentages specified by the Federal Reserve Board

[2]Board of Governors of the Federal Reserve System, *Annual Report*, 1959, pp. 26-27; *Federal Reserve Bulletin* (October 1966), p. 1451.

apply to *net demand deposits* and to the unadjusted gross amount of time deposits. Gross demand deposits include all accounts payable in less than 30 days–accounts of individuals, businesses, banks, governments, and others. Outstanding certified checks, officers' checks, and letters of credit or travelers' checks sold for cash are also included. Two rather large deductions are made from gross demand deposits to arrive at net demand deposits: (1) demand deposits due from banks (except Reserve banks and foreign banks), and (2) cash items in process of collection payable immediately upon presentation in the United States. Time deposits are defined to include all accounts payable after 30 or more days' notice. Legal reserves consist of balances at the Reserve Bank and cash in vault.

In order to provide a more representative base, the computation is made over weekly periods (ending on Wednesday) on an average daily basis. The calculation is expedited by using average-deposits and cash-in-vault figures for two weeks earlier, along with the average balance at the Reserve Bank for the current week. Thus, a bank may draw down its balance at the Reserve Bank below requirements for several days provided the balance is enough above on the other day (s) to meet the average requirement. A deficiency up to 2 percent of required reserves may be carried forward to the next reserve week. Penalties for average daily reserve deficiencies are assessed on a monthly basis at a rate of 2 percent above the Federal Reserve Bank discount rate–high enough to make their avoidance well worthwhile.[3]

RAISING RESERVE REQUIREMENTS

In order to emphasize the effects of raising legal-reserve requirements, first assume that excess reserves are large and that member banks have no indebtedness to the Reserve Banks; also that the average reserve requirement against demand deposits is raised from 10 to 15 percent. Under these circumstances, member banks would now have to maintain $15 of legal reserves to back up each $100 of demand deposits, instead of the previous $10. In contrast with sales of securities by Reserve Banks and reduction of member-bank borrowing, this change does not reduce total member-bank reserve balances. Rather, it converts existing excess reserve into *required* reserves. Such a change also differs significantly from the other two general instruments in that it reduces the *multiple* of bank-credit expansion. More concretely, when the reserve requirement is 10 percent and there is no change in currency and time deposits, the amount of demand deposits that can be supported by $1 of legal reserve in the banking system is about $10. But when the requirement is raised to 15 percent, the amount that can be supported is reduced to $6.67; if the

[3]*Federal Reserve Act,* Section 19; Board of Governors of the Federal Reserve System, Regulation D.

requirement is further raised to 20 percent, the amount is reduced to \$5. Thus, raising reserve requirements is like a double-edged sword. In the foregoing example, one edge reduces excess reserve held for each \$100 of demand deposits from, say, \$7 to \$2; the other edge reduces the coefficient of potential bank-credit expansion from 10 to 6.67, so that the remaining \$2 of excess reserve could support only \$13.34 of demand deposits. Before raising the requirement, the excess reserve of \$7 held for each \$100 of demand deposits could support a \$70 expansion $\left(\$7 \times \frac{100}{10}\right)$.

Results of raising reserve requirements are somewhat different if no excess reserves exist at the time. In terms of the illustration, assume that the requirement is raised another step to 20 percent. This would absorb the \$2 of remaining excess reserve and would create a reserve deficiency of \$3 for each \$100 of demand deposits. If no reserve money is forthcoming from Federal Reserve open-market purchases, or from other sources, member banks as a group then have only two broad alternatives. They may borrow from the Reserve Banks at the discount rate, which may have been raised to make the restrictive policy effective. Or they may reduce demand deposits by selling liquidity reserves and investments to nonbank interests and by reducing loans to the combined total of \$15 $\left(\text{that is, } \$3 \times \frac{100}{20}\right)$ for each \$100 of existing demand deposits. In practice, it is likely that the banks would employ both methods, so that the harshness of the contraction process would be cushioned by borrowing at the Reserve Banks. However, the latter might see fit to force contraction by rationing Reserve credit to members who seek to borrow. It should also be stressed that, insofar as borrowing at the Reserve Banks is induced by raising reserve requirements, there is an increase in total member-bank reserve balances—in contrast with the excess-reserve situation considered in the first example.

LOWERING RESERVE REQUIREMENTS

Despite the fact that the consequences of lowering reserve requirements are, in general, the opposite of raising them, it is desirable to carry the preceding example somewhat further. Suppose that the average member-bank reserve requirement is 20 percent against demand deposits, that the banks as a group are borrowing \$3 at the Reserve Banks per \$100 of demand deposits, and that there are no excess reserves. A reduction of the requirement to 17 percent would just enable the banks to repay their indebtedness, assuming no change in bank earning assets and in other factors affecting reserves. Such repayment would, at the same time, reduce total member-bank reserve balances by the same amount. If the requirement were dropped further to 15 percent, excess reserves of \$2 per \$100 of demand deposits would emerge; and if the requirement were reduced to

10 percent, $7 of excess reserves per $100 of deposits would appear. Thus, when member banks are out of debt to the Reserve Banks, a reduction in reserve requirements creates excess reserves but does not reduce total member-bank reserves. Instead, it converts previously required reserves to excess reserves.

Again, the influence on potential bank-credit expansion in the foregoing example needs emphasis. Not only are excess reserves of $7 per $100 of demand deposits created by reducing requirements from 20 to 10 percent, but the multiple of potential expansion is doubled–from 5 to 10. That is, $1 of legal reserves is now capable of supporting $10 of demand deposits in the banking system.[4]

USE OF CHANGES IN RESERVE REQUIREMENTS

Even though changes in reserve requirements are a powerful instrument of monetary management, they are not so well adapted to day-to-day and week-to-week adjustments as are open-market operations and the discount mechanism. Instead, their most appropriate use is to set the stage for effective employment of the other instruments of control. Frequent changes are not practicable for three reasons.

1. A small percentage change has a large effect on the liquidity position of member banks. For example, with member bank net demand deposits of $170 billion at midyear 1969, a change of $\frac{1}{2}$ percentage point would alter requirements by $850 million. This would have a massive effect in the money market which is sensitive to changes as small as $25 million. This limitation might be remedied in part by use of smaller gradations, but $\frac{1}{2}$ percentage point is the smallest ever utilized, and it is doubtful whether smaller and more frequent changes would be gracefully accepted by member banks.

2. Frequent changes constitute an unnecessary irritant. All member banks (or all in one reserve group) are directly affected by this method, and the hand of the Fed is clearly evident. Rather than being annoyed by frequent changes, banks much prefer some stability of the rules in administering their liquidity position. This aspect of the problem assumes larger importance in view of the fact that state-chartered banks, which represent two-fifths of commercial-bank resources, are not compelled by law to be members of the Fed. Frequent changes could become such a nuisance as to reduce membership by both withdrawals from the System and reductions in applications for membership.

3. Frequent changes in requirements are not consonant with existing institutional arrangements. The Board of Governors in Washington lacks intimate day-to-day contacts with the New York money market as well as the flexibility of organization to use this instrument effectively for short-term adjustments.

A further consideration in regard to use of this method may, at times,

[4]For simplification, it is here assumed that all bank expansion takes the form of demand deposits with no change in currency outside banks or in time deposits.

be relevant. Since changes in requirements are infrequent, member banks attach to them a considerable degree of permanence. Because of this, there is some reason to believe that their response to lowering reserve requirements is more immediate and of greater magnitude than to an equal increment of excess reserves created by open-market security purchases. Also, it is reasonable to expect a somewhat greater member-bank response to raising requirements than to open-market sales in enforcement of a policy of restraint. That is, members are more likely to adjust reserve deficiencies by sale of securities and reduction of loans than by borrowing at Reserve Banks.

A serious limitation of changes in reserve requirements exists because the Board is not in position to use it actively in curbing expansion under present banking laws. This follows from the point just made that state-chartered banks, representing two-fifths of banking resources and about two-thirds of the number of banks, are not required by law to be members. Hence, raising reserve requirements for member banks materially above requirements of nonmember banks constitutes a hazardous threat to membership. The fact is that this is but one of many reasons why all commercial banks should be required to be members of the Fed.[5] But until this constructive change is made, a weighty limitation on positive use of this method to prevent overexpansion will be present. It should be noted, however, that this point does not apply to the lowering of requirements as a means of fostering expansion. All banks usually welcome a move in this direction.

For the foregoing reasons, the Board of Governors is inclined to change reserve requirements only at infrequent intervals, usually with the aim of creating the proper environment for active use of open-market operations and discount policy. For example, only 17 changes were made during the 20-year period 1950-1970. Two of these were increases in early 1951 to combat inflationary developments during the Korean War; 9 were reductions to assist recovery from recession conditions; and 6 were small adjustments during the inflationary period 1965-1970. No increases in requirements were made in implementing policies of credit restraint when price inflation threatened in 1956-1957 and in 1959. In general then, this instrument is likely to be used only to absorb a sizable amount of existing excess reserves when there is danger of overexpansion, or to create excess reserves as a spur to business recovery; it is not likely to be used aggressively to force member banks to borrow reserve money.

COORDINATION OF GENERAL INSTRUMENTS

To this point, attention has been focused on the instruments individually in order to indicate their main characteristics. Effective monetary management,

[5]This is one of the recommendations of the Commission on Money and Credit. See *Report on Money and Credit* (Englewood Cliffs, N.J.: Prentice-Hall, 1961), pp. 76-77.

however, calls for their coordinated use, and for varying combinations under different circumstances.

features of instruments: summary

All three instruments have in common (1) a high degree of objectivity and generality, and (2) the fact that their influence is chiefly brought to bear on the reserve position of member banks by affecting the supply and cost of legal reserves.

The discount mechanism includes the discount rate and reserve-credit administration. Changes in the rate, unlike other methods, have no immediate effect on the reserve position of member banks. But given time, a rate change may significantly affect the attitude of banks toward borrowed reserves, and the amount of credit demanded by businesses and consumers. The discount rate is adapted to mild or vigorous use, and it can be changed frequently if conditions warrant. However, it is not so flexible for hourly and daily adjustments as open-market operations. Reserve credit administration can be applied whenever needed in the discretion of the authorities. It is likely to be used to limit the release of reserves through member-bank borrowing when inflationary dangers develop. The problem of rationing reserve credit is magnified when the discount rate is low in relation to Treasury bill rates and to the money-rate structure in general. A unique feature of member-bank borrowing is that reserve credit flows directly to banks that need reserve funds and is withdrawn directly from banks which no longer need them.

Open-market operations have the immediate effect of releasing or absorbing reserves of member banks, and, thereby, of influencing their net reserve position (excess reserves minus borrowings). This instrument is also distinctive in two respects: (1) demand deposits are changed dollar for dollar when the ultimate buyers or sellers of securities are nonbank interests; and (2) purchases and sales have a direct and immediate effect on the prices and yield structure of government securities (or bankers' acceptances). In contrast with member-bank borrowing, open-market operations do not release or withdraw reserves from individual banks that wish to borrow or to repay. Instead, the distribution of the increases or reductions of reserves is left to the market. The secondary effects of such operations are, however, far more important than the immediate influences. This follows from the fact that the released or withdrawn reserves form the basis of a multiple expansion or contraction of bank earning assets and deposits. Finally, this instrument is a highly flexible and sensitive one, adapted to making small daily and weekly adjustments in the money market as well as changes of large magnitude, including secular injections of reserves to support economic growth.

The effects of changing reserve requirements are similar in some respects, but different in others, from open-market operations. They are similar in that (1) both immediately change the net reserve position of member banks; (2) both may change total member-bank reserve balances; and (3) both set up secondary effects associated with multiple expansion and contraction of bank credit. The two instruments differ in that changes in reserve requirements (1) do not immediately affect total member-bank reserve balances when excess reserves are large; (2) do not immediately influence the amount of demand deposits; and (3) do not involve direct entry into the markets for U.S. securities and bankers' acceptances. They also differ in that changes in requirements (1) alter the multiple (coefficient) of bank-credit expansion and contraction; (2) are not so well adapted to short-term adjustments, nor to positive use in forcing banks to borrow reserves; and (3) affect all member banks, or at least all in one reserve group.

need for coordination

While the Fed authorities have relied much more heavily on open-market operations since the early 1920s, they have also made important use of the other two general instruments of control. The manner in which coordination has been realized can best be understood by an example drawn from the period 1953-1957.

When evidence accumulated in the spring of 1953 that a recession was developing, the authorities changed their policy from one of credit restraint to one of ease. During May and June, the Open-Market Committee purchased about $900 million of U.S. securities to enable member banks to reduce indebtedness to the Reserve Banks. This was followed in July by a reduction in reserve requirements on demand deposits which freed $1.2 billion of reserves. These steps, along with further substantial purchases of securities, made it possible for member banks to reduce borrowings by about $500 million by the year-end despite the expanding seasonal needs for currency and credit. Under these combined influences, open-market money rates declined steadily. The Treasury bill rate, which averaged 2.2 percent in May, dropped to about 1 percent by February 1954. At this point, after a delay of nine months, the Reserve Bank discount rate was lowered from 2 to 1 $\frac{3}{4}$ percent, and in April-May, it was further reduced to 1 $\frac{1}{2}$ percent. Then in July-August, reserve requirements were again reduced, freeing $1.5 billion more reserves. By this time, the liquidity of member banks had materially improved. Between midyear 1953 and midyear 1954, excess reserves increased about $300 million and Reserve Bank borrowing declined $900 million, representing a $1.2 billion improvement in net reserve position. In addition, member banks were enabled to increase liquidity reserves substantially as evidenced by the rise of U.S. security holdings from $48.3 to $53.1 billion. The response in money rates was indicated by a decline in the Treasury bill rate from 2.20 to 0.65 percent.

The July-August period also provides an interesting illustration of the use of open-market operations as a cushioning device. The release of $1.5 billion of reserves by reduction of reserve requirements would have created a sudden and undue increase of excess reserves. Consequently, this effect was offset by sale of about $1 billion of U.S. securities, part of which were repurchased in September and October. Thus, an action that at first glance might appear contradictory was, in fact, a carefully coordinated step designed to smooth out the massive effect of the reduced reserve requirement.

Without going into details, it will be helpful to carry the example on from midyear 1954 to midyear 1957. From the bottom of the recession, business recovery proceeded rapidly until practical full employment was reached in 1955, and inflationary dangers developed in 1956 and 1957. Under these circumstances, Federal Reserve policy was one of gradually increasing restraint. Reserve Bank holdings of U.S. securities were reduced about $2 billion, which, combined with increasing demands for currency and credit, materially reduced member-bank liquidity. Excess reserves declined $360 million and borrowings at Reserve Banks rose $840 million, so that net reserve position dropped by $1.2 billion. Also, liquidity reserves suffered heavily as indicated by a decline of $8.3 billion in member-bank holdings of U.S. securities. Beginning in April 1955, the Federal Reserve discount rate was raised in seven steps from $1\frac{1}{2}$ percent to $3\frac{1}{2}$ percent in August 1957. In each case, however, the upward adjustments in the discount rate lagged two or more months behind the upward course of the Treasury bill rate, which rose from 0.65 percent at midyear 1954 to nearly 4 percent in September 1957. The lagging discount rate made member-bank borrowing profitable, with the result that the problem of rationing Reserve credit was magnified. The reluctance of many banks to borrow had to be supplemented with active pressure on nonreluctant banks to limit borrowing. Without such pressure, borrowed reserves would have mounted well above the modest range of $700 to $1000 million, which usually marked their boundaries. Percentage-reserve requirements were not actively employed during this period to implement the policy of restraint. They were high enough at the outset to provide the proper environment for active use of the other more flexible instruments.

LEGAL-RESERVE REFORM

Legal-reserve reform should be considered in terms of the criteria of a good legal-reserve system. These are (1) contribution to effective control of the stock of money and bank credit by Federal Reserve authorities; (2) equitable distribution of the burden of holding nonearning reserves among all commercial banks; and (3) administrative simplicity and practicability.

The first criterion calls for adequate power and resources in the hands of the Fed to make effective and reasonably precise control of money possible. Adequate power implies complete discretion, or at least a broad range of latitude, for the Federal Reserve Board in setting required reserve percentages. The present legal range indicated on page 280 meets this requirement under foreseeable conditions. Adequate resources for effective control calls for changes in banking laws. All commercial banks, or at least all insured banks, should be required to join the Fed and thereby become subject to the same reserve requirements as member banks. At present, state-chartered banks, which represent about two-thirds of the number and two-fifths of total banking resources, join the Fed only on a voluntary basis. Nonmember state banks are subject to the varying, and usually more liberal, banking laws of the fifty separate states.

The second criterion of equity has never been well served by our banking laws. The location-basis for reserve requirements (reserve city and country banks) involves considerable discrimination. Many so-called country banks are larger than a substantial number of reserve city banks which are subject to a higher reserve requirement. Also, the philosophical question may be raised whether large banks should be penalized and small ones subsidized by legal-reserve requirements. It is difficult to support a case for departing from equality of treatment, where the same percentage requirement would apply to demand deposits, regardless of bank size. In addition, there is the problem of equity among all types of savings institutions. Reserve requirements against commercial-bank time and savings deposits should be no higher than those imposed on savings and loan associations, mutual savings banks, and credit unions. At present (1970), the Board has discretion within the range of a 3 and 10 percent reserve requirement for time deposits of member banks, whereas no legal requirement, or a more liberal requirement, exists for competitive institutions in most states.

While not a very important consideration, the existing legal-reserve system can doubtless be improved from the standpoints of simplicity and ease of administration. Uniform percentage requirements for all banks against the same type of deposits would contribute to simplicity as well as to equity. Also, one may question the complication of deductions of balances with other banks and cash items in process of collection from gross demand deposits in arriving at the reserve base of net demand deposits. It is doubtful whether more inequities would arise from using the simpler base of gross demand deposits.

Space precludes discussion of a number of proposals for legal-reserve reform, which have been made since the Fed was established in 1913.[6] But it is desirable to summarize a legislative change the Board has recommended for several years, although Congress has not yet responded. The bill would establish required reserve-percentage ranges and empower the Board to change require-

[6]For a description of the Board's proposal based on both amount and velocity of deposits, regardless of location or type of deposit, see Federal Reserve Board, *Report of Committee on Bank Reserves* (Washington, D.C., 1931). Also see Board of Governors of the Federal Reserve System, *Uniform Reserve Plan* (Washington, D.C., 1948); the special-asset reserve requirement of the Board proposed in 1947, *Federal Reserve Bulletin* (December 1947), pp. 1461-1463; and American Bankers Association, *Member Bank Reserve Requirements,* 1957.

ments within these ranges on a graduated basis according to the amount of a bank's deposits. The outmoded reserve city-country bank classification would be eliminated, and the requirements would be applicable to all federally insured banks—both of which would materially contribute to a more effective and equitable system. Whether equity would be fostered by graduated requirements is a controversial and philosophical question. The burden of proof rests on the advocates of any system that departs from equality of treatment of all banks regardless of size.[7]

MAXIMUM RATES PAYABLE ON TIME CERTIFICATES OF DEPOSIT AS A METHOD OF MONETARY CONTROL

A new method of general monetary control was utilized by the Board of Governors during the extremely stringent credit conditions which existed in 1966 and 1969, namely, control of maximum interest rates payable on time CDs. Maximum rates payable had been in effect since the mid-1930s (Regulation Q); hence there was nothing new concerning the authority to use this device. The new aspect pertained to its active use to restrain monetary expansion.

During the CD market's first four years, 1961-1965, the maximum rates payable by banks were set above the yields on competitive open-market instruments. In this favorable setting, the market made a phenomenal growth—from a nominal amount to over $17 billion at midyear 1966.

At this point, attention is called to Table 15-1, which shows the relation between the ceiling rate on CDs, the yield on open-market commercial paper, and the amount of CDs outstanding during the period 1965-1970. When the commercial-paper rate (a representative of competitive market rates) rose well above the maximum rate on CDs the banks could no longer freely compete with other short-term investment assets. Maturing CDs were not renewed as they matured, with the result that outstandings declined some $2 billion during the second half of 1966. From a monetary-control standpoint, this was in keeping with the desire of the Board. The liquidated CDs reappeared in the banking system as demand deposits which were subject to a substantially higher legal-reserve requirement. Thus, with diminished liquidity, the banks were forced to curtail loans and investments—their deposit-creating transactions.

During the economic slowdown in 1967, and in 1968, the financial environment again became favorable for issuance of CDs. Outstandings rose from $15.7 billion at the end of 1966 to $23.5 billion at the end of 1968. This was a welcome development to the Board, at least in 1967, when economic expansion was desired. The rapid growth of CDs took place because of a shift from demand deposits to time deposits, with an accompanying reduction in legal-reserve requirements. With released reserves at their disposal, the banks were in position

[7]Board of Governors of the Federal Reserve System, *Annual Report* (Washington, D.C., 1968), pp. 338-339; 1969, p. 300.

TABLE 15-1 / RELATION OF CEILING RATE ON CDs, COMMERCIAL PAPER RATE, AND AMOUNT OF CDs OUTSTANDING, 1965-1970

End of Period		CD Ceiling Rate (1)	Commercial-Paper Rate (2)	(2) – (1) (3)	Amount of CDs Outstanding (billions of dollars) (4)
1964	Dec.	4.50	4.17	–0.33	12.6
1965	March	4.50	4.38	–0.12	13.9
	June	4.50	4.38	–0.12	15.3
	Sept.	4.50	4.38	–0.12	16.3
	Dec.	5.50	4.65	–0.85	16.1
1966	March	5.50	5.21	–0.29	17.2
	June	5.50	5.51	+0.01	17.7
	Sept.	5.50	5.89	+0.39	17.0
	Dec.	5.50	6.00	+0.50	15.7
1967	March	5.50	5.24	–0.26	19.3
	June	5.50	4.65	–0.85	19.1
	Sept.	5.50	5.00	–0.50	19.9
	Dec.	5.50	5.56	+0.06	20.3
1968	March	5.50	5.64	+0.14	20.6
	June	6.00	6.25	+0.25	19.3
	Sept.	6.00	5.82	–0.18	22.3
	Dec.	6.00	6.17	+0.17	23.5
1969	March	6.00	6.82	+0.82	18.8
	June	6.00	8.23	+2.23	15.3
	Sept.	6.00	8.48	+2.48	11.7
	Dec.	6.00	8.84	+2.84	10.9
1970	March	6.75	8.33	+1.58	11.8
	June	6.75	8.21	+1.46	13.0
	Sept.	6.75	7.32	+0.57	22.2

Source: *Federal Reserve Bulletin,* various issues.

to expand loans and investments, and thereby deposits. This, in turn, fostered economic expansion.

A more aggressive use of this method of monetary control was made during 1969 and early 1970. The CD rate ceiling was held at 6 percent while market rates on competing instruments rose far above this level. For example, in December 1969, the commercial-paper rate was 2.8 percentage points higher than the ceiling on CDs. Under these circumstances, heavy liquidation of CDs occurred—from \$23.5 billion at the end of 1968 to \$10.9 billion at the end of 1969. For reasons explained above, this liquidation undermined bank liquidity; indeed, the banks were placed in the most illiquid position in over a century, and interest rates rose to the highest level since the Civil War.

After the first quarter of 1970, a more expansionary stance was taken by the Board, part of which was represented by raising the rate ceiling to $6\frac{3}{4}$ percent on CDs with maturities of 90-179 days and to $7\frac{1}{2}$ percent on maturities of 1 year or more, and by removing the ceiling entirely on maturities of 30-89 days. With market rates declining, conditions favorable to CDs were again restored and outstandings rose rapidly to near their former peak of $23.5 billion in 1968.

In retrospect, the use of Regulation Q as a method of monetary control was a serious mistake. For one thing, it undermined the essential conditions for issuance of CDs by the banks. Having given the CD market its blessing while the market grew to a position second only to Treasury bills, the Board straightway destroyed the market's foundations and forced wholesale liquidation. Because the CD market has demonstrated its potential to meet a real need for asset liquidity, an environment of certainty and stability should be provided. A healthy market cannot exist in the presence of the great uncertainty and wide variation associated with its use as a means of monetary control.

A second point pertains to the adequacy of the other general monetary controls of the Board of Governors. If these controls were so inadequate that effective monetary management could be realized only when supplemented by interest-rate ceilings, the conclusion would be quite different. In that event, sacrifice of a healthy CD market to the greater purpose of monetary management would be justified. But that is not the case. Open-market operations, supported by legal-reserve requirements and the discount mechanism, provide all the power necessary to control the money supply and the amount of bank credit. In view of this fact, the conclusion logically follows that continued use of interest-rate ceilings as a method of monetary management will be unwise—in fact, an egregious error.

It should be added that there was perhaps some justification in 1966 and 1969 for rate ceilings on passbook savings and other moderate-size time deposits of commercial banks as a protection against disintermediation in thrift institutions. But these ceilings provided no protection against withdrawals from these accounts to purchase government and corporate securities offering materially higher yields—a much larger alternative than that of shifting accounts to commercial banks. For this reason, a better method for protection against disintermediation could doubtless be devised, perhaps in the form of a temporary government subsidy for thrift institutions to enable them to meet competitive rates. The long-run solution appears to lie in requiring that rates on real-estate mortgages vary with some basic measure of current yields in the capital market. However, whatever justification existed for ceilings on small-saver accounts did not apply to ceilings on CDs because these large-denomination instruments did not provide an alternative for thrift accounts.

CONCLUSIONS

Consideration of the nature of these general instruments and their actual use leads to several conclusions.

1/No single instrument is adequate to the task; instead, all three need to be employed in proper combination.

2/Changing conditions require that the monetary authorities be empowered to use discretion in choosing the proper combination of instruments to achieve policy objectives. No rigid legal formula with respect to techniques of control can be expected to apply effectively to unknown future conditions.

3/While to a considerable extent the various instruments represent alternative methods of accomplishing the same purpose, different theories of central-bank control call for wide differences in techniques.

4/Those who would give the monetary authorities complete and rigid control of the stock of money would rely principally, or wholly, on open-market operations. They would not permit Reserve credit to be released at the initiative of member banks through the discount window, which they regard as a sieve through which reserve money escapes without control. Similarly, most of them would also advocate a 100 percent legal-reserve requirement against demand deposits in order to eliminate multiple expansion and contraction of credit in the commercial-banking system.

5/Another group, which views the problem mainly from the standpoint of the needs of the individual bank and its borrowing customers, would prefer that Reserve Bank credit be released and withdrawn largely through the discount window. They regard the discount mechanism as a safety valve which flexibly and directly meets bank liquidity requirements.

6/Those who are most concerned with controlling the character of bank assets, rather than the stock of money, tend to reject all the general instruments and to favor direct controls over different types of loans and investments.

7/The group that desires the freest possible market in U.S. securities looks with disfavor on open-market operations, especially transactions in intermediate and long-term issues, which affect the structure of yields. Changes in reserve requirements, discount rates, and Reserve credit administration are more to their liking. They would depend on a more active use of the discount rate to ration Reserve Bank credit automatically, and would advocate rationing of reserve credit only during the threat of seriously inflationary conditions.

8/The organization of the Fed is not well adapted to discriminating coordination of the general instruments of control. Open-market operations, the dominant current instrument, are under the aegis of the Federal Open-Market Committee. The other instruments are under final authority of the Board of Governors. It is therefore possible that the policies of the two bodies may fail to harmonize, or even negate each other. From the standpoint of effective organization, full responsibility for all policies and actions should be centered in one body.

9/While the techniques of control employed since 1951 have been effective, a good case can be made for more positive use of the discount rate. That is, changes in the rate might well be made more promptly in reflection of open-market changes; indeed, they might properly lead the market on occasion, instead of lagging two or three months. It is also believed that a moderate penalty rate (above yields on short-term U.S. securities) when general policy is one of restraint would serve a useful purpose. That is, it would utilize the cost-price mechanism to limit Reserve credit demands objectively. This would reduce the large administrative task of Reserve Bank rationing of reserve credit, which at best is somewhat arbitrary, inequitable, and productive of member bank ill-will.

10/A distinct advantage of the general instruments is the objective manner in which they influence the money and capital markets. In general, they are in harmony with the free-market system in which the price mechanism largely directs economic activity. In this respect, they are superior to direct selective controls which substitute judgments and decisions of officials for those of consumers and private businesses, and in addition, create major problems of enforcement. This advantage does not apply, however, to fiscal and debt-management controls which also have overall objective effects.

11/A disadvantage of vigorous use of the general instruments, which looms large in the eyes of critics, is the fact that the effects are not evenly distributed over the range of economic activity. Some sectors of the economy are responsive to tight (or easy) money conditions; others are not. The most sensitive sectors are residential construction; plant and equipment expenditures, particularly of smaller companies; and capital investments of state and local governments. Relatively insensitive sectors are consumer expenditures and speculative activities. Those who believe that this criticism is overdrawn point out that controls by nature must pinch, and that, in general, the effects fall on the most widely fluctuating sectors of the economy where control is most needed. They also point out that a rise in the level of interest rates has widely pervasive effects by tending, at given levels of income, to reduce investment and to increase savings; and that a decline in rates promotes investment and discourages savings.

12/The use of Regulation Q rate ceilings as a method of monetary management in 1966 and 1969 was unwise, and it will be a major tactical error to utilize this method in the years ahead.

REFERENCES

Ahearn, Daniel S., *Federal Reserve Policy Reappraised, 1914-1959* (New York: Columbia University Press, 1963).

Ascheim, Joseph, *Techniques of Monetary Control* (Baltimore: Johns Hopkins, 1961).

Board of Governors of the Federal Reserve System, *The Federal Reserve System: Purposes and Functions* (5th ed.; Washington, D.C., 1963), chaps. II, III, VII.

Studies Prepared for the Steering Committee for the Fundamental Reappraisal of the Discount Mechanism

Garvy, George, *The Discount Mechanism in Leading Industrial Countries Since World War II* (1968).

Holland, Robert C., and George Garvy, *The Redesigned Discount Mechanism and the Money Market* (1968).

Jones, David M., *A Review of Recent Academic Literature on the Discount Mechanism* (1968).

Meek, Paul, *Discount Policy and Open Market Operations* (1968).

Ormsby, Priscilla, *Summary of the Issues Raised at the Academic Seminar on Discounting* (1966).

Stackhouse, Benjamin, *Discount Policy and Bank Supervision* (1968).

Steering Committee, *Report of a System Committee* (1968).

Burgess, W. Randolph, *The Reserve Banks and the Money Market* (Rev. ed.; New York: Harper & Row, 1936) chaps. IV, XIV, XVI.

Commission on Money and Credit, *American Monetary Policy* (Englewood Cliffs, N.J.: Prentice-Hall, 1961), chap. 3.

Commission on Money and Credit, *The Federal Reserve and the Treasury* (Englewood Cliffs, N.J.: Prentice-Hall, 1963).

Commission on Money and Credit, *Monetary Management* (Englewood Cliffs, N.J.: Prentice-Hall, 1963).

Friedman, Milton, *A Program for Monetary Stability* (New York: Fordham University Press, 1960).

Goldfeld, Stephen M., and Edward J. Kane, "The Determinants of Member-Bank Borrowing: An Econometric Study," *Journal of Finance* (September 1966), pp. 499-514.

Holmes, Alan R., "A Day at the Trading Desk," Federal Reserve Bank of New York, *Monthly Review* (October 1970), pp. 234-238.

Horvitz, Paul M., *Monetary Policy and the Financial System* (2d ed.; Englewood Cliffs, N.J.: Prentice-Hall, 1969), chaps 19-21.

McKinney, George W., Jr., *The Federal Reserve Discount Window* (New Brunswick, N.J.: Rutgers University Press, 1960).

Meek, Paul, *Open Market Operations* (New York: Federal Reserve Bank of New York, 1969).

Meigs, A. James, *Free Reserves and the Money Supply* (Chicago: University of Chicago Press, 1962).

Prochnow, Herbert V., ed. *The Federal Reserve System* (New York: Harper & Row, 1960), chaps. 4-7.

Riefler, Winfield W., *Money Rates and Money Markets in the United States* (New York: Harper & Row, 1930).

Roosa, Robert V., *Federal Reserve Operations in the Money and Government Securities Markets* (New York: Federal Reserve Bank of New York, 1956), chaps. VI-X.

Simmons, Edward C., "A Note on the Revival of Federal Reserve Discount Policy," *Journal of Finance,* XI, no. 4 (December 1956), pp. 413-421.

Turner, Robert C., *Member-Bank Borrowing* (Columbus: Ohio State University Press, 1938).

U.S. Congress, Subcommittee on Economic Stabilization of the Joint Committee on the Economic Report Hearings, 83rd Congress, 2d Sess., *United States Monetary Policy: Recent Thinking and Experience* (Washington, D.C., 1954).

16

monetary management: selective methods

Selective methods of monetary management are members of the larger family of direct governmental controls of business operations. Legal regulation of this type is applied to production, prices, rationing, buying, selling, lending, borrowing, and other transactions. The free-market system is materially limited, or abolished. The best illustration is provided by World War II, when commodity prices, rents, and wages were brought under control, consumer goods were rationed, raw materials were allocated, and construction activities were regulated. After the war, these controls were removed one by one until by 1952 relatively free markets again prevailed. Selective credit controls have been applied in three areas in the United States, viz., security loans, consumer credit, and real-estate credit. But regulation of consumer and real-estate credit was abolished in 1952, so that in 1970 the only controlled sectors were security loans and international capital movements.

Consideration of selective credit controls raises several major questions among which are the following: Are such controls consistent with a free-market economy and with political democracy? Are they unnecessary in view of the fact that the general instruments of control are adequate under all conceivable circumstances? Are selective controls capable of serving as effective substitutes for general controls? Should selective controls be utilized more or less continuously to reenforce general controls? And finally, should selective controls be reserved only for war or other great emergencies when general controls are partially or wholly inoperative?

In addition to selective controls, another closely allied method, *moral suasion,* is discussed in this chapter. Unlike either general or selective methods, it depends on voluntary responses of lenders and borrowers to suggested policies in the public interest—even though the actions involve sacrifices of profits.

CRITERIA OF SELECTIVE CREDIT CONTROL

A striking contrast exists between the general instruments of control, discussed in the three preceding chapters, and selective controls. The former, it will be recalled, influence the overall conditions of supply and cost of credit. They affect the general money market environment objectively, and leave individual lenders and borrowers free to set their own terms and make their own choices in regard to amounts, types, and terms of loans. A selective control is quite different. It restricts the amount of credit that may be extended in individual transactions by setting the terms. Thus, aggregate demand for credit is held in check despite the ability and willingness of lending institutions to make additional loans.

The foregoing facts raise the basic question of criteria of successful selective credit regulation. The primary consideration is the degree of need for specific control. Is there convincing evidence that the general instruments are ineffective in controlling an important area of credit? If a strong case for such inadequacy cannot be made, the presumption is against establishment of a program of selective control. This follows from the fact that detailed regulation of decision-making violates a fundamental tenet of the private-enterprise system. Insofar as possible, business management and consumers should be free to decide what is best for them; and in general, government controls should be confined to the framework-types, which provide a proper economic environment.

But if there is convincing evidence of need for specific regulation, what are the criteria by which to judge the practicability of regulation of a particular credit sector? For one thing, the credit area in question should be susceptible to fairly accurate definition. It should be possible to fix credit boundaries with reasonable precision.

Second, the credit sector involved should be one of sufficient importance to justify the expense of establishing and maintaining an efficient regulatory organization. For example, consumer credit qualifies on this score, but loans to wholesale grocers do not. Third, practices in credit extension should be well standardized. That is, there should be a conventional structure in regard to types of loan, loan-value ratios, maturities, interest rates, and other contractual terms. Finally, the administrative problems and expenses of effective regulation, including enforcement, should be within reasonable bounds. For illustration, regulation of stock-market credit does not provide a very formidable administrative problem, but regulation of consumer credit at the retail level does so.

SECURITY-LOAN REGULATION

Security-loan regulation has the distinction of being the first selective credit control in the United States. Its primacy grew out of the heavy losses and the paralyzing business depression that followed the speculative orgy in stocks during 1928-1929. Its survival when other selective measures have been largely abolished, can doubtless be attributed to the general belief that a special need for regulation exists in the security markets.

need for regulation

While a reasonable amount of credit facilitates the constructive functions of the securities market, excessive credit may finance a speculative boom in stock prices that carries far beyond the realities of underlying values. Those who borrow to buy shares come under the spell of rising prices and seek further capital gains instead of earnings and dividends. This optimistic fever spreads to business management which overexpands, and to consumers who borrow and spend more freely. Under these conditions, the price-cost structure becomes distorted, basic resources are misused, and the capital market ceases to function properly. In addition, the forces producing commodity price inflation are stimulated.

In the end, the bubble bursts and speculators, interested in capital gains, begin to unload. The decline in prices feeds on itself as pessimism and fear replace overoptimism. Added momentum is provided by forced liquidation of securities held by brokers and banks as collateral for customer loans. If declining stock prices merely reflected business conditions and if the effects were confined to owners of shares, there would be little need for public concern. But such is not the case. The mood of pessimism spreads to business with the result that capital-goods outlays are curtailed and current operations are reduced. It also spreads to consumers who spend less freely. The higher-income groups are most directly affected as stockholders, but rising uncertainties about jobs and wages also alarm consumers in general who strive to reduce indebtedness. Recession may deepen to depression marked by unemployment, curtailed production, declining commodity prices, derangement of the price structure, reduced national income, and a rising rate of business failures. Thus, the excessive use of credit in security speculation provides fuel for an unhealthy boom which cannot be sustained and for commodity price inflation; the inevitable bust follows. Control of such credit is an important plank in any program of economic stabilization.

But why, it may be asked, is selective credit control necessary? Why are the general instruments inadequate? The answer is found in the inelasticity of demand for speculative credit. When the speculator expects large gains, perhaps 100 percent or more, he is not seriously deterred by the high cost of borrowed money. For example, brokers' loans continued to expand in 1929 even though call-loan rates ranged between 6 and 20 percent. The restrictive monetary policy then in force doubtless restrained business borrowing in some degree, but little response was evident in security loans. Perhaps these loans could have been curbed by more vigorous use of the general instruments, but such heavy-handed action would have developed more restraint than was desirable on business and consumers. This and other experiences demonstrate that effective control of security loans can be realized only by direct methods.

legal basis of regulation

With the disastrous events of 1929 to 1933—including the Bank Holiday—freshly in mind, Congress moved rapidly to establish effective controls of security markets and security loans. The Securities Exchange Act of 1934 directed the Board of Governors of the Fed to regulate security credit "for the purpose of preventing the excessive use of credit for the purchase or carrying of securities" and with attention to "accommodation of commerce and industry, having due regard to the general credit situation of the country. . . ."[1] In accordance with this directive, the Board issued Regulations T and U, which regulate margin requirements on loans for the purchase or carrying of stocks registered on national securities exchanges. The former applies to loans by brokers and dealers to their customers; the latter to security loans by banks to their customers. A new regulation (designated G), issued in February 1968, extended to other lenders the margin requirements on registered equity securities applicable to brokers, dealers, and banks. Also, margin requirements were applied for the first time to securities convertible into registered stock. However, the requirement was set at a lower percentage when the convertible security is a bond—50 percent compared with the current 70 percent on equities.

A further step toward more effective control was taken in July 1968 by an amendment to the Securities Exchange Act of 1934, extending margin requirements to loans that banks and other lenders make for the purpose of purchasing over-the-counter securities (those not registered on a securities exchange). This amendment was implemented in June 1969 by changes in Regulations G, T, and U, the thrust of which was to make margin requirements effective against a Federal Reserve list of over-the-counter stocks that are similar to registered stocks.[2]

The term "margin requirement" can best be understood from a simple example. When the requirement is 40 percent, a margin trader has to send $40 to his broker in order to buy $100 worth of stock (disregarding commission and taxes). The broker lends the remaining $60 at an agreed rate of interest. Thus, the margin requirement (customer's equity) is the difference between the current value of the securities and their maximum loan value. The broker is safeguarded by the collateral which, according to the loan agreement, can be sold by him to prevent loss.

[1]Securities Exchange Act of 1934, Section 7.
[2]Board of Governors of the Federal Reserve System, *Annual Report* (Washington, D.C., 1968), pp. 70, 334; 1969, pp. 78-79.

The margin requirement applies only to the initial purchase, not to the margin that must subsequently be maintained, which is governed by a rule of the stock exchange (25 percent for the New York Stock Exchange in 1970). In the example just mentioned, a 25 percent margin would be reached when the price of the stock declined to $80.[3] The broker must call for additional margin (cash or securities) if the price declines below $80. If the trader fails to meet the call, the broker must sell enough stock to bring the margin up to the 25 percent minimum. Thus, the cushion between the Board's requirement on initial purchases and the broker's minimum margin postpones forced liquidation in a declining market.

The Board of Governors is empowered to raise or lower margin requirements in its discretion as a means of controlling security loans and of effectuating general credit policies. Between 1934 and 1970, 18 changes were made, with requirements ranging from 40 to 100 percent. In November 1970, the requirement was 65 percent. In general, requirements were raised when there was evidence of excessive use of speculative credit as reflected in brokers' loans, customers' borrowing from brokers, heavy volume of trading, and rising stock prices. These steps were usually part of a restrictive general policy to dampen an inflationary expansion of the economy. Reductions in requirements were typically made during business recessions, as in 1962 and 1970.

One object of giving the Board power to change margin requirements was to prevent the chain reaction known as *pyramiding* which enlarged the speculative bubble in 1929. In terms of the example again, assume that the stock purchased for $100 rises to $200, so that the trader's equity becomes $140. This enables him to buy an additional $150 of securities with borrowed money, if he so desires, after which the value of securities in his account is $350 and his debit (borrowed) balance becomes $210. Thus, a rise of security prices creates more borrowing power, which the trader may use in progressive steps to bid prices still higher. But if the Board had raised margin requirements to 70 percent, the pyramiding process would have been forestalled because that is the trader's new margin; that is, his new equity of $140 is 70 percent of $200.

While control of margin requirements gives the Board large powers, the following types of security loans are exempted.

1/Loans for the purchase and carrying of bonds and other obligations, excepting registered bonds convertible into stocks.

2/"Nonpurpose" loans which are secured by stocks but whose purpose is not to purchase or carry stocks. Such loans are made for a wide range of purposes—for example, personal expenditures and financing business operations.

3/Loans to security dealers to finance the underwriting and distribution of new security issues.

[3]The loss reduces the customer's equity to $20, which is 25 percent of $80.

4/Brokers' loans secured by customers' collateral to enable a broker to lend to his customers.

5/Certain types of bank loans to brokers and dealers, mainly to finance very short-term transactions such as securities in transit, securities in process of delivery, and arbitrage operations.

In addition to margin requirements, security loans are subject to other controls. The Securities Exchange Act of 1934 provided that brokers on securities exchanges can borrow only from banks that comply with all federal laws pertaining to the securities business. This effectively brought brokers' loans under regulation. It also ended the practice of brokers' loans by "others," comprising mainly business corporations, investment companies, individuals, and foreign interests. At the peak in October 1929, these nonbank loans were nearly four-fifths of total brokers' loans, and their precipitate withdrawal was one of the causes of panicky liquidation of stocks in 1929 and 1930. Also, the Banking Acts of 1933 and 1935 gave the Board direct controls over security loans. It was empowered to "fix from time to time for each Federal Reserve district the percentage of individual bank capital and surplus which may be represented by loans secured by stock or bond collateral. . . ."[4] Further, the Board may deny all Reserve Bank borrowing privileges to a member bank that increases its security loans despite an official warning.[5] In practice, the Board has found no occasion for the use of either of these direct controls; changes in margin requirements have been sufficient to serve its purposes.

effectiveness of regulation

For more than two decades following establishment of controls in 1934, use of credit in the stock market presented little or no problem. This was partly a consequence of moderation in security speculation, and partly of high margin requirements set by the Board of Governors. But the great bull market during the period 1954-1961 questioned once again the effectiveness of security-credit regulation. The use of credit was actually very moderate in comparison with the late 1920s. For example, member brokers of the New York Stock Exchange were borrowing about $3 billion at the peak of stock prices in December 1961. This compared with $8.5 billion at the height of borrowing in October 1929, when total value of listed securities was less than one-fifth as large. In other words, brokers' loans in 1961 would have exceeded $40 billion if their proportion to value of securities had been the same as in 1929. Nevertheless, in recent years, borrowing to buy stock has increased materially, as evidenced by the fact that net debit balances of customers of New York Stock

[4]Federal Reserve Act, Section 1, par. 25.
[5]Ibid., Section 13, par. 8.

Exchange firms rose from $1.7 billion at the end of 1953 to $5.2 billion at midyear 1970.[6]

There was little reason for concern that security-loan credit was excessive during the late 1950s and early 1960s. As indicated, high margin requirements held such credit in check, and the Board could raise margins to 100 percent if need be. But since 1957, there has been increasing concern about unregulated lenders of security credit. These financial intermediaries have lent directly to individuals to buy stocks, with margins as low as 25 percent when the official requirement was 70 percent. Interest rates charged have been 15 to 36 percent, compared with 5 or 6 percent charged by brokers. One of the principal sources of funds of such lenders has been the nonpurpose bank loan. That is, the bank has accepted their statement that they were borrowing for a nonspeculative purpose; not to buy stock. Technically, this may have been true because they were borrowing to relend to others to buy stocks. Banks have lent them as much as 80 percent of the value of stock collateral, compared with 30 percent when the purpose was to purchase or hold stocks.

Unregulated lenders have not been the only offenders who have borrowed to speculate in stocks through the crevice of nonpurpose loans. Some businessmen have ostensibly borrowed to finance inventories with stock-secured loans. But in reality, they may have previously used inventory money to buy the stocks which they now use as collateral. Then, too, some professional men have used funds allocated for purchase of equipment to buy stocks; then they have used the stocks as collateral for bank loans to purchase equipment. Foreign financial institutions, which are not subject to margin requirements, have also lent to stock speculators. These are illustrations of the near impossibility of designing and administering a regulatory program free from loopholes. Credit, like gas under pressure, escapes through every fissure, and flows toward the most inviting vacuum. It is exceedingly difficult to apply regulation to one type of credit without extending control to other credit areas where freedom is desirable. Passage of the amendment to the Securities Exchange Act in 1968 and recent amendments by the Board of Regulations G, T, and U have significantly strengthened regulatory arrangements.

conclusions

Despite the general presumption against detailed government regulation, security loans present special problems which call for selective control. Excessive use of speculative credit undermines the smooth functioning of the capital market, accentuates business booms, fosters price inflation, and develops maladjustments in the economy. In the depression that follows, liquidation of stocks and of security loans actively promotes business decline. Because the

[6]*Federal Reserve Bulletin* (October 1970), p. A 36.

expectation of typical speculators is substantial capital gain, security loans are quite unresponsive to the general instruments of credit control. Therefore, effective control depends on a well-designed selective program. Since 1934, chief reliance has been placed on discretionary changes of margin requirements on security loans by the Board of Governors. This method has proved to be administratively practicable because the credit area is well defined, quite standardized practices prevail, and enforcement involves a manageable number of banks, brokers, and dealers. However, leakages of credit to finance security speculation have occurred in various ways, notably through nonpurpose loans to speculators.

CONSUMER-CREDIT REGULATION

In contrast with security-loan regulation which is generally regarded to be desirable, the control of consumer credit remains a highly controversial issue. Well-informed experts both within and outside the Fed differ widely with respect to its feasibility. With a view to resolving the issue, President Eisenhower directed the Board of Governors to make a broad study of the role of consumer credit in the economy, including the arguments for and against regulation. The result was a monumental six-volume work, published in 1957, which constitutes a major contribution to the factual and analytical background of the subject.[7] It was not the purpose, however, to make specific recommendations in regard to the advisability of granting permanent authority to the Board. Rather, the object was to provide relevant information needed to arrive at intelligent decisions on the question.

Consideration will now be given to the nature and functions of consumer credit, experiences with control, and the arguments for and against government regulation.

nature and functions

Consumer credit logically divides into three categories: (1) emergency credit, (2) convenience credit, and (3) installment credit. The first includes a large part of small installment personal loans and some single-payment loans, the purpose of which is to carry families through budget difficulties arising from illness, accidents, unemployment, and other emergencies. *Convenience credit* is represented by charge accounts at retail stores and by service credit mainly extended by electric, gas, telephone, and other public utilities. *Installment credit* is used chiefly to finance the purchase of automobiles and major durable household goods such as furniture, refrigerators, washing machines, stoves,

[7] Board of Governors of the Federal Reserve System, *Consumer Instalment Credit* (Washington, D.C., 1957).

vacuum cleaners, radios, and television sets. It is also used to finance home repairs and modernization. The general purpose of consumer credit is to enable consumers to enjoy products today and pay for them tomorrow. In contrast with a cash basis, where saving must precede purchase, the saving process takes place largely after purchase, and the peak of accumulated savings associated with a specific purchase may never exceed the downpayment. Periodic payments from income may just about cover the declining value of the product.

Installment credit contributes most to the economy by making possible mass consumption and mass production of major consumer durables whose unit prices are relatively high. The automobile is the best example. If the middle- and lower-income groups had to save the purchase price in advance, the automobile market would materially shrink.

Thus, a strong case can be made that installment credit contributes to economic growth and total output; that is, it does more than merely facilitate a diversion of demand from nondurable goods and services to durables. The argument is based on reduction of unit costs by mass production, increased desire for goods accompanied by greater efforts to enlarge personal incomes, and broadening the range of products available to consumers.

Some idea of recent developments in consumer credit is given by Table 16-1. Attention is called to the following: (1) total consumer credit exhibits a strong growth trend. The amount outstanding in 1970—$123.7 billion—was about 13 times as large as in 1941 and 22 times as large as it was at the end of

TABLE 16-1 / SHORT- AND INTERMEDIATE-TERM CONSUMER CREDIT OUTSTANDING ON SELECTED DATES, 1941-1970[a] (millions of dollars)

Type of Credit	1941	1945	1950	1955	1962	1967	1970
Installment credit							
Automobiles	2,458	455	6,074	13,437	17,039	30,724	36,908
Other consumer goods	1,929	816	4,799	7,641	11,256	22,395	27,801
Repair and modernization	376	182	1,016	1,693	3,084	3,789	4,104
Personal loans	1,322	1,009	2,814	6,112	11,325	24,018	31,047
Total	6,085	2,462	14,703	28,883	42,704	80,926	99,860
Noninstallment credit							
Single payment loans	845	746	1,821	3,002	5,056	8,428	9,294
Charge accounts	1,645	1,612	3,291	4,795	4,191	6,968	7,508
Service credit	597	845	1,580	2,127	3,729	5,810	6,993
Total	3,087	3,203	6,692	9,924	12,976	21,206	23,795
Grand total	9,172	5,665	21,395	38,807	55,680	102,132	123,655

[a]End of year, except 1970 which is at end of August.
Source: *Federal Reserve Bulletin* (October 1970), p. A 54.

World War II. This rapid increase is one of the reasons why peacetime control has been a live current issue. (2) Installment credit represents about four-fifths of total consumer credit, and its growth has been substantially more rapid than that of noninstallment credit. In fact those who favor regulation are mainly concerned with installment credit. (3) Automobile purchases generate nearly two-fifths of total installment credit. (4) It is of interest that installment credit was largely liquidated during the war when automobiles and other durables were not being produced, and that the postwar period has witnessed its most vigorous growth.

objectives of control

The first step in a program of consumer-credit control is a careful definition of goals. This is necessary to determine not only the nature and scope of the program but also its practical application. Authorities in this field emphasize the following objectives.

1/The most widely approved objective is that of contributing to economic stability. It is believed that a rapid expansion of consumer credit during the prosperity phase of the cycle is an important factor in generating an unsustainable rate of growth, and that in the readjustment period which follows, the liquidation of consumer debt magnifies the recession. Therefore, regulation is suggested to prevent excessive expansion of such credit.

2/It is desirable to prevent the added risks and losses of lenders that arise when competition leads to deterioration in credit quality as downpayments are reduced and maturities are extended. This purpose applies primarily to the protection of lenders and sellers, although by forestalling losses and insolvencies it also contributes to business stability.

3/Protection for buyer-borrowers from misrepresentations and excessive charges is important. Closely related to the second goal, this objective anticipates policing of trade practices.

4/Wide support exists for the use of consumer-credit control during war-created emergencies, when it can serve a multiple purpose. By restricting demand for durable goods, it assists in transferring productive resources to the war effort; it gives some protection to durable-goods consumers by checking the rise in prices of such goods; it aids in preventing a general price inflation; and it promotes personal savings to finance the war and to moderate a postwar depression. Moreover, during wartime the general instruments of monetary management are likely to be suspended, so that the regulation of consumer credit and other direct controls must assume a far greater burden.

While the foregoing objectives harmonize in some respects, they conflict in others. Prevention of excessive consumer-credit expansion in the interest of business stability would also serve to some extent the purposes expressed in the second objective. That is, the risks and losses of lenders and sellers would be minimized by raising lending standards. However, control might be needed to attain the second and third objectives when, from the standpoint of stability, it could well be removed. Seldom would the same degree of control be called for by the separate objectives; nor would the form and scope of control appropriate for one be entirely applicable to the others.

experience with regulation

The actual experience with consumer-credit control in the United States is confined to three periods under war or war-induced conditions. The first was during World War II and the subsequent reconversion; the second was in 1948-1949 when postwar price inflation was active; and the third was during the Korean War. In all three cases, general monetary controls were suspended or ineffective.

Regulation During World War II / The first regulation, based on an Executive Order of the President, became effective September 1, 1941. Control was placed in the hands of the Board of Governors. The main purposes as stated in the Order were to assist in the transfer of productive resources to war industries, to prevent price inflation, and to promote savings for the dual purpose of financing the war and creating consumer purchasing power to moderate a possible postwar depression. Regulation initially applied only to some 24 categories of consumer durable goods. It took the form of (1) minimum downpayments and (2) maximum maturities for installment contracts. Required downpayments ranged between 10 percent on furniture and $33\frac{1}{3}$ percent on automobiles. Maximum maturities were fixed at 18 months for all listed products. In general, requirements were in line with prevailing practices.

As the war progressed, controls were broadened and tightened. The list of regulated items was extended to include 48 categories, and both charge accounts and single-payment loans were brought under control. By the end of the war, the typical downpayment had been raised to one-third and the prevailing requirement on maturities had been reduced to 12 months. During the reconversion period, requirements were materially eased, including release from control of charge accounts and single-payment loans. Wartime regulation was terminated by Congress on November 1, 1947.

Regulation, 1948-1949 / Concerned about the strong upward movement of commodity prices, Congress provided for reinstatement of installment-credit control by a Joint Resolution approved in August 1948. The new regulation of the Board, which became effective in September, was substantially the same as the one in effect during reconversion. Minimum downpayments for automobiles were one-third and for major appliances were one-fifth. Maximum maturities ranged between 15 and 18 months. These limits were typical, so that the principal effects were to hold the line and to prevent further liberalization of terms. Shortly after the regulation became effective, evidences of recession began to appear, with the result that the Board relaxed the required terms in March-April before authority for control expired at the end of June 1949.

Regulation, 1950-1952 / The last period of regulation was associated with the Korean War. Congress once again authorized installment-credit control in the Defense Production Act of 1950.[8] The new regulation of the Board, effective September 18, 1950, followed the same lines as the former one, except that home-improvement loans were also included. In general, it conformed with current practices at the outset, and was only moderately restrictive. Minimum downpayments on automobiles were fixed at one-third and maximum maturities were set at 21 months. On major appliances, downpayments were 15 percent and maturities were 18 months. In mid-October, when the seriousness of the Korean situation became more evident, terms were materially tightened. They were eased at the end of July 1951, and control was entirely suspended in May 1952. Legal authority for installment-credit control was repealed as of June 30, 1952.

arguments for control

Although the abnormality and complexity of conditions during the war and postwar years make an appraisal of the effects of consumer-credit control difficult, several lessons can be learned from experience. The proponents of stand-by authority to regulate installment credit in peacetime advance a number of arguments which may be summarized, as follows:

1/The principal argument, which has several strands, is based on the promotion of business stability. The large wastes of resources and losses of welfare, together with the fluctuation of installment credits are important factors of instability. Consumer expenditures for durable goods vary much more widely than for nondurables, and, in turn, installment credit extended fluctuates to a greater degree than expenditures for durables. One form of argument places emphasis on the cycles in consumer inventories of durable goods. By the use of installment credit, consumers bunch purchases of durables and thereby build up their stocks at a more rapid rate than the increase of demand for the services of such goods. This process is followed by a decline in purchases, usually associated with a general recession, while demand absorbs the glut in durables on hand, and while installment debt is paid down to a more comfortable relation to income. Another approach underscores the influence of installment credit in magnifying variations of bank credit, aggregate demand, and economic activity. Total demand is augmented in periods of general expansion because additions to

[8]Federal Reserve Act, Section 601.

consumer credit beget increases in both the amount and velocity of money. The consequence may be an unsustainable boom, and perhaps also price inflation. For opposite reasons, contraction of installment credit accentuates declines in business activity and contributes to price deflation.

On the basis of the foregoing arguments, regulation of installment credit is advocated as a useful supplement to general monetary controls. It is believed that direct control of this disturbing factor would permit a more moderate use of the general instruments of control, and would make possible a more effective overall program of monetary management. The point is also made that restraint of installment credit during a boom reserves an important stimulant–liberalization of terms–for utilization during the ensuing recession.

2/Another argument for regulation is based on the insensitiveness of installment credit to restraints applied by the general instruments of monetary management. Consumer-borrowers, it is contended, think mainly in terms of the size of monthly payments rather than of interest charges or total indebtedness. Because interest represents only a small part, say, 10 percent, of the monthly payment–which includes repayment of principal, administrative costs, insurance, and commissions–a rise of interest rates causes a relatively small increase in payment. Moreover, the lender can avoid an accompanying increase in the monthly payment by a small extension in loan maturity. It is also believed that the profitability and safety of installment loans lead banks to shift credit in this direction at the expense of other types of loan during periods of restrictive credit policy. This shifting takes place both in their own installment loans and in their loans to large finance companies that are in position to compete strongly for bank loans.

3/Other proponents advocate regulation to protect both lenders and borrowers. They would safeguard the former against losses arising when competition produces excessively liberal credit terms. They would also police the terms of loan contracts in order to protect unsuspecting borrowers from misrepresentations and excessive charges. This argument is largely outside the realm of monetary management, except for the fact that maintenance of credit quality promotes business stability.

4/It is also argued that the existence of stand-by authority to regulate installment credit would, even though seldom utilized, exert a significant restraining influence on overexpansion of such credit. Faced with the regulatory threat, lenders would be less likely to depart from conservative standards in regard to downpayments, maturities, and other terms. They would be more inclined, individually and as a group, to police themselves with the aim of avoiding the inconveniences and restrictions that accompany government regulation.

5/Proponents contend that installment-credit regulation is practicable because this sector meets the tests of accepted criteria for direct control: (a) a well-defined credit area; (b) standardization of trade practices; (c) a large enough credit sector to be important from a regulatory standpoint; and (d) responsiveness to changes in downpayment and maturity terms.

arguments against control

Those who oppose stand-by authority to regulate installment credit in peacetime do so on the basis of three main arguments: (1) inconsistency with the principles that underlie our economic and political system; (2) lack of need in view of the adequacy of general monetary and fiscal controls; and (3) formidable problems of enforcement.

1/Those observers who place a high priority on individual freedom, the private competitive economic system, and political democracy see a strong presumption against detailed government controls in general, including installment-credit regulation. They fear the progressive nature of such controls, and contend that installment-credit control, to be effective and fair, calls for regulation of other forms of consumer credit; and that, in turn, plausible reasons can be found to extend the program of regulation to other types of loans. Therefore, insofar as possible, they prefer to rely on the guidance of individual choices as reflected in the market place, and to limit such controls as are necessary to the overall variety.

Considerable emphasis is also placed by this group on the misallocation of productive resources that is likely to result from regulation. They believe that a government agency's arbitrary decisions—often too rigid and confining—rather than consumer choices would determine the flow of resources into durable consumer-goods industries. More specifically, controls would operate to make these industries less attractive by limiting demand, so that less resources would be committed to them. Such restriction, it is held, would represent discrimination against producers, sellers, and lenders in the durable-goods field, and also against those who buy on credit as compared with cash purchasers. In answer to this charge, the proponents of regulation point out that waste of resources also occurs when overexpansion of installment credit intensifies demand for consumer durables. The direct effect is overinvestment in this area and the indirect effect, through the acceleration principle, is an unstabilizing stimulation of aggregate expenditures throughout the economy.

Opponents further call attention to the role of installment credit in promoting economic growth. Without the innovations and development of this form of credit in financing mass distribution, the rapid expansion of durable consumer-goods industries could not have occurred. The economies of large-scale production with the associated reduction in unit costs could not have been so fully realized. Some also stress the fact that the stimulus of installment credit is needed to finance expenditures in years of high prosperity—the periods when growth largely takes place. A further argument emphasizes the intolerable burdens that regulation would place on businesses subject to control. Inconveniences and expense would be imposed by required recordkeeping, the translation of regulations into operating procedures, the training of employees in regard to changing regulations, and the submission to periodic investigation. For the foregoing reasons opponents view regulation with alarm as a depressant of economic growth.

2/Those who oppose regulation also believe that there is little or no need for installment-credit control in peacetime in view of the adequacy of overall credit controls—the discount mechanism, open-market operations, legal-reserve requirements, federal fiscal policy, and debt management by the Treasury. What is needed, they say, is greater wisdom, skill, and courage in the coordinated use of these general controls, rather than an extension of direct regulation.

Another strand of this argument disputes the statement by proponents that installment credit is unresponsive to overall controls and should therefore be brought under selective control. When a policy of credit restraint is in force, banks curtail both direct lending to consumers and loans to finance companies. Direct consumer loans are usually restricted, despite the inducement of immediate profitability, in view of the primary responsibility of banks to meet borrowing needs of business customers who account for the greater part of demand deposits. Business loans are also immediately profitable, and they bear more directly on the bank's long-range success. While finance companies may also be depositors, they must compete for loan funds with other powerful business borrowers. There is, of course, no question about the higher priority of business borrowers compared with nondepositing finance companies which offer open-market short-term notes for subscription. Thus, faced with the necessity of borrowing more in the open capital market on less favorable terms, nonbank installment lenders restrict their consumer loans in various ways by raising rates, reducing dealer credit lines, raising loan standards, and increasing pressure on collections. For these reasons, opponents contend that a reasonable degree of responsiveness of installment credit to overall controls exists, and that selective control is therefore unnecessary.

3/A final objection to regulation relates to the formidable problems of administration, compliance, and enforcement. Some indication of the magnitude of the task is given by the fact that the number of organizations subject to installment-credit control is in the vicinity of 200,000. During the 1950-1952 period of control, the Federal Reserve made 111,956 investigations and 23,878 calls. Violations were found in 12 percent of the investigations, to which must be added an unknown number of undiscovered violations, evasions, and avoidances.[9] Experience shows that enforcement problems rise with the degree of restriction and with the length of the period of control; also that downpayment terms, largely because of trade-in values, are far more difficult to enforce than maximum maturities.

Violations, say opponents, would be widespread among the tens of thousands of smaller dealers who handle millions of pieces of paper. Even in the cases of large banks and finance companies, where enforcement is more manageable, there are numerous ways to avoid compliance. One of these is the

[9]Board of Governors of the Federal Reserve System, *Consumer Instalment Credit,* op. cit., Part I, Vol. I, pp. 302, 314.

nonpurpose bank loan in which the proceeds are actually used to buy consumer durables. A variant of this is use of the proceeds to meet the schedule of payments on a simultaneous installment loan. Still another device is the extension of maturities after the original loan is made, under the pretext that the borrower is not able to make payments as scheduled. In general, unless all forms of consumer credit are brought under control—a Herculean task—consumers would negate regulation of installment credit in large measure by single-payment loans, book credit, and other devices.

A practical aspect of this argument is the impossibility of maintaining an able and capable enforcement staff of several thousand persons for an intermittent assignment. Such a staff could not very well be retained without duties during years when regulation is unnecessary. But if disbanded at the conclusion of a period of regulation, these persons would move into permanent jobs and would not be available when needed at a later date. This staff problem is particularly serious because timeliness is a prime requisite of effective control. There is no doubt that an ineptly-administered program of regulation would do more harm than good.

4/Impressed with the likelihood of widespread violations, opponents view installment-credit control as a threat to the power and prestige of the Fed. They believe that noncompliance would reach such proportions as to undermine public respect for regulation. At this point, Congress, subjected to broadly-based political pressures, would no longer support the program. Then, having lost prestige and having developed powerful opposition, the Fed might well be stripped of part or all of its general powers of monetary management.

summary and conclusions

Several lessons can be learned from the war and postwar experience with consumer-credit regulation despite the abnormality and complexity of conditions in those years. First, such regulation is a useful and effective member of the family of direct controls that are necessary while the economy is dominated by the requirements of a major war. This conclusion would be accepted by most of the opponents of peacetime regulation.

Second, the tightening of credit terms is an effective method of reducing the rate of expansion, or of the amount, of installment credit. This was demonstrated beyond doubt by the experiences of both 1948 and 1950, when extensions were reduced and repayments were speeded after terms were tightened. This does not mean, however, that use of this method in peacetime is necessarily a wise policy. Costs may outweigh benefits, and in addition the general monetary and fiscal controls may be sufficient.

Third, regulation should be concerned primarily with changes of maturities rather than with downpayments. While not entirely free from evasion, the maturity contract is fairly definite and subject to check. In contrast, minimum downpayments depend on valuation of trade-ins and may also be indefinite because of variations in pricing. As a consequence, detection of violations becomes difficult.

Fourth, the scope of a control program tends to expand until all of consumer credit, and perhaps other types of credit, are included. For example, the initial regulation during the war covered only installment credit, but it was soon extended to include charge accounts and single-payment loans. This step was taken partly because of widespread evasion through these channels, and partly to eliminate discrimination among credit-using consumers. Beyond this, evasion by using the proceeds of nonpurpose loans to buy consumer goods may lead to regulation of other types of loan.

Finally, the problems of administration, compliance, and enforcement represent a major task, especially during peacetime when patriotic motives for compliance are absent and there is less public support of regulation. In fact, these problems alone render consumer-credit regulation at the retail level unwise in peacetime. If used at all in peacetime, the program should be limited to banks and finance companies of substantial size, so that the administrative problem is manageable.

REAL-ESTATE CREDIT REGULATION

With the outbreak of war in Korea, selective credit control was not only reinstated for consumer credit, but was also applied for the first time to residential real-estate credit. Some idea of the importance of this credit sector is given by the fact that the amount of mortgage loans outstanding on nonfarm 1-4-family houses at the end of 1950 was $45.1 billion. By comparison, total consumer installment credit outstanding at the same time was $20.8 billion. Thus, the program had special significance because it extended control to an important new area.

objectives of control

One of the main objectives of the program was to restrain price inflation, both in general and in the construction industry. Consumer and wholesale prices had risen materially during the first three quarters of 1950, and especially during the third quarter. Without control, it was feared that prices would continue their upward course when government demand for war goods was added to the existing high demands of consumers and businesses. Residential construction and the accompanying expansion of home mortgages were proceeding at record rates. Because commercial banks were large lenders of mortgage credit, continuation of this growth meant further increases in the amount of money and in other liquid assets. The flow of expenditures was also likely to be stimulated by increased velocity of money. It was believed that control of real-estate credit would assist in keeping these developments in bounds and that real-estate credit regulation could be a partial substitute, or a supplement to, general monetary and fiscal controls. General instruments of monetary control were not effective at the time in view of continuation of wartime support of U.S. security prices by the Reserve Banks. Pending return of these controls to the Fed, real-estate control could serve a substitutive role. When and if general controls were revived, real-estate credit control would serve usefully in a supplementary capacity. Others also regarded real-estate credit control as a partial substitute for, or supplement to, direct regulation of prices, wages, and rents. That is, the program would help to remove the need for fixing prices and wages. But if price and wage regulation became necessary, real-estate credit control would contribute to its effectiveness.

Still another important objective was to hasten the transfer of productive resources to production of war goods. Manpower, materials, and plants used in private construction industries had to be mobilized for the war effort. In expediting this reconversion process, real-estate credit control was viewed as a useful supplement to direct allocation of materials, and regulation of production.

A final, but less pressing purpose, was accumulation of a bank of deferred demand in the private construction field. Limitations on real-estate loans would permit these demands to become effective after the end of hostilities when productive resources were available, and when there might well be danger of a postwar depression.

origin and legal basis

Authority to regulate residential real-estate credit was granted the President by the Defense Production Act of 1950.[10] The President delegated this power to the Board of Governors of the Fed and the Housing and Home Finance Administrator. His Executive Order granted the Board authority over nongovernment-aided real-estate loans and gave the Housing Administrator control of government-aided real-estate credit. Concurrence of the Administrator was required in regulations of the Board, and in turn, regulations of the Administrator were to be comparable to the fullest practicable extent with those of the Board.

program of regulation

After extensive consultation with the real-estate finance and building industries, the Board of Governors, in cooperation with the Housing and Home

[10]Section 602.

Finance Administrator, issued Regulation X, effective October 12, 1950. With some exceptions, this regulation and its subsequent amendments applied to the financing of all nongovernment-aided residential construction. Parallel regulations applicable to government-aided programs were issued by the Administrator, so that the bulk of all residential construction was covered.

Regulation X took the form of specifications with respect to maximum amount of borrowing in relation to value of the project, maximum maturities, and minimum amortization requirements. For example, maximum loans on residential construction ranged from 90 percent of value in the $5,000-and-under value group to 50 percent in the $25,000-and-over category. Maximum maturities were restricted to 20 years, except in case of properties valued at $7,000 or less where maturity could be 25 years. In general, the regulation was framed with the aim of reducing residential building by about one-third below the current rate, or to not over 800,000 units in 1951.

Administration of Regulation X was decentralized among the Federal Reserve Banks and their branches. Enforcement was aided by cooperation from other federal agencies with examining staffs—Federal Deposit Insurance Corporation, Comptroller of the Currency, Home Loan Bank Board, Farm Credit Administration, and Federal Security Agency. Arrangements were also made for state officials or agencies to examine lenders subject to their supervision, including insurance companies, savings and loan associations, and noninsured banks. In all, about 50,000 lenders were registered and subject to control.

In conformity with acts of Congress,[11] Regulation X was relaxed substantially in September 1951 and again in June 1952. It was completely suspended in September 1952, and similar action was taken at the same time by the Housing and Home Finance Administrator. Suspension of regulation at this time was occasioned by the Defense Production Act amendment of 1952, which made effective control contingent on the rate of new housing starts.[12] Authority to regulate real-estate credit lapsed at the end of June 1953.

Most informed observers agree that Regulation X was effective in materially reducing the amount of residential construction after the first quarter of 1951, when preregulation commitments were largely out of the way. For example, between April and August 1951, the number of private residences started was over one-third below that of the corresponding period of the previous year. After relaxation of terms in September, the number of starts again moved upward. However, all credit for the decline in housing production cannot be given to real-estate credit control. The Treasury-Federal Reserve Accord in March 1951 made possible a more active use of the general instruments of monetary regulation. The sizable decline in prices of U.S. securities that followed made life insurance companies and banks less willing to make

[11]Defense Housing and Community Facilities and Services Act, August 28, 1951; Defense Production Act, amendment of 1952.

[12]Section 607 was amended to provide that if housing starts should fall below an annual rate of 1,200,000 in three successive months, downpayments required could not be in excess of 5 percent. This happened in June, July, and August 1952.

real-estate loans. In addition, allocations of building materials and various other factors affected the volume of construction. Also, the availability of real-estate credit is typically reduced during periods of high rates. The flow of savings to savings and loan associations, savings banks, and commercial banks may greatly decline, as in 1966 and 1969—when investors could realize a larger return by the purchase of government and corporate securities.

summary and conclusions

Several conclusions emerge from the foregoing brief experience with control of real-estate credit:

1/As with other detailed direct controls, there is a strong presumption against regulation of real-estate credit in peacetime because such regulation is not consistent with the basic principles of a free-market economy.

2/Direct regulation is not needed in this field in peacetime because the general instruments of monetary and fiscal control, if wisely and courageously used, are adequate to assure reasonable business stability. Moreover, real-estate loans are highly responsive to restrictive general credit measures. The demand for such credit declines as interest rates rise because interest is a large part of the schedule of installment payments that usually stretch over a period ranging between 15 and 30 years. Hence, an increase in the rate from, say, 5 to 7 percent, represents a significant increase in each installment and in total financing cost. In addition, the price of an income-bearing property tends to decline as interest rates rise because the price is, in large part, determined by capitalizing net income at the prevailing rate. With a decline in prices of existing properties, new construction and the associated loan demands are reduced.

3/In great emergencies, however, a well-designed program of real-estate credit control can serve useful purposes. It can be a partial substitute for, or a supplement to, general monetary controls; also, it can play a similar role with respect to direct control of prices, wages, materials, and production.

4/When and if employed, such a program should rely more heavily on changing the terms of downpayments than of maturities. This follows from the fact that the downpayment is a large hurdle in the case of a house. Moreover, there is usually no trade-in to give indefiniteness to the amount of the downpayment as in the case of automobiles and household durables. This does not mean, however, that control of maturities should be neglected. Shorter maturities, of course, present the obstacle of higher installment payments; longer maturities encourage construction and loans by reducing installment payments.

5/A limitation on real-estate credit control is the lag between application of regulation and its actual influence on the amount of new construction. Because such control would be employed, if at all, in a period of active building, there would be a large amount of advance commitments on the date of regulation. Moreover, if advance notice of pending regulation is given, an abnormal amount of commitments would be made just before the regulation date in order to avoid more restrictive terms. Because regulation can equitably be applied only to new loans, it would take several months to work off advance commitments. For example, it was not until the second quarter of 1951–five months after control was applied in October 1950–that tangible evidence of the effectiveness of Regulation X began to appear.

6/Enforcement of a regulatory program is a major task, although not so formidable as in the case of consumer credit. Even during the Korean War, strong pressures for relaxation of Regulation X were exerted on Congress, with the result that administrative powers of the Board and the Administrator were materially reduced in 1951, and were suspended in 1952. This experience strongly suggests that public and congressional support of such a program in peacetime, when patriotic fervor is lacking, cannot be reasonably expected. Moreover, if this be true, it would be a major mistake to threaten the prestige and the monetary powers of the Board of Governors by saddling it with administration of a foredoomed set of regulations.

MORAL SUASION

In addition to the general and selective credit controls previously discussed, the method of moral suasion has been employed from time to time. While utilized in a minor role during peacetime, its most important application was during the Korean War in the form of the voluntary credit-restraint program.

use in peacetime

In peacetime moral suasion embraces the entire range of activities of Federal Reserve authorities designed to develop support of credit policy by education, persuasion, and warning. Much staff-time of the Board and of the Reserve Banks is devoted to informational and educational projects. These include collection and publication of monetary, banking, and general economic statistics, publication of the *Federal Reserve Bulletin* and of annual reports by the Board, issuance of monthly reviews and annual reports by the Banks, and publication of books, pamphlets, and special studies. Efforts to persuade member banks and the public to support policies are made by public press releases, statements and speeches by Board members and other officials, memoranda to member banks, conferences of banking groups, and personal visits. Warnings against overexpansion of credit, the granting of speculative loans, excessive Reserve Bank borrowing, and other such matters are conveyed in a similar manner. While accurate measurement of results from these moral-suasion activities is impossible, they undoubtedly contribute at times to the effectiveness of prevailing monetary policy.

voluntary credit-restraint program

Moral suasion assumed a more systematic form when the Defense Production Act of 1950[13] provided for a program of voluntary credit restraint. Aside from being voluntary, it differed in scope from the other selective measures. Whereas they were directed to regulation of well-defined types of credit, the voluntary program covered the vague area of credit not essential for the Korean War effort. For this reason, it could be classified as a selective control only by broad definition. However, this program had even less resemblance to the general instruments of control. It was narrower in scope, and was concerned to a large extent with direction of credit demands, whereas the general instruments mainly regulated the overall supply and cost of credit.

Organization / Responsibility for implementation of the voluntary restraint program was given to the Board of Governors by an Executive Order of the President. Conferences with representatives of financial institutions developed an approved program which was announced in March 1951. Directing the program was a national voluntary-credit restraint committee composed of representatives of commercial banks, mutual savings banks, insurance companies, investment banks, and savings and loan associations. The chairman of this committee was a member of the Board of Governors. Administering the program were 43 regional subcommittees which were available for consultation with lenders in regard to decisions on specific loans. The final decision to approve or disapprove loans, however, rested entirely with each bank or other lending institution.

Objectives and Principles / The broad objectives of the program were to assist in containing overall inflationary tendencies, and in directing resources of manpower, materials, plants, and equipment to the war effort. More concretely, the purpose was to extend loans to finance war production and the essential needs of business and agriculture, and to curtail loans for nonessential projects. The basic criterion in passing upon a loan was: "Does it commensurately increase or maintain production, processing, and distribution of essential goods and services?" In applying this principle, certain types of nonessential loans were designated by the committee, as follows:

1/Loans to retire corporate stocks where no increase of production would result.

2/Loans for speculative purchases of securities, inventories, real estate, plants, or other property.

3/Loans to state and local governments to finance any project not urgently needed for preservation of health and safety or not directly related to the war effort.

[13] Defense Production Act, Section 708.

Under each of these headings more detailed tests were suggested to assist the subcommittees and lending institutions in distinguishing between essential and nonessential purposes.

Operation of the Program / Most observers say the program made a significant contribution to abatement of inflationary forces and to the direction of resources to war purposes. These results were achieved by providing lending officers and businessmen with bench-marks to judge the use of credit, and by strongly urging them to cooperate during the emergency of the Korean War.

Because the program was only one of several measures with similar purposes, it is not possible to isolate its influence in statistical terms. The experience during its operation, however, was favorable as evidenced by a lessening of inflationary pressures, a reduction of inventories, and an increase in personal savings. There was also evidence of postponement of numerous nonessential projects, and a shift in bank lending toward war-supporting industries. Furthermore, lending institutions' cooperation in supporting adverse recommendations by subcommittees on security issues or loans was nearly complete. Available information indicates that the program made a constructive contribution.

On recommendation of the national committee that conditions no longer justified continuance of voluntary credit restraint, the program was suspended on May 12, 1952. Legal authority for such a program was terminated at midyear 1952 by amendment of the Defense Production Act.

Conclusions / On the basis of experience with the voluntary credit-restraint program of 1951 to 1952, it may be concluded that such a program is capable of making a substantial contribution in great emergencies by curtailing nonessential loans and by restraining inflationary forces. There is, however, no place for a program of this nature in peacetime. Its success depends on suppression of individual self-interest by patriotic motives born in war or in some other great emergency. As these fervent motives subside, the extent of compliance rapidly deteriorates. Even those lenders who are willing to cooperate cannot afford to do so when noncomplying competitors are making the "nonessential" but credit-worthy loans. In fact, such a program in peacetime is not in harmony with the basic principle of a free competitive system in which enterprisers are expected to pursue their own interests within the framework set by law.

VOLUNTARY FOREIGN-CREDIT RESTRAINT PROGRAM

Another voluntary credit-restraint program was initiated by the Fed in 1965 as a part of President Johnson's program to restore equilibrium in the international balance of payments. The central focus was to diminish the outflow of capital from the United States as one way of reducing the deficit which had been accumulating for several years.

Guidelines for implementation of the program were issued by the Board of Governors in March 1965. Omitting details, the objective was to hold the increase in outstanding bank credit to foreigners to 5 percent of the amount at the end of 1964. Bona fide export credits were given the highest priority. Credits to less developed countries were favored over credits to developed nations. Certain countries heavily dependent on U.S. financing—Canada, Japan, the United Kingdom—were also favored. Cutbacks were recommended in credits to the developed countries in certain areas: third-country trade, local-currency expenditures outside the United States, and fixed or working capital needs. In 1968, the limit on foreign credits by commercial banks was further reduced to 103 percent of the 1964 base. The success of the program is attested by the fact that outstanding foreign credits of U.S. banks at the end of 1969 were about $75 million below the initial base, although part of this reduction resulted from the strong deflationary stance of Federal Reserve Policy in 1969.

In addition to restraint on foreign credits by banks, the Fed issued guidelines for nonbank financial institutions in 1965. Holdings of liquid funds in foreign countries were to be held to the amount at the end of 1964, and were to be reduced in orderly fashion to the amount at the end of 1963. This program was also successful in bringing about a substantial reduction in foreign assets of these institutions by the end of 1969.[14]

REFERENCES

general

Chandler, Lester V., *Selective Credit Control* (Washington, D.C.: Board of Governors of the Federal Reserve System, 1967).

Fforde, J. S., *Federal Reserve System, 1945-1949* (Oxford: Oxford University Press, 1954), chaps. 8, 18.

Prochnow, Herbert V., ed., *The Federal Reserve System* (New York: Harper & Row, 1960), chap. 7.

Saulnier, Raymond J., "An Appraisal of Selective Credit Controls," *American Economic Review*, 42 (May 1952), pp. 247-263.

Simmons, Edward C., "The Role of Selective Credit Control in Monetary Management," *American Economic Review*, 37 (September 1947), pp. 633-641.

security-loan regulation

Federal Reserve Bulletin (October 1934), pp. 629-634, 675-686; (April 1936), pp. 215-218, 250-253.

Thomas, Woodlief, "Use of Credit in Security Speculation," *American Economic Review*, 25 (March 1935), pp. 21-30.

Twentieth Century Fund, *Stock Market Control* (New York: Appleton-Century-Crofts, 1934).

U.S. Congress, Senate Committee on Banking and Currency, *Stock Market Study*, staff report, 84th Congress, 1st sess., Senate Report 376, chap. 3.

[14]*Federal Reserve Bulletin* (February 1965), pp. 256-257; (March 1965), pp. 371-376. See also Board of Governors of the Federal Reserve System, *Annual Report* (Washington, D.C., 1966), pp. 37-42; 1969, pp. 55-59.

consumer-credit regulation

American Bankers Association. *Basic Issues of Monetary Policy*. Monetary Study No. 6, 1954, pp. 7-10.

Bartels, Robert, "Justification for Direct Regulation of Consumer Credit Reappraised," *Journal of Finance,* 8 (May 1953), pp. 261-277.

Board of Governors of the Federal Reserve System, *Consumer Instalment Credit* (Washington, D.C., 1957), 6 vols.

Board of Governors of the Federal Reserve System, *Federal Reserve Bulletin* (September 1941), pp. 839-847; (April 1949), pp. 343-347; (December 1949), pp. 1442-1449; (November 1950), pp. 1427-1440; (July 1951), pp. 800-806; (October 1951), pp. 1244-1255; (May 1952), pp. 491-496.

Commission on Money and Credit, *The Consumer Finance Industry* (Englewood Cliffs, N.J.: Prentice-Hall, 1962).

Fauver, Clarke L., and Ralph A. Young, "Measuring the Impact of Consumer Credit Controls on Spending," *Journal of Finance,* 7 (May 1952), pp. 388-402.

Haberler, Gottfried, *Consumer Instalment Credit and Economic Fluctuations* (New York: National Bureau of Economic Research, 1942).

Shay, Robert P., *Regulation W: Experiment in Credit Control* (Orono: University of Maine Press, 1953).

U.S. Congress, House Committee on Banking and Currency, *Government Credit,* Hearings, 80th Congress, 1st sess., Part 2.

U.S. Congress, Joint Committee on Defense Production, *Annual Report,* 1951, pp. 245-265.

U.S. Congress, Senate Committee on Banking and Currency, *Defense Production Act Amendments of 1951,* Hearings, 82nd Congress, 1st sess., on S. 1397, pp. 311-355.

U.S. Congress, Senate Committee on Banking and Currency, *Defense Production Act Amendments of 1952*, Hearings, 82nd Congress, 2d sess., on S. 2594 and S. 2645, pp. 75-108.

real-estate credit regulation

Federal Reserve Bulletin (October 1950), pp. 1284-1286; (July 1951), pp. 777-799; (March 1952), pp. 244-250; (June 1952), pp. 620-637.

U.S. Housing and Home Finance Agency, *Facts About Housing Credit Controls* (Washington, D.C., 1951), 2 Parts.

U.S. Congress, Joint Committee on Defense Production, *Annual Report*, 1951, pp. 245-255; 1952, pp. 255-265.

U.S. Congress, Senate Committee on Banking and Currency, *Defense Production Act of 1950,* Hearings, 81st Congress, 1st sess., on S. 3936, pp. 355-408.

U.S. Congress, Senate Committee on Banking and Currency, *Defense Production Act Amendments of 1951,* Hearings, 82nd Congress, 1st sess., on S. 1397, pp. 311-355.

U.S. Congress, Senate Committee on Banking and Currency, *Defense Production Act Amendments of 1952,* Hearings, 82nd Congress, 2d sess., on S. 2594 and S. 2645, pp. 75-108.

U.S. Congress, Senate Committee on Banking and Currency, *Middle Income Housing,* Hearings, 81st Congress, 2d sess., on amendment of S. 2246, pp. 355-426.

voluntary credit-restraint program

Federal Reserve Bulletin (March 1951), pp. 263-266; (November 1951), pp. 1347-1355; (March 1952), pp. 251-253; (May 1952), pp. 501-502.

U.S. Congress, Joint Committee on Defense Production, *Annual Report,* 1951, pp. 245-255; 1952, pp. 255-265.

U.S. Congress, Senate Committee on Banking and Currency, *Defense Production Act Amendments of 1951,* Hearings, 82nd Congress, 1st sess., on S. 1397, pp. 311-355.

U.S. Congress, Senate Committee on Banking and Currency, *Defense Production Act Amendments of 1952,* Hearings, 82nd Congress, 2d sess., on S. 2594 and S. 2645, pp. 75-108.

17

fiscal management: monetary aspects

While monetary management is commonly viewed as a delegated prerogative of the Fed, this function is, in reality, shared with Congress (acting directly) and with the U.S. Treasury. That is, the general and selective credit controls, discussed in preceding chapters, have a Siamese twin in the form of fiscal and debt management. Potentially, at least, this twin is as strong and vigorous as its brother, as suggested by the prodigious size of both the federal budget and the federal debt during and since World War II.

Fiscal management has to do with the money-spending and money-collecting activities of the federal government. Federal debt management refers to the refunding, borrowing, and redemption operations of the Treasury. As indicated in the title of this chapter, we are mainly concerned at this point with the monetary aspects of fiscal and debt management.

FEDERAL FISCAL MANAGEMENT

Final responsibility for federal fiscal management, as provided in the Constitution of the United States, rests with the Congress. It holds the taxing power[1] from which revenues are principally derived. Similarly, the appropriations of Congress authorize all federal expenditures,[2] and it also holds the power to borrow money[3] in the event that revenues are insufficient to meet expenditures. Thus, whether the federal budget shows a surplus, a deficit, or a balance is largely a result of the policies, programs, and actions of Congress. Of course, Congress is strongly influenced by the proposed budget submitted annually by

[1]"The Congress shall have power to lay and collect taxes, duties, imposts, and excises . . ." Constitution, Article I, Section VIII, cl. 1.

[2]"No money shall be drawn from the Treasury, but in consequence of appropriations made by law . . ." Article I, Section IX, cl. 7.

[3]Article I, Section VIII, cl. 2.

the President, and by the attitudes of voters back home in regard to taxes, spending programs, and the federal debt. Also, whether a surplus or a deficit actually develops according to plan depends on the level of national income during the coming fiscal year. But in the final analysis Congress alone is responsible.

goals of fiscal policy

The broad goals of fiscal policy may be summarized as follows:

1/To provide for the optimum level of federal expenditures after consideration of all relevant facts pertaining to particular programs and to the grand aggregate. In terms of the nation's basic resources, this question becomes: What part of gross national expenditures (product) can best be spent by the federal government, and what part can best be spent by the private, state, and local sectors of the economy? In general, the presumption is in favor of private, state, and local activities, in view of the traditional (and prevailing) philosophy in this country to maximize individual freedom, private enterprise, and local responsibility. That is, federal programs and services should be undertaken only when they clearly promise to provide essential services that would not be provided at all, or that would be inferior, if furnished by private, state, and local institutions.

2/To raise revenues by a tax system that is equitable, that is based on ability to pay, and that causes a minimum of maladjustment, waste, and impairment of economic motivation.

3/To promote the broad economic objectives of the economy, viz., (a) high-level employment and production, (b) economic stability, (c) equitable distribution of income and wealth, (d) economic growth, (e) a relatively stable price level, and (f) reasonable equilibrium in the international balance of payments.

This chapter is mainly concerned with this third goal of fiscal policy. Little responsibility of this nature was assumed by Congress and the Treasury before the Great Depression of the 1930s. Since that time, and especially since the Employment Act of 1946, these responsibilities have been seriously recognized. Nevertheless, as subsequent discussion develops, fiscal and debt-management operations have only sporadically contributed to economic and price stability since World War II; in fact, on several occasions their influence has definitely been on the side of instability.

the federal budget

The federal budget summarizes the programs of expenditures and of revenues for the fiscal year. The process of budget-making is initiated by the

Bureau of the Budget which is in the Executive Office of the President. Shortly after the end of the fiscal year in June, the various departments and agencies submit budget requests to the Bureau. These are revised in conference, usually downward, to conform with the total budget figure set by the President. Meanwhile, the Treasury submits to the Bureau its estimates of anticipated revenues from existing taxes. During the first week of the regular session of Congress in January, the President is required to submit his proposed budget, accompanied by recommendations for revision of the tax structure to provide needed revenues. The budget is then referred to the proper committees of both the House and the Senate for their consideration and revision. Sometime before the beginning of the new fiscal year, Congress enacts the various appropriation bills and reenacts or revises the revenue bill. If the President approves, they become law.

Budget Expenditures / In order to provide a more tangible basis for discussion, federal expenditures by functions for fiscal 1970 are presented in Table 17-1. The huge size of the $197 billion budget first catches the eye. This

TABLE 17-1 / FEDERAL EXPENDITURES BY FUNCTION IN FISCAL 1970
(billions of dollars)

Function	Amount	Percent of Total
National defense	80.3	40.8
International affairs	3.5	1.8
Space research	3.7	1.9
Agriculture	6.5	3.3
Natural resources	2.5	1.3
Commerce and transportation	9.3	4.7
Community development and housing	3.1	1.6
Education and manpower	7.4	3.8
Health and welfare	56.5	28.7
Veterans	8.7	4.4
Interest	18.3	9.3
General government	3.4	1.7
Intragovernment transactions[a]	−6.4	−3.3
Total	196.8	100.0

[a]Government contributions for employee retirement and interest received by trust funds.
Source: *Federal Reserve Bulletin* (October 1970), p. A 41.

compares with $1 billion in 1915 and $9 billion in 1939—representative years, respectively, before World Wars I and II. In relative terms, 1970 expenditures amount to about 20 percent of GNP. From the standpoint of influence on economic conditions, it should be noted, the magnitude of the budget is highly significant. A change of 5 percent, for example, in a $200 billion budget amounts to $10 billion–enough to affect the economy appreciably. Another feature of the budget is that the lion's share–41 percent–is for national defense. Two other categories–health and welfare, and interest account for 38 percent, leaving only 21 percent for all other purposes.

The probable influence of an increase in federal expenditures depends on the state of business at the time and on the direction of spendings. When business is in a slump, added expenditures (assuming no change in tax rates) are likely to stimulate not only the industries directly affected but also the entire economy. New orders spread to many other industries which, in turn, increase their orders and employ more labor. Larger payrolls result in enlarged consumer expenditures which are followed by orders to distributors and manufacturers who may repeat the process and widen the circles of demand. At the same time, net profits of businesses are stimulated with a consequent increase of dividends, capital expenditures, and new security issues.

However, the method of raising revenues has much to do with the response of GNP. If taxation or noncommercial bank borrowing are the sources, spending in the private sector may be reduced as much as, more than, or less than government spending is increased. The response is indeterminate in advance. Private spending may be reduced more than the increase of government spending (1) if businessmen and consumers weight heavily the burden of higher taxes, (2) if federal expenditures take the form of competition with private enterprise, and (3) if business confidence is undermined by government policies that reduce the prospect for profits. Private spending may be reduced less than government expenditures are increased–with a net rise in GNP–when the three foregoing conditions are absent and when economic pessimism prevails. Under these circumstances, the government may spend existing money that would otherwise remain idle, and thereby provide a stimulus to output. But if revenues are raised by borrowing at commercial banks or the Reserve Banks, an almost certain increase in GNP will result. This is a money-creating process, and the new money in bank balances will tend to be spent on all manner of goods, services, and securities. It will also tend to lower interest rates which have a pervasive spending stimulus.

On balance, it is likely that properly directed federal spending during a slump will add appreciably more than its amount to real output; in other words, that the combined multiplier will exceed 1, and even be as high as 2 or 3 during the recovery period. At this stage of the cycle, the typical response is both in output and in prices, but with emphasis on the former. However, if added federal spending is undertaken under conditions of full employment, the response must be mainly in higher prices. At best, productive capacity cannot be enlarged on the average more than 3 or 4 percent annually, so that added demand must compete for scarce resources and final products.

In general, opposite influences are to be expected from a reduction of federal expenditures under boom conditions (assuming no change in tax rates). Upward pressure on prices and wages is removed directly by easement of government demands for goods and services. At the same time, the intensity of private demands may slacken. That is, when businesses, labor, and consumers become aware of the restrictive federal policy, they may be less impressed with the outlook for scarcities and higher prices. Beyond this, the accruing surplus in the federal budget may be used to retire debt held by the banks. If supported by restrictive monetary policy, this step will reduce the amount of money and other liquid assets, which, in turn, will restrain the flow of private expenditures.

While it is possible to increase federal expenditures in most categories of the budget, only a few of them are practicable candidates for countercyclical fiscal operations. National defense, international affairs, veterans' services, agriculture, general government, and interest on the public debt all represent programs whose size and scope are largely governed by other considerations. The two most likely avenues for such spending–public works (including housing) and public relief and welfare–are included under the classifications: Natural resources; Commerce and transportation; Community development and housing; and Health and welfare.

A countercyclical program of public works has occupied a prominent place in economic literature relating to stabilization. It was advocated during and after the depression of 1921-1922; it was utilized on a sizable scale during the Great Depression of the 1930s in this and other countries; and it was again advocated (and employed to some extent) in the recessions of 1958 and 1961. In bare outline, such a program contemplates that a shelf of projects–dams, bridges, highways, streets, parks, public buildings, sewerage systems, water facilities, airports, natural resource conservation, and so on–shall be planned ahead and prepared for immediate release when a recession develops. With the return of prosperity the program would be reduced, and if price inflation threatens it would be sharply curtailed.

The most serious limitation of a countercyclical public-works program is the difficulty–perhaps impossibility–of proper timing. "Heavy" public works such as large dams and bridges require two or more years of project planning and an even longer period of actual construction. Once begun, operations cannot be turned on and off like a spigot but must be carried through to completion. Even assuming careful preplanning of projects, six or more months must elapse before construction activities can significantly contribute to incomes. Also, the decision to expand public works must rest on a forecast of business conditions, a field in which there is always wide disagreement among influential experts. This means that such a decision must be deferred at least another half-year until it becomes certain that the downturn foreshadows a depression instead of a minor adjustment. Thus, it is very doubtful whether heavy works projects can be timed to promote business stability in view of (1) the interval of a year or more after the downturn begins before expenditures can reach a significant amount, and (2) the danger that they may carry over into the subsequent period of prosperity and generate an undesired inflationary boom. "Lighter" works projects–such as road-building, earth-moving, and public housing–are less suspect from a timing standpoint, but they are also subject to serious limitations on this score.

Another limitation on public works is that a program of sufficient magnitude to produce recovery is likely to prevent needed correction of downward adjustments in building costs and to develop new maladjustments in the economy. This is probable because construction activities concentrate demands on a limited number of products, require particular types of skilled labor, and cannot be evenly distributed geographically. A waste of national resources is difficult to avoid when public-works expenditures are raised well above their basic trend of growth. On the other side, when unsustainable expansion develops, expenditures on public facilities cannot reasonably be pared drastically as a means of checking it. Highway, street, water, sewerage, education, police, military, postal and other public services constitute essential components of a healthy and progressive economy. Undue restriction of their normal expansion is a high price for greater stability.

But despite these limitations, public-works policy should take cognizance of its relation to stability. At the minimum, the historic role of government expenditures in *accentuating* the business cycle should be changed. State and local governments have typically stepped up spending when incomes have increased, and have curtailed expenditures when incomes have declined. Before the 1930s, this pattern also applied to the federal government. In addition to eliminating this perversity, appropriate public-works programs can be effectively employed to exert a modest anticyclical influence. This assumes careful preplanning of useful projects, good timing, and efficient administration. But the size of practicable programs is limited compared with tax changes on the other side of the budget.

Aside from public works, federal expenditures designed to moderate the cycle would mainly take the form of *direct payments* to individuals. A wide variety of plans for such government transfer payments is conceivable. Most likely, payments would be made to families with low (or no) income, including the unemployed and the needy. Such a program would have a humanitarian aspect, and it would also contribute most certainly to mass consumer spending. Strong objections to direct relief payments are often voiced on the ground that the government gets nothing in return in contrast with public-works spending. But this is only partially true, and perhaps not true at all. One of the primary aims is to assist those in want, and the most certain way of accomplishing this aim quickly and economically is by direct payments. Another objective—the reduction of unemployment—is realized indirectly. The spending of relief money increases demand throughout the range of items in budgets of lower-income families with emphasis on services and basic necessities. The resulting orders by retailers to wholesalers, distributors, and manufacturers have a stimulating influence throughout the economy, including in some degree the capital-goods industries. Thus, a good case can be made for direct payments to the unemployed as compared with spending on public works. A dollar of relief money more certainly reaches the needy; it helps to reduce unemployment and does so more quickly; its stimulating effects are more pervasive and more in line with normal consumer demands; it is less likely to waste basic resources; and the amount of spending can be more flexibly expanded and contracted to meet changing conditions. Moreover, insofar as private capital-goods expenditures are stimulated, there are productive capital assets as a by-product to match the assets created by a public-works program. But on the other side, direct payments to the unemployed are less likely to have a multiple effect on national income than are public-works expenditures. This follows because direct payments tend to maintain demand in the necessity industries—food, apparel, services, and so on—with little direct effect on the depressed capital-goods industries, while public-works expenditures in large part constitute direct demand for cement, lumber, steel, and other capital goods.

Before leaving the expenditure side of the budget, some consideration should be given to the feasibility of countercyclical military spending. At first glance, this might seem to be a practicable approach, because this category is so large that a small percentage change amounts to billions of dollars. But, in fact, the rate of defense spending should be related only to changing military requirements as determined by our best informed military and civilian officials. The situation during the autumn of 1957 when Sputnik was launched into outer space provides a good illustration. A new appraisal of the character and size of the entire defense program was imperative. In the face of this threat, surely no reasonable person would have advocated a reduction of military expenditures in order to check the existing danger of further price inflation. Because the Executive Branch has large discretion in regard to the rate of spending appropriations for defense purposes, there is a strong temptation to vary this rate countercyclically. In fact, a few programs can doubtless be accelerated or decelerated at times without impairment of overall results. But the difficulty of isolating such programs is great indeed, and there is real danger of hasty selection. In this event, the consequences would be either complete waste or impairment of the entire defense posture—an unreasonable price for a small contribution to stability. For these reasons, there is a strong presumption against changes in the defense budget for cyclical purposes; other alternatives are more fruitful and less objectionable.

Budget Receipts / The principal sources of federal receipts for fiscal 1970 are presented in Table 17-2. Nearly one-half came from individual income taxes, 17 percent from corporate income taxes, and 23 percent from social insurance taxes and contributions. Most of the rest was derived from excises. Because net budget expenditures, including net lending of $1,784 million, were $196,572 million (Table 71-1) and net budget receipts were $193,844 million; the deficit in fiscal 1970 amounted to $2,908 million.

The probable effects of a reduction in taxes, as in the case of an increase in expenditures, depends on existing business conditions and on the character of the change. Assuming that federal expenditures remain the same,

TABLE 17-2 / FEDERAL RECEIPTS BY PRINCIPAL SOURCES IN FISCAL 1970
(billions of dollars)

Receipts	Amount	Percent of Total
Individual income taxes	90.4	46.7
Corporation income taxes	32.8	16.9
Excise taxes	15.7	8.1
Social insurance taxes and contributions	45.3	23.3
Estate and gift taxes	3.6	1.9
Customs duties	2.4	1.2
Miscellaneous receipts	3.6	1.9
Total net budget receipts	193.8	100.0

Source: *Federal Reserve Bulletin* (October 1970), p. A 41.

tax reduction increases the disposable incomes of consumers and businesses beyond what they would have been. Demands for goods and services are likely to rise all along the line for two reasons. First, people find themselves with larger money balances relative to disposable incomes than they are accustomed to hold. Second, they are also disposed to spend more freely as a consequence of the more optimistic outlook engendered by lower taxes. If substantial unemployment exists, the typical response largely takes the form of rising real output, accompanied by a small increase in prices. But if the economy is already at full capacity, the added demand results mainly in higher price tags. The influences just cited are more powerful if the Treasury finances its deficit by borrowing from the banks. This follows because the new money and liquid assets thereby created contribute to the ability and the inclination to spend more freely.

The effects of a tax reduction on the level of business do not, however, arise entirely from the amount of change. The character of the reduction also has an important bearing on results. In general, the maximum stimulus in the short run is to be expected from tax relief for individuals in the low- and middle-income groups. As applied to the tax structure, this means reduction in the lower brackets of the income tax and lower excise taxes on necessities. Less stimulus is immediately likely when the reduction applies to the upper-income groups. They can be expected to save an appreciable part of the released income, and there may be considerable delay before savings are spent for capital goods. But it is almost certain that income released to those at the bottom of the scale will be spent immediately on a broad range of necessities, and that little will be saved. It should be emphasized, however, that the foregoing conclusions are valid only for short cyclical periods. In the long run, economic growth is more likely to be spurred by reduction of tax rates of upper-income groups which will respond with increased savings and with higher incentives to produce. A good case can also be made for reduction of corporate income taxes. Such tax relief should foster recovery in business spending for plants, equipment, and inventories—the sector in which slumps are most pronounced. Apart from the incidence of tax reduction on income classes, it should also be noted that moderation of inequitable or incentive-killing taxes provides a definite spur to output. Examples are a high corporate income tax, a graduated tax on net profits of business, a tax on gross sales of business, and punitively high personal income tax rates in the upper brackets. Such taxes repress incentives and therefore constitute a drag on recovery and growth.

Almost the opposite influences follow from an increase in taxes. Disposable incomes are reduced so that demand is directly restrained. In addition, the outlook in regard to sales, net incomes, and prices becomes less optimistic, which provides further restraint on business and consumer expenditures. Moreover, if the Treasury in managing the debt applies its surplus to reduction of bank-held debt, demand will be even further curtailed by a reduction in the amount of money and near-money assets—provided the Fed does its part by absorbing the released legal bank reserves. When an inflationary boom is in progress, the initial effect of these restraints is to check the rise in prices. But if applied too vigorously, they may interrupt normal growth and precipitate a recession. A tax increase is usually most effective when applied to the lower- and middle-income groups which account for the bulk of consumer expenditures. But an increase in corporate income taxes also provides a check-rein on overinvestment which is a typical feature of boom conditions.

Tax Changes Versus Public Works / Tax changes have definite advantages over public-works expenditures as a method of moderating business fluctuations. First, tax changes are potentially more flexible. Proper timing is half the battle in cycle control and, as discussed above, this is perhaps the most serious drawback of a public-works program. Tax reduction, always popular, can often be brought about quickly. But tax increases, always unpopular, involve prolonged congressional hearings and much debate before a change in the law can be made effective, if indeed it can be made at all. Hence, under existing conditions, tax increases are a less flexible method of restraint than reduction of federal expenditures. But Congress could remove much of this difficulty by a grant of limited discretionary authority over tax rates to a responsible commission or to the President. This point is discussed more fully in a subsequent section of this chapter.

Second, tax changes are potentially a more powerful weapon than public works within the range of practicable action. The range of reasonable variation in public-works expenditures is comparatively limited. Third, the effects of tax changes on consumers are much more broadly distributed throughout the economy. A public-works program is necessarily spotty. Some commodities, industries, and areas are the chief beneficiaries—indeed may be overstimulated—while others are scarcely affected.

Finally, appropriate tax changes bring their influence to bear through the decisions of consumers and businesses. They involve no departure from the objective guidance of free markets. But this is not the case with public works. Decisions to release new projects are made by public officials with the resulting real danger that they may be made arbitrarily and hastily. There is also the hazard that decisions may be dictated by political considerations, with associated misallocation of resources, or even graft.

Tax Changes Versus Direct Payments / While at first glance flexible tax rates and variable direct payments seem poles apart as methods of fostering stabilization, they do have a number of features in common. For illustration, assume there is an economic recession with the federal budget in balance. Under these circumstances, a reduction in tax rates when expenditures remain constant would create a deficit which would necessitate Treasury borrowing. A similar result would follow from an increase of direct payments to the unemployed and needy when tax rates remain constant. Second, both approaches operate through decisions of consumers and businesses to spend, save, and invest. Both are, therefore, more consistent with the free-market system than is a program of public works, where each project decision is made by government officials. Finally, both methods are sufficiently powerful to have a substantial influence on the level of employment. Direct payments can always be increased enough to bring about full employment; similarly, at present high rates, taxes can be reduced enough to reach the same goal. Even if tax rates were low at the outset, there is no theoretical limit to negative taxes (refunds). In fact, negative taxes would be nothing more than a particular program of direct payments.

There are important differences, however, between the use of tax rates and direct payments for stabilization purposes. Perhaps the most significant one relates to incidence of the effects. Direct payments can be tailored to reach the unemployed and the needy, so that the social aspect is more certainly met as an incident to solving the economic problem. Tax reduction, however, can directly reach only those who are subject to the income tax or who purchase goods to which excises apply. In a depression, this excludes millions of unemployed and needy persons. Indirectly, tax reduction may eventually reach most of these people by way of new job opportunities. A second difference is that direct payments may pauperize a layer of the potential labor force. Doubtless, many people on half-pay would prefer leisure to a job; many more would choose leisure if the direct payment were as much as two-thirds of the prevailing wage. At the least, direct welfare payments present a difficult problem of efficient administration. This danger is not present in a program of tax reduction. Still another difference relates to flexibility. On this score, direct payments are superior. They can be changed on short notice, whereas it is extremely difficult under existing conditions to change tax receipts even semiannually. However, when and if Congress is willing to grant limited discretionary authority over tax changes, this method can become more flexible.

Fortunately, it is not necessary to choose between these two methods on an either-or basis. Both may be utilized with due regard for the good and bad features of each as part of an overall program. Direct payments may be employed modestly to assure relief without pauperization and to provide timeliness of action. Tax changes may be utilized to provide the additional budget adjustments required to stimulate or restrain the economy.

Theory of Federal Budget / Theories of the federal budget may conveniently be divided into three classes: (1) annual balance, (2) cycle balance, and (3) null balance. The annual-balance theory has been the traditional one in the United States. Before the 1930s few people questioned the rule that sound fiscal policy requires either a balance or a surplus in the annual budget during peacetime, and that a deficit is unhealthy and unsound. This rule was doubtless an extension of the prevailing view regarding sound personal and business finance. It was also reenforced by the observation that the disastrous price inflations of the past were all associated with large-scale deficits of the central government. The validity of this rule is not accepted by most authorities today, especially when capital outlays as well as operating expenditures are included in the budget. They reject the analogy between individual and federal financial policy. Moreover, the one-year interval is viewed as unduly arbitrary. Just why is one year a sacrosanct time interval as compared with, say, three or five years? Also, is it reasonable to adhere to an annual-balance policy when its influence is clearly to aggravate, rather than to moderate, economic fluctuations? Despite these limitations, however, the annual-balance standard has had a constructive aspect in protecting the value of the dollar. There is some danger, when the goal of annual balance is cast aside, that excessive federal borrowing from the banks may cause destructive price inflation.

The cycle-balance theory gained many adherents during the long depression of the 1930s. It is based on the proposition that fiscal policy is a strong force that should be utilized positively to promote stabilization. That is, depressions should be moderated by the stimulating effects of deficits, and overexpansion should be curbed by the restrictive influence of surpluses. The theory contemplates approximate balance in the budget from the peak of one business cycle to the next. Surpluses in good years should offset deficits of bad ones, so that over time the federal debt will remain about the same. The enlarged revenues of prosperous years may even permit some debt reduction from one cycle to the next. The opposite may also be true: The deficits of recession years may exceed the surpluses of good years with a resultant upward trend of debt.

A more liberal variant of the cycle-balance theory regards the budgetary balance from cycle to cycle relatively rather than absolutely. That is, the ratio of federal debt to GNP should at least be held constant. This would mean, assuming the same level of interest rates, that the costs of servicing the debt would represent the same proportion of GNP from cycle to cycle. In a growing economy, it would leave room over time for a considerable increase in both the amounts of federal debt and the interest payments thereon.

Those who support the null-balance theory of the budget deemphasize the significance of size of the debt and of whether the budget is in balance. In their view, the basic objectives of the economy should always be the governing criteria. That is, budget policy should be directed to foster full employment, growth, economic stability, reasonable equilibrium in the international balance of payments, and equitable distribution of income. Some proponents include a stable dollar in order to achieve these goals, while others advocate a slowly rising price level as a catalyst for high-level employment and growth.

All this raises questions in regard to the proper size of the federal debt. Is size inconsequential because "we owe it to ourselves"? What are the dangers, if any, of a huge and growing debt? And conversely, may the federal debt become too small for the best interest of the nation? These are complex questions which can here be accorded only summary consideration. The argument that size makes little difference because we owe it to ourselves is true in the sense that domestic investors own most of the outstanding federal securities; foreign interests hold only a small part. There is a valid contrast between the individual and the federal government as debtors. The individual always owes a debt to someone else; never to himself. But in the nation as a whole, tens of millions of people are taxed to pay interest on the federal debt, and at times to repay principal. On the other side, tens of millions, directly or indirectly, receive these payments. If both groups were identical and each person were equally a taxpayer and an interest receiver, there would be no great cause for concern. But this is not the case. Many people pay taxes but receive little or no interest. Others have large interest receipts in relation to taxes. Hence, size of the debt becomes a problem of equitable income distribution. Personal incomes may be significantly affected by changes in the amount of federal debt and by changes in interest payments of the Treasury. For example, a rise of the interest rate on federal securities from 4 to 6 percent would increase disposable incomes of security holders at the expense of taxpayers. It follows that the larger the debt and the interest thereon, the greater are the possible injustices from redistribution of income. The impact of this influence is magnified by burdensome inequities that creep into the tax system.

Another argument against a huge federal debt is the aversion to big government per se. Expenditures for services and projects that lead to a growing debt create big government. Heavy taxation is then necessary to meet expenditures, including interest on the debt. Big government tends to encroach on the private-enterprise system, to limit individual freedom, and to move toward some form of collectivism.

A final objection to a big federal debt arises from the hazards associated with its rapid growth. The Treasury borrows either current savings or bank credit. Absorption of savings reduces the flow of funds to business for capital investment, and may therefore check both investment and economic growth. When the Treasury borrows at the banks, new money and other liquid assets are created—a process that may proceed too rapidly and generate price inflation. Also, a fast-growing debt creates disturbances in the normal distribution of assets. The injection of billions of dollars of liquid federal securities has repercussions on all investment holdings, including stocks and real estate. A new structure of asset prices, reflecting decisions of investors, emerges. If new money is created, it too must find a home. This process works out through quickened buying and selling of securities and other property.

If the federal debt may grow too rapidly and become too large, there are also valid reasons why it may be too small. A widely accepted proposition is that much of the strength and stability of a democracy springs from a large middle class of property owners. With a personal stake in existing institutions, citizens are more likely to seek reform through evolutionary processes than by revolution. If this be true, a wide distribution of U.S. savings bonds among the people contributes to their "shareholder" interest in the national government, and thereby to national strength and stability. Another argument for savings-bond promotion is that it encourages mass savings. This, in turn, stimulates capital investment and contributes to a rising standard of living. In addition, the individual's economic independence is encouraged and the burden of social welfare is correspondingly reduced. To the extent that these arguments are well grounded, savings bonds should be conveniently available as a supplement to private savings facilities.

Another important function of federal debt is to provide the proper amount of short-term, marketable obligations to meet liquidity requirements of financial and nonfinancial businesses. Commercial banks, for example, need large liquidity reserves for protection against possible loss of deposits or increase of customer loan demands. The bulk of this requirement is met by short-term U.S. securities. In fact, commercial banks alone have held between $30 billion and $50 billion of such issues with maturity of under five years during the postwar period. Similarly, other financial institutions and nonfinancial businesses have large liquidity needs which can best be met by government short-terms. Determination of the proper amount of short-term federal securities is one of the tasks of debt management for which the Treasury is responsible. This topic is of such importance that it is the subject of the next chapter.

Beyond the savings-facility and liquidity functions, another layer of long-term federal debt is justified in order to meet investor requirements for marketable obligations of the highest possible quality. Trust funds, pension funds, insurance companies, savings banks, and endowment funds are the most conspicuous examples. There is no way to determine precisely the right amount, but it is certainly in the tens of billions.

In summary, there is a minimum below which it is unwise to reduce the federal debt, determined by the requirements of investors for adequate savings facilities, liquidity, and long-term securities of highest quality. This minimum is not fixed; instead it changes cyclically and with the growth of GNP.

Federal Budget as Automatic Stabilizer / Economists have long been challenged by the need for automatic methods to stabilize the economy at a high level, to control the price level, and to achieve other less ambitious aims. This is understandable in view of the mediocre record of those who undertake the complex task of forecasting business conditions, and in light of the practical difficulties of timely application of discretionary controls. Partly by design and partly by nature, the federal budget embodies certain stabilizing features—that is, attributes that tend to produce deficits during recessions and surpluses during booms. The conditions conducive to a strong stabilizing influence are (1) that the budget be relatively large so that a change in its amount will have a significant influence on national income; (2) that a liberal system of direct payments to individuals and businesses be provided during recessions—unemployment compensation, social security, relief subsidies, and so on; and (3) that the core of the tax system be a graduated personal income tax and a tax on corporate profits.

To a large degree, these very features characterize our federal budget. When a recession develops, unemployment compensation, social security, and relief payments increase. In addition, farm and other subsidy payments grow. On the revenue side, receipts from personal income taxes, corporate income taxes, excises, and employment taxes decline materially. Smaller declines are also registered in customs and miscellaneous receipts. The personal income tax (1970) is steeply graduated through 25 brackets, ranging (for married persons) from 14 percent on taxable income of under $1,000 to 70 percent on the portion of income exceeding $200,000. Hence, a decline in individual incomes not only reduces aggregate taxable income but also lowers the applicable tax rate. Because this tax is the source of between 40 and 50 percent of budget receipts, it is the primary stabilizing component. While the corporate income tax is not graduated, the rate is high (48 percent in 1970). Because percentage variations of pretax profits are two or three times larger than changes in GNP, and because corporate taxes account for about 17 percent of receipts, a substantial shrinkage in revenue from this source occurs as a recession develops. Thus, the combined effects of increased federal expenditures and reduced revenues tend to generate a budget deficit which grows as a recession deepens. If the Treasury borrows the deficit from banks, new money and other liquid assets are created, and an additional stimulus is given to private spending. Taken together, these influences automatically set limits on a business decline and open the way for the natural forces of recovery.

In general, these same influences are automatically brought to bear in opposite fashion to restrain an inflationary boom. Without change of tax rates, federal expenditures decline, and revenues rise at a more rapid rate than that of national income. A budget surplus is likely to emerge if the level of tax rates is set to balance the budget on the average. Moreover, if the surplus is used to retire securities owned by banks and if restrictive monetary policies are enforced, the amounts of money and other liquid assets are reduced. At the same time, the disposition to spend tends to decline.

This brings us to the question: What is the quantitative relation between deficits and surpluses in the federal budget and changes in GNP, assuming no change in tax rates or in the established bases of federal expenditures? Only a rough estimate is possible because many factors affect both series and there have been few years when tax rates and spending programs remained the same. But observation of postwar experience indicates that a decline of $100 million in GNP, other things equal, is typically accompanied by an increase in the deficit (or decrease in the surplus) of between $15 and $30 million. A similar rough relationship between increases in GNP and budget surpluses also prevails. Thus, the automatic stabilizing effects of the budget can be substantial.

Complete reliance on automatic stabilization is unwise for several reasons. (1) In a world of cold-war uncertainties, we are frequently confronted with the necessity of large changes in size and character of federal expenditures. The Korean situation in 1950, the Sputnik encirclement of 1957, the Cuban crisis of 1962, and the Vietnam War provide good illustrations. Every substantial change in size of expenditures upsets an automatic stabilization program unless it is balanced by a corresponding change in revenues. Such flexible adjustments of the tax system are difficult, if not impossible. (2) Automatic budget influences are at best inadequate to provide reasonable stability under all conditions. They are capable of moderating slumps and booms, but not always of confining them to tolerable limits. While they open the way for operation of natural forces and do provide stimulus or restraint, other more positive measures are usually desirable. (3) This or any other automatic device of economic control is bound to lack flexibility to meet changing conditions. No two booms and no two recessions are alike. For example, one recession may be initiated by downward adjustment of inventories, another by decline in capital expansion, still another by flagging consumer demand, and so on. Specific corrective measures need to be tailored to the particular conditions that emerge during a cycle.

Federal Budget Flexibility / The foregoing limitations on what can reasonably be expected from the automatic stabilizing influences of the budget illustrate the need for conscious action. How can greater flexibility of federal expenditures and revenues be practicably attained? Flexible budget management in coordination with monetary and debt management constitutes the one great hope for reasonable stability of the economy and of the price level. Without such flexibility and coordination, it is almost certain that we shall, as in the past, be plagued with recessions and inflationary booms. Hence, the attainment of budget flexibility is one of our most pressing politico-economic problems.

The primary problem of budget flexibility is one of political organization and delegation of discretionary power by Congress. Because timeliness and continuous expert supervision form the backbone of a successful program, direct administration by Congress is not feasible. This means that Congress should delegate limited discretionary power to an appropriate administrative agency or to the President. This question is discussed more fully in Chapter 19.

On the expenditures side of the budget, Congress might well delegate limited authority over the level of unemployment compensation, social security, relief payments, and selected subsidies. It might also delegate some power to activate already-approved public-works projects and to curtail current public-construction operations. However, as previously indicated, direct payments have greater promise than public works as a method of stabilization.

Of even greater importance than flexibility of expenditures is flexibility of federal revenues. Again, Congress should delegate limited discretionary authority. Flexibility of tax rates, however, is confronted with important political and administrative obstacles which should be removed.

In general, the direction of change would be to move further toward current tax collections and to speed up tax refunds. Substantial progress has, in fact, been made in recent years toward current collection of both the personal and corporate income taxes. For many years, employers have withheld income taxes from wages of employees and remitted directly to the Treasury. Also, individuals with appreciable income from sources other than wages (and therefore not subject to withholding) have been required to make current quarterly tax payments on the basis of estimated income for the current year. Corporations, in accordance with the Revenue Act of 1954, have gradually shifted to a quarterly basis, under which payments lag some six months, from the previous arrangement under which payments lagged about one year. Employment and social security taxes, being deducted from wages, are on a current basis; so are federal excise taxes which are paid by manufacturers at time of sale.

The most promising approach is for Congress to include alternative schedules in the tax law. One schedule would be the basic rate. A second schedule would set forth somewhat lower rates that might be made effective at the discretion of the chosen administrative agency. Such action would be taken to combat business recession. The third schedule would embody rates moderately above the basic schedule; it could be implemented by the agency as a means of curbing overexpansion. If desirable in light of experience, the law could, of course, provide for more alternative schedules. At the outset, this arrangement could be confined experimentally to one tax—that is, personal income. Later on, appropriate flexible features could be adapted to other taxes.[4]

[4]Flexibility of tax rates to promote stability was advocated by President Kennedy who recommended in 1961 that Congress grant him authority to adjust personal income-tax rates downward by as much as 5 percentage points, subject to legislative veto, as a means of promoting recovery from the recession. After much delay, the largest tax cut in the nation's history was achieved when Congress passed the $11.5 billion tax cut bill and President Johnson signed it in early 1964.

Another notable proposal for discretionary changes in tax rates was included in the Report of the Commission on Money and Credit in 1961, pages 133-137. In brief, the Commission recommended that Congress grant the President power to make temporary changes of 5 percentage points upward or downward in the first bracket (20 percent) of the personal income tax. Exercise of this power, however, was to be subject to a legislative veto by a concurrent resolution of both houses of Congress.

Space does not permit consideration of details of alternative tax schedules. There are of course numerous possibilities. For example, an alternative schedule for the personal income tax might apply to all brackets, be confined to selected brackets, or apply only to changes in exemptions. If the aim is to influence consumer expenditures directly, changes in rates should apply to the lower- and middle-income brackets. If the purpose is to affect the flow of personal saving, changes should mainly apply to above-average incomes. When stimulation or suppression of business investment is desired, a change should be made in the corporate income-tax rate. Regardless of where changes are made, important monetary effects on the level of private spending are generated by alterations in the budget surplus or deficit.

The most formidable obstacle to achieving adequate budget flexibility is the political one. Congress has never delegated discretionary power over taxes and would doubtless be extremely reluctant to do so. However, the President already has considerable leeway in the rate at which appropriated funds shall be spent. Also, there are precedents in the authority of the President to change tariff rates, and in the delegation of monetary-management powers to the Board of Governors. In fact, the needed discretionary authority over the budget is less sweeping and far-reaching than existing Federal Reserve powers. By altering the cost and availability of bank credit, it will be recalled, the Reserve authorities can significantly influence the welfare of every citizen and business in the country. In the broad sense, there is no logical difference between delegation of authority over taxes and delegation of authority over bank credit. Both are integral parts of any rounded economic stabilization program; both are essential to realization of the goals of the Employment Act of 1946. Only inertia, therefore, stands in the way of governmental changes that hold high promise of contributing materially to the stability of production, employment, and the price level.

FISCAL AND MONETARY ACTION: RELATIVE IMPORTANCE

From the late 1930s to the mid-1960s, fiscal policy received far greater attention as a method of economic stabilization than monetary policy. This was largely a consequence of the wide acceptance of the model of the economy developed by Lord Keynes in his classic book, *The General Theory of Employment, Interest and Money,* published in 1936. Fiscal policy was given center stage and monetary policy was relegated to a minor role as influences on output, employment, and prices. In the Keynesian system, money exerted only an indirect influence on the economy through affecting the money rate of interest. Economists were also impressed by the seeming impotence of abundant excess bank reserves and low interest rates to provide the needed stimulus for recovery from the Great Depression. Federal government spending on a huge scale to finance World War II was required to spur the economy to full employment.

Again in 1964, belief in the potency of fiscal policy was strengthened when business recovery followed after a large reduction of over $11 billion in federal taxes.

But serious doubts about the strength and efficiency of fiscal policy developed during the inflationary boom of 1965-1969. The inflexibility of this method was demonstrated when Congress delayed action to increase taxes for one and one-half years while price inflation gained momentum. Then, when the tax bill was finally enacted in mid-1968, the upsurge of business and prices continued unabated throughout the year. Consumers were disposed to spend more and save less, and business maintained its high rate of capital investment. This was a disillusioning blow to the proponents of fiscal policy.

In the meantime, events in the academic world were strengthening the position of the still large group which believed that "money matters a great deal." Most important was the publication in 1963 of a classic book, *A Monetary History of the United States, 1867-1960* by Milton Friedman and Anna J. Schwartz.[5] In this exhaustive study of cyclical movements of money, Professor Friedman concluded that swings in the amount of money have been the predominant influence causing swings in output and prices after a lag on the average of some 14 months. On the basis of this study, Friedman developed his famous proposal that the stock of money be increased at a steady rate designed roughly to stabilize the price level. This simple monetary rule, he contended, was the best hope for viable economic and price stability. He also concluded that such a rule would have produced a materially higher degree of stabilization in the past than the actual policies of the Federal Reserve authorities–on whose mistakes he blamed a goodly portion of economic instability, including the Great Depression.[6]

By this time, the school of monetary thought emanating from Professor Friedman and the University of Chicago was rapidly expanding, and members became generally known as *monetarists.* Within the Fed, the St. Louis Bank has been the focal point of research and influence. Several prominent economists of commercial banks, notably A. James Meigs of the First National City Bank and Beryl Sprinkel of the Harris Trust and Savings Bank, have also espoused the cause.

One of the most influential studies is that of Anderson and Jordan.[7] In a convincing statistical analysis, the authors refute three commonly held propositions: (1) that fiscal actions exert a larger influence on economic activity than do monetary actions; (2) that the response of economic activity to fiscal actions is more predictable than the response to monetary influence; and

[5]Milton Friedman and Anna J. Schwartz, *A Monetary History of the United States, 1867-1960* (New York: National Bureau of Economic Research, 1963).

[6]See Milton Friedman, *A Program for Monetary Stability* (New York: Fordham University Press, 1960), especially chap. 4.

[7]Leonall C. Anderson and Jerry L. Jordan, "Monetary and Fiscal Actions: A Test of Their Relative Importance in Economic Stabilization," Federal Reserve Bank of St. Louis, *Review* (November 1968), pp. 11-24.

(3) that the influence of fiscal actions on economic activity occurs faster than that of monetary actions. In fact, their study indicates just the opposite: that monetary actions are at once more influential, more predictable, and faster than fiscal actions in their effects on GNP.

Space precludes more than a summary of results of the Anderson and Jordan study which develops a regression of changes in GNP on changes in monetary and fiscal actions during the period 1952-1968. Changes in the amount of money and of the monetary base resulted in a highly significant change in GNP during the current and three following quarters. However, changes in various measures of fiscal action—high employment budget surplus, expenditures, and receipts—had no significant effect on GNP during the same period. The authors conclude:

> Evidence found in this study suggests that the money stock is an important indicator of the total thrust of stabilization actions, both monetary and fiscal. First, changes in the money stock reflect mainly what may be called discretionary actions of the Federal Reserve System as it uses its major instruments of monetary management—open market transactions, discount rate changes, and reserve requirement changes. Second, the money stock reflects the joint actions of the Treasury and the Federal Reserve System in financing newly created Government debt. Such actions are based on decisions regarding the monetization of new debt by Federal Reserve actions, and Treasury decisions regarding changes in its balances at Reserve Banks and commercial banks. According to this second point, changes in Government spending financed by monetary expansion are reflected in changes in the monetary base and in the money stock.[8]

Thus, they conclude that fiscal actions are relatively unimportant when receipts come from taxes or nonbank borrowing. Government expenditures are then only substituted for private spending with no assurance that total spending will be increased. Fiscal actions are important only when they result in budget deficits which are financed by money creation through borrowing at commercial banks or Federal Reserve Banks. Hence, the predominent factor causing changes in GNP is changes in the stock of money, whether brought about by fiscal actions, Federal Reserve actions, or private-sector demands.

As a consequence of extensive research by the monetarists[9] and of recent events, a substantial shift toward rediscovery of money has occurred among economists since the mid-1960s. Many have joined the ranks; many others have opened their eyes to the unique importance of money and monetary

[8]Anderson and Jordan, op. cit., pp. 22-23.

[9]See also these articles which appeared in the *Review* of the Federal Reserve Bank of St. Louis: Karl Brunner, "The Role of Money and Monetary Policy" (July 1968), pp. 9-24; David I. Fand, "Some Issues in Monetary Economics" (January 1970), pp. 10-27; and Leonall C. Anderson and Keith M. Carlson, "A Monetarist Model for Economic Stabilization" (April 1970), pp. 7-25.

policy. This change in attitude has likewise pervaded the Fed as evidenced by the policy directives of the Federal Open-Market Committee. Beginning in 1970, the Committee began to include the rate of growth of money in its operating directive to the manager of the Open-Market Account at the Federal Reserve Bank of New York. Also, Arthur F. Burns, Chairman of the Federal Reserve Board, indicated the large importance of monetary growth rates in determination of policy in a statement before the Joint Economic Committee in July 1970, as follows:

> Looking back from our present vantage point, it seems to me that we have achieved the middle course with regard to monetary aggregates that we sought. During the second quarter of this year, the money supply grew at an annual rate of about $4\frac{1}{2}$ percent, compared with a rate of about $3\frac{3}{4}$ percent in the first quarter and virtually no growth over the preceding 6 months. . . . In the second quarter, growth of bank credit advanced to an annual rate of about $5\frac{1}{2}$ percent.[10]

But having expressed the purpose of maintaining orderly quarterly or semiannual rates of monetary expansion as one goal, Mr. Burns hastened to add:

> An impression seems to have prevailed in some quarters that the Federal Reserve had decided to pursue fixed target rates of growth in the monetary aggregates on a more or less continuous basis. This was a misreading of our intent. We believe that the Nation would be ill served by a mechanical application of monetary rules.[11]

In conclusion, the monetarists have succeeded in reducing the emphasis on fiscal actions and increasing the emphasis on monetary actions as methods of economic stabilization. They have also succeeded in elevating the position of money among the various financial and economic variables which Federal Reserve authorities monitor as guides to credit policy. But they have not yet achieved their purpose of making steady growth in the stock of money at a rate consistent with a stable price level the *sole* target of the Federal Reserve authorities. This compromise is probably just as well until more can be learned by further analysis and observation of the relation of money to output and prices.

REFERENCES

See references at the end of Chapter 19.

[10] *Federal Reserve Bulletin* (August 1970), p. 623.
[11] Ibid., p. 624.

18

federal debt management: monetary aspects

In its broad context, fiscal management—discussed in the preceding chapter—includes debt management. But prevailing usage treats debt management as a separate method or technique in its own right. There are, in fact, two good reasons to justify this dichotomy. First, Congress bears final responsibility for the budget and the size of the federal debt—that is, for the amount and character of expenditures and revenues, and hence for the size of surpluses and deficits. But there its fiscal job ends for the most part. At that point, the Treasury takes over the responsibilities of managing the outstanding debt, of raising funds to meet a current deficit, of retiring debt in the event of a surplus, and of administering government cash and deposits. Performing these functions is known as debt management. Second, the great size and complexity of the federal debt raises the task of management to a new dimension, which further justifies separate treatment. When the debt was small, the Treasury could proceed without giving much attention to the general economic effects of its operations—much as the treasurer of a large corporation approaches management of the company's debt. But management of a \$380 billion debt is a huge task with widespread repercussions on the money market; the level and structure of interest rates; the flow of funds into corporate, state, and municipal investment; the stock of money; and the amount of other liquid assets. Moreover, through these channels Treasury operations influence expenditures for output, the level of employment, the value of the dollar, and the international balance of payments.

FEATURES OF THE FEDERAL DEBT

As background for consideration of debt management, it is necessary to call attention to a few basic features of the federal debt, viz., types of securities outstanding, ownership, and maturity distribution, Table 18-1 presents the types of securities that made up the interest-bearing public debt at the end of June 1970. Total marketable issues—those that can be bought and sold—amounted to $232.6 billion, or almost two-thirds of the grand total. The remaining one-third

TABLE 18-1 / U.S. GOVERNMENT INTEREST-BEARING PUBLIC DEBT, JUNE 30, 1970 (billions of dollars)

Type of Security	Amount	Percent of Total
Marketable		
Bills	76.2	20.6
Notes	93.4	25.3
Bonds	63.0	17.1
Total marketable	232.6	63.0
Nonmarketable		
Savings bonds	51.3	13.9
Bonds, investment series	2.3	0.6
Special issues[a]	82.8	22.5
Total nonmarketable	136.4	37.0
Grand total	369.0	100.0

[a]Includes "depositary bonds" of $103 million, foreign series of $4,755 million, and other obligations of $1,656 million.
Source: *Treasury Bulletin* (September 1970), p. 23.

was represented by nonmarketable issues—those that must be held by the owner until maturity or redemption by the Treasury. Bills, whose maturities are restricted to 1 year or less, are utilized for short-term borrowing. Notes are used for intermediate-term borrowing (1-7 years), and bonds are used when maturity exceeds 7 years. In 1970, the longest maturity was 1998—a $3\frac{1}{2}$ percent bond outstanding in the amount of $4.1 billion.

Savings bonds outstanding in the amount of $51.3 billion constitute the second largest category of nonmarketables. They are currently issued in two series, E and H, to individuals to yield $5\frac{1}{2}$ percent if held to maturity. The special issues, the largest class of nonmarketables, are held by various government trust funds, the largest of which—$26 billion—is the Old-Age and Survivors Insurance Trust Fund.

Little needs to be added to the summary of ownership of the federal debt presented in Table 18-2. Over two-fifths was held by nonbank private investors, with 22 percent in the hands of individuals. Nearly one-third was held by commercial and Federal Reserve Banks, the monetized portion. The remaining one-fourth resided in government investment accounts.

The maturity distribution of marketable federal securities in 1970 is shown in Table 18-3. Nearly one-half had maturities within 1 year; over four-fifths within 5 years. Maturities of 10 years or more comprised only 9 percent of the total.

TABLE 18-2 / ESTIMATED OWNERSHIP OF FEDERAL SECURITIES, JUNE 30, 1970 (billions of dollars)

Type of Owner	Amount	Percent of Total
Private nonbank investors		
Individuals	82.5	22.3
Corporations	11.1	3.0
State and local government	24.6	6.6
Foreign and international	14.8	4.0
Insurance companies	6.8	1.8
Mutual savings banks	2.9	0.8
Miscellaneous investors	22.0	5.9
Total nonbank	164.7	44.4
Banks		
Commercial banks	53.3	14.4
Fed Banks	57.7	15.5
Total bank	111.0	29.9
U.S. government investment accounts	95.2	25.7
Grand total	370.9	100.0

Source: *Federal Reserve Bulletin* (October 1970), p. A 42.

TABLE 18-3 / MATURITY DISTRIBUTION OF MARKETABLE FEDERAL SECURITIES, JUNE 30, 1970

Due or First Callable	Billions of Dollars	Percent of Total
Within 1 year	105.5	45.5
1-5 years	89.6	38.5
5-10 years	15.9	6.8
10-20 years	10.5	4.5
20 years and over	11.0	4.7
Total	232.5	100.0

Source: *Federal Reserve Bulletin* (September 1970), p. A 43.

GOALS OF DEBT MANAGEMENT

The overriding aim of debt management is that of fostering the broad economic objectives of the economy, viz., stable production and employment at a high level, economic progress, a relatively stable price level, and a viable equilibrium in the balance of international payments. All other aims are subsidiary and should be advanced only insofar as they are in harmony at the time with these basic objectives. The subsidiary criteria are, nevertheless, very important as guides for the Treasury's highly technical management task, and attention is now directed to them.

1/There is the aim of minimizing the cost of borrowing. Some idea of the magnitude of this problem is given by the fact that interest on the federal debt amounted to $19.3 billion in fiscal 1970. With debt in the vicinity of $380 billion, a change of 1 percent increases or decreases interest cost by $3.8 billion. Therefore, other things equal, the Treasury obviously should tailor its current offerings of securities with a view to borrowing at the lowest rates in the money market. In fact, this aim has historically been the dominant one, frequently with little consideration given either to basic objectives or to other subsidiary goals. It should be noted that pennies saved on interest may cost the nation dollars if easy money leads to price inflation. A rise in interest cost to the Treasury is often erroneously regarded to be synonymous with a rise in cost to the nation. This view disregards the fact that there are two sides to the coin. Almost as many people receive interest on the debt, directly and indirectly, as pay taxes. Moreover, the Treasury recaptures over one-third of its interest outlays by high income-tax rates and through holdings of federal securities by U.S. agencies and trust funds, and Federal Reserve Banks.

2/Debt management should give due consideration to the liquidity needs of the economy. Commercial banks largely depend on short-term Treasury obligations to provide needed liquidity reserves. In lesser degree, other financial institutions, businesses, and individuals also hold such securities for liquidity purposes. A substantial shift from short-term to long-term issues may unduly reduce asset liquidity and at the same time cause a decline in short-term rates in relation to long-term rates. A move in this direction has a repressive effect on business and prices. On the other side, large-scale refunding of long-terms into short-terms may create a greater measure of liquidity than is justified. This would raise short-term yields relative to long-term yields, and in general would be a stimulative influence on production and prices.

3/Another aspect of maintaining proper balance between liquid and nonliquid assets relates to monetary management by Federal Reserve authorities. If holdings of short-term Treasury issues by commercial banks and others are abnormally large, the effectiveness of general monetary instruments to restrain credit is weakened. This follows from the fact that funds to make additional loans are forthcoming from maturities, or by sale of, liquidity-reserve assets. However, large holdings of long-term bonds and small holdings of short-terms strengthen Federal Reserve powers of restraint. A tightening of the reserve position of commercial banks then leads to a more ready response in rising interest rates and reduced credit availability. The accompanying decline in bond prices generates losses in bond accounts of commercial banks, savings banks, life insurance companies, and other lenders. As book losses grow, these institutions become increasingly reluctant to sell bonds as a source of funds to make additional loans.

4/An additional aim of debt management is to develop a structure of types and maturities of federal securities that promises a stable pattern of ownership. In other words, insofar as possible the outstanding securities and new issues should be tailored to investor requirements. This implies that the amount of short-term issues should be adequate for liquidity needs and that intermediate- and long-term securities be outstanding in sufficient volume and variety of maturities to meet investment demands for highest-grade obligations. A rough test of proper distribution by maturities is provided by the shape of the yield curve. In an average period, the yield-maturity curve would be expected to rise gently as maturities lengthen. In easy-money periods, an upsweeping curve usually prevails, with a sharp rise in the earlier years. But in tight-money periods, the curve would be expected to follow a downward course. Any material departure from the expected pattern, considering the state of the money market, may well indicate a disregard of a stable pattern of ownership.

This last aim raises the questions: What structure of security types and maturities gives promise of stable ownership? Is it some fixed proportion between marketable and nonmarketable issues? Is it an equal distribution of amount over the various maturity classes? The answer to the last two questions is definitely in the negative. There is no ideal structure that remains constant over time. Instead, the division between marketables and nonmarketables and the maturity distribution should be flexibly adapted to continuously changing requirements. While nonmarketable, redeemable savings bonds meet a special need of the small saver for protection against bond-price fluctuations, there is a strong presumption against other public issues of nonmarketables. The reason lies in the desirability of having a broad, active market in all maturities of federal securities. Such a market significantly contributes to liquidity needs and to the flexibility of investors' positions. In regard to maturities, it would be purely coincidental if an even distribution should meet investor demands at the time, and therefore give the greatest assurance of stable ownership. At one time, investor preferences may be dominantly for short-term issues; at another time, the pendulum may swing back toward intermediate- and long-term bonds.

5/Another consideration is to manage the debt so that current financing problems will be simplified. This would call for departure from an equal distribution of maturities only to the extent necessary to realize overall purposes. If maturities of a \$380 billion debt were evenly spread over 40 years, the size of annual refundings would be \$9.5 billion. At the other extreme, if all maturities were one year, the Treasury would have to come to market annually for the entire amount.

6/A final aim is the maintenance of the Treasury bank balance within a reasonable range in relation to requirements. In the last few years, this has been roughly between \$3 and \$8 billion. When the balance drops below \$3 billion, the

Treasury may be temporarily embarrassed for lack of funds. If the balance becomes excessive, the Treasury incurs unnecessary interest costs.

As with all multiple criteria, there is at times bound to be conflict among them, so that overall policy should constantly seek a balanced compromise. Attention has already been called to the fact that arbitrarily low rates on Treasury borrowing cannot be reconciled with effective control of inflationary overexpansion. Another example of possible conflict is the fact that provision of the desired amount of short-term issues for liquidity purposes may weaken Federal Reserve controls.

DEBT MANAGEMENT WHEN INFLATION THREATENS

Debt-management operations to moderate an inflationary boom vary somewhat depending on the state of the cash budget—whether it shows a surplus, a deficit, or is in balance. First assume that Congress seriously desires to curb an overexpansion, and therefore develops a budget surplus which is used to retire securities. As the following illustrations show, the effects on the stock of money and on spending depend on ownership of the retired securities. For this purpose owners, like Gaul, may be divided into three divisions: (1) Federal Reserve Banks, (2) commercial banks, and (3) all other investors.

retirement of debt held by reserve banks

On the assumption that a cash surplus of $5 billion is utilized to retire securities held by the Reserve Banks, the effects on their statement and that of member (commercial) banks as a group would be as follows:

CASE I

Member (Commercial) Banks

Assets	*Liabilities*
	(1) Demand deposits – 5
	(1) U.S. deposits + 5
(2) Reserve with Federal Reserve Banks – 5	(2) U.S. deposits – 5

Federal Reserve Banks

Assets	*Liabilities*
	(2) Deposits – U.S. Treasury + 5
	(2) Deposits – member banks – 5
(3) U.S. securities – 5	(3) Deposits – U.S. Treasury – 5

In step 1, individuals and businesses pay taxes to Uncle Sam whose tax-and-loan account is correspondingly increased. Step 2 shows the shift of the Treasury's balance to its active checking account in the Reserve Banks. In the last step, the Treasury draws on its balance to retire securities owned by the

Reserve Banks. The net effect on the commercial banks is to extinguish both demand deposits (money) and legal reserves by $5 billion. If legal reserves of commercial banks just met requirements at the outset and we assume a 15 percent legal reserve, this operation would create a deficiency of $4.25 billion. In the event that member banks are denied more Reserve Bank credit and do not gain reserves from other sources, their only alternative would be to liquidate loans and investments, and thereby deposits, to the amount of $28.3 billion, that is, (100/15 × 4.25). Adding this to the initial $5 billion gives a total reduction of $33.3 billion in deposit money—doubtless considerably more than would be desirable. Of course, the extent of multiple contraction could, and probably would, be modified by release of Reserve Bank credit to member banks through the discount window, or by open-market purchases of securities.

retirement of debt held by commercial banks

Next, consider the case of the retirement of federal securities held by member (commercial) banks. The effects would be as follows:

CASE II

Member (Commercial) Banks

Assets	*Liabilities*
(2) Reserve with Federal Reserve Banks – 5	(1) Demand deposits – 5
	(1) U.S. deposits + 5
(3) Reserve with Federal Reserve Banks + 5	(2) U.S. deposits – 5
(3) U.S. Securities – 5	

Federal Reserve Banks

	Liabilities
	(2) Deposits – U.S. Treasury + 5
	(2) Deposits – member banks – 5
	(3) Deposits – U.S. Treasury – 5
	(3) Deposits – member banks + 5

As in the first case, steps 1 and 2 cover tax collection and transfer of the Treasury balance to the Reserve Banks. In step 3, the Treasury draws on this balance to retire securities held by member banks, and thereby returns the reserves which were initially drawn down in the transfer process. Thus, the net monetary result is a reduction of demand deposits accompanying a corresponding decline of member-bank investments. There is no change in total member-bank reserve balances, but required legal reserves are released to the amount of $.75 billion, that is, (15/100 × 5). In the absence of absorption of these excess reserves by Federal Reserve action, they would provide the base for a subsequent expansion of member-bank loans and investments, and thereby of deposits, to replace the $5 billion initially destroyed. Consequently, there would be a check on inflationary spending for a time, but this would be removed if and when subsequent bank expansion replaced the deposits. In fact, if the replacement process is one of loan expansion, there is reason after a time lag to expect a net inflationary result. This follows from the fact that borrowers are likely to spend immediately, so that the new deposits will probably be more active than the original deposits at least on the first round of spending. Thus, because these are offsetting influences, the retirement of federal securities owned by commercial banks may be neutral in its effect on total spending for output in the absence of absorption of the released reserve of $.75 billion by the Fed.

retirement of debt held by nonbank investors

Assume finally that the securities retired are owned by individuals or other nonbank investors.[1]

CASE III

Member (Commercial) Banks

Assets	*Liabilities*
	(1) Demand deposits – 5
	(1) U.S. deposits + 5
(2) Reserve with Federal Reserve Banks – 5	(2) U.S. deposits – 5
(3) Reserve with Federal Reserve Banks + 5	(3) Demand deposits + 5

Federal Reserve Banks

	Liabilities
	(2) Deposits – U.S. Treasury + 5
	(2) Deposits – member banks –5
	(3) Deposits – U.S. Treasury – 5
	(3) Deposits – member banks + 5

Steps 1 and 2 again show the process of tax collection and transfer of Treasury deposits to the Reserve Banks. In step 3, the Treasury draws on its account in the Reserve Banks to redeem securities owned by individuals. In turn, these individuals deposit the Treasury checks in commercial banks which send them to the Reserve Banks for collection by credit to their reserve balances. Thus, after the cycle is completed, there is no change in the stock of money or in the reserve positions of member banks or Reserve Banks. In this sense, retirement of securities held by nonbank investors is neither inflationary nor deflationary, aside from the temporary effect during the interval between tax collection and debt retirement.

However, the influence on consumer and business expenditures is likely

[1]In this usage, "nonbank" means other than commercial banks and Reserve Banks.

to be a depressing one because the greater part of federal taxes is collected, directly and indirectly, from personal and corporate income. But the money returned to security owners constitutes part of their capital funds rather than income. Hence, it will largely be used to purchase other investment securities instead of consumer goods. It is true that under conditions of intense demand for capital goods these funds may finance expansion and thereby contribute as much currently to national income as an equivalent amount of consumer expenditures. But this expectation may not be realized in the face of flagging consumer demand which is a direct consequence of a level of taxation designed to produce a budget surplus.

In summary, the use of a budget surplus to retire debt held by Reserve Banks has the strongest deflationary effect because both member-bank reserves and demand deposits are extinguished by the amount of debt retirement. In addition, if supported by Federal Reserve action, a multiple contraction of deposit money is set in motion. Next in order of restraining power is retirement of debt owned by commercial banks because demand deposits are reduced at once by the amount of retired debt. But given time, the released member-bank reserves may support bank expansion and replacement of the extinguished deposits. However, this subsequent expansion process may be nipped in the bud by a restrictive Federal Reserve policy. The mildest restraint of all arises from retirement of debt owned by nonbank investors. This does not change deposits or reserves at all, but tends to depress national income by checking consumer and business expenditures during the tax-collection process.

shifts in federal debt ownership

Regardless of whether the budget shows a surplus, deficit, or balance, debt management can exert a powerful restraining influence by promoting shifts in ownership of existing federal securities. The following illustrations of these techniques first view a shift of securities from the Reserve Banks to nonbank investors, and second, a shift from commercial banks to nonbank investors.

Assume that the Treasury sells $100 million of savings bonds to individuals and uses the proceeds to retire securities owned by the Reserve Banks. The changes would be as follows:

CASE IV

Member (Commercial) Banks

Assets	*Liabilities*
	(1) Demand deposits – 100
	(1) U.S. deposits + 100
(2) Reserve with Federal Reserve Banks –100	(2) U.S. deposits – 100

Federal Reserve Banks

Assets	*Liabilities*
	(2) Deposits – U.S. Treasury + 100
(3) U.S. securities – 100	(2) Deposits – member banks – 100
	(3) Deposits – U.S. Treasury – 100

In step 1, individuals purchase savings bonds and the checks are deposited in the Treasury's tax and loan accounts with commercial banks. Step 2 indicates the transfer of deposits to the Reserve Banks with an associated reduction in member-bank reserve balances. In step 3, the Treasury draws on its account to redeem securities held by the Reserve Banks. The net result is destruction of both legal reserves and demand deposits of member banks by the full amount of the shift. This is precisely the same result, it will be recalled, that followed from use of a budget surplus to retire debt owned by the Reserve Banks. Collection of taxes, however, is a greater deterrent to consumer expenditures than sale of an equal amount of savings bonds. Tax receipts do not contribute to one's wealth, but bonds do. The disposition to spend current income increases as the backlog of savings grows.

Assume now that the proceeds of savings bond sales are used to retire securities owned by commercial banks. The changes would be as follows:

CASE V

Member (Commercial) Banks

Assets	*Liabilities*
	(1) Demand deposits – 100
	(1) U.S. deposits + 100
(2) Reserve with Federal Reserve Banks – 100	(2) U.S. deposits – 100
(3) Reserve with Federal Reserve Banks + 100	
(3) U.S. securities – 100	

Federal Reserve Banks

	Liabilities
	(2) Deposits – U.S. Treasury + 100
	(2) Deposits – member banks – 100
	(3) Deposits – U.S. Treasury – 100
	(3) Deposits – member banks + 100

Once again, steps 1 and 2 refer to the Treasury's receipt of deposits from individuals and transfer to the Reserve Banks. In step 3, the Treasury draws on its account to redeem securities held by commercial banks whose reserves are correspondingly increased. The net result is a reduction in demand deposits and in securities of commercial banks–the same as that which followed from use of a budget surplus to retire debt held by commercial banks. The immediate effect is deflationary in view of destruction of deposits. But given time, the associated excess reserves may be utilized to support a new bank-credit expansion which may replace the destroyed deposits. However, a tight Federal Reserve policy could hold the line and forestall this subsequent expansion.

While these illustrations of deflationary shifts in debt ownership require increased sales of savings bonds to individuals, similar results can be realized by shifting federal securities from banks to any type of nonbank investors–whether they be insurance companies, mutual savings banks, pension funds, businesses, or others. By selling long-term bonds to this broad market and using the money to retire issues held by banks—largely short- and intermediate-term issues—powerful restrictive influences can be brought to bear. But, in fact, little use has been made of this technique because the Treasury usually faces a dilemma during inflationary booms. Private demand for loans typically exceeds current savings so that borrowers eagerly seek bank loans to fill the gap. But due to previous loan expansion and to restrictive Federal Reserve policy, the banks are not in position to meet all demands. The consequences are rising interest rates and declining bond prices. Under such conditions, the Treasury is extremely reluctant to issue long-term bonds, and indeed is more likely to borrow on short-term.

The reasons for this attitude are not hard to understand. Officials shrink from committing the Treasury to pay high rates for the next 15 to 40 years, and in addition they are under real pressures not to compete with private enterprise for long-term money. As a result, the Treasury's action has more often been perverse than supportive of the prevailing monetary policy of restraint. A good illustration may be drawn from the period 1956-1957, when practically all Treasury borrowing was at short-term in the presence of Federal Reserve efforts to restrain inflation. This all raises the question whether under such conditions the Treasury should not exhibit more courage and give greater weight to its monetary responsibilities. The real issue is whether the goals of stable business and a steady price level are more or less important than the aim of borrowing at low cost. Previous analysis has established the overriding priority of the former when conflict arises between them. If this conclusion be accepted, there remains not the slightest doubt in regard to proper debt-management policy. The blunt fact is that the only way to restrain credit aside from direct control is to follow policies that do so. If the Treasury is to assume a positive role in this enterprise, it must at the same time face the unpleasant necessities of paying higher rates on both short- and long-term issues and of competing with private borrowers for funds. These are important building blocks in the control structure.

Even more important, when inflation threatens, the Treasury should avoid actions that positively spur spending and prices. The best illustration is provided by the period 1946-1951, when interest rates were maintained at an artificially low level in face of a sharp rise in the price level. The Treasury dominated the Federal Reserve authorities and negated restrictive monetary controls by insisting that Reserve Banks purchase federal securities whenever yields rose above the fixed ceilings. This unwise policy was ended by the Treasury-Federal Reserve Accord in March 1951. Another bias of the Treasury in these years, and in some degree since, was to overestimate the demand for new security offerings. With an eye to cheap borrowing, coupon rates were sometimes set too low with the result that the Reserve Banks were forced to save the day by open-market purchases or by subscriptions. Such action was, of course, not consistent with efforts to contain price inflation. From all this, the conclusion may be drawn that the Treasury should ever bear in mind that a somewhat higher interest charge on the debt is a small price to pay for avoidance of the inequitable and disorganizing effects of price inflation.

administration of treasury cash and deposits

The Treasury also possesses significant powers of monetary restraint in administration of its cash and deposit balances. There are four ways in which these powers may be implemented.

1/Treasury deposits held by commercial banks may be shifted to the Reserve Banks. It will be recalled that the bulk of Treasury deposits–usually between $3 and $8 billion–is held in the tax and loan accounts of some 11,000 depositary commercial banks; also that the Treasury's active checking account–between $500 and $1,200 million–is in the Reserve Banks. A decision to raise the average level of the balance in the Reserve Banks by, say, $500 million, would correspondingly reduce member-bank reserve balances. On the assumptions that member-bank excess reserves equal borrowings at Reserve Banks, and that the member-bank reserve requirement is 15 percent, this step would create a legal-reserve deficiency of $425 million. There is no legal reason to prevent the Treasury from transferring *all* its deposits to the Reserve Banks, and thereby creating a member-bank reserve deficiency of several billion dollars. This power is so great that an easy Federal Reserve policy could be negated by the Treasury at will. But, in fact, the Treasury has not exercised this latent power to tighten the money market, and it is unlikely to do so in view of its desire to minimize interest costs. Instead, it has worked closely with the Reserve Banks to keep its balance with them in the vicinity of $750 to $1,100 million in recent years. Nevertheless, the potentiality for conflict exists.

A variant of this method by which the Treasury may accomplish about the same result is that of borrowing and depositing the proceeds with the Reserve Banks. Member-bank reserves would be reduced by the amount of increase in Treasury deposits at the Reserve Banks. This method differs in that it involves a decision in regard to where newly created Treasury deposits, rather than existing deposits, shall be kept.

2/The Treasury may sterilize the effects of imports or domestic purchases of gold on member-bank reserves. Treasury purchases of gold from private interests normally increase member-bank reserves dollar for dollar. That is, the Treasury checks drawn on the Reserve Banks are deposited in commercial banks which receive reserve credit on collection. No permanent change in the Treasury's deposit balance is involved because on receipt of the gold it deposits an equal amount of gold certificates in the Reserve Banks. But the Treasury need not deposit the gold certificates; instead it may borrow to replenish its balance. In this event, the process becomes the same as that described in the preceding paragraph, and is, in fact, only a specialized case of borrowing to build up Treasury deposits in the Reserve Banks. It will be observed that gold sterilization is a hold-the-line method of preventing member-bank reserves from rising as a consequence of increases in the stock of gold.

3/The Treasury may administer the cash position of trust funds and other agencies with a view to monetary restraint. Some idea of the sweep of its power in this area is given by the facts that government investment accounts held $97.7 billion of federal and agency securities at midyear 1970. Trust-account receipts alone exceeded $45 billion in fiscal 1970.[2] The cash position of these funds can be built up by a lagging investment of current receipts and by sales of securities from portofolios. If the increased balances are left with commercial banks, the effect is to impound active private balances. But if the balances are shifted to the Reserve Banks, member-bank reserves are correspondingly reduced. In practice, with few exceptions, trust-fund and agency balances are part of the general deposit accounts of the Treasury. Current receipts are usually invested promptly and cash balances are kept at a minimum. But again, a significant credit-control power resides in the administration of these funds.

4/A final restraining technique involves Treasury borrowing from nonbank investors in advance of needs in order to build up its deposit balances at commercial banks. This results in a transfer of demand deposits of investors to the tax and loan accounts of the Treasury. Because these accounts are not checked upon to make payments, the effect is that of impounding a part of the active stock of money. The borrowing must be from nonbank investors because borrowing from banks creates new money and is positively inflationary. The cost of this procedure to the Treasury is the additional amount of interest on the debt. Moreover, because a far more powerful response can be expected from transferring Treasury deposits to the Reserve Banks, the Treasury is not well advised to use this more expensive method of restraint.

DEBT MANAGEMENT WHEN RECESSION THREATENS

While the techniques of debt management when recession threatens are, in general, just the opposite of those designed to suppress overexpansion, there are enough differences in application to justify a few illustrations. We may assume that fiscal policies of Congress permit, or actively create, a deficit in the federal budget.

borrowing from reserve banks

If the deficit of, say, $5 billion, is borrowed from the Reserve Banks, the following are the results.

[2]*Treasury Bulletin* (August 1970), pp. 2, 3, 20.

CASE I

Federal Reserve Banks

Assets	*Liabilities*
(1) U.S. securities + 5	(1) Deposits – U.S. Treasury + 5
	(2) Deposits – U.S. Treasury – 5
	(2) Deposits – member banks + 5

Member (Commercial) Banks

Assets	*Liabilities*
(2) Reserve with Federal Reserve Banks + 5	(2) Demand deposits + 5

In step 1, the Reserve Banks give the Treasury deposit credit for the amount of purchased securities. Step 2 indicates the effects that follow when the Treasury spends the borrowed money. The businesses and individuals who receive checks deposit them in commercial banks. The banks then present the checks for collection and receive reserve credit. Thus, both demand deposits (money) and member-bank reserves are shortly increased by the amount of Treasury borrowing. Beyond this, $4.25 billion of the new reserves are in excess of requirements (assuming a 15 percent requirement and a net reserve position of zero). These excess reserves have the effect of making loans readily available at low rates, and of encouraging the banks to purchase investments—a financial climate favorable to business recovery. Moreover, spending is fostered by the initial creation of $5 billion in demand deposits, and by the additional deposits that may be generated later by loan and investment expansion. This procedure, it will be noted, is the equivalent of an open-market operation (purchase) at the initiative of the Reserve Banks.

borrowing from commercial banks

Next, assume that the deficit is borrowed from commercial banks:

CASE II

Member (Commercial) Banks

Assets	*Liabilities*
(1) U.S. securities + 5	(1) U.S deposits + 5
(2) Reserve with Federal Reserve Banks – 5	(2) U.S. deposits – 5
(3) Reserve with Federal Reserve Banks + 5	(3) Demand deposits + 5

Federal Reserve Banks

	Liabilities
	(2) Deposits – U.S. Treasury + 5
	(2) Deposits – member banks – 5
	(3) Deposits – U.S. Treasury – 5
	(3) Deposits – member banks + 5

In step 1, commercial banks purchase the new offering of federal securities and give the Treasury credit to its tax and loan account. Step 2 shows the transfer of these deposits to the Reserve Banks, accompanied by an equivalent reduction in member-bank reserve balances. When the Treasury spends the deposits in step 3, demand deposits of businesses and individuals are increased, and collection of the checks rebuilds member-bank reserves. Thus, the net result is a $5 billion expansion of demand deposits (money), associated with an equal increase in U.S. securities of member banks. At the same time, required legal reserves would rise and excess reserves would decline by $.75 billion to support the new deposits (assuming a 15 percent requirement and the presence of excess reserves). If excess reserves were not present, the Reserve Banks would have to provide the required reserves in one way or another, or member banks would have to dispose of $5 billion of loans and investments.

borrowing from nonbank investors

Should the Treasury borrow the $5 billion from nonbank investors (other than Federal Reserve or commercial banks), there would be no resulting change in either demand deposits or member-bank reserve balances. It is probable, however, that aggregate expenditures in the economy would be stimulated by an increase (or less decrease) in the velocity of money. That is, the government is likely to spend the borrowed funds immediately, and thereby generate a train of private spending that would otherwise take place in smaller volume, or not occur at all.

To recapitulate, the most powerful influences against recession follow when the Treasury borrows the deficit from the Federal Reserve Banks. This step creates an equivalent amount of new demand deposits and member-bank reserves, and the bulk of the latter provide the base for substantial further monetary expansion. Next in order of influence is borrowing the deficit at commercial banks. This procedure, like the previous one, immediately generates new demand deposits, but leaves aggregate member-bank reserves unchanged—except for borrowing, if necessary, to meet a reserve deficiency. The weakest effect is exerted when the Treasury borrows from nonbank investors because neither demand deposits nor bank reserves are increased. The stimulus, if any, must then come from increased spending that is financed by a rise in velocity of money.

shifts in federal debt ownership

Regardless of whether Congress creates a budget deficit, the Treasury can exert a strong influence against recession by shifts in ownership of existing federal debt. In general, the procedure is to move federal debt from nonbank investors to Federal Reserve Banks and commercial banks—that is, to money-creating institutions. The most potent response follows from shifting debt from individuals, insurance companies, pension funds, businesses, and other nonbank investors to the Reserve Banks. This step increases both demand deposits and member-bank reserve balances by the amount shifted. The increase of the latter consists mostly of excess reserves[3] which form the base for subsequent multiple expansion of loans and investments, and of deposits. Moreover, the excess reserves foster subsequent expansion by augmenting credit availability at lower rates. Incidentally, the reader will recognize this transaction as the equivalent of a Federal Reserve open-market purchase of securities, and therefore as a concrete illustration of the oneness of monetary (narrowly defined) and debt-management policies.

While the effect of moving federal securities from nonbank investors to commercial banks is not so great, it is nevertheless substantial. New demand deposits in equivalent amount are created. Because a net reserve surplus usually exists under these conditions, the process is typically one of putting excess reserves to work. In any event, the additional deposit money is likely to provide a spur to both consumer and investment expenditures. Considering the huge size and varied maturities of the federal debt, frequent opportunities arise for action along these lines. For example, $105.5 billion of marketable debt were due within one year as of midyear 1970.[4] Other issues could be purchased by the Treasury in the open market. The funds with which to make these redemptions and retirements could be raised by offerings of new issues especially attractive to commercial banks.

administration of treasury cash and deposits

Just as the administration of Treasury cash and deposits can be directed toward restraint, so in opposite fashion this power can be utilized to promote recovery. The master technique involves a reduction in the amount of Treasury deposits at the Reserve Banks or in Treasury cash, both of which lead to an increase of member-bank reserve balances and of demand deposits. When the Treasury draws checks on its balance at the Reserve Banks, the recipients deposit them in commercial banks which gain reserves upon collection. Important use of this method would require a preparatory buildup of the Treasury's balance at Reserve Banks to an amount substantially above the working minimum of around $700 million, say, to $1.7 billion. This would then provide a possible reduction of $1 billion to provide more legal reserves for member banks. A special aspect of Treasury deposits at the Reserve Banks is the balances of trust funds and of government agencies. A reduction of these balances by purchasing

[3]This assumes a net reserve position of zero at the outset.
[4]*Treasury Bulletin* (August 1970), p. 68.

federal securities in the market, or by other expenditures in excess of receipts, augments member-bank deposits and legal reserves.

If the Treasury holds unexpended cash, this may be spent in order to increase member-bank reserves and the stock of money. Possession of a sizable amount of cash may be the result of devaluation of the gold dollar, as in 1934, when the Treasury's profit was $2.8 billion, or of previous sterilization of gold purchases, as in 1936-1937. But regardless of the source of Treasury cash, it may be deposited in the Treasury's account with the Reserve Banks, thereby increasing at the same time the latter's gold-certificate account or other-cash account. Then as the Treasury subsequently spends the new deposits, member-bank reserves and deposits are enlarged.

MATURITY DISTRIBUTION OF THE FEDERAL DEBT

A relatively even maturity distribution of the federal debt has been a traditional goal of the Treasury even though this pattern has seldom characterized the actual distribution. The advantages of such a distribution are (1) simplification of the Treasury's problem of refunding by avoiding concentration of maturities, (2) assurance of financing at average interest costs, and (3) satisfaction of investor requirements for a wide range of maturities of highest-grade, marketable obligations.

This traditional aim, however, must be submerged whenever the dominant goal of debt management becomes economic stabilization. The supporting reasons for an orderly maturity distribution then become relatively minor matters of good housekeeping and smooth administration of the Treasury Department. Instead of being a mere department with narrowly defined functions, the Treasury then becomes a powerful institution in the area of monetary management. In this setting, the ideal maturity distribution of debt in peacetime is the one that makes the largest contribution to stable growth in output and to a steady value of the dollar. The same can be said for the interest rate paid by the Treasury and for ownership distribution of the debt.

These facts raise the questions: What does all this mean in more specific terms with respect to changes in the maturity distribution during succeeding stages of the business cycle? When can maturities consistently be lengthened; and when can they consistently be shortened? The answers depend mainly on whether it is desirable at the time to shift debt from banks to nonbank investors, or in the opposite direction. In addition, the answers depend on the probable effects on the money and capital markets of substantial cyclical changes in maturity distribution of the huge marketable federal debt. In this regard, consideration must be given to investment preferences as reflected by the actual ownership distribution of U.S. securities. More specifically, investments of commercial banks and holdings of nonfinancial corporations are mainly in the short-term category to meet liquidity needs. However, life insurance companies, mutual savings banks, pension funds, trust funds, and individuals have a general preference for intermediate- and long-term obligations. In view of this considerable degree of compartmentalization, the mobility of investment funds along the maturity scale is limited. Hence, large shifts in the maturity distribution may be expected to generate material changes in yield-maturity relationships, as well as some change in the average rate level.

Positive countercyclical action to moderate an inflationary condition calls for some refunding of maturing issues to intermediate- and long-term securities. Because banks are the largest holders of short-terms, this will have the effect of reducing demand deposits (money) if supported by a restrictive Federal Reserve policy. It will also absorb long-term funds in the capital market and prevent their use to finance overexpansion of private investment. In addition, the associated rise of long-term rates will provide further restraint on investment, and the general decline of asset liquidity will have a repressive effect on expenditures by businesses and consumers.

In opposite fashion, countercyclical debt management during recession requires that maturing issues be refunded into short-term securities, and that deficit financing be done by short-term offerings. This will provide a boost to the economy in several respects. For one thing, more money will be created insofar as banks buy the new securities, and the general state of liquidity will be increased by larger holdings of short-term issues. For another, long-term investment funds will be released to finance business investment, residential construction, and state and local capital improvements. Also, investment expenditures will be encouraged by the lower rates that emerge because of Treasury forbearance to compete in the capital market.

While most authorities agree on the nature of countercyclical debt management, there are wide differences of opinion concerning the program that should actually be adopted. Many economists believe that debt management should definitely assume a positive role. They feel that this goal far transcends the lesser aims of minimizing interest cost of the debt, and of developing an even distribution of maturities. In addition, debt management should share the responsibility in the overall program of economic stabilization with fiscal management, and with monetary management. These economists are particularly disturbed by debt-management policies that have tended to magnify cyclical swings in the past, and to negate monetary and fiscal policies designed to promote stability.

Some economists hold that the principal consideration of the Treasury should be minimization of interest cost of the debt. They advocate a program of maturity extension during recessions when rates are low, and of short-term borrowing during prosperous years when rates are high. While they place less emphasis on maturities, a by-product of their prescription would doubtless be a longer average maturity than would exist under the positive program of the first group. The following are the reasons and beliefs underlying this point of view.

First, the interest cost of the federal debt should be minimized because it is—aside from national defense, health and welfare expenditures—the largest item in the budget. On a $380 billion debt, a rise of 1 percent amounts to $3.8 billion additional cost. The added tax burden involves both inequities and a drag on economic incentives. Second, it is difficult, or impossible, for the Treasury to borrow substantial sums in the long-term market during the tight-money conditions of a boom, except at higher rates than can be justified for a long commitment. Third, the demand for credit is quite inelastic to changes in interest rates. That is, high rates do not greatly deter the demand for long-term funds during prosperity, and low rates do not induce material increases in demands for credit during recessions. Fourth, there is no clear evidence that enlarged asset liquidity leads to a greater propensity to spend during recessions, or that a reduction in asset liquidity during prosperity dampens the disposition to spend. Finally, fiscal management and monetary management—with emphasis on selective controls—are better adapted to effective stabilizing actions, and are capable of assuming the added burden of offsetting perverse debt-management operations.[5]

Other economists take the middle position that treasury debt management should be neutral with respect to economic stabilization. They hold that as a practical matter, institutional limitations are too great for the Treasury to make a positive contribution to stabilization. The traditional aims of borrowing at lowest rates and of lengthening and spacing maturities are too deep-seated to be abandoned or reversed. In their view, the best that can reasonably be expected is that the Treasury cease to accentuate cyclical swings by shortening maturities during tight-money markets, and lengthening maturities during recessions when rates are low. Some members of this group suggest that Treasury neutrality be attained by accepting the existing proportions of debt in broad maturity classes as a standard for future financing. They would create as much certainty in the market as possible by spacing maturities evenly within these broad classes, and by announcing a definite long-range rollover program in which maturing issues are always refunded into the longest maturity of their class. Such a program would eliminate money and capital market disturbances that arise from the uncertainties surrounding all large Treasury financing operations, when dealers and investors try to guess the nature of the package to be offered, including amounts of certificates, notes, and bonds; maturities; and other terms.[6]

NEW TECHNIQUES OF DEBT MANAGEMENT

In administering the huge federal debt, the Treasury has developed certain new

[5]For a full statement of this viewpoint see Warren L. Smith, *Debt Management in the United States,* Study Paper No. 19, Joint Economic Committee of Congress (Washington, D.C., 1960), especially chap. VI.

[6]For the most complete statement of this viewpoint see Tilford C. Gaines, *Techniques of Treasury Debt Management* (New York: Free Press, 1962), especially chap. VIII.

techniques which have a significant bearing on the money market. The most important of these is known as *advance refunding.* Others include the offering of longer Treasury bills at more frequent intervals, the offering of *strips* of bills, and the use of competitive bidding for intermediate- and long-term securities.

advance refunding

In an advance refunding, the Treasury offers owners of federal obligations the opportunity to exchange them before maturity for longer-term issues which usually bear a higher coupon rate and give a moderately higher yield to maturity. Three types of such operations are distinguished: senior refunding, junior refunding, and prerefunding. A senior refunding involves the offer to exchange outstanding issues in the intermediate range of about 5 to 10 years for long-term bonds (15 to 40 or more years). Junior refunding refers to the exchange of issues maturing in 1 to 5 years for bonds in the intermediate range of 5 to 10 years. Prerefunding applies to the exchange of securities maturing in under 1 year for new issues in the intermediate range of 5 to 10 years. This last device was first used in September 1962, when $8 billion of securities maturing in 8 months or less were exchanged for issues maturing in the 5-10-year range.

The advance refunding program of the Treasury was begun in June 1960, after a change in income-tax legislation in 1959, applying to capital gains and losses, made it practicable. Many advance refunding operations were completed in the following decade in which holders of over $130 billion of securities were given the opportunity to exchange them for longer-term issues. By spreading and lengthening maturities, there is less risk of future disturbance to the money market and of interference with monetary policy from bunching of Treasury financing.

An important advantage of the advance-refunding technique is that maturities are lengthened with appreciably less effect on the market than would result from cash offerings of the same securities. For this reason, it was especially adapted to operation twist, which was designed to hold down long-term interest rates as a spur to the economy, but at the same time to maintain short-term rates as a means of checking the persistent deficit in the balance of payments. If the Treasury waits until maturity to refund long-term issues, it loses many of its original long-term investors. They are likely to sell their holdings before maturity to others who want highly liquid assets, and who are not interested in new long-term issues. Considerable churning of the market occurs while dealers move the maturing securities (rights) into the hands of investors who want the new long-terms, and while the new securities sold for cash find their way to permanent investors. During this digestive process, yields are likely to rise appreciably above what they would be under advance refunding. This technique enables the Treasury to hold its long-term investors by offering attractive exchanges before they sell to investors who seek liquidity.

other new techniques

Another new debt-management technique is the offering of a strip of Treasury bills, maturing over a series of consecutive weeks. This device was first employed in June 1961, when a $1.8 billion offering to mature serially over an 18-week period was made. At that time it was used to achieve the maximum firming effect on rates and thereby prevent short-term funds from flowing abroad. This effect results from the tendency to increase dealer inventories when they are offered a package of weekly maturities at one time, instead of a comparable increase in weekly offerings of regular Treasury bills.

Still another new technique was the offering of long-term Treasury bonds at competitive bidding. The first such offering was made in January 1963–a $250 million issue of 30-year bonds with a 4 percent coupon. Four large syndicates of dealers submitted bids which were surprisingly close together. The winning syndicate, headed by C. J. Devine and Company, bid $99.85111 per $100 of face amount, while the next highest bid, by the Morgan Guaranty group, was $99.85100, only $275 less.[7] The operation was generally regarded to be successful because the bonds were sold out quickly at par, and then moved to a premium within the next few days. A second offering on a competitive basis was made in April 1963–$300 million of bonds of 1989-1994 with a $4\frac{1}{8}$ percent coupon. Again, pricing by the three bidding syndicates was close–with interest costs in a range of $\frac{1}{100}$ of 1 percent. While the Treasury expressed satisfaction with the results, the purchasing group was not so fortunate. The bonds moved out slowly in a declining market, and the syndicate was terminated some two weeks later when only about half were sold and when the market price was $\frac{6}{32}$ below the price paid.[8] The failure of this second experiment from the underwriters' standpoint apparently discouraged further use of this method; no bonds were offered at competitive bidding between 1963 and 1970.

REFERENCES

See references at the end of Chapter 19.

[7]U.S. Treasury Department, news release, January 8, 1962.
[8]U.S. Treasury Department, news release, April 9, 1963.

19

coordination of monetary, fiscal, and debt management

The weakest link in the chain of cyclical controls is not lack of power, nor of intelligence to exercise it, but rather the failure to coordinate existing powers into an effective overall program. Federal Reserve authorities are responsible for part of monetary management; Congress, with counsel from the Administration, is responsible for the monetary aspects of fiscal policy; and the Treasury is charged with the monetary aspects of debt management. This chapter draws together the discussion in this and the preceding six chapters by summarizing the features of a coordinated program of cyclical control (1) when an inflationary boom threatens, and (2) when a business recession impends.

CONTROL OF INFLATIONARY BOOMS

When an inflationary expansion develops, the Federal Reserve authorities may take restrictive monetary measures, as follows:

GENERAL INSTRUMENTS

1/Raise the discount rate and ration reserve credit among member banks that wish to borrow. This restrains the expansion of money and of spending by reducing the availability of credit and by raising its cost.

2/Reduce Reserve Bank holdings of U.S. securities and bankers' acceptances. This action absorbs member-bank reserves and forces them either to borrow at the higher discount rate or to undertake multiple contraction of bank credit.

3/Raise legal-reserve requirements. This step converts excess member-bank reserves into required reserves, and if pressed further, it creates legal-reserve deficiencies. In turn, these deficiencies must be repaired by borrowing at the higher rate or by multiple contraction of loans and/or investments, and thereby of deposits.

4/In addition, as in 1966 and 1969, the Board may fix maximum rates payable on time deposits (Regulation Q) below competitive market rates. This step tends to restrain the expansion of bank credit.

All these general instruments, it should be emphasized, operate to restrict spending by a reduction in the amount of money and in the disposition to spend existing money.

SELECTIVE INSTRUMENTS

1/Raise margin requirements on security loans. This step limits or reduces borrowing by speculators to purchase and carry stocks.

2/Moral suasion to restrict speculative loans.

In contrast with general instruments, selective methods are designed to restrain particular types of credit. Consumer credit and real-estate credit were subject to control during the postwar period, but these powers lapsed in 1952 and 1953. Also, a voluntary credit-restraint program was instituted during the Korean War and again in 1965 to reduce the outflow of investment funds to other countries.

When inflation threatens, Congress, assisted by the Administration, may undertake deflationary fiscal steps, as follows:

1/Decrease federal expenditures for public works, subsidies, and other programs susceptible to curtailment. This directly reduces demand in the markets, and may have a multiple restraining influence on private spending.

2/Establish a tax structure that automatically applies the check rein as a boom gains momentum. With a rise in national income, this would produce, without change in tax rates, an even faster rate of increase in revenues. A graduated personal income tax and a tax on corporate profits are best adapted to this purpose.

3/Raise tax rates in order to increase revenues and to curtail private spending. This, combined with reduction in expenditures, should produce a budget surplus which can be applied to debt reduction.

4/Reduce the scope and liberality of programs of insurance or guarantee of private loans. The outstanding examples are insurance of home loans by the FHA and guarantee of housing loans to veterans.

Finally, the Treasury may bring further restraining influences to bear by federal debt-management operations, as follows:

1/Use the budget surplus, if it exists, to redeem federal securities owned by Federal Reserve and commercial banks, rather than securities owned by nonbank investors. This procedure, if supported by restrictive Federal Reserve policy, reduces the stock of money and puts a damper on spending.

2/Shift part of the existing federal debt from the banks to nonbank investors. This similarly reduces the amount of money and restrains spending if supported by a Federal Reserve policy of restraint.

3/Borrow long-term rather than short-term. This reduces liquidity in the economy and the availability of long-term funds to the private sector for expansion of investment.

4/Increase the average amount of Treasury cash and deposits at Federal Reserve Banks. While there are several aspects of this operation, the general effect is to suppress private spending by reducing bank reserves and the stock of money.

CONTROL OF DEPRESSIONS

When depression threatens or exists, the various methods of combating an inflationary expansion may in general be reversed. The Reserve authorities may take monetary steps to promote recovery as follows:

GENERAL INSTRUMENTS

1/Lower the discount rate, and lend more liberally to member banks.

2/Purchase U.S. securities and bankers' acceptances. This releases legal reserves so that member banks may repay indebtedness and build up excess reserves with which to buy securities and make loans at lower rates.

3/Lower legal-reserve requirements. This action converts required reserves into excess reserves, and also increases the multiple by which bank credit may be expanded on the basis of each $1 of legal reserve.

All three of these steps have the effects of lowering interest rates, raising bond prices, and encouraging expenditures by businesses, consumers, and state and local governments.

SELECTIVE INSTRUMENTS

1/Margin requirements on security loans may be lowered, so that speculators may borrow more freely to purchase and carry stocks.

2/Moral suasion may be employed to encourage commercial banks to lend more generously at lower rates.

3/Other selective controls, if in force, may be relaxed or removed.

Congress, aided by the Administration, may undertake positive fiscal measures to stimulate the economy, as follows:

1/Increase federal expenditures on public works, subsidies, unemployment compensation, and direct payments to the needy. Such expenditures contribute directly to demand and may also have a multiple effect on private spending.

2/Establish a tax structure that automatically reduces tax receipts more rapidly than the rate of decline in national income. This releases disposable income and stimulates private spending.

3/Lower tax rates in order to augment private disposable income and thereby encourage spending. Also a budget deficit, which may arise from either lower revenues or increased expenditures, activates federal borrowing. If the Treasury sells its securities to the commercial banks, new money is created and enlarged private expenditures are likely to follow.

4/Expand and liberalize programs of federal insurance and guarantee of private loans, such as FHA and VA residential construction loans.

Finally, debt-management operations of the Treasury may be directed toward expansion, as follows:

1/Borrow the budget deficit from Federal Reserve and commercial banks rather than from nonbank investors. This is a money-creating process; money holdings are enlarged and private spending is stimulated by increased incomes and a greater willingness to spend.

2/Move part of existing federal debt from nonbank investors to Federal Reserve and commercial banks. This also is a money-creating process which spurs private spending.

3/Decrease the average level of Treasury cash and deposits at the Federal Reserve Banks. The general effect of this operation is to activate spending by increasing the amount of bank reserves and the stock of money.

The foregoing summary, it should be noted, is nothing more than a systematic listing of control methods that may be employed to moderate cyclical fluctuations; it is not in itself an integrated program. Such a program should utilize a combination of techniques that promises to realize the most effective and equitable results under existing conditions. In a border skirmish, a company of soldiers armed with rifles and grenades may be sufficient to quell the disturbance; so, in the early phase of business decline, a lower discount rate and a moderate easing of bank reserves may be sufficient unto the day. But in all-out war, the most powerful weapons of the armed forces must be brought to bear. Similarly, in an all-out fight against depression or inflation, the big guns of fiscal policy must be aimed and fired. To carry the analogy further, war against a strong enemy cannot be won without close coordination between the army, navy and airforce. Similarly, the conquest of stability cannot be successful without an overall plan of action that calls for effective coordination between Congress, the Treasury (Administration), and the Fed—which brings us to the important problem of political organization.

ORGANIZATION FOR EFFECTIVE COORDINATION

The observation is often made that organization structure is a relatively unimportant consideration; that able and courageous men will transcend a poor organization; and that incapable people will fail despite perfect organization. This is only a half-truth because notable achievement is most likely to be a joint product of ability and good organization. Thus the present organization for monetary, fiscal, and debt management requires critical scrutiny.

organizational defects

One of the tragedies of our time is the lack of proper organization for exercise of monetary and fiscal powers by Congress, the Treasury, and the Fed. Each body possesses vast monetary powers and responsibilities that are closely interwoven; yet there is no official system of coordination. Without such a system, effective coordination is out of the question in view of diverse interests. The most that can be expected is sporadic and passive cooperation in periods when broad-minded officials and legislators make great efforts to this end. Part of the time, unfortunately, opposing policies must be anticipated—that is, negation of the actions of one body by operations of another. The tragedy arises from the fact that we have within our grasp techniques of control that, if intelligently coordinated, are capable of providing a degree of stability hitherto unknown. Yet we permit these organizational obstacles to block an integrated, effective program.

What, in fact, should be done to overcome organizational defects, so that they will facilitate, rather than obstruct, coordination? The most exhaustive recent study of the problem is that of the Commission on Money and Credit. Their main conclusions may be summarized, as follows:[1]

1/Congress is not equipped to coordinate monetary-fiscal policy directly, so that some delegation of authority in the interest of cyclical control is a prime requisite. This follows from the fact that a leading characteristic of Congress is dispersion of power, between the House and the Senate, and among committees and individual members. Moreover, the task is a highly specialized one which requires continuous technical research. Pressed by a broad range of problems, members of Congress have neither time nor technical knowledge to administer a program of monetary-fiscal management.

2/The organizational focus of coordination should be lodged in the executive branch and center on the President, with Congress ultimately responsible for legislative guidance.

3/Congress should delegate limited power to the President to raise and

[1]Report of the Commission on Money and Credit, *Money and Credit, Their Influence on Jobs, Prices, and Growth.* © 1961, by permission of Prentice-Hall, Inc., Englewood Cliffs, N.J.

lower certain federal tax rates in order to promote economic stability. The personal income tax is selected as best adapted to this purpose. Cyclical changes in the first bracket rate are preferred over proportional adjustments throughout the rate structure, and over variations in personal exemptions. More specifically, it is suggested that the President be empowered to raise or lower the rate on the first $2,000 of taxable income by up to 5 percentage points, to become effective 60 days after announcement unless vetoed within that period by a concurrent resolution of Congress. According to the Commission's estimate, full use of this power would, in 1960, have added or taken away about $5 billion of disposable personal income.[2]

4/Congress should provide for discretionary variation of federal public-works expenditures by the Executive Branch insofar as cyclical flexibility can reasonably be introduced into such programs. To this end, it is suggested that Congress approve a capital budget for a number of years in advance, and that the President be given a measure of flexibility in timing particular projects. It is also suggested that incentives be given state and local governments, mainly by short-run grants and loans, to vary their expenditures countercyclically.[3]

5/Somewhat closer ties of the Fed to the President are recommended in order to promote coordination. In particular, it is suggested that the President designate the chairman and vice-chairman from among the membership of the Board of Governors, to serve four-year terms corresponding with that of the Presidency; also that the terms of office of members be arranged to enable the President to appoint one new member shortly after his inauguration. In addition, the prestige of the Board as a whole and of individual members should be raised by centering Federal Reserve powers more fully in the Board, by reducing membership from seven to five, by raising qualifications of competence, and by raising compensation to the highest salary available for appointive offices. Thus, while a measure of independence of the Board from the Treasury and from the President is preserved, the balance of monetary power and policy is shifted in the direction of the President.[4]

6/Having recommended a material increase in the power of the President to take countercyclical measures, the Commission makes further suggestions designed to assure prompt and decisive action on his part. They conclude that the most feasible approach is to strengthen procedures established by the Employment Act of 1946 which is already a milestone on the road to coordination of economic policies.

7/More specifically, the Commission suggests that the Employment Act be amended, as follows:

(a) " . . . to formulate the goals of a low level of unemployment, an adequate rate of economic growth, and reasonable price stability as applicable to

[2]Ibid., pp. 133-137.
[3]Ibid., pp. 138-141.
[4]Ibid., pp. 82-90.

all Federal agencies administering economic programs" (identical provisions should be incorporated in the Federal Reserve Act);[5] and

(b) to provide that whenever the current economic situation shows a tendency counter to the foregoing goals, the President shall supplement his annual *Economic Report* with an analytical report on the unfavorable tendencies, on steps being taken by him, including the Fed, to remedy the situation, and on any congressional action that he deems advisable; further, that such supplementary reports be made quarterly thereafter as long as the unfavorable situation prevails.[6]

8. A final recommendation of the Commission is that the President strengthen his organization for coordination by appointment of an *advisory board* to assist in coordinating economic policies and actions along the lines set forth in amendments to the Employment Act. This board should be broadly based, with high-level representatives from the Treasury Department, the Federal Reserve Board, the Council of Economic Advisers (CEA), the Bureau of the Budget, and from other departments or agencies vitally concerned. A favored possibility is that the CEA Chairman serve as a chairman of the board, and with assistance from his staff, call weekly meetings, set up agenda, and report conclusions. A prime requisite for success of such a board is that the President frequently attend meetings and that the agenda include consideration of significant matters pertaining to economic stabilization and growth.[7]

Recognizing the great need for coordination of cyclical controls, a number of alternative suggestions have been made in recent years. One is that a new super monetary-fiscal commission be created, charged with the responsibility of adopting and implementing policies that foster stabilization of production, high-level employment, growth, and a steady price level. The commission would be granted limited discretion to vary federal tax rates and expenditures, and to coordinate fiscal, monetary, and debt management, and other related programs such as the amounts and terms of federal grants and loans. While such a commission would necessarily be influenced by the political administration in power, safeguards would be set up to protect it from current pressures of private and public self-interest groups. In keeping with the great responsibilities, the commission should embody, individually and collectively, abilities and experience of the highest order. Conditions of membership should be such as to attract men of this caliber. Like the Federal Reserve Board, the new commission should be responsible to Congress, rather than to the President. Another suggestion has been that, instead of setting up a new supercommission, the Board of Governors be granted the necessary discretionary powers to coordinate cyclical controls, and that attractiveness of membership be enhanced in keeping with the greater responsibilities. Philosophically, this suggestion is very similar to the preceding one. The chief difference is an attempt to adapt

[5] Ibid., pp. 263-264.
[6] Ibid., p. 273.
[7] Ibid., pp. 274-277.

existing institutions, rather than to create still another board or commission.

Those who prefer a monetary-fiscal commission along the foregoing lines, or reconstitution of the Board of Governors as the coordinating agency, do not look with favor on granting larger discretionary authority to the President over fiscal and monetary policies. They feel that current pressures from private and political self-interest groups would be more likely to influence decisions and that Treasury influence would be overweighted at the expense of wise monetary policy. Also, as a practical matter, they believe that a new organization for coordination has a greater chance of realization because Congress would be more reluctant to delegate discretionary powers over the federal budget to the President than to a commission responsible to Congress. Another difference between the suggestions of this group and those of the Commission on Money and Credit relates to breadth of the coordinated program. One of the reasons for the Commission's choice of the Presidency as the focus for coordination is the wide-ranging power in his hands to adapt all relevant federal policies and operations to the stated national goals.

MONETARY, FISCAL, AND DEBT MANAGEMENT: SUMMARY AND COMPARISONS

In this and the preceding six chapters, attention has been focused individually on the various methods of monetary, fiscal, and debt management. It remains to take an overall view of these methods by way of summary and comparison. We shall first examine them under the assumption of model conditions of control, and subsequently under conditions that presently exist.

assume model conditions

Model conditions of control are defined as a setting in which regulatory authorities are in position to realize basic objectives as nearly as can reasonably be expected. More specifically, it is assumed that the authorities have well-defined goals, that they are intelligent experts with the courage to adopt and activate proper policies, that they have been granted adequate powers, that regulatory organization is designed to foster a well-coordinated program, and that operations are not hampered by pressures from private or political self-interest groups. Each method will be appraised from the standpoints of (1) inherent power, (2) flexibility, and (3) incidence of effects.

Inherent Power / By far the most potent method of control, at least in the short run, is that of changes in the federal budget. There are two principal ways in which the various methods of control influence national income: (a) by directly affecting disposable incomes of individuals and businesses, and (b) by changing the amount of money and the degree of liquidity in the entire asset structure. The second way affects disposable incomes *indirectly,* and sometimes with considerable delay, by influencing the amount of spending. Changes in the state of the budget operate powerfully through *direct* effects on disposable incomes, but they also have potent indirect effects. In contrast Federal Reserve and Treasury techniques have little direct effect on disposable incomes; their influence is mainly brought to bear indirectly through changes in the amount of money, the degree of liquidity, and the disposition to spend (or to hold) money.

To be more specific, an increase of federal expenditures on public works immediately finds its way into personal and business incomes; the same is true of direct payments to the unemployed and needy. On the other side, a cut in taxes leaves more spendable income in the hands of the beneficiaries of tax relief. At the same time, the amount of money is increased if the deficit is borrowed at the banks, and asset liquidity is further enhanced by issuance of Treasury securities. The opposite effects may be brought to bear on an inflationary expansion by curtailment of federal expenditures and by an increase of taxes. Massive power is available for either stimulation or restraint of the economy.

Federal Reserve and Treasury techniques operate mainly through easing or tightening the reserve position (liquidity) of commercial banks and by affecting the amount of money. For example, purchase of U.S. securities from nonbank investors by the Reserve Banks builds up excess legal reserves of member banks and creates an equivalent amount of deposit money in the process. The banks are then in position to expand earning assets and deposits by a multiple of their excess reserves. If the demand for loans does not rise despite lower rates, the banks typically add to investments as long as attractive securities are available, and thereby create new deposits. But it will be noted that disposable incomes are not directly increased. The new deposits arising from additional loans are likely to generate income almost immediately as they are spent. But this result is by no means certain with respect to the new deposits arising from bank investments. The nonbank investor from whom they were purchased finds himself with deposits which he is likely to reinvest, and the same applies to succeeding sellers in the chain of security transactions. At some point–and perhaps with considerable delay–the securities purchased may be a new issue to finance business or personal expenditures that generate incomes.

Changes in the federal budget apply with about equal force to the control of booms and slumps, but this is not the case with Federal Reserve and Treasury techniques. Their operations are capable of restraining an inflationary expansion, unless budget policies negate their effects, by raising the cost and reducing the supply of loan money. But Federal Reserve and Treasury operations are far less effective in combating a major depression, particularly after the downward spiral has gained momentum. They can create a favorable financial environment for recovery by making loanable funds abundant at low rates, by increasing the amount of money, by stimulating prices of bonds and other fixed-income assets, and by encouraging spending instead of saving. But because these conditions for the most part do not affect disposable incomes directly, the stimuli may not be sufficient to overcome mounting pessimism, and may therefore not produce an actual increase in spending. Under these circumstances, the forces of recovery need an additional boost from a budget deficit.

While there is no doubt about the combined powers of fiscal, monetary, and debt management to contain booms and slumps within a moderate range of fluctuation in peacetime, the authorities should always weigh short-term against long-term considerations. A quick recovery from recession might be achieved by a huge federal deficit combined with inflationary steps by the Fed and the Treasury. But the aftermath of such overvigorous action would be the maladjustments and inequities during a subsequent inflationary expansion. The application of controls should seek a nice balance between speed of recovery and future equilibrium.

Flexibility / Because timeliness of action is half the battle, methods of control should also be appraised from the standpoint of flexibility. A powerful method is inappropriate unless it can be applied with reasonable flexibility. In order of flexibility the various techniques may be arrayed as follows:

1/Open-market operations. (Fed)

2/Administration of Treasury cash balances. (Treasury and Fed)

3/Discount rate and administration of discounts and advances. (Fed)

4/Debt management—new borrowing, refunding, and redemptions. (Treasury)

5/Changes in legal-reserve requirements. (Fed)

6/Changes in federal budget.

Because these techniques have previously been discussed in detail, only summary comments are needed at this point. Open-market operations are by far the most flexible instrument. In a matter of hours, the reserve position of commercial banks can be altered objectively by purchase or sale of U.S. securities. Shifts of Treasury cash balances between commercial and Federal Reserve Banks can be made on any business day to or from the large Class C depositary banks.

Change in the Federal Reserve Bank discount rate comes up for consideration at two-week intervals, and can be made more frequently. However, the average interval has actually been several months. A new program of rationing Reserve credit to member banks requires several weeks of preparation before it can become effective. Similarly, the techniques of federal debt management as applied to borrowing, refunding, and redemptions require weeks or months.

Legal-reserve requirements of member banks could, if necessary, be changed often and by small amounts. But institutional limitations have led the Board to use this method infrequently to produce sizable alterations in reserve position.

Changes in the federal budget are the least flexible of the various methods, even under model conditions of control. There are, however, considerable differences in flexibility among the programs that affect the budget. A change in the amount of direct payments to the unemployed and needy can be made within a few weeks. But activation of a public-works program requires six months or more. Changes in tax rates can be made effective in a shorter period than alterations in expenditures on public works, but administrative difficulties preclude frequent use of tax-rate changes and also prevent their immediate application.

No one of the instruments of control under model conditions—unless it be heavy public works—is so inflexible that it cannot be utilized in an overall program of control. In such a program, the more flexible devices may be employed first. If they prove inadequate to the task, budgetary changes may be brought to bear.

Incidence of Effects / Federal Reserve controls are sometimes criticized because their effects are concentrated heavily on certain sectors of the economy, especially residential and other construction, state and local capital improvements, small business, and high-grade bond prices. These sectors are most sensitive to the cost and the availability of bank credit, which are the main channels through which these controls influence economic activity. At the same time, other areas of the economy, notably consumer expenditures, may scarcely be affected. This uneven distribution of the burden constitutes a practical limitation on the extent to which Federal Reserve controls can wisely be applied. While this criticism is a valid one, it is often exaggerated because these sectors of the economy are especially sensitive to changes in conditions, whatever the origin. They would doubtless feel a heavier impact than the rest of the economy from restraint or stimulation by any method of control. The concentration of influence of Federal Reserve controls is also overdrawn by failure to recognize the pervasive effects of changes in the amount of money. For example, when a policy of restraint is being applied, there are various ways in which the amount of money is held to a lower level than it would be in the absence of controls. Commercial-bank loans are restricted or reduced; commercial-bank investments are reduced; Reserve Bank open-market sales to nonbank investors directly reduce demand deposits as well as primary reserves; and higher interest rates induce savings at the expense of consumption expenditures.

A canvass of debt-management techniques leads to the conclusion that there is little difference in the incidence of effects of Treasury and Federal Reserve monetary operations. When the Treasury borrows from or repays commercial banks, and when it shifts security ownership between commercial bank and nonbank investors, the principal effects are to change the amount of money without affecting total member-bank reserve balances. But shifts in Treasury balances between commercial and Reserve Banks, borrowing from or repayment to Reserve Banks, and shifts of security ownership to and from Reserve Banks all affect the amount of member-bank reserves and the stock of money. Thus, within a considerable range of monetary action, incidence of effects are the same for the Treasury and the Fed.

Fiscal controls have the potential advantage of the broadest distribution of effects; that is, they are least subject to the criticism that by nature their influence is unduly concentrated. If desired, a program of direct payments can be designed to increase disposable incomes of all consumers and businesses. Public-works expenditures have a more spotty effect, which is one of their serious limitations; however, their secondary, or multiple, effects spread rather widely throughout the economy. Also if desired, income-and excise-tax changes may contribute to, or reduce, incomes of all spending units subject to taxation. In addition to these direct effects on disposable incomes, budget changes exert broad monetary effects. A deficit borrowed from the banks creates new money and a surplus used to redeem bank-held debt extinguishes money if supported by a monetary policy of restraint. Moreover, the disposition to spend or to save may be significantly influenced. Any one of these federal budget programs can be designed to concentrate heavily on certain sectors, much more so, in fact, than Federal Reserve operations. In the final analysis, however, the potentiality of broad distribution of effects is a distinctive feature of fiscal controls.

Thus, under model conditions of control, the authorities should first employ the most flexible techniques in a timely manner. This suggests an appropriate combination of the general controls of the Fed supported by the debt-management methods of the Treasury. Budget policies should then be adapted to the control objective as soon as possible, especially if the state of the budget is in conflict with current aims. In the early stage, the budget should ordinarily exert a relatively neutral influence. But if Federal Reserve and Treasury controls prove to be inadequate, the proper budgetary weapons should be utilized. This follows from the facts that they are more powerful, at least in the short run, and that a broader and more even distribution of effects may be realized. A tight federal fiscal policy should be enforced when price inflation threatens in order to avoid the necessity for, and the disturbing effects of, an excessively restrictive monetary policy. In opposite circumstances, an expansionary fiscal policy should be employed in recessions to preclude the need for, and the unwanted repercussions of, an excessively easy monetary policy.

control under existing conditions

It remains to summarize the status of monetary, fiscal, and debt management under existing conditions. Obviously, responsible public officials must face up to the regulatory environment as it is, not as it should be under model conditions. Pending reforms, the overall program must utilize the various control techniques with full recognition of all practical obstacles. The most important limitation is the lack of organization to foster, or even permit, effective coordination of the separate powers of the Fed, the Congress, and the Treasury. Another serious limitation is the fact that fiscal policy is undependable and inflexible. Congress cannot be expected to manage the budget directly according to requirements of cyclical control. Seldom can the timing or extent of change be harmonious with a well-coordinated stabilization program. Occasionally, especially when price inflation threatens, it is realistic to expect an adverse fiscal influence, i.e., a deficit in the budget which stimulates the economy. Still another limitation until recently has been the failure of the Treasury to take a broad-gauge view of its debt-management responsibilities. Instead of using its powers in neutral fashion or to promote stability, it has frequently been most concerned about borrowing cheaply and about developing an orderly distribution of debt maturities. Since 1961, however, the Treasury has demonstrated much greater awareness of its responsibility to foster stability and growth.

As long as these limitations remain, it is an illusion to expect too much from the Employment Act of 1946. It is probable that the principal burden of regulation will be borne by the Fed, instead of a well-rounded program of control. With inadequate powers to achieve stability, the degree of its success must depend on the nature and extent of help from Congress, the Administration, and the Treasury. Lacking material assistance, or even confronted with counteractions, the Fed is placed in an untenable position. It is popularly held responsible for maintenance of stability, and it is likely to respond with more vigorous changes in the availability and cost of credit than would be necessary or proper in a well-balanced program.

Control of Recessions / The position of the Fed is more comfortable but not so effective under conditions of recession. Ineffectiveness arises from the passive response of businesses and individuals to abundant credit at low rates. The comfortable environment exists because all groups hope for recovery and favor an easy-money policy. In addition, a sizable federal deficit is almost certain to develop automatically, and Congress is likely to lend support in time by larger expenditures, lower tax rates, or both. For reasons previously stated, Treasury cooperation cannot be counted on; in fact, debt-management operations may inhibit recovery, as witness the sale of long-term bonds during the first quarter of 1958, when recession was gaining momentum, and reliance on short-term borrowing during the inflationary expansion of 1966-1969.

With these facts in mind, and assuming no improvement in organization for control, what are the prospects for moderation of cyclical declines and for avoidance of price inflations? There are valid reasons to believe that in the future we may avoid a decline of the magnitude of 1929-1933, when GNP declined 46 percent; industrial production, 52 percent; factory employment, 45 percent; and wholesale commodity prices, 37 percent. The most important reason for this expectation is the formal acceptance of responsibility by the federal government to maintain relatively full employment in the Employment Act of 1946. In contrast with the situation prior to the 1930s, both major political parties are committed to the use of budgetary and other powers to moderate cyclical declines. A second reason is the existence of the social security program which provides direct payments to retired, needy, and unemployed persons during a slump. Third, Federal Reserve powers to meet financial emergencies have been materially extended. Fourth, operation of the Federal Deposit Insurance Corporation removes the likelihood of loss of confidence in the banking system. Fifth, federal guarantee or insurance of a large part of real-estate loans removes much of the depressing influence of defaults in this area. Sixth, the farm subsidy program, though economically unjustified, does give support to a segment that is, by nature, extremely vulnerable to cyclical decline. Finally, the proportion of total expenditures represented by stable components of GNP—notably services, nondurables, and government expenditures—has appreciably increased since the 1920s.

In view of the foregoing institutional changes, it is unrealistic to expect at worst a cyclical decline in GNP in excess of 15 percent, and of industrial production in excess of 25 percent from peak to valley. Such a decline would be nearly twice as severe as the recessions that have occurred since World War II, but only half as serious as the 1929-1933 experience.

Control of Price Inflation / Control of price inflation becomes a major problem in peacetime at the height of a business expansion, and an even more stubborn problem in the event of major war. These two cases require separate consideration.

Even in peacetime, there is a net inflationary bias in the economy that is unlikely to be entirely curbed under present regulatory arrangements. The upward bias is the consequence of various factors that lead to the creation of money and other highly liquid assets at a more rapid rate than the growth of real output. Under these conditions, effective monetary demand exceeds production, and prices are bid upward by buyers. Most of the inflationary factors involve large federal government outlays which are unlikely to be balanced by increases in tax revenues. Spending programs are, by nature, far more popular politically than compensating tax programs. The resulting budget deficits are inflationary, particularly when they are met with new money borrowed from commercial banks or the Fed. The program most responsible for heavy federal outlays are (1) health and welfare, (2) farm subsidies, (3) veterans administration, (4) road building and other public works, and (5) defense expenditures.

An important reason for expecting excessive creation of money and other liquid assets arises from overuse of monetary, fiscal, and debt-management instruments during the preceding period of recession. In view of the cumulative pessimism that develops during a slump, the disposition of businesses and consumers to spend undergoes a marked decline. The demand for money and liquid assets to hold rises and the velocity of money declines. These circumstances greatly magnify the problem of producing recovery by governmental measures. Moreover, the magnitude of a requisite program mounts rapidly as pessimism cumulatively gains momentum. All this means large federal deficits and excess bank reserves, which in turn create excessive amounts of money and liquid assets. The money remains in existence, and indeed is likely to be increased by bank-loan expansion as recovery progresses. The next villain is the rise in velocity of money which returns to normal and then rises well above normal during the last stage of prosperity. The combined effect of the excessive increment of new money circulating at above-normal velocity raises effective demand above the supply of goods at existing prices with the result that prices move upward. Monetary authorities then face the problem of containing an inflationary overexpansion.

While the dominant cause of inflationary bias arises from excessive effective demand (demand-pull inflation), inflation also develops at times from the cost side (cost-push inflation). For example, the strong bargaining position of union labor may result in wage rate increases that exceed the rise in productivity per man-hour. Faced with narrowed profit margins, businesses may then mark up selling prices. Moreover, because interbusiness sales represent costs to others, the original price increases actuate a train of others. Higher prices of consumer goods subsequently provide the basis for another round of wage-price increases, with the process of mutual interactions repeating itself in a sort of spiral. Cost-push inflation of this nature can occur, however, only when supported by rising effective demand for goods and services—that is, in the optimistic environment of a business boom. If the demand to purchase the economy's output at higher prices is insufficient, unsold inventories will rise, business profits will decline, and a recession will be generated. Prices will then stop rising or recede, and wage rates will cease to rise or will decline.

Whether cost-push inflation can stick depends in large measure on monetary policies. If the rise in prices leads to restrictive monetary, fiscal, and debt-management actions that prevent expansion of the stock of money, effective demand will not support a cost-push inflation for long. For a time, the process may be sustained by a continued rise in the velocity of money. But experience demonstrates that velocity has a cyclical limit which provides a real barrier to expansion of expenditures. However, if the monetary and fiscal authorities—fearing unemployment more than higher prices—permit monetary expansion, they may validate the cost-push inflation and the higher price level can be maintained. Because such validation is probable at times, inflation initiated from the cost side is a stubborn reality that tends to erode the value of the dollar.

A powerful check on the rise of prices during the recovery stage is the increase of production and unit productivity as unemployed labor and other idle resources are utilized. But when full employment is reached, the power of this restraining force is largely spent. Further increases of production must then come from real secular growth alone—not more than 3 or 4 percent per annum. It is at this point that the greatest threat of a cyclical rise of prices begins. Overoptimism may lead spending to increase at a more rapid rate than production with a consequent rise in the price level.

Because most of the burden of control falls on the Fed, and because its problems may be intensified by Congress and the Treasury, the outlook for a stable price level is not favorable. While the Fed possesses powerful instruments, it is unlikely to apply them vigorously enough to halt the inflationary process until it has made headway. In the first place, there is usually a time lag before restrictive measures are applied. The monetary authorities never wish to disturb the happy condition of full employment until evidence of an unhealthy boom is convincing. This necessarily requires time because the various bits of evidence are usually conflicting in the early stages, and because a majority of the Board and the Open-Market Committee must see eye-to-eye on a change in policy. Second, to the extent that higher prices appear to be a consequence of cost-push inflation, the authorities are faced with a dilemma. How much unemployment are they willing to face, if necessary, to prevent higher prices that stem largely from a union-induced hike in wage rates? Third, the vigor with which Federal Reserve instruments are used is limited by the uneven incidence of their effects. High interest rates and restrictions on credit availability impinge most heavily on the construction industry, small-business interests, durable consumer-goods industries, investment bankers, and state and local financing. The extent to which these sensitive sectors should be impaired for overall welfare raises real questions to which answers are not clear. Finally, a policy of active restraint by the Fed gives rise to strong private and political pressures for relief from those who are adversely affected. A barrage of criticism tends to undermine Federal Reserve prestige, and may even threaten its existence. Extraordinary courage is required under these circumstances to stand fast on principles and policies. While the Board has on occasion demonstrated remarkable courage, notably during 1956-1957 and in 1969, there is no doubt that these potent pressures limit the effectiveness of a program of restraint.

There is, of course, no absolute answer to the extent of net inflationary bias in the economy. One can only arrive at a rough judgment by appraising the strength of opposing forces. In a peacetime era, inflationary forces appear to prevail moderately, with the probability that the long upward trend of the general price level will be somewhere between 2 and 4 percent per annum. The crucial factor bearing on the rate of increase will doubtless be the size of defense expenditures.

If estimation of net inflationary bias in the economy is difficult in peacetime, it becomes a matter of pure conjecture in the event of war. History records that there is no instance of a major war, involving this or any other nation, in which prices did not rise precipitately. They approximately doubled in the United States during and following both World War I and World War II. Inflation was far more severe in most other countries, and in some the value of monetary units nearly vanished. Illustrations abound of all gradations of war inflation. The basic cause was that war expenditures of central governments were financed in more or less degree by creating new money, instead of by taxation and borrowed savings. Swiftly rising outlays of governments, businesses, and consumers collided with limited or reduced supplies of goods and services.

In this new age of hydrogen bombs, missiles, and other weapons of mass destruction, it may appear idle to raise questions concerning such a relatively insignificant problem as war inflation. This is, of course, true if we assume a case of total war, and if total war means total destruction. But the possibilities also include all gradations of limited war and partial destruction—in which event, war inflation becomes a problem of great practical moment.

What then are the main factors that determine the probable extent of price inflation in the event of war? They may be summarized as follows:

1/The dimensions of the war as measured by the amount of federal expenditures and the proportion of such expenditures to GNP. The total amount of expenditures is of course a product of the rate of spending and the duration of the war.

2/The extent to which production is crippled by physical destruction, disorganization, restrictions, trade barriers, and other war-created impediments.

3/War finance policies. The greater the reliance on money-creating methods of war finance, the greater the inflationary stimulus. Conversely, the larger the proportion of government expenditures met by tax revenues and borrowed savings, the less the inflationary stimulus. It should be noted, however, that prices may rise moderately even though the war is financed without additions to the amount of money. This may occur as a consequence of more rapid spending of existing money and/or a reduction in normal physical production and trade.

4/The character and extent of government regulation. Inflationary pressures may be materially lessened by a broad and effectively administered program of price-fixing, wage control, rationing, and material allocations. If prices and wage rates are held in check, the amount of war expenditures and the Treasury deficit will be reduced. However, if money-creating methods of finance are employed, price ceilings and rationing can only suppress the effects. When controls are removed in the postwar period, prices will rise in a free market if effective demand exceeds supply at existing prices. That is what happened after World War II.

REFERENCES

books

Abbott, Charles C., *The Federal Debt: Structure and Impact* (New York: Century Fund, 1953).

Commission on Money and Credit, *Money and Credit, Their Influence on Jobs, Prices, and Growth* (Englewood Cliffs, N.J.: Prentice-Hall, 1961).

Commission on Money and Credit, *The Federal Reserve and the Treasury* (Englewood Cliffs, N.J.: Prentice-Hall, 1963).

Gaines, Tilford C., *Techniques of Federal Debt Management* (New York: Free Press, 1962).

Lewis, Wilfred, Jr., *Federal Fiscal Policy in Postwar Recessions* (Washington, D.C.: Brookings Institution, 1963).

Maxwell, James A., *Fiscal Policy, Its Technique and Institutional Setting* (Rev. ed.; New York: Holt, Rinehart & Winston, 1955).

Mayer, Thomas, *Monetary Policy in the United States* (New York: Random House, 1968).

Murphy, Henry C., *National Debt in War and Transition* (New York: McGraw-Hill, 1950).

Musgrave, Richard A., *The Theory of Public Finance* (New York: McGraw-Hill, 1959), chaps. 17-24.

Stein, Herbert, *The Fiscal Revolution in America* (Chicago: University of Chicago Press, 1969).

Taylor, Philip E., *The Economics of Public Finance* (3d ed.; New York: Macmillan, 1961), chaps. 4-9.

articles and other materials

Anderson, Leonall C., and Keith M. Carlson, "A Monetarist Model for Economic Stabilization," Federal Reserve Bank of St. Louis, *Review* (April 1970), pp. 7-25.

Anderson, Leonall C., and Jerry L. Jordan, "Monetary and Fiscal Actions: A Test of Their Relative Importance in Economic Stabilization," Federal Reserve Bank of St. Louis, *Review* (November 1968), pp. 11-24.

Cohen, Jacob, "A Theoretical Framework for Treasury Debt Management," *American Economic Review,* XLV, no. 3 (June 1955), pp. 320-344.

Eisner, R., "Fiscal and Monetary Policy Reconsidered," *American Economic Review,* 59 (December 1969), pp. 897-905.

Fand, David I., "A Monetarist Model of the Monetary Process," *The Journal of Finance,* XXV (May 1970), pp. 275-289.

Foley, D. K., et al., "Optimal Fiscal and Monetary Policy and Economic Growth," *Journal of Political Economy,* 77, part 2 (July 1969), pp. 698-719.

Jones, R. W., "Monetary and Fiscal Policies for an Economy with Fixed Exchange Rates," *Journal of Political Economy,* 76, part 2 (July 1968), pp. 921-952.

Niehans, J., "Monetary and Fiscal Policies in Open Economies Under Fixed Exchange Rates," *Journal of Political Economy,* 76, part 2 (July 1968), pp. 893-920.

Rolph, Earl R., "Principles of Debt Management," *American Economic Review,* XLVII, no. 3 (June 1957), pp. 302-320.

Smith, Warren L., *Debt Management in the United States,* Study Paper No. 19, Study of Employment Growth, and Price Levels, Joint Economic Committee of Congress (Washington, D.C., 1960).

Tokayama, A., "Effects of Fiscal and Monetary Policies Under Flexible and Fixed Exchange Rates," *Canadian Journal of Economics,* 2, (May 1969), pp. 190-209.

U.S. Congress, Hearings before the Subcommittee on Monetary, Credit and Fiscal Policies of the Joint Committee on the Economic Report, 81st Congress, 1st sess. (Washington, D.C., 1950).

U.S. Congress, Subcommittee on General Credit Control and Debt Management, Joint Committee on the Economic Report, 82nd Congress, 2d sess. (Washington, D.C., 1952).

U.S. Congress, Hearings Before the Committee on Finance, U.S. Senate, 85th Congress, 1st sess. (Washington, D.C., 1957).

20

monetary, fiscal, and debt management, 1914 to 1941

It is no exaggeration to say that passage of the Federal Reserve Act at the end of 1913 marked a new epoch in the financial history of the United States. This is so chiefly because provision was made in the new Fed for management of the nation's money by a government agency. It will be recalled that the lack of this feature in the old national banking system was its most serious weakness. Inelasticity of money and the absence of an agency responsible for control of money, bank credit, and the money market were the main reasons for the periodic financial crises which had plagued the nation since the 1830s.

In the six decades that have followed establishment of the Fed–including World War I, the prosperous 1920s, the depressing 1930s, World War II, and the prosperous postwar era–the objectives and methods of monetary management have gradually evolved. The Reserve authorities, to be sure, could draw on the long credit-control experience of the Bank of England and of other European central banks. But this proved of limited value because of the wide differences between the United States and foreign countries in central and commercial-banking organization and in the structure of money markets. In large measure, therefore, the Reserve authorities had to develop their own aims and techniques within the framework of the Federal Reserve Act as amended from time to time.

A summary of the evolution of monetary and fiscal management in the United States will contribute materially to the understanding of current problems. Exposition will be facilitated by dividing the period as follows: (1) 1914 to 1920–the formative years, including World War I, before the Fed could actively engage in monetary management; (2) first quarter 1920 to 1929–the postwar depression and the prosperous 1920s; (3) 1929 to 1941–the Great Depression; (4) 1942 to 1945–World War II; (5) 1946 to 1951–the early postwar years when the Fed remained in bondage; and (6) 1951 to 1970—when the Fed played a positive role in monetary management.

THE FORMATIVE YEARS, 1914 to 1920

The initial period, 1914 to 1920, may well be designated the *formative years* because the dominant problems were those of organization to perform central-banking functions, and experimentation with various methods of controlling credit conditions. There was, in fact, little opportunity for the Fed to assume an active role in monetary regulation in view of the necessity of cooperating fully with the Treasury in financing World War I.

from 1914 to April 1917

The Reserve Banks opened their doors in November 1914, after the outbreak of the European war in August. Thus, while the United States did not declare war on Germany until April 1917, the Fed was born and organized in the midst of the abnormal economic repercussions of war. Serious financial disturbances immediately arose from mass selling of foreign-held securities, which led to closure of the New York Stock Exchange, and from cessation of international gold shipments accompanied by gyrations in foreign-exchange rates. Export trade came to a standstill, which precipitated a sharp decline in business activity. But with the opening of sea lanes in 1915, the pressing demands of the Allies for our products ushered in a surge of war-induced prosperity. Bank loans and the money supply expanded rapidly as did also the velocity of money. Active bidding for goods resulted in a rise of about 60 percent in wholesale prices between the first quarter of 1916 and April 1917, when the United States entered the war.

Until active American participation in the war, there was little need for borrowing by member banks at the Reserve Banks, despite the sharp rise of both production and prices. This was mainly a consequence of two factors that contributed to the lending power of member banks. The gold stock nearly doubled between December 1914 and April 1917—rising from \$1.5 billion to \$2.9 billion as foreign countries paid for expanding U.S. exports. Also, legal-reserve requirements of member banks were appreciably reduced under the Fed, thereby releasing excess reserves for support of multiple credit expansion. There was, however, some use of the discount window at all Reserve Banks during 1915 and 1916. Discount rates on eligible paper varied somewhat among the Reserve Banks, usually being lowest in New York. The prevailing practice was to post differential rates, rising along with maturities. The rates set were well below average rates realized by member banks on customer loans, and in the vicinity of, or below, the open-market rate on prime, 4-6-month commercial paper. The Reserve Banks thus departed somewhat from the traditional practice of the Bank of England of posting a penalty rate—doubtless in their desire to encourage member banks to use the new discount mechanism.

Open-market operations were also of small proportions before American entry into the war. United States securities held averaged less than $50 million in 1916 and under $90 million in 1917. Their amount was exceeded both by holdings of bankers' acceptances and municipal warrants. The motive for purchases was principally that of income to cover expenses and dividends because the small amount of bills discounted was inadequate for this purpose, and because there was no need to provide additional reserves for member banks. As a matter of fact, Fed officers had little understanding at this time of the powerful effects of open-market operations on the reserve position of commercial banks, and hence of their potential as a weapon of control. They could not foresee that within a few years these operations were to emerge as the most important single method of monetary management.

April 1917 to first quarter 1920

During World War I and the early postwar years, monetary considerations were dominated by the fiscal policies of Congress and the Administration. The Fed cooperated fully by assisting the Treasury in borrowing funds needed beyond tax revenues at relatively low rates of interest. Despite the Treasury's counsel of conservatism, fiscal policies were highly inflationary. Less than 30 percent of federal expenditures was met by taxation; the rest was borrowed, in part from current savers, but in far greater measure by the creation of additional bank credit. The strategy was to borrow as much as possible from individuals and other nonbank investors, and to sell as few securities as possible directly to commercial banks and the Fed. The Liberty Bond drives made strong patriotic appeals for current savings and also urged people "to borrow to buy" bonds. Commercial banks were enlisted in the sales effort to induce customers to borrow freely for this purpose. Rates charged on loans with Treasury securities as collateral were the same as bond coupon rates, so that people could be patriotic without cost. In turn, the Fed stood ready to lend liberally at low discount rates to commercial banks in need of reserves.

There was, in reality, no substantial reason for this cumbersome method of indirect borrowing at the banks. The expansion of commercial-bank loans to customers creates the same amount of new deposits as direct bank purchases of Treasury securities. Hence, at the outset the indirect method was equally inflationary. Treasury officials believed, however, that postwar price inflation would be less serious if the people, instead of the banks, owned the securities. They visualized bank-credit contraction as loans were repaid from income, and they held that government debt owned by the people would more likely be reduced than if owned by the banks. There is little of substance in either of these contentions. Whether bank credit and the federal debt were to be reduced depended chiefly on the character of monetary and fiscal policies in the postwar years, not on the nature of bank assets and ownership of the debt.

A more tangible understanding of the sweeping financial changes in this period is best conveyed by a statistical summary. Between the end of 1916 and the end of 1919, the federal debt rose from less than \$1 billion to a peak of nearly \$26 billion. Total loans and investments of commercial banks expanded from \$20.4 billion at midyear 1916 to \$36.3 at midyear 1920. The money supply (demand deposits and currency outside banks) climbed from \$12.8 to \$23.7 billion, or by 72 percent. In support of this enormous monetary expansion, Reserve Bank credit rose from an average of only \$163 million in 1916 to \$3.4 billion in 1920.[1] The bulk of this high-powered money flowed out through the discount window because purchases of U.S. securities were relatively small. The inevitable consequence of this outpouring of money and other liquid assets was a sharp rise in commodity prices. Wholesale prices, which had risen nearly 70 percent in the prewar years, moved up 20 percent further during the war and another 23 percent before they reached a peak in May 1920. The overall price increase between 1914 and the peak was about 150 percent.

The question may well be raised: Where were the Federal Reserve authorities during the postwar boom which was marked by seething speculation in commodities and real estate as well as by rising prices? As indicated, they could do nothing during the war beyond warning the banks against making nonessential and speculative loans. Full cooperation in war finance called for a liberal discount policy at low rates which ranged between 3 and $3\frac{1}{2}$ percent during the first half-year of the war, and between 4 and $4\frac{3}{4}$ percent during 1918 as market rates increased. Treasury expenditures during the nine months following the Armistice were as large as those of the preceding nine months, so that a year elapsed before the Fed felt free to take restrictive action. Discount rates were raised moderately in November 1919, and in January-February 1920, they were set uniformly at 6 percent. Then, in early June, the rate was raised to 7 percent in New York and in three other Federal Reserve districts. But despite this and direct pressure on member banks, borrowings at the Reserve Banks continued to rise until the end of 1920, even though member banks were urged to repay indebtedness, and business, employment, and prices declined sharply after midyear. The steps taken followed conventional central-bank policy of raising the discount rate to protect gold reserves. The reserve ratio of the Reserve Banks nearly touched the legal minimum in late 1919 and early 1920 under the combined influence of expanding credit and gold export. There was also the aim of preventing member banks from extending unsound, speculative loans.

If restrictive action was tardy in regard to discounts, it was more adverse in regard to open-market operations. Holdings of bankers' acceptances

[1] Board of Governors of the Federal Reserve System, *Banking and Monetary Statistics* (Washington, D.C., 1943), pp. 34, 368.

and U.S. securities both rose substantially between November 1918 and midyear 1920. Altogether, Reserve Bank credit contributed about $1 billion to member-bank reserves in this period. In passing judgment, however, one should recall that open-market operations were not entirely understood at this time and were still carried on autonomously by the separate Reserve Banks, and that the Reserve Banks were attempting to stimulate the infant acceptance market by setting a favorable (low) buying rate of discount.

The liberal credit policies of the Fed resulted in a moderate decline in interest rates during the first three quarters of 1919. But the restrictive steps beginning in November, combined with other factors reducing bank liquidity—loss of gold, increase of currency in circulation, and growth of loans—led to a sharp upturn in rates that reached a peak at midyear. For example, the yield on open-market commercial paper rose from 5.25 percent in November 1919 to 8.13 percent in July 1920.

Most critics are in agreement that in face of the rapid rise in commodity prices and evidence of speculative excesses, the Reserve authorities should have applied restrictions soon after the first quarter of 1919. This would have moderated the inflationary expansion and the subsequent depression. In any event, the Fed cannot be credited with contributing to price or business stability in this first real opportunity to exercise its powers. In fairness, however, one should not pass judgment too harshly in view of the complicated nature of the problem. Peacetime objectives were not yet well defined; the Fed was inexperienced in the use of its new weapons of control; many able economists expected deflation, rather than inflation, during the reconversion period; its political position was none too secure; it was attempting to bring nonmember banks into the fold; and its hands were tied during most of 1919 by requirements of Treasury finance. In fact, the basic cause of the postwar inflation is to be found on the doorsteps of Congress, the Administration, and the general public. They were unwilling to increase taxes to meet the bulk of war expenditures. Treasury funds were provided in large part by the inflationary method of borrowing at the banks. Thus, responsibility rests largely on fiscal policies instead of on the new Fed.

FIRST QUARTER 1920 TO 1929

This period includes the postwar depression and the prosperous years that followed until the last half of 1929. Minor recessions that require some comment occurred in 1924 and 1927.

postwar depression: first quarter 1920 to 1922

A major postwar depression got underway during the first half of 1920 from which full recovery was not achieved until the end of 1922. Industrial production declined by over 25 percent by January 1921, and remained at this low level until recovery began in the fourth quarter. Manufacturing, employment, and payrolls followed a similar course. Wholesale prices tumbled 44 percent between May 1920 and June 1921; farm-product prices, by 53 percent. Business failures mounted as profits turned to losses. Hardest hit were the concerns with speculative inventories bought at high prices. The agricultural areas suffered even more severely than industry. Farmers had borrowed heavily to buy land at high prices and at high interest rates; many lost their farms when farm-product prices declined more sharply than costs. The amount of money (demand deposits and currency) shrank by 12 percent and the velocity of demand deposits declined about 15 percent between midyear 1920 and midyear 1921.

This was the first major depression encountered by Federal Reserve authorities. How did they conduct themselves? When evidence of an impending depression became clear, alert monetary management would have promptly reduced discount rates and would have contributed to bank liquidity by Reserve Bank purchases of securities. But action in these directions was inexplicably tardy because of concern over the U.S. gold position. It was not until May 1921—after the bottom of the depression had been reached—that Reserve Bank discount rates were lowered from the 6-7 percent range established a year earlier at the peak of prices. They were still at 5 to 6 percent when recovery began in the last quarter of 1921, and, as recovery proceeded, were then lowered by steps to 4 percent by mid-1922. Similarly, open-market operations were used adversely. Instead of being increased, holdings of U.S. securities and acceptances were steadily reduced during the business decline—by over $300 million. It was not until recovery was well underway in the first quarter of 1922 that holdings of U.S. securities were enlarged. In fairness, it should be stated that the liquidity of commercial banks was increased during 1921 by a moderate gold inflow and a decrease of currency in circulation. But the fact remains that the actions of Reserve authorities tended to magnify, rather than to moderate, the depression.

Meanwhile, government fiscal policy similarly tended to accentuate the cyclical decline. In the fiscal year ended midyear 1921, federal receipts exceeded expenditures by over $500 million. Consequently, the conclusion emerges that business recovery in 1921 and 1922 was a result of natural forces, unaided, and even impeded, by monetary and fiscal management.

credit restraint in 1923

Recovery of production and employment proceeded rapidly throughout 1922 and into the spring of 1923, which marked another peak. The Board's index of production rose 60 percent above the 1921 low point. Wholesale prices also rose steadily, but little more (about 13 percent) than would be expected during such a strong recovery. Moderate expansion similarly took place in bank credit and in the money supply. By the turn of 1923, the Reserve authorities became apprehensive lest further credit expansion would generate an inflationary expansion. Certain restraining measures were therefore taken. In February-March, the discount rate was raised from 4 to $4\frac{1}{2}$ percent where it remained at all Reserve Banks the rest of 1923. This was more a gesture of policy than a curb on member-bank borrowing. More important, Reserve Bank holdings of U.S. securities were reduced with little interruption throughout the year—from $421 million in January to $83 million in November. This forced members to borrow more heavily, subjected the money market to mild pressure, and caused firmer money rates.

The foregoing open-market operation was particularly significant because it represented the first coordinated use of this instrument. In previous years, the Reserve Banks entered the open market individually, with earnings their main consideration. But experience demonstrated the fact that purchases tended to increase member-bank reserves dollar for dollar, and that sales had the opposite effect. It was also observed that discounts and advances moved inversely with holdings of U.S. and other securities. These operations, therefore, were recognized as having national and international repercussions instead of merely local effects. Accordingly an informal open-market committee, composed of the heads of the twelve Reserve Banks, took steps to coordinate operations in mid-1922. In the spring of 1923, a new committee—although with the same membership—was appointed to function under supervision of the Federal Reserve Board. The guiding principle was stated by the Board, as follows: "That the time, manner, character, and volume of open-market investments purchased by Federal reserve banks be governed with primary regard to the accommodation of commerce and business and to the effect of such purchases or sales on the general credit situation."[2] These steps established open-market policy on the same basis as discount policy. Henceforth, the two methods were to be used in coordination to achieve desired conditions in the money market.

This period marked the emergence not only of a new *method* of credit control, viz., open-market operations, but also of new criteria for monetary management. The traditional guide of central-bank policy—the ratio of gold reserves to central-bank note and deposit liabilities—was no longer useful. The logic of its use was based on conditions of the prewar international gold standard with its automatic adjustments of price levels, interest rates, and balances of payments among countries. These conditions no longer prevailed because the United States was the only important nation that had returned to this standard. Moreover, an unprecedented shift of gold to the United States had taken place—roughly $1 billion before American entry into the war and another $1 billion after the war. The $4.2 billion gold stock at the end of 1923 was more

[2]Federal Reserve Board, *Annual Report* (Washington, D.C., 1923), p. 16.

than double U.S. holdings in 1914, and constituted about two-fifths of the total monetary gold stock in the world. Also, under these circumstances, the reserve ratio of the Reserve Banks had risen from 39.6 percent (near the legal minimum) at the end of 1919 to 72.5 percent at the end of 1922, and to 75.3 percent at the end of 1923—despite the policy of paying gold out into circulation. Thus, the use of the reserve ratio as a guide would have promoted an enormous inflationary expansion of bank credit. Clearly, new criteria to guide policies were needed.

The new "guides to credit policy," which were explained at some length in the 1923 annual report of the Board,[3] represented an interpretation of the broad principle set forth in the Federal Reserve Act that Federal Reserve credit should be used only for "agricultural, industrial, or commercial purposes," and not for purposes "covering merely investments or . . . carrying or trading in stocks, bonds, or other investment securities. . . ."[4] The following is a summary of these guides.

1/Fed credit should be utilized only for *productive* purposes; not for investment nor speculation.

2/Credit for short-term, nonspeculative operations in agriculture, industry, and trade—that is, credit to finance the movement of goods through any one of the successive stages of production and distribution into consumption—is productive credit.

3/Nonproductive uses of credit are present when the effect is to impede the forward movement of goods from producer to consumer, to accumulate goods for an anticipated rise in price (speculation), or to finance long-term, fixed-capital investment.

4/The amount of bank credit will be in harmony with credit needs when credit is used for productive purposes; the nonproductive use of credit breeds unwarranted increase in its amount, leads to maladjustment between production and consumption, and causes price changes and other economic disturbances.

5/Each Reserve Bank should administer the direction of credit to productive uses among its member banks, and to this end should be familiar with their loan policies.

6/The Federal Reserve Board is concerned not with detailed transactions but with the total volume of commercial-bank and Reserve Bank credit and the overall effects of such credit on the economy.

7/The Board must look for guidance primarily to the whole range of information concerning the state of industry, trade, consumption, prices, and credit. Analysis and interpretation of these data, along with elusive qualitative factors, must form the basis for judgment and discretion in determination of broad credit policies.

[3]Ibid., pp. 29-39.
[4]Federal Reserve Act, Sections 13, 14.

8/While price changes should be considered along with other relevant information, stabilization of the price level should not be set up as the sole guide to credit policies.

The foregoing productive-credit theory enunciated by the Board, it should be emphasized, was an extension to central banking of the then widely accepted commercial-loan theory of commercial banking. These guiding criteria formed the main basis of Fed policies for over a decade.

recessions and easy money in 1924 and 1927

Although moderate business recessions occurred in 1924 and 1927, the period as a whole was characterized by relatively full employment and by normal economic progress. The amount of money (demand deposits and currency), except for an interruption in 1926, increased at approximately the rate of real growth—$3\frac{1}{2}$ percent per annum. Wholesale prices exhibited relative stability, ending the period slightly lower than at the beginning—the net result of a moderate rise in farm product prices and a decline in prices of other commodities. The influx of gold, begun in late 1920, ended by mid-1924. Only moderate changes followed, with the result that the overall increase in the gold stock was some $200 million. A feature of financial developments was the large increase of common-stock prices which more than doubled between mid-1924 and the end of 1927. The accompanying growth of three-fifths in member-bank security loans became a matter of concern to the Reserve authorities.

A recession from the peak of business activity in the second quarter of 1923 followed its downward course until midyear 1924. Production, employment, and prices all experienced declines. Agriculture was particularly hard hit by the greater decline in farm-product prices than in other commodities. Faced with these developments, the Reserve authorities acted promptly and decisively. Holdings of U.S. securities were increased steadily—from $118 million in January to $588 million in November. These purchases, along with the rising gold stock, enabled member banks to repay nearly $500 million of debt to Reserve Banks. The improved liquidity position of commercial banks was reflected by a sizable decline in the commercial-paper rate—from 5 percent at the end of 1923 to 3.13 percent in the autumn of 1924—and by expansion of both bank loans and investments. Lagging downward adjustments of Reserve Bank discount rates were also made between April and August, 1924—from $4\frac{1}{2}$ to 3 percent. Business recovery was rapid after midyear, and relatively full employment was attained by the end of 1924, at least partly in consequence of timely monetary management.

Little comment is required on developments during 1925, 1926, and the first quarter of 1927. Production maintained a high level, prices drifted slowly downward, and interest rates were relatively stable. In general, Reserve authorities followed a policy of neutrality. But during the second quarter of 1927, evidences of recession once more began to appear. Also, international monetary conditions presented a case for easing the money market. England was losing gold to the United States and was having difficulty in maintaining the gold standard to which she had returned in 1925. Lower money rates in New York would tend to direct international funds to London. But the sharp rise in stock prices and the expansion of security loans argued against such a change. Perhaps this was the main reason for delayed Reserve action. In any event, open-market purchases of U.S. securities were undertaken in June 1927 and continued throughout the year—an addition of about $300 million. This action, along with reduction in money in circulation, improved the reserve position of member banks despite a sizable decline in gold stock during the second half of the year. In addition, the Reserve Banks reduced their discount rates from 4 to 3½ percent in July-August. As a consequence of these actions, open-market money rates declined moderately. The business decline, which had not been severe, ended in the last quarter, followed by rapid recovery.

Much adverse criticism has been leveled at the Fed for its 1927 policy on the ground that easy money provided the fuel for the rise in stock prices that culminated in the orgy of speculation in 1929. But in view of the declining tendencies in business and commodity prices, and of England's plight, it is hard to find fault with the moderate steps taken, unless it be that action was too long delayed.

the 1928-1929 boom

The major problem that confronted the Fed during 1928 and 1929 was the continued upsurge of common-stock prices and the enormous expansion of security credit associated with it. Having more than doubled between 1923 and 1927, the industrial common-stock average rose another 60 percent before reaching its peak in September 1929.[5] Security loans of member banks in leading cities rose from just over $4 billion in 1923 to over $6 billion in 1927 and to $7.7 billion in September 1929. The rise of brokers' (stock-exchange) loans was even more spectacular—from $1.6 billion in 1923 to $8.5 billion in September 1929. The rising tide of security speculation was also reflected in the number of shares traded on the New York Stock Exchange, which rose fivefold between 1923 and 1929.

In contrast with security speculation, there was little in the general economic situation to cause concern. It is true that industrial production was above normal and was expanding at a rate that could not be sustained. But there appeared to be no reason for alarm because wholesale prices were at the same time drifting slowly downward. This would lead to the conclusion that physical output was even more than keeping pace with effective demand. Federal Reserve

[5]Standard and Poor's Corporation index.

authorities were therefore confronted with a puzzling dilemma. Should they use measures of restraint in order to dampen speculative excesses, but at the risk of depressing employment and production? Or should they adopt a relatively neutral policy so as not to disturb the full-employment situation, but at the risk of permitting a spread of stock-price inflation to the commodity markets? If the former course were followed, there were also the questions of appropriate methods, and of proper degree of restraint.

For reasons discussed below, a policy of monetary restriction was adopted. Between January 1928 and October 1929, U.S. security holdings of the Reserve Banks were reduced by $450 million. This program soon forced member-bank borrowing up to the $1 billion level for the rest of the period. Also, beginning in January-February 1928, the Fed raised discount rates by successive steps from $3\frac{1}{2}$ percent to 6 percent by August 1929. Buying rates on bankers' acceptances were similarly increased by steps from 3 to $5\frac{3}{4}$ percent by March 1929, so that acceptance holdings were reduced by some $100 million. But a strange compromise in the restraint program occurred in July-August 1929. Faced after midyear with a renewed burst of speculation, rising stock prices, and increasing demand for security loans, the discount rate of the New York Reserve Bank was raised in August from 5 to 6 percent. However, confronted with the autumn increase in currency and loan requirements, the buying rate on acceptances was reduced in July-August by $\frac{1}{4}$ percent to a level well below the discount rate. This opened the acceptance door to Reserve credit, so that acceptance holdings rose about $300 million—more than was needed for seasonal requirements. As a consequence, an easier money market developed. A decline took place in rates on both acceptances and stock-exchange call money. This experience demonstrated that Reserve credit dollars, once released through whatever channel, become unidentifiable in the money market. Having entered member-bank reserves, they then provide support for credit expansion in directions to be determined by market forces.

The stringent Federal Reserve policy enforced during 1928 and the first three quarters of 1929, combined with active credit demand—especially for security loans—led to a sharp increase in interest rates. For example, the commercial-paper rate rose from 4 percent at the beginning of 1928 to $6\frac{1}{4}$ percent in September 1929; and the call-money rate increased from about 4 percent to as high as 15 percent in the spring of 1929.

While the Reserve Banks had used the method of *moral suasion* in some degree in 1920, it was applied so much more vigorously in 1929 as to justify calling it a new technique. Not wishing to raise discount rates and interest rates higher in early 1929, the Board instructed the Reserve Banks to prevent further use of Reserve credit to make speculative loans. This rationing technique was effective in bringing about some reduction in brokers' loans of member banks until the stock-market crisis in September. However, as already noted, it was powerless to halt the rise in brokers' loans by nonbank lenders.

This brings us to further consideration of the guiding criteria of Federal

Reserve policy during 1928 and 1929. Were the authorities applying the productive-credit theory enunciated in 1923, or did they develop a new standard for policy? The record suggests that a new criterion was evolved. While the 1923 pronouncement specifically stated that Reserve credit should not be used to support speculative operations, it was necessary to justify the 1928-1929 actions by further elaboration of the theory of Reserve credit in relation to security prices and speculation. This was done in numerous official statements which require brief discussion. In its 1929 annual report the Board stated:

> The year 1929 opened with total reserve-bank credit outstanding in larger volume than in any year since the post war crisis. Security loans of member banks and brokers' loans had attained new peaks. Collateral indications derived principally from the intense activity of the securities markets and the unprecedented rise of security prices gave unmistakable evidence of an absorption of the country's credit in speculative security operations to an alarming extent. There was nothing in the position of commercial credit or of business to occasion concern. The dangerous element in the credit situation was the continued and rapid growth of the volume of speculative security credit.[6]

In a similar vein the Board wrote to the Federal Reserve Banks in early 1929:

> The extraordinary absorption of funds in speculative security loans . . . deserves particular attention lest it become a decisive factor working toward a still further firming of money rates to the prejudice of the country's commercial interests.[7]

And further:

> Loans to brokers by non-banking lenders, although they do not directly involve member banks, have nevertheless an effect on the banking situation, both because the banks are aware of the necessity of taking over such loans in case an emergency develops and because their existence and employment results in a much more active use of bank deposits.[8]

Thus, it is apparent that the cardinal purpose of Federal Reserve policy in 1928-1929 was control of stock-market credit. The Board was alarmed by the large increase in "security loans of member banks and brokers' loans, . . . the intense activity of the securities markets and the unprecedented rise of security prices. . . ." The stated reasons for concern were: (1) use of Reserve Bank credit to support speculative activity is forbidden by the Federal Reserve Act; and (2) speculative activity absorbs credit and thereby makes it (a) less available and (b) more costly for legitimate industrial, commercial, and agricultural uses. That

[6]Federal Reserve Board, *Annual Report* (Washington, D.C., 1929), pp. 1-2.
[7]Ibid., p. 3.
[8]Ibid., p. 7.

the second reason was largely erroneous has already been discussed. It would have been better simply to say that the excessive expansion of speculative credit involves the danger of promoting a rate of investment and current spending that will lead to an inflationary expansion, followed by a recession.

The policies and actions of Reserve authorities during the 1928-1929 stock-market boom have elicited almost every possible shade of criticism. One group takes the position that the Fed, by its measures of restraint, was largely responsible for the years of deepening depression that followed. They point to the slowly declining level of commodity prices as evidence that effective demand was not excessive, and conclude therefore that Reserve policy should have been neutral, not restrictive. At the other extreme, another group condemns the authorities for failure to take stronger measures at an earlier date. Others feel that the Board acted with intelligence and good judgment with the inadequate weapons at its disposal. Whatever one's appraisal, the chief lesson to be learned from this experience was the need for direct power to control the amount of stock-market credit. The general instruments of control were clearly not adequate to cope with a surge of security speculation. This fact was recognized in the legislation of 1933 and 1934 which conveyed this power to the Board.

fiscal policy, 1920 to 1929

Fiscal policies of the 1920s were not determined with an eye to fostering business stability at a high level. Rather, the object was one of so-called sound finance, which called for a surplus in the federal budget each year and gradual retirement of the war-created public debt. The level of taxes was such that a surplus—ranging between $291 million and $1,155 million—was realized in every fiscal year, 1920 to 1930. From its peak of $25.8 billion at the end of 1919, the federal debt was reduced to $16.3 billion at the end of 1929. It is of special interest that the largest surpluses were recorded in 1924 and 1927, the two recession years when a compensatory fiscal policy would have called for deficits. As it worked out, the easy Reserve credit policies in those years, combined with the strength of natural forces, were sufficient to prevent serious slumps and to produce speedy recovereis despite the drag of adverse fiscal policies. It is also significant that the period of healthy economic growth, 1922-1929, was achieved when surpluses in the budget permitted a 37 percent reduction in the federal debt.

THE GREAT DEPRESSION, 1929 TO 1941

The Great Depression of the 1930s, which had its beginnings in the early fall of 1929, persisted until the enormous demands of World War II evoked full employment of labor and other resources. This was a worldwide phenomenon of unprecedented length and severity. For purposes of exposition the period may conveniently be divided into (1) fall 1929 to spring 1933–descent from the height of the economic and speculative boom to the depths which culminated in the Bank Holiday; (2) 1933 to midyear 1937–years of gradual economic improvement; (3) midyear 1937 to fall 1939–depression within a depression; and (4) 1940 to 1941–prelude to Pearl Harbor and U.S. entry into World War II. Only highlights of these eventful years can be sketched here as a background for developments in monetary and fiscal management.

descent into the maelstrom: fall 1929 to spring 1933

While people stood in a state of shock and disillusionment during the stock-market crash in 1929, few realized that this was only a prelude to the deepest and longest depression on record. Some idea of the extent of this great liquidation is given by the declines in the following selected factors: national income, 55 percent; industrial production, 52 percent; manufacturing employment, 44 percent; wholesale commodity prices, 37 percent; and common-stock prices, 81 percent. One of the most powerful contributing factors was the loss of confidence in the banking system. Over 9,000 commercial banks–two-fifths of all banks–failed. Failures, currency-hoarding, and shifts of deposits from weak to strong banks mutually interacted until all banks were officially closed in March 1933. Demand deposits declined by 37 percent and their velocity by 50 percent. Currency in circulation rose by about 60 percent as a consequence of hoarding, despite the enormous reduction in retail trade and payrolls.

What actions were taken by the Federal Reserve authorities in face of these disastrous developments? In general, their policy was one of monetary ease as expressed by purchases of U.S. securities, and lowering of discount rates. The aim was to provide member banks with excess reserves, so that they, in turn, could repay indebtedness, make loans freely at low rates, and purchase investment securities–although there were occasions when the Fed lost sight of this goal. In this way it was hoped to moderate the decline, and in time to spur recovery. Attention is now directed to a summary of leading developments.

Beginning in late October 1929–a month after the stock-market crash–the Reserve Banks began to build up holdings of U.S. securities. This continued steadily until the end of 1930, when the portfolio amounted to over $700 million–an increase of some $550 million. Combined with a gold inflow, this permitted member banks to reduce debt to Reserve Banks from about $1 billion to approximately $150 million in April-May 1931, and to accumulate substantial excess reserves. Also, beginning in November 1929, the discount rate of the New York Reserve Bank was reduced from 6 to 5 percent, and by successive steps to $1\frac{1}{2}$ percent in May-September 1931. Meanwhile, the buying rate on bankers' acceptances was reduced from 5 to 1 percent. These steps, along with a large reduction in demand for loans, caused a precipitous decline in money rates. For example, the commercial-paper rate dropped from $6\frac{1}{4}$ percent in 1929 to 2 percent in mid-1931.

Events took a decided turn for the worse during the fall of 1931. There had been no letup in the pace of decline of production, employment, commodity prices, and stock prices. Currency-hoarding and bank failures, mutually interacting, had continued to gain momentum. Then came the further blow in September of England's suspension of the gold standard, accompanied by similar action in the entire sterling bloc. With international confidence shattered, the dollar next became the object of suspicion, with the result that the United States lost over $700 million of gold in the next six weeks. This, in turn, accentuated domestic currency-hoarding. Under these influences, bank reserves were drawn down sharply and member banks were forced to borrow heavily at the Reserve Banks (over $1 billion at year-end) and to seek liquidity by reduction in loans and investments.

While Federal Reserve policy and actions during the depression were, in general, praiseworthy up to this time, they suffered a regrettable lapse until the spring of 1932. Instead of adhering courageously to their policy of easy money and abundant bank reserves, the authorities drew back and reverted to conventional central-bank policy during periods of gold outflow. In October-November 1931 the New York Reserve Bank raised the discount rate from $1\frac{1}{2}$ to $3\frac{1}{2}$ percent, and the buying rate on bankers' acceptances from 1 to $3\frac{1}{8}$ percent. At the same time, they chose to release no more reserves by additions to holdings of U.S. securities. Under these circumstances, the money market tightened materially as reflected by the doubling of commercial-paper rates—from 2 to 4 percent. Thus, the Fed must at this stage be charged with positively abetting the headlong course of liquidation and business decline. Some analysts may defend them on the ground that they protected the gold standard, but the argument is weak. The gold outflow was clearly occasioned by panicky loss of confidence and was therefore insensitive to the level of money rates. Moreover, if a choice were necessary, the dangers of deepening depression and a breakdown of the financial system were infinitely graver than departure from the gold standard. But, in fact, a choice was not necessary, and it can be cogently argued that maintenance of the policy of abundant reserves would, by moderating wholesale liquidation, have been more effective in saving the gold standard.

It was not until the spring of 1932 that the Reserve authorities positively resumed their general policy of easy money. At this time they began a program of sizable weekly additions to U.S. security holdings. By August, the portfolio was increased by $1,000 million to about $1,850 million, where it remained until early 1933. This positive program was made possible by the Glass-Steagall Act, approved in February 1932, which permitted the use of U.S. securities as collateral for Federal Reserve Notes, and thereby released gold from this use. In addition, the New York Reserve Bank reduced the discount rate during the first half of 1932 from $3\frac{1}{2}$ to $2\frac{1}{2}$ percent and lowered the buying rate on acceptances from 3 to 1 percent. These steps, together with some return flow of currency and a gain of about $600 million in gold, restored ease in the money market during the second half of 1932. Member banks were enabled to reduce indebtedness materially and to build up sizable excess reserves. The commercial-paper rate dropped from 3.88 percent in February 1932 to 1.38 percent a year later. Meanwhile, business activity, after reaching a low point at midyear, recovered appreciably in the fall and gave rise to hope that the worst was over. But this was not destined to be the case. Business slumped again at year-end, and after the turn of the new year a renewed wave of both bank failures and currency-hoarding developed. Bank holidays were declared by most states during February, so that practically all banks were closed or operating under restrictions by Inauguration Day. One of the first official acts of President Roosevelt was a proclamation on March 6 declaring a nationwide bank holiday until emergency legislation could be passed and a program for reopening sound banks could be devised. The enormous increase in currency-hoarding just before the bank holiday was met in part by Reserve Bank purchases of acceptances and U.S. securities, but mainly by member-bank borrowing which soared to $1.4 billion. The money market tightened and rates rose sharply.

We must now examine the nature of fiscal policy during the steep business decline of 1929-1933. The record reveals that the traditional goal of annual balance in the federal budget prevailed. The idea of reducing taxes and/or increasing expenditures as methods of promoting recovery had not yet become respectable. In the midst of the near-panic conditions late in 1931, the Secretary of the Treasury stated:

> It is not easy for any people to determine to assume a large additional burden at a time when their resources are depleted through business depression, but in the long run they will best serve their own interests by doing whatever is required to maintain the finances of their government on a sound basis.[9]

He then went on to recommend increases in tax rates and reduction in expenditures. Following this counsel, Congress raised tax rates appreciably in the Revenue Act of 1932. It is also well to recall that President Roosevelt supported a platform in 1932 calling for a balanced budget, sound money, and maintenance of the gold standard, and that his first actions as President were in the direction of reduced expenditures and increased taxes. Thus, while there were deficits in the federal budget during the fiscal years 1931-1933, they arose despite higher tax rates and vigorous efforts to hold expenditures to a minimum. Fiscal policies, therefore, tended to magnify, rather than to moderate, the steep decline in business. Had they been employed courageously in the opposite direction, it is likely that this nation and many others would have been saved from the ravages of forced liquidation that followed midyear 1931.

[9]Secretary of the Treasury, *Annual Report* (Washington, D.C., 1931), p. 28.

partial recovery: spring 1933 to midyear 1937

This subperiod may well be labeled one of "partial recovery" because although progress was steady and the level of production surpassed that of 1929, the economy fell far short of capacity output. This is evidenced by the fact that at the top of recovery in the first half of 1937 over 15 percent of the civilian labor force was unemployed. With the reopening of sound banks after the bank holiday and the various emergency measures taken, confidence in the financial system was speedily restored. Over \$2 billion of hoarded currency returned to the banks by the end of August 1933, including about \$800 million of gold and gold certificates. With this relief of pressure on reserves, member banks rapidly reduced borrowing at Reserve Banks and built up excess reserves. To be more specific, between the bank holiday and the end of 1933, net free reserves improved from a negative \$1,285 million to a positive \$704 million. This was, of course, reflected in a rapid decline of money rates.

From the standpoint of Federal Reserve policy, few additional comments are needed for the years 1934 and 1935 and the first half of 1936. The keynote was gradual development of an easier money market. Member-bank borrowing was virtually absent and excess reserves piled up to the \$3 billion level by mid-August 1936. The discount rate of the New York Reserve Bank was reduced by steps from $3\frac{1}{2}$ to $1\frac{1}{2}$ percent in early 1934, where it remained. However, this had only psychological significance in view of the virtual absence of borrowing needs. Money rates declined to the lowest level in history. The yield on bankers' acceptances was only 0.13 percent during and after the last quarter of 1934, and dealers quoted 3-month Treasury bills at 0.15 to 0.20 percent. The main cause of this unprecedented situation was devaluation of the gold dollar at the end of January 1934, following passage of the Gold Reserve Act. The attractive new price (\$35 per ounce compared with the former \$20.67) drew gold from hoards and mines the world over. As a consequence, the U.S. gold stock rose from \$7 billion in early February 1934 to \$10.7 billion by mid-August 1936. The Fed not only permitted this gold to augment member-bank reserves but contributed further by the addition of about \$600 million to holdings of U.S. securities. As would be expected, the enormous excess reserves induced expansion of bank loans and investments, and therefore of deposits. Because of prevailing pessimism, loan expansion was small, but commercial banks added nearly \$9 billion to investments between midyear 1932 and 1936—mostly in U.S. securities. Total deposits rose by \$16 billion.

During 1936 and the first half of 1937, the course of events prompted significant actions by both the Fed and the Treasury. In general, the easy-money policy prevailed in recognition of the fact that the economy was still operating far below capacity. But the rapid rise of production and prices—especially of stock prices—in 1936 and the mounting volume of excess bank reserves became matters of concern. The first step taken related to the stock market. Margin requirements on security loans by banks and brokers were raised from 45 to 55 percent in early 1936. This new selective power, it will be recalled, had been conferred upon the Board by the Securities and Exchange Act of 1934. It enabled them to do what was impossible in 1928-1929—that is, to restrict the amount of security loans without at the same time restricting the amount of cheap bank credit available for industry and trade. The second action taken brought excess reserves of member banks down to a manageable level. Legal-reserve requirements were raised in two steps—one in August 1936, the other in the following spring—to twice their former level.[10] This absorbed over $2 billion of excess reserves and reduced their level to the $700-$900 million range. This step also halved the multiple of potential bank expansion on the basis of remaining excess reserves.

Another significant move in monetary management was made by the Treasury near the end of 1936. This was the so-called sterilization of further increases in the gold stock, whether from imports or from domestic production. Current gold purchases under this program were set aside in an inactive account so that they were withheld from entering either Reserve Bank or member-bank reserves. After accumulating about $1.4 billion in this account, the program was abandoned in April 1938, when the Treasury deposited gold certificates in this amount with the Reserve Banks. Member-bank reserves were then increased as the Treasury drew on its balance with the Reserve Banks. This episode calls attention to the vast monetary powers of the Treasury. Fortunately, they were used in this instance in harmony with Federal Reserve policy but, as we shall see, this was not to be the case for a period of time following World War II.

A further important development of this period related to Federal Reserve aims and objectives. For the first time, the Board recognized that "the increased importance of bonds as a medium of investment for idle bank funds makes the maintenance of stable conditions in the bond market an important concern of banking administration."[11] United States bond prices, which reached a historic peak in late 1936, declined sharply during the spring of 1937. With a view to preventing a disorderly market, the Open-Market Committee gave direct support to long-term issues by increasing Reserve Bank holdings. Successive deficits in the federal budget since fiscal 1930 had brought the gross debt to a new peak of about $35 billion, of which over $32 billion consisted of marketable securities. As a consequence, U.S. securities represented a highly important sector of the money market, and Reserve authorities felt obliged to assume a measure of responsibility for their prices. This development foreshadowed Federal Reserve policy in regard to federal-security prices during World War II and until the spring of 1951.

Also, in August 1937, the Board made a further statement on policy objectives as follows: ". . . to promote economic stability, which means the maintenance of as full employment of labor and of the productive capacity of

[10]From 10 to 20 percent (average) of net demand deposits; and from 3 to 6 percent of time deposits. The Board was granted this power by the Banking Act of 1935.

[11]Federal Reserve Board, *Annual Report* (Washington, D.C., 1937), p. 7.

the country as can continuously be sustained."[12] While recognizing the disastrous effects of wide fluctuations in the price level, the Board went on to reject price stabilization as an adequate single objective. Although maintenance of stable conditions in the government security market was not recognized as a principal objective, it was definitely a secondary aim at this time.

depression within a depression: midyear 1937 to 1939

An exceedingly sharp business decline got underway during the last half of 1937. Industrial production dropped one-third and factory employment one-fourth by midyear 1938. All the hard-earned recovery since 1934 was erased in a few months. Prices also moved downward: wholesale commodity prices by 11 percent, and industrial common stocks by about 50 percent. Recovery was rapid during the second half of 1938, but the 1937 peak was not reattained until the last quarter of 1939.

While the Board of Governors and most monetary economists believed at the time that the 1937-1938 depression was caused by nonmonetary factors, the opposite position is taken by Friedman and Schwartz.[13] In their view, the absorption of $2 billion of excess reserves by doubling legal-reserve requirements of member banks prior to the downturn of the economy was the major cause. They contend that even though excess reserves were not reduced below the $700-$900 million range, the demand for liquidity by banks was so great that they were unwilling to lend and invest. As a consequence, the rate of expansion of the money stock declined materially between midyear 1936 and 1937, followed by an absolute decline of 2.4 percent between midyear 1937 and 1938. This interpretation would doubtless be accepted by most economists of the monetarist persuasion today. Other causes of the depression which should be included are the restrictive effects of the Treasury's gold-sterilization program and the deflationary fiscal policy of the Administration and Congress during fiscal 1938.

Confronted with a new depression within a depression, the monetary authorities belatedly adopted measures to assure abundant bank reserves and record low rates of interest. In the fall of 1937, the New York Reserve Bank reduced its discount rate to 1 percent–lowest on record–and the other Reserve Banks lowered rates to $1\frac{1}{2}$ percent. Also, bank reserves were augmented by release of $300 million from the inactive gold account of the Treasury and by additions to Reserve Bank holdings of U.S. securities. Then, in the spring of 1938, two further moves were made. The Treasury discontinued its inactive gold account, releasing it to enter member-bank reserves shortly by depositing the amount ($1.4 billion) in its balance at the Reserve Banks. In addition, the Board reduced

[12]Ibid., p. 221.

[13]See Milton Friedman and Anna J. Schwartz, *A Monetary History of the United States* (Princeton: Princeton University Press, 1963), pp. 520-545.

legal-reserve requirements of member banks by about $750 million. Taken together, these steps, plus a sizable increase in gold stock, brought about a continuous rise of member-bank excess reserves—to $1 billion in the last quarter of 1937; to $3 billion at midyear 1938; and to $4.3 billion at midyear 1939. Meanwhile, money rates, which had risen moderately during the first half of 1937, sank to new lows. The range of dealers' quotations on 3-month Treasury bills during 1938 and 1939 was 0.02 to 0.13 percent; in fact, the rate on new issues was zero or below on occasion because of the rights value of bills in subscriptions to forthcoming longer-term issues.

prelude to war: 1939 to 1941

The national economy became increasingly dominated in the years 1939-1941 by the European conflict which entered the shooting stage in September 1939, and spread progressively until America was drawn into actual combat in December 1941. After midyear 1939, the levels of production, employment, and national income rose rapidly until at the end of 1941 we were approaching a full-employment situation for the first time in twelve years. The Great Depression, which had stubbornly defied all peacetime recovery measures, was finally being erased by war demands. To be more specific, between midyear 1939 and the end of 1941, industrial production rose 63 percent and factory employment increased 40 percent. Wholesale prices did not begin their sharp ascent until the fall of 1940, but between August 1940 and December 1941, they rose 25 percent—fostered by an accelerated expansion of the money supply.

In this setting, little positive action was undertaken by the Reserve authorities until the autumn of 1941, when the inflationary impact of the defense program caused concern. Prior to that time, the policy of monetary ease prevailed because it served both to encourage economic recovery and to spur defense production. The dominant monetary influence through the third quarter of 1941 was the huge influx of gold, occasioned by the enormous demands of the Allies for war goods and the flight of capital from Europe. The gold stock rose $6.7 billion between midyear 1939 and the beginning of the last quarter of 1941, to a peak of $22.8 billion. As a direct consequence, excess reserves of member banks piled up to the staggering amount of nearly $7 billion—almost as large as required reserves. During 1941, however, the course of excess reserves was downward. Until November, this was mainly a result of increasing currency needs, but on November 1, the Board absorbed $1.2 billion of reserves by raising percentage requirements to the maximum. The purpose of this move was to establish closer Federal Reserve contact with the money market and to reduce the inflationary potential. Despite this action, excess reserves remained above $3 billion.

Two further significant actions were taken by Reserve authorities during this period, viz., stabilizing operations in the government-security market, and the direct control of consumer credit. With the outbreak of war in Europe in 1939, U.S. bond prices declined abruptly from their abnormally high level. In line with a policy of maintaining orderly conditions in this market, the Fed purchased nearly $475 millions in September. Later in the year, as prices recovered, some bonds were sold. Further stabilizing operations on a smaller scale were taken during the period, notably purchases in the spring of 1940, when Norway, Denmark, and the Low Countries were invaded, and sales later in the year as the market recovered. Direct control of consumer credit was assumed for the first time by the Board in September 1941. Regulation W, which prescribed minimum downpayments and maximum maturities on credit to finance installment sales, was issued in accordance with an executive order of the President.

fiscal policy, 1933 to 1941

The philosophy of federal fiscal policy underwent a revolution during the 1930s. Previously, sound fiscal policy was thought to require annual balance of the budget in years of depression even though an increase in tax rates was required. Fiscal 1932 provides an illustration; taxes were raised despite mounting unemployment and panicky asset liquidation. The inevitable consequence of such action was to magnify the depth and length of the depression. But beginning about midyear 1933, the theory of a compensatory federal budget gained increasing acceptance—that is, planned deficits to moderate depression and planned surpluses to dampen inflationary expansion. This philosophy was officially accepted in the Employment Act of 1946, which was passed by a large majority of both political parties; it continues to prevail up to the present time (1971) among both statesmen and economists.

During the eight fiscal years 1934-1941, the average annual federal deficit was about $3.5 billion. This result was brought about principally by enlarged expenditures for public works, unemployment relief, and agricultural and other subsidies. The method of tax-rate reduction was not employed; in fact, a moderate increase in tax rates took place. In terms of national income and budgets in recent years, the deficits of the 1930s appear inconsequential. But they were not small in relation to GNP during that period—4 percent on the average. Applied to the 1970 GNP of about $985 billion this proportion would have meant a deficit of $39.4 billion—a substantial sum indeed. The only attempted departure during this period from budget deficits occurred in fiscal 1938. The policy goal was a balanced budget to be achieved by reduction of expenditures and a moderate rise in tax rates. Although the goal was not attained, the deficit was materially reduced to $1.8 billion. The deflationary effect of this rather abrupt change in budget policy is regarded by many economists as one of the important causes of the 1938 depression.

The question may well be raised at this point: Why were the sizable federal deficits during the 1930s so ineffective in producing business recovery? The answer is that *under the circumstances* they were too small. The federal spending program was undertaken only after the crippling effects of the deepest business decline on record had taken their toll, involving wholesale liquidation, widespread bankruptcies, real-estate foreclosures, and the collapse of the financial system. Once such heavy blows shattered both business and consumer confidence, quick recovery could not reasonably be expected. Had fiscal policy been teamed with a more aggressive monetary policy in 1930-1931 to promote recovery, it is probable that the depths of 1932 and 1933 could have been avoided, and that full recovery could have been realized at a much earlier date.

21

monetary, fiscal, and debt management, 1942 to 1951

While the outbreak of World War II increasingly stimulated the American economy in 1939 and 1940, it became a major influence during 1941. After Pearl Harbor, when the United States was catapulted into armed conflict, the watchword became "total war." All-out conversion from peace to war production was then pursued with all possible vigor. We shall now review the highlights of monetary and fiscal policies.

MONETARY AND FISCAL POLICIES DURING WORLD WAR II

Under conditions of total war, monetary policies were merged with, and submerged by, fiscal policies. Canons of sound monetary action in peacetime were necessarily relegated to a minor role for the duration. The main task of the Fed became that of assisting the Treasury to borrow all needed funds and to manage the growing debt in the best interests of the nation. The day after Pearl Harbor the Board of Governors officially accepted this responsibility in a public statement, as follows:

> The System is prepared to use its powers to assure that an ample supply of funds is available at all times for financing the war effort and to exert its influence toward maintaining conditions in the United States Government security market that are satisfactory from the standpoint of the Government's requirements.[1]

[1]*Federal Reserve Bulletin* (January 1941), p. 2.

The record shows that the Fed did, in fact, live up to this statement; it cooperated fully with the Treasury in all phases of war finance.

objectives and methods of war finance

The broad wartime economic objective was maximum output of needed war goods within the limits of a tolerable standard of life for the civilian population whose morale and efficiency had to be maintained. Basically, this meant a massive conversion of all nonessential production to war purposes—including residential and other nonessential construction and production of automobiles and other consumer durables. The financial goal then became that of promptly raising the money needed in such manner as to foster maximum war output, but at the same time to minimize the inequities and disorganization of price inflation during and after the war.

The methods by which the Treasury can raise money to meet expenditures fall into three broad categories: (1) taxation, (2) borrowing current savings and idle funds from nonbank sources, and (3) borrowing or issuing newly created money. Congress holds final responsibility for the federal budget. It sets the levels of both tax rates and expenditures, and therefore of the budget deficit or surplus. Of course, the Executive Branch exerts a strong influence through recommendations and political pressures, and it has some discretion in regard to timing of expenditures, but Congress is responsible for the end product. It determines the amount of borrowing that must be done by the Treasury, or the amount of debt repayment that can be made.[2] Taxation is the least inflationary method of raising funds because spending power is not increased, but is merely transferred to the government by private interests which receive tax receipts. In the early part of the war, the Secretary of the Treasury and other public officials expressed the intention of meeting at least two-thirds of expenditures by taxation in order to forestall price inflation.

When borrowing is confined to the flow of current savings and to existing idle money, the effect may be little, if any, more inflationary than from taxation. Here again, money already on hand is transferred to the Treasury. But in this case, the Treasury hands out interest-bearing investment securities instead of merely tax receipts. With greater wealth and liquidity, the private sector is likely to spend more freely than under the tax method. Investment of current savings in Treasury securities may be voluntary, semivoluntary, or compulsory. It was, in fact, kept on a voluntary or semivoluntary basis during the war, although serious consideration was given to compulsory lending.

If tax revenues and sale of securities to nonbank investors fail to produce sufficient funds, the creation of *new money* becomes necessary. That is, the funds must be borrowed from Federal Reserve or commercial banks, or

[2]This assumes a constant Treasury cash balance.

Treasury currency (noninterest-bearing obligations) must be issued. While Treasury currency notes were not issued, a vast amount of new money was, in fact, created by selling securities to the banking system. Borrowing from commercial banks creates an equivalent amount of money in the form of demand deposits. Borrowing from Reserve Banks also creates deposits, but goes a long step further by originating an equivalent amount of member-bank reserves. These balances, in turn, provide the basis for an additional multiple expansion of bank loans, investments, and deposits, unless forestalled by raising member-bank reserve requirements. Thus, the Treasury's alternatives in raising funds may be listed in ascending order of inflationary potential, as follows: (1) taxation, (2) borrowing from nonbank investors, (3) borrowing from commercial banks, (4) borrowing from Reserve Banks, and (5) issuance of Treasury currency notes. The Treasury and Fed designed their program to raise as much as possible from nonbank investors; only the remainder from commercial banks and Reserve Banks, with emphasis on the former. This was as far as they were in position to go in protecting against inflationary dangers.

financial record of world war II

A few statistics are necessary to visualize the actual financial record of the war. Total federal expenditures rose from $12.7 billion in fiscal 1941 to $100.4 billion in 1945. Total expenditures during the six-year period 1941-1946 amounted to $382.5 billion; total receipts, to $176.3 billion; and the total budget deficit, to $206.2 billion. The interest-bearing federal debt rose in this period from $42.4 to $268.1 billion, or by $225.7 billion.[3] Individuals and other nonbank investors lent the Treasury $135.4 billion, and the remaining $90.3 billion was borrowed from the banking system—$69 billion from commercial banks and $21.3 billion from Reserve Banks. Thus, about 45 percent of total expenditures was met by taxes, and 55 percent was borrowed. In turn, 60 percent of borrowed funds came from nonbank investors and the remaining 40 percent from the banking system by money creation. Mainly as a consequence, the total money stock (demand deposits and currency outside banks) increased from $38.7 to $106 billion, or by 174 percent. With the stream of income and spending power so greatly enlarged, and with growing scarcities of consumer goods and materials, there was a tremendous upward pressure on prices. Despite price and wage controls, wholesale prices advanced by 45 percent and the cost of living by one-third.

Two further financial developments require comment because of their important bearing on postwar conditions, viz., (1) the enormous increase in nonmoney liquid asset holdings and (2) the decline in velocity of money. Between midyear 1940 and 1946, nonmoney holdings (time and savings deposits

[3]Federal debt rose more than the deficit because of a rise in the cash balance of the Treasury.

and U.S. securities) of individuals and businesses increased from $38.7 billion to $134 billion. This was principally a result of purchases of U.S. securities by nonbank investors. The velocity of money dropped during the war to less than half its level of the 1920s, and even well below the depression years of the 1930s. For example, the annual rate of turnover of demand deposits in 100 leading cities (excluding New York) was about 17 during the war and remained at that level until 1946. In contrast, the annual turnover in these cities averaged 35 during the 1920s and over 23 during the 1930s. This large decline in velocity was a joint product of the enormous increase in the amount of money and the lack of consumer and other goods on which to spend it because of rationing, allocation of materials, and price control. Thus, the wartime accumulation of savings in liquid assets, the abnormally low velocity of the huge stock of money, and scarcities of consumer durables and capital goods all combined to provide a highly inflationary postwar setting.

federal reserve policies

Federal Reserve policy during the war was one of complete cooperation with the Treasury. Excess reserves of member banks were kept in the vicinity of $1 billion in order to keep commercial banks in position to purchase the succeeding issues of Treasury securities, and to make needed loans in support of the war economy. This required an expansion of Reserve Bank credit of nearly $23 billion, most of which occurred by purchase of U.S. securities. The dominant factor that drew down member-bank reserves was the $20 billion rise of currency in circulation, but there was also a decline of $2 billion in the gold stock. In addition, required reserves of member banks rose by about $7 billion, mainly because of the huge expansion of deposits. Until mid-1942, rising requirements were met by existing excess reserves. But henceforth, with excess reserves at the desired minimum, further increases in needs were provided principally by Reserve Bank purchases of Treasury securities. These rising needs were also met in part by reducing required reserves in central-reserve cities and by freeing Treasury deposits from reserve requirements. The large increase of currency in circulation was closely related to the rapid increase of national income which, in turn, resulted from both rising prices and growing physical output. More specifically, currency needs were linked to expansion of retail trade and payrolls, and to the special requirements of those who left their communities to work in war industries and to enter the armed forces. The sizable loss of gold was a result of net payments to foreign countries, chiefly for purchase of war goods.

Early in 1942, the Fed agreed to maintain the existing pattern of yields on U.S. securities for the duration. Henceforth, they stood ready to buy all securities offered at yields ranging from $\frac{3}{8}$ percent on 90-day Treasury bills and $\frac{7}{8}$ percent on 12-month certificates to $2\frac{1}{2}$ percent on long-term bonds. This, of course, meant that yields could not rise above this level. The main purposes were to facilitate Treasury borrowing at low rates, and to protect investors from the danger of depreciation in security values. In the case of bills, the Reserve Banks were also committed to sell at $\frac{3}{8}$ percent, so that this yield was fixed. There was, however, no agreement to sell certificates, notes, and bonds on a predetermined yield basis. Consequently, the yields of these securities could fall below (prices rise above) the established maximum yield pattern.

Adoption of the foregoing policy had important implications from the standpoint of monetary management. It meant that the Fed lost control of the amount of member-bank reserves. All holders of marketable government securities, whether bank or nonbank, possessed demand options on reserve money. Their decisions, and not those of the Fed, determined the size of Reserve Bank holdings, and hence the amount of bank reserves. But this was not all; Reserve Banks also lost control of types of securities and of the maturity distribution of their holdings. The adopted yield pattern became the monetary fulcrum—in one sense, a new monetary standard.

An interesting and unforeseen development grew out of maintenance of the wide spread between yields on Treasury bills and on notes and bonds. The latter, if purchased at par or below, not only possessed as much liquidity as bills—because the Reserve Banks provided an unlimited market—but also offered materially higher yields. Commercial banks and other investors, therefore, preferred bonds and notes, especially after midyear 1943. Bills, and to a lesser extent, certificates gravitated to Reserve Banks while their bond and note holdings declined. Astute government security investors enjoyed a heyday "playing the pattern" of rates. Because market yields declined as maturities approached, the prices of intermediate-term securities rose above par with the passage of time and afforded almost certain capital appreciation. Thus, investors subscribed to new issues at par and sold them later at a profit, meanwhile enjoying the higher coupon rate. After mid-1944, the strong demand for intermediate- and long-term securities drove their yields sharply downward, so that the spread was appreciably reduced. At the low point in the first quarter of 1946, yields on long-term Treasury bonds and on 7-9-year issues dropped to 2.2 and 1.6 percent, respectively.

Three significant changes in legal-reserve requirements were made during the war: (1) reduction of the percentage requirement in central-reserve cities, (2) exemption of Treasury deposits with member banks from reserve requirements, and (3) reduction of the minimum reserve requirement of Federal Reserve Banks. With regard to the first, it will be recalled that reserve requirements of members were raised to the legal maximum in the last quarter of 1941 in order to absorb part of the then-existing mountain of excess reserves. As Treasury borrowing, taxes, and expenditures mounted in 1941 and 1942, an uneven distribution of bank reserves developed. New York City and Chicago banks lost reserves because Treasury expenditures in those centers were less than borrowings and tax receipts. In order to alleviate this situation, which was interfering with war finance and disturbing the money market, the Board reduced the reserve requirement of central-reserve city banks in the autumn of 1942 from 26 to 20 percent.[4] Requirements of reserve city and country banks remained at the maximum for the duration, with the result that the Reserve Banks had to purchase larger amounts of U.S. securities.

Treasury deposits with member banks, known as war-loan accounts, were exempted from reserve requirements in the spring of 1943. This step had a double purpose. The Treasury wished to encourage use of war-loan accounts as a means of facilitating war finance. Payment by banks and their customers for new issues could conveniently be made by credits to these accounts. In addition, it was anticipated that the disturbing effects of Treasury transactions on the money market would be reduced by avoidance of unnecessary transfers to the Treasury's balance at Reserve Banks. While some disturbances were doubtless avoided by this action, the net result was to magnify effects of war finance, and perhaps also to promote inflationary expansion of bank credit. Subscriptions to succeeding war loans involved large transfers from deposit accounts of individuals and institutions, which were subject to reserve requirements, to Treasury accounts against which no legal reserve was needed. With enlarged excess reserves, member banks were encouraged to purchase securities for their own account and to make loans to customers for such purchases. Speculation on the "free ride" was thereby fostered; that is, banks and their customers subscribed to new issues with the expectation of selling at a profit within a few days or weeks—a procedure which usually paid off. Afterward, as the Treasury checked on its balance and returned deposits to the private sector, reserve requirements rose again. The banks then sold securities to adjust reserves. Reserve Banks, in turn, purchased the overflow at pegged prices and thereby released new reserves capable of supporting multiple credit expansion. Thus, the exemption of war-loan accounts from reserve requirements resulted in a sort of inflationary ratchet action, as well as alternately creating tighter and easier conditions in the money market.

The last change in reserve requirements pertained to the Federal Reserve Banks. On recommendation of the Board, Congress reduced the minimum requirement in June 1945 to 25 percent in gold certificates against combined Federal Reserve Note and deposit liabilities. This change was sought because the ratio had dropped rapidly as a result of both a decline in the gold-certificate reserve and a large increase in notes and deposits. The previous minimum ratios were 40 percent against notes and 35 percent against deposits. Thus, the reduction added materially to potential monetary expansion.

Another measure taken by the Fed was reduction of discount rates. In the spring of 1942, the rate was dropped $\frac{1}{2}$ percentage point to a uniform 1 percent for the rest of the war period. Then, in the autumn, a preferential rate of $\frac{1}{2}$ percentage point was established on advances secured by U.S. securities

[4]This required an amendment to Section 19 of the Federal Reserve Act, which became law in July 1942. It enabled the Board to take separate action on reserve requirements of the different classes of member banks. Previously, this was not legally possible.

maturing or callable within one year. The object of this change was to enable member banks to adjust reserve positions by low-cost borrowing instead of sale of U.S. securities. As things worked out, the low preferential rate was not very significant because most banks could adjust reserves more favorably by sale of bills and certificates; borrowing at Reserve Banks was moderate in amount. The preferential rate was discontinued with cessation of hostilities.

In addition to the foregoing actions involving the general instruments of control, the Board employed selective regulation of stock-market and consumer credit. Margin requirements on stock-exchange security loans remained at 40 percent until the last year of the war. From their low point in 1942, common-stock prices made a strong recovery accompanied by increased buying on margin. Concerned with this speculative development, the Board raised margins to 75 percent in two steps in 1945, and to 100 percent in early 1946. These measures curbed expansion of stock-market credit but did not prevent an accelerated rise of stock prices.

The program of direct consumer-credit control, applied for the first time in the autumn of 1941, was broadened and tightened the following spring. Regulation W of the Board, which originally related only to installment sales, was extended to charge accounts and single-payment loans. The maximum length of most installment contracts was reduced to one year, with minimum downpayments of one-third the purchase price. With only minor changes, these controls continued effectively throughout the war. Partly as a consequence, consumer credit declined from a peak of about $10 billion in 1941 to $5 billion in early 1944. Other influences, however, were more important in causing the decline. Automobiles and other consumer durables became virtually unavailable. Also, the rise in incomes and savings fostered repayments and cash purchases. The main purposes of consumer-credit control were to prevent a marked rise in the cost of living, and to assist in conversion of productive resources to wartime purposes. Most authorities agree that the program made a positive contribution to the system of wartime controls.

A final feature of war finance was the effort to borrow needed funds from nonbank investors. Treasury and Federal Reserve authorities cooperated fully in this endeavor with the aim of minimizing war and postwar price inflation. They rightly stressed that this method transferred *existing* money to the Treasury, and thereby curbed the spending of current income and idle funds, and that, in contrast, borrowing from commercial and Reserve banks created *new* money and additional spending power. The actual program involved vigorous promotion of a variety of securities designed for different classes of nonbank investors. The War Savings staff of the Treasury promoted sale of Series E bonds to small savers by payroll-deduction plans. Series F and G nonmarketable bonds were offered to larger savers and nonbank institutions. A Victory Fund Committee was set up in each Reserve district under Treasury and Federal Reserve auspices to promote successive war-loan drives among nonbank investors. In addition, commercial-bank subscriptions to offerings were usually limited, and they were not permitted to purchase issues with maturity of over ten years. As a result of these efforts, three-fifths of Treasury borrowing was from nonbank investors; the remaining two-fifths came from the banking system.

appraisal of fiscal and monetary policies

In retrospect, the fiscal and monetary policies of World War II deserve both commendation and censure. Certainly, they were superior in most respects to those of World War I, when only about 30 percent of expenditures (compared with 45 percent) was covered by tax receipts, and a larger proportion of borrowed funds came from the banking system. Both the Treasury and the Fed merit praise for waging a vigorous campaign to raise funds from nonbank investors in order to avoid creation of new money. Also praiseworthy was Federal Reserve administration of the consumer-credit control program. In addition, the systems of price control and rationing unquestionably served constructively to contain inflation and to lessen inequities.

On the other side, the worst mistake of Congress and the Administration was that of being too soft on the civilian public. They, too, should have borne heavy sacrifices along with the armed forces; civilian conscription was a logical counterpart of military conscription from the standpoints of both equity and effective war output. Instead, the real standard of civilian life rose during the war. In terms of fiscal policy, the mistake was that of raising too small a part of funds by taxation and nonbank borrowing, and too large a proportion by the inflationary method of borrowing from banks. It would have been possible, without breaking morale or sacrificing production, to have raised at least 60 percent (instead of 45 percent) by taxes and another 30 percent by nonbank borrowing. This would have reduced the proportion of bank borrowing to 10 percent instead of the actual one-fourth. Such a degree of austerity could not have been attained, however, without resort to compulsory lending—a method that, unfortunately, was not utilized.

The major error of the Treasury and the Fed was that of freezing interest rates at an absurdly low level. The rate structure in 1942 reflected depression conditions and a money market with over $3 billion of excess reserve in member banks. It would have been far wiser to have fixed maximum yields at a more normal level, say, about $3\frac{1}{2}$ percent. This would have avoided much of the postwar dilemma of whether to maintain government-security prices at their abnormally high level by Federal Reserve support, or to let them decline in a relatively free market. The fact that the former course was followed until 1951—the sixth postwar year—meant nullification of the general instruments of monetary control, one of the main defenses against the steep rise of commodity prices.

While not so important as the level of rates, maintenance of the wide spread in rates—from $\frac{3}{8}$ percent on bills to $2\frac{1}{2}$ percent on long-term bonds—also contributed to price inflation. This rate differential provided a speculative opportunity to "play the rate pattern" with the result that commercial banks were more avid holders of intermediate- and long-term securities than they would otherwise have been. Thus, bank-credit expansion was encouraged and inflation was invited.

The objection may be raised that the interest cost of borrowing at $3\frac{1}{2}$ percent, instead of the actual cost of less than 2 percent, would have been unjustifiable if not prohibitive. But the answer is that the higher interest cost would have been a small price to pay for abatement of inflationary pressures, and for the opportunity to return to traditional monetary management soon after the end of hostilities. Moreover, the gross increase in interest cost to the Treasury would not have been a real cost to the nation. Federal income taxes recapture in the vicinity of one-third of interest received by private investors, and about two-fifths of gross interest is paid to government trust accounts and the Federal Reserve Banks. But more important, higher interest payments represent mainly a redistribution of income between taxpayers and interest receivers, many of whom wear both shoes.

FEDERAL RESERVE IN BONDAGE, 1946 TO SPRING 1951

For more than five years after World War II the Fed lived in a state of bondage. This was necessarily the case during the war when fiscal considerations were paramount, but not so with the return of peace. In fact, the highly inflationary postwar setting called for prompt restoration and implementation of monetary objectives. These goals, however, remained largely submerged while Congress, the Administration (including the Treasury), and the Reserve authorities took only token measures to prevent the destructive upward course of commodity prices. Federal Reserve actions alone could not have contained the inflation, but they could have substantially reduced it. Instead, following the false aim of maintaining low yields on government securities, they added fuel to the fire.

What accounts for this supine attitude of the monetary authorities? With benefit of hindsight, several reasons may be seen. In the first place, after five war years of subservience, it was not easy to recapture authority. This was particularly true under the circumstances. The Secretary of the Treasury, Mr. Snyder, believed that above all else the high prices of government securities must be maintained, and in this he had the support of President Truman. The political position of the Fed was not powerful enough to overcome a policy strongly advocated by the Administration.

Second, depression psychology prevailed in the early postwar years. Many people held the mature-economy theory that was popular during the depression of the 1930s, and believed that peace would be accompanied by chronic unemployment. More immediately, they anticipated large-scale unemployment during reconversion. They did not believe that private industry could absorb over ten million persons from the armed forces and reconvert some three-fifths of factory capacity to peacetime without a major depression.

Third, fiscal and monetary authorities were confronted with management of a federal debt of almost astronomical proportions. In the vicinity of $260 billion, it was ten times that of World War I, nearly seven times the prewar level, and it represented three-fifths of total private and public debt. Moreover, the bulk of the marketable debt was short-term, so that the Treasury faced a huge refunding problem, and until maturities could be lengthened, it had to redeem or exchange annually between $60 and $75 billion of securities. It is therefore not surprising that stability of government-security prices appeared to be a "must." A large decline in these prices would have meant heavy losses to individual and institutional investors who had responded to successive war-loan appeals. In addition, it might have threatened the solvency of commercial banks, insurance companies, and other financial institutions, and might have led to panicky liquidation. Equally important, the accompanying rise of interest rates would have added materially to the Treasury's cost of borrowing, which was already a major item in the budget—about $5 billion. Each 1 percent increase would eventually have meant another $2.5 billion. So went the argument.

Finally, the attitude of the authorities was influenced by the view that henceforth low interest rates would have to be maintained to promote full employment and economic growth. This was a corollary of the chronic-unemployment thesis. In other words, the major economic problem of the future was regarded to be avoidance of unemployment rather than the danger of price inflation.

But the foregoing factors can only soften criticism of the authorities' passive attitude. In fact, in light of economic conditions and prospects, little perspective was displayed. The amount of money and other liquid assets had approximately trebled during the war; the income velocity of money was almost one-third below its average during the depressed 1930s, and only one-half that of 1929; there were huge backlogs of demand for capital goods and durable consumer goods; vast foreign needs and demands for our exports were in prospect; commodity price inflation had been suppressed by wartime controls; and the limited productive capacity of peacetime products could not be rapidly expanded. In short, all the ingredients for a great price inflation were present. The situation called for vigorous fiscal and monetary restraints, but instead policies were permissive and expansionary.

postwar inflationary boom, 1946 to 1948

Background Developments / The most spectacular development of the early postwar years was the upsurge of prices. Between V-J Day and August 1948, wholesale prices rose 60 percent and consumer prices, 35 percent. Thus, two-thirds of the depreciation in the value of the dollar after 1940 took place in the three postwar years, and only one-third during the war. Reconversion proceeded much more rapidly than most economists and public officials believed possible. Industrial production dropped sharply until the first quarter of 1946, but thereafter made a strong recovery to the autumn of 1948. GNP rose by one-third between the first quarter of 1946 and the third quarter of 1948, but the increase came mainly from higher prices. Total real output showed little gain, although there was a marked shift toward consumer goods. The moderate nature of the decline during reconversion, as well as the sharp rise of prices, was largely a consequence of the intense demand for consumer goods. Private domestic investment also expanded rapidly, but its magnitude was only one-fourth that of consumer expenditures. Together, the increases of consumer spending and of private investment far more than compensated for the large decline in federal purchases—from $90 billion during the war to $16 billion in 1947.[5]

More strictly in the financial area, the amount of money (demand deposits and currency) rose between August 1945 and August 1948, from $100 to $109.4 billion—no more than a normal growth. But the velocity of money (measured by turnover of demand deposits) rose by over one-third. A significant change also took place in the composition of bank assets. Loans of commercial banks nearly doubled, whereas holdings of U.S. securities decreased by $24 billion. With partial release of control, interest rates rose appreciably, but they remained abnormally low even at the peak of the inflationary boom.

Removal of Price and Product Controls / Price controls, wage controls, and rationing were reasonably effective in moderating the rise of commodity prices during the war. They also reduced materially the factors that might generate postwar inflation. That is, they limited private incomes and spending, increased personal and business savings, reduced the federal deficit by holding the price line, and moderated the increase in money and liquid assets. Nevertheless, the United States emerged from the war in a state of "suppressed" inflation. In other words, the vast reservoir of newly-created spending power had been in part contained, but under mounting pressures. Release of controls in free markets before scarcities were relieved could have only one result: a speculative rise of prices. This was just what happened. Wage controls were first relaxed immediately after the end of hostilities in August 1945 and were further liberalized in October. The substantial wage increases that followed forced the Office of Price Administration to approve upward price adjustments. This mutually propelling process continued until November 1946, when all wage controls and most price controls were terminated by an Executive Order of the President.

[5]For a more comprehensive analysis of developments in this period, see Lester V. Chandler, *Inflation in the United States, 1940-1948* (New York: Harper & Row, 1951), chap. XI. The above summary is based in large part on this excellent study (by permission).

Few would disagree that the impatient removal of price and wage controls was one of the major postwar mistakes in policy. They should have been retained, especially in the durable-goods field, until production had time to relieve scarcities. This was, however, almost a political impossibility. Tired of war and the harness of controls, the public demanded return of peacetime freedoms. But the nation paid dearly for this spending spree by the disruptions and inequities associated with rapid price inflation.

Fiscal Policies / While the federal budget registered surpluses in both fiscal 1947 and 1948, Congress made two tax rate reductions during the period which largely nullified fiscal restraints. The Revenue Act of November 1945 repealed the excess-profits tax, reduced rates on both individual and corporate incomes, and made other minor reductions. Altogether, the reductions were estimated to be $6 billion. The reasons for this action were similar to those that account for removal of price controls and rationing. Public pressure to lower the high rates was tremendous and legislators saw an opportunity to please their constituents. Also, there was genuine fear of a serious depression during the period of reconversion, and rapid reduction of defense expenditures. The second rate reduction was made in the Revenue Act of April 1948, which lowered individual income-tax rates enough to reduce annual revenues by an estimated $5 billion. Full responsibility for this action rested on Congress because it mustered a two-thirds majority to pass the act over a Presidential veto. Two earlier bills of similar nature had been vetoed by the President in June and July of the previous year. The lack of wisdom of this legislation is affirmed by the fact that it was passed in the midst of sharply rising commodity prices.

Federal expenditures declined more rapidly than revenues—from nearly $100 billion in fiscal 1945 to $33.8 billion in 1948. The reduction took place entirely in defense spending; in fact, expenditures rose in all other major categories. The net result of these large changes in revenues and expenditures was a cash surplus of $6.7 billion in fiscal 1947 and another of $8.9 billion in 1948. These surpluses were particularly noteworthy because they were the first in 17 years. Yet in retrospect one must conclude that they were too small. Less reduction in tax rates combined with selected economies in expenditures would have been powerful weapons to combat the inflation. Larger tax collections would have limited the increase of private disposable incomes, and decreased expenditures would have removed an increment of demand. In addition, larger budget surpluses could have reduced the amount of money and other liquid assets by redemption of bank-held federal debt.

Debt-Management Policies / In addition to the antiinflationary effects of surpluses during this period, Treasury debt management was employed to the same end by (1) retirement of federal securities held by Reserve Banks, and (2) shifting federal debt from banks to nonbank investors. Control potentialities in this area were very large, because of the Treasury's enormous cash balance—

almost $26 billion–which accrued as a result of the Victory Loan early in 1946. Added to this balance was a Treasury cash surplus by mid-1948 of nearly $15 billion. Most of these funds were kept in the war-loan deposit accounts of commercial banks. Hence, by drawing on these accounts to retire federal securities held by Reserve Banks, member-bank reserve balances could be extinguished dollar for dollar. As a matter of fact, almost $11 billion of securities held by Reserve Banks were retired. Another $17 billion was used to redeem U.S. securities owned by commercial banks, and $10 billion to retire securities held by nonbank investors. Neither of the last two steps, however, had an antiinflationary influence; in fact, the effect of the last was probably inflationary. Retirement of securities held by commercial banks did not change either member-bank reserve requirements[6] or the amount of money owned by the public because war-loan deposit liabilities of banks were used to retire investments in U.S. securities. Retirement of securities held by nonbank investors involved a transfer from the Treasury's war-loan deposits to demand deposits of individuals and businesses–an increase in the amount of money. However, because war-loan accounts were not subject to legal-reserve requirements, the transfer involved an increase in required reserves. This could have had a deflationary effect, but under the circumstances it was largely nullified by the ease with which banks could meet reserve deficiencies by selling U.S. securities to the Reserve Banks at supported prices. Thus, the net effect of redeeming securities of nonbank investors by drawing on war-loan accounts, created by previous bank borrowing, was probably inflationary.

The Treasury also attempted to exert an antiinflationary influence by shifting ownership of federal securities from banks to nonbank investors. If the shift is from Reserve Banks, both member-bank reserve balances and demand deposits are reduced correspondingly; if from commercial banks, demand deposits are extinguished. However, in the latter case legal-reserve requirements are reduced, so that member banks either hold larger excess reserves or repay borrowings from Reserve Banks. Given time, therefore, the released excess reserves may be utilized to support subsequent expansion of loans, investments, and deposits. If so, the immediate contractive effect is eventually counteracted. But if the excess reserves are absorbed by accompanying operations of the Treasury or Fed, the deflationary effect can be sustained. With this goal in view, the Treasury vigorously promoted savings bonds and offered attractive marketable and nonmarketable issues to other nonbank investors. The proceeds of these sales could then be applied to redemption of bank-held debt. This program undoubtedly had some measure of success, although it is not possible to appraise the result in quantitative terms.

In summary, we may conclude that in some respects debt management was employed from the end of the war to the autumn of 1948 as an antiinflationary influence. The Treasury cash balance, built up by overborrowing

[6]War-loan deposits were exempt from legal-reserve requirements.

and budget surpluses, was utilized to redeem federal securities held by Reserve Banks, and strong efforts were made to shift bank-held debt to nonbank investors. However, the deflationary effects were annulled by another aspect of debt management—Federal Reserve support of U.S. securities at par or above. Low-cost reserve money was provided so liberally to the banks that the overall influence was to foster, rather than restrain, price inflation.

Federal Reserve Policies / In the larger sense, it is a misnomer to speak of Federal Reserve policy during this period, in view of dominance by the Treasury. Nevertheless, token efforts were made to moderate price inflation even though doomed to failure in the framework of the controlling criterion: maintenance of low interest rates on federal securities.

The first departure from the wartime open-market policy came in July 1947, when the Open-Market Committee discontinued the practice of buying and selling Treasury bills at the fixed rate of $\frac{3}{8}$ percent. This was followed in August by withdrawal of support of certificates at the $\frac{7}{8}$ percent rate. Both rates rose immediately and by year-end, bills were quoted at 1 percent and certificates slightly higher, where they remained until the autumn of 1948. Then, in December 1947, the Open-Market Committee lowered its support prices on intermediate- and long-term federal securities to par. Following this, a wave of liquidation of U.S. bonds by insurance companies and other institutional investors gained momentum. Support of prices required purchase of over $10 billion of bonds by Reserve Banks between the end of November 1947 and November 1948. However, total holdings increased only $1 billion because of offsetting sales of bills, certificates, and notes. The inconsistency of this support program is confirmed by the fact that excess reserves of member banks rose appreciably at a time when inflationary developments called for restraint.

As part of the general policy of permitting short-term yields on government securities to rise, moderate increases were made during this period in discount rates of the Reserve Banks. The first step was discontinuance in the spring of 1946 of the preferential rate of $\frac{1}{2}$ percent on advances for which the collateral was short-term U.S. securities. This raised the effective borrowing rate to 1 percent, where it remained for nearly two years. Two increases were made in 1948—to $1\frac{1}{4}$ percent in January, and to $1\frac{1}{2}$ percent in August. These changes were mostly symbolic because few member banks needed to borrow. They did encourage banks to repair reserve deficiencies by sale of short-term government securities rather than by borrowing at Reserve Banks. Yields on these issues were below the discount rate so their sale was less costly than borrowing. Reserve adjustments could be made in this way because most banks held large amounts of short terms.

With member-bank reserve requirements at the maximum, except in central-reserve cities, the Fed had little room to utilize this instrument of restraint. It did, however, raise requirements in central-reserve cities by 4 percentage points (about $1 billion) during the first half of 1948. Then in

August, after repeated requests, Congress granted the Board temporary power to raise requirements above the former legal limits.[7] This power was promptly exercised in September, when requirements were raised another $1.5 billion, to the highest percentages in Federal Reserve annals.[8] This reflected the desire to keep member-bank reserves under maximum pressure consistent with support of government security prices. But again the action was largely futile. Member banks met the new requirements by selling U.S. securities, most of which gravitated to Reserve Banks. In the two weeks following increase of requirements, Reserve Bank holdings rose over $2 billion. While excess reserves declined somewhat, discounts and advances remained at the same level, and only a minor firming of interest rates occurred.

The Fed made full use of its powers of direct control over credit during this period, but the scope of these powers was strictly limited. Margin requirements on security loans, which had been raised from 40 to 75 percent in 1945, were placed at 100 percent in January 1946. This was in response to the sharp rise in stock prices, which had been fostered by expansion of security loans. But after the sizable decline in stock prices in the last half of 1946, margin requirements were cut back to 75 percent in February 1947, where they remained for over two years. Little liberalization of wartime regulation of consumer credit occurred until November 1947. But at that time, Congress terminated the Board's authority. The rapid growth of such credit continued in 1948, with the result that Congress temporarily restored the Board's authority in August. Regulation W was reissued in September 1948, but was lifted prior to termination of legal control at midyear 1949.

There is no doubt that the selective controls applied during this period exerted a restraining influence. Curtailment of security loans dampened the speculative rise of stock prices as well as bank-credit expansion, and thereby moderated the inflationary boom. Similarly, until the autumn of 1947, regulation of consumer credit reduced the demand for consumer goods, especially durables, at a time of pronounced scarcities. But these influences were submerged by the flood of buying power that entered the markets. It was unfortunate that consumer-credit regulation was terminated before production could more nearly match demands. It was also regrettable that real-estate credit control was not applied in these years of housing scarcity. The too liberal credit terms contributed to the steep rise of costs and prices. Downpayments could have been increased and loan maturities could have been shortened without much sacrifice of the volume of construction. Had it been possible to apply general monetary controls effectively, the direct control of consumer and real-estate credit would not have been so necessary. But with virtually no control

[7]By 4 percentage points against demand deposits and 1½ points against time deposits; power to expire June 30, 1949.

[8]Against demand deposits: central-reserve cities, 26 percent; reserve cities, 22 percent; country banks, 16 percent. Against time deposits: 7½ percent.

over total bank credit, selective regulation was justified until general controls could be restored.[9]

recession of 1949

The first postwar recession got underway during the last quarter of 1948 and reached bottom during the second and third quarters of 1949. Recovery proceeded rapidly throughout 1950. From peak to trough, industrial production declined 17 percent; factor employment, 11 percent; wholesale prices, 11 percent; and GNP 6 percent. It was thus a mild and short-lived decline, occasioned mainly by excessive accumulation of inventories at rising prices during 1947 and 1948.

Federal Reserve Policies / When evidences of a developing recession became clear, the Fed changed its policy from one of moderate restraint to one of ease. While scope for restraint had been narrowly limited, there was room to move in the opposite direction and to provide more abundant credit at lower cost. Selective controls were first modified. Margin requirements on security loans were reduced in the spring from 75 to 50 percent. Consumer-credit regulations were also liberalized and eventually repealed before their legal termination at midyear. The most decisive action was taken in regard to member-bank reserve requirements. Successive reductions were made during May-September, amounting in aggregate to $3.8 billion.[10] This move represented not only a cyclical adjustment but also a realignment of relationship between this instrument and open-market operations. That is, the release of reserves was much larger than desired for current purposes, so that a large compensatory reduction in holdings of U.S. securities was an essential part of the overall program. In fact, Reserve Bank holdings were reduced by $5.4 billion between November 1948 and November 1949. Despite this large reduction, net free reserves of member banks eased by some $200 million as a consequence of declines in Treasury deposits with Reserve Banks, currency in circulation, and member-bank deposits as well as an increase in the gold stock. Member-bank liquidity was enhanced not only by more free reserves but also by their addition of over $5 billion short-term U.S. securities and by a sizable reduction in loans. Thus, member banks absorbed the bulk of U.S. securities sold by the Reserve Banks. The net effect of the foregoing changes was a moderate decline in interest rates during 1949, especially yields on long-term issues.

[9] See Chandler, op. cit., chaps. XI-XIII, for a more comprehensive treatment of fiscal and monetary policies during this period. This author has drawn heavily on the latter work (by permission) in preparing this section.

[10] The overall reductions were as follows: Against demand deposits: central-reserve cities from 26 to 22 percent; reserve cities from 22 to 18 percent; country banks from 16 to 12 percent. Against time deposits: from 7½ to 5 percent.

An interesting aspect of open-market operations during this period was the conflict between the goals of stabilization of government-security prices and stabilization of business. Federal Reserve authorities would probably have created larger net free reserves and lower rates had they not been committed to a fixed interest-rate pattern. That is, Reserve Banks sold more securities to prevent an excessive rise in bond prices than was in harmony with promotion of business recovery. The dilemma was brought out sharply in the following public statement by the Federal Open-Market Committee at midyear 1949.

> The Federal Open-Market Committee, after consultation with the Treasury, announced today that with a view to increasing the supply of funds available in the market to meet the needs of commerce, business, and agriculture it will be the policy of the Committee to direct purchases, sales, and exchanges of Government securities by the Federal Reserve Banks with primary regard to the general business and credit situation. The policy of maintaining orderly conditions in the Government security market, and the confidence of investors in Government bonds, will be continued. Under present conditions the maintenance of a relatively fixed pattern of rates has the undesirable effect of absorbing reserves from the market at a time when the availability of credit should be increased.[11]

The foregoing statement constituted some departure from maintenance of a fixed rate pattern when confronted with a business decline. It did not state, however, that the fixed pattern would be modified under opposite conditions—that is, to permit a rise of rates when confronted with an inflationary expansion. Nevertheless, this pronouncement was significant as another small breach in the sacred postwar doctrine of stable interest rates, foreshadowing its rejection in early 1951.

fiscal and debt-management policies

The difficulty under existing arrangements of using the federal budget to promote economic stability was well illustrated during the 1949 recession. As previously indicated, Congress took adverse action in 1948. The Revenue Act of 1948, providing for tax reductions estimated at $5 billion, was passed over the President's veto, and appropriations were made calling for about $3 billion additional expenditures. This was at a time when the boom was at its peak. But as events fortuitously worked out, the tax cut became a blessing in disguise, at least in the short run. The federal cash budget surplus of $8 billion in calendar 1948 was transformed into a $1.7 billion deficit in 1949, the first calendar year

[11]Board of Governors of the Federal Reserve System, *Annual Report* (Washington, D.C., 1949), p. 28.

in which tax reduction registered its delayed effects.[12] This was one of the strongest moderating forces in the recession, yet it was a result of Congress doing the right thing at the right time for the wrong reasons. No important change in tax rates was made in 1949, so that Congress can at least be given negative credit for not raising rates during recession with a view to balancing the budget.

Debt-management operations during 1949 were in harmony with Federal Reserve policies and contributed to business recovery. Maturing and callable bonds were refunded into short-term certificates and notes. This step provided more short-term securities for bank purchase and therefore tended to increase the money supply; it also withheld Treasury competition with business in the long-term capital market. In addition, the Treasury reduced its deposits with Reserve Banks by about $1 billion—a move that released a corresponding amount of reserves to member banks.

business recovery and war in korea—1950 to spring 1951

Business recovery proceeded rapidly throughout 1950 and until the peak was reached in the spring of 1951. Natural forces were largely responsible until June 1950, but thereafter the pace was quickened by the outbreak of war in Korea. Between the last quarter of 1949 and the first quarter of 1951, industrial production increased by $33\frac{1}{3}$ percent; factory employment, by 18 percent; wholesale prices, by 22 percent; and GNP, by 24 percent. The amount of money (demand deposits and currency) rose by a modest 3.6 percent, but the velocity of demand deposits in leading cities increased by 22 percent. The rise in prices was intensified by speculative consumer and business spending. Fearing that renewed warfare would mean scarce goods at higher prices, consumers bought heavily, especially in the third quarter of 1950 and the first quarter of 1951. Businesses built up inventories at rising prices and also enlarged capital expenditures. What, under these conditions, was the character of monetary and fiscal policies?

Federal Reserve Policies / Alarmed by rising prices and the rapid expansion of loans, the Fed used its narrowly limited powers to restrain credit beginning in August 1950. Reserve Bank discount rates were raised from $1\frac{1}{2}$ to $1\frac{3}{4}$ percent, and insofar as possible open-market operations were used to limit bank reserves. However, it was necessary to support large Treasury refunding operations in the third quarter and to make heavy purchases of bonds after November. Otherwise, sales by insurance companies, banks, and other institutions would have driven prices downward and created a disorderly market. The

[12] *Economic Report of the President* (January 1950), p. 136.

net result was that Reserve Bank holdings of U.S. securities increased about $5 billion between the last quarter of 1949 and the first quarter of 1951. Approximately $2 billion of this was accounted for by a rise in member-bank reserve requirements which became effective gradually during January 1951;[13] the rest mainly by a $2.5 billion reduction in gold stock and a sizable rise in member-bank deposits. The overall consequence was a considerable decline in commercial-bank liquidity as evidenced by a moderate decline of net free reserves, a large increase in loans, and a material reduction in holdings of U.S. securities. As would be expected under these circumstances, interest rates rose moderately.

In addition to use of general instruments, the Fed applied selective controls in the fields of consumer credit and real-estate credit under new powers conferred by the Defense Production Act of 1950. Regulation W, establishing minimum downpayments and maximum maturities on installment credit extended for the purchase of major consumer durable goods, was made effective in September. This form of credit had risen by an unprecedented amount since termination of controls at midyear 1949. The new controls were designed to reduce demand in an area from which resources should be diverted for defense production. Regulation X, restricting residential real-estate credit by prescribing maximum borrowing limits and maximum maturities, became effective in October. Housing construction and the increase of mortgage loans had set new records in 1950. As in the case of consumer credit, the aim was to curb price inflation and to assist in diversion of resources to military production.

fiscal debt-management policies

Congress and the Administration took decisive actions in 1950 to meet the growing war expenditures with tax revenues. Two major revenue measures were passed—the Revenue Act of 1950 and the Excess Profits Tax Act of 1950. Taken together, they were estimated to add $9.3 billion to revenues at the level of incomes in 1951. On the other side, nondefense outlays were cut by over $3 billion. The net result was a budget surplus of $3.5 billion in fiscal 1951, compared with a $3.1 billion deficit in the preceding year. Net cash operating income (surplus) of the Treasury in fiscal 1951—a more significant item for this purpose—was $7.6 billion. Thus, fiscal policy operated as a powerful restraining force. Federal debt-management operations, however, exerted little influence in either direction during the period.

End of Federal Reserve Bondage: Treasury-Federal Reserve Accord, March 1951 / While Federal Reserve authorities became increasingly restive in

[13]Requirements were raised by 2 percentage points against demand deposits and 1 point against time deposits. This placed them at the legal maximum except in central-reserve cities, where they became 24 percent.

their subordinate role following World War II, disagreement with Treasury policies did not come to a head until the last of 1950 and early 1951. As time went on, the shortsightedness of supporting government-security prices in the face of rapidly rising commodity prices became evident to an increasing number of people both inside and outside the Fed. The most influential development in this regard was the series of congressional hearings and the report of the Douglas Committee during the last half of 1949 and early 1950. The report of this committee stated:

> ... Timely flexibility toward easy credit at some times and credit restriction at other times is an essential characteristic of a monetary policy that will promote economic stability rather than instability. . . . we believe that the advantages of avoiding inflation are so great and that a restrictive monetary policy can contribute so much to this end that the freedom of the Federal Reserve to restrict credit and raise interest rates for general stabilization purposes should be restored even if the cost should prove to be a significant increase in service charges on the Federal debt and a greater inconvenience to the Treasury in its sale of securities for new financing and refunding purposes. . . . We recommend that Congress by joint resolution issue general instructions . . . that it is the will of Congress that the primary power and responsibility for regulating the supply, availability, and cost of credit in general shall be vested in the duly constituted authorities of the Federal Reserve System, and that Treasury actions relative to money, credit, and transactions in Federal debt shall be made consistent with the policies of the Federal Reserve.[14]

After the outbreak of war in Korea in June 1950, both the Treasury and the Fed agreed that price inflation should be minimized by increased taxes, restraint on nondefense expenditures, promotion of savings, and selective credit controls. But sharp disagreement developed in regard to use of general instruments of monetary management. The Treasury held the view that maintenance of stable government-security prices was of paramount importance. The Fed believed that the time was overdue for restoration of traditional methods of credit restraint. This involved termination of the all-out support of U.S. securities, declining bond prices, and rising interest rates. Open-market operations could then be used to place member banks under the pressure of borrowing a part of required reserves from Reserve Banks at penalty discount rates. Restraint could be brought to bear on the existing engine of inflation whereby Reserve Banks bought all government securities offered at support prices. These purchases created a new bank reserves which became the basis of subsequent multiple expansion of deposit money.

The divergence of policies took a dramatic turn in connection with the

[14]U.S. Senate, 81st Congress, 2d sess., Report of the Subcommittee on Monetary, Credit, and Fiscal Policies of the Joint Committee on the Economic Report, 1950 (Senator Paul H. Douglas, Chairman), pp. 17-18.

Treasury's $13.5 billion refunding program announced in August 1950. A rate of $1\frac{1}{4}$ percent was fixed for two 13-month note issues offered in exchange. Three days later, the Fed took action to raise the discount rate from $1\frac{1}{2}$ to $1\frac{3}{4}$ percent, and open-market operations permitted short-term rates to rise to levels inconsistent with the Treasury offering. As a result, the refunding operation became a fiasco of the first order. Cash redemptions amounted to $17\frac{1}{2}$ percent compared with a normal 5 percent, and they would have exceeded three-fourths had the Fed not purchased over $8 billion of maturing securities from private holders. A few months later, another refunding program for $8 billion of securities maturing in December 1950 and January 1951 encountered almost equally poor reception. Even though the Fed bought $2.5 billion of maturing securities, only 51 percent was exchanged by private holders, and cash redemptions amounted to $14\frac{1}{2}$ percent.[15]

By this time, the controversy was making headlines and was evoking wide public discussion. In an effort to settle the issue, officials of the Treasury and the Board of Governors met twice with the President during January, and there were other conferences with the banking committees of Congress. In the end, representatives of the Treasury and the Fed were designated to work out a compromise, which resulted in the following joint announcement on March 4, 1951.

> The Treasury and the Federal Reserve System have reached full accord with respect to debt-management and monetary policies to be pursued in furthering their common purpose to assure the successful financing of the Government's requirements and, at the same time, to minimize monetization of the public debt.

The foregoing statement reflected more specific agreements relating to four problems. First, it was agreed that a large part of outstanding marketable long-term bonds would be exchanged for a higher-yielding nonmarketable $2\frac{3}{4}$ percent, 29-year bond, convertible at the holder's option into a $1\frac{1}{2}$ percent, 5-year marketable Treasury note. The purpose was to encourage investors to hold long-term bonds and to reduce the amount of such issues overhanging the market. Second, it was agreed that during the exchange operation the Fed would purchase, if necessary, a limited amount of the marketable bonds to ensure an orderly market. Third, it was agreed that the Fed would reduce purchases of short-term issues, and would permit short-term rates to rise to a level at which banks would choose to adjust reserve positions by borrowing at the Fed; also that the Fed would assure the success of refunding the short-term issues maturing in the near future. Finally, it was agreed that the Treasury and Fed would collaborate more closely in working out programs of government financing and in maintaining an orderly U.S. security market.

Thus, March 4, 1951, the date of the Treasury-Federal Reserve Accord, is a highly significant one in recent monetary and banking annals. At long last,

[15]U.S. Senate, 82nd Congress, 2d sess., Document 123, Part 1, pp. 70-72.

after over a decade of eclipse, the Fed was emancipated. The Treasury recognized that regulation of the money supply, the level and structure of interest rates, and general money-market conditions were primarily Federal Reserve prerogatives. At the same time, the Fed recognized that the various aspects of federal debt management were in the province of the Treasury. Both were keenly aware of the interwoven nature of their respective responsibilities and of the imperative need for close and continuous cooperation.

22

monetary, fiscal, and debt management, 1951 to 1958

The entire period, 1951-1958, is characterized by the Fed's freer hand and more positive role. Analysis will be facilitated by consideration of subperiods: (1) high-level production, first quarter 1951 to mid-1953; (2) second postwar recession, mid-1953 to last quarter of 1954; (3) business recovery and boom, fourth quarter 1954 to mid-1957; and (4) third postwar recession mid-1957 to mid-1958.

HIGH-LEVEL PRODUCTION, FIRST QUARTER 1951 TO MID-1953

In general this period was one of high-level production and employment with stable commodity prices. Fed policy was characterized by moderate restraint which, combined with strong demand for loans, resulted in a marked rise of interest rates.

background developments

A summary of economic and financial developments is required as background for analysis of monetary, fiscal, and debt-management policies. This is found in Table 22-1. Appreciable growth of the economy in real terms is evident from the gain of 11 percent in industrial production, of 6 percent in nonagricultural employment, and of 17 percent in GNP–but with little change in the general price level. The amount of money increased 10 percent–enough to provide for growth at a stable price level. Loans of commercial banks increased \$11.1 billion and investments by \$1.3 billion. All types of bank loans

TABLE 22-1 / SELECTED MEASURES OF ECONOMIC CHANGES, 1951-1953

Measures	1951	1953	Increase (percent)
Gross national product (billions of dollars)	319.5 (Q1)	372.4 (Q2)	16.6
Industrial production (Board of Governors; 1947-1949 = 100)	222.0 (Mar.)	240.0 (June)	10.8
Employment (nonagricultural) (BLS; 1947-1949 = 100)	106.3 (Mar.)	112.7 (June)	6.0
Amount of money (billions of dollars)[a]	113.4 (Mar. 28)	124.3 (June 24)	9.6
Bank loans and investments (billions of dollars)	125.7 (Mar. 28)	138.1 (June 24)	9.9
Wholesale prices (BLS; 1947-1949 = 100)	116.5 (Mar.)	109.5 (June)	−6.0
Consumer prices (BLS; 1947-1949 = 100)	110.3 (Mar.)	114.5 (June)	3.8
Rate on Treasury bills (3-month; percent)	1.4 (Mar.)	2.2 (June)	57.1

[a] Adjusted demand deposits and currency outside banks.

participated, but loans to consumers showed the largest increase, followed in order by business loans and real-estate loans. It will also be observed that wholesale prices and consumer prices moved in opposite directions, so that little change took place in the overall price level. Wholesale prices reflected a decline in prices of farm products and of other basic raw materials, which reached a speculative peak in early 1951.

federal reserve policies and actions

The tone for a Federal Reserve policy of moderate restraint was set by open-market operations. A substantial amount of bonds was purchased by the Fed in support of the major exchange, beginning in April, of nonmarketable $2\frac{3}{4}$ percent bonds for outstanding marketable issues. This Treasury operation removed \$13.6 billion of the $2\frac{1}{2}$ percent bonds of 1967-1972 from the market. It is significant that this support was given on a scale downward, which permitted a decline in price of over 3 percent in long-term issues by the end of 1951. Material support was also given to Treasury refundings during the remainder of 1951 and during 1952. Purchases of maturing issues, however, were largely offset by sale of other issues, so that the net increase in Federal Reserve holdings was moderate. Aside from maintenance of orderly conditions, the Fed weaned the U.S. bond market at the end of 1951. Support for short-term issues was largely withdrawn some nine months earlier, at the time of the Treasury-Federal Reserve Accord.

A highly significant change in policy and procedures, designed to create a freer, more self-reliant U.S. security market, was announced by the Open-Market Committee in March 1953. The various aspects of this change may be summarized, as follows:

1/Transactions of the Open-Market Account would be administered with a view, among other things, "to correcting a disorderly situation in the government securities market" instead of, as previously, "to maintaining orderly conditions in the government securities market." This change set the stage for a "hands-off" policy toward the market except in emergency situations.

2/Operations of the Open-Market Account would be confined to short-term issues, with the exception of transactions required to correct disorderly conditions. As a corollary, there would be no effort to maintain any fixed pattern of prices and yields for different issues and maturity classes.

3/The Committee would "refrain during a period of Treasury financing from . . . purchasing 'rights' evidenced by maturing issues, when-issued securities, and outstanding securities of comparable maturity to those being offered for exchange," except to correct disorderly conditions.

4/Operations in U.S. securities would be "solely to effectuate the objectives of monetary and credit policy."[1]

Thus, taken together these changes (1) materially strengthened open-market operations as a positive instrument of monetary management, and (2) created a freer and more self-reliant U.S. security market in which many of the uncertainties, arising from frequent positive interventions by the Fed, were eliminated.

While holdings of U.S. securities of Reserve Banks rose about $1.8 billion between March 1951 and June 1953, the net result was a policy of moderate pressure on the reserve position of member banks. Other factors—largely an increase in currency and of required reserves against higher deposits—reduced member-bank liquidity more than it was increased by open-market purchases. Consequently, member banks were forced to borrow a larger part of required legal reserves from the Reserve Banks. Discounts and advances rose from $242 million in March 1951 to $1,633 million in December 1952, and averaged about $1,300 million during the first half of 1953. There was also an appreciable decline in overall excess legal reserves. These changes in relationship between credit demand and supply were reflected in rising interest rates. For example, the 3-month Treasury bill rate rose from 1.4 percent in March 1951 to 2.2 percent in June 1953, and the 4-6-month commercial-paper rate rose from 2.03 to 2.75 percent.

Little use was made of the other general instruments of control during

[1]Board of Governors of the Federal Reserve System, *Annual Report* (Washington, D.C., 1953), pp. 87-90.

this period. Legal-reserve requirements had already been raised to the legal maximum in January 1951, except in central-reserve cities, so that little room for action remained. The Federal Reserve discount rate rested at $1\frac{3}{4}$ percent until January 1953 when it was raised to 2 percent. This move, however, was nothing more than a passive adjustment to the rising level of open-market rates. Treasury bill rates were appreciably higher than the discount rate after mid-1952. Why the discount rate was administered so gently and in such a laggard fashion remains a mystery—particularly in view of the major problem of Reserve credit rationing that arose because bank reserve deficiencies could be repaired more cheaply by borrowing than by the sale of short-term U.S. securities.

Selective credit controls were utilized to restrain credit expansion during the early months of this period, but thereafter they played a minor role. Congress curtailed the Board's power to regulate consumer credit by the 1951 amendment of the Defense Production Act, and withdrew this power entirely, effective June 30, 1952. As a consequence, Regulation W was a minor influence after its liberalization at the end of July 1951. Similarly, Congress reduced the Board's power to regulate real-estate credit in 1951 and 1952. In line with these legal changes, the Board eased Regulation X in June 1952, and suspended it entirely in September 1952. The relatively high margin requirement of 75 percent on stock-exchange security loans, established in January 1951, remained in effect until February 1953, when it was reduced to 50 percent.

A more detailed summary of the changes that occurred during the period following the Treasury-Federal Reserve Accord is given in Table 22-2. By way of interpretation, attention is called to strategic changes, as follows: (1) The legal-reserve position of member banks was tightened by a decrease of $122 million in excess reserves and an increase of $713 million in borrowed reserves; that is, the net reserve position deteriorated by $835 million. (2) This deterioration arose principally from (a) an increase of money in circulation of $2,698 million, (b) an increase in required reserves of $812 million, and (c) a Federal Reserve policy of moderate pressure, which refrained from increasing holdings of U.S. securities enough to compensate for (a) and (b), after allowing for the sizable increase of gold and other factor changes. Thus, member banks were forced to borrow a larger portion of required reserves which were higher because of the growth in deposits. (3) The ascendancy of credit demand over credit supply, as evidenced by the foregoing changes, led to appreciably higher interest rates.

fiscal policies

A summary of the federal budget for the years 1951-1953 is given in Table 22-3 as background for consideration of fiscal policies. When the Korean crisis occurred, it became evident that a large increase in expenditures for military purposes would be necessary. President Truman publicly recommended

TABLE 22-2 / MEMBER-BANK RESERVES AND FACTORS OF CHANGE, MARCH 1951 AND MAY 1953 (millions of dollars)

	March 1951	May 1953	Factors of Increase	Factors of Decrease
Factors of supply				
Reserve Bank credit				
Discounts and advances	242	955	713	
U.S. securities	22,333	23,973	1,640	
Float and other	1,088	754		334
Gold stock	21,909	22,557	648	
Treasury currency	4,639	4,843	204	
Factors of demand				
Money in circulation	27,171	29,869		2,698
Treasury cash and deposits	1,892	1,635	257	
Foreign and nonmember deposits	1,212	902	310	
Other Federal Reserve accounts	730	779		49
Total factors of increase			3,772	
Total factors of decrease				3,081
Member-bank reserve balances	19,207	19,897	690[a]	
Required reserves	18,494	19,306		
Excess reserves	713	591		
U.S. Treasury 3-month bill rate	1.4%	2.2%		
Commercial-paper rate, 4-6-month	2.0%	2.7%		

[a]Discrepancy of 1 million arises from rounding of figures.
Source: *Federal Reserve Bulletin* (April 1952), p. 404; (December 1953), p. 1336.

TABLE 22-3 / FEDERAL CASH BUDGET FOR FISCAL YEARS ENDED JUNE 30, 1951-1953 (millions of dollars)

Year	Net Receipts	Total Expenditures	Surplus or Deficit	Cash Surplus or Deficit
1951	47,568	44,058	+3,510	+7,715
1952	61,391	65,408	–4,017	+ 287
1953	64,825	74,274	–9,449	–5,062

Source: Secretary of the Treasury, *Annual Report* (Washington, D.C., 1955), pp. 350-351, 395.

a pay-as-you-go policy, and emphasized that higher taxes were our best weapon against the developing inflationary pressure. The Revenue Act of 1950 (September), which embodied most of the Treasury's suggestions, raised individual and corporate income-tax rates, and provided about $6 billion additional annual revenue. Then, in January 1951, another $4 billion was provided by the Excess Profits Tax Act which imposed a tax of 30 percent on corporate profits above a designated normal base.[2] In his tax message to Congress in February 1951, the President again recommended a tax increase sufficient to preserve a balanced budget, and shortly afterward the Treasury proposed changes to yield about $10 billion of annual revenue. Congress, however, provided for only a $5.4 billion increase in the Revenue Act of 1951. Individual income-tax rates were raised to a range of between 22.2 and 92 percent; the corporate rate was raised to 52 percent, so that the marginal rate, including the excess-profits tax, became 82 percent. Increases were also made in the excise and capital-gains taxes, but the bulk of the burden fell on individual and corporate income. No further significant changes affecting the level of taxes were made up to midyear 1953.

A closer view of Table 22-3 shows that the Revenue Act of 1950 provided a surplus of $7.7 billion in the cash budget in fiscal 1951. In 1952, there was a near balance in the cash budget. But in 1953, the continued rise of expenditures outstripped the modest increase of revenues, so that the cash budget registered a sizable deficit of $5.1 billion.

All this raises the question: Did fiscal policy positively contribute to, or did it obstruct the realization of, basic monetary objectives—high-level production without price inflation—in these years? Both the President and the Treasury deserve a clean bill of health, at least with respect to the level of taxation. Had their recommendations been followed, there would have been a surplus in both budgets over the three-year period. The record of Congress is not so praiseworthy. It should be commended for quick passage of the Revenue Act of 1950 and the Excess Profits Tax Act, which together provided the budget surplus in 1951. But Congress' subsequent failure to provide sufficient revenues constituted a strong inflationary force which contributed to the 1952-1953 inflationary expansion and the reaction that followed. Moreover, had tax policy been positive or neutral instead of in opposition, the burden on the Fed to check overexpansion would have been materially lightened.

federal debt management

On the whole, the debt-management operations of the Treasury made a positive contribution to the Federal Reserve policy of moderate restraint during this period. First, thrift was encouraged by actively promoting sale of U.S. savings bonds. In addition to encouraging systematic saving by payroll deductions and in other ways, yields on Series E bonds were raised, both in the intermediate stage and at maturity, effective May 1, 1952. Also, a new current-income savings bond, Series H, was offered beginning June 1, 1952. The

[2]The base was 85 percent of the three highest base-period years 1946-1949. The Revenue Act of 1951 reduced this percentage to 83 and limited the maximum excess-profits tax to 18 percent of total net income.

yield on both Series E and Series H bonds, if held to maturity ($9\frac{2}{3}$ years), was fixed at 3 percent.

Second, the Treasury attempted to shift ownership of federal debt from the banks to nonbank holders, and thereby, with Federal Reserve support, to reduce the amount of deposit money. This was done in various ways. One was promotion of savings bonds as just described. Another was a systematic effort to offer types of securities and terms that would meet investment needs of other classes of nonbank investors. For example, offerings included long-term issues to appeal to life insurance companies and mutual savings banks, and tax-savings notes, tax-anticipation bills, and regular bills to meet the needs of corporations for short-term investments. In the three fiscal years 1951-1953, bank-held federal debt declined about $300 million despite an increase of $8.7 billion in total debt outstanding.

Finally, in line with the Treasury-Federal Reserve Accord, the Treasury recognized the primacy of the Fed in determination of monetary policies and money market conditions. It cooperated more fully in harmonizing debt-management operations and monetary policies. This was evident both by the absence of countering actions and by positive assistance in implementing monetary policies even though it might mean higher interest costs. A first step in creating a more favorable environment for Federal Reserve freedom of action was the offer in March 1951 to exchange nonmarketable $2\frac{3}{4}$ percent bonds, due April 1, 1980, for two marketable issues outstanding in the amount of $19.7 billion. Exchanges amounted to $13.6 billion. In May 1952, the offer of nonmarketable $2\frac{3}{4}$ percent bonds was reopened for cash subscription and for exchange of four outstanding long-term, marketable issues. Cash subscriptions were $450 million and exchanges were $1,307 million. The object was to withdraw part of the large volume of long-term marketable issues and thereby reduce the Fed's problem of maintaining orderly conditions during the transition to a freer government-security market.

The second step involved extension of maturities of the federal debt, so that Federal Reserve regulatory action would have a more immediate and more powerful response in the money market. That is, the reduction of short-term issues in the hands of banks and other lenders would modify their ability to expand loans by disposing of such holdings. The Treasury also desired to lengthen maturities in order to simplify its refunding problem, as evidenced by the fact that in calendar 1953, maturities and redemptions exceeded $60 billion—nearly one-fourth of the entire federal debt. The intermediate- and long-term bond offerings were as follows: A 7-year, $2\frac{3}{8}$ percent bond was issued in March 1952 in the amount of $927 million in exchange for a maturing issue. This was followed in July by a 6-year, $2\frac{3}{8}$ percent bond offered for cash and issued in the amount of $4,245 million. Then followed two bond offerings under the Eisenhower Administration which declared the lengthening of maturities to be one of its major financial goals. A 5-year, 10-month, $2\frac{1}{2}$ percent bond was issued February 15, 1953 to the amount of $620 million in exchange for maturing issues. The second offering was a 30-year, $3\frac{1}{4}$ percent bond issued May 1, 1953 to the amount of $1,606 million. This was the longest issue since 1941. Thus, with increasing tempo, the Treasury aided the Federal Reserve policy of restraint by offering intermediate- and long-term securities in the capital market.[3]

RECESSION, MID-1953 TO FOURTH QUARTER 1954

By midyear 1953, it became apparent that the expansion phase had reached its zenith, and as time moved on that the immediate danger was one of business recession. This called for a major change in monetary, fiscal, and debt-management policies. In the section that follows, these policy changes are explored in the light of changing economic conditions.

economic developments

The last year of the expansion which culminated at midyear 1953 was marked by rising military expenditures and by expanding private-investment outlays. A strategic element of private investment was accumulation of business inventories which grew at the annual rate of $8.8 billion in the second quarter. After midyear, the pace of inventory accumulation slackened. Then the Korean truce in July led to sharply reduced military orders and expenditures, which, in turn, resulted in further curtailment of business spending.

Table 22-4 shows the course of selected measures of recession between the high points of 1953 and the low points of 1954. It will be noted that the declines of industrial production and of manufacturing employment were in the range of 10 to 12 percent, and that GNP declined only 4 percent. The largest decline took place in federal expenditures—23 percent—and the next largest occurred in private investment—19 percent. Only nominal changes were registered in the amount of money and the level of commodity prices. The business decline was arrested in the first quarter of 1954, after which it reached bottom during the second and third quarters; definite progress toward recovery was made in the last quarter. Thus, the second postwar recession was a minor cycle in terms of both depth and length. Consumer expenditures and residential construction were the strong components that moderated the decline and sparked the recovery.

[3]The statistical information with respect to fiscal and debt-management operations in the sections above is drawn largely from Secretary of the Treasury, *Annual Report* (Washington, D.C., 1951, 1952, 1953).

TABLE 22-4 / MEASURES OF RECESSION, MID-1953 TO FOURTH QUARTER 1954

Measures	High Point, 1953	Low Point, 1954	Change (percent)
Industrial production (FRB; 1947-1949 = 100)	137.0 (July)	123.0 (Aug.)	−10.2
Employment in manufacturing (BLS; 1947-1949 = 100)	114.0 (June)	99.7 (Aug.)	−12.5
Gross national product (billions of dollars)	369.9 (Q1)	355.5 (Q3)	− 3.9
Gross private domestic investment (billions of dollars)	55.9 (Q2)	45.3 (Q3)	−19.0
Federal expenditures (billions of dollars)	62.2 (Q3)	47.9 (Q3)	−23.0
Amount of money (billions of dollars)[a]	124.3 (June 24)	125.2 (June 30)	+ 0.7
Wholesale prices (BLS; 1947-1949 = 100)	110.9 (July)	109.7 (Oct.)	− 1.1
Consumer prices (BLS; 1947-1949 = 100)	114.7 (July)	114.5 (Oct.)	− 0.2
Yield on Treasury bills (percent)	2.23 (June)	0.65 (June)	−71.3

[a]Adjusted demand deposits and currency outside banks.
Source: *Federal Reserve Bulletin,* various issues.

federal reserve policies

This brings us to the question: What changes in monetary policies were made by the Fed in response to impending recession? In general, the policy of restraint, which had been applied with increasing force during the last half of 1952 and into May 1953, was quickly reversed and was soon transformed to one of active ease. The purpose was to check business decline and to speed recovery by making credit abundantly available at low rates. All general instruments of control were coordinated to this end.

Open-market operations initiated the change in policy in May 1953 and set the tone of money market conditions. Between April and October 1953, Reserve Bank holdings of U.S. securities were increased by about $1.5 billion—a step that released an equivalent amount of member-bank reserves. After this time, the amount of such holdings declined moderately in order to compensate for sizable reductions in legal-reserve requirements.

The strongest easing action was exerted by lowering legal-reserve requirements of member banks. This was done in two steps. The first, in early July 1953, reduced requirements by about $1.2 billion; the second, in late July 1954, lowered them by another $1.6 billion—in all a total of $2.8 billion.[4]

[4]Taken, together, these changes reduced requirements from 24 to 20 percent in central-reserve cities, from 20 to 18 percent in reserve cities, and from 14 to 12 percent in country banks. Requirements against time deposits were lowered in all member banks from 6 to 5 percent.

These steps not only converted required reserves into excess reserves but also appreciably increased the multiple of bank-credit expansion on the basis of each dollar of excess reserves. The reduction of reserve requirements in July 1954 provides an interesting illustration of the compensatory use of open-market operations. In the absence of other changes, the reduction of requirements would have created an excessively easy money market. Consequently, the Reserve Banks reduced their holdings of U.S. securities by an amount sufficient to maintain the desired balance between supply and demand. This involved a reduction of over $1 billion in their security portfolio between July and September.

Changes in the Federal Reserve discount rate played a minor role during the 1954 recession. The rate was reduced in two steps from 2 to 1½ percent—the first from 2 to 1¾ during the first half of February; the second from 1¾ to 1½ percent in April-May. These represented delayed adjustments to lower open-market rates which had already emerged largely as a result of the other Federal Reserve actions just described. Because most banks had no borrowing needs, the level of the discount rate was, in general, a matter of indifference.

A summary review of monetary developments indicates aggressive Federal Reserve action to combat the 1953-1954 recession. The combined effects of purchases of U.S. securities and reduction in reserve requirements brought about a marked increase in liquidity of commercial banks. Member banks were enabled to repay over $1,000 million of indebtedness to Reserve Banks and at the same time to increase excess reserves by more than $300 million—a net improvement in legal-reserve position of about $1.3 billion. Also, they were able to improve their liquidity-reserve position substantially, as evidenced by the fact that holdings of U.S. securities—mainly short-term issues—increased almost $11 billion between the end of May 1953 and the end of October 1954. This increase occurred despite a rise of both total loans and other securities in the combined amount of $3.2 billion. The response of the money market to such an impressive improvement in bank liquidity was a sharp decline of interest rates. The Treasury bill rate dropped from 2.20 percent in May 1953 to 0.65 percent in June 1954, and between the same dates the open-market commercial-paper rate declined from 2.75 to 1.56 percent.

There is no doubt that the timely and vigorous antirecessionary steps of the Fed were a major force in checking the business decline and fostering quick recovery. As previously noted, the amount of money actually increased, instead of declining as in most previous recessions. In fact, some critics of Federal Reserve policies, including the chairman of the board, hold the view that reserve money was made excessively abundant for too long a time, with the result that the groundwork was laid for the ensuing inflationary expansion.

fiscal policies

Whether by design or by chance, fiscal policies and operations significantly reenforced Federal Reserve antirecessionary actions. The largest tax reduction in the country's history up until that time—$7.4 billion—became effective during fiscal 1954. Expiration of the excess-profits tax at the end of 1953 meant a saving of about $2 billion, and reversion of individual income-tax rates to the basis that prevailed before the Revenue Act of 1951 accounted for another $3 billion; the remaining $2.4 billion of the reduction came from lower excise taxes and structural changes in the tax system.

A more concrete understanding of the state of the federal budget in fiscal 1954 and 1955 can be gained from Table 22-5. Net receipts in 1954 were

TABLE 22-5 / THE FEDERAL BUDGET, FISCAL 1954 AND 1955 (millions of dollars)

Fiscal Year	Net Budget Receipts	Total Expenditures	Surplus or Deficit	Cash Surplus or Deficit
1954	64,655	67,772	−3,117	− 232
1955	60,390	64,570	−4,180	−2,712

Source: Secretary of the Treasury, *Annual Report* (Washington, D.C., 1955), pp. 350-351, 395.

not much lower than in the previous year because of the high level of income in 1953. The economy drive of the Eisenhower Administration resulted in a reduction of $6.5 billion in total expenditures, distributed throughout the budget, but with about two-thirds of the savings in the categories of "National security" and "International affairs and finance." The net result was an administrative budget deficit of $3.1 billion and a cash deficit of $232 million. While expenditures were reduced further in 1955, receipts declined even more, due to the full impact of lower tax rates and the lower level of income. Consequently, the federal deficit was running at a higher rate during the second half of calendar 1954 than during fiscal 1954.

federal debt management

The role of debt management during fiscal 1954 and the last half of calendar 1954 was a neutral or passive one. At first glance, one might easily reach the conclusion that Treasury operations exerted a significant influence in opposition to the Federal Reserve policy of monetary ease. The objective of lengthening the average maturity of marketable issues was frequently reiterated in public statements, and the savings-bond program was aggressively promoted. Neither of these policies was consistent with the positive use of debt management to stem the cyclical decline—which called for borrowing at the banks and shifting debt from nonbank holders to the banks. In fact, the average maturity of the debt was extended from 4 to $4\frac{1}{2}$ years during this period. But all marketable issues offered, aggregating $88.7 billion, were short- and intermediate-term securities appropriate for commercial-bank investment, and were purchased in large volume by banks.

BUSINESS EXPANSION, FOURTH QUARTER 1954 TO THIRD QUARTER 1957

Recovery from the 1954 recession, which began during the autumn of the year, proceeded with only minor interruptions until, by the end of 1955, the economy again approached capacity output. From this point on until the third quarter of 1957, effective demand exceeded supply, with the result that control of rising prices became a major national problem. Under these conditions, the Fed reversed its easy-money policy of 1954 and adopted a policy of restraint, mild at first but with increasing pressure, especially during the first three quarters of 1957. A more complete review of economic developments and of monetary-fiscal policies follows.

economic developments

Table 22-6 provides a summary view of the extent and character of expansion between the last quarter of 1954 and the third quarter of 1957. Industrial production increased 15 percent and nonagricultural employment rose 10 percent. The most dynamic factors accounting for the 23 percent increase of GNP were the 34 percent expansion of private investment and the 28 percent rise in expenditures of state and local governments. However, the dominant factor in absolute terms was the 19 percent increase in personal-consumption expenditures. Monetary controls held the increase in money to only 3.6 percent, but rising velocity of money permitted an increase in the general price level of about 7 percent. When allowance is made for rising prices, the growth of total output was in the vicinity of 11 percent.

Other significant developments were that (1) the initial stimuli of recovery came from outlays for consumer durable goods which focused on automobiles and housing; (2) after the second quarter of 1955, the dynamic influences became investment outlays of business, consumer spending for nondurables and services, state and local expenditures, and increased exports; (3) automobiles and home-building lagged during 1956 and 1957, but this was more than offset by the rise of other types of construction and the influences just listed; (4) the rise of wholesale prices began in mid-1955 and progressed steadily thereafter; and (5) consumer prices remained steady until mid-1956, after which the rise was continuous.

TABLE 22-6 / MEASURE OF RECOVERY, 1954-1957

Measures	Low Point, Fourth Quarter 1954		High Point, Third Quarter 1957		Change (percent)
Industrial production (FRB; 1947-1949 = 100)	126.0	(Oct.)	145.0	(Aug.)	+ 15.1
Nonagricultural employment (BLS; 1947-1949 = 100)	110.3	(Oct.)	120.8	(Aug.)	+ 9.5
Gross national product (billions of dollars)	362.0		445.6		+ 23.1
Consumer expenditures (billions of dollars)	237.7		283.6		+ 19.3
Gross private domestic investment (billions of dollars)	49.5		66.5		+ 34.3
Federal expenditures (billions of dollars)	45.9		50.6		+ 10.2
State and local expenditures (billions of dollars)	28.2		36.1		+ 28.0
Amount of money (billions of dollars)[a]	130.0	(Oct. 27)	134.7	(Aug.)	+ 3.6
Wholesale prices (BLS; 1947-1949 = 100)	109.7	(Oct.)	118.4	(Aug.)	+ 7.9
Consumer prices (BLS; 1947-1949 = 100)	114.3	(Dec.)	121.1	(Sept.)	+ 5.9
Yield on Treasury bills (percent)	0.93	(Nov.)	3.58	(Sept.)	+284.9

[a]Adjusted demand deposits and currency outside banks.
Source: *Federal Reserve Bulletin,* various issues.

federal reserve policies

As the evidences of recovery became more numerous in the last quarter of 1954, the Fed retreated from its policy of "active ease," at first by open-market operations. Net surplus reserves, which exceeded $600 million in the third quarter, were permitted to decline to $300 million in December and to an average of about $100 million through July 1955. From that point on through 1957, net borrowed reserves appeared as Federal Reserve holdings of U.S. securities were reduced. That is, member banks were forced to borrow increasing amounts until borrowings exceeded excess reserves. From April through September 1957, net borrowed reserves were in the vicinity of $500 million. The marked deterioration in bank liquidity and the increasing demand for bank loans resulted in a sharp rise of interest rates.

As market interest rates rose, the Federal Reserve discount rate was increased promptly, in rough correspondence with the yield on Treasury bills. The first increase—from $1\frac{1}{2}$ to $1\frac{3}{4}$ percent—became effective in April 1955. After that there were six further increases which culminated in a rate of $3\frac{1}{2}$ percent in August 1957—three in 1955, two in 1956, and one in 1957. It is significant that the discount rate was employed much more promptly and actively than in the previous boom of 1952-1953, when the only increase was $\frac{1}{4}$ percentage point to 2 percent in January 1953. No change in legal-reserve requirements was made during this period.

Margin requirements on security loans were raised twice—from 50 to 60 percent in early January 1955, and from 60 to 70 percent in late April—where they remained throughout 1956 and 1957. Because the power to regulate consumer credit and real-estate credit lapsed in 1952 and 1953, respectively, the change of margin on security loans was the only selective instrument available. From time to time, moral suasion was utilized through communications with member banks and by public statements which counseled conservatism in extension of speculative credit.

A more definite summary of the change during this period in reserve position of member banks and the factors responsible therefore is given in Table 22-7. By way of interpretation, attention is called to the following: (1) member banks borrowed $824 million more at the Fed in September 1957 than in

TABLE 22-7 / CHANGES IN RESERVE POSITION OF MEMBER BANKS BETWEEN SEPTEMBER 1954 AND SEPTEMBER 1957 (millions of dollars)

Factors of Change	September 1954	September 1957	Changes Increasing Member-Bank Reserves	Changes Reducing Member-Bank Reserves
Source factors				
Reserve Bank credit				
U.S. securities	23,941	23,325		616
Discounts and advances	170	994	824	
Float and other	726	1,170	444	
Gold stock	21,809	22,627	818	
Treasury currency	4,967	5,121	154	
Use factors				
Currency in circulation	29,991	31,143		1,152
Treasury cash and deposits	1,337	1,310	27	
Foreign and other deposits	953	649	304	
Other Federal Reserve accounts	929	1,180		251
Member-bank reserve balances	18,403	18,956		553
Required reserves	17,628	18,434		
Excess reserves	775	522		
Rate on U.S. Treasury bills (percent)	1.01	3.58		
Rate on 4-6-month commercial paper (percent)	1.31	4.00		

Source: ***Federal Reserve Bulletin*** **(April 1955), pp. 373, 395; (December 1957), pp. 1368, 1385; averages of daily figures.**

September 1954, while at the same time their excess reserves declined $253 million—a deterioration of $1,077 million in reserve liquidity; (2) stated differently, a net reserve surplus of $605 million deteriorated to a net reserve deficit of $472 million; (3) the reduction in bank liquidity combined with rising demand for credit resulted in a sharp rise of interest rates to the highest level since 1929; (4) Treasury bill rates rose from 1.01 to 3.58 percent, and the rate on open-market commercial paper increased from 1.3 to 4 percent; (5) the main factors responsible for reduced liquidity of member banks were (a) increase of currency, (b) rise of required reserves, which was a result of expansion of deposits, and (c) reduction of Federal Reserve holdings of U.S. securities; and (6) member banks were forced to draw down excess reserves and to borrow heavily despite sizable additions to their reserves from (a) gold stock, (b) float, and (c) reduction of foreign and other deposits at Fed Banks.

While Table 22-7 shows the reduction of bank liquidity in terms of legal-reserve position, it conveys only a partial view of the overall deterioration in the proportion of liquid asset holdings. Between the third quarter of 1954 and the third quarter of 1957, holdings of U.S. securities (largely short-term) of all commercial banks declined about $13 billion, and total loans increased over $26 billion. This marked reduction in liquidity reserves and change in character of assets must also be weighed heavily in explaining the sharp rise of rates.

In retrospect, the restraining actions of the Fed were not sufficient to prevent a rise of prices of about 7 percent during 1956 and 1957. The incoming tide of business investment, consumer expenditures, and state and local outlays was too strong to contain. Nevertheless, there is no doubt that Federal Reserve restraints significantly contributed to stability. Without them, the rise of prices and other excesses in the economy would have been materially greater, and the ensuing recession would have been more serious.

fiscal policies

As in the preceding period, fiscal policies and operations were in harmony with Federal Reserve objectives. Table 22-8 shows that federal budget receipts exceeded expenditures in both fiscal 1956 and 1957. As a consequence, it was possible to reduce the public debt by $1.6 billion and $2.2 billion,

TABLE 22-8 / THE FEDERAL BUDGET, FISCAL 1956 AND 1957 (millions of dollars)

Fiscal Year	Net Budget Receipts	Total Expenditures	Surplus or Deficit	Cash Surplus or Deficit
1956	68,165	66,540	+1,626	+4,471
1957	71,029	69,433	+1,596	+2,099

Source: Secretary of the Treasury, *Annual Report* (Washington, D.C., 1957), pp. 338-339, 400.

respectively. This policy of budget conservatism provided a check rein on the inflationary business expansion. That is, expenditures by individuals and businesses were restricted by taxation, and the budget surplus could be used to retire bank-held debt, and thereby reduce the amount of money.

Strong leadership was given by the President to defer tax reduction until the national security program would permit a sufficient decline in expenditures to preserve a balanced budget. This recommendation encountered wholehearted support by conservative members of Congress, but it met with vigorous opposition by those who supported tax reduction. The most crucial political struggle on this issue took place in early 1955, after the following Presidential recommendations: (1) that the corporate income tax be maintained at the 52 percent rate instead of being permitted to revert to 47 percent on April 1—a drop of about \$2 billion in revenue—and (2) that excise-tax rates on alcoholic beverages, cigarettes, automobiles, gasoline, and other commodities also be maintained rather than be permitted to decline automatically on April 1—a drop of another \$1 billion in revenue. The House of Representatives passed a bill denying these recommendations and providing, in addition, a cut in individual income taxes of some \$2.3 billion—a total tax reduction of about \$5.3 billion. But the Senate supported the President, and in the end the corporate income-tax rate and the excise rates were extended one year, and individual income-tax rates were not altered in the tax bill approved in March 1955.

Congress gave stronger support to the President's recommendations in both January 1956 and 1957 that the corporate income-tax rate of 52 percent and the excise rates be extended another year. As previously indicated, this program provided sufficient revenues to meet expenditures, and in addition, created modest budget surpluses in 1956 and 1957.

In conclusion, fiscal policy made a positive contribution to business stability during the period under review in that budget surpluses limited private spending and permitted reduction in the rate of growth of money. The only justifiable criticism of fiscal policy as related to economic stability is one of degree. With benefit of hindsight, a somewhat higher level of taxation, combined perhaps with reduction of selected items of expenditure, would have suppressed the inflationary expansion of 1956-1957. At the same time, a more active fiscal policy in this direction would have lessened the burden of control that was faced by the Fed.

federal debt management

Analysis of Treasury debt management during this period reveals that some operations contributed to economic stability whereas others tended to magnify the boom. On the side of stability, the Treasury applied cash surpluses to retirement of U.S. securities owned by commercial banks. This gave an assist to the Fed in its efforts to check increases in the money supply. But Treasury operations with respect to maturities were expansionary when they should have exerted restraint. In the interest of stabilization, maturities should have been lengthened. But instead, they were appreciably shortened with a resultant contribution to asset liquidity. More specifically, between midyear 1955 and September 30, 1957, the amount of federal marketable securities maturing within one year rose from $51.2 to $77.8 billion, or from 32.9 to 48.1 percent of the total; furthermore, the amount maturing within five years rose from $97.6 to $124.3 billion, or from 62.8 to 76.8 percent of the total. At the other end of the scale, the amount maturing in over ten years declined from $11.9 to $8.1 billion, or from 9.7 to 5.1 percent of the total.[5] In addition to augmenting the liquidity of the economy, these operations tended to lower long-term interest rates in relation to short-term rates, and made long-term funds more readily available to finance the private investment boom. In short, the Treasury placed the objective of low-cost borrowing above the goals of economic stability and price-level stability.

Viewing fiscal policies and debt management together, one is led to the conclusion that the major error was in the former. Had Congress and the Administration increased tax rates and reduced federal expenditures, this powerful weapon could have assumed its proper share of the control program, with the result that Treasury debt management and Federal Reserve operations would not have been confronted with such formidable problems.

BUSINESS DECLINE, THIRD QUARTER 1957 TO SECOND QUARTER 1958

The strong cyclical upswing which began in the third quarter of 1954 came to an abrupt end in the third quarter of 1957. Business investment in plant, equipment, and inventories—the most active force in the expansion—had built up excess capacity in many industries. Retail sales of durable goods began to lag in late summer and early autumn, and federal spending and new orders for defense purposes were curtailed during the summer. In this atmosphere, business spending and inventory policies experienced a sharp reversal. Later in the year, the decline in domestic activity was further aggravated by a material decline in exports to foreign countries. Faced with a developing recession, Federal Reserve policy shifted, beginning in October, from one of restraint to one of monetary ease.

measures of business decline

Table 22-9 provides a more specific view of the decline between the third quarter of 1957 and the second quarter of 1958. The drop in industrial

[5]Secretary of the Treasury, *Annual Report* (Washington, D.C., 1958), p. 475; *Treasury Bulletin* (December 1957), p. 39.

TABLE 22-9 / MEASURES OF RECESSION, THIRD QUARTER 1957 TO SECOND QUARTER 1958

Measures	High Point Third Quarter 1957	Low Point Second Quarter 1958	Change (percent)
Industrial production, total (FRB; 1947-1949 = 100)	145.0 (Aug.)	126.0 (Apr.)	−13.1
Durable goods	163.0	131.0	−19.6
Nondurable goods	132.0	125.0	− 5.3
Manufacturing employment (BLS; 1947-1949 = 100)	103.3 (Sept.)	92.3 (May)	−10.6
Gross national product (billions of dollars)	445.6	430.4	− 3.4
Consumer expenditures	288.3	288.3	0
Gross private domestic investment	66.7	50.7	−24.0
Change in business inventories	+2.2	−6.5	
Federal expenditures	50.9	50.7	− 0.4
State and local expenditures	36.1	39.1	+ 8.3
Amount of money (billions of dollars)[a]	134.7 (Aug.)	135.0 (Apr.)	+ 0.2
Wholesale prices (BLS; 1947-1949 = 100)	118.4 (Aug.)	119.2 (June)	+ 0.7
Consumer prices (BLS; 1947-1949 = 100)	121.1 (Sept.)	123.7 (June)	+ 2.1
Yield on Treasury bills (percent)	3.58 (Sept.)	0.83 (June)	−76.8

[a]Adjusted demand deposits and currency outside banks.
Source: *Federal Reserve Bulletin,* various issues.

production which centered in durable goods was 13 percent; manufacturing employment declined 11 percent, disregarding an appreciable reduction in hours worked per week. The number of unemployed rose from 2.5 to 5.2 million—from 3.9 to 7.7 percent of the civilian labor force. The sharp decline of 24 percent in private domestic investment more than accounted for the drop of 3.4 percent in GNP. Consumer expenditures remained steady, and positive support was given by enlarged state and local outlays. The amount of money remained about the same as a consequence of Federal Reserve additions to bank reserves, which enabled the banks to increase investment holdings. A notable feature of the period was the rise of prices, even though moderate. This was in contrast with all previous recessions of this magnitude, which were marked by declining prices.

fed policies

Moving cautiously because of the continued rise of commodity prices, the Fed began to ease restraints on bank expansion in mid-October 1957. As usual, the first instrument employed was open-market operations. Holdings of U.S. securities were gradually increased by about $2 billion until member-bank net surplus reserves reached the desired maximum during April-July 1958. In mid-November 1957, a decisive change in policy was signaled when the Federal Reserve discount rate was reduced from $3\frac{1}{2}$ to 3 percent. In three more steps after the turn of the year, the discount rate was lowered to $1\frac{3}{4}$ percent by mid-April 1958. Reserve requirements were also reduced beginning in late February 1958 by about $1.5 billion.[6] The combined effects of open-market purchases and lower reserve requirements conspicuously eased the net reserve position of commercial banks. For example, member-bank borrowing at Reserve Banks declined from $1,000 million in mid-October 1957 to an average of $125 million in April-July 1958. At the same time, excess reserves rose from $530 million to around $650 million. Thus, net borrowed reserves of $470 million were converted to net surplus reserves of $525 million—an overall improvement in legal-reserve liquidity of $1 billion. As one would expect under these conditions of abundant liquidity and slackened demand for credit, interest rates dropped precipitately, and bond prices rose. Treasury bill rates declined from 3.58 percent in October 1957 to 0.83 percent in June 1958; the commercial-paper rate dropped from 4.10 to 1.50 percent; and yields on long-term U.S. bonds declined from 3.73 to 3.19 percent.

fiscal policies

Aside from the automatic stabilizing features of the federal budget, no concerted fiscal program was undertaken to stem the recession and to promote recovery. Early in 1958, a powerful congressional group from both major parties sponsored a reduction in taxes on the theory that without such action the sharp downturn was likely to become cumulative and to develop into a major depression. Many of the same group also favored quick action on a public-works program. But the Administration held fast against a cut in taxes, at least until it became more certain that the economy would not respond to natural forces aided by easy money and automatic budget influences. In the end, Congress took no significant action on taxes.

On the expenditures side, three noteworthy steps were taken. Congress and the Administration speeded up the large national highway-construction program. Actual outlays, however, did not begin to increase until the summer and autumn of 1958, well after the spring upturn. This was still another illustration of the inflexibility of public works as a method of cyclical control. In addition to its lagging initial influence, there was a real danger that the maximum impact might occur after full employment had been reached. The

[6]Requirements against demand deposits were reduced, as follows: central-reserve cities from 20 to 18 percent; reserve cities from 18 to 16½ percent; country banks from 12 to 11 percent. The requirement against time deposits was left unchanged at 5 percent. This reduction established the lowest requirements since February 1937.

second step was designed to stimulate residential construction. Congress provided enlarged appropriations for public housing and also extended the authority of the FNMA to purchase FHA and VA mortgages. In addition the Housing and Home Finance Agency liberalized borrowing terms under insured and guaranteed home loans. The third step was a speed-up in orders for aircraft, missiles, and other military equipment. Effects of this program, however, were only indirect and psychological in regard to initial recovery. Actual expenditures for military purposes through August 1958 were about $350 million less than during the corresponding period of 1957. Thus, except for the relatively moderate action taken with respect to residential construction, the initial phase of recovery cannot be ascribed to fiscal changes beyond those inherently present in the budget.

But there is no doubt that the automatic stabilizing effect of the federal budget was a powerful force in stemming the decline and in producing the cyclical upturn. As a consequence of the decline of private incomes, federal receipts from the public during fiscal 1958 dropped $.2 billion, and cash payments rose $3.4 billion largely because of additional social welfare outlays. The net result was that the 1958 cash budget showed a deficit of $1.5 billion compared with a surplus of $2.0 billion in 1957.

A more comprehensive view of the key importance of the automatic stabilizing influence of the federal budget is provided by the national income accounts. Government transfer payments to private sectors of the economy—largely unemployment and social security payments—were at the annual rate of $22.5 billion during the first quarter of 1958, and $24.6 billion during the second quarter. These payments exceeded those of the corresponding quarters of 1957, respectively, by $4.1 billion and $4.7 billion.[7] Mainly as a consequence, both disposable personal income and personal consumption expenditures were higher in the second quarter of 1958 than in the same quarter of 1957. Being the dominant component of GNP, personal consumption expenditures provided solid support while inventory, price, and cost adjustments were taking place.

federal debt management

Once again, Treasury debt operations tended to accentuate, rather than to moderate, the business cycle. Maturities of the debt were lengthened with a resultant reduction of asset liquidity in the economy. Thus, the disposition of businesses and consumers to spend was restrained in a period of recession when outlays should have been encouraged.

More concretely, federal marketable securities with maturities under 5 years declined between the end of September 1957 and 1958 from $124.3 to $120.7 billion, or from 76.8 to 71.9 percent of the total. The largest increases

[7] *Federal Reserve Bulletin* (October 1958), p. 1222.

were in the 5-10-year category—from \$29.4 to \$38.6 billion—and in the over-20-year category—from \$4.3 to \$5.6 billion. The lengthening of maturities was accomplished by issuance of 6 bonds to the total of \$16.2 billion, with average maturity of about 11 years. These offerings of bonds in the capital market were in competition with private borrowers. Business firms desiring to finance capital investment found less long-term funds available and at higher cost than otherwise would have been the case. Had the Treasury borrowed short-term funds from commercial banks, the amount of money would have been increased, asset liquidity in general would have been enhanced, and private expenditures would have been stimulated.

23

monetary, fiscal, and debt management, 1958 to 1961

The next period under review is marked by the presence of a new international development which had been only a remote consideration since establishment of the Fed in 1914. Reference is to the steady decline of the U.S. gold stock from nearly $23 billion in early 1958 to $17.4 billion in the first quarter of 1961. This decline was basically associated with a persistent overall deficit in the international balance of payments, which built up dollar claims of foreigners. The so-called dollar shortage of the first decade following World War II gradually subsided as the economies of western Europe and Japan recovered. After about 1958, the revival of their exports, combined with high levels of U.S. foreign investment and foreign aid, created an increasing "dollar surplus." Under these circumstances, the problem of safeguarding the dollar as the standard monetary unit in the international payments system became one of the major goals of monetary and fiscal policies.

For purposes of analysis, it is convenient to separate this period into two subperiods: (1) business recovery, mid-1958 to first quarter 1960; and (2) fourth postwar recession, mid-1960 to first quarter 1961.

BUSINESS RECOVERY, MID-1958 TO FIRST QUARTER 1960

economic developments

While the decline in production and employment during late 1957 and early 1958 was rapid, the recession proved to be shorter than the two preceding postwar recessions—about 9 months compared with 11 months in 1948-1949, and 13 months in 1953-1954. Recovery began in the late spring of 1958 by virtue of resilient natural forces with strong assists from an easy Federal Reserve policy and the automatic stabilizing effects of the federal budget. As indicated in the preceding chapter, tax rates were not reduced and additional federal outlays were modest. The recovery was a notably vigorous one during the last half of 1958 and the first half of 1959. In addition to strong revival of residential construction, which led the upturn, the most dynamic influence was the shift from heavy liquidation of business inventories to their speculative accumulation. Inventory liquidation during the first quarter of 1958 was at the annual rate of $6.4 billion, but by the second quarter of 1959, the rate of accumulation rose to $9.2 billion. This large change in inventories accounted for almost two-fifths of the increase of GNP. However, a substantial part of inventory accumulation during the first half of 1959 was in anticipation of the steel strike which began in mid-July and was not settled until nearly four months later, in November. After this serious interruption, the general recovery, supported by strong consumer demands, reached a plateau-like level during the first half of 1960. The level attained, however, fell appreciably short of capacity output, with about 5 percent of the labor force still unemployed.

A more comprehensive view of the extent and nature of this recovery period is given by Table 23-1 and figures 20 and 21. Industrial production rose by one-third, with durable-goods output, as usual, exhibiting a larger increase than nondurables. Manufacturing employment increased by 10 percent. Gross national product expanded by 16.5 percent, with private domestic investment providing the strongest relative contribution of 56.4 percent. Virtually all the increase of GNP was in real output, because the rise of commodity prices during the period was small—0.7 percent in wholesale prices and 1.6 percent in consumer prices. The tight rein of the Fed is also evident. Monetary expansion was only 3.7 percent, and the growth of total loans and investments of commercial banks was held to 7 percent. In fact, in order to meet strong loan demands, the banks had to reduce investments by over 5 percent. In this setting of restricted supply and vigorous demand for credit, the Treasury bill rate moved upward from 0.83 percent to 4.35 percent. Indeed, the whole structure of money rates reached the highest level since 1929.

fed policies

The Fed shifted its policy from monetary ease to restraint more promptly in 1958 than in any previous recovery period. This was, in part, a result of the prevailing view that the rapid bank-credit expansion permitted in 1954-1955 was a principal cause of the inflationary expansion of 1956-1957. But prompt action was more immediately sparked by the inflationary psychology that developed during the late summer and early fall of

20 MEASURES OF BUSINESS CONDITIONS, 1948-1963.
Source: U.S. Department of Commerce, *Business Cycle Developments* (September 1963)

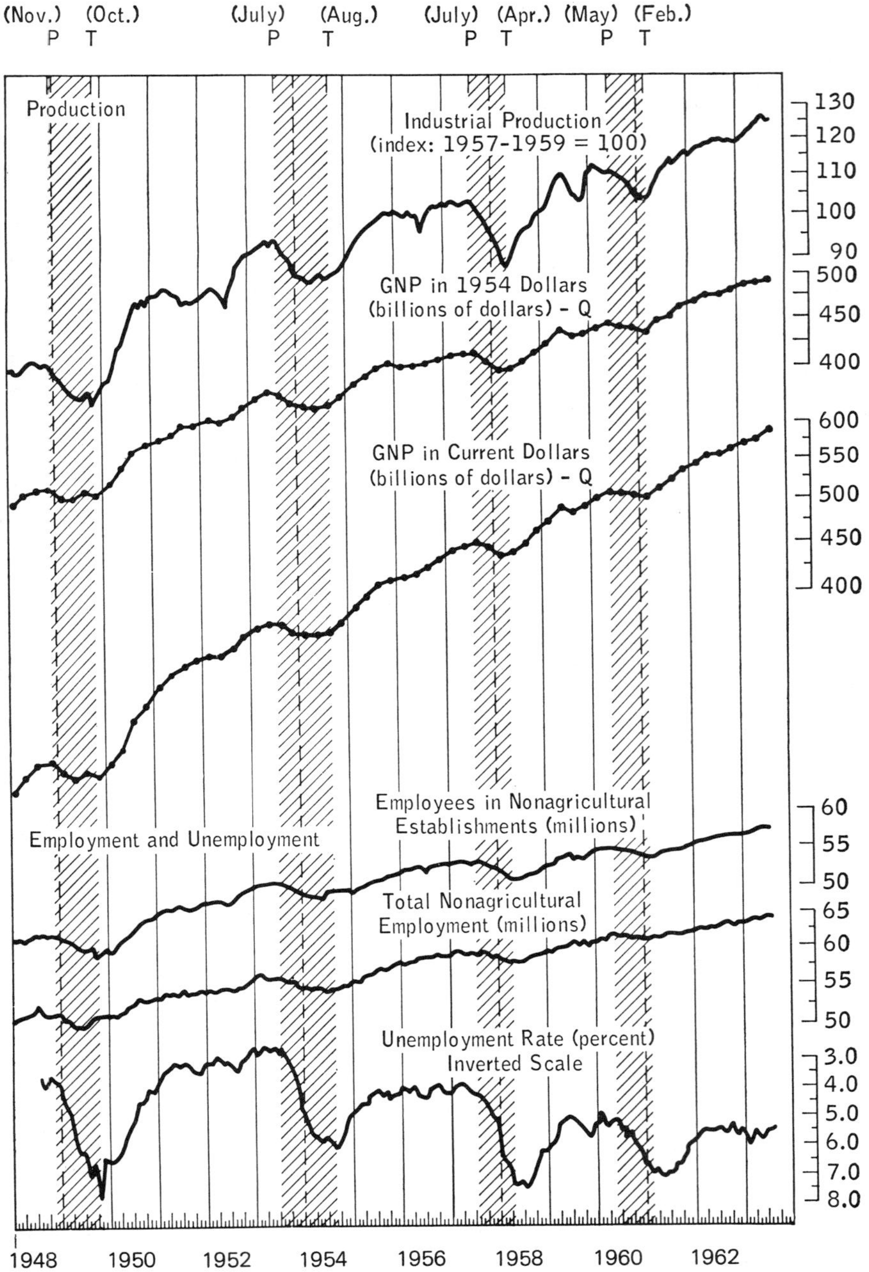

21 MEASURES OF FINANCIAL CONDITIONS, 1948-1963.
Source: U.S. Department of Commerce, *Business Cycle Developments* (September 1963)

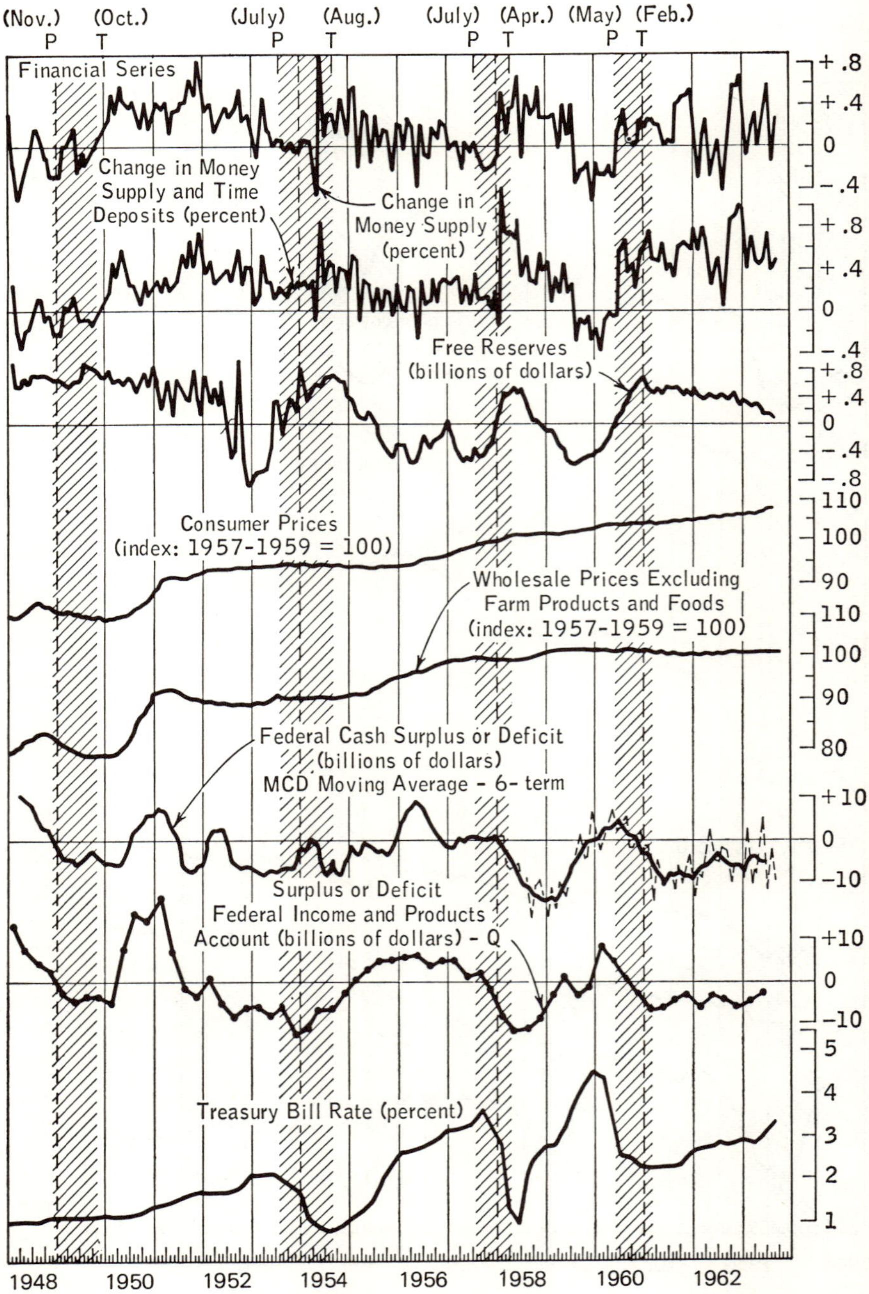

TABLE 23-1 / MEASURES OF RECOVERY, SECOND QUARTER 1958 TO FIRST QUARTER 1960

Measures	Low Point, Second Quarter 1958	High Point, First Quarter 1960	Change (percent)
Industrial production			
(FRB; 1947-1949 = 100)	126.0 (Apr.)	168.0 (Jan.)	+ 33.3
Manufacturing, durable	131.0	180.0	+ 37.4
Manufacturing, nondurable	125.0	159.0	+ 27.2
Manufacturing employment			
(BLS; 1947-1949 = 100)	92.3 (May)	101.4 (Feb.)	+ 9.9
Gross national product			
(billions of dollars)	430.4	501.3	+ 16.5
Consumer expenditures	288.3	323.3	+ 12.1
Gross private domestic investment	50.7	79.3	+ 56.4
Change in business inventories, annual rate	−6.5	+11.4	
Federal expenditures	50.7	51.8	+ 2.2
State and local expenditures	39.1	45.7	+ 16.9
Amount of money			
(billions of dollars)[a]	135.0 (Apr.)	140.0 (Jan.)	+ 3.7
Loans and investments of commercial banks (billions of dollars)	175.4 (May)	187.8 (Jan.)	+ 7.0
Loans	92.9	109.6	+ 18.0
Investments	82.5	78.2	− 5.2
Wholesale prices			
(BLS; 1947-1949 = 100)	119.2 (June)	120.0 (Mar.)	+ 0.7
Consumer prices			
(BLS; 1947-1949 = 100)	123.7 (June)	125.7 (Mar.)	+ 1.6
Yield on Treasury bills			
(percent)	0.83 (June)	4.35 (Jan.)	+424.1

[a]Demand deposits adjusted and currency outside banks, seasonally adjusted.
Source: *Federal Reserve Bulletin,* various issues.

1958. Business recovery was anticipated by a bull market in stocks which began in early 1958 and continued until the third quarter of 1959. Speculators, who had bought bonds heavily and bid up their prices during the recession, reversed their positions during the summer. Panicky selling drove bond prices down until the Fed intervened in July by purchasing $1.2 billion of bonds and notes to prevent disorderly conditions. Fearing inflationary developments associated with vigorous recovery and the large federal deficit, speculators shifted from bonds to stocks. As a consequence, common-stock yields dropped well below high-grade bond yields—historically a rare phenomenon that persisted through 1970.

With broadening evidence of robust revival, accompanied by strong demands for bank credit, the Fed began measures of restraint in August 1958, despite the fact that seasonally adjusted unemployment stood at the recession peak of 7.6 percent of the labor force. As usual, open-market operations were first utilized to change the credit situation. Net surplus reserves of member banks, which had been maintained in the vicinity of $500 million through July, were reduced materially in August-September to under $100 million, and by the end of the year they were transformed to net borrowed reserves. The market was tightened steadily until by mid-1959 net borrowed reserves rose to over $500 million. This condition was maintained throughout the recovery period, although member banks were permitted to reduce borrowings at Reserve Banks month by month during 1960.

While Federal Reserve discount rates were not used aggressively to restrain expansion, they were kept in rough alignment with rising market rates. This was done in five steps during the period: the first in August-September 1958, when rates were raised from $1\frac{3}{4}$ to 2 percent; the last in September 1959, when they were raised from $3\frac{1}{2}$ to 4 percent. However, upward adjustments lagged behind market rates, with the result that member-bank borrowing became increasingly profitable. This was notably true during the last half of 1959 and the first quarter of 1960, when yields on short-term Treasury securities rose well above the discount rate (see figure 21). This situation, of course, magnified the problem of rationing discounts and advances at the Reserve Banks. It is noteworthy that the third principal quantitative method of control, increase of member-bank reserve requirements, was not utilized in the program of restraint.

Aside from exhortations and warnings, the only other restrictive method employed was margin requirements on loans for purchasing or carrying listed stocks. The first move in this direction was made in August 1958, when the requirement was raised from 50 to 70 percent of market value of securities; the second step came two months later, in October, when the requirement was boosted to 90 percent. This action was taken during the bull market in stocks when increasing amounts of security credit were being used.

Additional monetary aspects of the period are brought out by Table 23-2 which presents changes in member-bank reserves and the factors responsible therefore between June 1958 and January 1960. The gold outflow of over $2 billion and the increase of currency in circulation of nearly $1 billion were the dominant factors of decrease in bank reserves. While Federal Reserve authorities desired to tighten the money market, they did not wish the full impact of these factors to be felt. Despite material assistance from less important factors, it was still necessary to add nearly $1.2 billion to Reserve Bank holdings of U.S. securities as an offset. Even then, member banks found it necessary to increase borrowed reserves by $763 million and to reduce excess legal reserves by $82 million. Their net reserve position changed from +$484 million to –$361 million. Commercial banks sold over $5 billion of securities to meet customer loan requirements, and money rates rose to new postwar highs.

fiscal policies

Fiscal policies were not utilized aggressively to spur recovery from the 1958 recession. There was no reduction in federal individual and corporate

TABLE 23-2 / MEMBER-BANK RESERVES AND FACTORS OF CHANGE, JUNE 1958 AND JANUARY 1960 (millions of dollars)

	June 1958	January 1960	Factors of Increase	Factors of Decrease
Sources of funds				
Reserve Bank credit				
Discounts and advances	142	905	763	
U.S. securities	24,749	25,934	1,185	
Float and other	960	1,397	437	
Gold stock	21,490	19,454		2,036
Treasury currency	5,203	5,315	112	
Uses of funds				
Currency in circulation	31,039	32,008		969
Treasury cash holdings	701	419	282	
Treasury deposits with Fed Banks	442	534		92
Foreign and other deposits with Fed Banks	631	638		7
Other Fed accounts	1,132	838	294	
Total factors of increase			3,084	
Total factors of decrease				3,115
Member-bank reserves with Fed Banks	18,600	18,568	32[a]	
Member-bank cash reserves	0	310		
Total member-bank reserves	18,600	18,878		
Required legal reserves	17,974	18,334		
Excess legal reserves	626	544		
Addenda				
Net surplus (+) or borrowed (−) reserves	+ 484	− 361		
U.S. Treasury 3-month bill rate	0.83%	4.35%		

[a]Discrepancy of 1 million arises from rounding figures.
Note: All figures are averages of daily figures.
Source: *Federal Reserve Bulletin* (February 1959), p. 156; (January 1961), p. 40.

income-tax rates, despite strong political support for a program of tax reduction. Similarly, excise taxes on alcohol, cigarettes, and manufacturers were generally maintained, although there were miscellaneous reductions in 1958 and 1959, which taken together reduced estimated receipts by over $1 billion annually. These were offset, however, by an increase of nearly $600 million in taxes on motor fuel. Thus, in general, tax rates were not lowered to help recovery, and they were not raised during 1959 to restrain expansion.

Similarly, changes in federal expenditures attributable to stabilization were modest. Additional spending to assist recovery included acceleration of public-works projects, advances to states for extension of unemployment compensation, and purchases of mortgages by the FNMA. These outlays, which aggregated some $2 billion, occurred largely during the last three quarters of

TABLE 23-3 / FEDERAL GOVERNMENT RECEIPTS AND EXPENDITURES IN THE NATIONAL INCOME ACCOUNTS, 1958-1960 (billions of dollars)

Calendar Quarter		Receipts	Expenditures	Surplus or Deficit
1958:	I, II	76.0	85.4	−9.5
	III, IV	81.2	90.7	−9.4
1959:	I	87.4	90.1	−2.7
	II	91.6	91.1	0.5
	III	89.1	91.6	−2.5
	IV	89.6	92.0	−2.4
1960:	I	98.9	90.8	8.1
	II	98.4	92.9	5.5

Note: Figures are seasonally adjusted annual rates.
Source: *Economic Report of the President* (January 1961), p. 189; (January 1962), p. 275; (January 1963), p. 241.

1958 and the first quarter of 1959. From that point on through the first half of 1960, these programs were cut back as a measure of restraint.

But the fact that fiscal policy was not used aggressively does not mean that the influence of the federal budget was unimportant during the recovery period. This is brought out by Table 23-3, which presents federal receipts and expenditures in the national income accounts. The peak of the deficit of $9.5 billion (annual rate) came during the low point of the recession in the first half of 1958. As recovery proceeded, the deficit continued to impart stimulation through 1959, although to a decreasing extent. The budget surplus reached a maximum of $8.1 billion in the first quarter of 1960, when most measures of business activity registered high points. At this level, the surplus exerted a repressive influence on the economy. It should be noted that reduction of the deficit and emergence of the surplus were largely a consequence of increases in receipts as personal and corporate incomes rose. Expenditures, beginning with the second half of 1958, were stabilized within the narrow range of $90 to $92 billion (see figure 21 for the record of the federal cash budget). This period provides one of the best illustrations of the automatic stabilizing effect of the federal budget. With no significant change in tax rates and with modest countercyclical expenditures, the budget moved from a $9.5 billion deficit to a surplus of $8.1 billion—a change of $17.6 billion, or about 20 percent of the level of expenditures. This powerful gyroscopic force is built into the tax structure and, to a lesser degree, into expenditure programs.

federal debt management

Analysis of the Treasury's debt-management operations reveals that once again their influence was to magnify, rather than to moderate, the cycle.

TABLE 23-4 / MATURITY DISTRIBUTION OF FEDERAL MARKETABLE SECURITIES ON SELECTED DATES, 1958-1960 (millions of dollars)

	August 31, 1958		March 31, 1960	
Maturity Classes	*Amount*	*Percent*	*Amount*	*Percent*
Within 1 year	70,477	41.6	72,721	39.2
1-5 years	49,559	29.3	72,934	39.3
5-10 years	14,347	8.5	19,931	10.8
10-20 years	27,642	16.3	12,659	6.8
20 years and over	7,208	4.3	7,193	3.9
Total	169,233	100.0	185,437	100.0
Average maturity	5 years, 1 month		4 years, 4 months	

Source: *Economic Report of the President* (January 1960), p. 213; (January 1962), p. 271.

This fact is clearly evident from Table 23-4, which compares the maturity distribution of marketable U.S. securities in August 1958 with that of March 1960. These dates approximately define the period during which Federal Reserve credit policy was vigorously directed toward bank-credit restraint. It may be noted that the amount of securities with maturity under 5 years rose from \$120 billion to \$146 billion, and that their proportion of total securities increased from 71 to 79 percent. Also, at the long end of the distribution, the amount with maturity of 10 years and over declined from \$34.8 to \$19.9 billion, and their proportion of the total dropped from 20.6 to 10.7 percent. The average maturity of marketable securities was reduced from 5 years, 1 month to 4 years, 4 months. Debt-management operations contributed materially to asset liquidity, and thereby to the inflationary potential of the economy, when both monetary and fiscal policies were directed toward restraint.

In this instance, however, the Treasury was able to place the blame for these destabilizing operations on the Congress. After midyear 1959, the $4\frac{1}{4}$ percent ceiling on the coupon rate of federal securities with maturities over five years prevented longer-term borrowing. Market yields rose above this rate, so that issues bearing a $4\frac{1}{4}$ percent coupon could be sold only below par—a procedure the Treasury regarded as illegal. Both the President and the Secretary of the Treasury repeatedly requested Congress to remove this ceiling, and in January 1960, this request was formalized in a proposed bill which was presented to both the House and the Senate. Congress debated the question at length but took no action.

In these circumstances, the Treasury minimized the inflationary effects of its operations as much as possible by issuing securities with maturities in the 4-5-year range instead of obligations with shorter maturities. But this could be little more than a gesture because there is a very high degree of liquidity in all marketable federal securities with maturities under 5 years, and the passage of time constantly augments their liquidity. There is no doubt that Congress erred in refusing the Administration's request to remove the rate ceiling which served no useful purpose, and definitely prevented the Treasury from pursuing a well-balanced, flexible financing program. But even if Congress had acceded to the request, it is doubtful whether the Treasury's operations would have been substantially different—at least if one may judge on the basis of actions taken in earlier postwar years. In the two preceding expansion periods of 1952-1953 and 1956-1957, it will be recalled, the Treasury similarly contributed to liquidity and inflation by borrowing largely in the short-term market. In neither case did the rate ceiling constitute a practical obstacle to longer-term borrowing because it was well above market yields.

summary and appraisal

Looking back at the 1958-1960 recovery, three points in regard to cyclical controls stand out in bold relief. First, the Fed assumed the dominant role of restraining a potential inflationary development. They began to move in this direction in August 1958, soon after broad evidence of an upturn in the economy was at hand. Their response set a new record for promptness, and with the exception of 1928-1929, for degree of restraint. The rein was held so taut that interest rates rose to the highest level in thirty years. Second, aggressive fiscal policies were not utilized either to spur recovery or to check overexpansion. The positive actions taken were in harmony with Federal Reserve policy, but they were modest in character. However, the federal budget automatically exerted a powerful stabilizing influence because of the existing structure of taxation and expenditure programs. Finally, Treasury debt-management operations were expansionary during the last half of the recovery period, when monetary and fiscal policies were designed to check inflation. This, of course, increased the burden of the Fed, and partly accounts for the extremely tight money-market situation in which rates in the 1-5-year range rose well above yields on long-term U.S. securities.

As usual, appraisals of control policies cover the whole spectrum. Those who regard price inflation to be one of the most serious threats to the economy believe that controls were not strict enough because they should have prevented any rise in the general price level. Another group holds that the net effects of regulation were about right because the rise of prices was moderate, and no more than would be expected during recovery. Many others, who stress the goals of full employment and economic growth, believe that both monetary and fiscal policies were too repressive. They point to the fact that the Fed began its move toward restraint when the rate of unemployment was at the peak of 7.6 percent; that because of excessive restrictions, this rate averaged well over 5 percent during the peak zone of recovery; and that the danger of an unhealthy rise in prices was remote in the presence of unused labor and other productive resources. The facts give convincing support to this criticism.

FOURTH POSTWAR RECESSION, MID-1960 TO FIRST QUARTER 1961

The buoyant optimism that prevailed in late 1959 faded during the first half of 1960 as evidence began to accumulate that the fourth postwar recession was underway. The business peak from which the decline began was in May 1960, and the trough was reached in February 1961, according to the comprehensive analysis of the National Bureau of Economic Research. This nine-month recession proved to be the mildest one of the postwar period, and approximately the same length as its predecessor in 1957-1958. In general, Federal Reserve policy moved rather rapidly from restraint toward active ease—which, combined with slackened demands for credit, resulted in a sharp decline of interest rates.

TABLE 23-5 / MEASURES OF RECESSION, MID-1960 TO FIRST QUARTER 1961

Measures	High Point, First Half 1960		Low Point, First Quarter 1961		Change (percent)
Industrial production					
(FRB; 1947-1949 = 100)	168.0	(Jan.)	155.0	(Feb.)	− 7.7
Manufacturing, durable	180.0	(Jan.)	153.0	(Feb.)	−15.0
Manufacturing, nondurable	159.0	(Jan.)	155.0	(Jan.)	− 2.5
Employment, manufacturing					
(BLS; 1947-1949 = 100)	101.4	(Jan.)	92.5	(Feb.)	− 8.8
Gross national product					
(billions of dollars)	506.4	(Q2)	500.8	(Q2)	− 1.1
Consumer expenditures	329.9		330.7		+ 0.2
Private domestic investment	74.6		59.8		−19.8
Change in business inventories,					
annual rate	+ 10.8	(Q2)	− 3.6	(Q1)	
Federal purchases	52.9		54.7		+ 3.4
State and local purchases	46.8		50.3		+ 7.5
Amount of money					
(billions of dollars)[a]	140.0	(Jan.)	140.6	(Jan.)	+ 0.4
Loans and investments of commercial					
banks (billions of dollars)	188.8	(Apr.)	197.0	(Jan.)	+ 4.3
Loans	113.0	(Apr.)	114.2	(Jan.)	+ 1.1
Investments	75.8	(Apr.)	82.8	(Jan.)	+ 9.2
Wholesale prices					
(BLS; 1947-1949 = 100)	120.0	(Mar.)	119.9	(Mar.)	− 0.1
Consumer prices					
(BLS; 1947-1949 = 100)	125.7	(Mar.)	127.5	(Mar.)	+ 1.4
Yield on Treasury 3-month bills					
(percent)	4.74	(Jan.)	2.47	(Jan.)	−47.8

[a]Demand deposits adjusted and currency outside banks, seasonally adjusted.
Source: *Federal Reserve Bulletin,* various issues.

economic developments

As Table 23-5 indicates, the pattern of decline was very similar to former postwar recessions, and particularly to that of 1957-1958. The 8 percent drop in production centered in manufacturing of durable goods, which declined 15 percent. Manufacturing employment declined nearly 9 percent; unemployment rose from 5.1 percent to 6.9 percent of the civilian labor force. For the most part, these developments reflected a pause to adjust for excessive accumulation of inventories. In fact, the annual rate of inventory build-up declined from $10.8 billion in the first quarter of 1960 to a negative $3.6 billion in the first quarter of 1961. This overall change of $14.4 billion was over twice the decline in GNP which was moderated by increased government expenditures. The money supply remained about the same, because the increase of bank loans and investments found its outlet largely in time deposits. Wholesale prices were unchanged, but consumer prices rose moderately. (See also figures 20 and 21, pp. 447-448.)

fed policies

As inflationary expectations subsided in early 1960, Federal Reserve policy moved progressively from one of restraint toward easier money. All general instruments of control were employed in this direction. Policy determination encountered a dilemma in the form of conflicting requirements for domestic and international conditions. The developing recession called for abundant credit at low rates, while the deficit in the international balance of payments and the associated gold outflow called for relatively high interest rates. For the most part, this conflict was resolved in favor of the domestic situation. All general instruments—open-market operations, reserve requirements, and the discount rate—were employed at one time or another to create easy credit and to stem the business decline.

The Reserve Banks added about $1.5 billion to their holdings of U.S. securities between March 1960 and March 1961. In addition, the reserve position of member banks was eased to the extent of $1.9 billion by permitting them to count vault cash as legal reserves in accordance with legislation enacted in July 1959. This was done in two steps—one in August 1960, which released $.5 billion of reserve funds, the other in November, which released $1.4 billion. The net effect of these actions enabled member banks to reduce their borrowings at Reserve Banks from around $800 million in early 1960 to under $100 million a year later, and at the same time to add some $200 million to excess reserves. Stated differently, member banks moved from a position of net borrowed reserves of some $400 million to one of net surplus reserves of around $500 million (see figure 21). As indicated in Table 23-5, this permitted banks to increase investments by $7 billion, and was largely responsible for the drop in yield on Treasury bills from 4.7 to 2.5 percent. In line with these developments, the Reserve Bank discount rate underwent two downward adjustments—one in June 1960 from 4 to $3\frac{1}{2}$ percent; the other in August-September from $3\frac{1}{2}$ to 3 percent.

One further credit-easing move was made by the Board of Governors in the area of selective credit regulation. Margin requirements on loans for purchasing or carrying securities were reduced in July 1960 from 90 to 70 percent of market value. This was in recognition of some decline in stock-market credit, and of the reduced likelihood of excessive security speculation. While this change was only a facilitating one, it was followed by a strong upward movement of common-stock prices, which reached a new peak at the end of 1961.

fiscal policies

Federal budget programs designed to stimulate the economy were unimportant during the 1960-1961 recession. In accordance with the President's recommendation, Congress enacted legislation at the end of June 1960 to extend the 52 percent tax rate on corporate profits and the existing excise tax rates until July 1, 1961. Had the corporation tax rate been permitted to drop to 47 percent at midyear 1960 according to schedule, tax receipts would have declined by an estimated $1.2 billion; and had the scheduled reductions in excise taxes become effective, tax receipts would have been curtailed further by $1.3 billion—an aggregate reduction of $2.5 billion.[1] But federal tax rates remained virtually unchanged, so that the economy received no stimulus from this quarter.

While some positive actions were taken on the side of expenditures, they were relatively unimportant. A minor stimulus was given to residential construction by the FNMA in the form of more liberal financing terms. There were also efforts to speed up highway construction and to accelerate military contract awards and federal construction projects. But these steps were on a rather small scale and, for the most part, did not become effective until well after the business upturn in the first quarter of 1961.

However, the absence of substantial programs of stimulation does not mean that the influence of federal finance was unimportant in promoting recovery. On the contrary, the effects of automatic stabilizers built into the fiscal system were highly significant: tax receipts were reduced and expenditures were increased. More specifically, the federal budget surplus in the first quarter of 1960, according to national income accounts, was at an annual rate of $8.1 billion. From that point on, the surplus diminished steadily, was converted to a deficit of $.4 billion by the fourth quarter, and to a deficit of $6.3 billion in the first quarter of 1961. Thus, the overall stimulative change in the federal budget during the period was $14.4 billion.[2]

[1]Secretary of the Treasury, *Annual Report* (Washington, D.C., 1960), p. 50
[2]*Economic Report of the President* (January 1963), p. 193. See also figure 21 for the record of the federal cash budget.

federal debt management

The influence of Treasury debt management on the course of the 1960-1961 recession was also of minor significance. This is evident from Table 23-6, which compares the maturity distribution of marketable federal securities at the end of April 1960 with the distribution at the end of February 1961. A positive contribution of debt management to business recovery would call for shifts to short maturities in order to increase the liquidity of the economy. Also, borrowing in the long-term market would be avoided in order to promote a favorable capital market for private borrowers. In fact, some Treasury operations enhanced liquidity, particularly the material increase in both the amount and proportion of securities with maturities of less than 1 year. But this was offset by reduction of the 1-5-year category, and by increase of securities with maturities of 10 years and over. The overall average result was a 3-month lengthening of maturities. However, the lengthening process was accomplished by the advance refunding technique which minimizes the effect on the capital market. Thus, all in all, the influence of debt management on the recession appears to have been neutral.

TABLE 23-6 / MATURITY DISTRIBUTION OF MARKETABLE FEDERAL SECURITIES ON SELECTED DATES (millions of dollars)

	April 30, 1960		February 28, 1961	
Maturities	*Amount*	*Percentage Distribution*	*Amount*	*Percentage Distribution*
Within 1 year	72,807	38.7	80,054	42.2
1-5 years	75,133	39.9	67,007	35.3
5-10 years	19,930	10.6	18,683	9.8
10-20 years	12,649	6.7	13,203	7.0
20 years and over	7,629	4.1	10,973	5.8
Total outstanding	188,147	100.0	189,919	100.0
Average maturity	4 years, 3 months		4 years, 6 months	

Source: *Treasury Bulletin* (January 1961), p. 22; (December 1961), p. 23.

24

a review of monetary and fiscal policies, 1961 to 1970

The final period under review represents the longest sustained economic expansion in the annals of the nation—eight and one-half years, from 1961 to 1969. The first half of the period, 1961-1965, was marked by growth in real output with relative price stability. But during the second half, 1965-1970, the price level rose at an increasing rate, and control of inflation became a major economic and political issue. In fact, the real growth of the economy would doubtless have continued through 1970 had President Nixon's Administration not undertaken a determined program of monetary and fiscal restraint in 1969, which induced a recession.

For purposes of analysis, it is desirable to divide the period into three subperiods, as follows: (1) noninflationary expansion, first quarter 1961 to first quarter of 1965; (2) inflationary expansion, first quarter 1965 to third quarter 1969; and (3) attempted control of inflation, 1969-1970.

ECONOMIC EXPANSION, FIRST QUARTER 1961 TO THIRD QUARTER 1969

An overall view of the record expansion is provided by Table 24-1 and figures 22 and 23. Attention is called to several significant developments. First, the real output of the economy grew by almost one-half in this period—at an annual rate of 4.4 percent. Part of this represented cyclical recovery from a recession when unemployment was 6.8 percent of the labor force and only 78.5 percent of manufacturing capacity was being utilized. Nevertheless, the secular trend

TABLE 24-1 / MEASURES OF ECONOMIC EXPANSION, 1961-1969

Measures	Low Point, First Quarter 1961	High Point, Third Quarter 1969	Change (percent)
Gross national product (billions of dollars)	500.8	942.8	+ 88.3
Gross national product (1958 prices)	497.2	730.6	+ 46.9
Industrial production (FRB, 1957-1959 = 100)	103.4	174.6	+ 68.9
Capacity utilization in manufacturing (percent)	78.5	84.2	+ 7.3
Employment, nonagricultural (1957-1959 = 100)	100.4	134.2	+ 33.7
Unemployment (percent of labor force)	6.8	3.5	– 48.5
Wholesale prices (BLS, 1957-1959 = 100)	101.0	113.4	+ 12.3
Consumer prices (BLS, 1957-1959 = 100)	103.9	128.7	+ 23.9
Money supply (billions of dollars)[a]	142.4	211.8	+ 48.7
Velocity of money (income)	3.03	3.85	+ 27.0
Demand deposits (billions of dollars)	111.9	150.5	+ 34.5
Time deposits (billions of dollars)	61.4	195.5	+218.4
Bank loans and investments (billions of dollars)	199.3	405.9	+103.7
Loans	116.7	280.7	+140.5
Investments	82.6	125.2	+ 51.6
Yield on 3-month Treasury bills (percent)	2.42	7.00	+189.3
Yield on long-term U.S. bonds (percent)	3.81	6.02	+ 58.0
Yield on Aaa corporate bonds (percent)	4.27	6.97	+ 63.2

[a]Demand deposits adjusted and currency outside banks, seasonally adjusted, series revised upward, November 1970.
Source: *Federal Reserve Bulletin,* various issues.

compared favorably with that of the previous 100 years, which had been in the vicinity of 3.3 percent (see figures 22 and 24). Second, nearly half the increase in GNP (current dollars) resulted from the rise of prices. Consumer prices rose 24 percent and wholesale prices, 12 percent. Most of the price inflation, however, occurred during the second half of the period–after 1964 (see figure 25). Third, commercial-bank loans and investments more than doubled, rising from \$199 to \$406 billion; four-fifths of this increase took place in loans (see figure 26). On the liabilities side of the balance sheet, the expansion was evidenced by a large growth of deposits, mainly in the form of time deposits, which increased 218 percent compared with demand-deposit growth of 35 percent. Fourth, the stock of money rose at a notably slower rate than bank credit and GNP–39 percent compared with 104 percent and 88 percent, respectively. The velocity of money rose by one-fourth and thus played a substantial role in financing the growth of GNP. Last, interest rates rose precipitously as a consequence of robust demand for credit combined with Federal Reserve restrictions on supply, especially in 1966 and 1969. Short-term yields doubled and long-term yields rose by approximately two-thirds (see figure 27).

NONINFLATIONARY EXPANSION, FIRST QUARTER 1961 TO FIRST QUARTER 1965

With the background of an overall view of the expansion period 1961-1969, it is desirable to analyze events in more detail with special reference to monetary, fiscal, and debt-management policies. Initial consideration is given to the first half of the period when the rise in prices was modest and most of the growth in GNP was real. Wholesale prices rose only nominally, and consumer prices increased at the moderate annual rate of 1.3 percent (see figure 25). Real GNP and industrial production expanded, respectively, at annual rates of 4.6 percent and 6.2 percent (see figures 22 and 24).

monetary policies

With unemployment nearly 7 percent at the outset and above 5 percent until the last quarter of 1964, the Fed properly adopted an expansionary monetary policy. Net surplus reserves of member banks were held in the range of

22 GROSS NATIONAL PRODUCT, 1963-1971.
Source: Federal Reserve Bank of St. Louis

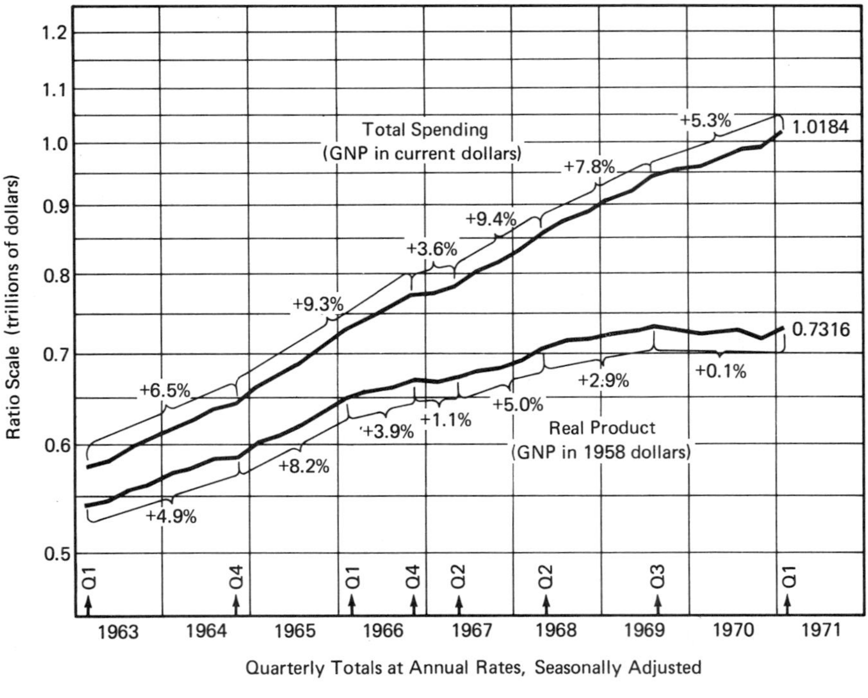

23 THE STOCK OF MONEY IN THE UNITED STATES, 1966-1971.
(percentages are annual rates of change for periods indicated)
Sources: Board of Governors of the Federal Reserve System; Federal Reserve Bank of St. Louis

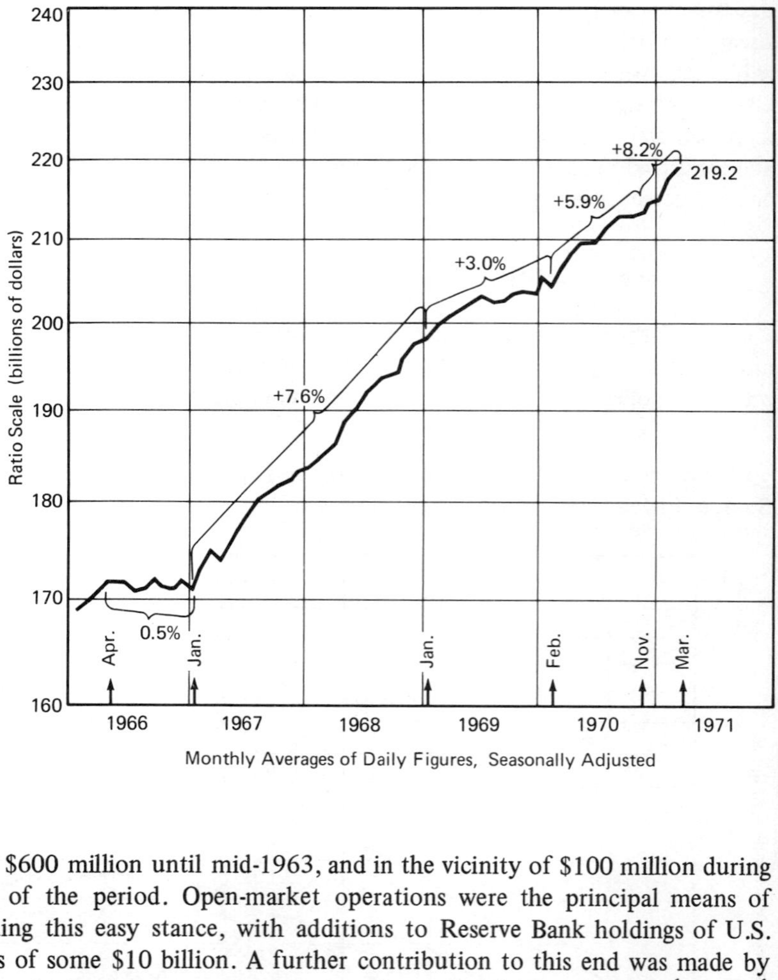

\$250 to \$600 million until mid-1963, and in the vicinity of \$100 million during the rest of the period. Open-market operations were the principal means of maintaining this easy stance, with additions to Reserve Bank holdings of U.S. securities of some \$10 billion. A further contribution to this end was made by reductions in legal-reserve requirements of member banks—from $17\frac{1}{2}$ to $16\frac{1}{2}$ percent against demand deposits of central-reserve city banks in December 1960, and from 5 to 4 percent against time deposits of all member banks in October 1962. The Reserve Bank discount rate, which had been reduced from $3\frac{1}{2}$ to 3 percent in the third quarter of 1960, was held at this low level until July 1963. Subsequently, it was raised rather passively in two steps to 4 percent in line with the firming of short-term money rates. Margin requirements for the purchase of stocks were reduced from 70 to 50 percent in July 1962, in response to the sharp decline in stock prices during the second quarter. But after the strong market recovery, the requirements were returned to their former level of 70 percent in November 1963.

Reflecting business recovery, the demands for credit by businesses, consumers, and governments were large. Total bank credit grew at an annual rate of nearly 9 percent and bank loans at a rate of over 12 percent (see figure 26). However, the growth of the money supply was more modest—at an annual rate of about $3\frac{1}{2}$ percent. In this setting of economic expansion, short-term interest rates rose beginning in late 1961. But long-term bond yields were quite stable (see figure 27). While monetary policy was expansive throughout the period, the efforts of the Fed in this direction were limited by the annual deficits in the international balance of payments, which ranged between $2.4 and $3.6 billion on a liquidity basis. This situation was responsible for operation twist, an attempt to keep short-term interest rates high in relation to long-term rates by purchase of fewer short-term issues and more intermediate- and long-term bonds by the Reserve Banks.

24 INDEX OF INDUSTRIAL PRODUCTION, 1962-1970. (percentages are annual rates of change for periods indicated)
Sources: Board of Governors of the Federal Reserve System; Federal Reserve Bank of St. Louis

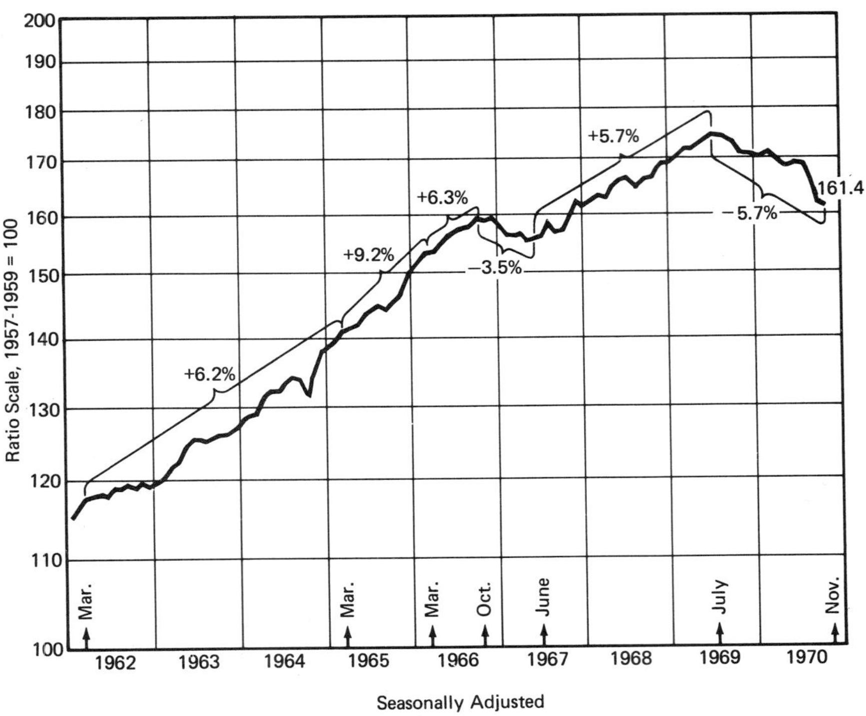

fiscal policies

The expansive monetary policies just described were properly supported by expansive fiscal policies. There were deficits in the unified federal budget in every fiscal year, 1961-1965, ranging between \$1.6 and \$7.1 billion and aggregating \$22.8 billion. The deficits were smaller on a national income accounts basis, ranging between \$1.2 and \$2.7 billion during fiscal 1961-1964, and showing a surplus of \$2 billion in fiscal 1965.[1]

25 INDEXES OF CONSUMER PRICES AND WHOLESALE INDUSTRIAL PRICES, 1963-1971. (percentages are annual rates of change for periods indicated)
Sources: U.S. Department of Labor; Federal Reserve Bank of St. Louis

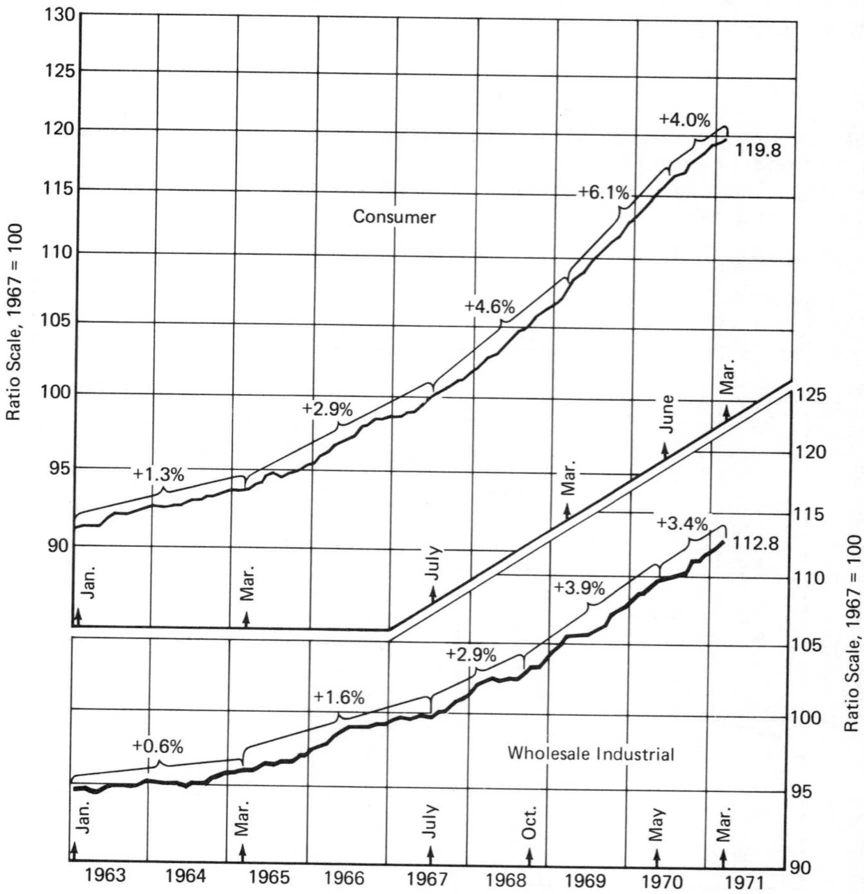

[1]*Economic Report of the President* (February 1970), pp. 249, 253.

Three significant fiscal steps designed to spur economic expansion were taken during the period: (1) liberalization of depreciation allowances, (2) the investment tax credit; and (3) a reduction of federal tax rates. A summary of these taxation changes follows.

1/The Treasury issued new guidelines with respect to depreciation allowances on about 75 broad classes of business assets in July 1962. On the average, the new ruling permitted the lifespan of these assets to be shortened by 30 to 40 percent, and more rapid depreciation was allowed on 70 to 80 percent of machinery and equipment. Tax reductions on businesses were estimated by the Treasury to be in the vicinity of $1.5 billion.[2] The effect of using more rapid rates of depreciation was, of course, to reduce net taxable income correspondingly, and thereby to lessen the current tax burden. However, the decision to adopt more rapid rates involved estimates of the value of a current tax saving compared with the present value of higher taxes in the years ahead—when net taxable income would be higher after existing assets became fully depreciated. In

26 COMMERCIAL-BANK LOANS AND INVESTMENTS, 1962-1970. (gross data are averages of end of current and preceding month. This series replaces the daily average series previously reported. Percentages are annual rates of change for periods indicated. Latest data plotted: November 1970)
Sources: Board of Governors of the Federal Reserve System; Federal Reserve Bank of St. Louis

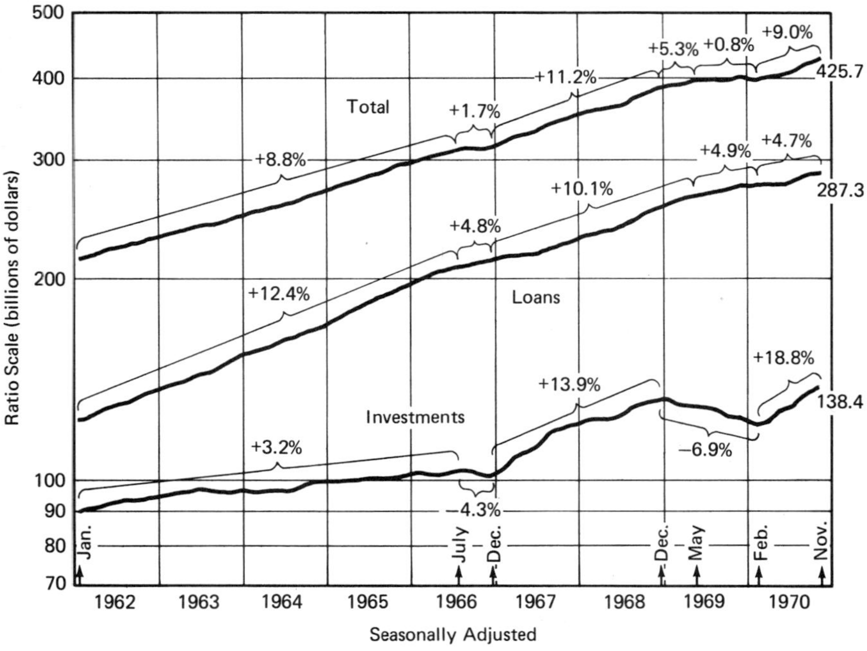

[2]Secretary of the Treasury, *Annual Report* (Washington, D.C., 1962), p. 69.

fact, most businesses chose to adopt more rapid rates of depreciation with a consequent current tax saving, and a tendency to promote investment outlays.

2/An investment tax credit was first proposed to the Congress by President Kennedy in his message of April 1961. After extensive hearings, a modified version of his proposal was incorporated in the Revenue Act of October 1962. A tax credit of 7 percent (3 percent for certain public utilities) of investment made in depreciable machinery and equipment was established. The tax credit could be offset in full against tax liability up to $25,000, but only against one-fourth of tax liability above $25,000. A three-year carryback and a five-year carryforward was provided for unused credits. Most analysts agree that the investment tax credit was a significant stimulant to business investment. A controversy developed between those who believed that the tax credit should be a permanent feature of the law and those who held that it should be employed

27 MONEY MARKET RATES, 1962-1970.
Source: Federal Reserve Bank of St. Louis

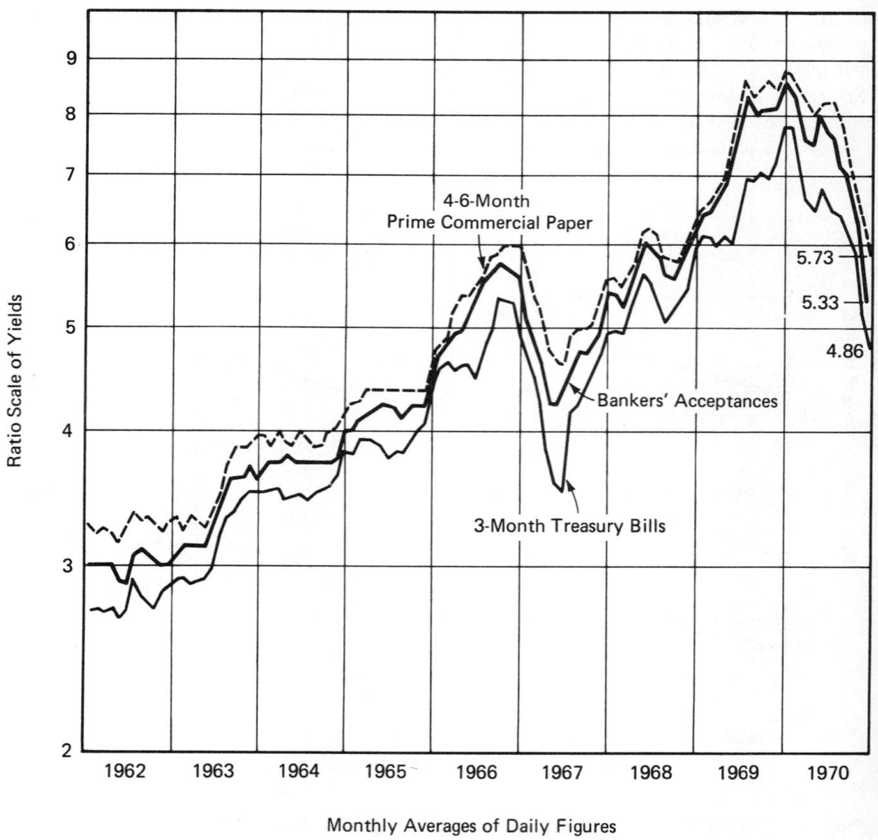

cyclically to stimulate investment when recession threatens and to restrain investment during overexpansion. The latter group has thus far prevailed. During the threatened inflationary expansion of 1966, the investment credit was suspended in November. But it was restored in June 1967 (effective in March), when evidences of an economic slowdown were apparent. Then, in August 1970, it was again repealed as a means of curbing the investment boom.[3]

3/The largest tax reduction ever made was enacted in February 1964, as part of the Revenue Act. It provided an annual reduction of $11.5 billion in federal income-tax liabilities—$9.1 billion for individuals and $2.4 billion for corporations. The rate scale for individuals, which previously ranged from 20 to 91 percent, was reduced to a range of 14 to 70 percent. The corporate tax rate was reduced from 52 to 48 percent.[4] The unique feature of this program was that for the first time in history, tax rates were lowered substantially during a period of sizable deficits in the unified federal budget, ranging between $3.4 and $7.1 billion between fiscal 1961 and fiscal 1964. The program was first proposed by President Kennedy in a message to Congress in January 1963, with the objective of stimulating the economy when chronic unemployment of about 5.5 percent of the labor force persisted.[5]

A majority of economists believe that this active fiscal strategy was primarily responsible for the strong expansion of the economy in 1965. Real GNP rose 5.6 percent, and industrial production increased 8 percent. By the year-end, the rate of unemployment had dropped to about 4 percent and the output of the economy had attained its full potential (see figure 28). However, the monetarist school of thought, including Professor Friedman of the University of Chicago, disagrees. They prefer to explain the economic expansion more in terms of increases in money and in bank credit. The money supply increased 5 percent in 1965; bank credit, 10 percent; and time deposits, 16 percent.

debt-management policies

The broad objectives of federal debt management were fully enunciated and accepted by the Treasury for the first time in 1961:

> First, to raise the money required to meet the Government's obligations.
>
> Second, to borrow as cheaply as possible, consistent with meeting other debt management objectives.
>
> Third, to make sure that the Government carries out its borrowing in a way that fosters, rather than inhibits, economic stability and sustained growth of the economy.

[3]Secretary of the Treasury, *Annual Report* (Washington, D.C., 1967), p. 29.
[4]Secretary of the Treasury, *Annual Report* (Washington, D.C., 1964), pp. 37-38.
[5]Secretary of the Treasury, *Annual Report* (Washington, D.C., 1963), pp. 293-332.

Fourth, to conduct debt operations in such a way as to try to avoid significant international interest rate differentials, which can lead to large and disruptive flows of short-term funds.

Fifth, to work toward a balanced debt maturity structure, in order to facilitate the orderly managing of the debt in future years. This requires maintenance of both a reasonable volume of long-term securities and a sufficient supply of short-term securities to meet the needs of the economy.[6]

While there is always some conflict among the foregoing objectives, the Treasury deserves commendation for its order of priorities during the period 1961-1965. In the early stages of cyclical recovery, the liquidity of the economy should be enlarged by increasing near-money assets. This was done by a steady increase of Treasury bills, while keeping the total of obligations maturing within

28 ACTUAL AND POTENTIAL GROSS NATIONAL PRODUCT, 1948-1970 (in 1958 dollars). (trend line of 3.5 percent per year—intersecting actual line in middle of 1955—from 1st quarter 1952 to 4th quarter 1962; 3.75 percent from 4th quarter 1962 to 4th quarter 1965; 4 percent from 4th quarter 1965 to 4th quarter 1969; and 4.3 percent from 4th quarter 1969 to 3rd quarter 1970)
Source: U.S. Department of Commerce, *Business Conditions* (November 1970)

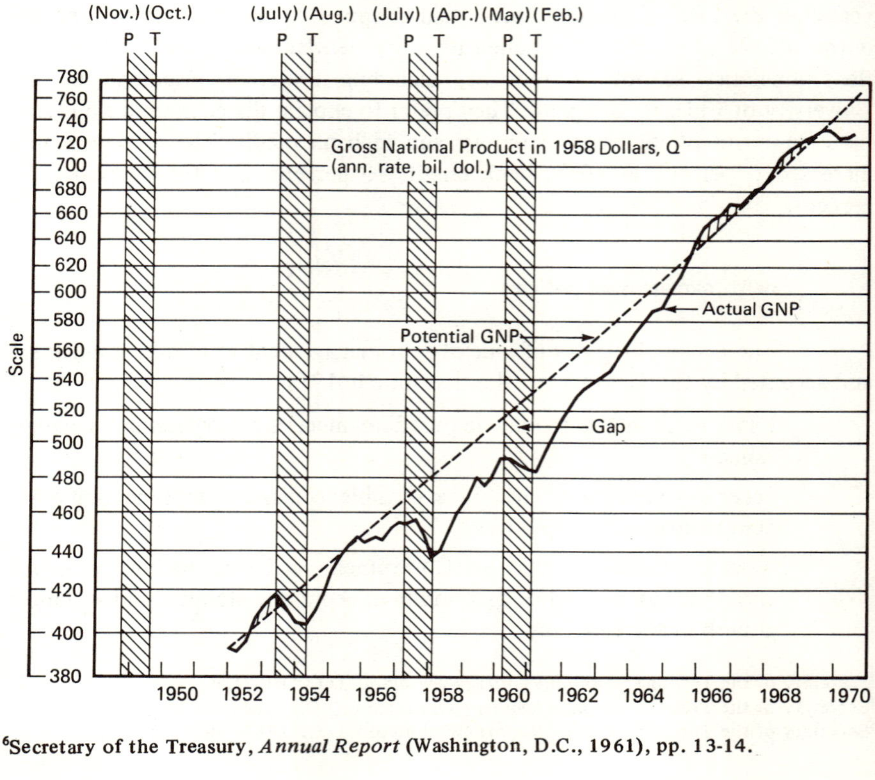

[6]Secretary of the Treasury, *Annual Report* (Washington, D.C., 1961), pp. 13-14.

one year steady at between $81 and $89 billion. At the same time, the goal of lessening the deficit in the international balance of payments was served—by increasing the outstanding amount of Treasury bills from $32.4 billion at the end of 1960 to $53.7 billion at midyear 1965. This strategy complemented that of the Fed to keep short-term yields high in relation to long-term yields as a means of discouraging the outflow of liquid capital. Meanwhile, the Treasury refrained from competing for long-term funds with corporations, the mortgage market, and state and local governments. This is evidenced by the fact that the yield on U.S. 20-year bonds remained in the vicinity of 4 percent while the yield of 3-month Treasury bills rose from about $2\frac{1}{4}$ percent in 1961 to $3\frac{3}{4}$ percent in early 1965.

The Treasury also exhibited imagination and ingenuity by experimenting with new techniques of debt management. Advance refunding was used on several occasions: prerefunding to exchange securities with maturity under 1 year for new issues in the 3-7-year intermediate range; junior refunding to exchange 1-5-year issues for new securities with maturities in the 5-10-year range; and senior refunding to exchange 5-10-year securities for long-term bonds. Another new technique was used for the first time in June 1961, viz., offering a strip of $1.8 billion of Treasury bills maturing in series over an 18-week period. It was used subsequently on several occasions for the purpose of firming money rates and preventing the outflow of short-term capital. Still a further experiment was tried in January 1963, when $250 million of 30-year bonds were offered at competitive bidding. The success of this first offering led to a second one in April 1963, for $300 million. But this issue moved out slowly, with a substantial loss by the underwriting syndicate. There was no further use of this method through 1970 because of unfavorable market conditions. But it may again be revived when bond prices are stable or rising as a means of borrowing at the lowest possible rate.

INFLATIONARY EXPANSION, FIRST QUARTER 1965 TO THIRD QUARTER 1969

The principal difference between the first and second halves of the $8\frac{1}{2}$-year expansion was the behavior of prices. As already indicated, the value of the dollar remained steady during the first period. But during the second, its value shrank at an accelerating rate; that is, the price level rose. In general, this was an outgrowth of an overheated economy in which effective demand exceeded productive capacity at existing prices. In the sections that follow, it will be helpful to analyze fiscal, monetary, and debt-management policies to seek explanations for inflationary developments.

measures of expansion

An overall view of the extent of economic expansion is presented in Table 24-2 and in figures 22 to 29. Gross national product rose at an average

TABLE 24-2 / MEASURES OF ECONOMIC EXPANSION, 1965-1969

Measures	First Quarter 1965	Third Quarter 1969	Change (percent)
Gross national product (billions of dollars)	641.1	942.8	+47.1
Gross national product (1958 prices)	600.3	730.6	+21.7
Industrial production (FRB, 1957-1959 = 100)	139.2	174.6	+25.4
Capacity utilization in manufacturing (percent)	87.5	84.2	– 3.8
Employment, nonagricultural (1957-1959 = 100)	113.6	134.2	+18.1
Unemployment (percent of labor force)	5.0	3.5	–30.0
Wholesale prices (BLS, 1957-1959 = 100)	101.2	113.4	+12.1
Consumer prices (BLS, 1957-1959 = 100)	108.9	128.7	+18.2
Money supply (billions of dollars)[a]	161.3	202.6	+25.6
Velocity of money (income)	3.36	3.85	+14.6
Bank loans and investments (billions of dollars)	275.7	405.9	+47.2
Loans	175.5	280.7	+59.9
Investments	111.7	125.2	+12.1
Yield on 3-month Treasury bills (percent)	3.93	7.00	+78.0
Yield on long-term U.S. bonds (percent)	4.16	6.02	+44.7
Yield on Aaa corporate bonds (percent)	4.41	6.97	+58.0

[a]Demand deposits adjusted and currency outside banks, seasonally adjusted; series revised upward, November 1970.
Source: *Federal Reserve Bulletin,* various issues.

annual rate of about 9 percent (including a pause during the first half of 1967) until the second quarter of 1968, after which it slowed to a rate of 7.8 percent. Over half this growth, however, was attributable to the rise of prices. Real product increased at an average annual rate of approximately 4 percent (see figures 22 and 28). Apart from the interruption during the first half of 1967, industrial production grew steadily at an average annual rate of about 5 percent (see figure 24). Price inflation accelerated during the period. Consumer prices rose at an annual rate of 2.9 percent until mid-1967, at 4.6 percent until early 1969, and thereafter at over 6 percent. Wholesale industrial prices increased less rapidly, but were rising at an annual rate of 3.9 percent during the terminal year (see figure 25). Before the restraint of 1969, growth of the money stock accelerated from a 2 percent annual rate in the 1953-1965 period, to 4 percent in 1965-1967, and to over 7 percent during 1967-1968. The rise in the velocity of money also played an important role in financing the growth of GNP. Interest rates rose rapidly in 1965 and 1966, and after the interruption of 1967, they increased even more in 1968 and 1969 to the highest level in over a century (see figure 27).

fiscal policies

Fiscal policies were strongly expansionary during the period 1965-1968. The federal deficit increased each year—from a modest $1.6 billion

TABLE 24-3 / THE FEDERAL BUDGET, FISCAL 1965-1969 (billions of dollars)

		Unified Budget Basis			National Income Accounts Basis
		Receipts	*Outlays*	*Surplus or Deficit (−)*	*Surplus (+); Deficit (−)*
1965		116.8	118.4	− 1.6	+ 2.0
1966		130.9	134.7	− 3.8	+ 0.9
1967		150.0	158.3	− 8.7	− 7.2
1968		153.7	178.8	−25.2	−11.5
	Q1	(annual rates; seasonally adjusted)			− 8.4
	Q2				− 9.5
	Q3				− 2.8
	Q4				− 0.1
1969		187.8	184.6	3.2	+ 6.0
	Q1				+10.1
	Q2				+13.5

Source: *Economic Report of the President* (February 1970), pp. 249, 253.

in 1965 to the huge figure of $25.2 billion in fiscal 1968. Outlays rose from $118.4 billion in 1965 to $178.8 billion in 1968 (see Table 24-3). Acceleration of defense expenditures to finance the Vietnam War was a principal cause—from $50.1 billion in fiscal 1965 to $78.7 billion in 1968. But social welfare outlays also increased enormously—from $5.7 billion in fiscal 1965 to $40.7 billion in 1968—almost twice as much as the increase in defense.[7] The insistence on both guns and butter in wartime was clearly the dominant cause of inflationary developments.

While President Johnson was jointly responsible for the large increase in federal expenditures, Congress must shoulder the blame for the lagging increase of revenues. Two significant tax changes were made during the period: (1) restoration and extension of certain excise taxes, and (2) establishment of a surtax on personal and corporate income.

1/The Tax Adjustment Act of March 1966 restored the excise-tax rate on automobiles to 7 percent and on telephone service to 10 percent for a two-year period. (Under the Act of June 1965, these two taxes were being gradually phased out.) This action added $1.2 billion to revenues in fiscal 1967 and $2.7 billion by 1969.

2/In January 1967, and again in August, President Johnson recommended a surtax on corporate and individual income-tax liabilities, first of 6 percent and later of 10 percent. Immediate action was imperative, but Congress delayed a year and one-half—until June 1968—before passing the Revenue and Expenditure Control Act of 1968. The surtaxes were estimated to augment

[7]Secretary of the Treasury, *Annual Report* (Washington, D.C., 1965), pp. 11, 506; 1968, Statistical Appendix, p. 24.

revenues by $11.6 billion in fiscal 1969. This incident, which accounted for a large part of the $25.2 billion deficit in 1968 with its strong inflationary influence, illustrates the inflexibility of fiscal policy as a method of cyclical control—without some discretionary power in the hands of the President or in some administrative agency.

monetary policies[8]

Along with fiscal policy, monetary policy must share responsibility for the inflationary developments of the period. Aside from restrictive actions in 1966, it was basically expansive until early 1969. As in the past, open-market operations were the principal method of providing member banks with reserve money. Between the ends of 1964 and 1968, the increase in holdings of U.S. securities accounted for most of the increase in total Reserve Bank credit—$15.4 billion compared with $1.3 billion from other sources. Total member-bank reserves, the base of multiple bank-credit expansion, rose by $5.6 billion between the same dates. The $5 billion reduction in gold stock and the $10.9 billion increase of currency in circulation were the main factors offsetting the expansion of Reserve Bank credit.

The degree of pressure or relaxation of the money market is best reflected in the net reserve position of member banks and by the behavior of interest rates. By March 1965, net surplus reserves, which had been maintained in the range $100 to $500 million since 1961, were absorbed and a net reserve deficit appeared. This persisted in the range of $100 to $400 million throughout the remainder of 1965 and 1966. At the same time, interest rates moved up sharply in response, on the one side, to strong credit demands and, on the other, to curtailment of supply by Reserve authorities. For example, the Treasury bill rate rose from 3.8 percent in December 1964 to 5.3 in the last quarter of 1966. The Federal Reserve discount rate was adjusted to the rising market rate structure—from $3\frac{1}{2}$ to 4 percent in November 1964, and from 4 to $4\frac{1}{2}$ percent in December 1965.

No change was made in percentage-reserve requirements for member banks until the last half of 1966, when the requirement against time deposits in excess of $5 million was raised from 4 to 5 percent in July and to 6 percent in September.

An important controversy developed in the last quarter of 1965 between those who wished to prevent interest rates from rising and those who were willing to accept higher rates as a necessary cost of preventing an inflationary boom. President Johnson and Representative Wright Patman of Texas were the most vocal of the former group. The Board of Governors in a 4-3

[8]It is suggested that the reader utilize figures 22 to 29 frequently while reading this section in order to gain perspective with respect to developments.

decision cast their lot on the side of restraint on December 5, 1965, when they approved an increase of the discount rate from 4 to $4\frac{1}{2}$ percent. This represented an act of great courage by Chairman Martin and three other members in upholding the independence of the Board against strong pressure from the Administration. The move was the beginning of a policy of vigorous restraint during 1966.

A significant restrictive influence was exerted by the Fed in 1966 through control of maximum interest rates payable on time deposits by commercial banks (Regulation Q). Rate ceilings were held well below yields on competitive market instruments with the result that time deposits declined sharply. For example, in 1966, the maximum rate payable on savings deposits was 4 percent and on other time deposits $5\frac{1}{2}$ percent, whereas the yields on prime commercial paper and bankers' acceptances rose to 6 percent and $5\frac{3}{4}$ percent, respectively. Under these circumstances, CDs of large commercial banks declined from $18.6 billion in August 1966 to $15.4 billion in December, or by 17 percent.

By November 1966, it became evident that the restrictive Federal Reserve policy was curbing excessive demands of consumers and of state and local governments, and that the upsurge of capital spending was being brought under control. As a consequence, Federal Reserve policy was modified and remained on the easy side until the last quarter of 1967. The main method employed was purchase of U.S. securities by the Reserve Banks whose holdings increased by $4.7 billion between November 1966 and November 1967. The member banks' net reserve deficit of over $400 million was converted to a net reserve surplus in the range of $200 to $300 million after March 1967. Interest rates declined sharply—the Treasury bill rate from 5.3 percent in November 1966 to 3.5 percent at midyear 1967; the commercial-paper rate, from 6 to 4.6 percent.

Encouraged by abundant reserves, commercial-bank credit expanded by 11 percent in 1967; demand deposits, by 7 percent; and time deposits, by 16 percent. The money stock increased 6.5 percent. It is also significant that labor productivity increased by only 1 percent, compared with 3 percent in 1966 and an average annual rate of 4 percent during 1960-1965. Hourly wage rates rose 5.1 percent with the result that unit labor costs went up 4.7 percent. Wholesale prices rose only fractionally, but consumer prices increased 2.7 percent. Price inflation was not out of hand, but it was gaining momentum.

Monetary management presented confusing and difficult problems in 1968. The economy was expanding with vigor, but under conditions of overemployment and excessive price inflation. Unemployment averaged only 3.6 percent of the labor force and dropped to 3.3 percent in late 1968; consumer prices rose 4.2 percent; wholesale prices, 2.5 percent; and unit labor costs, 4.2 percent. These conditions clearly called for a policy of restraint. But the appropriate degree of restraint depended on whether and when a restrictive fiscal policy would be forthcoming from Congress. It will be recalled that President

Johnson had proposed a 10 percent surtax on corporate and individual income-tax liabilities in 1967, along with other minor methods of increasing federal revenues, and that Congress delayed action on the tax bill over a year–until June 1968. This circumstance compounded the complexities facing the Fed. If no increase of tax rates were forthcoming, a more restrictive monetary policy would be needed to curb existing inflationary conditions which were being fostered by a large federal deficit. But if a prompt and substantial increase in tax rates could be expected, monetary restrictions might well be moderated in coordination with fiscal restraint.

The policy actually followed was one calling for tight money-market conditions during the first half of 1968, a move toward ease after the tax bill was passed in June, and a return to greater restraint in the last quarter. More specifically, a net reserve surplus of $144 million in January 1968 was converted to a net reserve deficit in the range of $300 to $400 during the remainder of the first half. This was accomplished mainly by increasing the Reserve Bank portfolio of U.S. securities at a slower rate than necessary to offset the loss of gold and the increase of currency in circulation. Also, legal-reserve requirements were increased on demand deposits by $\frac{1}{2}$ percentage point in January 1968, and the Federal Reserve discount rate was raised in two steps from $4\frac{1}{2}$ to $5\frac{1}{2}$ percent in March and April. In this setting and with vigorous demands for credit, money rates moved on upward. For example, the Treasury bill rate rose from 4.72 percent in November 1967, to 5.52 percent in June 1968, and during the same period the commercial-paper rate increased from 5.28 to 6.25 percent.

With passage of the 10 percent surtax bill in June 1968, Federal Reserve policy became less restrictive. This was deemed advisable because of the anticipated deflationary influence of higher taxes. A net reserve deficit was maintained in member banks, but the amount was cut back some $200 million. Also, the discount rate was reduced from $5\frac{1}{2}$ to $5\frac{1}{4}$ percent in August. But as time passed, it became evident that the higher tax rate was not sufficient to restrain the rampant overoptimism and the inflationary expectations of individuals and businesses. Even though disposable income of consumers was reduced, they maintained and increased their spending by saving less and borrowing more. Likewise, the business investment boom persisted. Faced with these facts, Federal Reserve policy again shifted toward restraint, which was destined to become the harshest monetary control ever experienced in the nation.

At this point, a short digression is required to explain a sharp controversy between the monetarists and the traditionalists both within and outside the Fed. The traditional approach is to define a tight and restrictive money market in terms of market conditions–in which an increasing proportion of required bank reserves is borrowed from the Reserve Banks, the amount of the net reserve deficit is high, and interest rates are high. An easy or expansionary money market is the reverse–one in which member-bank borrowing at the Reserve Banks is minimal, excess reserves are substantial, a sizable net reserve surplus exists, and interest rates are low. In contrast, the monetarists, who regard the stock of money to be the key factor determining the price level and business conditions, deemphasize money market conditions in their definition of a restrictive or expansionary monetary policy. To them a restrictive (deflationary) policy is one that produces relatively slow growth, or a decline, in the stock of money. An easy (inflationary or expansive) policy is just the opposite—one that produces relatively rapid growth in the stock of money.

In the preceding discussion of the 1967-1968 period, the traditional definitions of tight- and easy-money markets were used as a basis for preliminary analysis. It is now desirable to characterize Fed policies through the eyes of the monetarists. With the stock of money growing at an annual rate of 7.6 percent during 1967-1968, compared with a noninflationary normal rate of $3\frac{1}{2}$ to 4 percent, they would label monetary policy as strongly expansive or inflationary. The traditionalists, however, would designate the same policy as tight, restrictive, or deflationary—with an eye on the level of net borrowed reserves and the rising level of interest rates. Both are correct within the framework of their own definitions. Caring little for the immediate targets of net reserve position and the level of money rates, and placing primary emphasis on changes in the stock of money, the monetarists are correct in labeling the policy an expansionary one. They point out that the traditionalists failed to recognize the intense character of the demand for credit when inflationary expectations became firmly implanted. Under these conditions, no preconceived idea of the height of net borrowed reserves and of interest rates associated with deflation is relevant. A deflationary monetary policy exists, in their view, only when the rate of increase in bank reserves and the stock of money are brought down to normal or below normal rates—despite what happens to interest rates and to net borrowed reserves.[9] Since 1968, the views of the monetarist school have been given much more official credence by Federal Reserve authorities. The Open-Market Committee has recently couched its current economic directives to the Fed Bank of New York in terms of the behavior of money as well as with reference to money market conditions. For example, the directive from the meeting in September 1970, concluded:

> In light of the foregoing developments, it is the policy of the Federal Open-Market Committee to foster financial conditions conducive to orderly reduction in the rate of inflation, while encouraging the resumption of sustainable economic growth and the attainment of reasonable equilibrium in the country's balance of payments.
>
> To implement this policy, the Committee seeks to promote some easing of conditions in credit markets and *moderate growth in money and attendant bank credit expansion* over the months ahead. System open-

[9]See Alan H. Meltzer, "Controlling Money," Federal Reserve Bank of St. Louis, *Review* (May 1969), pp. 16-24; also, Richard C. Davis, "How Much Does Money Matter?" Federal Reserve Bank of New York, *Monthly Review* (June 1969), pp. 119-131.

market operations until the next meeting of the Committee shall be conducted with a view to maintaining bank reserves and money market conditions consistent with that objective.[10]

debt management

The influence of debt management during the period 1965-1969 was not very significant, but the thrust of policy was in opposition rather than helpful to the goal of economic stabilization. In order to exert an antiinflationary influence, which was needed in these years, financial liquidity should have been reduced. Instead, as indicated in Table 24-4, liquidity was increased. The proportion of marketable federal debt maturing within 1 year rose from 41.6 percent in 1964 to 46.8 percent in 1969, and the proportion maturing in under 5 years increased from 71.7 to 74.2 percent. Also the average maturity of the marketable debt declined from 5 years to 3 years, 11 months. In part, the Treasury may be absolved because of the desire to overcome the deficit in the international balance of payments by keeping short-term interest rates high in relation to long-term rates. Also, the Congress may be blamed for refusing to repeal the ancient law that prohibits issuing U.S. bonds with coupon rates exceeding $4\frac{1}{4}$ percent. Moreover, the Treasury did make several attempts at maturity extension: 2 advance refundings in fiscal 1965, 2 prerefundings in fiscal 1967, a prerefunding and an exchange to 7-year notes in fiscal 1968, and an exchange to a 6-year note in 1969. But these efforts were not sufficient to offset the shortening of maturities that automatically occurred from the passage of time.

TABLE 24-4 / DISTRIBUTION OF MARKETABLE FEDERAL DEBT BY MATURITIES, 1964 AND 1969 (millions of dollars)

Maturities	December 31, 1964	Percentage Distribution	July 31, 1969	Percentage Distribution
Within 1 year	88,451	41.6	107,416	46.8
1-5 years	64,007	30.1	62,763	27.4
5-10 years	36,421	17.2	34,837	15.2
10-20 years	6,108	2.9	8,372	3.6
20 years and over	17,467	8.2	16,194	7.0
Total	212,454	100.0	229,581	100.0
Average length	5 years		3 years, 11 months	

Source: *Treasury Bulletin* (February 1965), p. 27; (May 1970), p. 22.

[10]*Federal Reserve Bulletin* (December 1970), p. 927; italics mine. The statistical data cited in the foregoing section are drawn from the *Federal Reserve Bulletin*, various issues.

Thus, despite these efforts of the Treasury, a shortening of maturities actually occurred—with the result that its influence was inflationary at a time when a policy of restraint was in order. This adverse action could have been avoided by a more aggressive effort to issue intermediate- and long-term obligations. It was, quite simply, a question of priorities—whether domestic economic stabilization should take precedence over minimization of the cost of borrowing and some reduction of the balance-of-payments deficit. Treasury officials chose the latter, whereas the majority of economists, including the author, would have preferred a higher priority for stabilization.

INFLATION CONTROL, 1969-1970

The Administration of President Nixon, which was inaugurated in January 1969, faced a very difficult and complex domestic problem: the defusing of price inflation without generating intolerable unemployment. As already indicated, the expansionary fiscal and monetary policies in the four preceding years had firmly entrenched inflationary expectations in the minds of businessmen and consumers. This is understandable because the rise of prices had steadily accelerated until both the consumer price index and the general price index were rising at annual rates of over 4 percent during the last half of 1968. The official level of full employment (96 percent) had been exceeded for three years, and by December, the rate of unemployment had declined to 3.3 percent of the labor force. Both consumer spending and business investment in fixed capital were especially strong, having risen over 8 percent above the levels of the preceding year. It was clear that the most pressing economic issue was that of breaking the inflationary spiral.

The game plan of the President, the Council of Economic Advisers, and the Federal Reserve Board was one of gradualism. It called for increasing fiscal and monetary restraint to suppress the boom. However, the brakes were to be applied gradually—with enough pressure to decrease the rate of price increase to a tolerable level during the two or three years ahead, but with not so much that they would grab and send the economy into a severe recession. The mechanical tools were at hand in the forms of adequate monetary and fiscal powers. The screws could be tightened a few turns at intervals, meanwhile watching alertly the economic response. But they were dealing with an organism, not a mechanism. Success would depend on controlling mass psychology as well as on purely economic factors. Could the surging overoptimism and the deeply imbedded inflationary expectations be broken without a swing to mass pessimism and a resultant recession? The previous postwar recessions had all involved unemployment rates of between 6 and 8 percent, which had been necessary to bring approximate stability to the price level. Could this record be improved?

It should be added that the game plan envisaged no direct interference with the free market. There was not to be a revival of the Office of Price Administration (OPA), nor of legal wage controls. The wage-price guideposts of the previous Administration were rejected, as was also the use of "jawboning" tactics by the President and other high officials to interfere in particular price and wage decisions. Free market forces would be relied on to bring about a slowdown or elimination of price inflation. In brief, fiscal restraint would be expected to limit disposable individual and corporate income. Monetary restraint would be expected to reduce the availability of credit, to curb the rate of monetary expansion, and to raise interest rates. This would lead, in turn, to a slowdown in the rates of expansion of business investment and of consumer expenditures, especially for housing and other durables. Unemployment would rise, unused plant capacity would develop, inventories would rise, and corporate profits would decline. Hopefully, in this environment, wage settlements would be more in line with increases in productivity, and the rate of price inflation would be suppressed, if not eliminated.

the record, 1969-1970

Fiscal restraint was applied in mid-1968 and strong monetary restraint became effective in early 1969, but economic expansion continued apace during the first half of 1969 and was not curbed until the third quarter. After that, the economy entered a recession phase which continued throughout 1970. Attention is called to Table 24-5, which indicates the extent of change in selected measures of business conditions between the third quarters of 1969 and 1970. A small decline took place in real GNP, industrial production fell by 5 percent, and the rate of unemployment rose from 3.6 to 5.5 percent. Also, the ratio of

TABLE 24-5 / SELECTED MEASURES OF ECONOMIC CHANGE, 1969-1970

Measures	Third Quarter 1969	Third Quarter 1970	Percentage Change
Real GNP (1958 prices, billions of dollars)	730.9	727.4	− 0.5
Industrial production (FRB, 1957-1959 = 100)	174.6	165.8	− 5.0
Rate of unemployment (BLS, percent)	3.6	5.5	+52.8
Consumer prices (BLS, 1957-1959 = 100)	128.2	136.6	+ 6.5
Wholesale prices (BLS, 1957-1959 = 100)	113.3	117.8	+ 4.0
GNP deflator (1958 = 100)	129.0	135.5	+ 5.1
Basic commodity prices (BLS, 22 commodities; 1957-1959 = 100)	110.9	110.6	− 0.3
Wage rates (average hourly wage of non-agricultural establishment; dollars)	3.11	3.28	+ 5.5
Labor cost per unit of output in manufacturing (BLS, 1957-1959 = 100)	113.7	122.3	+ 7.6
Output per man-hour, nonagricultural	5.2	5.3	+ 2.0

Source: *Survey of Current Business,* various issues.

inventories to sales rose materially to approximately the height of previous postwar recessions. But the responses of prices and wage rates were disappointing. The broad price indexes rose between 4 and 6.5 percent, wage rates increased 5.5 percent, and labor cost per unit of output in manufacturing rose 7.6 percent. The only encouraging evidences that price inflation was being brought under control were the facts that the rate of increase of wholesale prices had been halved by the last quarter of 1970, that basic commodity prices were stable, and that a considerable improvement in labor productivity was underway.

monetary policies

The principal method of monetary control was again open-market operations. Net borrowed reserves of member banks were increased from $310 million in December 1968 to a range of $700 to $1,200 million until midyear 1970, after which they were permitted to decline gradually toward zero. The Reserve Bank discount rate was raised in December 1968, from $5\frac{1}{4}$ to $5\frac{1}{2}$ percent, and again in April 1969, to 6 percent where it remained until November 1970. After that, it was reduced to 5 percent in January 1971, by a series of $\frac{1}{4}$ point reductions. Changes in member-bank reserve requirements were used sparingly. In April 1969, they were increased by $\frac{1}{2}$ percentage point against net demand deposits where they remained throughout 1970. However, in October 1970, when Federal Reserve policy was being moderated, the requirement against time deposits of over $5 million was lowered from 6 to 5 percent. Only one change was made in margin requirements for the purchase or carrying of stock-exchange securities. This requirement, which had been raised from 70 to 80 percent in June 1968, was reduced to 65 percent at the bottom of the bear market in May 1970.

The highly restrictive monetary policy initiated in early 1969 had important repercussions in the financial system. Growth in the stock of money, which had been at an annual rate of 7.6 percent during 1967-1968, was reduced to 5.1 percent in the first half of 1969, and to only 0.6 percent in the second half. With the moderation of Federal Reserve policy in 1970, the rate of growth was accelerated to 5.5 percent (see figure 23). The annual rate of growth of commercial-bank loans, which was over 10 percent during 1967-1968, declined to about 5 percent in 1969, and to 4.7 percent in 1970 (see figure 26). Banks were able to increase loans in 1969 only by liquidating investments heavily, by borrowing from Fed Banks, by borrowing in the Fed funds market, the Eurodollar market, and the commercial-paper market, and by selling loans under repurchase agreements. Their liquidity dropped to the lowest point in this century, which brought on near-crisis conditions. The combination of restricted supply and intense demand for credit drove interest rates at the end of 1969 and at midyear 1970 to the highest level since the Civil War, and sent bond prices to their lowest level. Rates drifted downward during the third quarter of 1970 and declined sharply in the last quarter (see figure 27).

fiscal policies

It will be recalled that the 10 percent federal surtax became law in June 1968—following the series of federal deficits since 1961, which culminated in the huge $25.2 billion deficit in fiscal 1968. This, along with extension of excises and the imposition of certain expenditure controls, produced a budget surplus of $3.2 billion in fiscal 1969—a deflationary swing in one year amounting to $28.4 billion. In terms of the national income accounts, the budget surplus in calendar 1969 was about $10 billion compared with a $5 billion deficit in 1968. Attention is also called to figure 29 which presents the high-employment federal budget, 1962-1970. Between the second quarters of 1968 and 1969, the budget moved from a deficit (stimulus) of $15 billion to a surplus (restraint) of $10 billion. This was strong disinflationary medicine.

Three significant tax changes took place in 1969. The 10 percent surtax was extended through the second half, was reduced to 5 percent during the first half of 1970, and was eliminated at midyear. Next, the 7 percent investment tax credit was repealed, effective in April 1969. Also, Social Security tax rates were increased from 8.8 to 9.6 percent at the beginning of 1969, adding thereby about $3 billion to revenues.

In April 1969, the Nixon Administration announced its intention to hold expenditures in fiscal 1970 to $192.9 billion. Reductions in a wide range of federal programs were made immediately, aggregating some $4 billion, and the budget was cut another $3 billion in September. But these were not enough to offset the shortfall of revenues below their predicted level as a consequence of the economic slowdown. Instead of an intended budget surplus of $3 to $5 billion, fiscal 1970 ended with a deficit of $2.8 billion. Thus, the influence of the federal budget moved from restraint in 1969, first to neutrality, then to stimulus in 1970 and on to stronger stimulus in 1971 when the deficit was $23 billion.

With the rate of unemployment at 6.2 percent and capacity utilization of plant down to 72 percent in December 1970, the Administration decided that the danger of deeper recession transcended the problem of suppressing price inflation. Having dampened the confidence of consumers and businessmen in the upward course of the economy, it turned to rebuilding confidence on various fronts. The most important reversal was in the field of fiscal policy. As already indicated, the budget began to be expansionary during the last half of 1970. A further stride in this direction was announced by President Nixon in his State of the Union message to the Congress on January 22, 1971, as follows:

> To achieve this (full employment), I will submit an expansionary budget this year—one that will help stimulate the economy and thereby open up new job opportunities for millions of Americans.

29 COMPARISON OF HIGH-EMPLOYMENT AND NATIONAL INCOME ACCOUNTS; FEDERAL BUDGETS, 1962-1970 (Surplus +, Deficit –).
Source: Federal Reserve Bank of St. Louis

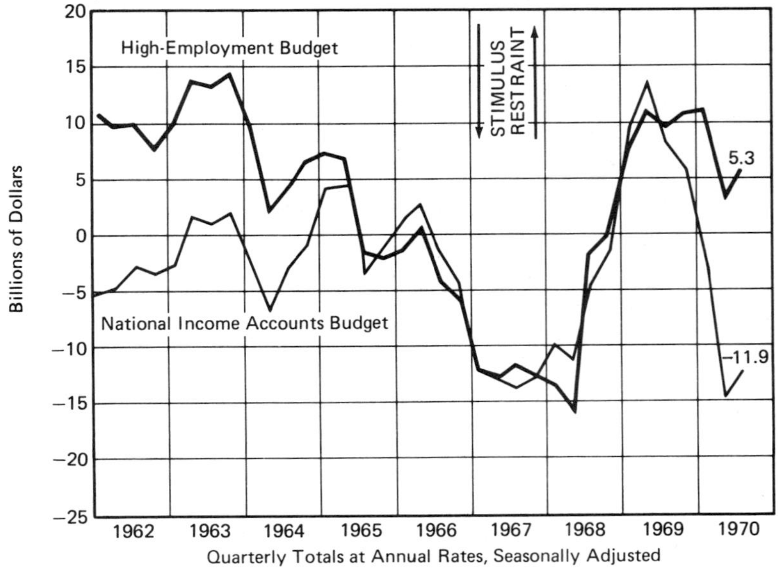

It will be a full-employment budget, a budget designed to be in balance if the economy were operating at its peak potential. By spending as if we were at full employment, we will help to bring about full employment.

I ask the Congress to accept these expansionary policies–to accept the concept of the full-employment budget.

At the same time, I ask the Congress to cooperate in resisting expenditures that go beyond the limits of the full employment budget. For as we wage a campaign to bring about a widely-shared prosperity, we must not re-ignite the fires of inflation and so undermine that prosperity.

Federal outlays in fiscal 1972 are estimated in the budget submitted to Congress in late January 1971 to be $229.2 billion compared with $211.4 billion in 1971–an increase of 8.4 percent. Receipts are estimated at $217.6 billion with a resultant deficit of $11.6 billion.

However, predicted receipts are based on a rather optimistic rise of GNP to $1,065 billion, an increase of 9 percent–of which 5 percent is real product and 4 percent is attributable to price inflation. The consensus of private forecasts is that GNP will be well below this figure. If they prove to be correct, the federal deficit in fiscal 1972 will, of course, be substantially larger.

Another fiscal step on the revenue side was announced in early January 1971, in the form of a 20 percent more liberal allowance for depreciation on equipment placed in service after the end of 1970. According to Treasury estimates, the potential tax saving for corporations will amount to $2.6 billion in 1971 and rise to $4.1 in 1976. This change is expected to provide stimulus to plant and equipment outlays which are projected to increase only 1.4 percent in 1971 by the Department of Commerce survey.[11]

The President also made public in his message the pledge of the monetary authorities to support an overall expansionary policy:

> With the stimulus and discipline of a full-employment budget, with the commitment of the independent Federal Reserve System to provide fully for the monetary needs of a growing economy; and with a much greater effort by labor and management to make their wage and price decisions in the light of the national interest and their own long-run best interests—then for the worker, the farmer, the consumer, and for Americans everywhere we shall gain the goal of a new prosperity: more jobs, more income and more profits, without inflation and without war.

It will be recalled that gradual liberalization of the taut monetary stance in 1969 began in the first quarter of 1970, when Arthur Burns became chairman of the Federal Reserve Board. The annual rate of increase in the stock of money, which was only 0.6 percent in the last half of 1969, increased to 5.5 percent in 1970. At the same time, net borrowed reserves of member banks declined from a $1 billion level at midyear to a small net surplus position at the year-end. This, along with the sluggish demand for credit, enabled commercial banks to rebuild their liquidity substantially. The consequence was one of the sharpest declines of interest rates in history. Treasury bill rates halved between January 1970 and January 1971—from 8 to 4.2 percent. Prime commercial paper dropped from 8.8 to 5.4 percent. The prime rate of commercial banks (loan rate to best customers) was lowered by $2\frac{1}{2}$ percentage points—from $8\frac{1}{2}$ to 6 percent—between March 1970 and January 1971 (see figure 27). The decline in long-term bond yields was also large but less precipitate—between 1 and 2 percentage points. Whether monetary policy will be eased further in 1971 in support of an expansionary fiscal policy remains to be seen, but current probabilities point in that direction. For example, Paul W. McCracken, Chairman of the Council of Economic Advisers, recommends that the money supply should increase between 6 and 8 percent to be consistent with the 9 percent growth of GNP projected by the Administration.[12]

Another notable change in Administration policy began to emerge in the last quarter of 1970, viz., a retreat from the strict laissez-faire attitude toward price and wage determination. Although an incomes policy was espoused by some advisers—notably Arthur Burns—this approach was rejected by the

[11] *Business Week* (January 16, 1971), pp. 22-23.
[12] *New York Times* (February 2, 1971), p. 49.

President as unworkable until early January 1971. Then came his public condemnation of Bethlehem Steel's 11.5 percent rise in structural steel prices, with the threat of lifting quotas on imported steel. A few days later, when U.S. Steel announced a smaller increase–between 6 and 8 percent–Bethlehem retreated to meet the competitive level. Next, the President attacked the excessive wage increases (about 16 percent) in the construction industry and appointed a commission to study the problem and to make recommendations for action.

Temporary standby authority to regulate prices, wages, salaries, and rents was given the President in the Economic Stabilization Act of 1970, approved August 15, as follows:

> The President is authorized to issue such orders and regulations as he may deem appropriate to stabilize prices, rents, wages, and salaries at levels not less than those prevailing on May 25, 1970.[13]

As this is being written, the President is requesting the Congress for a two-year extension of the Stabilization Act. This represents a marked reversal in position since passage of the Act in August, when he stated that he had no intention of utilizing the powers granted. Also, the Council of Economic Advisers has just issued its third inflation alert which focuses on coming wage-price decisions in the construction, lumber, and steel industries. These departures from a hands-off policy appear to signal a much more active role by the Administration in price and wage determination. Such a role may be undertaken as a complementary safeguard against renewed inflation from current expansionary fiscal and monetary policies. Because tangible progress has been made in the first quarter of 1971 in moderating the rate of price inflation, it can only be hoped that the mistakes in previous postwar recession periods will not be repeated–that is, pressing too hard for quick recovery by expansive monetary and fiscal policies. If this road is again taken, the almost certain costs will be renewed price inflation, with its disrupting and inequitable consequences, followed by another period of restrictive monetary-fiscal controls and the application of undesired direct price-wage regulation.

[13] 84 Stat. 799 and 800.

APPENDIX

multiple expansion and contraction of bank credit

The processes of multiple bank-credit expansion and contraction have many theoretical and practical facets. A thorough understanding of these processes and their implications is imperative for all who are in responsible financial positions, whether in public or private life. Prior to the 1930s, there was a great deal of misunderstanding and confusion on the part of both financial economists and practical bankers in regard to bank expansion and contraction. Since that time, these issues have been clarified, but due to their complexity some professional confusion still exists. One of the objects of this appendix is to analyze these issues and to present them in understandable form. Several major questions command attention:

1/What factors govern credit expansion and contraction in the commercial-banking system?

2/Does it make a difference if expansion takes the form of demand deposits, time deposits, or currency?

3/How does expansion and contraction of Federal Reserve Bank credit influence commercial-bank credit and the stock of money?

4/In what respects does the position of the *individual* commercial bank differ from that of the commercial-banking *system* in the processes of expansion and contraction?

THE COMMERCIAL-BANKING SYSTEM

From the standpoint of national economic policies, including monetary policies, the multiple expansion and contraction of bank credit is a problem that relates to commercial banks as a group—that is, to the banking system. At the outset, therefore, we ignore the position of the individual bank and focus attention only on the banking system. Later on, consideration is given to the role of the individual bank, especially because its position is for the most part antithetical to that of the system.

Bank expansion takes different forms which appear on both sides of the combined statement of all commercial banks. On the asset side, expansion appears as an increase in the various types of loans and investments. Qualities and maturities of new loans and investments are immaterial except insofar as quality and maturity standards influence the quantity of bank credit. On the liability side of the statement, expansion is evidenced by deposits–demand deposits which represent about four-fifths of active money, and time deposits which constitute an important form of personal savings and of near-money.

The term "multiple expansion of bank credit" has been used rather loosely to convey a general idea, and therefore requires definition. When applied to the commercial-banking system it means the number of dollars of loans and investments that can be made on the basis of one dollar of legal reserve. The ratio between these two items is known as the *coefficient of expansion.* Such a multiple is possible because banks need, and are required, to hold only a fraction of reserve money to back up their deposit liabilities. Because an integral part of the expansion process is creation of new deposit liabilities, we may alternatively view potential expansion in terms of deposits–that is, the amount of total deposits (demand and time) that can be supported by one dollar of legal reserve. It should also be noted that the term "multiple expansion" applies not only to the commercial-banking system but also to the Federal Reserve Banks, which may expand credit by a multiple of their gold-certificate and Special Drawing Rights reserves. When expansion takes the form of Reserve Bank deposits belonging to member banks (legal reserves), it is aptly labeled *high-powered money*. This emphasizes that one dollar of such reserves provides the base for a multiple expansion of member-bank credit. Attention is first given to multiple expansion and contraction of commercial banks, then to the Reserve Banks.

potential expansion of demand deposits

For the sake of simplicity, we begin with the assumption that expansion of bank loans and investments takes the form of demand deposits and that no change whatever takes place in either currency or time deposits. Under these circumstances, what is the potential amount of expansion that can be generated on the basis of a primary deposit of $100 million of reserve money in member banks when the legal-reserve requirement is 15 percent?[1] The answer is that member banks can expand loans and investments, and thereby create new

[1]It is here assumed that all commercial banks are members of the Fed. Actually, nonmember commercial banks account for about one-fifth of total commercial-bank assets. Because state regulations in regard to legal reserves are generally less rigorous than federal regulations, this assumption leads to an understatement of potential credit expansion and contraction in the U.S. banking system.

demand deposits, in the amount of $567 million; that is, $\frac{85}{.15} = 567$. The original excess reserves of $85 million ($100 million deposit less $15 million required reserves) will, at this point, be entirely utilized in support of the new deposits, with the result that member-bank reserves become just sufficient to meet legal requirements. The coefficient of expansion in this case is thus 6.67; that is, $\frac{100}{15}$. In general, the coefficient depends on the percentage legal-reserve requirement that can be changed within limits by the Board of Governors. When the reserve requirement is 10 percent, the coefficient is 10, and when the requirement is 20 percent, the coefficient is 5.

Such an expansion will in fact take place only if the banks desire to lend to borrowers who seek loans and/or the banks are disposed to purchase federal, municipal, and corporate obligations in the market. Motivation of bank officers to utilize excess reserves is strong because such assets yield no income. Under most conditions, the availability of earning assets combines with the desire to lend and invest, so that expansion actually occurs if excess reserves above the operational minimum exist. A conspicuous exception, however, occurred during the Great Depression, when there was a dearth of credit-worthy borrowers and of securities appropriate for bank investment. During most of this period, excess reserves of member banks ranged between $2 and $6 billion.

potential expansion of currency

Next, let us assume that the entire expansion of bank loans and investments takes the form of currency, and that no change occurs in either demand deposits or time deposits. In this event the coefficient of expansion would be only 1. The original $85 million of excess reserves would be used up dollar for dollar as borrowers took the proceeds of loans in currency and as banks paid for investment securities with currency. Thus, to the extent that the general public decides to hold the newly created money as currency instead of deposits, the expansion coefficient is reduced and approaches its minimum value of 1.

potential expansion of time deposits

Now assume that the entire expansion of bank loans and investments is in time deposits, and that no change occurs in demand deposits or in currency. This is a rather unrealistic situation although it was approximated in 1962 when time deposits increased by $15 billion, adjusted demand deposits by $1.2 billion, and currency by $1 billion. Such a development could occur only if the demand deposits originally created by expansion of bank loans and investments were all shifted by their holders to time deposit accounts. In this case the $85 million excess reserves would support expansion of $1,308 million (that is, 85/.065) and the coefficient of expansion would be 15.38 (that is, 100/6.5). This assumes a median legal reserve requirement of $6\frac{1}{2}$ percent against time deposits. If the minimum requirement of 3 percent is used, the coefficient is 33.33, and if the maximum requirement of 10 percent is used the coefficient becomes 10. Thus, because of the lower reserve requirement applying to time deposits, the potential expansion of bank loans and investments increases when the public chooses to hold a larger part of the proceeds in the form of time deposits.

normal potential expansion

Finally, and more realistically, let us assume that the expansion of loans and investments occurs as demand deposits, time deposits, and currency in the proportions which obtained at midyear 1970—when the amounts were demand deposits, $155.9 billion; time deposits of commercial banks, $201 billion; currency outside banks, $47.8 billion; grand total, $404.7 billion. In other words, each $100 of the combined total was composed of demand deposits, $38; time deposits, $50; and currency, $12. How much, under these average conditions, is the potential expansion of bank loans and investments on the basis of $85 million excess reserves? This question can be answered most readily by calculating the legal reserve needed to support each component of total expansion:

Expansion Component		Percentage Reserve Requirement	Amount of Reserve Required
Demand deposits	$ 38	15.0	$ 5.70
Time deposits	50	5.0	2.50
Currency outside banks	12	100.0	12.00
Total	$100		$20.20

If $20.20 of reserve is required to support the combined expansion of $100, the coefficient of such expansion is 4.95 (that is, 100 ÷ 20.20 = 4.95).

It is also of interest to break down the overall coefficient of 4.95 into subcoefficients for each component. These are demand deposits, 1.88; time deposits, 2.48; currency, 0.59.[2] Thus, $85 million in excess reserves would support $159.8 million in demand deposits, $210.8 million in time deposits, and $50.2 million in currency outside banks—a total of $420.8 million. However, as a consequence of the currency drain of $50.2 million, the potential expansion of bank deposits would be only $370.6 million ($420.8-$50.2 = $370.6 million).

The foregoing analysis of potential bank expansion under fairly typical conditions controverts an error that currently prevails, namely, a disposition to overstate the size of the coefficient of expansion. For example, when the Board

[2]That is, 4.95 X .38 = 1.88; 4.95 X .50 = 2.48; and 4.95 X .12 = .59.

of Governors announced a liberalization of legal-reserve requirements in August 1960, Federal Reserve officials were reported to have said that, "the three moves will make available about $600 million of additional bank reserves. Because each dollar of reserves can be used to make up to $6 in loans, the potential expansion of funds lent by banks is $3.6 billion."[3] Similar announcements have accompanied previous steps to free bank reserves.[4] The method of determining the multiple appears to be that of dividing the released reserves by the average required reserve against demand deposits in member banks. Thus, the important limiting effect of the associated rise of currency outside banks and the influence of growth in time deposits are ignored. As the illustration above shows, it would be more realistic to use a coefficient of about $4\frac{1}{3}$, rather than 6, under prevailing conditions to indicate the potential expansion of bank loans and investments, and of total bank deposits.

Writers in the field of money and banking also frequently leave an erroneous impression with most readers when discussing bank-credit expansion. The coefficient is usually stated in terms of demand deposits by dividing the amount of excess reserve by the required reserve ratio applying to demand deposits—under the assumption that there is no change in currency and time deposits. Such statements are misleading unless properly qualified because changes in currency are second only to Federal Reserve credit as a factor affecting potential expansion and money market conditions. A currency drain reduces member-bank reserve balances dollar for dollar. This forestalls further multiple bank-credit expansion and offsets Federal Reserve actions to enlarge bank reserves and create monetary ease. Conversely, a return flow of currency to the banks provides new reserves on which multiple expansion may be based, and therefore offsets Federal Reserve steps to tighten the money market.

A warning is needed at this juncture against the inclination to treat conclusions that follow from assumed conditions as if they were realities. We have already noted the popular error of overstatement of the coefficient of expansion. But in a similar manner, a significant error may be committed by applying conclusions drawn on the basis of *average* conditions assumed in the above illustration. While average conditions in a representative period provide the best basis for realistic conclusions, they will seldom actually exist in the period ahead. In fact, it is almost certain that future conditions will be different. More specifically, the conclusion that the overall coefficient of expansion under typical conditions is between 4 and 5 is a reasonable generalization. But this expectation is not realistic if future conditions depart materially from the past. Deviations are more likely for short periods of a few months than for

[3] *Wall Street Journal* (Chicago ed.; August 9, 1960), p. 3.

[4] *New York Times* (February 20, 1958), p. 1: "Theoretically, the $500,000,000 (released reserves) can mount to $3,000,000,000 as it is loaned and re-loaned."

Ibid., (June 22, 1954), p. 35: "This action will release from reserves more than $1,500,000,000, which means that the entire system theoretically may expand its loans and investments by $9,000,000,000."

Ibid., (March 19, 1958), p. 1: "The effect of the move was to release about $400,000,000 in reserves. This in turn would make possible an expansion by member banks of just under $3,000,000,000 in their loans and investments."

longer periods of three to five years, which provide time for adjustments to work out. The two most important factors responsible for variation in the coefficient are (1) changes in legal-reserve requirements and (2) changes in preferences of people as between demand deposits, time deposits, and currency.

Legal-reserve requirements may be changed substantially, both by law and administration of existing law. In 1970, the Federal Reserve Act set the minimum and maximum reserve requirements for demand deposits at 7 percent and 22 percent, respectively, and for time deposits at 3 percent and 10 percent. These limits have been changed in the past, and will doubtless be altered by Congress in the future. Moreover, the Board of Governors holds discretionary power to change requirements within the stated limits which means that they also have power to change the coefficient of bank-credit expansion.

While the habits of the community in regard to use of demand deposits and currency have been quite stable, the proportion of currency outside banks to total money has varied appreciably over the years. The record of year-to-year changes shows that in about two-thirds of the years since 1914, changes in demand deposits have been accompanied by currency changes in the same direction. This represents a high degree of positive correlation. Nevertheless, their movements were in opposite directions about one-third of the time, and in all years their rates of change were different. During the 1920s, there was a persistent shift toward demand deposits. In fact, demand deposits rose from \$19.6 billion at midyear 1920 to \$22.5 billion in 1929, whereas currency declined from \$4.1 billion to \$3.6 billion. Again in the early 1930s, the two series moved in opposite directions as the Great Depression brought heavy credit liquidation and currency hoarding. Between midyear 1930 and 1933, demand deposits declined from \$21.7 billion to \$14.4 billion, whereas currency rose from \$3.4 billion to \$4.8 billion.[5] But since 1933, demand deposits and currency have increased together in every three-year period without exception. The generalization may be made that in relatively short periods demand deposits and currency usually move inversely. This follows from their direct relationship as alternative forms of money. When the total money stock remains the same, an increase in currency outside banks necessarily reduces demand deposits by the same amount, and a decrease in currency augments demand deposits. But in longer periods—say, five years or more—both forms of money typically change in the same direction along with the aggregate stock of money.

A complication arises at this point, in view of the definition of active money, which includes currency and demand deposits but excludes time deposits. Hence, the coefficient of "monetary" expansion is only 2.47; that is, 1.88 plus 0.59, under the foregoing conditions compared with 4.36 for total deposits, and 4.95 for total loans and investments. From this it follows that if people choose to hold a larger proportion of bank-credit expansion as time deposits, the potential expansion of total loans and investments (or of total deposits) is

[5]Board of Governors of the Federal Reserve System, *Banking and Monetary Statistics* (Washington, D.C., 1943), p. 34.

thereby enlarged. But at the same time, the potential expansion of active money is thereby reduced because the additional time deposits use up part of the excess legal reserve; less reserve remains to support monetary expansion in the strict sense. This point may be further illustrated by noting the effect of a shift of $100 from demand deposits to time deposits. Immediately, the obvious reduction of demand deposits and the corresponding increase of time deposits would reduce legal-reserve requirements by $10 (that is, $15 – $5). Subsequently, when the banks utilize the released reserve to expand loans and investments (assuming that they can and do), new demand deposits are created in the amount of $66.67 (that is, $10/.15). Thus, the ultimate net result is an *increase* of $66.67 in *total deposits*—an increase of $100 in time deposits and a *reduction* of $33.33 in demand deposits (money).

In summary, as a consequence of the structure of legal-reserve requirements, a given amount of excess reserve will support a larger amount of total bank loans and investments (and of total deposits) as the general public chooses to hold smaller proportions of the expansion as currency and demand deposits and a larger proportion as time deposits. But in terms of monetary expansion proper, a given amount of excess reserve will support a larger amount of money (currency and demand deposits) as the community chooses to hold smaller proportions in currency and in time deposits and a larger proportion in demand deposits.

multiple contraction of bank credit

The opposite side of the multiple-expansion coin is multiple contraction. Let us therefore pose the question of how much contraction would be forced on member banks if Federal Reserve policies and actions should create a legal-reserve deficiency of $85 million—a situation that might develop by sale to nonbank interests of $100 million of U.S. securities by the Reserve Banks. This step would reduce both member-bank deposits and legal reserves $100 million, and would thereby create the $85 million reserve deficiency if reserve requirements were 15 percent. Assume also that all sources of reserve money are closed, so that member banks can repair the deficiency only by credit contraction. Under the conditions described in normal potential expansion, the overall contraction coefficient would be 4.95; hence, extinguishment of $420.8 million of total loans and investments (and of currency, demand deposits, and time deposits) would be necessary. Using the proportions at midyear 1960—12 percent, 38 percent, and 50 percent, respectively—this would mean reductions as follows: currency, $50.2 million; demand deposits, $159.8 million; and time deposits, $210.8 million.

Similarly, the amounts of bank-credit contraction required under each of the foregoing assumptions to repair the $85 million reserve deficiency would be the same as the corresponding amounts of potential expansion on the basis of

$85 million of excess reserves. That is, if all liquidation should take place in demand deposits, the required contraction would be $567 million; if all contraction were in time deposits subject to a 5 percent reserve requirement, the amount would be $1,700 million.[6]

Under actual conditions, the multiple-contraction process operates infrequently because a growing economy requires a roughly corresponding growth in money in order to prevent a decline in the general price level and in output. Monetary policies have generally allowed for normal growth, and they are likely to do so in the future. In addition, largely as a consequence of war finance, money has been created faster than real output, with the result that the average annual increase in the wholesale price level since 1900 has been slightly over 2 percent. Under these circumstances, multiple expansion of credit has been the rule and multiple contraction the exception. The most notable exception since establishment of the Fed was the headlong contraction in 1931-1932 as the economy plunged to the low point of the Great Depression. Multiple contraction took place when bank reserves were drained by currency hoarding and gold exports. However, in view of institutional changes—including enlarged powers of the Fed, federal deposit insurance, and the Employment Act of 1946—forced liquidation is unlikely to confront the banks in future recessions or depressions. Monetary and fiscal policies will almost certainly be utilized to cushion and counteract destructive liquidation. In fact, deposit expansion took place in the recessions of 1954, 1958, and 1961 largely in response to easy-money policies of the Fed. Moreover, contrary to prewar precedent, demand deposits declined between midyear 1959 and midyear 1960 and again in 1969—the prosperity phase of the cycle. A restrictive monetary policy was mainly responsible.

In conclusion, it may be helpful to note that with respect to multiple expansion and contraction the banking system as a whole is analogous to a single consolidated commercial bank with branches throughout the country. Reserve money is not lost (nor gained) domestically by expansion (or contraction) of loans and investments by the consolidated bank. Shifts of deposits and reserves from one office reappear in another branch. The same is true for the banking system: Deposits and reserves lost by one bank reappear in another, and are not lost by the system. But the position of the individual bank stands in sharp contrast because it tends to lose (gain) reserves to *other* banks when it increases (decreases) loans and investments. This point will be developed more fully later.

equations of expansion and contraction of bank credit

While the essence of multiple expansion and contraction of bank credit is understandable in written terms, there are definite advantages in a more

[6]The coefficients of contraction are 6.67 for demand deposits, 1 for currency, and 20 for time deposits.

mathematical approach. Formulas summarizing the influences and relationships of relevant factors, provide a basis for generalization of specific cases, and permit a higher order of precision. Therefore, we now reconsider the previous illustrations in terms of a few simple algebraic equations.

In all cases, the generalized equations are

$$R = rL$$

or

$$L = \frac{R}{r}$$

also,

$$L = D + C$$

where L represents potential expansion of member-bank loans and investments; R is an increment of member-bank legal reserves; r is the ratio of required legal reserves to deposits of member banks; D represents total deposits, the sum of demand deposits (D_d) and time deposits (D_t), and C is currency outside banks.

Also, in all cases, the coefficient of expansion of member-bank loans and investments, (E), is

$$E = \frac{L}{R}, \text{ or } \frac{1}{r}$$

In Case I—potential expansion of demand deposits—the assumptions are made that no change takes place in either currency or time deposits, that member-bank excess reserves and borrowings at Reserve Banks are zero, that a primary deposit of $100 million of reserve money (D_1) is made in member banks, and that the member-bank reserve requirement is 15 percent. Under these circumstances, $R = D_1(1 - r)$, or $85 million. Substituting in the equations,

$$L = \frac{R}{r} \text{ and } E = \frac{L}{R}, \text{ we have:}$$

$$L = \frac{85}{.15} = \$566.7 \text{ million}$$

and $$E = \frac{566.7}{85} = 6.67$$

It should be noted that the coefficient of expansion (E) is expressed as a multiple of excess reserves (R), not of the primary deposit (D_1) which equals the addition to total member-bank legal reserves. The reserve requirement of $15 million ($D_1r$) must be subtracted from total new reserves in order to determine the amount of excess reserves. Thus, including the primary deposit, the total increase of deposits is $667 million compared with an increase of $567 million in loans and investments, and of loan-derived deposits.

In Case II—potential expansion of currency—it is assumed that no change in demand and time deposits occurs and that the entire reserve deposit (D_1) is withdrawn in currency—so that the entire expansion of bank loans and investments takes the form of currency outside banks.

Substituting in the equations, $L = \frac{R}{r}$ and $E = \frac{L}{R}$, we have:

$$L = \frac{85}{1} = \$85 \text{ million}$$

and $$E = \frac{85}{85} = 1$$

Under these conditions, borrowers take the proceeds of loans in currency and banks pay for securities with currency which remains outside the banks. This case illustrates the important factor of people's choices concerning the forms of money they wish to hold on the problems of bank-credit expansion and of monetary management. An increase of currency absorbs reserves dollar for dollar, whereas an increase of deposits absorbs reserves only by the fractional amount of the reserve requirement.

Case III—potential expansion of time deposits—assumes no change in demand deposits and currency, so that the entire expansion takes the form of time deposits. A legal-reserve requirement of 5 percent against time deposits is also assumed. Substituting in the equations, $L = \frac{R}{r}$ and $E = \frac{L}{R}$, we have

$$L = \frac{85}{.05} = \$1700$$

and $$E = \frac{1{,}700}{85} = 20$$

Using the minimum-reserve requirement of 3 percent, the coefficient (E) is 33.3, and using the maximum requirement of 10 percent, it becomes 10.

This case is useful in demonstrating the small absorption of bank reserves in support of a given amount of time deposits as compared with demand deposits, and especially, with currency. It is somewhat unrealistic in the sense that the proceeds of a new loan expansion are not initially taken in the form of time deposits. But it is more realistic when time is allowed for savers to make the shift from demand to time deposits—a process which releases required reserves.

Case IV—normal potential expansion—assumes that expansion of bank loans and investments takes the forms of demand deposits (D_d), time deposits (D_t), and currency (C) in the proportions that existed in midyear 1970—38 percent, 50 percent, and 12 percent, respectively. If these proportions are used to weight the assumed percentage reserve requirements—demand deposits, 15 percent; time deposits, 5 percent; and currency, 100 percent—the weighted average reserve requirement (r_w) is 20.2 percent as shown in the following table.

Expansion Element (1)	Reserve Requirements (percent) (2)	Weights (3)	(2) X (3) (4)
Demand deposits	15.0	38	570
Time deposits	5.0	50	250
Currency	100.0	12	1,200
		100	2,020

$$\frac{\text{Sum of (4)}}{\text{Sum of (3)}} = \frac{2{,}020}{100} = 20.2\%$$

Hence, substituting in the equations, $L = \frac{R}{r}$ and $E = \frac{L}{R}$, we have:

$$L = \frac{85}{20.2} = \$420.8 \text{ million}$$

and $$E = \frac{420.8}{85} = 4.95$$

MULTIPLE EXPANSION OF RESERVE BANK CREDIT

A far more explosive aspect of monetary expansion than that of commercial banks is multiple expansion by central banks—represented in this country by the Federal Reserve Banks. This is so because a large part of Reserve Bank credit—45 percent in 1970—takes the form of legal reserves of member banks. Such reserves, as we have just seen, constitute high-powered money in the sense that, because of fractional reserve requirements, one dollar is capable of supporting several dollars of member-bank deposits. But the Reserve Banks have traditionally been subject to a fractional reserve requirement—between 1942 and 1965 a minimum of 25 percent in gold certificates behind liabilities in the forms of deposits and Federal Reserve Notes. That is, \$100 in gold certificates provided the reserve money base for \$400 of legal-reserve balances of member banks, or of \$400 in Federal Reserve Notes, or a combination of the two—an expansion coefficient of

4. Thus, if member-bank reserve balances are called high-powered money, gold-certificate reserves of the Reserve Banks may well be designated *super money*.

expansion in member-bank reserve balances

First, consider the case of Reserve Bank expansion which takes the form of member-bank reserve balances. This could be brought about by additions to holdings of U.S. securities on the initiative of the Reserve authorities, or by increases in discounts and advances on the initiative of borrowing member banks. For illustrative purposes, the question may well be raised: How much total expansion of member-bank credit could be supported under these conditions by $100 of gold-certificate reserve in the Reserve Banks? The answer can be readily calculated by use of the already-determined coefficients of expansion, as follows:

1/If all member-bank expansion took the form of demand deposits and member-bank reserve requirements were 15 percent, total potential expansion would be $2,667 $\left(\text{that is, } 100 \times \frac{100}{25} \times \frac{100}{15}\right)$; if member-bank reserve requirements were 10 percent, the potential amount would be $4,000; and if member-bank reserve requirements were 20 percent, the answer would be $2,000.

2/If member-bank expansion of loans and investments took the monetary proportions at midyear 1970—demand deposits, 38; time deposits, 50; currency, 12—and if reserve requirements against demand deposits were 15 percent and against time deposits were 5 percent, total potential expansion would be $1,980 $\left(\text{that is, } 100 \times \frac{100}{25} \times 4.95\right)$. The potential expansion of money (demand deposits and currency), however, would be only $988 $\left(\text{that is, } 100 \times \frac{100}{25} \times 2.47\right)$[7].

expansion in federal reserve notes

Next, consider the case of Reserve Bank expansion which took the form of Federal Reserve Notes. Here the total potential expansion of $100 of gold-certificate reserve would be only $400 $\left(\text{that is, } 100 \times \frac{100}{25}\right)$. No sub-

[7]Sum of coefficients of demand-deposit expression (1.88) and of currency expansion (0.59).

sequent expansion of member-bank credit follows under the assumptions that Federal Reserve Notes are passively paid out by Reserve Banks only in response to member-bank requests for currency, and that member banks, in turn, make such requests only when the general public withdraws currency from them. Under these conditions, which are close to reality, the new increment of Federal Reserve Notes merely passes through the hands of member banks as currency distributing agencies. Obviously, Federal Reserve Notes "outside banks" and held by the general public cannot serve as a reserve base for further bank expansion.

Although the foregoing assumptions closely correspond to reality during the period 1942-1965, some qualification is required by the 1959 amendment of the Federal Reserve Act pertaining to legal-reserve requirements. Under this amendment all, or part of, cash in vault of member banks may, at the discretion of the Board of Governors, be counted as legal reserve. Thus, it would be possible for a new increment of Federal Reserve Notes to be retained as legal-reserve cash in vault. Such an increment of notes would serve as a basis for further bank-credit expansion to the same extent as a member-bank deposit at the Reserve Bank. But it is unlikely that this change in the Federal Reserve Act will significantly shift legal reserves from Reserve Bank deposits to Federal Reserve Notes held as cash in vault. Member banks are likely to continue the practice of minimizing currency holdings because (1) insurance costs are thereby reduced, (2) dangers of robbery and defalcation are not so great, (3) expensive vault space is saved, and (4) a deposit at the Reserve Bank is a more convenient and more acceptable means of payment in the money market than are Federal Reserve Notes.

While the legal-reserve requirement for Federal Reserve Banks has historically provided an upper limit on expansion of member-bank reserves and Federal Reserve Notes, this has ceased to be true since 1968 as a result of two amendments to the Federal Reserve Act. The first, passed in March 1965, eliminated the 25 percent reserve requirement against member-bank reserve balances; the second, passed in March 1968, removed the requirement against Federal Reserve Notes. As a consequence, the only limit on expansion of Federal Reserve credit is the discretionary judgment of the Federal Reserve authorities. In peacetime, this limit is presumably an amount that is consistent with the basic objectives of the economy—stable growth, practical full employment, a relatively stable price level, reasonable equilibrium in the international balance of payments. Under war conditions, the primary consideration would become a war-finance program designed to assure victory and a minimum of disorganization and injustice in the postwar economy. If the financial record of all previous major wars is indicative, this would mean an enormous expansion of Reserve Bank credit, commercial-bank credit, and the stock of money. This, in turn, would lead to a rise in the price level of unknown dimensions, depending on the magnitude, character, and length of the war.

POSITION OF THE INDIVIDUAL BANK

If the commercial-banking *system* can develop a multiple expansion on the basis of a given amount of excess legal reserve, can the *individual* bank similarly indulge in multiple expansion to the same extent, in lesser degree, or not at all? Before the mid-1920s, monetary economists frequently erred in treating expansion by the individual bank as if it were identical with expansion by the banking system as a whole.[8]

It is not surprising that this error was quite general because it was an easy one to make. Fully aware that the banking system was capable of generating multiple expansion, and somewhat unfamiliar with problems of bank management, economists concluded that the individual bank could lend several dollars on the basis of each dollar of excess reserve. Support for this conclusion was also provided by individual bank statements of condition which showed total loans and investments and total deposits to be several times larger than legal reserves. Thus, there was a superficial plausibility attached to this erroneous conclusion–a fact that undoubtedly explains its long persistence. In the 1920s, several monetary economists–notably Chester A. Phillips and Robert G. Rodkey[9]–discovered the error and developed the correct analysis of the individual bank's place in the expansion process.

The basic point developed by these new analyses was that the positions of the banking system and of the individual bank are in the main antithetical instead of identical with respect to the expansion process. Whereas the causation for the banking system is from loans and investments to deposits, the reverse is true for the individual bank–that is, from the receipt of primary deposits (and thereby reserve money) to loans and investments. That is, with rather minor exceptions, the individual bank cannot in the short run build up its own deposits by expanding its own loans and investments. The immediate task before us is to develop the reasons why this proposition is true.

[8]The first systematic presentation of this error to the author's knowledge was made by the distinguished British economist, Henry Dunning Macleod, who was a professor at Trinity College, Cambridge. After giving a specific example of how a banker holding £10,000 in cash could lend £40,000 and thereby create an equivalent amount of new deposits, he summarized the analysis as follows:

> Hence we see that the business of a "banker" does not consist in lending out money, as is so often supposed, but in buying securities of different sorts, with Credit. When he sees that one tenth in specie is sufficient to meet his liabilities, of course he may create liabilities, or Credit, to the amount of ten times the amount of specie he has. He therefore buys bills, and creates liabilities several times exceeding the basis of bullion; and, as he charges exactly the same price for this Credit as if it were cash, it is seen how this Credit is Capital to him; and the creation of such a Credit, or Right of action is an "issue" or *exitus.*

See *The Theory and Practice of Banking* (3d ed.; London: Longmans, Green, 1875), p. 275.

The foregoing erroneous pattern set by Macleod was accepted, and frequently cited with approval, by academic writers in the United States until the early 1920s. Notable examples are as follows: Charles F. Dunbar, *The Theory and History of Banking* (3d ed.; New York: Putnam's, 1917), p. 32; Eugene E. Agger, *Organized Banking* (New York: Holt, Rinehart & Winston, 1918), pp. 32-33; Horace White, *Money and Banking* (3d ed.; Boston: Ginn, 1908), pp. 194-195; H. G. Moulton, *The Financial Organization of Society* (Chicago: University of Chicago Press, 1921), pp. 476-477.

[9]Chester A. Phillips, *Bank Credit* (New York: Macmillan, 1920), chaps. I-IV; Robert G. Rodkey, *The Banking Process* (New York: Macmillan, 1928), chap. XV.

primary and derivative deposits

A first step in the analysis requires a distinction between primary and derivative deposits of the individual bank. *Primary* deposits are built up by the receipt of currency and, far more importantly, by receipt of checks drawn on *other* banks. In either case, when a deposit is made, primary reserves are correspondingly increased. Currency deposits immediately augment legal reserve cash, and currency in excess of working needs is usually shipped to the Reserve Bank for credit in the legal-reserve account. Checks drawn on other banks are quickly converted to legal reserves by collection—mainly through Reserve Bank channels but also through clearing houses and correspondent banks. Competition among banks for primary deposits is very keen because they constitute the chief source of funds, and hence the chief source of earning power. After allowance for needed primary reserves, all primary deposits can usually be converted to income-bearing assets—loans and investments (including liquidity reserves).

In contrast with primary deposits, *derivative* deposits of a bank arise from loans to depositor-borrowers. When a loan is made, the customer's account is typically credited with the proceeds. If the customer should leave these proceeds untouched during the life of the loan, the derivative deposit would obviously equal the amount of the loan (disregarding interest). However, if the customer draws out the proceeds immediately and does not rebuild his account in anticipation of repayment, the amount of derivative deposits becomes zero. Between these two extremes there is the possibility that checks drawn on the proceeds by the borrower will not return through collection channels for a few days; that the borrower may increase his balance a few days before the loan matures in preparation for repayment; and that the bank may insist that a small part of the derivative deposit be left in the account as a compensatory balance. Under these circumstances, the amount of derivative deposits may be important; so the next question before us becomes: How significant are such deposits in the individual bank?

significance of derivative deposits

Analysis of bank lending and investing operations leads to the conclusion that the amount of derivative deposits in the individual bank is of rather minor importance; that is to say, deposits of the individual bank belong, for the most part, in the primary category. The principal reason for this conclusion is that business firms and individuals borrow only when they have debts to pay. Only the foolish or grossly-careless borrower would arrange for a loan at a cost of between 4 and 9 percent per annum and leave the proceeds untouched in his account. Certainly, in the typical case, the proceeds are checked away almost immediately. Corporate treasurers often order immediate transfer of the proceeds to creditors as part of the borrowing transaction.

Borrowers also frequently allow for collection time, so that even checks sent to distant creditors return shortly after loan proceeds are credited. Most of the checks drawn on a derivative deposit (loan proceeds) are deposited in *other* banks, not in the lending bank. Moreover, there is no assurance that checks deposited in the lending bank by payees represent a permanent addition to the lending bank's deposits. To the extent that such deposits raise payees' balances above normal, they may reside there only temporarily because they constitute unwanted liquidity. Undesired increments in deposit accounts are likely to be checked upon to purchase earning assets or consumers' goods, and thus indirectly to find their way to other banks.

If derivative deposits are relatively unimportant during the initial period of a new loan, are they significant during the period just preceding maturity and repayment? In other words, does the typical borrower substantially build up his balance during the days preceding maturity date in order to repay his debt? The answer is in the negative; on the average, there is not an important build-up of balances at this time. Because his checking account yields no interest, the borrower avoids accumulation above a working minimum. If his account rises materially above this minimum from the flow of income or sale of assets, he either prepays the loan or invests in liquid earning assets such as Treasury bills. Thus, while specific cases of derivative deposit build-up prior to loan payment can be cited, they represent the exception, not the rule.

Another possible avenue by which derivative deposits may assume importance is the prevailing practice of banks to insist that customers maintain an average compensating balance of between 15 and 20 percent of their borrowed funds. That is, assuming all other relevant factors to be favorable, a business firm with an average deposit balance of $20,000 may expect to be able to borrow between $100,000 and $133,000. Now if the average balance of the firm should decline to $10,000, the bank might insist that it be restored to $20,000 in order to maintain the peak borrowing power of $100,000. If this adjustment is made by borrowing $10,000 from the bank, it is proper to regard the deposit as derivative from the loan. More or less permanent derivative deposits sometimes arise when a loan is associated with the opening of a new deposit account. If the new customer shifts $10,000 from other banks (primary deposit) and desires a line of credit of $100,000, the bank may insist that he leave an additional $10,000 of the loan proceeds in his account. Another special case is the intermittent borrowing by large finance companies not having a permanent account at the bank. The bank, for example, may agree to lend $1,000,000 if the company will maintain an average balance of, say, $100,000, during the life of the loan.

Incidentally, loans that give rise to untouched derivative deposits in a bank yield handsome returns because they can be made to a multiple of excess reserves. Under average conditions, $100 of excess reserve can support about $400 to $500 of new loans and derivative deposits. If the rate on loans is 7 percent, the yield realized on excess reserves is 28 to 35 percent (7 percent × 4 or 5).

Despite these exceptions, the amount of derivative deposits in a single bank is a very small part of its total deposits. Compensating balance requirements are met for the most part, not by borrowing, but by shifting funds from other banks or by selling liquid assets. Bank borrowing by a business firm is not the source of the basic portion of its current assets; instead, a healthy current asset position, including cash assets, is one of the important conditions to borrowing ability. Thus, the insistence by banks that an average balance of 15 to 20 percent of the borrowed funds be maintained becomes one of their standards to determine whether, and to what extent, a prospective borrower is credit-worthy. Such insistence is far more important as a method of drawing primary deposits than as a means of creating derivative deposits.

Finally, a better view of the significance of derivative deposits in the individual bank is provided by actual loan and investment statistics. At the end of 1969, earning-asset categories in which derivative deposits are infinitesimal constituted 72 percent of total loans and investments of all commercial banks in the United States. These were: investments, $126.1 billion; real-estate loans, $70 billion; consumer loans, $70.6 billion (including "other loans"); loans to financial institutions, $17.6 billion; loans for purchasing or carrying securities, $9.8 billion; and Federal funds sold, $9.9 billion. Commercial and agricultural loans of all commercial banks, the only earning-asset category in which derivative deposits have any importance whatever, were $118.8 billion, or 28 percent of total loans and investments.[10] On the liberal hypothesis that derivative deposits arising from commercial and agricultural loans amount to 10 percent of such loans, the proportion of derivative demand deposits in the average commercial bank at the end of 1969 would be only 6.9 percent.[11] Thus the conclusion emerges that derivative deposits in the average individual bank are relatively insignificant, even though, in the banking system as a whole, almost all deposits have been created by loan and investment expansion.

While derivative deposits in the average bank are relatively unimportant, some banks enjoy a much higher proportion of such deposits than others. The conditions that give rise to maximum derivative deposits in a bank may be listed, as follows: (1) a high proportion of commercial loans to total loans and investments; (2) a loan portfolio marked by short maturities; (3) strong insistence on customer maintenance of generous compensating deposit balances–a factor that becomes most important during tight-money markets; (4) low interest rates on loans; and (5) holding of a substantial part of total demand deposits in a major trade area and in the nation. These conditions are almost self-explanatory. Short-term commercial loans represent the only earning-asset category in which derivative deposits are significant. Such deposits are virtually nonexistent in business term loans, mortgage loans, consumer loans, security loans, open-market commercial paper, and security investments. Low interest

[10] *Federal Reserve Bulletin* (October 1970) p. A 24.

[11] Commercial and agricultural loans were $118.8 billion; adjusted demand deposits, $172.1 billion.

rates are conducive to derivative deposits because borrowers have less incentive to keep deposit accounts at the working minimum. Finally, the ratio of retained derivative deposits in a bank tends to rise along with its proportion of total demand deposits in the country. All derivative deposits would be retained under present assumptions if there were only a single consolidated bank with offices throughout the nation. At the other extreme, the ratio is insignificant in a small bank operating competitively in a system of many thousands of banks, as in the United States. The ratio is doubtless quite significant in the Bank of America, the largest bank in the country, with a statewide branch system in California. The ratio is still more important in a bank that is one of a few large nationwide branch systems, such as the Midland Bank in England, and the Royal Bank of Canada.

For the bank whose derivative deposits are well above average, it may be useful to compute the coefficient of loan expansion on the assumption that other banks are neither expanding nor contracting loans and investments. The formula for determination of a bank's potential loan expansion on the basis of a given amount of excess reserve is,

$$L = \frac{R}{1 - b + br_d}$$

Dividing by R, we have the coefficient of expansion, where

$$E_d = \frac{L}{R} = \frac{1}{1 - b + br_d}$$

and where R is the amount of excess reserve; L is the amount of possible loan expansion; b is the ratio of derivative deposits to new loans; r_d is the ratio of required legal reserves to demand deposits; and E_d is the coefficient of potential expansion in the form of demand deposits. For example, if b has a value of 20 percent and r_d is 15 percent, we have

$$E_d = \frac{1}{1 - .20 + .03} = 1.2$$

By way of explanation, the potential new loans (L) of a bank rise in relation to excess reserve (R) as the proportion of retained derivative deposits (b) rises. That is, if no derivative deposits are retained, $b = 0$ and $L = R$; if $b = 10$ percent and $R = 1$, $L = \frac{1}{(1 - .10)} = 1.11$; if $b = 20$ percent, $L = \frac{1}{(1 - .20)} = 1.25$; if $b = 30$ percent, $L = \frac{1}{(1 - .30)} = 1.43$; and so on. But legal reserve must be held against the retained derivative deposits, allowance for which is made by adding br_d to $(1 - b)$ in the denominator, so that $L = \frac{R}{(1 - b + br_d)}$. The factor br_d, being a fraction times a fraction, has a low value which rises as b increases, thereby limiting somewhat the decline in value of $(1 - b)$ and the rise in value of L.

For most U.S. banks, the above formula for determination of their coefficient of expansion is not a useful management tool. The assumed conditions seldom if ever fit the reality of the moment. Variation from the average ratio of retained derivative deposits is wide, and other banks are always changing their loans and investments. Bank officers seldom count on retention of a portion of derivative deposits from the typical loan in any category, including commercial loans. They are aware that the average does not apply to the individual case. Hence, in general, they proceed on the day-to-day basis that reserves will be lost to the full amount of net additions to loans and investments. If, in fact, a portion of derivative deposits is retained, the associated increment of reserves can be committed to earning assets in the days ahead.

MULTIPLE EXPANSION OF COMMERCIAL-BANK CREDIT

At this point, we are confronted with what seems to be a stubborn paradox. The banking system as a whole can expand loans and investments (and thereby deposits) by a multiple of excess reserves We have just found this multiple to be 4 or 5 under average conditions. However, the analysis reached the conclusion that the individual bank, like any ordinary business firm, can lend and invest no more (or very little more) than the amount of excess reserve it holds or borrows. How can the whole represent more than the sum of the parts? Resolution of this paradox is our next task.

For the sake of clarity, several assumptions are made in the subsequent illustration: (1) All commercial banks are members of the Fed; (2) the legal-reserve requirement against net demand deposits is 15 percent; (3) all bank-credit expansion takes the form of demand deposits; (4) both excess legal reserves and member-bank borrowing at Reserve Banks are zero; (5) a strong demand prevails for loans at existing rates; and (6) banks are willing to lend all excess reserves. In addition, assume that the expansion process is initiated by the First National Bank of Chicago which receives on deposit an officer's check of the Federal Reserve Bank to the amount of $100, issued to purchase U.S. securities from a bond dealer. The abstracted entries on the statements of First National Bank, and of succeeding groups of banks participating in the expansion process, would be as follows:

At the outset the First National Bank holds $85 of excess reserve after setting aside $15 of legal reserve to back up the new primary deposit. In step 2 the bank lends $85 to customers and credits their deposit accounts with the proceeds. Then shortly (assume immediately) the borrowers' checks, drawn on the new deposits to pay debts, return for collection through the Federal Reserve Bank or the local clearing house. That is, in step 3, the First National loses all the

First National Bank of Chicago (Bank I)

Assets				*Liabilities*			
Required reserves	+ $15	(1)		Deposits (primary)	+ $100	(1)	
Excess reserves	± 85	(1)	(3)				
Loans	+ 85	(2)		***Deposits (derivative)***	± 85	(2)	(3)
		Group II (assume 10 banks)					
Required reserves	+ $12.75	(3)		Deposits (primary)	+ 85	(3)	
Excess reserves	± 72.25	(3)	(5)				
Loans	+ 72.25	(4)		***Deposits (derivative)***	± 72.25	(4)	(5)
		Group III (assume 100 banks)					
Required reserves	+ 10.84	(5)		Deposits (primary)	+ 72.25	(5)	
Excess reserves	± 61.41	(5)	(7)				
Loans	+ 61.41	(6)		***Deposits (derivative)***	± 61.41	(6)	(7)
To Group IV				To Group IV			

All Succeeding Groups

Group	*Required Reserves*	*Excess Reserve*	*Loans*	*Deposits*
IV	$ 9.21	$ 52.20	$ 52.20	$ 61.41
V	7.83	44.37	44.37	52.20
VI	6.66	37.71	37.71	44.37
VII	5.60	32.11	32.11	37.71
VIII	4.82	27.29	27.29	32.11
IX	4.09	23.20	23.20	27.29
X	3.48	19.72	19.72	23.20
Other Banks	19.72	111.41	111.41	131.13
Total for all banks	$100.00	$567.00	$567.00	$667.00

derivative deposits and all its excess reserve. Thus, the net result is an increase of primary deposits ($100), of reserve ($15) to support the deposit, and of loans ($85); the italicized items cancel out.

This brings us to the banks in Group II, in which the checks drawn on First National are deposited. Some members of Group II, assumed to be 10 banks, are located in the Chicago trade area, but others are widely scattered, depending on the location of creditors. Step 3 brings them $85 of *primary* deposits and an equal amount of reserves of which $12.75 are required. Loans are then increased by the amount of excess reserves ($72.25) and customers' accounts are then credited in step 4. In step 5, the borrowers spend the new deposits, and when the checks return for payment, Group II banks lose both the derivative deposits and their excess reserves.

The same process is repeated by Groups III, IV, V, and so forth until in the end all excess reserves have been utilized and transformed into required reserves supporting the new structure of demand deposits. Each bank has loaned only the amount of its excess reserve, but by working together, the banks as a system have loaned a multiple (6.67) of the initial excess reserve ($85), or $567, and in the process an equal amount of new demand deposits has been created. When the initial primary deposit of $100 is added, aggregate new deposits amount to $667. In the illustration, it will be noted that the amount of excess reserve in the hands of each succeeding group is diminished by the required reserve of 15 percent against the primary deposit it receives. The excess reserve in the hands of Group X, the last one calculated, is only $19.72. Theoretically, there are an infinite number of groups and the process goes on and on, finally subdividing the residual into cents, mills, and fractions thereof.

Actually, the illustration is oversimplified in order to highlight the essential features of the process. In reality, the succeeding groups are not mutually exclusive; that is, First National Bank of Chicago may be a member of several other groups, and so may any other individual bank. The process may be likened to that of dropping myriad stones of gradually diminishing size into a pool. The concentric circles form crisscross patterns that finally envelop the entire surface; so it is with the numerous increments of excess reserves dispersed throughout the banking system.

Several additional observations are suggested by the illustration.

1/The First National Bank can pay the proceeds of loans in currency, rather than in deposit credit, without basically altering its liquidity position. In both cases, the loss of primary reserve approximates the amount of new loans. There is, however, a big difference in the two cases with respect to bank-credit expansion. If loan proceeds are paid in currency that remains outside the banks, reserves are drawn from the whole banking system as well as from the First National Bank. The expansion process is stopped in its tracks and never goes beyond the initial stage. But if, as the illustration shows, loan proceeds take the form of deposit credit, the legal reserve remains somewhere in the banking system and can support a multiple credit expansion.

2/The question may be raised: Why cannot the First National Bank extend loans well beyond the $85 of excess reserves, say, by $285? At first glance, this might appear plausible because $85 represents a 30 percent reserve against $285, and indeed, represents 15 percent of $567. But this line of thought overlooks the fact that borrowers would check away the $285 of derivative deposits, with the result that First National would be confronted with a reserve deficiency of about $200. Such a deficiency can be adjusted only by borrowing reserves or by disposing of liquidity reserves and other assets.

3/Students sometimes express doubt that the First National is in position to lend even as much as $85 because required reserves against the new derivative deposit amount to $12.75. But this contention fails to associate the loss of derivative deposits with the loss of reserves. That is, as long as the derivative deposits remain on the books, there is no draining away of reserve money, but only the reduction of $12.75 in excess reserves. However, if all derivative deposits are checked away, the bank is in position to lend at least $85, and concomitantly, to lose an equal amount of reserves.

4/One occasionally encounters the argument that when all banks are expanding together, the proposition that a single bank can lend no more than its excess reserves is invalidated. More specifically, if First National should gain $85 in primary deposits from *other* banks' loans while losing $85 in derivative deposits, the amount of its legal reserve would remain unchanged. Its gain in reserves would exactly offset its loss in reserves; legal-reserve requirements would increase $12.75 because of the net rise of $85 in deposits. Such a result is theoretically possible if all banks are expanding loans in step, but this does not invalidate the original proposition, which assumed "other things being equal." One of the principal "other things" was an unchanged amount of loans and investments of other banks. As a practical matter, the individual banker typically proceeds with loan expansion on the basis of "other things being equal," even though he may be aware that the banking system is expanding. He follows this course because he can never be certain when and whether he will receive a share of yesterday's expansion by other banks; he usually waits to see what happens to his primary reserves. If new primary deposits and reserves come his way, he puts the excess reserves to work; if not, he stands pat unless he chooses to face a reserve deficiency.

5/The antithetical positions in the expansion process of the individual bank and the banking system represent extremes between which stand groups of banks in specified areas with positions on the scale depending largely on the size of the area. For example, the banks as a unit in Boston occupy a position far more like the individual bank. That is, if they should expand loans substantially while banks elsewhere in the United States make no change in total earning assets, Boston banks would lose reserves heavily to the rest of the country. But an appreciable part of the new derivative deposits would remain in Boston, so that–unlike the individual bank–loans could be increased appreciably more than excess reserves without creating a reserve deficiency. As the size of the area and the number of banks in the group increase–say, first to the Boston Federal Reserve district, then step by step to include the other eleven districts–the coefficient of expansion gradually rises until it equals that of the entire banking system.

6/The multiple expansion depends on the percentage of required reserves which, in turn, depends on banking laws, Federal Reserve regulations, liquidity policies of banks, and the decisions of people in regard to the relative amounts of demand deposits, time deposits, and currency they wish to hold. The expansion coefficient of 6.67 in the illustration depends, of course, on the given assumptions; it would be different under other assumptions. As already indicated, if required reserves are 10 percent, the coefficient becomes 10; if 20 percent, the coefficient becomes 5. When the general public shifts part of demand deposits to time deposits, required reserves are released, so that the coefficient of expansion of *total* deposits increases. However, because time deposits require reserves–even though small–the coefficient of demand-deposit expansion is thereby reduced. When people wish to hold a larger part of money in currency, the expansion is reduced because new currency withdrawals reduce bank reserves dollar for dollar, the initial base of the expansion.

7/The point needs to be stressed that the mere existence of excess bank reserves does not assure their immediate utilization by loan and deposit expansion. Credit-worthy borrowers must demand the available amount of potential loans at current rates and other terms, and banks must be willing to lend as much as excess reserves will support. In any event, the lending process takes time so that some lag must be expected between appearance and utilization of excess reserves. Since World War II, banks have put reserves to work rather promptly by lending and investing. But such was not the case during the Great Depression. Excess reserves then ranged between $2 and $6 billion. Income prospects for businesses and consumers were so bleak that the demand for loans was low, and on the supply side, banks were unwilling to assume normal credit risks. Furthermore, appropriate liquidity-reserve securities were either not to be found, or if available, yields were so low that banks preferred to hold nonearning excess reserves.

While the illustration of multiple expansion has been carried through in terms of loans, the process may also take place by purchase of open-market investments—bonds, notes, and other obligations. In fact, the vast amount of new deposits—over $65 billion—created during World War II came into being in just this way as banks purchased Treasury securities to finance the war effort. Under the same general assumptions, let us record the effects of the process on the statements of First National Bank, and of succeeding groups of participating banks, as follows:

First National Bank of Chicago (Bank I)

Assets				*Liabilities*		
Required reserves	+$ 15	(1)		Deposits (primary)	+$100	(1)
Excess reserves	± 85	(1)	(2)			
Municipal bonds	+ 85	(2)				
Group II (assume 10 banks)						
Required reserves	+ 12.75	(2)		Deposits (primary)	+ 85	(2)
Excess reserves	± 72.25	(2)	(3)			
Municipal bonds	+ 72.25	(3)				
Group III (assume 100 banks)						
Required reserves	+ 10.84	(3)		Deposits (primary)	+ 72.25	(3)
Excess reserves	± 61.41	(3)	(4)			
Municipal bonds	+ 61.41	(4)				
All Succeeding Groups						
Required reserves	+ 61.41	(4)		Deposits (primary)	+ 409.42	(4)
Excess reserves	+ 348.01	(4)				
Municipal bonds	+ 348.01					
Total for All Banks						
Required reserves	+$100.00			Deposits	+$667.00	
Excess reserves	+ 567.00					
Municipal bonds	+ 567.00					

By way of explanation, the First National Bank, having received $100 in primary deposits in step 1, purchases municipal bonds from dealers in step 2 to the amount of excess reserves ($85). The dealers then deposit the checks, drawn on the Federal Reserve Bank, in Group II banks. The latter, after setting aside required reserves, purchase bonds in step 3 to the amount of excess reserves ($72.25). The dealers deposit the checks in Group III banks, and the process repeats itself through succeeding groups until the excess reserves of $85 are entirely utilized by addition of $567 to bond holdings of the banking system. Including the initial deposit, total deposits rise by $667.

Thus, from the standpoint of deposit creation, bank expansion by purchase of open-market securities reaches the same result as expansion by loans to customers. The chief difference is that payment for a loan is made by deposit credit to the customer's account, whereas payment for a security is made by a check on the Federal Reserve Bank, so that *derivative* deposits do not initially appear in the individual bank. This fact sometimes leads students as well as some practical bankers to the erroneous conclusion that the purchase of investments by the banking system does not create new deposits. The confusion arises from failure to see beyond the individual bank; transactions of other banks in the system, lying beyond the horizon, are overlooked.

time deposits and multiple expansion

The place of time deposits in the multiple-expansion process requires further consideration. Those who classify time deposits as money are disposed to lump them with demand deposits in analyzing the expansion process, and to deal only with aggregate deposits. However, those who regard time deposits not as money, but as one form of near-money, are inclined to treat time deposits quite separately in the analysis. For the following reasons, the author subscribes to the latter view.

To begin with, there are convincing reasons for excluding time deposits from money because they perform neither of the traditional primary functions of money, namely, to serve as a medium of exchange and as a standard measure of values. True, time deposits serve the liquidity function, but so do many other forms of near-money—U.S. savings bonds, mutual savings bank deposits, share accounts of savings and loan associations, short-term Treasury obligations, and others. There is no logical place to draw the line separating money from other liquid assets if one goes beyond checkbook money. Time deposits are not subject to check, with the result that they must be converted to demand deposits or currency before a money payment is made.

Also, time deposits come into being as a consequence of an entirely different set of decisions from those that give rise to demand deposits. The expansion of loans and investments in the banking system initially creates an equivalent amount of *demand deposits.* People borrow at the banks in order to make payments. No rational person borrows at 6 to 9 percent in order to build up a time-deposit account which pays 4 or 5 percent. Time deposits emerge from subsequent decisions in regard to (1) current savings and (2) administration of existing liquid assets. Decisions with respect to current savings have to do with (a) the choice between savings and consumption expenditures and (b) choices among various alternative commitments of current savings such as time deposits, U.S. savings bonds, savings-and-loan share accounts, and other investments. If this overall choice of time deposits in a given year is 10 percent of personal and business savings of $70 billion, then approximately $7 billion of demand deposits are shifted to time deposits. Furthermore, in administering existing liquid assets, funds may be shifted to time deposits from alternative commitments listed above to the amount of $1 billion. If so, these transactions involve an additional shift of this amount from demand deposits to time deposits, and the total increase of time deposits during the year becomes $8 billion.

At this point, the question arises: How do the foregoing decisions to commit savings to time deposits, other factors remaining the same, affect the amount of potential bank-credit expansion? The shift of $7 billion of demand deposits to time deposits in connection with current savings decisions releases required reserves to the amount of $.7 billion, assuming a 15 percent requirement against net demand deposits and a 5 percent requirement against time deposits. This, in time, permits new loan and investment expansion, and thereby demand-deposit expansion, of $4.67 billion; that is, $\frac{.7}{.15}$. Thus, after this expansion, demand deposits (money) are $2.33 billion less than before, time deposits are $7 billion larger, and total deposits are $4.67 billion larger. The second case of shifting $1 billion of existing liquid assets to time deposits from alternative types of investment, say, Treasury notes, is somewhat different. The notes are sold and payment of $1 billion is received in demand deposits which, in turn, are converted to time deposits. Using the same reserve requirements–15 percent and 5 percent, respectively–there is a release of $.1 billion in requirements, which, in time, permits $.67 billion of subsequent demand-deposit expansion; that is, $\frac{.1}{.15}$. Thus, the shift has a deflationary influence, mainly because legal reserves must be held against time deposits, whereas there is no reserve requirement for Treasury obligations. The immediate effect is to reduce demand deposits by $1 billion and to leave total near-money assets the same. Later on, if and when the released excess reserves are fully utilized, total demand deposits (money) are rebuilt by $.67 billion, so that their net reduction becomes $.33 billion.

The place of time deposits in the multiple-expansion process may now be summarized, as follows:

1/The potential expansion of total loans and investment (and total deposits) in the banking system on a given base of reserve money rises as demand deposits are shifted to time deposits. However, all initial bank expansions take the form of demand deposits, and conversion of these to time deposits rests on subsequent decisions of savers.

2/The potential expansion of demand deposits (money) rises when time deposits are shifted to demand deposits. This follows from the fact that there is a reserve requirement, however small, against time deposits.

3/As a corollary of (2), the potential expansion of demand deposits (money) rises as time deposits become less attractive than alternative commitments for savings. This follows from the fact that there is a legal-reserve requirement against time deposits but none against Treasury obligations and other such liquid assets.

4/Analysis of the bank expansion process should discriminate between demand deposits (money) and time deposits (near-money) because of their marked difference in economic influence. The average demand-deposit dollar has a large *multiple* influence, representing in the course of a year effective demand for goods and services to the amount of $20 to $35. In contrast, the average time-deposit dollar turns over less than twice per year; it is used only in exceptional cases directly in making payments.

MULTIPLE CONTRACTION OF COMMERCIAL-BANK CREDIT

Because multiple contraction in the banking system is, in general, the converse of multiple expansion, a less comprehensive analysis should suffice. However, just as in mountain climbing one encounters new vistas when following the return trail, so there are new aspects of multiple contraction. For illustration, assume that, as a consequence of the sale of U.S. securities by Federal Reserve Banks, the First National Bank of Chicago loses $100 of deposits and an equal amount of legal reserves. Assume further that net excess reserves are zero, and that no additional reserve money is available. Again, it is helpful to note changes on the abstracted statements of succeeding groups of banks, as follows:

In step 2, the First National Bank repairs its reserve deficiency of $85 by selling U.S. securities to dealers who have deposit accounts in Group II banks. Collection of checks given by dealers reduces deposits of Group II by $85, and also reduces reserves equally of which $12.75 represents reduced requirements, and $72.25 represents reserve deficiency. Group II banks then adjust their deficiency by sale of $72.25 of U.S. securities in step 3, thereby drawing reserves from Group III. This liquidation process continues throughout the banking system until in aggregate the $85 reserve deficiency has been eliminated by sale of $567 of U.S. securities. Total deposit reduction, including the initial withdrawal from First National, amounts to $667.

Liquidation of U.S. securities is chosen in the illustration because sale of liquidity reserve assets is the most likely method of adjusting the reserve position. The same quantitative effect, however, takes place by liquidation of

First National Bank of Chicago (Bank I)

Assets				*Liabilities*		
Required reserves	–$ 15	(1)		Deposits	–$100	(1)
Reserve deficiency	± 85	(1)	(2)			
U.S. securities	– 85	(2)				
Group II (assume 10 banks)						
Required reserves	– 12.75	(2)		Deposits	– 85	(2)
Reserve deficiency	± 72.25	(2)	(3)			
U.S. securities	– 72.25	(3)				
Group III (assume 100 banks)						
Required reserves	– 10.84	(3)		Deposits	– 72.25	(3)
Reserve deficiency	± 61.41	(3)	(4)			
U.S. securities	– 61.41	(4)				
All Succeeding Groups						
Required reserves	– 61.41	(4)		Deposits	– 409.42	(4)
Reserve deficiency	– 348.01	(4)				
U.S. securities	– 348.01					
Total for All Banks						
Required reserves	–$100			Deposits	–$667	
Reserve deficiency	– 567					
U.S. securities	– 567					

any earning asset–whether bonds or loans. Instead of actual sale, open-market securities may not be replaced when redeemed at maturity. Similarly, some loans may not be renewed, and some loans may be called.

Adjustment of a reserve deficiency by loan liquidation requires further analysis. At one extreme, one may assume that all loan maturities of First National Bank are met by checks drawn on other banks, so that loan liquidation has no effect on First National's deposits. In this case, the only alteration in the statement is substitution of "loans" for "U.S. securities." At the other extreme, the unrealistic assumptions may be made that all loan and deposit liquidation takes place at the First National Bank, and that no deposits and reserves are drawn from other banks. In this event, the statement changes are substitution of "loans–$567" for "U.S. securities–$567" and insertion of "deposits–$667" on the liabilities side. The first case is much nearer reality than the second. That is to say, loan liquidation by one bank, other things being equal, draws reserves mainly from *other* banks and forces them, in turn, to call loans. But the first case is also unrealistic in assuming that checks to repay loans of First National are drawn on other banks; rather, such checks are typically drawn on the lending bank. However, just before loan repayments, deposits and reserves of First National increase at the expense of *other* banks as customers prepare to meet their obligations. Deposits are then drawn down as loan payments are made.

REFERENCES

books

Chandler, Lester V., *The Economics of Money and Banking* (5th ed.; New York: Harper & Row, 1969), chap. 4.

Phillips, Chester A., *Bank Credit* (New York: Macmillan, 1920), chaps. III, IV.

Pritchard, Leland J., *Money and Banking* (2d ed.; Boston: Houghton Mifflin, 1964), chap. 6.

Rodkey, Robert G., *The Banking Process* (New York: Macmillan, 1928), chap. XV.

monographs and articles

Angel, J. W., and K. F. Ficek, "The Expansion of Bank Credit," *Journal of Political Economy* (February 1933), pp. 1-32; (April 1933), pp. 152-193.

Board of Governors of the Federal Reserve System, *The Federal Reserve System* (Washington, D.C.: Board of Governors, 1963), chap. IV.

Crick, W. F., "The Genesis of Bank Deposits," *Economica* (June 1927), pp. 191-202.

Federal Reserve Bank of Chicago, *Modern Money Mechanics* (May 1961).

McDonald, Stephen L., "The Internal Drain and Bank Credit Expansion," *Journal of Finance* (December 1953), pp. 407-421.

Orr, D., and W. G. Mellon, "Stochastic Reserve Losses and Expansion of Bank Credit," *American Economic Review*, LI (September 1961), pp. 614-623. Reply with rejoinder, H. L. Miller, *American Economic Review*, LII (December 1962), pp. 1118-1122.

INDEX

72 73 74 75 76 9 8 7 6 5 4 3 2 1